CIVIL JUSTICE, PRIVATIZATION, AND DEMOCRACY

TREVOR C.W. FARROW

Civil Justice, Privatization, and Democracy

UNIVERSITY OF TORONTO PRESS
Toronto Buffalo London

Toronto Buffalo London
www.utppublishing.com
Printed in Canada

ISBN 978-1-4426-4578-3

Printed on acid-free, 100% post-consumer recycled paper with vegetable-based inks.

Library and Archives Canada Cataloguing in Publication

Farrow, Trevor C.W., author
Civil justice, privatization, and democracy / Trevor C.W. Farrow.

Includes bibliographical references and index.
ISBN 978-1-4426-4578-3 (bound)

1. Dispute resolution (Law)—Canada. 2. Justice, Administration of—Political aspects—Canada. 3. Privatization—Canada. 4. Dispute resolution (Law). 5. Justice, Administration of—Political aspects. 6. Privatization. I. Title.

KE8615.F37 2014 347.71'09 C2013-907275-6
KF9084.F37 2014

This book has been published with the help of a grant from the Federation for the Humanities and Social Sciences, through the Awards to Scholarly Publications Program, using funds provided by the Social Sciences and Humanities Research Council of Canada.

University of Toronto Press acknowledges the financial assistance to its publishing program of the Canada Council for the Arts and the Ontario Arts Council.

Canada Council for the Arts Conseil des Arts du Canada

ONTARIO ARTS COUNCIL
CONSEIL DES ARTS DE L'ONTARIO
50 YEARS OF ONTARIO GOVERNMENT SUPPORT OF THE ARTS
50 ANS DE SOUTIEN DU GOUVERNEMENT DE L'ONTARIO AUX ARTS

University of Toronto Press acknowledges the financial support of the Government of Canada through the Canada Book Fund for its publishing activities.

For Joseph, Morley, and Mary

[T]hat grounded maxim,
So rife and celebrated …
that to the public good
Private respects must yield. …

John Milton[1]

Publicity is the very soul of justice.

Jeremy Bentham[2]

1 John Milton, *Samson Agonistes* (1671) in *The Poetical Works of John Milton*, with a memoir, and critical remarks on his genius and writings, by James Montgomery (London: Tilt and Bogue, 1843) vol. ii, p. 110.

2 Jeremy Bentham, "Draught of a New Plan for the Organization of the Judicial Establishment in France: With Critical Observations on the Draught Proposed by the National Assembly Committee, in the Form of a Perpetual Commentary" (1790) in *The Works of Jeremy Bentham*, published under the superintendence of his executor, John Bowring (Edinburgh: Tait, 1843) vol. iv, p. 316.

Contents

Figure and Tables

Figure

Tables

Preface

Almost twenty years ago, prior to becoming an academic, I was a litigator in a case that changed my view of the civil justice system. The case involved a dispute over a contract for a computer system and computer services. The parties were located in the United States. The contract provided that any dispute between the parties would be resolved by way of arbitration, which is essentially a trial that is private, funded by the parties and presided over by a neutral person selected by the parties (an arbitrator). The case took several years to prepare, culminating in a week-long hearing. The result, in my view, was a travesty of justice. Fairness was not accomplished, justice was not served, and poor, unethical – and potentially fraudulent – conduct was permitted to persist. Seeing first-hand how a modern private dispute resolution regime could run rough-shod over well-established rule of law values in a case involving informed clients, sophisticated counsel, a senior and experienced lawyer-arbitrator, and important corporate law principles was, put simply, shocking.

Although there were potentially several reasons for the unfairness of the result in that case (which, as outlined in Chapter 1, I call the "Dealership case"), the fact that the dispute was resolved pursuant to a private justice regime, to me, was a root cause of the problem. The procedural safeguards, at least for one party, were not adequate. The problematic conduct at issue in the case, which affected many more people and organizations than those directly involved in the dispute, was permitted to persist. And, because of the private and confidential nature of the proceeding, no one could talk about it. From that point on, I became increasingly concerned about the state of our justice system, which is actively pushing for more, not less, privatization of civil dispute resolution.

In addition to telling the story of the Dealership case (which returns from time to time throughout this book), as I outline in Chapter 1, this book is designed to provide a general account and critique of the privatization of civil justice and its potential ramifications for democracy. Privatization is rapidly and increasingly occurring at all levels of the public justice system, including courts, tribunals, and state-sanctioned private dispute resolution regimes. This reform movement is driven by a widespread ethos of efficiency-based civil justice reform. There are many sound reasons for these privatization trends, including reduced costs, increased speed and efficiency, privacy, enhanced participation and autonomy through increased party choice within and control over dispute resolution processes, and improved access to the tools of justice. However, these trends also have a number of costs in the form of negative impacts on the development of the common law, potential procedural unfairness, power imbalances between disputants, and a potential negative impact on systems of democratic governance. Civil society is publicly regulated largely through legislation and adjudication. To the extent that we are actively privatizing how we do adjudication, we are in effect actively privatizing a large part of the way we govern ourselves in modern democracies.

Current procedural reforms and practices designed to improve the efficiency of and access to civil courts and tribunals – through processes of privatization – have the potential to do a lot of good in terms of improving our systems of civil justice. However, left unchecked and unexamined, these processes also have the serious potential to damage some of the core values underlying the institutional structure that makes up our modern democracies. The purpose of this book is to look critically at the positive and negative aspects of those tools of privatization.

This book represents the confluence of my early days as a practicing litigation lawyer and my subsequent and ongoing career as a full time academic, as well as my research and teaching interests in political theory, globalization, ethics, and the administration of civil justice. In my view, there is a necessary interdisciplinarity to the topic of civil justice reform because in the end, through the tools of law, we are really talking about the pursuit of justice in the name of democracy. I have been fortunate to raise these concerns and to think about some potential solutions on a couple of previous occasions. My first direct attempt at formulating an early and brief articulation of these issues was published in 2006. Subsequently, I developed these ideas and published them in the proceedings of the 2007 annual conference of the Canadian Institute for the Administration of Justice (CIAJ), and further as the culmination of my doctoral work. This book draws on much of that previous thinking, as well as on subsequent comments and debates from and with colleagues and students over the past number of years.

Although I certainly feel that I have pushed my thinking much further because of those earlier publications, I also acknowledge that a primary goal of this book is not necessarily to finally answer all questions, but rather is to identify a number of important challenges and, in particular, to open further debates and encourage further research about both the positive and negative aspects of the privatization movement. These are important issues with direct implications for the way we govern ourselves in modern democracies. As such, I hope that this book is of interest to social, legal, and political theorists and practitioners. By engaging with past and present practice, policy, and academic conversations on these issues, my hope is that, in addition to adding to those conversations, this project will directly contribute to the shaping of the future trajectory of our modern systems of civil justice.

In terms of the overall focus of the book, my interest is squarely on the privatization movement in the context of civil dispute resolution. As discussed further in Chapter 1, it does not directly take up the issue of privatization in the contexts of criminal law, family law, Aboriginal law, or religious or other ethnocultural contexts (although having said that, some of the discussion will certainly be relevant for aspects of those contexts). In terms of the jurisdictional reach of this book, I hope it will be of interest to an international audience. Although many of the examples and procedural contexts are drawn from the Canadian experience, there is also a significant amount of research and material from other jurisdictions included in the book. And because the privatization of civil justice is a phenomenon that is being experimented with around the world, I am hopeful that this book will be of assistance not just in the context of Canadian reform initiatives, but also more generally in those international efforts as well.

T.C.W.F.
September 2013
Toronto, Canada

Acknowledgments

Acknowledging that it "takes a village" to produce a book like this feels like a major understatement. Many generous people have provided me with significant help, support, and encouragement along the way.

As mentioned in the Preface, this book draws heavily on my doctoral research. For comments and guidance on that earlier work, I am grateful to Judith Garber, James Lightbody, David Kahane, Catherine Kellogg, Ian Urquhart, George Pavlich, and Gerald Baier.

In terms of research assistance for several civil justice and related projects over the past number of years that have both directly and indirectly influenced and assisted me with the writing of this book, I would like to thank Bart Danko, Patricia Hania, Ada Ho, Alan Melamud, Ziad Reslan, Jason Sacha, Ian Smith, Anton Tabuns, Karolina Wisniewski, and Hannah De Jong. The Canadian Forum on Civil Justice has been very supportive and helpful in terms of research and editing. Thanks to Nicole Aylwin, Sabreena Delhon, Diana Lowe, Q.C., and Kim Taylor. In addition, I am grateful for the assistance that members of the Osgoode Hall Law School Information Technology department provided me in connection with the survey that I conducted for this book. I am also grateful for administrative assistance from Denise Jagdeosingh-Martinez, Jody-Ann Rowe-Butler, Tania Gittens, and Jacqueline Dwyer.

Other important influences – former and current students who have constantly pushed me to think about civil justice in fresh and progressive ways; judges and lawyers with whom I have worked in a number of educational, development, and rule of law contexts (domestically and internationally) and who have helped to shape the way I think about the administration of civil justice; and a number of fellow academics with whom I continue to collaborate in the ongoing project of civil justice reform – can be seen on many of the pages throughout this book.

The research that ultimately formed the basis of this book was also greatly assisted by generous financial support from several organizations and institutions over a number of years. Specifically, I would like to thank the Social Sciences and Humanities Research Council of Canada for awarding me a doctoral fellowship and for its support of the *Cost of Justice: Weighing the Costs of Fair and Effective Resolution to Legal Problems* project (a Community-University Research Alliance grant awarded to the Canadian Forum on Civil Justice, for which I am the Award Holder/Principle Investigator), which has provided research assistance for this book; the Canadian Institute for the Administration of Justice for awarding me the Charles D. Gonthier Research Fellowship; Borden Ladner Gervais, LLP for the opportunity to act as a BLG Research Fellowship Directing Professor on two occasions; the University of Alberta for several generous research fellowships and grants; York University for support from the Research at York funding program; and Osgoode Hall Law School for generous research fellowship and grant support. This book has been published with the help of a grant from the Federation for the Humanities and Social Sciences, through the Awards to Scholarly Publications Program, using funds provided by the Social Sciences and Humanities Research Council of Canada.

I am very grateful for assistance provided by the University of Toronto Press, and in particular Daniel Quinlan for his excellent editorial guidance. Two anonymous readers, together with the members of the Manuscript Review Committee of the University of Toronto Press, also provided extremely helpful and detailed comments and suggestions, many of which influenced my thinking in this book. Mae Lum and David Zielonka have also provided very helpful manuscript assistance.

On a more personal note, thanks to Jane Birdsell, Dale Birdsell, David Birdsell, Jill Farrow, Grant Farrow, Susan Farrow, Blake Hutcheson, and Ruth Peterson – all of whom, in their own ways, had an important influence on this book. Further, thanks to my kids, Morley and Joseph, for the joy they bring to my days, for their constant curiosity, and ultimately for being the reason why I care so much about the future of society and our systems of justice and democracy. Finally, thanks to my spouse, Mary Birdsell, for supporting, encouraging, and believing in me at every step of this process – I could not have done it without you.

For all of that generous assistance and support I am incredibly grateful.

Chapter One

Introduction

The Dealership Case[1]

For almost fifty years, John, who immigrated to the United States when he was very young, operated a dealership in the Midwest. He sold merchandise made exclusively by one of the biggest and most familiar manufacturers in United States history (the "Manufacturer"). John was an extremely popular dealer who won sales awards in almost all categories. He was a true American success story. Late in his career, John was asked – purportedly by the local representative for the Manufacturer's computer service division (whom John had known and dealt with for years) and as part of the overall obligations and expectations set out in his dealership agreement – to purchase a new computer system and computer service package. Doing, as he always did, what the computer representative suggested and what he understood to be what the Manufacturer required, John agreed to purchase, without doing any research or comparison shopping, the full computer system and a long-term service package (the "Contract").

1 The Dealership case, which has dramatically influenced my thinking and driven my concerns in this book, is a case in which I was directly involved at one point in my life. In my previous career as a litigator, I was co-counsel on the case. As such, I have a very close, inside perspective on it. For the same reason, I am also limited in what I can reveal about the case both because of basic solicitor–client confidentiality obligations and because of a strict confidentiality agreement that binds the parties and their counsel. However, although I have changed and omitted names and facts to comply with all of my professional, ethical, and legal obligations, the Dealership case is a case that actually happened. For an earlier account of the Dealership case, see Trevor C.W. Farrow, "Public Justice, Private Dispute Resolution and Democracy," in Ronalda Murphy and Patrick A. Molinari, eds., *Doing Justice: Dispute Resolution in the Courts and Beyond* (Montréal: Canadian Institute for the Administration of Justice, 2009), 301 at 305.

As it turned out, the computer representative did not work for the Manufacturer but rather for a newly reorganized, separate, and privately held multinational corporation (the "Corporation"). Notwithstanding the change in corporate structure, ownership, and employment relationship, the representative's uniform, business card, and letterhead continued – as they always had – to use the Manufacturer's logo. The computer system that the representative recommended, and that John purchased, was designed for a much bigger dealership (or group of dealerships) than what John operated. Further, the cost of the equipment and services was vastly higher than the cost of the same equipment and services found on the open market. Finally, there was no Manufacturer requirement under John's dealership agreement to purchase the equipment or services. Put simply, the Corporation, relying on John's good faith, history of service, relationship with the representative, and unquestioning loyalty to the Manufacturer, sold John an incredibly overpriced computer system and unreasonably lengthy service package that he did not need or in fact want.

Subsequently, when John discovered the truth about the Corporation, the computer equipment and the service package, he decided to stop further payments and seek to resolve the matter with the Manufacturer and the Corporation. Because of the separate ownership structure of the Corporation, the Manufacturer wanted nothing to do with the dispute. The Corporation, for its part, was not willing to make any concessions. Further, based on the clear wording of the Contract and on John's refusal to pay, the Corporation proceeded to take legal action. Because the Contract provided that "all disputes" arising under the Contract were to be resolved pursuant to the commercial arbitration rules of a major U.S. arbitration association, the Corporation initiated arbitration proceedings against John.[2]

The Corporation's claim was simple: John should make the payments owed under the Contract. John argued in his defence and counterclaim, in a nutshell, that because the costs of the system and services were not only unreasonably high but were based on what amounted to at least an unreasonable contract of adhesion,[3] if not actual fraud, the Contract

2 For a further discussion of contract-based mandatory dispute resolution clauses, see, for example, infra Chapters 4 and 5. See also Chapter 2.

3 A contract of adhesion is a contract in which one party is given little or, more typically, no choice as to its terms. These types of contracts often involve standard forms as well as unequal bargaining positions.

should be set aside and he should be compensated for his losses. Those losses essentially amounted to the payments that he had made to that date under the Contract. An animating and aggravating factor for John's defence and counterclaim was the fact that, given the system's incompatibility for a smaller dealership, it did not function for John as advertised (or really at all). After a lengthy and costly pre-hearing process that involved extensive document gathering, depositions in various cities in various states and numerous pre-hearing motions, the dispute proceeded to arbitration. The hearing lasted for a week, at the conclusion of which the arbitrator found for the Corporation and dismissed John's counterclaim. Notwithstanding several years of preparation, volumes of documentary discovery, and weeks of depositions (several problematic parts of which I discuss further in this book[4]), the arbitrator – consistent with the arbitration association's practices, rules, and guidelines – provided no oral or written reasons at all for his judgment. And because of the terms of the Contract, John had no right of appeal.

Reasonable people can always disagree, particularly in hindsight, as to what the correct result should have been in a given case. Although I am convinced – as one of John's two lawyers in that case[5] – that the arbitrator in the Dealership case got it wrong, I do not think that he acted in bad faith. However, as I discuss later in this book,[6] I am of the view that the business practices of the Corporation that led to the dispute were at least unfairly aggressive, were likely pursued – at least by some – in bad faith, were part of a systematic and nation-wide approach of the Corporation to target similarly situated dealers through deceptive business practices, and, as a result, likely amounted to fraud. Further, in addition to the questionable conduct on the part of the Corporation, I am also of the view that the lawyers for the Corporation, as I also discuss later in this book,[7] acted on numerous occasions unprofessionally and in bad faith.

Unfortunately, the private dispute resolution regime in which we were working – state-sanctioned confidential commercial arbitration – protected the conduct of the Corporation and its lawyers from being properly discovered, made public, prohibited or sanctioned. Part of the reason, as I discuss further elsewhere,[8] was the system's lack of

4 See infra Chapter 6.
5 See supra note 1.
6 See infra Chapter 6.
7 Ibid.
8 Ibid.

meaningful procedural safeguards. The more significant reason, in my view, was the curtain of secrecy, provided for by strategically drafted and wide-ranging contractual confidentiality provisions, that shielded the systematically suspect conduct of the Corporation and its lawyers in our proceeding, and in all of the similar proceedings with other dealerships in which they were involved and about which we knew but could do nothing about. As such, because no reasons for judgment were ever written, let alone published, and because the entire proceedings were shrouded in secrecy, the Corporation was free to continue its problematic pattern of present and future dealings with other dealerships across the country. Further, any similarly situated corporation would not have the burden (or benefit) of a public precedent that could guide its future conduct or curb its future misbehaviour.

Privatizing Civil Justice

As an English literature teacher once told me, there are often two ways to come at a discussion. You can start widely, with the big picture, and work towards the finer points, or you can start narrowly, with the details, and work your way out. Put differently, you can look at a room through a wide-open door or through the narrow opening of a key hole. They are very different vantage points providing very different perspectives. In the end, typically, it is the combination that is often most instructive. In approaching this research, I have tried to come at it from both the narrow as well as the broad. It is a project about an individual dispute: the Dealership case. It is also a project about the entire civil justice system. By telling John's story, I seek to raise some specific and problematic aspects of private justice. Then, by linking his story to the theory and practice of everyday civil justice, I hope to provide a critical account of the purpose, current privatizing trends within, and future directions of civil justice as a process of societal regulation. My main focus of consideration is the privatization movement that has engulfed the practice and reform of modern civil justice. Specifically, I am concerned that, through the increasing privatization of civil justice, a key aspect of how democratic governance is realized in society – public adjudication – is jeopardized. What the Dealership case highlights is the potentially negative impact that privatized processes can have on the immediate dispute resolution interests of particular litigants, as well as the future regulation of potentially large sectors of society. These are the issues that – framed in a discussion of the role of courts and other dispute resolution processes in our systems of democratic governance – are at stake in this book.

Privatization is occurring at a rapid rate in all levels of the public justice system. First, in the civil justice system, there is an increasing and overwhelming tendency to resolve disputes through mechanisms other than the traditional public court process. For example, mandatory court-based mediation rules, judicial dispute resolution initiatives, case management regimes, pre-trial conferences, and cost-based settlement incentives have all become central pillars of the modern civil justice system and its reform. Each of these mechanisms, either directly or indirectly, and in different ways, encourages the resolution of disputes through methods that are outside of the formal, public trial process. Second, alongside civil court initiatives, privatization is occurring in the administrative system as well. Tribunals and other administrative processes are increasingly experimenting with formal and informal alternatives to their traditional hearing-based processes. Third, legislative regimes – typically arbitration statutes – also continue to sanction (and encourage) the resolution of civil disputes outside the formal court system. The Dealership case was governed by this kind of regime. Fourth, privatization is also occurring in parts of the criminal justice system. Although the state is always an essential part of the criminal process, plea-bargaining, community-based diversion programs, and restorative justice initiatives have been, and are increasingly becoming significant alternatives (or complements) to the more formal, public trial–based criminal dispute resolution system. Finally, all of these state-based privatized (or privatizing) systems – civil, administrative, legislative, and criminal – operate in addition to the already robust, millennia-old tradition of resolving the vast majority of virtually all disputes through mechanisms entirely separate from formal state processes (private negotiations, religious and community-based dispute resolution tools, etc.).

There are many sound reasons for these privatization trends, including reduced costs, increased speed and efficiency, privacy, enhanced participation and autonomy through increased party choice within and control over dispute resolution processes, and improved access to the tools of justice. That such benefits can result from privatization of dispute resolution is relatively well documented.[9]

9 See, for example, Farrow, "Public Justice," Private Dispute Resolution and Democracy" in Murphy and Molinari, eds., *Doing Justice: Dispute Resolution in the Courts and Beyond*, supra note 1.

However, these trends also have a number of costs in the form of negative impacts on the development of the common law, potential procedural unfairness, and power imbalances between disputants. These costs are all reasons enough, in themselves, to be concerned about these wide-ranging trends. However, my main concern, which is the driving concern behind this book, is the larger question of the negative impact that the privatization of public dispute resolution processes has on systems of democratic governance. Civil society is publicly regulated largely through the twin pillars of legislation and adjudication. The adjudicative function is clearly a central pillar of democratic processes of government. To the extent that we are actively privatizing how we do adjudication, we are in effect actively privatizing a large part of the way we govern ourselves in modern democracies. Put differently, the more we actively and systematically move the resolution of disputes like the Dealership case out of public civil justice and related dispute resolution processes and into private regimes, the less democratic control and scrutiny we will have over the regulation of and influence over large sectors of both our public and private lives.

Unlike the benefits of privatization about which people have been actively talking for some time, there is comparatively very little discussion or debate about the costs of privatizing civil justice. As one commentator has noted, although the move to privatize the justice system and its results are being "recently discovered," they are certainly "still not understood."[10] This lack of understanding is of particular concern given the ongoing and significant institutional reforms that are presently occurring in civil justice systems the world over and the fundamental public interest values that are at stake. However, having raised these concerns, I also want to make it very clear at the outset that the overall goal of this project is *not* to do away with privatization of civil justice all together. There are many sound legal and policy reasons, as supported by the voices of practicing stakeholders from all corners of the dispute resolution system, to support some aspects of current privatization initiatives. As such, the difficult question becomes one of balance: how to think about and harness aspects of the privatization movement without jeopardizing the underlying civil justice system.

---

10 Tracy Walters McCormack, "Privatizing the Justice System" (2006) 25 *Rev. of Lit.* 735 at wpt. i. See further Eric K. Yamamoto, "ADR: Where Have the Critics Gone?" (1995–6) 36 *Santa Clara L. Rev.* 1055.

To develop my overall analysis in this book, I primarily look at three parts of the justice system (see Figure 1.1). The primary focus of attention is the public civil court system. In addition, I also look at both the administrative law system and legislative initiatives (typically including arbitration statutes) that actively sanction the resolution of

Figure 1.1. Potential dispute resolution process alternatives

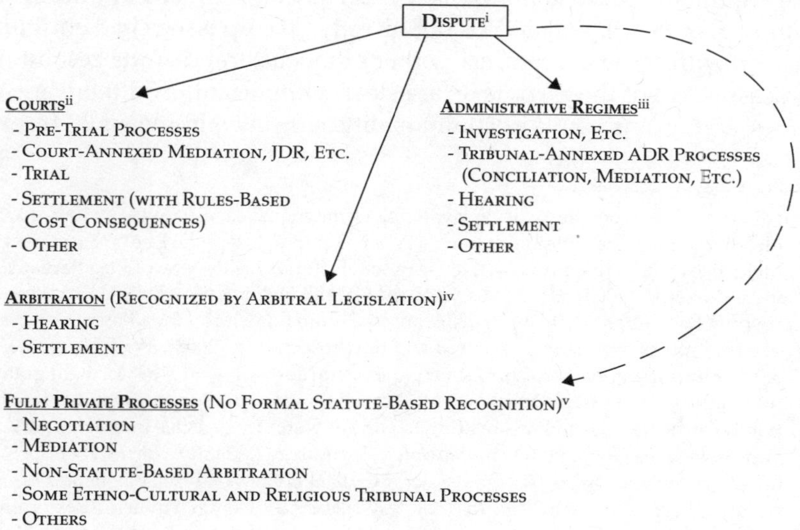

i The nature of a dispute, at least as between courts and administrative regimes, will often determine in which dispute resolution process it will proceed. Private dispute resolution contractual clauses also play an increasingly determinative jurisdictional role.

ii See, for example, Nova Scotia Supreme Court, Ontario Superior Court of Justice, Supreme Court of British Columbia, and so on. For various discussions of superior courts, see, for example, Chapters 2 and 3.

iii See, for example, Québec Human Rights Tribunal, Alberta Environmental Appeals Board, Commission for Public Complaints Against the RCMP, and so on. For a discussion of administrative regimes, see, for example, Chapter 4.

iv For a discussion of state-recognized arbitration regimes, see, for example, Chapter 4. I recognize that some state-recognized commercial mediation legislation is now also in force. See Chapter 4.

v The processes listed here – negotiation, mediation, and so on – are examples of separate private processes, not steps in a single proceeding. I recognize that fully private processes can, and often do, occur alongside public processes (e.g., concurrent settlement negotiations, discussed, e.g., in Chapters 3 and 5).

non-criminal – primarily civil – disputes outside of the public court and administrative law regimes. This book also touches on the entirely private system (including negotiation and mediation for example) to the extent that the private system is annexed directly or indirectly by the public stream through the court system, the administrative system, and/or legislative initiatives (again see Figure 1.1).

This book does not focus on privatizing initiatives in the criminal justice system,[11] nor does it focus heavily on family law (although many of the arguments made in this book are directly or indirectly applicable to family disputes[12]). It also does not directly take up issues in Aboriginal law or, with some exceptions,[13] other ethnocultural dispute resolution processes. All of those contexts are clearly important. And there are, at times, significant points of commonality. However, in the end – from a

11 For commentary on alternative, privatizing criminal justice initiatives, including plea-bargaining and other initiatives, see, for example, Joseph Di Luca, "Expedient McJustice or Principled Alternative Dispute Resolution? A Review of Plea Bargaining in Canada" (2005) 50 *Crim. L.Q.* 14; and Gabriel Hallevy, "Is ADR (Alternative Dispute Resolution) Philosophy Relevant to Criminal Justice? – Plea Bargains as Mediation Process between the Accused and the Prosecution" (2008), available online: SSRN <http://papers.ssrn.com/sol3/papers.cfm?abstract_id=1315984>. I am grateful to James Stribopoulos and Mary M. Birdsell for assistance on this criminal law point. For further discussions relating to various restorative justice initiatives and approaches, see George Pavlich, *Governing Paradoxes of Restorative Justice* (London: GlassHouse Press, 2005); George Pavlich, "Critical Policy Analysis, Power and Restorative Justice" (March 2009) 75 *Crim. Just. Matters* 24; George Pavlich, "Restorative Justice and Its Paradoxes" (Winter 2005–6) 22 *Connections* 1; Jennifer Llewellyn, "Doing Justice: New Directions in Restorative Justice" in Murphy and Molinari, eds., *Doing Justice: Dispute Resolution in the Courts and Beyond*, supra note 1 at 191; Annalise E. Acorn, *Compulsory Compassion: A Critique of Restorative Justice* (Vancouver: UBC Press, 2004); and Bruce P. Archibald, "Progress in Models of Justice: From Adjudication/Arbitration through Mediation to Restorative Conferencing (and Back)" in Murphy and Molinari, eds., *Doing Justice: Dispute Resolution in the Courts and Beyond*, supra note 1 at 129. See also Mary-Ellen Turpel-Lafond, "Justice for Aboriginal Communities: Sharing the Ways" in Murphy and Molinari, eds., *Doing Justice: Dispute Resolution in the Courts and Beyond*, supra note 1 at 211. For further general discussions, see George Pavlich, "The Law of Subaltern Discipline" in Augustine Brannigan and George Pavlich, eds., *Governance and Regulation in Social Life: Essays in Honour of W. G. Carson* (Abingdon, Oxon, and New York: Routledge-Cavendish, 2007), c. 8; Kevin Stenson, "Reconstructing the Government of Crime" in Gary Wickham and George Pavlich, eds., *Rethinking Law, Society and Governance: Foucault's Bequest* (Oxford, UK, and Portland, OR: Hart Publishing, 2001), c. 6.

12 See, for example, Chapters 3, 4, 6, and 7.

13 See, for example, Chapters 6 and 7.

procedural perspective – they are sufficiently distinct to warrant separate treatment (or, put differently, to warrant not being lumped into the general civil justice terrain on which this book is largely focused). And although I certainly do look at the relevant preferences for, influences on, and justifications for privatization,[14] this book does not deal directly with some of the underlying influences of or debates in the general public policy literature[15] or some of the important and underlying sociological questions raised by general conflict theory.[16]

By focusing on the primary elements of the civil justice system, coupled with further discussions of the Dealership case as it relates from time to time to broader themes and discussions, this book in

---

14 See, for example, generally infra Chapter 5.

15 Although the public policy literature and its treatment of actors and processes are clearly related to the general governance issues at stake in this book, I do not need to take it up head on in order to develop my specific arguments. For background sources, see, for example, Laurent Dobuzinskis, Michael Howlett, and David Laycock, eds., *Policy Analysis in Canada: The State of the Art* (Toronto: University of Toronto Press, 2007); Francis G. Castels, *Comparative Public Policy: Patterns of Post-war Transformation* (Cheltenham, UK: Edward Elgar, 1998); Paul A. Sabatier, ed., *Theories of the Policy Process*, 2nd ed. (Boulder, CO: Westview Press, 2007); Maarten Hajer and Hendrik Wagenaar, eds., *Deliberative Policy Analysis: Understanding Governance in the Network Society* (Cambridge, UK: Cambridge University Press, 2003); and Michael Moran, Martin Rein, and Robert E. Goodin, eds., *The Oxford Handbook of Public Policy* (Oxford, UK: Oxford University Press, 2006).

16 A significant body of literature concerns itself directly with conflict, which is obviously a precondition to conflict resolution. Important elements to that research include, among other areas, the identification and understanding of the roots and sources of conflict and disputes; conflict management and prevention; elements, sources, and courses of conflict; historical and political perspectives; international dimensions; and personal and social issues, including race, gender, culture, power, communication, personality, emotional challenges, and ethics. For a sampling of conflict theory materials, see, for example, Robert A. Baruch Bush and Joseph P. Folger, "Changing People, Not Just Situations: A Transformative View of Conflict and Mediation" in Robert A. Baruch Bush and Joseph P. Folger, *The Promise of Mediation: Responding to Conflict through Empowerment and Recognition* (San Francisco: Jossey-Bass, 1994); Clyde H. Coombs and George S. Avrunin, *The Structure of Conflict* (Hillsdale, NJ: Lawrence Erlbaum, 1988); Herbert C. Kelman and V. Lee Hamilton, *Crimes of Obedience: Toward a Social Psychology of Authority and Responsibility* (New Haven, CT: Yale University Press, 1989); Ronald J. Fisher, *Interactive Conflict Resolution* (Syracuse: Syracuse University Press, 1997); Michael S. Lund, *Preventing Violent Conflicts: A Strategy for Preventive Diplomacy* (Washington, DC: United States Institute of Peace Press, 1996); Bernard S. Mayer, *The Dynamics of Conflict Resolution: A Practitioner's Guide* (San Francisco: Jossey-Bass, 2000); Dean G. Pruitt and Peter J. Carnevale,

turn has three main goals. First, it seeks to bear witness to the modern and wide-ranging privatization initiatives that are currently defining the way we think about and resolve almost all non-criminal disputes. Given its importance, we need to publicize, politicize and ultimately, I argue, temper (although not eliminate) this ever-increasing move to the private. Second, this book seeks to articulate the benefits and costs of these privatizing initiatives, particularly including their potential negative impacts on the way we publicly regulate ourselves in modern democratic societies. Third, this book makes recommendations for future thinking about, and approaches to, these initiatives. In so doing, it calls on academics, jurists, civil justice reformers, elected representatives, practitioners, and citizens to engage in a robust debate about all aspects of the privatization of civil justice, the future of which will have a fundamental impact on our public processes of democracy.

Outline

The purpose of this introductory chapter has been to tell the story of the Dealership case as well as to start identifying the larger procedural landscapes in which the Dealership case was, and other civil disputes are as

---

Negotiation in Social Conflict (Buckingham, UK: Open University Press, 1993); Dean G. Pruitt, Jeffrey Z. Rubin, and Sung Hee Kim, *Social Conflict: Escalation, Stalemate, and Settlement*, 2nd ed. (New York: McGraw-Hill, 1994); and Thomas L. Saaty and Joyce M. Alexander, *Conflict Resolution: The Analytic Hierarchy Approach* (New York: Praeger, 1989). See also Lon L. Fuller, "Mediation – Its Forms and Functions" (1971) 44 *S. Cal. L. Rev.* 305, reprinted in Kenneth I. Winston, ed., *The Principles of Social Order: Selected Essays of Lon L. Fuller*, rev. ed. (Oxford, UK: Hart Publishing, 2001) at 141; and Thomas C. Schelling, *The Strategy of Conflict* (Cambridge, MA: Harvard University Press, 1960, reprinted 1997) at 119–61. For Canadian collections of materials on conflict and conflict theory, see Colleen M. Hanycz, Trevor C.W. Farrow, and Frederick H. Zemans, *The Theory and Practice of Representative Negotiation* (Toronto: Emond Montgomery, 2008) at cc. 5–10; Julie Macfarlane, gen. ed., *Dispute Resolution: Readings and Case Studies*, 3rd ed. (Toronto: Emond Montgomery, 2010) at c. 1; Catherine Bell and David Kahane, *Intercultural Dispute Resolution in Aboriginal Contexts* (Vancouver: UBC Press, 2004); Desmond Ellis and Dawn Anderson, *Conflict Resolution: An Introductory Text* (Toronto: Emond Montgomery, 2005) at cc. 1, 4–7; and L. Michelle LeBaron and Venashri Pillay, eds. *Conflict Across Cultures: A Unique Experience of Bridging Differences* (Boston: Intercultural Press, 2006). See further Trevor C.W. Farrow, "Dispute Resolution and Legal Education: A Bibliography" (2005) 7:1 *Cardozo J. Confl. Resol.* 119.

well played out. A critical discussion of those landscapes now becomes the primary focus of the balance of this book, the outline for which proceeds as follows. Following this introductory chapter, Chapter 2 looks at the public court system, including its history, functions, and central role in democracy. Only with an understanding of the place and role of the public court system, amounting to what the chief justice of Canada described as an "essential condition of democracy,"[17] can we start to understand the important and far-reaching ramifications stemming from the privatization movement that is going on within and around it. The chapter first looks at superior courts and their general jurisdictional reach. It then takes up the primary functions of superior courts, including dispute resolution and societal regulation, and the theoretical and constitutional underpinnings of those functions.

Chapters 3 and 4 examine the privatization movement in several dispute resolution contexts (largely as identified earlier in Figure 1.1). Chapter 3 provides a detailed account of the privatization movement that has strongly taken hold of the public court system. The chapter begins with a general treatment of "privatization" and then situates and defines the current aspects of that movement that relate specifically to the civil justice system. After acknowledging its historical roots, the chapter proceeds to document many of the current influential international and domestic examples of the privatization of civil justice. A relatively comprehensive look at this landscape is provided in order to establish the power, scope, and depth of the movement. The chapter ends with a discussion of the "vanishing trial" phenomenon that is increasingly occurring, at least in large measure, as a result of the privatization movement. Chapter 4 examines the privatization movement in two other specific contexts: the administrative law system (federal and provincial) and alternative, legislatively sanctioned private dispute resolution processes (largely including arbitration). Both of these procedural areas have become increasingly popular and powerful parts of the overall justice sector.

---

17 Rt. Hon. Beverley McLachlin, P.C., "Judges in a Multicultural Society" (paper presented at Chief Justice of Ontario's Advisory Committee on Professionalism, First Colloquium on the Legal Profession, "Inaugural Colloquium on the Legal Profession," 20 October 2003, Faculty of Law, University of Western Ontario) at 3–6, available online: LSUC <http://www.lsuc.on.ca/media/mclachlin_judges_multicultura_society.pdf>. See also infra Chapter 2.

Chapter 5 then discusses the important bases on which the privatization of civil justice (which is largely documented in Chapters 3 and 4) is premised. It looks specifically at key privatizing preferences and influences, including those of governments, judges, lawyers, clients and the academy. A survey of lawyers done in connection with this project to look at the preferences of lawyers and clients on this issue is discussed. With these preferences and influences in mind, Chapter 5 proceeds to explore the movement's primary justifications, specifically including the business case and the access to justice case for privatization.

By this point in the book, I have tried to essentially set up the clearest and most persuasive evidence of, and arguments for, the privatization of civil justice. Put simply, in order to critique the movement, it is necessary first fully to understand it. Providing that understanding is the main purpose of Chapters 3 through 5. Chapters 6 and 7 are largely designed to articulate my own analysis of the landscape. Specifically, Chapter 6 sets out my five main concerns regarding the privatization of civil justice. Those concerns include my arguments that the movement: overstates some of its benefits, contributes to an impoverished development of the common law, results in a system of dispute resolution that lacks adequate procedural protections, has a negative impact on democracy (drawing largely on the procedural landscape set up in Chapters 2 and 3), and is aggravated by globalization. With those concerns in mind, I then, in Chapter 7, conclude by responding to several main challenges to my arguments, specifically including challenges based on efficiency and access to justice premises. Notions of justice and proportionality in the civil justice system are discussed. I then start to sketch out some directions for future thinking in the context of the practice, teaching, research, and reform of our systems of civil justice. Finally, I have also included a relatively extensive and inclusive bibliography, which I hope will be useful to those who are interested in further pursuing both the practical and the theoretical issues raised in this book.

Chapter Two

Courts and Democracy

Superior Courts

Modern provincial superior courts throughout Canada are the primary public venues in which Canadians resolve their disputes.[1] The system is *public* in the sense that it is largely funded by governments (through taxpayer money), is – at least in theory – potentially available to all people for all disputes, is open to the public and the press, and provides judgments that are of interest not just to disputing parties but also to society as a whole. I say in theory because formally *open* courts may be; widely *accessible* they are not. As the Irish judge Sir James Mathew reportedly stated about the English courts many decades ago, "justice is open to all – like the Ritz Hotel."[2] Pursuing the resolution of disputes through traditional public litigation processes, particularly with the assistance of legal counsel, presents a series of challenges for most Canadians.[3] As the chief justice of Canada has acknowledged, "many

1 For a further discussion of other courts in Canada (including small claims courts, courts of appeal, and the federal court) and recent reform initiatives in those courts, see infra Chapter 3. For further discussions of other state-based or sanctioned tribunals, see infra Chapter 4.

2 Sir James Mathew (1830–1908) cited in Susan Denham, "Launch of the Report on Multi-Party Litigation" (The Court Services of Ireland, 27 September 2005) at conclusion, available online: <http://www.courts.ie/courts.ie/library3.nsf/16c93c36d3635d5180256e3f003a4580/97b4a7362c75858f8025708f002f964e?OpenDocument>.

3 See Trevor C.W. Farrow, "Sustainable Professionalism" (2008) 46:1 *Osgoode Hall L.J.* 51 at 96; Trevor C.W. Farrow, "Dispute Resolution, Access to Civil Justice and Legal Education" (2005) 42 *Alta. L. Rev.* 741; Trevor C.W. Farrow, "What is Access to Justice?" (2014) *Osgoode Hall L.J.* (forthcoming). For further access to justice discussions, see, for example, George C. Pavlich, *Justice Fragmented: Mediating Community Disputes*

Canadian men and women find themselves unable, mainly for financial reasons, to access the Canadian justice system."[4] This lack of access to the tools of civil justice, which has, at least significantly, fuelled the engine of privatization, is addressed later in this book.[5]

However, notwithstanding these significant challenges, it is also important to acknowledge that we continue to maintain a very active and robust public court system in this country. Again according to the chief justice of Canada, "Canada has a strong and healthy justice system. Indeed, our courts and justice system are looked to by many countries as exemplary."[6] The animating historical spirit of that system – of openness

---

under Postmodern Conditions (London and New York: Routledge, 1996), c. 2; Roderick A. Macdonald, "Access to Justice and Law Reform" (1990) 10 *Windsor Y.B. Access Just.* 287; Roderick A. Macdonald, "Whose Access? Which Justice?" (1992) 7 *Can. J.L. & Soc.* 175; Roderick A. Macdonald, "Access to Justice in Canada Today: Scope, Scale and Ambitions" in Julia Bass, W. A. Bogart and Frederick H. Zemans, eds., *Access to Justice for a New Century – The Way Forward* (Toronto: Law Society of Upper Canada, 2005), at 19–31, 99–101; Marc Galanter, "Access to Justice as a Moving Frontier" in *Access to Justice for a New Century*, at 147–52; Michael Trebilcock, "Report of the Legal Aid Review 2008" (2008) at 61–70, available online: Legal Aid Ontario <http://www.legalaid.on.ca/en/publications/downloads/advisorygroups/transform-poverty_trebilcock.pdf>; Ab Currie, "A National Survey of the Civil Justice Problems of Low- and Moderate-Income Canadians: Incidence and Patterns" (2006) 13 *Int'l J. Legal Prof.* 217; Lorne Sossin, "The Public Interest, Professionalism, and Pro Bono Publico" (2008) 46:1 *Osgoode Hall L.J.* 131 at 134, n. 5 and accompanying text; and Law Society of Upper Canada, "Accessing the Justice System: Exploring Perceptions" (Focus article on access to justice) *Gazette* 16:1 (Winter 2012), 5. For media coverage, see, for example, John Intini, "No Justice for the Middle Class" *Maclean's* (10–17 September 2007), 68. For an historic discussion of some of these issues, including systemic inequalities, see W. Bogart, *Courts and Country* (Toronto: Oxford University Press, 1994), 107–24, cited in Janet Walker, gen. ed., et al., *The Civil Litigation Process: Cases and Materials*, 6th ed. (Toronto: Emond Montgomery, 2005) at 36–44. See also Allan C. Hutchinson, ed., *Access to Civil Justice* (Toronto: Carswell, 1990). For a relatively recent collection of articles on the topic of access to justice, see Patricia Hughes and Janet E. Mosher, guest eds., "Access to Justice," Special Issue, (2008) 46:4 *Osgoode Hall L. J.* For recent national initiatives, see, for example, the work of the Action Committee on Access to Justice in Civil and Family Matters (materials for which are available online, CFCJ <http://www.cfcj-fcjc.org/collaborations>). For further discussions, see infra Chapters 5 and 7.

4 Rt. Hon. Beverley McLachlin, P.C., "The Challenges We Face" (remarks presented at Empire Club of Canada, Toronto, 8 March 2007), available online: Supreme Court of Canada <http://www.scc-csc.gc.ca/court-cour/judges-juges/spe-dis/bm-2007-03-08-eng.aspx>.

5 See, for example, infra Chapters 5 and 7.

6 Rt. Hon. Beverley McLachlin, P.C., "The Challenges We Face," supra note 4.

to all parties and to all disputes – can be found very early on, for example, in the following promise from the *Magna Carta*: "To. ... none will we deny, to none will we delay right or justice."[7] In modern times, it is the state's court system that, at least in large measure, is provided to make good on this promise of justice. In the year of Canada's confederation, Brooke J.A. of the Ontario Court of Appeal commented (with reference to Justice Willis in *Manor of London v. Cox*[8]) that "nothing shall be intended to be out of the jurisdiction of a superior Court, but that which specifically appears to be so."[9] As such, as with the corresponding Queen's Bench courts in England, if a "right exists, the presumption is that there is a Court which can enforce it."[10]

Modern superior courts in this country enjoy the plenary jurisdiction, power and authority at law and in equity that were historically exercised by the courts of common law and equity in England and subsequently in early Canada[11] and in many of the states in the United

---

7 *Magna Carta*, or *The Great Charter of King John* (15 June 1215) at cl. 40. For a discussion of the *Magna Carta* in the context of early civil procedural reforms, see Adolph J. Rodenbeck, "The New Practice in New York" (1916) 1:2 *Cornell L.Q.* 63 at 76.

8 (1867), 1 E. & I. App. 239 at 259.

9 *80 Wellesley St. East Ltd. v. Fundy Bay Builders Ltd. et al.*, [1972] 2 O.R. 280, Brooke J.A. (C.A.) (QL). See also *Canada (Attorney General) v. TeleZone Inc.*, 2010 SCC 62, [2010] 3 S.C.R. 585 at paras. 42–46, where the Court reemphasizes the wide jurisdictional reach of the superior courts. For a recent general discussion of the court's jurisdiction, see Janet Walker and Lorne Sossin, *Civil Litigation*, 7th ed. (Toronto: Irwin Law, 2010) at 9.

10 *80 Wellesley St. East Ltd. v. Fundy Bay Builders Ltd. et al.*, supra note 9 (referring to Viscount Haldane in *Board v. Board* (1919), 48 D.L.R. 13 at 17–18, [1919] A.C. 956 (P.C.)). For recent discussions of superior court jurisdiction, see *Canada (Attorney General) v. TeleZone Inc.*, supra note 9; *Donaghy v. Scotia Capital Inc./Scotia Capitaux Inc.* (2009), 93 O.R. (3d) 776 (C.A.), leave to appeal to S.C.C. refused, 33068 (May 28, 2009), [2009] S.C.C.A. No. 92 (QL).

11 See, for example, Ontario *Courts of Justice Act*, R.S.O. 1990, c. C.43, s. 11(2); Alberta's *Judicature Act*, R.S.A. 2000, c. J-2, pts. 1–2; Alberta's *Court of Queen's Bench Act*, R.S.A. 2000, c. C-31, s. 2. See also *Constitution Act, 1867*, 30 & 31 Victoria, c. 3 (U.K.), ss. 92(13)–(14), 96–100, 129. For accounts of early Canadian courts, see, for example, William R. Riddell, *The Early Courts of the Province* (Toronto?, 1916? [specific publication details unknown]); William R. Riddell, *Some Early Legislation and Legislators in Upper Canada* (Toronto: Carswell, 1913); William R. Riddell, *The Bar and the Courts of the Province of Upper Canada, or Ontario* (Toronto: Macmillan, 1928); William R. Riddell, *How the King's Bench Came to Toronto* (Toronto? [specific publication details unknown]); William R. Riddell, *The Court of King's Bench in Upper Canada, 1824-1827* (Toronto? [specific publication details unknown]); William R. Riddell, "The

States.[12] This plenary jurisdiction provides courts with "all the powers that are necessary to do justice"[13] (typically within the province[14]). This jurisdiction is generally "unlimited and unrestricted in substantive law in civil matters."[15] Further, it is limited only "where provided specifically to the contrary" by a "special law."[16] A "special law" could, for example, include a law that refers a certain kind of case to the federal

---

Prerogative Court in Upper Canada" in Ontario Historical Society, *Papers and Records* (Toronto: Ontario Historical Society, 1926) at vol. xxii, p. 397; William R. Riddell, "The First Court of Chancery in Canada" (1922) 2 *B.U.L. Rev.* 231; Gerald E. Hart, *The Québec Act, 1774* (Montréal: Gazette Printing, 1891) at 8; Margaret A. Banks, "The Evolution of the Ontario Courts, 1788–1981" in David H. Flaherty, ed., *Essays in the History of Canadian Law*, vol. 2 (Toronto; Buffalo, NY; London: University of Toronto Press, 1983), c. 9, William N. T. Wylie, "Instruments of Commerce and Authority: The Civil Courts in Upper Canada, 1789–1812" in Flaherty, *Essays in the History of Canadian Law*, vol. 2, supra, c. 1; Christopher English, "From Fishing Schooner to Colony: The Legal Development of Newfoundland, 1791–1832" in Louis A. Knafla and Susan W. S. Binnie, eds., *Law, Society, and the State: Essays in Modern Legal History* (Toronto, Buffalo, London: University of Toronto Press, 1995) at c. 3; G. Blaine Baker, "The Reconstitution of Upper Canadian Legal Thought in the Late-Victorian Empire" (1985) 3 *L.H.R.* 219; M.H. Ogilvie, "Recent Developments in Canadian Law: Legal History" (1987) 19 *Ottawa L. Rev.* 225 at 241–46; John Delatre Falconbridge, "Law and Equity in Upper Canada" (1914) 63:1 *U. Pa. L. Rev.* 1; and Sidney T. Miller, "The Development of the Canadian Legal System" (1913) 61:9 *U. Pa. L. Rev.* 625 at 637–42.

12 See, for example, Rodenbeck, "The New Practice in New York," supra note 7 at 65. For accounts of early American courts, see, for example, ibid. at passim; Lawrence M. Friedman, A *History of American Law*, 3rd ed. (New York: Simon & Schuster, 2005) at 7–23, 79–101, 279–92; Kermit L. Hall, *The Magic Mirror: Law in American History* (New York, Oxford: Oxford University Press, 1989); and Deborah A. Rosen, "The Supreme Court of Judicature of Colonial New York: Civil Practice in Transition, 1691–1760" (1987) 5 *L.H.R.* 213. See further Morton J. Horwitz, *The Transformation of American Law, 1780–1860* (Cambridge, MA: Harvard University Press, 1977).

13 *80 Wellesley St. East Ltd. v. Fundy Bay Builders Ltd. et al.*, supra note 9.

14 For rules regarding the service of originating processes both within and without a province, see, for example, Ontario *Rules of Civil Procedure*, R.R.O. 1990, Reg. 194, as amended, rr. 16–17. For a discussion of the extraterritorial application of a provincial superior court's jurisdiction, see Janet Walker, gen. ed., et al., *The Civil Litigation Process: Cases and Materials*, 7th ed. (Toronto: Emond Montgomery, 2010) at 249–71. See also *Club Resorts Ltd. v. Van Breda*, 2012 SCC 17.

15 *80 Wellesley St. East Ltd. v. Fundy Bay Builders Ltd. et al.*, supra note 9. See also *Canada (Attorney General) v. TeleZone Inc.*, supra note 9; *Board v. Board*, supra note 10. For a brief history of the courts in Canada, see *The Civil Litigation Process*, supra note 14 at 18–44.

16 *80 Wellesley St. East Ltd. v. Fundy Bay Builders Ltd. et al.*, supra note 9. See also *Black v. Canada (Prime Minister)* (2001), 54 O.R. (3d) 215 at paras. 66–76 (C.A.).

court of Canada or perhaps to a provincial or federal tribunal.[17] Arbitration legislation also permits parties to agree, by way of arbitration contracts, to put jurisdiction for a given case in the hands of an arbitrator and not the court.[18] Further, forum selection clauses in modern contractual relations also allow parties to limit a court's jurisdiction over certain matters (in favour of a foreign jurisdiction).[19]

Functions of Superior Courts

Retrospective Function: Dispute Resolution

A typical, but incomplete, understanding of the purpose of a civil justice system is that courts exist primarily to resolve disputes. For example, according to Berlins and Dyer, the "courtroom" has for "centuries ... been the setting for the final settlement of disputes."[20] Similarly, according to a more recent treatment of civil justice systems and reform by Alon Klement and Zvika Neeman, the "main goal of the court system is to differentiate between those who obeyed the law and those who did not, and to administer the disputes that are brought before it according

17 For examples of contrary jurisdictional legislation, see Ontario's *Courts of Justice Act*, supra note 11 at s. 148 or Alberta's *Judicature Act*, supra note 11 at s. 27 (recognizing the jurisdiction of the federal court of Canada or the Supreme Court of Canada for certain "controversies"); Ontario *Human Rights Code*, R.S.O. 1990, c. H.19, s. 39 (providing that "[t]he Tribunal has the jurisdiction to exercise the powers conferred on it by or under this Act and to determine all questions of fact or law that arise in any application before it"). See further *Black v. Canada (Prime Minister)*, supra note 16.

18 See, for example, *Commercial Arbitration Act*, R.S.C. 1985 (2nd Supp), c. 17 or, provincially, Alberta's *Arbitration Act*, R.S.A. 2000, c. A-43 (and other similar provincial statutes), all discussed further infra Chapter 4. See also *TeleZone Inc. v. Canada (Attorney General)*, 2008 ONCA 892, 94 O.R. (3d) 19 at 28, para. 5 (aff'd *Canada (Attorney General) v. TeleZone Inc.*, supra note 9), in which the Court of Appeal for Ontario comments specifically on the relationship between arbitration clauses and the court's general jurisdictional reach.

19 See, for example, *Z.I. Pompey Industrie v. ECU-Line N.V.*, [2003] 1 S.C.R. 450; *Expedition Helicopters Inc. v. Honeywell Inc.* (2010), 100 O.R. (3d) 241 (C.A.).

20 Marcel Berlins and Clare Dyer, *The Law Machine*, 3rd ed. (London: Penguin, 1989) at 18. Similarly, when describing the British system of government, Anthony Birch makes only passing reference to the role of courts in the overall process of governing. See Anthony H. Birch, *The British System of Government*, 7th ed. (London: Allen & Unwin, 1986) at 221–4. For a useful background discussion, see Garry D. Watson, "The Structure and Purpose of Civil Procedure" in Walker, gen. ed., et al., *The Civil Litigation Process: Cases and Materials*, 7th ed., supra note 14 at 66.

to substantive law."[21] These descriptions focus on the retrospective function of the judicial system. The court looks backward in time to understand what happened in a given dispute, based on the "facts" of a case, and decides what should have been done, or at least what should now be done, in order to make things right for the immediate parties involved according to settled law. Of course, Klement and Neeman as well as Berlins and Dyer are correct (at least in part): dispute resolution is clearly one of the purposes of a civil justice system. However, it certainly is not its only purpose and, further, is not necessarily always its most important purpose.

Prospective Function: Societal Regulation

There are many aspects to the ways in which we order ourselves and our affairs in society. At the personal level, custom, religion, morality, and tradition, for example, all often play significant roles. These factors and forces help shape what Roberto Unger, borrowing from Charles Fourier, refers to as the "micropolitics of personal relationships."[22] However, once we step out of the spheres of the personal and into the light of a more generalized civil society,[23] increasingly generalized and systematic regimes of rules for governance – largely in the form of laws and legal rules – have been required. As W.H. Jennings has pointed out,

> As soon as man began to live in groups, rules became necessary to govern his relations with his fellows. Even in the most primitive forms of society both the rights of the individual and the common interests of the community were bound to emerge and create a need for governing social relationships.[24]

---

21 Alon Klement and Zvika Neeman, "Civil Justice Reform: A Mechanism Design Framework" (2008) 164 *J. of Institutional and Theoretical Econ.* at 1, available online: SSRN <http://papers.ssrn.com/sol3/papers.cfm?abstract_id=998028>.

22 Roberto M. Unger, *Democracy Realized: The Progressive Alternative* (London and New York: Verso, 1998) at 254. See further Roberto M. Unger, *The Self Awakened: Pragmatism Unbound* (Cambridge, MA, and London: Harvard University Press, 2007), passim.

23 For a discussion of various treatments of the notion of civil society, see Jürgen Habermas, *Between Facts and Norms: Contributions to a Discourse Theory of Law and Democracy*, trans. by William Rehg (Cambridge, MA: MIT Press, 1996) at § 8.3.2, pp. 366–73. See also Charles Taylor, *Philosophical Arguments* (Cambridge, MA; London: Harvard University Press, 1995), c. 13 ("Liberal Politics and the Public Sphere").

24 W.H. Jennings, *Canadian Law: For Business & Personal Use* (Toronto: The Ryerson Press, 1951), 1–2.

The regulation, by laws and legal institutions, of humans – as "political animal[s]"[25] who choose "to live in groups"[26] – is clearly a central concern of political and legal theory that pervades the work, in different ways and to different degrees, throughout the canonical tradition. For example, in his shift from an ideal state in the *Republic* to a law-governed state (albeit still idealized) in *The Laws*, Plato sketched a political theory in which law, conceived of as "the sacred and golden cord of reason,"[27] is "the master of the government."[28] Aquinas, in *Summa Theologica*, discussed a vision of "human" law,[29] "regulated by reason," that "must have as its proper object the well-being of the whole

---

25 Aristotle, *The Politics*, trans. by Carnes Lord (Chicago and London: The University of Chicago Press, 1984) at bk. I, c. 2, 1253a1. For different translations, see, for example, Aristotle, *The Politics*, ed. by Richard McKeon (New York: Random House, 1941); Aristotle, *The Politics*, ed. by Stephen Everson (Cambridge, UK: Cambridge University Press, 1988); Aristotle, *The Politics* in *The Politics of Aristotle*, ed. and trans. by Ernest Barker (Oxford, UK: Oxford University Press, 1969); and Aristotle, *The Politics*, trans. by William Ellis (Buffalo, NY: Prometheus, 1986).

26 Jennings, *Canadian Law: For Business & Personal Use*, supra note 24 at 1–2.

27 Plato, *The Laws*, in *The Dialogues of Plato*, trans. by B. Jowett, vol. v, 3rd ed. (London: Oxford University Press, 1931 imp.) at § 645, 23.

28 Plato, *The Laws*, trans. by Trevor J. Saunders (London: Penguin, 1970) at § 715, 174. For a useful discussion of the distinction between Plato's treatment of law and government in his early and later writings, see George H. Sabine, A *History of Political Theory* (New York: Henry Holt, 1948) at 67–76, 85–6. See also Leo Strauss and Joseph Cropsey, eds., *History of Political Philosophy*, 3rd ed. (Chicago and London: The University of Chicago Press, 1987) at 78–87.

29 Aquinas distinguishes "human law" from "eternal law," "natural law," and "divine law." See, for example, St. Thomas Aquinas, *Summa Theologica*, pt. I.5–11, qu. 91–7, in A.P. D'Entrèves, ed., *Aquinas: Selected Political Writings*, trans. by J. G. Dawson, 6th imp. (Oxford, UK: Basil Blackwell, 1974), at 113–47. See also *St. Thomas Aquinas on Politics and Ethics* (selections from the works of St. Thomas Aquinas), trans. and ed. by Paul E. Sigmund (New York and London: Norton, 1988), at 44–56. For a useful treatment of Aquinas in the context of a modern defense of natural law, see John Finnis, *Natural Law and Natural Rights* (Oxford, UK: Clarendon, 1980). According to Finnis,

> The central case of law and legal system is the law and legal system of a complete community, purporting to have authority to provide comprehensive and supreme direction for human behaviour in that community and to grant legal validity to all other normative arrangements affecting the members of that community.

Finnis, *Natural Law and Natural Rights*, supra at c. X.1, 260. See also generally ibid. at c. X. See further Catherine Kellogg, "Ideas of Justice: Natural and Human" in Austin Sarat et al., eds., *Law and the Humanities, An Introduction* (Cambridge, UK: Cambridge University Press, 2010), c. 5.

community" and the "ordering of the common good."[30] Subsequently, theorists born of the Enlightenment developed a vision of positive law that was part of the necessary architecture of an increasingly complex and secular civil society.[31] That Enlightenment vision of law, and its developing relationship with rights-based procedural and substantive justice, still largely animates the theories of modern liberal democratic legal and political scholars.[32]

Notwithstanding the continued complex and pluralistic nature of the private and public aspects of modern society and its sources of regulation,[33] our social relationships at the level of civil society – contemplated

---

30 Aquinas, *Summa Theologica*, pt. I.4, qu. 90, arts. 1–3, supra note 29 at 111.

31 Hobbes, for example, contemplated a notion of civil law that bound humans once freed from a "solitary" state of nature and as members of a commonwealth. According to Hobbes, "By Civil Lawes, I understand the Lawes, that men are therefore bound to observe, because they are Members, not of this, or that Common-wealth in particular, but of a Common-wealth." Thomas Hobbes, *Leviathan*, ed. by Richard Tuck (Cambridge, UK: Cambridge University Press, 1991) at §§ 62 and 137 (pt. I, c. XIII, p. 89, c. XXVI, p. 183). According to Locke, the "great instrument and means" of making good on the "great end of Mens entering into Society, being the enjoyment of their Properties in Peace and Safety" are "the Laws establish'd in that Society." John Locke, *The Second Treatise of Government: An Essay Concerning the True Origin, Extent, and End of Civil Government* in John Locke, *Two Treatises of Government*, ed. by Peter Laslett, stud. ed. (Cambridge, UK: Cambridge University Press, 1990) at c. XI, § 134.

32 See, for example, John Rawls, *A Theory of Justice*, rev. ed. (Cambridge, MA: Belknap, 1999); John Rawls, *Justice as Fairness: A Restatement*, ed. by Erin Kelly (Cambridge, MA, and London: Belknap Press, 2001); H.L.A. Hart, *The Concept of Law*, 2nd ed. (Oxford, UK: Clarendon Press, 1994); Joseph Raz, *The Authority of Law: Essays on Law and Morality* (Oxford, UK, and New York: Oxford University Press, 1986); Ronald Dworkin, *Law's Empire* (London: Fontana, 1986); R.M. Dworkin, "Is Law a System of Rules?" in R.M. Dworkin, ed., *The Philosophy of Law* (Oxford, UK: Oxford University Press, 1977) at c. II; Ronald Dworkin, *Freedom's Law: The Moral Reading of the American Constitution* (Cambridge, MA: Harvard University Press, 1996); Ronald Dworkin, *A Matter of Principle* (Cambridge, MA: Harvard University Press, 1985); and Ronald Dworkin, *Taking Rights Seriously* (London: Duckworth, 1977).

33 As Rawls correctly points out, other powerful regulating institutions include social rituals, markets, and so on. See *A Theory of Justice*, supra note 32 at §10, p. 48. For further discussions of legal pluralism, particularly from an historical perspective, see, for example, Louis A. Knafla and Susan W.S. Binnie, "Beyond the State: Law and Legal Pluralism in the Making of Modern Societies" in Knafla and Binnie, *Law, Society, and the State: Essays in Modern Legal History*, supra note 11 at c. 1; H. Robert Baker, "Creating Order in the Wilderness: Transplanting the English Law to Rupert's Land, 1835–51" (1999) 17:2 *L.H.R.* 209; Rosen, "The Supreme Court of Judicature of Colonial

earlier for example by Jennings[34] – continue to be governed by two primary regulatory legal tools: legislation and adjudication. As supported by additional public institutions, including the executive branch and increasingly important legislatively created administrative agencies,[35] legislation and adjudication can be seen as the fundamental public law making and resolving mechanisms for societal regulation.[36] They are what Hart and Sacks referred to as the "institutionalization of procedures for the settlement of questions of group concern,"[37] or as the Supreme Court of Canada more recently recognized, the "institutional … aspect" of democracy.[38] Further, according to Raz,

> [L]egal philosophers have been agreed that one of the defining features of law is that it is an institutionalized normative system. Two types of

---

New York: Civil Practice in Transition, 1691–1760" supra note 12 at 235–45. See also generally John McLaren, Hamar Foster, and Chet Orloff, eds., *Law For The Elephant, Law For The Beaver: Essays in the Legal History of the North American West* (Pasadena, CA: Ninth Judicial Circuit Historical Society, 1992); Hall, *The Magic Mirror: Law in American History*, supra note 12; G.R. Rubin and David Sugarman, *Law, Economy and Society, 1750–1914: Essays in the History of English Law* (Oxford, UK: Professional Books Limited, 1984); L.C. Green, *Law and Society* (Dobbs Ferry, NY: Oceana Publications, 1975) at c. 1; and Farrow, "Sustainable Professionalism," supra note 3 at 90–3.

34 See supra note 24 and accompanying text.

35 For a further discussion of administrative agencies, particularly their dispute resolution function, see infra Chapter 4. For a general discussion of the interaction of the branches of government in the context of societal regulation, see, for example, Henry M. Hart, Jr. and Albert M. Sacks, *The Legal Process: Basic Problems in the Making and Application of Law*, ed. by William N. Eskridge, Jr. and Philip P. Frickey (Westbury, NY: Foundation Press, 1994) at c. 1, sec. 1, pp. 3–6; c. 1, sec. 2, pp. 158–74; c. 6, secs. 1–3. See further Albert P. Malone and Allan Karnes, *The American Legal System: Perspectives, Politics, Processes, and Policies*, 2nd ed. (Lanham, MD: Rowman & Littlefield Publishers, 2008). See also Habermas, *Between Facts and Norms*, supra note 23 at c. 5, pp. 194–7; c. 6, p. 238; c. 9, § 9.3.2, 438–43.

36 Blackstone similarly recognized that the "municipal law of England, or the rule of civil conduct prescribed to the inhabitants of this kingdom, may with sufficient propriety be divided into two kinds; … the unwritten or common law; and the … written or statute law." William Blackstone, *Commentaries on the Laws of England* (Oxford, UK: Clarendon Press, 1765–9), elec. ed. (Novi, MI: Lonang Institute, 2005) at intro., sec. 3, available online: Lonang <http://www.lonang.com/exlibris/blackstone/>. See similarly Friedman, A *History of American Law*, supra note 12 at 3.

37 Hart and Sacks, *The Legal Process: Basic Problems in the Making and Application of Law*, supra note 35 at c. 1, sec. 1, pp. 3–4.

38 *Reference re Secession of Québec*, [1998] 2 S.C.R. 217 at para. 61.

> institutions were singled out for special attention: norm-applying institutions such as courts, tribunals ... etc., and norm-creating institutions such as ... parliaments, etc.[39]

Of these two tools, adjudication – the focus of this book – clearly plays a central function in our regulatory state. Indeed, again according to Raz, "the existence of norm-creating institutions though characteristic of modern legal systems is not a necessary feature of all legal systems, but ... the existence of certain types of norm-applying institutions is."[40] Key to this discussion, however, is the recognition that the conceptual distinction between norm-creation and norm-application does not always, or indeed necessarily, map directly onto two distinct institutional tools. Although legislatures only act as norm-creating institutional tools,[41] modern common-law courts – in effect – act as both. Judges apply norms (typically laws) to facts in order to resolve disputes. They also, however, create norms by interpreting and applying existing laws, in the form of precedential judgments, for regulating the future behaviour and the future outcome of similarly situated parties in similarly situated cases or negotiated settlements.

This dual role of the courts was described by de Tocqueville, as follows, in his observations of the U.S. judicial system:

> [J]udicial power ... pronounces on particular cases and not on general principles. [However] [i]f a judge, in deciding a particular question, destroys a general principle, because one is quite sure that all consequences deriving from that principle will be alike undermined, and so the principle becomes barren, he stays within the natural sphere of his authority. ... An American judge can pronounce a decision only when there is litigation. He never concerns himself with anything except a particular case, and to act he must have cognizance of the matter. ... Nevertheless he is invested with immense political power. ... [T]he American judge is dragged in spite of himself onto the political field. He only pronounces on the law because he has to judge a case, and he cannot refuse to decide the case. The political question he has to decide is linked to the litigants' interests, and to refuse to

39 Joseph Raz, *The Authority of Law: Essays on Law and Morality*, supra note 32 at 105.

40 Ibid.

41 I recognize that in some circumstances legislatures delegate significant powers, including norm-creating and norm-applying powers, to administrative agencies, which are further discussed in the following. See infra at Chapter 4.

> deal with it would be a denial of justice. It is by fulfilling the narrow duties imposed on his status as a judge that he also acts as a citizen.[42]

Similarly, John Stuart Mill, when describing English law and its "adaptation of barbarous laws to the growth of civilised society," recognized that much of this legal development was done by "stealth" through the court system.[43] These "adaptations," according to Mill, were "generally made by the courts of justice, who could not help reading the new wants of mankind in the cases between man and man which came before them; but who, having no authority to make new laws for those new wants, were obliged to do the work covertly."[44]

More recently, Mirjan Damaška described the "two faces of adjudication" as including "conflict-solving" and "policy-implementing" functions.[45] Similarly, Habermas recognizes the dual – retrospective and prospective – aspects of the public adjudicative role as framed by modern rules of civil procedure: "The institutionalized self-reflection of law promotes individual legal protection from two points of view, that of achieving justice in the individual case and that of consistency in the application and further development of law."[46] Ronald Dworkin has also recognized the norm-creating function of the court (in addition to its dispute resolution function): "judicial decisions affect a great many … people … because the law often becomes what judges say it is."[47] Duncan Kennedy pushes this judicial norm-creation discussion further by fully recognizing not only the "judicial law making" function but also its history as an active "vehicle of ideological projects."[48]

In these norm-creation senses, then, courts play a central role in public governance structures. Numbers of commentators have made this

---

42 Alexis de Tocqueville, *Democracy in America*, trans. by George Lawrence, ed. by J.P. Mayer (New York: Perennial, 2000) at 100, 103.

43 John Stuart Mill, "Bentham" (August 1838) *London and Westminster Review* in John Stuart Mill, *Utilitarianism, On Liberty, Essay on Bentham*, ed. by Mary Warnock (New York: Meridian, 1962) 78 at 108.

44 Ibid. For a further background discussion of the various roles and functions of courts, see Hart and Sacks, *The Legal Process: Basic Problems in the Making and Application of Law*, supra note 35 at c. 3, pp. 341–4.

45 Mirjan R. Damaška, *The Faces of Justice and State Authority: A Comparative Approach to the Legal Process* (New Haven, CT: Yale University Press, 1986) at 88.

46 Habermas, *Between Facts and Norms*, supra note 23 at § 5.3.4, p. 236; § 6.1.2, pp. 244–6.

47 Ronald Dworkin, *Law's Empire*, supra note 32 at 2.

48 Duncan Kennedy, A *Critique of Adjudication (fin de siècle)* (Cambridge, MA: Harvard University Press, 1997) at 1. See further ibid. at *passim*. See also Horwitz, *The Transformation of American Law, 1780–1860*, supra note 12.

point in various ways. For example, as Héctor Fix-Fierro comments, courts "participate openly in the constitutional and political process" and have become a "real branch of government, at least in the sense that they now play an important role in shaping the general direction of society."[49] Similarly, again according to de Tocqueville, when commenting on the nineteenth-century U.S. judicial system, "Judicial institutions exercise a great influence on the fate of the Anglo-Americans; they have a very important place among their political institutions properly so called. ... [C]ourts are the most obvious organs through which the legal body influences democracy."[50] Miguel Schor has also recently commented, particularly with respect to courts that wield modern U.S.-style powers of judicial review (which fuel ongoing debates about "judicial activism"), that "courts ... are powerful political as well as legal actors."[51]

---

49 Héctor Fix-Fierro, *Courts, Justice and Efficiency: A Socio-Legal Study of Economic Rationality in Adjudication* (Oxford, UK, and Portland, OR: Hart Publishing, 2003) at 14–15. For further discussions, see Ian Greene, "The Courts and Democracy" in Ian Greene, *The Courts* (Vancouver: UBC Press, 2006) at c. 6; Peter H. Russell, *The Judiciary in Canada: The Third Branch of Government* (Toronto: McGraw-Hill Ryerson, 1987); Peter H. Russell, "Judicial Power in Canada's Political Culture" in F.L. Morton, ed., *Law, Politics and the Judicial Process in Canada* (Calgary: University of Calgary Press, 1989) at c. 2; and Paul Weiler, *In the Last Resort: A Critical Study of the Supreme Court of Canada* (Toronto: Carswell, 1974) at cc. 2–3.

50 *Democracy in America*, supra note 42 at 138, 269. Further, according to de Tocqueville, "[a]n American judge, armed with the right to declare laws unconstitutional, is constantly intervening in political affairs. He cannot compel the people to make laws, but at least he can constrain them to be faithful to their own laws and remain in harmony with themselves." Ibid. at 269. The same observation could essentially be made today, both of U.S. judges and of Canadian judges.

51 Miguel Schor, "Judicial Review and American Constitutional Exceptionalism" (2008) 46:3 *Osgoode Hall L.J.* 535 at 537. See also Gerald Baier, *Courts and Federalism: Judicial Doctrine in the United States, Australia, and Canada* (Vancouver: UBC Press, 2006).

Debates continue as to the extent and propriety of "judge-made law" (as opposed to law made by a majority of the people through their elected officials), which some criticize as improper judicial activism. This issue is taken up further in Chapter 6. For previous comments of mine on this issue, see, for example, Trevor C.W. Farrow, "Re-Framing the Sharia Arbitration Debate" (2006) 15:2 *Const. Forum Const.* 79 at 82, n. 50 and accompanying text. For an early but useful commentary, see John Austin, *The Province of Jurisprudence Determined* in *The Province of Jurisprudence Determined Etc.* (London: Weidenfeld and Nicolson, 1954) lecture v, "Note," 184 at 191, in which Austin – when disagreeing with Bentham's criticism of "judge-made" law – stated,

Finally, similar descriptions of the role of courts in our regulatory state come from judges of the Supreme Court of Canada as well as other courts. Judges very much see themselves as a legitimate part of this democratic landscape. For example, according to Justice LeBel of the Supreme Court of Canada, "courts play a key role in a democracy."[52] Alberta's former chief justice stated that "what happens in the courthouse has a profound impact upon what happens in the community. And when I say 'community,' I am not just referring [to] the legal community, but rather the community at large."[53] Similarly, according to the

---

> I by no means disapprove of what Mr. Bentham has chosen to call by the disrespectful, and therefore, as I conceive, injudicious, name of judge-made law. For I consider it injudicious to call by any name indicative of disrespect what appears to me highly beneficial and even absolutely necessary. I cannot understand how any person who has considered the subject can suppose that society could possibly have gone on if judges had not legislated, or that there is any danger whatever in allowing them that power which they have in fact exercised, to make up for the negligence or the incapacity of the avowed legislator. The part of the law of every country which was made by judges has been far better made than that part which consists of statutes enacted by the legislative. Notwithstanding my great admiration for Mr. Bentham, I cannot but think that, instead of blaming judges for having legislated, he should blame them for the timid, narrow, and piecemeal manner in which they have legislated, and for legislating under cover of vague and indeterminate phrases.

For Bentham's concerns about the role and function of the judiciary, see, for example, Jeremy Bentham, *Principles of Judicial Procedure, with the Outlines of a Procedural Code*, cc. ii, iv in *The Works of Jeremy Bentham*, ed. by John Bowring, vol. 2 (Edinburgh: William Tait, 1843) in Online Library of Liberty ed., online: Liberty Fund <http://oll.libertyfund.org>. For a useful discussion of Bentham's concerns about judge-made law, see Neil Duxbury, *The Nature and Authority of Precedent* (Cambridge, UK and New York: Cambridge University Press, 2008) 43. See generally Albert Venn Dicey, *Lectures on the Relation between Law and Public Opinion in England during the Nineteenth Century*, 2nd ed. (London: Macmillan, 1919); John Austin, *Lectures on Jurisprudence Or the Philosophy of Positive Law*, rev. ed. by Robert Campbell (London: John Murray, 1885); William B. Hornblower, "A Century of Judge-Made Law" (1907) 7:7 *Colum. L. Rev.* 453; Oliver Wendell Holmes, "Law and the Court" (1913) in Oliver Wendell Holmes, *Collected Legal Papers* (New York: Peter Smith, 1952) 291 at 296; and John Hart Ely, *Democracy and Distrust: A Theory of Judicial Review* (Cambridge, MA: Harvard University Press, 1980).

52 *Named Person v. Vancouver Sun*, [2007] 3 S.C.R. 252, para. 85.

53 Hon. Allan H. J. Wachowich, "Opening of the Court 2009" (Address by Chief Justice of Court of Queen's Bench of Alberta, 7 January 2009, Courtroom 317, Edmonton Law Courts, Alberta) at 4, available online: Alberta Courts <http://www.albertacourts.ab.ca/LinkClick.aspx?fileticket=lf4Lt8v3cmA%3d&tabid=69&mid=704>.

chief justice of Canada, "[j]udges give effect to our laws and give meaning to our rights and duties as Canadians. Courts offer a venue for the peaceful resolution of disputes, and for the reasoned and dispassionate discussion of our most pressing social issues."[54] This "discussion" includes reviewing the law in light of current societal expectations. Again according to the chief justice of Canada,

> "Judges can and should adapt the common law to reflect the changing social, moral and economic fabric of the country." It is implicit in this duty that the courts will, from time to time, take a fresh look at the common law and re-evaluate its consistency with evolving societal expectations through the lens of *Charter* values.[55]

An "Essential Condition of Democracy"[56]

So where does all of this leave us? Taken together, the previous historic, academic, and judicial discussions, in sum, clearly see a dual role for courts, which is to provide a robust, retrospectively looking public dispute resolution system, as well as a predictable, accessible, and just prospectively looking common law-based regulatory regime. As such, superior courts clearly play a central regulatory role in rule-of-law-based democracies. They have done so for some time now. For example, when referring to the development of the modern courts in England after the passing of the *Judicature Acts* of 1873–1875 and into the twentieth century, R.M. Jackson argued that the "growth and expansion of the King's Courts was doubtless an excellent thing for the building of a uniform law and standard of justice."[57] Similarly, in this country, courts provide an adjudication tool that has, as several commentators have noted, played and continues to play an "instrumental"

54 Rt. Hon. Beverley McLachlin, P.C., "Welcome," available online: Supreme Court of Canada <http://www.scc-csc.gc.ca/home-accueil>.

55 *Grant v. Torstar*, 2009 SCC 61, [2009] 3 S.C.R. 640 at para. 46, citing *R. v. Salituro*, [1991] 3 S.C.R. 654 at 670, Iacobucci J.

56 See infra note 60 and accompanying text.

57 J.R. Spencer, ed., *Jackson's Machinery of Justice* (Cambridge, UK: Cambridge University Press, 1989) at 8. At the same time, however, Jackson does acknowledge that uniformity of courts in England did come potentially at the price of "competing courts which were perhaps more suitable for poor litigants and small cases." Ibid.

role in the "historical development of Canada" and in its "economic growth"[58] and that, therefore, continues to be "an essential component of our democratic form of government."[59] Again according to Chief Justice Beverley McLachlin (when characterizing the role of courts in the democratic process),

> [C]ourts are seen as ways of compensating for the weaknesses of electoral decision-making and contributing to deliberative democracy by providing a forum where citizens can test laws for conformity to the fundamental values upon which the society is premised – the shared commitments and values that constitute the deeper community constitutional morality. ... These values may be at risk of being overlooked or overridden in the short-term perspective of elected legislators. Yet they are fundamental to deliberative democracy, the goal of which is decisions that best represent the interests of the community as [a] whole. Independent courts thus emerge as an essential condition of democracy.[60]

The specific procedural mechanisms used by courts, which in turn enable them to operate effectively in their role as an "essential condition of democracy," create power at both the retrospective and prospective levels of the judicial function. As I have stated elsewhere, when speaking about the specific processes and impacts of civil procedure (domestically and internationally),

58 M.H. Ogilvie, "Recent Developments in Canadian Law: Legal History" (1987) 19 *Ottawa L. Rev.* 225 at 237, 239.

59 Wayne D. Brazil, "Hosting Mediations as a Representative of the System of Civil Justice" (2007) 22 *Ohio St. J. Disp. Resol.* 227 at 241. For comments that these progressive values were more present in U.S. than in Canadian courts in the 1800s and early 1900s, see Ogilvie, "Recent Developments in Canadian Law: Legal History," supra note 58 at 250–1. See also Bogart, *Courts and Country*, supra note 3. Regardless, the influence of the courts on the development of economic and social relations in Canada, particularly over the past twenty-five years, is undeniable.

60 Rt. Hon. Beverley McLachlin, P.C., "Judges in a Multicultural Society" (paper presented at Chief Justice of Ontario's Advisory Committee on Professionalism, First Colloquium on the Legal Profession, "Inaugural Colloquium on the Legal Profession," 20 October 2003, Faculty of Law, University of Western Ontario) at 3-5–3-6, available online: LSUC <http://www.lsuc.on.ca/media/mclachlin_judges_multicultura_society.pdf>. For a further discussion of deliberative democracy, see, for example, Habermas, *Between Facts and Norms*, supra note 23.

> Civil procedure is, in the end, about power. It is about power – albeit often retrospectively – to regulate individual and corporate behaviour. It is about power to manage efficiently and resolve expectations, transactions, and disputes. And, ultimately, it is about power to access meaningful substantive rights and remedies in a fair and fulsome way. In the context of globalization and international human rights, far from merely being a tool of parochial domestic process, civil procedure has become a gatekeeper in this era of modern commerce and social intercourse: a gatekeeper to the access of meaningful justice – through the protection and/or the recognition of basic rights and liberties – for parties involved in civil matters with global contacts.[61]

There is no doubt, given the challenges posed by the realities of the cost and inaccessibility of modern superior courts, that the procedural power at stake here often militates in favour of parties who already enjoy a power advantage in society (financial or otherwise). In this sense, courts can be seen as venues that simply distribute power to power. Although the public justice system is becoming increasingly inaccessible to ordinary people for several reasons, the primary barriers largely stem from the significant costs of the court process as well as, often, from the financial inequalities of potential users of the system. These challenges, as mentioned earlier, provide significant justifications for the privatization movement discussed in the following chapter and again in Chapter 5. However, as I discuss later on,[62] the answer is not simply always to acquiesce to (or indeed to encourage) the current privatization trajectory (as we currently do). Doing so potentially further aggravates imbalances of power by simply taking the imbalances that exist in the public sphere and shifting them behind closed doors to unregulated private venues.[63] Parties will typically retain the choice to make those moves to the private, which is sometimes a good thing. However, we need a balance. Because, as I also argue, there are many disputes for which the court system, guided by fair procedures administered under the watchful eye of the public, is more appropriate for

61 Trevor C.W. Farrow, "Globalization, International Human Rights, and Civil Procedure" (2003) 41 *Alta. L. Rev.* 671 at 673 [footnote omitted].

62 See generally infra Chapters 6 and 7.

63 For an earlier comment on this move to the private, see Trevor C.W. Farrow, "The Rule of Law in Developing Countries Is Not Just about Courts" 26:31 *The Lawyers Weekly* (15 December 2006) 11.

redressing power imbalances and resulting injustices that can have far-reaching implications for disputants as well as the wider community. Privatization, therefore, does not always flatten power imbalances (by providing, for example, more informal processes that might be more accessible to more people). In fact, in some cases, such as in the Dealership case that I discuss further later on, it can aggravate them.

In addition to power issues between litigants, often – but not exclusively – seen most sharply at the dispute resolution level of the court's operations (either by parties having less money or inadequate representation, or simply by being excluded altogether because of cost or other access issues that I discuss later on in this book), there is another form of power at stake here, this time at play largely at the prospective, societal regulation level. This is a shared institutional power[64] along the lines of what I earlier identified as the power for citizens to "access meaningful justice,"[65] or put differently, what the chief justice of Canada identified as the court's role in "contributing to deliberative democracy by providing a forum where citizens can test laws for conformity to the fundamental values upon which the society is premised – the shared commitments and values that constitute the deeper community constitutional morality."[66] What I am talking about here, at heart, is the court's democratic institutional role, or what makes the court, according to the chief justice of Canada, "an essential condition of democracy."[67]

Liberal democratic theorists and legal positivists – clearly influenced by rights-based Enlightenment sensibilities but firmly entrenched in modern, robust, rule-of-law values (values that I discuss further later) – take the view that the role of law, including the law developed by courts, is essentially to frame a landscape in which fair contests of rights can take place. Formal institutional structures, including laws and courts, are put in place to regulate the relationships and distributional choices of citizens in social life. For example, according to Joseph Raz,

64 For a useful discussion of institutional power and process, see Habermas, *Between Facts and Norms*, supra note 23 at § 8.3.1, p. 363.

65 Farrow, "Globalization, International Human Rights, and Civil Procedure," supra note 61 at 673.

66 Rt. Hon. Beverley McLachlin, P.C., "Judges in a Multicultural Society," supra note 60.

67 Ibid.

> The law provides the general framework within which social life takes place. It is a system for guiding behavior and for settling disputes which claims supreme authority to interfere in any kind of activity. It also regularly either supports or restricts the creation and practice of other norms in the society. By making these claims the law claims to provide the general framework for the conduct of all aspects of social life and sets itself up as the supreme guardian of society.[68]

Similarly, according to Rawls, "the law defines the basic structure within which the pursuit of all other activities takes place."[69]

Important to this liberal vision of the role of law and courts is a requirement that, subject to some basic procedural and constitutional requirements (discussed below), citizens must be free to pursue their own notion of the good life. Courts – premised on a procedural architecture that acts as a precondition, or gatekeeper, to substantive justice – are largely there to provide citizens with the procedural tools with which to realize their substantive rights and interests. The state, which directly or indirectly appoints judges and operates (although importantly does not control) the courts is neutral vis-à-vis the parties' substantive claims, provided that their claims are at least within the bounds of what the state has predetermined as a minimally acceptable landscape on which to participate. Beyond that, the parties are free to conduct their affairs, pursuant to fulfilling their life interests, in any way they choose. For example, parties are welcome to make and contest good or bad bargains; they are not, however, welcome to make or contest illegal ones. As such, the state, under this liberal notion of democratic participation, prioritizes the right over – or at least as a precondition for – the good. In the specific context of the civil justice system, citizens are free to pursue their legal rights and interests largely unconstrained by any particular obligations stemming from what the state might think about those rights and interests.[70]

Intimately connected to this overall liberal premise of the system are the substantive core values that animate that system, specifically

68 Joseph Raz, *The Authority of Law: Essays on Law and Morality*, supra note 32 at 120–1.
69 John Rawls, *A Theory of Justice*, supra note 32 at §38, p. 207. See further John Rawls, *Justice as Fairness: A Restatement*, supra note 32 at §4.
70 See further Trevor C.W. Farrow, "The Good, the Right, and the Lawyer" (2012) 15:1 *Legal Ethics* 163 at 165.

including robust notions of constitutionalism and the rule of law.[71] These values typically delineate, in essence, what I described earlier as the "minimally acceptable landscape" on which the court process plays out. Again, courts are central to the development and maintenance of those core values. Without these core values, any amount of preference for an open – public – system would not advance the project and the legitimacy of liberal democracy. What is at stake here, in essence, is what Rawls contemplates as the difference between a procedural democracy and a constitutional democracy. For Rawls, a procedural democracy is one "in which there are no constitutional limits on legislation and whatever a majority ... enacts is law, provided the appropriate procedures ... are followed."[72] In contrast, a constitutional democracy, according to Rawls, is one "in which law and statutes must be consistent with certain fundamental rights and liberties."[73]

A useful place to look for the court's understanding and treatment of these underlying core values that animate the adjudicative elements of democracy's "institutional ... aspect[s],"[74] including its own understanding of its place and legitimacy in the constitutional process, is the Supreme Court of Canada's judgment in *Reference re Secession of Québec*.[75] To contextualize the importance of these underlying values, the court first looked at the place of democracy, which it described as "a fundamental value in our constitutional law and political culture."[76]

71 The concept of the "rule of law" is enshrined in Canada's constitutional documents as an animating principle on which the country is founded. See *Canadian Charter of Rights and Freedoms, Part I of the Constitution Act, 1982*, being Schedule B to the *Canada Act 1982* (U.K.), 1982, c. 11, pt. 1, preamble, which provides that "Canada is founded upon principles that recognize the supremacy of God and the rule of law." For further treatments of the concept of the "rule of law," see infra notes 80–5 and accompanying text.

72 See Rawls, *Justice as Fairness*, supra note 32 at § 44.1, p. 145.

73 See ibid. When thinking about Rawls' articulation of political theory and justice, it is important to recall that his arguments are framed in the context of tiers – or levels – of justice. Specifically, he distinguished between "levels" of justice: "local," "domestic," and "global." He was primarily concerned with the "domestic" level of justice, which contemplated "principles applying to the basic structure of society," and then, secondarily, with the other levels of justice. See ibid. at § 4.2.

74 *Reference re Secession of Québec*, supra note 38 at para. 61.

75 Ibid.

76 Ibid.

The court understood and accepted the democracy principle very much as informing the contours of our constitutional regime. The principle does so, according to the court, by acting as "an essential interpretive consideration" in the form of "a baseline against which the framers of our Constitution, and subsequently, our elected representatives under it, have always operated."[77] With this baseline vision in mind, the court proceeded to articulate its vision of democracy's connection to the fundamental substantive goals of society. Key to this discussion is the court's articulation of an institutional framework – clearly including the judiciary – that fosters the achievement of those substantive goals. According to the court, democracy "is not simply concerned with the process of government. On the contrary ... democracy is fundamentally connected to substantive goals."[78]

In order to make sense of these institutional requirements of a democratic process, the court pointed to the underlying and fundamental preconditional principles of the rule of law and constitutionalism, which are found at the core of a democratic system of government. For the court, democracy "cannot exist without the rule of law."[79] The rule of law, the specific elements of which are discussed further below,[80] provides – at its core – that law is supreme over the acts of both governments and private persons[81] and that citizens are protected from arbitrary state action.[82] Further, it is required for the notion of the sovereign will to be realized and implemented, as well as to legitimize the institutional arrangements that are pursued under a constitutional regime.[83] According to the court, the rule of law – at what it described as its

77 Ibid. at para. 62.

78 Ibid. at para. 64. The Court went on to hold that "[i]n considering the scope and purpose of the *Charter*, the Court in *R. v. Oakes*, [1986] 1 S.C.R. 103, articulated some of the values inherent in the notion of democracy (at p. 136): 'The Court must be guided by the values and principles essential to a free and democratic society which ... embody ... faith in social and political institutions which enhance the participation of individuals and groups in society ...'." *Reference re Secession of Québec*, ibid. at para. 64.

79 Ibid. at para. 67.

80 See infra at notes 98–106 and accompanying text.

81 According to the Court, "[t]here is, in short, one law for all." Ibid. at para. 71.

82 Ibid. at para. 70.

83 According to the Court,

> The consent of the governed is a value that is basic to our understanding of a free and democratic society. Yet democracy in any real sense of the word cannot exist without the rule of law. It is the law that creates the framework within which the 'sovereign will' is to be ascertained and implemented. To be accorded

"most basic" level – "vouchsafes to the citizens and residents of the country a stable, predictable and ordered society in which to conduct their affairs."[84] The court went on to provide, however, that "adherence to law alone" is not adequate.[85] Not unlike Rawls's distinction between a procedural democracy and a constitutional democracy,[86] the court very much sees the legitimacy of a system of government to be bound up with its democratic underpinnings, which reflect the "aspirations of the people."[87] However, even this is not enough fully to establish the legitimacy of law and the regime by which it is created. Settled procedures, which militate to the benefit of the majority, are not always necessarily legitimate per se in a constitutional democracy. Other values, those which the court referred to as "moral values," many of which it holds "are imbedded in our constitutional structure," are necessary in order for a law and legal regime to claim legitimacy.[88] Otherwise, as the court warns, it "would be a grave mistake to equate legitimacy with the 'sovereign will' or majority rule alone, to the exclusion of other constitutional values."[89]

Clearly, this model of the constitutional and rule of law premises for Canada's system of democratic government, as largely articulated by the court, is consistent with a liberal democratic vision of law and courts as regulatory tools in society.[90] With this articulation in hand, the

---

legitimacy, democratic institutions must rest, ultimately, on a legal foundation. That is, they must allow for the participation of, and accountability to, the people, through public institutions created under the Constitution. ... The principles of constitutionalism and the rule of law lie at the root of our system of government. The rule of law, as observed in *Roncarelli v. Duplessis*, [1959] S.C.R. 121, at p. 142, is "a fundamental postulate of our constitutional structure."

See ibid. at paras. 67 and 70.

84 Ibid. at para. 70.

85 Ibid. at para. 67.

86 See supra note 72 and accompanying text.

87 *Reference re Secession of Québec*, supra note 38 at para. 67. According to the Court, "a system of government cannot survive through adherence to the law alone. A political system must also possess legitimacy, and in our political culture, that requires an interaction between the rule of law and the democratic principle. The system must be capable of reflecting the aspirations of the people." Ibid.

88 Ibid.

89 Ibid.

90 For other treatments of the role of law and courts as central aspects to the democratic process, see supra notes 36–60 and 64–73 and accompanying text.

court has proceeded to drill deeper by discussing the specifics of the principle of "constitutionalism,"[91] as well as that principle's difference from, and connection to, the "rule of law" principle. According to the court, the constitutionalism principle "bears considerable similarity to the rule of law, although they are not identical."[92] Constitutionalism, which it identifies as being embodied in s. 52(1) of the *Constitution Act, 1982*,[93] requires that all acts of government comply with Canada's constitution.[94] The rule of law, although similar, requires specifically that all acts of government comply with the law, which includes Canada's constitution.[95] A key element of the Supreme Court's treatment of the rule of law is its recognition that the principles of constitutionalism and the rule of law, together, exist as a necessary precondition to the institution of democracy. Constitutional supremacy, as backstopped by the rule of law, allows for the proper functioning of political decision making in a liberal democracy. Put simply, constitutionalism and the rule of law, as operationalized through a public court system, are pivotal for a functioning democracy.[96] According to the court,

> [W]ith the adoption of the *Charter*, the Canadian system of government was transformed to a significant extent from a system of Parliamentary supremacy to one of constitutional supremacy. ... It might be objected. ... that constitutionalism is. ... incompatible with democratic government. This would be an erroneous view. Constitutionalism facilitates – indeed, makes possible – a democratic political system by creating an orderly framework within which people may make political decisions. Viewed correctly,

91 For further, non-judicial treatments of "constitutionalism" and the fundamental norms underlying that concept, see, for example, Rawls, *Justice as Fairness: A Restatement*, supra note 32 at §44; Finnis, *Natural Law and Natural Rights*, supra note 29 at § X.4, pp. 272–3. See also generally Hart, *A Concept of Law*, 2nd ed., supra note 32 at c. vi.

92 *Reference re Secession of Québec*, supra note 38 at para. 72.

93 *Constitution Act, 1982*, being Schedule B to the *Canada Act 1982* (U.K.), 1982, c. 11, s. 52(1), which provides that "[t]he Constitution of Canada is the supreme law of Canada, and any law that is inconsistent with the provisions of the Constitution is, to the extent of the inconsistency, of no force or effect."

94 According to the Court, "[s]imply put, the constitutionalism principle requires that all government action comply with the Constitution." *Reference re Secession of Québec*, supra note 38 at para. 72.

95 Ibid.

96 Ibid. at para. 78.

> constitutionalism and the rule of law are not in conflict with democracy; rather, they are essential to it.[97]

In terms of the actual specific elements of the rule of law, the court recognized that it is a "highly textured" concept and includes "many things."[98] For the purpose of this book, which is largely focussed on process, several of those "many things," according to the court, include "a sense of orderliness, of subjection to known legal rules and of executive accountability to legal authority."[99] Further, it requires "the creation and maintenance of an actual order of positive laws which preserves and embodies the more general principle of normative order,"[100] and that "the exercise of all public power must find its ultimate source in a legal rule"[101] (or, put differently, that "the relationship between the state and the individual must be regulated by law"[102]). Without publicity of societal rules, through published laws and open judicial processes,[103] key aspects of the rule of law are missing. And taken together, these considerations make up, for the court, what it describes as a "principle of profound constitutional and political significance."[104]

A different treatment of the principle of the rule of law comes from John Finnis. Without needing to adopt his natural law theory of law, I do find that his multi-faceted articulation of the concept of the rule of law is particularly clear as well as particularly instructive for the purpose of this book. Finnis, like the Supreme Court of Canada, acknowledges

---

97 Ibid. at paras. 72 and 78. For further commentary regarding judicial review and potential concerns surrounding the notion of judicial activism, see supra note 51 and accompanying text. See also infra at Chapter 6.

98 *Reference re Secession of Québec*, supra note 38 at para. 70 [reference omitted].

99 Ibid. [reference omitted].

100 Ibid. at 71 [reference omitted].

101 Ibid. [reference omitted].

102 Ibid.

103 Discussed further infra.

104 *Reference re Secession of Québec*, supra note 38 at para. 71. See further *British Columbia (Attorney General) v. Christie*, [2007] 1 S.C.R. 873, paras. 19–21; *British Columbia v. Imperial Tobacco Canada Ltd.*, [2005] 2 S.C.R. 473, paras. 57–77; and *Charkaoui v. Canada (Citizenship and Immigration)*, [2007] 1 S.C.R. 350, para. 134; *Re: Resolution to amend the Constitution*, [1981] 1 S.C.R. 753 at 805–6; *Manitoba Language Rights Reference*, [1985] 1 S.C.R. 721 at 747–52; *Provincial Judges Reference*, [1997] 3 S.C.R. 3 at para. 10. See generally *Sauvé v. Canada (Chief Electoral Officer)*, 2002 SCC 68, [2002] 3 S.C.R. 519.

that there are a number of aspects to the concept. According to Finnis, a legal system "exemplifies" the rule of law to the extent that

- "its rules are prospective, not retroactive," and "are not in any other way impossible to comply with";
- "its rules are promulgated," "clear," and "coherent one with another";
- "its rules are sufficiently stable to allow people to be guided by their knowledge of the content of the rules";
- "the making of decrees and orders applicable to relatively limited situations is guided by rules that are promulgated, clear, stable, and relatively general";
- "those people who have authority to make, administer, and apply the rules in an official capacity" are "accountable for their compliance with rules applicable to their performance" and "do actually administer the law consistently and in accordance with its tenor";
- its judiciary is "independent";
- it maintains an "openness of court proceedings";
- its courts have "the power. ... to review the proceedings and actions not only of other courts but of most other classes of official"; and
- its courts are accessible "to all, including the poor."[105]

---

105 Finnis, *Natural Law and Natural Rights*, supra note 29 at § X.4, pp. 270–1. In Finnis's discussion, he identifies "eight desideratum" (elements) of the rule of law, together with "further desiderata" derived from "histori[c] experience." See ibid. The set of considerations that I have cited earlier from Finnis collapses the "eight" and "histori[c]" desiderata into one list.

For further, non-judicial discussions of the principle of the "rule of law," see, for example, Rawls, *A Theory of Justice*, supra note 32 at § 38; Rawls, *Justice as Fairness: A Restatement*, supra note 32 at § 4, p. 10 (discussing society's "basic structure," which, according to Rawls, "secures what we may call background justice") and ibid. at § 9.3, p. 28; Lon Fuller, *The Morality of Law*, rev. ed. (New Haven, CT, and London: Yale University Press, 1969) at c. II; Joseph Raz, *The Authority of Law: Essays on Law and Morality*, supra note 32 at c. 11; Joseph Raz, *Ethics in the Public Domain: Essays in the Morality of Law and Politics* (Oxford: Clarendon Press, 1994) at c. 16; Dworkin, *Law's Empire*, supra note 32 at 93; and Habermas, *Between Facts and Norms*, supra note 23 at Postscript (1994), § 3, p. 455.

For an earlier treatment, see Benjamin Constant, "Liberty of the Ancients Compared with That of the Moderns" (1819) in Benjamin Constant, *Political Writings*, trans. and ed. by Biancamaria Fontana (New York: Cambridge University Press, 1988), cited in Rawls, *Justice as Fairness: A Restatement*, supra note 32 at § 1.1, n. 1 and accompanying text. According to Constant, the "liberties of the moderns" – derived from Locke – included the freedom of thought and liberty of conscience, certain

There is clearly overlap between the treatment of the rule of law by the Supreme Court of Canada and the treatment by Finnis. Again, for modern civil justice systems, specific attention must be paid to Finnis's articulation that the rule of law requires that a society

- has rules that are "clear," "prospective" and not "retroactive";
- has rules that "allow people to be guided by their knowledge of. … the rules";
- maintains an "openness of court proceeding"; and
- has courts that are "accessible."[106]

Although all these aspects of the rule of law identified by Finnis are distinct elements, they do have a common thread that joins them: they contemplate a public system through requirements of openness, knowledge, and accessibility. It is this notion of "public" that is at the heart of this book. Put differently, it is the idea that, by privatizing significant sections of the adjudicative function, we are systematically – and knowingly – treading on key rule of law protections and thereby are at risk of impoverishing a significant aspect of the democratic process.

I will shortly turn to the open nature of the court system. Before doing so, however, it is important to recognize that the rights-based sense of liberalism that I have been discussing – what Taylor refers to as the "popular" or "dominant" sense of liberalism[107] – and the resulting role for law and courts contemplated by that vision (that clearly

---

basic personal and property rights, and the rule of law. The "liberties of the ancients," in contrast – derived from Rousseau – included equal political liberties and values of public life. See Rawls, *Justice as Fairness: A Restatement*, ibid.

For various (and diverse) foundational accounts, see, for example, Aristotle, *The Politics*, trans. by Lord, supra note 25 at bk. 4, c. 4, 1292a30; Aquinas, *Summa Theologica*, pt. I.10, qu. 96, in D'Entrèves, ed., *Aquinas: Selected Political Writings*, trans. by J.G. Dawson, supra note 29 at 138; Niccolo Machiavelli, *Discourses*, intro. by Max Lerner (New York: Random House, 1950) at 103; Hobbes, *Leviathan*, supra note 31 at § 137 (pt. 2, c. XXVI, p. 183); Locke, *The Second Treatise of Government*, supra note 31 at cc. IX–XV; Adam Smith, *An Inquiry into the Nature and Causes of the Wealth of Nations*, ed. by Edwin Cannan (Chicago: The University of Chicago Press, 1967) at vol. 2, bk. V, c. I, pt. II ("Of the Expense of Justice"), p. 244; and John Stuart Mill, *Utilitarianism* (1863) in John Stuart Mill, *Utilitarianism, On Liberty, Essay on Bentham*, ed. by Warnock, supra note 43 at c. v; Albert Venn Dicey, *Introduction to the Study of the Law of the Constitution*, 10th rev. ed. (London: Palgrave Macmillan, 1961).

106 Finnis, *Natural Law and Natural Rights*, supra note 29 at § X.4, pp. 270–1.

107 Charles Taylor, "Cross Purposes: The Liberal-Communitarian Debate" in Charles Taylor, *Philosophical Arguments*, supra note 23 at c. 10, p. 186.

plays itself out in our modern court system today) is certainly not the only story of law and the judicial process. For example, both forerunners[108] and beneficiaries (of all stripes) of Marx[109] have taken issue, in various ways and to varying degrees, with the "illusion" of law's basis in individual rights, liberties, freedom, and "free will."[110] Given the inequities – natural, financial, sociological, historical, and so on – that exist between individuals and groups in pluralistic societies, the idea that a procedural architecture that is largely agnostic to the values that animate its participants or the outcomes it produces has the potential to fly in the face of a sense of justice that sees substantive equality as its ultimate end game. As Rousseau argued,

> [I]nequality. ... becomes stable and legitimate by the establishment of property and laws. ... This is enough to determine what we ought to think, in this respect, of the kind of inequality that prevails in all civilized

---

108 See, for example, Jean-Jacques Rousseau, *Discourse on the Origin and Basis of Inequality Among Men* (1754) in *The Essential Rousseau*, trans. by Lowell Bair (New York: Meridian, 1974) at 125. A fundamental aspect of social contract theory was, according to Rousseau, that in "the state of society [as opposed to the 'state of nature'] all rights are fixed by law." Jean-Jacques Rousseau, *The Social Contract or Principles of Political Right* in Jean-Jacques Rousseau, *The Social Contract and Discourses*, trans. by G.D.H. Cole, rev. by J.H. Brumfitt and John C. Hall (London and Melbourne: J. M. Dent, 1973) at bk. II, c. 6, pp. 210–11.

109 See, for example, Max Horkheimer and Theodor W. Adorno, *Dialectic of Enlightenment*, trans. by John Cumming (London and New York: Verso, 1979); Herbert Marcuse, *Eros and Civilization* (London: Sphere Books, 1969). The liberal conception of law has also been robustly critiqued by others, including critical legal studies and critical race theory scholars. See, for example, Duncan Kennedy, A *Critique of Adjudication (fin de siècle)*, supra note 48; and Richard Delgado and Jean Stefancic, *Critical Race Theory: An Introduction* (New York and London: New York University Press, 2001).

110 This general "illusion" critique by Marx, of the bourgeois approach to law and justice, is taken from his specific critique of the relation of law and property. See Karl Marx, *The German Ideology* (1845–6) at pt. 1.B.2 ("The Relation of State and Law to Property") in Robert C. Tucker, ed., *The Marx-Engels Reader*, 2nd ed. (New York and London: W.W. Norton, 1978) 146 at 187 [emphasis omitted]. See further ibid. at 186–8. More generally, see Karl Marx, "On the Jewish Question" (1843) and "Critique of the Gotha Program" (1875) in Tucker, ed., *The Marx-Engels Reader*, supra at 26 and 525, for Marx's critique, among other things, of bourgeois rights-based notions of justice. Similarly, see Karl Marx and Friedrich Engels, *Manifesto of the Communist Party* (1848) in Tucker, ed., *The Marx-Engels Reader*, ibid. at 487.

nations, because it is obviously contrary to the law of nature ... for a handful of people to wallow in luxury while the starving multitude lacks the necessities of life.[111]

Communitarians, for example, reviving Aristotle's sense of the good life in the context of what counts as important for citizens in their deliberations about life choices at the personal and the political level, have pushed the idea that democracy must contemplate more than a procedural shell of justice if it is to make sense of what is important to people, families, and communities living in modern societies. Personal and group notions of the good, on these readings, do play a determining role of who we are and therefore must take a front seat in how we interact and govern ourselves through modern democratic institutions.[112] In this sense, courts provide a place for the citizenry to debate what is most important to them as situated individuals, or – borrowing a phrase from the chief justice of Canada – a place "where citizens can test laws for conformity to ... the shared commitments and values that constitute the deeper community constitutional morality."[113]

For the purpose of this discussion of the court's regulatory function as a central mechanism of liberal democracy, perhaps the most useful counterpoise to the Rawlsian notion of rights-based liberal democracy

111 Rousseau, *Discourse on the Origin and Basis of Inequality Among Men*, supra note 108 at 200–1.

112 See, for example, Michael J. Sandel, "Political Liberalism," Review Essay (1994) 107 *Harv. L. Rev.* 1765; Michael J. Sandel, *Liberalism and the Limits of Justice* (Cambridge, UK: Cambridge University Press, 1982); and Michael J. Sandel, *Democracy's Discontents: America in Search of a Public Philosophy* (Cambridge, MA: Belknap, 1996). See further Michael J. Sandel, *Justice: A Reader* (Oxford, UK, and New York: Oxford University Press, 2007); Michael J. Sandel, *Justice: What's the Right Thing to Do?* (New York: Farrar, Straus and Giroux, 2009). For different accounts associated with communitarianism, see, for example, Michael Walzer, *Spheres of Justice: A Defence of Pluralism and Equality* (New York: Basic Books, 1983); Michael Walzer, "The Communitarian Critique of Liberalism" (1990) 18 *Political Theory* 6; Alisdair MacIntyre, *After Virtue*, 2nd ed. (Notre Dame, IN: University of Notre Dame Press, 1984); Alisdair MacIntyre, *Whose Justice? Which Rationality* (Notre Dame, IN: University of Notre Dame Press, 1988); and Charles Taylor, "Cross Purposes: The Liberal-Communitarian Debate," supra note 107. For a general introduction, see, for example, Will Kymlicka, *Contemporary Political Philosophy: An Introduction*, 2nd ed. (Oxford, UK: Oxford University Press, 2002), c. 6.

113 Rt. Hon. Beverley McLachlin, P.C., "Judges in a Multicultural Society," supra note 60.

is Habermas' treatment of deliberative democracy. As will be seen, these two thinkers clearly come at the project of understanding the process of democracy quite differently. However, they are both – in different ways – sympathetic to the liberal tradition of taking the role and the moral agency of individuals in society seriously. Both thinkers, influenced by Locke, Kant, and others, contemplate an empowered citizenry with a significant rational capacity for moral deliberation.[114] In this way, as Frank Michelman has quipped, the views of Rawls and Habermas – both engaged in a project of "liberal justification of politics" – are not radically different, with the differences that do exist being described as something akin to "family quarrels"[115] as opposed to out-and-out war.

In Habermas, we clearly see an understanding of judicial institutions, as tools of democracy – or as what the chief justice of Canada contemplated by referring to the courts' "ways of ... contributing to deliberative democracy"[116] by offering "a venue for ... the reasoned and dispassionate discussion of our most pressing social issues"[117] – come alive not simply through the provision of value neutral laws and procedures, but rather by facilitating a discursive environment in which citizens participate in the making of the laws that regulate their lives. The citizenry, on this account, is intimately connected to the law making function. As such, through this form of institutionally provided deliberative participation, the law derives its legitimacy. According to Habermas, through the "procedure of lawmaking" – including the processes of civil dispute resolution – law receives its "full normative sense" and its "legitimacy,"[118] and further, this proceduralist sense of law and legal institutions therefore "privileges the communicative presuppositions and procedural conditions of democratic opinion- and will-formation as the sole source of legitimation."[119] Legitimacy, simply

114 See Frank I. Michelman, "Democracy and Positive Liberty" (1996) 21 *Boston Rev.* 3 at § iv.

115 Frank I. Michelman, "W(h)ither the Constitution?" (1999–2000) 21 *Cardozo L. Rev.* 1063 at 1065, n. 2 and surrounding text.

116 Rt. Hon. Beverley McLachlin, P.C., "Judges in a Multicultural Society," supra note 60.

117 Rt. Hon. Beverley McLachlin, P.C., "Welcome," supra note 54.

118 Habermas, *Between Facts and Norms*, supra note 23 at § 4.1.1, p. 135 [emphasis omitted].

119 Ibid. at "Postscript" (1994), § 1, p. 450. See also Jürgen Habermas, "Paradigms of Law" (1996) 17 *Cardozo L. Rev.* 771; Habermas, *Between Facts and Norms*, supra note 23 at c. 9 ("Paradigms of Law").

put, comes from the fact that parties to a proceeding move from simple disputants to agents of law and law making. Objects and subjects of law and legal process now also become its creators. According to Habermas, "the modern legal order can draw its legitimacy only from the idea of self-determination: citizens should always be able to understand themselves also as authors of the law to which they are subject as addressees. … [T]he legal community constitutes itself not by way of social contract but on the basis of a discursively achieved agreement."[120] Similarly, again according to Habermas,

> Law can be preserved as legitimate only if enfranchised citizens switch from the role of private legal subjects and take the perspective of participants who are engaged in the process of reaching understanding about the rules for their life in common. … [T]he structures of a vibrant civil society and an unsubverted political public sphere must bear a good portion of the normative expectations, especially the burden of a normatively expected democratic genesis of law.[121]

As such, courts – as public law-making and applying venues – matter, not simply to know what the law is or to make sure it is being applied fairly, but as central features of public norm generation and legitimation, which guide the formation and understanding of relationships in pluralistic and democratic societies.

These generalized accounts of law and legal process[122] – rights-based and deliberative – provide different visions of the role of the individual and individual rights vis-à-vis each other and the collective. Asking

---

120 Habermas, *Between Facts and Norms*, supra note 23 at "Postscript" (1994), § 1, p. 449. For useful discussions of Habermas' deliberative approach to political-legal theory, see Frank I. Michelman, "Constitutional Authorship by the People" (1999) 74 *Notre Dame L. Rev.* 1605 at 1626; Frank I. Michelman, "Democracy and Positive Liberty," supra note 114; and Frank I. Michelman, "Morality, Identity and 'Constitutional Patriotism'" (2001) 14 *Ratio Juris* 253. For a collection of general discussions, see James S. Fishkin and Peter Laslett, eds., *Debating Deliberative Democracy* (Malden, MA: Blackwell, 2003). See also Bruce Ackerman, "Why Dialogue?" (1989) 86 *J. Phil.* 5.

121 Habermas, *Between Facts and Norms*, supra note 23 at "Postscript" (1994), § 5, p. 461. See also Jürgen Habermas, *Legitimation Crisis*, trans. by Thomas McCarthy (Boston: Beacon Press, 1975) at 98–102. For a further discussion of Habermas, in the context of my discussion of access to justice, see infra Chapter 7.

122 Of course, much more could be said, and has been said, about liberalism and its various critics. For various accounts, see further, for example, Rawls, supra note 32; Dworkin, supra note 32. Additionally, see Will Kymlicka, *Liberalism,*

citizens to become object, subject, and author of law – as a legitimating process – allows for a grander vision of citizenship than the one championed by either "night-watchman" libertarians[123] or even robust, rights-based democrats.[124] However, notwithstanding their differences, these two accounts do share a sense, albeit in clearly different ways, that courts are key sites for law-making in modern democratic societies. Citizens claim, protect, deliberate about, and create rights and law that, in turn, regulate their life choices and activities. Limiting, curtailing, or impoverishing this democratic mechanism through processes of privatization (which I take up in the next chapter), again on either account, will therefore clearly have dramatic repercussions for the ways in which we regulate our individual and collective wellbeing. Doing so will also, again on both accounts, have implications for the system's legitimacy. And while the purpose of this book is not ultimately to provide an account or defence of democracy, linking the civil justice system to the core of the democratic process (on any account) brings into sharp relief what is at stake when I talk about the privatization of the civil justice system as a regulatory process of democracy.

Community and Culture (Oxford, UK: Clarendon Press, 1989). See further Trevor C.W. Farrow, "The Good, the Right, and the Lawyer," supra note 70 at 165. There are many varied sources of historical roots of liberalism. See, for example, Locke, supra note 31; Smith, infra note 105. For Marxist and Continental critiques and treatments of liberalism, see, for example, Marx, supra note 110; Horkheimer and Adorno, supra note 109; and Marcuse, supra note 109. For a modern natural law critique, see, for example, Finnis, supra note 29. For a discourse theory critique, see further, for example, Habermas, supra note 23. And for communitarian critiques of liberalism and its typical prioritizations of the right over the good, see, for example, Sandel, supra note 112 and accompanying text. Although a comprehensive treatment of liberalism and its critics is not the focus of this book, because this project does take issue with current challenges to and changes within the public civil justice system, it is important to keep in mind the normative political underpinnings of that system. See further George Pavlich, "The Art of Critique or How Not to be Governed Thus" in Gary Wickham and George Pavlich, eds., *Rethinking Law, Society and Governance: Foucault's Bequest* (Oxford, UK, and Portland, OR: Hart Publishing, 2001), c. 9.

123 See, for example, Robert Nozick, *Anarchy, State, and Utopia* (New York: Basic Books, 1974) 25, 26–7.

124 For a useful discussion of the differences between these political theories, see Habermas, *Between Facts and Norms*, supra note 23 at Postscript (1994), § 3, p. 457.

Open and Public Process

Open Courts

As Chief Justice Beverley McLachlin recently stated, "justice is a process."[125] Without meaningful process, infused with core constitutional and rule of law values, there is little hope of any kind of meaningful participation or sustained justice. In this sense, process creates order, which – as the Supreme Court of Canada has acknowledged – is a "precondition" to justice.[126] Various levels of procedure facilitate the operation of the public court system. However, key to this procedural regime for the purpose of this book – and, as we saw, central to any notion of the rule of law – is its open and public nature. In addition to the general rules and procedures that guide lawyers and parties through all steps of the court-based dispute resolution process,[127] orders of the court[128] are entered in the entry book of a provincial registrar,[129] precedents are published,[130] and "all court hearings shall be open to the public."[131] In line with the spirit of openness of these provisions, any "person is entitled to see" the "list maintained by a court of civil proceedings commenced or judgments entered" as well as "any document filed in a civil proceeding in a court" (subject only to limited exceptions).[132] Put simply, when speaking about the civil justice system in

125 Rt. Hon. Beverley McLachlin, P.C., "Lawyers' Professional Obligations, Public Service and Pro Bono Work (remarks made during a question-and-answer session following her presentation at the University of Alberta, Faculty of Law, 19 September 2008) [archived with author].

126 See *Tolofson v. Jensen; Lucas (Litigation Guardian of) v. Gagnon*, [1994] 3 S.C.R. 1022, para. 56, La Forest J. (QL).

127 See, for example, Ontario *Courts of Justice Act*, supra note 11; and Ontario *Rules of Civil Procedure*, supra note 14.

128 The term order typically includes "orders" and "judgments." See, for example, Ontario *Rules of Civil Procedure*, supra note 14 at r. 1.03(1) at "order."

129 See, for example, ibid. at r. 59.05.

130 For a useful discussion of the history of reported precedents and Bentham's influence on that system, see Neil Duxbury, *The Nature and Authority of Precedent* (Cambridge and New York: Cambridge University Press, 2008) 43, n. 57 and accompanying text. See a further discussion of Bentham and "judge-made" law, infra at note 51 and accompanying text.

131 See, for example, Ontario *Courts of Justice Act*, supra note 11 at s. 135(1) (subject to the limited exceptions provided for in s. 135(2)).

132 See, for example, ibid. at s. 137.

Canada, the court-based system is an open, publicly accessible system. As Archibald, Killeen, and Morton have commented, the "general rule provides for full access to and disclosure and publication of court proceedings ... covertness is the exception and openness the rule."[133]

The importance of the requirement of openness of the public court system cannot be overstated. As Justice Fish of the Supreme Court of Canada has recognized, "[w]hat goes on in the courts ought ... to be, and manifestly is, of central concern to Canadians."[134] Court proceedings need to be open to the public, the materials by which cases are resolved need to be accessible, and the media need to be able to access what goes on in courts. This last point is important because, in general (and practical) terms, it is through the media that scrutiny of judicial proceedings largely occurs.[135] These elements of openness and access (through the media) were raised in the Supreme Court of Canada's judgment in *Canadian Broadcasting Corp. v. New Brunswick (Attorney General) (Re R. v. Carson)*.[136] The case engaged s. 2(b) of the *Charter*, which provides that "[e]veryone has the following fundamental freedoms: ...

---

133 Hon. Justice Todd Archibald *et al., Ontario Superior Court Practice,* 2008 ed. (Markham, Ontario: LexisNexis, 2008) at 286 ("Practice Notes," § 1); 288 ("Practice Notes," § 1). See similarly *Canadian Broadcasting Corp. v. New Brunswick (Attorney General) (Re R. v. Carson)* [1996], 3 S.C.R. 480 at para. 22, discussed further in notes 138–46.

134 *Toronto Star Newspapers v. Ontario,* [2005] 2 S.C.R. 188, para. 2. See also *Vancouver Sun (Re),* [2004] 2 S.C.R. 332 at paras. 22–31; *A.B. v. Bragg Communications Inc.,* 2012 SCC 46.

135 According to Justice Iacobucci of the Supreme Court of Canada,

> In our country, courts are the institutions generally chosen to resolve legal disputes as best they can through the application of legal principles to the facts of the case involved. One of the underlying principles of the judicial process is public openness, both in the proceedings of the dispute, and in the material that is relevant to its resolution. ... The importance of public and media access to the courts cannot be understated, as this access is the method by which the judicial process is scrutinized and criticized. Because it is essential to the administration of justice that justice is done and is seen to be done, such public scrutiny is fundamental.

Sierra Club of Canada v. Canada (Minister of Finance), [2002] 2 S.C.R. 522 at paras. 1 and 52 [citations omitted]. See also ibid. at para. 36. See further *Canadian Broadcasting Corp. v. Canada (Attorney General),* 2011 SCC 2.

136 See supra note 133. See also *Canadian Broadcasting Corp. v. Canada (Attorney General),* supra note 135.

(b) freedom of thought, belief, opinion and expression, including freedom of the press and other media of communication."[137] Justice La Forest extensively discussed the elements of openness and access in a series of foundational passages in that case.[138] One of the key aspects of that judgment is the important link it makes between representative democracy, which I discussed in the preceding section of this chapter, and meaningful access to the judicial process through open courts. As Justice La Forest put it, "a democracy cannot exist without … freedom to … put forward opinions about the functioning of public institutions. The concept of free and uninhibited speech permeates all truly democratic societies and institutions."[139] As such, according to Justice La Forest, it "cannot be disputed that the courts … play a critical role in any democracy."[140] The basis for the link is the court's recognition that, practically speaking, not all citizens have the opportunity actually to access court proceedings. It is through the press by which most – if not essentially all – public access to the judicial process is derived.[141] And

---

137 *Canadian Charter of Rights and Freedoms*, supra note 71 at s. 2(b).

138 See generally *Canadian Broadcasting Corp. v. New Brunswick (Attorney General) (Re R. v. Carson)*, supra note 133 at paras. 17–22. See also *Dagenais v. Canadian Broadcasting Corp.*, [1994] 3 S.C.R. 835; *MacIntyre v. Nova Scotia (Attorney-General)*, [1982] 1 S.C.R. 175; *R. v. Mentuck*, [2001] 3 S.C.R. 442 and its companion case *R. v. O.N.E.*, [2001] 3 S.C.R. 478; *Named Person v. Vancouver Sun*, supra note 52; *Canadian Broadcasting Corp. v. Canada (Attorney General)*, supra note 135.

139 *Canadian Broadcasting Corp. v. New Brunswick (Attorney General) (Re R. v. Carson)*, supra note 133 at para. 19 [reference omitted]. See also ibid. at para. 18.

140 Ibid. at para. 20.

141 As Justice Cory stated in *Edmonton Journal v. Alberta (Attorney General)*, [1989] 2 S.C.R. 1326 at 1339–40, cited in *Canadian Broadcasting Corp. v. New Brunswick (Attorney General) (Re R. v. Carson)*, supra note 133 at para. 23,

> [A]s listeners and readers, members of the public have a right to information pertaining to public institutions and particularly the courts. Here the press plays a fundamentally important role. It is exceedingly difficult for many, if not most, people to attend a court trial. Neither working couples nor mothers or fathers house-bound with young children, would find it possible to attend court. Those who cannot attend rely in large measure upon the press to inform them about court proceedings – the nature of the evidence that was called, the arguments presented, the comments made by the trial judge – in order to know not only what rights they may have, but how their problems might be dealt with in court. It is only through the press that most individuals can really learn of what is transpiring in the courts. They as "listeners" or readers have a right to receive this

because public understanding,[142] scrutiny,[143] and criticism[144] of the judicial process, together, are essential parts of democracy, so too is the notion that court procedures need to be open and accessible to the public.

The importance of the open court principle and its link to democracy is central to the arguments that I make in this book. The ability to deliberate about, generate, understand, scrutinize, and disseminate legal principles, binding on both disputants and on society as a whole, is what the public court system is designed to provide. This ability also makes the court system – including all types of cases that are involved in the system[145] – a key part of society's regulatory framework.[146] Access to that system, through the open court principle, as made meaningful

---

> information. Only then can they make an assessment of the institution. Discussion of court cases and constructive criticism of court proceedings is dependent upon the receipt by the public of information as to what transpired in court. Practically speaking, this information can only be obtained from the newspapers or other media.

See further *Canadian Broadcasting Corp. v. New Brunswick (Attorney General) (Re R. v. Carson)*, ibid. at para. 17.

142 *Canadian Broadcasting Corp. v. New Brunswick (Attorney General) (Re R. v. Carson)*, ibid. at para. 22.

143 Ibid. at para. 21.

144 Ibid. at paras. 18 and 23.

145 Many of the cases involved in the various publication ban judgments of the Supreme Court of Canada, some of which are discussed above in this part of this chapter, involve criminal proceedings. See also *R. v. Carswell*, [2008] O.J. No. 4242 (Ont. C.J.), paras. 96–112, N.A. Dawson J.; and *R. v. Baltovich [re Canadian Broadcasting Corp.]*, [2008] O.J. No. 2307 (Ont. Sup. Ct. Just.), para. 6, J.D. McCombs J. However, as the Ontario Superior Court of Justice confirmed, "the principles expressed apply to all civil and criminal proceedings which involve restrictions on freedom of expression and freedom of the press." See *Moore v. Bertuzzi* (2007), 88 O.R. (3d) 499 at para. 32 (Master). Similarly, according to Justice Bastarache of the Supreme Court of Canada, the open court principle "is clearly a broad principle of general application to all judicial proceedings." *Named Person v. Vancouver Sun*, supra note 52 at para. 34. For a discussion of the *Moore* case, see Ryder Gilliland, "Public Access Trumps Confidentiality for Filed Transcripts" 28:4 *The Lawyers Weekly* (23 May 2008) 11. For a further media discussion of the balance of privacy, fair trials, and open courts, see Kirk Makin, "One Law, Many Views on Keeping the Public Informed," *The Globe and Mail* (25 May 2010) A10.

146 See *Canadian Broadcasting Corp. v. New Brunswick (Attorney General) (Re R. v. Carson)*, supra note 133 at para. 24. See further *Canadian Broadcasting Corp. v. Canada (Attorney General)*, supra note 135.

by a robust notion of freedom of the press,[147] is an essential part of that structure.[148] Of particular importance to this discussion is the open court principle vis-à-vis the specific law-recognizing and law-making aspects of the judicial process (its norm-creation function). As we have seen, courts resolve disputes by determining what the law is – or what the rights or equities are – in a given case. This judicial norm-applying function is of immediate concern to the interested parties in any given case. Courts also determine what the law, rights, and equities might be in future cases for future parties. This potentially norm-creating function is not of limited but rather of general concern to all citizens in a democracy. It follows then, as Justice Cory of the Supreme Court of Canada recognized, that citizens have a "right to information pertaining to public institutions and particularly the courts" in order "to know not only what rights they may have, but how their problems might be dealt with in court."[149] Similarly, as summarized by John Godfrey Spragge, the public court system, which is "built upon precedent and authority," is established by the state "so that a man may, with reasonable certainty,

147 For a further, historical – but still powerful – defense of the fundamental importance of a free press, see John Stuart Mill, *On Liberty* in John Stuart Mill, *Utilitarianism, On Liberty, Essay on Bentham*, ed. by Mary Warnock (New York: Meridian, 1962) at c. II ("Of the Liberty of Thought and Discussion"):

> If all mankind minus one were of one opinion, and only one person were of the contrary opinion, mankind would be no more justified in silencing that one person, than he, if he had the power, would be justified in silencing mankind. … [T]he peculiar evil of silencing the expression of an opinion is, that it is robbing the human race; posterity as well as the existing generation; those who dissent from the opinion, still more than those who hold it. If the opinion is right, they are deprived of the opportunity of exchanging error for truth: if wrong, they lose, what is almost as great a benefit, the clearer perception and livelier impression of truth, produced by its collision with error.

Ibid. at 142–3. For a different historical take on the issue, see de Tocqueville, who commented that "freedom of the press … modifies mores as well as laws." Alexis de Tocqueville, *Democracy in America*, supra note 42 at 180. He defines "mores" as covering "the sum of the moral and intellectual dispositions of men in society." Ibid. at 305, n. 8. For his further general discussion of the principle of a free press and its place in U.S. history, see ibid. at 180–8.

148 For a different and useful background discussion of "fair and open" trials, see John Rawls, *A Theory of Justice*, supra note 32 at § 38, p. 210.

149 *Edmonton Journal v. Alberta (Attorney General)*, supra note 141 at 1339–40.

know what the law is, and govern himself accordingly."[150] Open courts, put simply, play a defining role in how citizens understand their rights and obligations and in how those citizens relate to one another in complex, pluralistic societies.

Legitimacy

To the extent that the legitimacy of the system is bound up in the citizenry's ability to participate, openness, and the public nature of the deliberative process is again key to the system. According to Habermas,

> [T]he public sphere is not conceived simply as the back room of the parliamentary complex, but as the impulse-generating periphery that surrounds the political center: in cultivating normative reasons, it affects all parts of the political system. … [A] publicly mobilized critique of judicial decisions imposes more-intense justificatory obligations on a judiciary engaged in further developing the law.[151]

Although certainly in favour of protecting the "intimate sphere" from "intrusive forces and the critical eyes of strangers," for Habermas, to "talk about something is not necessarily the same as meddling in another's affairs" and, further, "not everything reserved to the decisions of private persons is withdrawn from public thematization and protected from criticism."[152] Rather, for Habermas, "every affair in need of political regulation should be publicly discussed, though not every legitimate object of public discussion will in fact be politically regulated."[153] These are not uncontroversial statements. The more sympathetic one is to the libertarian branches of the liberal family tree, the

150 John Godfrey Spragge, "A Letter on the subject of the Courts of Law of Upper Canada addressed to the Attorney General and Solicitor General" (1847) in Falconbridge, "Law and Equity in Upper Canada," supra note 11 at 13–15, discussed further in *The Civil Litigation Process*, supra note 14 at 20. These comments were made by Spragge when advocating – before becoming chancellor of Upper Canada and later the chief justice – for an early court of equity in Upper Canada. See also David B. Read, Q.C., *The Lives of the Judges of Upper Canada and Ontario, From 1791 to the Present Time* (Toronto: Rowsell & Hutchison, 1888), c. XXIII.

151 Habermas, *Between Facts and Norms*, supra note 23 at § 9.3.2, p. 442 [emphasis omitted].

152 Ibid. at § 7.2.2, p. 313.

153 Ibid.

less sympathetic one will be with Habermas' view of deliberation that treads into the private.[154] However, assuming even a minimum level of citizen participation in the norm-generating aspect of the judicial process, if the adjudicative process is increasingly privatized, then – taking a phrase from Michelman – the "law that people would regularly confront would increasingly be law with whose creation they have had nothing whatsoever to do."[155]

Whereas the legitimacy of the retrospective – dispute resolution – aspect of the court's function is increased from its openness, clearly seeing courts as public venues for meaningful debate and deliberation is fundamental to the legitimacy of the prospective – societal regulation – function of the court in democratic societies. Both Rawlsian and Habermasian notions of democratic judicial process contemplate such openness. Similarly, from the court's perspective, as recognized by LeBel J., "stress has been laid on the relationship between open courts and the promotion of democracy."[156] Open information about the courts is, therefore, clearly tied to the court's legitimacy and norm-creation function. As Justice Bastarache remarked,

> Information is at the heart of any legal system ... lawyers and witnesses present information to courts; juries and judges make decisions based on that information; and those decisions, reported by the popular and legal press, make up the basis of the law in future cases. In Canada, as in any truly democratic society, the courts are expected to be open, and information is expected to be available to the public.[157]

An open court system, animated by strong constitutional and rule-of-law values, is clearly what is contemplated and promised by the modern Canadian judicature[158] and the courts of justice legislation.[159] Such a court system plays, as the Supreme Court of Canada has acknowledged, a key role in realizing a form of democracy that is "fundamentally

---

154 For a much fuller treatment of Habermas' use of and distinction between the "public sphere" and the "private sphere" and their roles in deliberative politics and his procedural concept of democracy, see, for example, ibid. at c. 7.

155 Michelman, "W(h)ither the Constitution?," supra note 115.

156 *Named Person v. Vancouver Sun*, supra note 52 at para. 85.

157 Ibid. at para. 1.

158 See, for example, Alberta's *Judicature Act*, supra note 11.

159 See, for example, Ontario's *Courts of Justice Act*, supra note 11; and Alberta's *Court of Queen's Bench Act*, supra note 11.

connected to substantive goals" including "the promotion of self-government through the democratic process."[160] It is also the justice system that facilitates democracy's ability to "accommodate[] cultural and group identities."[161] To the extent that the civil justice system is being actively privatized by modern court reform initiatives, as I discuss in the following chapter, its role and legitimacy as an "essential condition of democracy"[162] get called into question. Democracy itself, in turn, is potentially impoverished. That is what is at stake in this discussion.

160 *Reference re Secession of Québec*, supra note 38 at para. 64 [reference omitted].
161 Ibid. [reference omitted].
162 See supra note 60.

Chapter Three

Privatization of Civil Courts

Privatization

Background

As a basic starting point, privatization, broadly defined, is any shift from the public to the private. In theory, privatization can involve a number of different contexts, including, for example, an increased preference to keep personal or family issues away from public scrutiny, transforming a company from a publicly traded corporation to a privately held asset, or downloading government services to a private service provider. In the latter sense, privatization, generally speaking, involves shifting the provision of government services or assets to various non-state (for-profit) entities. In this sense, "government" is being equated with "public" and "non-state" is being equated with "private." Of course, things are not always that simple. There is a significant space outside of the immediate personal or family sphere, but that is not part of the formal government sphere, which is typically thought of as "public." One only needs to look as recently as the "Occupy Movement" to think of the public space that is taken up by members of civil society, occupying public spaces and engaging with others in a very public way. Public corporations and the market, non-governmental organizations (NGOs) and other non-governmental charitable organizations, religious and community groups, and so on all can fairly locate their roots in the "public," although they would not be characterized as part of "government." And in the digital age, the new commons – the Internet – provides a vast new terrain for public presence and public discourse.

The literature on privatization is wide ranging, and often confusing,[1] given the broad scope of issues, interests, problems, and solutions that are potentially at stake when it comes to talking about privatization. Part of the confusion often stems from definitional debates, in which commentators describe and conceive of "privatization" as meaning different things. Various concepts have been used to define privatization, including "contracting for services," "denationalization," "commercialization," "marketization," "asset sale," "managed competition," and other processes.[2] As a general starting point, to "privatize," according to Savas, means "to rely more on the private institutions of society and less on government to satisfy people's needs."[3] According to Brodie and Trimble, "privatization ... makes the claim that services and assets initially created or regulated in and through the public service are better delivered and maintained through market mechanisms and the price system."[4] Similarly, according to Savas, privatization is "the act of increasing the role of the private sector, or decreasing the role of government, in an activity or in the ownership of assets."[5] It has also been defined as a "process aimed at shifting functions and responsibilities, in whole or in part, from the government to the private sector";[6] "privatiz[ing] ... the ownership and control of state-owned enterprises";[7] and "the deliberate sale by a government of state-owned enterprises ... or assets to private economic agents."[8] Privatization is

1 E. S. Savas, "A Taxonomy of Privatization Strategies" (1989–90) 18:2 *Pol'y Stud. J.* 343 at 343 [citation omitted].

2 Ibid. See also United States General Accounting Office (GAO), Report to the Chairman, House Republican Task Force on Privatization, "Privatization: Lessons Learned by State and Local Governments" (GAO/GGD-97-48) (Washington, DC: March 1997) at 1, available online: Government of United States <http://www.gao.gov/archive/1997/gg97048.pdf>.

3 Savas, "A Taxonomy of Privatization Strategies," supra note 1 at 344–5.

4 Janine Brodie and Linda Trimble, "Reinventing Canada, An Overview" in Janine Brodie and Linda Trimble, eds., *Reinventing Canada: Politics of the 21st Century* (Toronto: Prentice Hall, 2003) 1 at 7.

5 Savas, "A Taxonomy of Privatization Strategies," supra note 1 at 345. See further Deborah S. Ballati, ed., *Privatizing Governmental Functions* (New York: Law Journal Press, 2001).

6 GAO, "Privatization: Lessons Learned by State and Local Governments," supra note 2 at 1.

7 Paul Bennell, "Privatization in Sub-Saharan Africa: Progress and Prospects during the 1990s" in *World Development*, vol. 25, no. 11 (Brighton: Elsevier Science, 1997) 1785 at 1785.

8 William L. Megginson and Jeffry M. Netter, "From State to Market: A Survey of Empirical Studies on Privatization" (2001) 39:2 *J. Econ. Lit.* 321 at pt. 1.

also not necessarily an either-or phenomenon: "mixed public-private" arrangements are also part of this discussion.[9]

A mixture of – and shift between – state and private ownership or provision of public assets and services has been part of the thinking and workings of society from ancient Greece[10] through the Enlightenment[11] and the Industrial Revolution;[12] the Great Depression[13] and the Keynesian Revolution;[14] and the post-war break-up of colonial empires.[15] More recently, modern privatization trends can be seen as anchoring the economic theories of Friedrich von Hayek[16] and Milton Friedman[17] and located in the economic policies of post-war Adenauer and subsequent governments in Germany and certainly with the Thatcher government of the late 1970s and 1980s in the United Kingdom.[18] According to Kikeri

9 See, for example, GAO, "Privatization: Lessons Learned by State and Local Governments," supra note 2 at 1. See also Roberto M. Unger and Cornel West, *The Future of American Progressivism: An Initiative for Political and Economic Reform* (Boston: Beacon Press, 1998), 89–90. Compare Stuart Murray, "Value for Money? Cautionary Lessons about P3s from British Columbia" (Summary), available online: Canadian Centre for Policy Alternatives, B.C. Office <http://www.policyalternatives.ca/sites/default/files/uploads/publications/BC_Office_Pubs/bc_2006/P3_vfm_summary.pdf>.

10 For an historical summary of privatization, see, for example, Megginson and Netter, "From State to Market: A Survey of Empirical Studies on Privatization," supra note 8 at pt. 2.

11 See, for example, Adam Smith, *An Inquiry into the Nature and Causes of the Wealth of Nations* (1776), ed. by Edwin Cannan (Chicago: The University of Chicago Press, 1967) at vol. 2, bk. V, c. II, pt. II ("Of the Sources of the General or Public Revenue of the Society"), pp. 348–9.

12 See, for example, Megginson and Netter, "From State to Market: A Survey of Empirical Studies on Privatization," supra note 8 at pt. 2.

13 See, for example, ibid.

14 See, for example, John Maynard Keynes, *The General Theory of Employment, Interest and Money*, new ed. (New York: Palgrave Macmillan, 2007). For a useful introductory discussion, see Daniel Cohn, "Changing Conceptions of the Public Interest" in Brodie and Trimble, eds., *Reinventing Canada: Politics of the 21st Century*, supra note 4 at c. 4.

15 See, for example, Megginson and Netter, "From State to Market: A Survey of Empirical Studies on Privatization," supra note 8 at pt. 2.

16 See, for example, Friedrich A. von Hayek, *The Road to Serfdom* (London: Routledge Press; Chicago: The University of Chicago Press, 1944).

17 See, for example, Milton Friedman, *Capitalism and Freedom* (Chicago: The University of Chicago Press, 1962).

18 See, for example, Megginson and Netter, "From State to Market: A Survey of Empirical Studies on Privatization," supra note 8 at pt. 2. For related and influential libertarian political theories, see, for example, Robert Nozick, *Anarchy, State and Utopia* (New York: Basic Books, 1974). Foundationally, see, for example, John Locke, *Second Treatise of Government* (1690), ed. by C.B. Macpherson (Indianapolis, IN: Hackett Publishing,

and Nellis, "privatization has become a central element of the structural reform agenda in developed and developing countries alike."[19] Commentators have described current characteristic privatization trends as "worldwide,"[20] "accelerating,"[21] "extensive,"[22] "activ[e],"[23] "ambitious,"[24] and "growing,"[25] descriptors that are all supported by various economic indicators. For example, the annual privatization revenues for divesting governments went from approximately US$38 billion in 1988 to US$180 billion in 2000.[26] The result of divesting revenues, framed as the total global proceeds from privatization between 1990 and 1999, amounted to US$850 billion.[27] And notwithstanding government

---

1980) at c. v. Further, contrast John Rawls, A *Theory of Justice*, rev. ed. (Cambridge, MA: Belknap, 1999); Michael J. Sandel, *Democracy's Discontents: America in Search of a Public Philosophy* (Cambridge, MA: Belknap, 1996); Michael J. Sandel, "Political Liberalism," Review Essay (1994) 107 *Harv. L. Rev.* 1765; and Michael J. Sandel, *Liberalism and the Limits of Justice* (Cambridge, UK: Cambridge University Press, 1982). For a further useful collection of relevant materials, see Michael J. Sandel, *Justice: A Reader* (Oxford, UK, and New York: Oxford University Press, 2007). For a further discussion of Neoliberal economic approaches, see Janine Brodie, "Reforming Social Justice in Neoliberal Times" (2007) 1:2 *Studies in Social Just.* 93.

19 Sunita Kikeri and John Nellis, "Privatization in Competitive Sectors: The Record to Date" (World Bank Policy Research Working Paper 2860, June 2002), available online: World Bank <http://www-wds.worldbank.org/servlet/WDSContentServer/WDSP/IB/2002/08/02/000094946_02072209183311/Rendered/INDEX/multi0page.txt> 1 at 1. See further ibid. at 2. See also Tim Jenkinson and Colin Mayer, "The Privatisation Process in France and the U.K." (1988) 32 *Eur. Econ. Rev.* 482; and Josef C. Brada, "Privatization Is Transition – Or Is It?" (1996) 10:2 *J. Econ. Perspectives* 67.

20 Megginson and Netter, "From State to Market: A Survey of Empirical Studies on Privatization," supra note 8 at pt. 1.

21 Sunita Kikeri, John Nellis, and Mary Shirley, *Privatization: The Lessons of Experience* (Washington, DC: World Bank, 1992) at 1.

22 Kikeri and Nellis, "Privatization in Competitive Sectors: The Record to Date," supra note 19 at 1–2.

23 Ibid.

24 Eytan Sheshinski and Luis F. López-Calva, "Privatization and Its Benefits: Theory and Evidence" (2003) 49:3 *CESifo Econ. Stud.* 429 at 429.

25 Ibid. See also Janice Gross Stein, *The Cult of Efficiency* (Toronto: House of Anansi Press, 2001) at c. 2.

26 Megginson and Netter, "From State to Market: A Survey of Empirical Studies on Privatization," supra note 8 at fig. 1. See further Sheshinski and López-Calva, "Privatization and Its Benefits: Theory and Evidence," supra note 24 at 429–30.

27 Kikeri and Nellis, "Privatization in Competitive Sectors: The Record to Date," supra note 19 at 2. See also ibid. at fig. 1. For more-recent regional and sector-specific data, particular for developing regions, see World Bank, "Privatization Database" [archived

statements and news reports[28] about the current global economic crisis and policy moves by the United States, Canadian, European, and other governments around the world to combat the crisis, privatization-related reports argue that the private sector, through privatization, which continues to be viewed as an "accepted ... legitimate – often core – tool of statecraft,"[29] will continue to "drive[] ... modernization efforts."[30] For example, as Leonard Gilroy has commented, "[p]rivatization remains a key policy focus as public officials grapple with deteriorating fiscal conditions."[31] Clearly privatization continues to be widespread and on the rise.

The widespread trend of modern privatization is typically driven by several primary objectives. These include a strengthened private sector, improved financial health of the public sector, freedom to reallocate public resources, and – most notably for this book – efficiency.[32] According to Sheshinski and López-Calva, for example, privatization is "fundamentally" about efficiency.[33] Similarly, according to Megginson and

---

with author]. See also Reason Foundation, "Privatization Trends and Statistics" [archived with author]. See further Sunita Kikeri and Verena Phipps, "Privatization Trends: A Record Year in 2006" (13 January 2008), available online: World Bank <http://rru.worldbank.org/documents/publicpolicyjournal/317Kikeri_Phipps.pdf>.

28 For various news reports and perspectives, see, for example, Shawn McCarthy and Greg Keenan, "Ottawa Jumps into the Car Warranty Business" *The Globe and Mail* (8 April 2009) A1; Karen Howlett, "Auto Bailout Pushes Ontario $4-Billion Deeper into the Red" *The Globe and Mail* (2 June 2009) A1; and Adam Nagourney and Megan Thee-Brenan, "Outlook on Economy is Brightening, Poll Finds" *The New York Times* (6 April 2009) [archived with author].

29 Megginson and Netter, "From State to Market: A Survey of Empirical Studies On Privatization," supra note 8 at pt. 1.

30 See Shirley Ybarra, "Even during the Recession Private Companies Are Investing in Ports" (19 March 2009) [archived with author].

31 Leonard C. Gilroy, "Reason Foundation's 22nd Annual Analysis of Privatization and Outsourcing" (1 August 2008) [archived with author]. For example, according to one report, "[n]o government asset is being spared scrutiny as the Harper government considers auctioning off holdings while it grapples with record deficits. ... Ottawa aims to generate up to $4-billion through privatizations or sales in this fiscal year." See Steven Chase, "Ottawa Considering Asset Sales, from VIA Rail to Royal Canadian Mint" *The Globe and Mail* (2 June 2009), A4.

32 See, for example, Sheshinski and López-Calva, "Privatization and Its Benefits: Theory and Evidence," supra note 24 at 430. See also ibid. at 432, 440, and 450–1. See further Kikeri and Nellis, "Privatization in Competitive Sectors: The Record to Date," supra note 19 at 6–7.

33 Sheshinski and López-Calva, "Privatization and Its Benefits: Theory and Evidence," supra note 24 at 430.

Netter, "the goal of government is to promote efficiency."[34] This kind of efficiency can be realized in both competitive and non-competitive – infrastructure – sectors.[35] A focus on efficiency, in the context of privatization, is not new for scholars and policy makers. For example, Adam Smith, when writing about societal revenues and funds of sovereigns, argued that

> In every great monarchy of Europe the sale of the crown lands would produce a very large sum of money, which, if applied to the payment of the public debts, would deliver from mortgage a much greater revenue than any which those lands have ever afforded to the crown. … When the crown lands had become private property, they would, in the course of a few years, become well-improved and well-cultivated.[36]

Modern privatization scholars continue to focus heavily on efficiency. For example, according to Kikeri and Nellis, "[t]here is now a wealth of information from a wide range of countries showing that privatization is associated with … efficiency,"[37] and further, "private firms are found to be more efficient than state enterprises."[38] According to Megginson and Netter, "research … supports the proposition that privately owned firms are more efficient and more profitable than otherwise-comparable state-owned firms."[39] Further, according to those two commentators,

---

34 Megginson and Netter, "From State to Market: A Survey of Empirical Studies on Privatization," supra note 8 at pt. 3.1.

35 Sheshinski and López-Calva, "Privatization and Its Benefits: Theory and Evidence," supra note 24 at 449–50.

36 Smith, *An Inquiry Into the Nature and Causes of The Wealth of Nations*, supra note 11 at vol. 2, bk. V, c. II, pt. II ("Of the Sources of the General or Public Revenue of the Society"), pp. 348–9. For further reference to Smith, see Sheshinski and López-Calva, "Privatization and Its Benefits: Theory and Evidence," supra note 24 at 432.

37 Kikeri and Nellis, "Privatization in Competitive Sectors: The Record to Date," supra note 19 at 7.

38 Ibid. at 14. This observation by Kikeri and Nellis about the efficiency of private firms was made specifically "[i]n terms of growth," and "especially in competitive industries." See ibid.

39 Megginson and Netter, "From State to Market: A Survey of Empirical Studies on Privatization," supra note 8 at pt. 9.1(2). When speaking about their research into the empirical realities of privatization, scholars such as Megginson and Netter acknowledge that "[t]o a large extent we ignore the arguments concerning the importance of equitable concerns. … The effect[] of privatization on productive efficiency … is the focus of most of the empirical literature we review." Ibid. at pt. 3.1.

"[w]e know that privatization 'works,' in the sense that divested firms almost always become more efficient."[40] Similarly, according to Sheshinski and López-Calva, "private ownership has advantages over public ownership in terms of being inherently more efficient."[41] From these comments, we can see that, as a general matter, privatization is very much viewed as a process for creating economic efficiencies.

Systems of Civil Justice

At specific issue in this book is the increasing and widespread privatization of one particular aspect of the state's infrastructure: the civil justice system. In the last chapter, I commented that

> Modern provincial superior courts throughout Canada are the primary public venues in which Canadians resolve their disputes. The system is public in the sense that it is largely funded by governments (through taxpayer money), is – at least in theory – potentially available to all people for all disputes, is open to the public and the press, and provides judgments that are of interest not just to disputing parties but also to society as a whole.[42]

It is this dispute resolution system that is becoming subject to an increasingly widespread and aggressively pursued trend of privatization through modern court reforms.[43]

This acknowledgment by Megginson and Netter is qualified by their further statement that "[w]e do so not because they [arguments concerning the importance of equitable concerns] are unimportant, but because they are beyond the scope of this review." Ibid.

40 Ibid. at pt. 9.1(5).

41 Sheshinski and López-Calva, "Privatization and Its Benefits: Theory and Evidence," supra note 24 at 432. See also ibid. at 438, 440, 445, and 451.

42 See supra Chapter 2, note 1 and accompanying text [footnote and emphasis omitted].

43 For earlier commentary, see Trevor C.W. Farrow, "Public Justice, Private Dispute Resolution and Democracy" in Ronalda Murphy and Patrick A. Molinari, eds., *Doing Justice: Dispute Resolution in the Courts and Beyond* (Montréal: Canadian Institute for the Administration of Justice, 2009) at 301; Trevor C.W. Farrow, "Privatizing our Public Civil Justice System" (2006) 9 *News & Views Civ. Just. Reform* 16; Trevor C.W. Farrow, "Re-Framing the Sharia Arbitration Debate" (2006) 15:2 *Const. Forum Const.* 79; Trevor C.W. Farrow, "The Rule of Law in Developing Countries Is Not Just About Courts" 26:31 *The Lawyers Weekly* (15 December 2006) (QL); and Trevor C.W. Farrow, "Dispute Resolution, Access to Civil Justice and Legal Education" (2005) 42 *Alta. L.*

Before proceeding to a more detailed examination of the range of privatization efforts in Canada's systems of civil justice (both past and – increasingly – present), I first discuss with more detail the basic idea of privatization as it specifically applies to the public justice system. Of course, the state's public dispute resolution institutions – courts[44] (as well as administrative tribunals[45]) – continue to exist and function under the public authority of the state. In this sense, there clearly continues to be a well-functioning public justice system. However, both separate from and as part of the administration of that public system, large elements of the state's civil justice regime are increasingly shifting away from the traditional public court process and towards a range of other – private – processes. And notwithstanding earlier private elements and alternatives that have certainly existed for centuries (which

---

Rev. 741 at 797–8. See also Andrew Pirie, "Critiques of Settlement Advocacy" in Colleen M. Hanycz, Trevor C.W. Farrow, and Frederick H. Zemans, *The Theory and Practice of Representative Negotiation* (Toronto: Emond Montgomery, 2008) at c. 11; Harry W. Arthurs and Robert Kreklewich, "Law, Legal Institutions, and the Legal Profession in the New Economy" (1996) 34 *Osgoode Hall L.J.* 1 at 25–6; Kim Kerelis, "Private Justice: How Civil Litigation is Becoming a Private Institution – The Rise of Private Dispute Centres" (1993–4) 23 *Sw. U. L. Rev.* 621; Martin H. Malin and Robert F. Ladenson, "Privatizing Justice: A Jurisprudential Perspective on Labor and Employment Arbitration from the *Steelworkers Trilogy* to *Gilmer*" (1992–3) 44 *Hastings L.J.* 1187; Lewis L. Maltby, "Private Justice: Employment Arbitration and Civil Rights" (1998–9) 30 *Colum. Hum. Rts. L. Rev.* 29; Bryant G. Garth, "From Civil Litigation to Private Justice: Legal Practice at War with the Profession and its Values" (1993–4) 59 *Brook L. Rev.* 931; Bryant G. Garth, "Privatization and the New Formalism: Making the Courts Safe for Bureaucracy" (1988) 13 *Law & Soc. Inquiry* 157 at 160–2; Jack B. Weinstein, "Some Benefits and Risks of Privatization of Justice through ADR" (1996) 11 *Ohio St. J. Disp. Resol.* 241; and Jack B. Weinstein and Catherine Wimberly, "Secrecy in Law and Science" (2001–2) 23 *Cardozo L. Rev.* 1 at 24–6. For a contrary view, in which the move to incorporate ADR in the public court system is seen as a move to expand the public dispute resolution sphere, rather than privatize it, see Richard C. Reuben, "Public Justice: Toward a State Action Theory of Alternative Dispute Resolution" (1997) 85 *Cal. L. Rev.* 577. Finally, for a useful treatment of changes in public and private space, see Law Commission of Canada, ed., *New Perspectives on the Public-Private Divide* (Vancouver: UBC Press, 2003).

44 See further supra Chapter 2.

45 I discuss the issue of the privatization of administrative processes further in Chapter 4.

are discussed elsewhere in this book[46]), the current privatization moves in the civil justice system are active, aggressive, increasing and extremely far-reaching. What does this form of civil justice privatization entail? There are several elements to it, including jurisdictional, informational, and financial aspects, to which I now turn.

JURISDICTION

Historically, sovereigns, prior to modern governing systems with a robust separation of powers, largely maintained the judicial authority.[47] In this early context, the first jurisdictional move – in recognition of what Adam Smith commented on as the "increasing business of … society, in consequence of its increasing improvement"[48] as well as what James Madison described as the tendencies towards "tyranny" of this retained sovereign authority[49] – came with the development of separate and independent judicial powers.[50] The result was a robust,

---

46 See, for example, further below in this chapter. For discussions of early attempts at ADR in the United States, see, for example, Lawrence M. Friedman, A *History of American Law*, 3rd ed. (New York: Simon & Schuster, 2005) at 13–14, 22–3, and 405; Kermitt L. Hall, *The Magic Mirror: Law in American History* (New York; Oxford, UK: Oxford University Press, 1989) at 27, 86, 228, and 296; and William R. Riddell, *The Early Courts of the Province* (Toronto?, 1916? [specific publication details unknown]) at 8. For references to early arbitration in Ontario, see William R. Riddell, *The Bar and the Courts of the Province of Upper Canada, or Ontario* (Toronto: Macmillan, 1928) at 184 (commenting on an action in the Queen's Bench being "settled by reference to arbitration" at Cobourg in 1843). See also ibid. at 48. For a useful historical discussion of arbitration and other processes in England, see Harry W. Arthurs, "Special Courts, Special Law: Legal Pluralism in Nineteenth Century England" in G.R. Rubin and David Sugarman, *Law, Economy and Society, 1750–1914: Essays in the History of English Law* (Oxford, UK: Professional Books Limited, 1984) at 380. For a brief worldwide review of the ancient roots of some alternative dispute resolution tools – specifically mediation – see Jay Folberg, "A Mediation Overview: History and Dimensions of Practice" (1983) 1 *Mediation Q.* c. 1, p. 3 at 3–7.

47 See, for example, Adam Smith, *An Inquiry into the Nature and Causes of the Wealth of Nations*, supra note 11 at vol. 2, bk. V, c. I, pt. II, p. 236 (discussed further infra).

48 Ibid. at 243.

49 See, for example, James Madison, "The Particular Structure of the New Government and the Distribution of Power among its Different Parts" *The New York Packet* (1 February 1788) in *The Federalist* (New York: J. and M. McLean, 1788) ("*The Federalist Papers*") at "Federalist No. 47" in *The Federalist Papers*, ed. by Clinton Rossiter (New York: Mentor, 1961) 300 at 301.

50 For a discussion of this development, see, for example, Adam Smith, *An Inquiry into the Nature and Causes of the Wealth of Nations*, supra note 11 at vol. 2, bk. V, c. I, pt. II, p. 244.

independent public court system.[51] It is this public court system, as modified and modernized, that still exists and functions today.[52]

Over time (as I discuss further below), calls to improve the efficiency and lower the costs of state-funded and state-run dispute resolution processes (civil courts and, more recently, administrative tribunals) have resulted in initiatives that take cases or parts of cases out of the full-blown public dispute resolution process and move them into more nimble, streamlined, and private arenas (both separate from and increasingly as part of the overall state-funded system). Arbitration legislation, as increasingly supported by private arbitration dispute resolution providers,[53] was an early (and continuing) example of the kind of reform initiative that actively seeks to move cases out of the public arena and into a fully private stream (although still legislatively contemplated, sanctioned, and increasingly encouraged). This move has led to what the Supreme Court of Canada has recently described as the creation of a "private justice system."[54] This form of privatization, in particular, was at issue in the Dealership case: a forum selection clause in the Corporation's standard form Contract, in the form of a mandatory arbitration agreement, which ousted the jurisdiction of a court in favour of a private (for-profit) arbitration regime.[55] Equally significant, privatizing initiatives have also been pursued for some time *within* the publicly funded dispute resolution system. Early mandatory mediation efforts, in a very different way and as part of the public court system, still had the effect of moving disputes – at an early stage of development – off the public court track and, significantly, away from the eyes of the press and into private and confidential venues for early and confidential resolution (again, all as legislatively contemplated, sanctioned, and increasingly encouraged).

Recently, these trends have not only continued but also significantly increased. As I discuss more fully later in this chapter, modern civil

51 Discussed generally supra Chapter 2.

52 Ibid.

53 See, for example, American Arbitration Association (AAA), available online: AAA <http://www.adr.org/>; ADR Chambers, available online: ADR Chambers <http://adrchambers.com/ca/>. Private arbitration is discussed further in the following. See, for example, infra Chapter 4.

54 *Dell Computer Corp. v. Union des consommateurs*, 2007 SCC 34, [2007] 2 S.C.R. 801 at para. 132 [reference omitted]. See also *Seidel v. Telus Communications Inc.*, 2011 SCC 15, [2011] 1 S.C.R. 531. I discuss the *Dell* and *Seidel* cases further in Chapter 4.

55 See supra Chapter 1.

justice reform has taken off like wildfire across the common law world. Here at home, as will be seen, there is no jurisdiction in Canada at the moment that is not in the midst of, is just coming out of, or is contemplating continued civil justice reform. Over the last several years alone, four provinces and one territory have adopted new or essentially new sets of civil justice rules of court.[56] This modern reform movement, as I call it, is expressly promoted by members of all stakeholders in the public civil dispute resolution system, including governments, courts and judges, law societies, bar associations, lawyers, clients, and law schools. These groups generally share a strong ethos of reform. And the result has been a continued and increasing push towards using private processes such as mandatory mediation, judicial dispute resolution, arbitration, settlement negotiations, and so forth, rather than the publicly scrutinized open-court aspects of the public system. This collection of varied reform-oriented procedures, taken together, is the jurisdictional aspect of privatization to which I am referring.

Now before going on, it is important, to avoid any misunderstandings or immediate objections, to underscore two points. First, I recognize that jurisdictional privatization in the civil justice system is not new. As I have said, and as I discuss further below, various efforts involving various different processes have been in place for some time. However, the current, active and widespread initiatives – taken together in what I have called the modern civil justice reform movement – amount to an entirely new wave of privatization that, given its sheer volume, is at least different in degree if not different in kind to earlier, piecemeal efforts. Second, it is important also to acknowledge that the processes through which privatization is happening – case management, judicial dispute resolution, arbitration, mediation, cost-shifting incentives, and so forth (that I discuss in more detail below) – are all very different processes, which operate in very different ways and in different circumstances, one from the other. There is no doubt of that. However, for my purpose in this book, the remarkable phenomenon now at work is the overall jurisdictional privatization that happens when all of these processes are seen, as a collective of a privatizing whole, acting together in concert. So although I certainly identify, discuss, and make use of many different civil justice reform processes in the context of this book, it is their collective force that lights up this discussion.

---

56 These jurisdictions include British Columbia, Alberta, Saskatchewan, Nova Scotia, and Yukon.

PRIVACY

In addition to the issue of jurisdiction, privatization also has a significant impact on the amount of information about civil disputes that is available to the public (i.e., beyond the immediate disputing parties). As I discussed in Chapter 2, a central element of the public court system is its open and informationally accessible nature. As we saw, the court's effectiveness and legitimacy as an institution of societal regulation depends on its transparency. The following statement by Justice Bastarache that I raised in Chapter 2 bears repeating:

> Information is at the heart of any legal system ... lawyers and witnesses present information to courts; juries and judges make decisions based on that information; and those decisions, reported by the popular and legal press, make up the basis of the law in future cases. In Canada, as in any truly democratic society, the courts are expected to be open, and information is expected to be available to the public.[57]

In direct opposition to this open and transparent sensibility, one of the central goals of the privatization movement – from an informational perspective – is typically to move disputes out of the public eye and into confidential, or at least largely private, *in-camera* settings. This aspect of privatization is generally part of the confidential processes that operate *within* the publicly funded justice and administrative law systems (e.g., mandatory or voluntary mediation programs that increasingly form part of both of those publicly funded systems). It is also typically a defining badge of private processes (e.g., private mediation, commercial arbitration, etc., all of which I discuss later in the "Alternative Dispute Resolution" section in this chapter). Again, this informational aspect of privatization was at issue in the Dealership case. A key motive of the Corporation in that case was clearly to keep its affairs out of the eyes of the public. And as we will see in Chapter 6, many parties – including public authorities – actively favour these private venues specifically because they are off-limits to public scrutiny and public debate.

Before moving off this point, it is important to recognize that there is a relatively large and loosely defined body of law that governs the privacy (and confidentiality) of information in the dispute resolution setting. Although a full treatment of that law is not necessary for the arguments that I am making in this book, I do make a few comments

57 *Named Person v. Vancouver Sun*, [2007] 3 S.C.R. 252, para. 1.

about it now in this section to further contextualize the privacy arguments that I am making throughout this book.

As a general matter, what goes on in a public court, including the litigation material that is generally filed at the courthouse (as discussed earlier in Chapter 2), is considered to be public (i.e., available for all to see and access). Subject to limited exceptions, citizens can come to court and listen to court proceedings and they can attend at the court clerk's office and generally access documents that are available in court files. The press, again subject to limited exceptions, can also report on the proceedings. In contrast, the processes of privatization that I am discussing in this book, involving mediation, arbitration, and so on, are generally assumed to be private, meaning specifically that members of the public are not typically allowed to attend. The key here is agreement. Unless the parties agree otherwise, these sorts of processes are typically assumed to be or implied to be private affairs. In the specific context of arbitrations, as Mason C.J. of the High Court of Australia recognized in the case of *Esso Australia Resources Ltd. and Others v. Plowman (Minister for Energy and Minerals) and Others*, parties submitting their disputes to arbitration may assume that such hearings will not be conducted in public.[58] And the assumed private nature of these processes

---

58 According to Mason C.J.,

> Subject to any manifestation of a contrary intention arising from the provisions or the nature of an agreement to submit a dispute to arbitration, the arbitration held pursuant to the agreement is private in the sense that it is not open to the public. ... It does not matter much whether this characteristic of privacy is an ordinary incident of the arbitration, that is, an incident of the subject matter upon which the parties have agreed, or whether it is an implied term of the agreement. For the most part, the authorities refer to it as an implied term. But, for my part, I prefer to describe the private character of the hearing as something that inheres in the subject matter of the agreement to submit disputes to arbitration rather than attribute that character to an implied term. That view better accords with the history of arbitrations. In *Hassneh Insurance Co of Israel v. Mew* [[1993] 2 Lloyd's Rep. 243 at 246–7], Colman J. said,
>
> > If the parties to an English law contract refer their disputes to arbitration they are entitled to assume at the least that the hearing will be conducted in private. That assumption arises from a practice which has been universal in London for hundreds of years and [is], I believe, undisputed. It is a practice which represents an important advantage of arbitration over the courts as a means of dispute resolution. The informality attaching to a hearing held in private and the candour to which it may give rise is an essential ingredient of arbitration. ...

is seen not simply as a descriptive fact but also as a normative commercial advantage for the parties involved. Further, according to the court, without the advantage of privatization, the benefit of arbitration will be damaged or potentially "defeated."[59]

Privacy clearly plays a central role in the arbitral process. However, taking the issue of information availability further, the question then becomes whether a private mediation or arbitration and the information dealt with at one of those proceedings is assumed to be confidential (meaning that not only does the public not have access to the proceeding, but the parties also are not permitted to discuss it with any third party). Most people assume that the information and materials relating to a private process are to be kept confidential. However, again, the key here is agreement, although this time the assumption may be reversed. The parties must agree (explicitly) to this further layer of secrecy (which they often do), or otherwise, information may be disclosed. And further, in some circumstances – including, for example, statutory financial reporting obligations, insurance reporting obligations, judicial scrutiny of an arbitral proceeding, and so on – the parties may not have a choice.[60]

> As the statement just quoted makes clear, the efficacy of a private arbitration as an expeditious and commercially attractive form of dispute resolution depends, at least in part, upon its private nature. Hence the efficacy of a private arbitration will be damaged, even defeated, if proceedings in the arbitration are made public by the disclosure of documents relating to the arbitration.

See (1995) 128 A.L.R. 391 at 398–9 [references omitted].

59 Ibid.

60 As Mason C.J. provided in *Esso Australia Resources Ltd.*,

> On the other hand … while it is one thing to say that the hearing is private in the sense that strangers are excluded, it is another thing to say that it is confidential. …
>
> Moreover, it has to be acknowledged that, for various reasons, complete confidentiality of the proceedings in an arbitration cannot be achieved. First, it is common ground between the parties that no obligation of confidence attaches to witnesses who are therefore at liberty to disclose to third parties what they know of the proceedings. Second, there are various circumstances in which an award made in an arbitration, or the proceedings in an arbitration, may come before a court involving disclosure to the court by a party to the arbitration and publication of the court proceedings. … Third, there are other circumstances in which an arbitrating party must be entitled to disclose to a third party the existence and details of the proceedings and the award. An arbitrating party may be bound

There is therefore a distinction to be drawn between the privacy of a proceeding and its confidentiality. One is deemed to be essentially automatic; the other is not (subject to various rules of court and privilege issues, discussed further below). However, just because courts have made this informational distinction[61] does not mean that confidentiality is not generally expected (which in fact was a significant part of the argument in the *Esso Australia Resources* case[62]). Confidentiality is possible and is, in fact, typically expected, particularly with respect to sensitive information such as financial information or trade secrets, as well as with respect – often – to the results of a proceeding. Other disclosure requirements, which amount to exceptions to typical confidentiality expectations – including specific financial reporting, and insurance reporting, among others – are often more limited (disclosure to an insurance company is not disclosure to the world), and they are, in any event, certainly much less the norm than the exception. Put simply, it is normally expected that private dispute resolution processes will largely be kept confidential. However, and regardless, to ensure (as far as possible) their confidential treatment, parties typically provide for such confidentiality in their dispute resolution agreements.[63]

> under a policy of insurance to disclose to the insurer matters involved in the arbitration proceedings which are material to the risk insured against. Likewise, an arbitrating party may be obliged to disclose the existence and nature of arbitration proceedings as well as the award made in the proceedings because the disclosure is necessary in order to state accurately what are the assets and liabilities of the party or to give an indication of its future prospects. Such a disclosure may be necessary in order to comply with the statutory requirements regulating the provision of financial information by corporations or with stock exchange requirements or simply because a company considers that it is desirable that its shareholders and the market should have up-to-date information concerning the company's affairs.
>
> The illustrations just given are but some of the instances in which a party to an arbitration could legitimately and justifiably disclose the proceedings, or some aspect of the proceedings, of an arbitration. …

Ibid. at 400–1 [references omitted].

61 See, for example, ibid.

62 Ibid.

63 Again according to Mason C.J. in the *Esso Australia Resources* case, in the context of arbitrations,

> An obligation not to disclose may arise from an express contractual provision. If the parties wished to secure the confidentiality of the materials prepared for or used in the arbitration and of the transcripts and notes of evidence given, they

In Canada, federal and provincial arbitration statutes deal specifically with these confidentiality issues. The federal *Commercial Arbitration Act*, for example, provides that the "parties are free to agree on the procedure to be followed" in the proceeding and that, absent such agreement, the panel may conduct an arbitration "in such a manner as it considers appropriate."[64] It is the general practice in Canada, as elsewhere, to conduct arbitrations (as well as other dispute resolution processes such as negotiations and mediations) in private. However, applicable governing legislation and rules of court (in the context of arbitrations as well as mediations and other judicial dispute resolution processes in some jurisdictions) provide room for alternatives and, as such, express agreement as to the privacy of a process and the extent of its confidentiality are usually discussed and agreed on ahead of time by disputing parties.[65]

Finally, a further layer of secrecy can be relevant in this context. Confidential information that is also thought to be "privileged" is typically secret for most purposes and must therefore not be disclosed. Examples of this kind of information include most information exchanged between a party and a lawyer for the purpose of seeking legal advice (solicitor and client privilege), information a lawyer (or a party) puts together in order to prosecute or defend a proceeding (litigation privilege), and information that the parties may exchange in the context of

---

> could insert a provision to that effect in their arbitration agreement. Importantly, such a provision would bind the parties and the arbitrator, but not others. Witnesses, for example, would be under no obligation of confidentiality.
>
> Absent such a provision … I do not consider that … having regard to the various matters to which I have referred, we are justified in concluding that confidentiality is an essential attribute of a private arbitration imposing an obligation on each party not to disclose the proceedings or documents and information provided in and for the purposes of the arbitration.

Ibid. at p. 401 [citations omitted].

64 R.S.C. 1985, c. 17 (2nd Supp.) at art. 19.

65 The Supreme Court of Canada's decision in *Seidel v. Telus Communications Inc.*, supra note 54 generally recognizes the private sensibility of arbitration. In the context of commercial mediation, some jurisdictions have enacted commercial mediation statutes, which include specific disclosure, confidentiality and admissibility provisions. See e.g. the relatively new Ontario *Commercial Mediation Act, 2010*, S.O. 2010, c. 16, sched. 3 at ss. 8–9. See further the various provincial rules of court that deal with this issue in the context of court-annexed dispute resolution processes (infra note 66).

attempts to settle a dispute (settlement privilege). Information in these categories, which often come up in the context of civil dispute resolution, is typically deemed not to be available for disclosure, unless the person entitled to the privilege waives it. And there are other sorts of privileged information and communications as well. As a general matter, it has been held in Canada that privileges that are available in litigation proceedings are available in alternative dispute resolution proceedings as well.[66]

Further, if the parties to a private dispute (typically arbitrations) agree to a process that involves documentary or oral discovery (a process whereby parties exchange relevant documents and information in preparation for a hearing or trial), as with its public, court-based counterpart, arbitral discovery is typically thought to be deemed or implied to be confidential and for the use of that proceeding only. Parties will often expressly contemplate this issue in their dispute resolution agreements or in the context of formulating a procedural regime with the arbitral panel.[67] Again, the Dealership case, set out in Chapter 1, provides an example of this kind of scenario.

---

66 For discussions of various privileges, see, for example, *Pritchard v. Ontario (Human Rights Commission)*, 2004 SCC 31, [2004] 1 S.C.R. 809; *Blank v. Canada (Minister of Justice)*, 2006 SCC 39, [2006] 2 S.C.R. 319; *A.M. v. Ryan*, [1997] 1 S.C.R. 157; *Sable Offshore Energy Inc. v. Ameron International Corp.*, 2013 SCC 37. See further *Ontario (Liquor Control Board) v. Magnotta Winery Corp.*, 2010 ONCA 681, 102 O.R. (3d) 545, in which the Court of Appeal for Ontario found that parties (in this case including a government agency) could take advantage of the solicitor and client privilege in the context of a mediation. In that case, the court held that alternative dispute resolution (which I discuss further below) "now forms an integral part of the civil litigation process in Ontario." See para. 36. In this discussion, the court specifically included various alternative dispute resolution processes, including mediation and settlement discussions. Ibid. The court held that while that case related to solicitor and client privilege, "many of the same considerations apply to settlement privilege." See ibid. at para. 38. Further, some provincial rules of court also speak to this issue. See *e.g.*, *Alberta Rules of Court*, Alta. Reg. 124/2010 at r. 4.20; *Civil Procedure Rules of Nova Scotia* (effective 1 January 2009) at r. 10.16(1), available online: Courts of Nova Scotia <http://www.courts.ns.ca/Rules/toc.htm>. Finally, whether all court-connected settlement discussions (*e.g.*, case planning conferences) are both confidential and privileged, in jurisdictions in which rules of court do not specifically speak to this issue, has been seen as an open question. For a discussion of this issue, see *Parti v. Pokorny*, 2011 BCSC 955, [2011] B.C.J. No. 1362 (B.C.S.C.).

67 For a discussion of discovery and confidentiality in arbitration, see, for example, *Esso Australia Resources Ltd. and Others v. Plowman (Minister for Energy and Minerals) and Others*, supra note 60. The general approach to discovery in public proceedings,

My reasons for including the foregoing discussion on aspects of the law governing privacy, confidentiality, and privilege in this context essentially include two purposes: first, the section is designed to acknowledge that these issues are part of the technical legal landscape forming the backdrop to this privacy discussion. As such, it is important to acknowledge their application to this context. Second, having said that, I also want to make it clear that a full treatment and understanding of the law relating to privacy, confidentiality, and privilege are not necessary for the arguments that I am making in this book. That is because, as indicated, the parties that engage in the kinds of privatized proceedings that I am discussing typically either assume or agree that the proceedings will be private. It is the expectation and the practice in Canada and elsewhere that these sorts of tools will include a major element of secrecy (whether always technically required or not). So if parties are engaging in these sorts of processes, they, of course, typically think about this issue. However, as far as my argument goes with respect to the general trajectory of these processes in Canada (and indeed around the world), privacy and confidentiality are the norm; publicity is the exception (which is opposite to what was discussed in the context of the public court system earlier in Chapter 2).

FINANCING

Another element to current privatization trends in the civil justice system involves at least a partial shift of financial responsibility. When parties engage the public civil justice system to resolve their disputes, they typically pay for any legal assistance they receive in terms of their own legal fees.[68] Unless people choose to represent themselves in court (which, I acknowledge, is increasingly occurring, and certainly not

---

including the "deemed" or "implied" undertaking rule (a rule that deems discovery information to be confidential and for the use of the immediate proceeding only) has been codified by provincial discovery rules. See, for example, Ontario's *Rules of Civil Procedure*, R.R.O. 1990, Reg. 194, as amended at r. 30.1. See also *Juman v. Doucette*, 2008 SCC 8, [2008] 1 S.C.R. 157, in which the Supreme Court of Canada discussed the implied undertaking rule.

68 In jurisdictions in which fee-shifting occurs (i.e., there are loser-pay rules with respect to at least part of a winning party's legal expenses), there may be additional "costs" to pay. These may include, for example, at least part of the legal expenses of the winning party. See, for example, Ontario's *Courts of Justice Act*, R.S.O. 1990, c. C.43 at s. 131; Ontario's *Rules of Civil Procedure*, supra note 67 at r. 57.

always by choice[69]), the process of retaining and paying for legal representation is part and parcel of modern self-regulatory legal regimes in which the bar enjoys virtually a monopoly over the provision of legal services.[70] But for being represented by a legal aid lawyer (either by a clinic lawyer or, unlikely in the case of a civil dispute, a lawyer being paid by the state through some form of legal aid certificate program),[71] the typical options for legal representation in superior court civil matters amount to either self-representation or private lawyer representation. In this sense, then, a large part of the system involves a self-regulating, for-profit private bar, and has for some time now. Although this self-regulatory regime brings with it a number of access to justice ramifications that are in need of further discussion, those are not my focus of attention here.[72]

However, what I am now talking about is not directly focused on the fees paid for legal representation, but rather the financial arrangements of the underlying dispute resolution institutions. Other than court administration fees (e.g., nominal filing fees), the state's dispute resolution costs, including court house expenses, judicial and court administrative salaries, and so forth are all paid for by the state. When the regular citizen goes to court, other than his or her own lawyer's fees (which clearly are often not insignificant) and nominal filing fees, he or she does not expect also to pay for the services that are provided at the courthouse (such as the judge's salary, for example). The cost of those services is the cost to the taxpayer of running a public court system.

In contrast, when parties choose to resolve their disputes using non-state-based tribunals (e.g., private mediation or arbitration regimes such as are provided by the AAA[73] or the ADR Chambers[74]), they still

---

69 See, for example, Trevor C.W. Farrow et al., *Addressing the Needs of Self-Represented Litigants in the Canadian Justice System*, a white paper prepared for the Association of Canadian Court Administrators (ACCA) (Toronto and Edmonton: ACCA, 2012) at pt. II, available online: ACCA <http://www.acca-aajc.ca/portals/0/repository/Addressing%20the%20Needs%20of%20SRLs%20ACCA%20White%20Paper%20March%202012%20Final%20Revised%20Version.f4bd3c5b-e062-4678-aff2-7fd2ac0c6772.pdf>.

70 See, for example, *Law Society Act*, R.S.O. 1990 c. L.8, s. 26.1.

71 See, for example, *Legal Aid Services Act, 1998*, O. Reg. 107/99, as amended by O. Reg. 151/10.

72 For earlier comments on this issue, see Trevor C.W. Farrow, "Sustainable Professionalism" (2008) 46:1 *Osgoode Hall L.J.* 51 at 96.

73 See supra note 58.

74 See ibid.

pay for their own legal fees. In addition, however, they also pay for the private provider's fees, which consist of mediator or arbitrator services, filing and administration fees, and boardroom rental, among others. Those fees are not insignificant. According to the AAA, for example, rates for AAA mediators range from $125 to $800 USD an hour.[75] And although fees and rates for AAA arbitrators vary depending on the arbitrator and the type and complexity of the case,[76] those fees are certainly at least no lower than those charged by their mediating counterparts.[77] Even in the context of private procedures *within* the public system (e.g., court-based mandatory mediation), additional fees, including, for example, mediator fees, are often incurred. In Ontario, for example, the mandatory mediation rules[78] provide for a default mediator fee scale – for mediators on the county mediation coordinator's list (or "roster") of mediators[79] – of a total of $600 to $825 for one-half hour of preparation time for each party plus up to three hours of actual mediation time.[80] However, to the extent that the parties choose a non-roster mediator,[81] or in any event, even with a roster-based mediator, if the mediation exceeds three hours, additional fees will apply (as determined, on consent of the parties, by the mediator).[82] These fees can be based on market rates and are often significantly higher than the scheduled fees allowed for roster-based mediators for the first three hours of a mandatory mediation session.[83]

75 See AAA, "Fees," available online: AAA <http://www.adr.org/aaa/faces/services/fileacase/fees?_afrLoop=14636197386440&_afrWindowMode=0&_afrWindowId=pl43mdtyc_141#%40%3F_afrWindowId%3Dpl43mdtyc_141%26_afrLoop%3D14636197386440%26_afrWindowMode%3D0%26_adf.ctrl-state%3Dpl43mdtyc_193>.

76 See ibid.

77 For example, the reported pre-hearing hourly rate for one of the arbitrators in the Vulcan arbitration, which I discuss in Chapter 6, was $610 USD. See Vulcan's Motion to Vacate Arbitration Award, filed in the Superior Court for the State of Washington, County of King (8 March 2010), pt. II.C (together with underlying declaration materials), discussed further infra Chapter 6.

78 See Ontario's *Rules of Civil Procedure*, supra note 67 at r. 24.1, discussed further infra.

79 Ibid. at r. 24.1.08(1).

80 The range is determined by the number of parties involved in the dispute. See "Mediators' Fees (rule 24.1, *Rules of Civil Procedure*)," O. Reg. 451/98 at s. 4(1).

81 For example, a mediator from the ADR Chambers in Toronto (see supra note 53).

82 See Ontario's *Rules of Civil Procedure*, supra note 67 at r. 24.1.08(2); "Mediators' Fees (rule 24.1, *Rules of Civil Procedure*)," ibid. at s. 4(3).

83 According to the ADR Chambers, for example, mediators' fees range from $150 to $700 CAD an hour. See ADR Chambers, "Mediation, Fees," available online: ADR Chambers <http://adrchambers.com/ca/mediation/>.

OVERALL RESULT

The overall result of this form of infrastructural privatization, including its jurisdictional, informational, and financial aspects, is a systematic increase in the number of disputes that are being dealt with – albeit in many different ways and using many different processes – in private; using private funding; by private negotiators, mediators, and/or adjudicators; with no public informational access; and without necessarily any (or at least all) of the procedural safeguards that are typically provided for by public court or tribunal systems.[84] Privatization is also encouraged (and at times mandated) by all justice system stakeholders, including the state. It is happening, through the use of many different dispute resolution tools, in all sectors and at all levels and stages of the civil court system, the administrative system, and through statutorily encouraged private dispute resolution initiatives.[85] This form of privatization is also involving all kinds of civil disputes, including, for example, commercial manufacturing and service disputes (such as the Dealership case), employment disputes (such as the Vulcan case that I discuss in Chapter 6), pay-equity disputes, police complaints, human rights complaints, and so forth. In sum, this form of wide-ranging privatization animates the various arguments that I make in this book.[86]

ALTERNATIVE DISPUTE RESOLUTION

Before looking further at specific aspects of privatization in the civil justice system, I spend a moment here discussing the terminology of this

---

84 For earlier discussions on this point, see, for example, Farrow, "Public Justice, Private Dispute Resolution and Democracy," supra note 43; Farrow, "Re-Framing the Sharia Arbitration Debate," supra note 43.

85 For a summary diagram of these collected processes (courts, tribunals and private initiatives), see supra Chapter 1, Figure 1.1.

86 Although many of the arguments that I make are also directly applicable to privatizing initiatives in family law, this book does not specifically focus on dispute resolution in the family law context. For some useful treatments of privatization in the family law context, see, for example, Jana B. Singer, "The Privatization of Family Law" (1992) *Wis. L. Rev.* 1443; Kelly Browe Olson, "Lessons Learned from a Child Protection Mediation Program: If at First You Succeed and Then You Don't ..." (2003) 41:4 *Fam. Ct. Rev.* 480; Martha J. Bailey, "Unpacking the 'Rational Alternative': A Critical Review of Family Mediation Claims" (1989) 8 *Can. J. Fam. L.* 61. For a recent collection of materials, see Julie Macfarlane, "Mediating Family Disputes" in Julie Macfarlane, gen. ed., et al., eds., *Dispute Resolution: Readings and Case Studies*, 3rd ed. (Toronto: Emond Montgomery, 2010) 329–36; and see further (earlier), Julie Macfarlane, "Mediating Family Disputes" in Julie Macfarlane, gen. ed., et al., eds., *Dispute Resolution: Readings and Case Studies*, 2nd ed. (Toronto: Emond Montgomery, 2003) 396–410.

kind of privatization and its relation to the terminology of alternative dispute resolution. As with privatization literature generally, terminology in the context of the privatization of civil justice can be equally problematic and confusing.

Many of the tools by which the civil justice system is being privatized include, for example, negotiation, private and/or court-annexed mediation, judicial dispute resolution, arbitration, and so on. And there are others. The format and motivation for each of these processes are different.[87] Speaking very generally, negotiation involves direct discussions between the disputing parties themselves. It is totally voluntary and private and involves no outside authority or assistance. Mediation is a form of assisted or facilitated negotiation. Again, it is typically voluntary and private. The parties, by agreement, choose a neutral third party to assist with their negotiation discussions. The third party has no binding authority. As with negotiation, the parties can always walk away.[88]

---

87 These processes are discussed in greater detail later in this chapter. See also generally infra Chapters 4 and 5. For a general useful overview of different dispute resolution techniques, see D. Paul Emond, "Alternative Dispute Resolution: A Conceptual Overview" in D. Paul Emond, ed., *Commercial Dispute Resolution* (Aurora, ON: Canada Law Book, 1989) 20–2, rep'd in Macfarlane et al., eds., *Dispute Resolution: Readings and Case Studies*, 3rd ed., supra note 86 at 96–8.

88 There is an extensive and growing body of mediation literature generally, partly as a result of the extensive and growing domestic and international mediation programs. For some examples, see Julie Macfarlane, ed., *Rethinking Disputes: The Mediation Alternative* (Toronto: Emond Montgomery, 1997); Macfarlane et al., eds., *Dispute Resolution: Readings and Case Studies* (2010), supra note 86 at c. 3; Genevieve A. Chornenki and Christine E. Hart, *Bypass Court: A Dispute Resolution Handbook*, 3rd ed. (Toronto: Butterworths, 2005) at cc. 3, 8; Laurence Boulle and Kathleen J. Kelly, *Mediation: Principles, Processes, Practice*, Cdn. ed. (Toronto and Vancouver: Butterworths, 1998); Hon. George W. Adams, *Mediating Justice: Legal Dispute Negotiation* (Toronto: CCH Canadian Limited, 2003) at cc. 5–7; Cheryl Picard et al., *The Art and Science of Mediation* (Toronto: Emond Montgomery, 2004); Cinnie Noble, L. Leslie Dizgun, and D. Paul Emond, *Mediation Advocacy: Effective Client Representation in Mediation Proceedings* (Toronto: Emond Montgomery, 1998); Marcus Stone, *Representing Clients in Mediation* (London, Edinburgh, and Dublin: Butterworths, 1998); Andrew J. Pirie, *Alternative Dispute Resolution: Skills, Science, and the Law* (Toronto: Irwin Law, 2000) at c. 4; Michael P. Silver, *Mediation and Negotiation: Representing Your Clients* (Toronto; Vancouver: Butterworths, 2001) at pt. II; Desmond Ellis and Dawn Anderson, *Conflict Resolution: An Introductory Text* (Toronto: Emond Montgomery, 2005) at c. 3; Stephen B. Goldberg et al., eds., *Dispute Resolution: Negotiation, Mediation, and Other Processes*, 4th ed. (New York: Aspen Law & Business, 2003) at cc. 3, 6; and Katherine V. W. Stone, *Private Justice: The Law of Alternative Dispute Resolution* (New York: Foundation Press, 2000) at c. 2.

Mediation that is "court-annexed" refers to a process that has been developed as part of the public civil justice system. In a nutshell, in jurisdictions in which court-annexed mediation is available, parties – before proceeding to trial – can (and in some jurisdictions must) attempt to mediate their dispute. Mediators are typically non-judges and can be part of a state-provided roster of mediators and/or the private sector. Judicial dispute resolution (or JDR) is – very loosely – a form of court-annexed mediation, although it has grown up from much more voluntary roots (and is typically thought of as its own process, separate from mediation). JDR typically involves parties seeking the assistance, voluntarily, from judges who act as third party neutrals with a view to assisting the parties to settle their disputes. Experience has shown that the voice and experience of a judge can be particularly persuasive to parties in deciding what might be a fair result in the context of a given dispute. JDR is becoming an increasingly popular option in Canadian jurisdictions.[89] Finally, arbitration is basically a private trial. Agreement between the parties to proceed to this form of dispute resolution process is again required. Such agreement can come at the time a dispute arises, or it can come at the front end of the parties' relationship (typically in the form of a mandatory dispute resolution clause in a commercial contract, as was the situation in the Dealership case). Arbitration requires the appointment of a private judge (arbitrator) who, by agreement, has the power to provide a binding decision on the parties. Arbitration is usually used in situations in which parties cannot come to a resolution of their dispute on their own or with the assistance of a neutral mediator. As to common threads between these various processes, they are all designed to resolve disputes, they do not involve the public trial process, they are typically premised on an agreement between the parties to engage in the process, and they are all – again typically – confidential.

All of these procedures fall within the broad ambit of what has come to be commonly referred to, together, as "alternative dispute resolution"

---

89 For a set of useful materials on dispute resolution in Canada, including various court-annexed and JDR initiatives, see Association of Canadian Court Administrators (ACCA), "Dispute Resolution," materials collected in *Can. Ct. Communiqué* (Winter 2011). For federal provisions relevant to Canadian federal judges acting in a settlement capacity pursuant to provincial settlement regimes, see *Judges Act*, R.S.C. 1985, c. J-1 at ss. 55–6. Further materials relating to these (and other) specific ADR tools are discussed throughout this book (see, for example, further discussions in this chapter as well as generally infra Chapters 4 and 5).

or "ADR." Defining ADR is not a simple task. As I have discussed elsewhere with respect to ADR: there is "significant debate" over its meaning.[90] As Andrew Pirie has commented when discussing ADR, "there continues to be a complicated fascination with what lies behind these three words."[91] Part of this debate comes from the view that, given its prevalence, "ADR is no longer 'alternative.' Many theorists and practitioners now refer to ADR, in its current form, simply as 'Dispute Resolution' or 'DR.'"[92] Another reason for this definitional challenge is the fact that many different types of processes (briefly discussed earlier) have been loosely collected under this broad label: from very collaborative and consensus-based processes of negotiation all the way through to highly scripted and adversarial arbitral procedures. Complicating things further is the inclusion, again under the same ADR tent, of both court-based (e.g., court-annexed mediation) and non-court-based (e.g., private arbitration) ADR procedures.

However, in this book, I use the term ADR – for simplicity and consistency – as it "has come to be commonly used in legal scholarship and practice."[93] This means that I include a wide range of procedures

---

90 Farrow, "Dispute Resolution, Access to Civil Justice and Legal Education," supra note 43 at 742–3, n. 7 and accompanying text, quoting – in turn – Trevor C.W. Farrow, "Thinking about Dispute Resolution," Review Essay (2003) 41 Alta. L. Rev. 559 at 559, n. 1.

91 Pirie, *Alternative Dispute Resolution: Skills, Science, and the Law*, supra note 88 at 1.

92 Farrow, "Dispute Resolution, Access to Civil Justice and Legal Education," supra note 43 at 742, n. 7, quoting again – in turn – Farrow, "Thinking About Dispute Resolution," supra note 90 at 559, n. 1. Reference is also made there to Macfarlane, *Dispute Resolution: Readings and Case Studies* (2003), supra note 86; Goldberg et al., eds., *Dispute Resolution: Negotiation, Mediation, and Other Processes*, supra note 88; John S. Murray, Alan Scott Rau, and Edward F. Sherman, *Processes of Dispute Resolution: The Role of Lawyers*, 3rd ed. (Westbury, NY: The Foundation Press, 2002). See also Trevor C.W. Farrow, "Negotiation, Mediation, Globalization Protests and Police: Right Processes; Wrong System, Issues, Parties and Time" (2003) 28 *Queen's L.J.* 665 at 688–9, nn. 90, 94; Trevor C.W. Farrow, "Dispute Resolution and Legal Education: A Bibliography" (2005) 7 *Cardozo J. Conflict Resol.* 119; Hon. George W. Adams and Naomi L. Bussin, "Alternative Dispute Resolution and Canadian Courts: A Time for Change" (1995) 17 *Advocates' Q.* 133 at 135–41; Alison E. Gerencser, "Alternative Dispute Resolution Has Morphed into Mediation: Standards of Conduct Must Be Changed" (1998) 50 *Fla. L. Rev.* 843 at 844–6; and Alberta Law Reform Institute (ALRI), Consultation Memorandum No. 12.6, "Promoting Early Resolution of Disputes by Settlement" (Edmonton: ALRI, July 2003) at 9–10, available online: ALRI <http://www.law.ualberta.ca/alri/>.

93 Farrow, "Dispute Resolution, Access to Civil Justice and Legal Education," supra note 43 at 743, n. 7, quoting Farrow, "Thinking About Dispute Resolution," supra note 90 at 559, n. 1.

under the ADR label (recognizing, again, that the processes themselves that I am collecting are often very different, one from the other). However, more important, for the purpose of my argument, is the fact that although privatization and ADR are not synonymous terms or concepts, many of the methods by which privatization in the civil justice system is occurring involve various ADR processes.

Privatization of Civil Courts

Many of the far-reaching privatization initiatives discussed in this book have been developed in the context of modern civil justice reform initiatives. As discussed in the next section of this chapter (as well as further in Chapter 5), there have been several reasons articulated for these reform initiatives. A primary reason has been cost. Over the millennia, the cost of justice has been both a source of revenue and, more recently, an issue of concern for sovereigns and governments. Adam Smith, for example, when discussing a sovereign's "duty of establishing an exact administration of justice" for "protecting, as far as possible, every member of the society from the injustice or oppression of every other member of it," discussed at length the "expense of justice."[94] As discussed briefly earlier,[95] early sovereigns, prior to a meaningful separation of judicial and executive branches, maintained the "judicial authority," which, "far from being a cause of expence [*sic*], was for a long time a source of revenue."[96] Subsequently, judges began receiving fixed salaries rather than "the ancient emoluments of justice,"[97] which

94 Smith, *An Inquiry into the Nature and Causes of the Wealth of Nations*, supra note 11 at vol. 2, bk. V, c. I, pt. II, p. 231.

95 Supra part 1.

96 Smith, *An Inquiry into the Nature and Causes of the Wealth of Nations*, supra note 11 at vol. 2, bk. V, c. I, pt. II, p. 236. For Smith's discussion of the "separation of the judicial from the executive power" over the centuries, including its increasing independence from the executive power, see ibid. at vol. 2, bk. V, c. I, pt. II, pp. 243–4. For a general foundational commentary on the importance of the separation of powers, see, for example, Madison, "Federalist No. 47," supra note 49 at 301: "The accumulation of all powers, legislative, executive, and judiciary, in the same hands, whether of one, a few, or many, and whether hereditary, self-appointed, or elective, may justly be pronounced the very definition of tyranny." For a recent discussion of judicial independence, particularly in the context of the United States, see Judith Resnik, "Interdependent Federal Judiciaries: Puzzling about Why & How to Value the Independence of Which Judges" (2008) 137 *Daedalus* 28.

97 Smith, *An Inquiry Into the Nature and Causes of The Wealth of Nations*, supra note 11 at vol. 2, bk. V, c. I, pt. II, p. 239.

was an effort to improve on those "ancient governments" whose "administration of justice appears for a long time to have been extremely corrupt."[98] Increased taxes were levied for the purpose of defraying the sovereign's judicial expenses. It was in that context in which "[j]ustice was then said to be administered gratis."[99] However, even so, as Smith also recognized, "[j]ustice … never was in reality administered gratis in any country. Lawyers and attornies [*sic*], at least, must always be paid by the parties,"[100] and those payments were part of the significant and "necessary expense of a law-suit."[101] As such, almost since their inception, concerns over the high cost of public justice processes have led to continued reform efforts.

In addition to cost, other related concerns have been (and continue to be) raised, including low efficiency and imperfect access to public court systems (all of which I discuss further at length in Chapters 5 and 7). These primary concerns continue to drive reform efforts. And it is largely in the context of these reform efforts, discussed later in this chapter, in which we find many of the modern privatization of civil justice initiatives.[102]

---

98 Ibid. at 238.

99 Ibid. at 239.

100 Ibid.

101 Ibid. at 240. With respect to at least some of the costs of a lawsuit, Smith commented that

> [i]t has been the custom in modern Europe to regulate, upon most occasions, the payment of the attornies and clerks of court, according to the number of pages which they had occasion to write; the court, however, requiring that each page should contain so many lines, and each line so many words. In order to increase their payment, the attornies and clerks have contrived to multiply words beyond all necessity, to the corruption of the law language of, I believe, every court of justice in Europe. A like temptation might perhaps occasion a like corruption in the form of law proceedings.

Ibid. at 242–3.

102 For a collection of comparative discussions, see Adrian Zuckerman, *Civil Justice in Crisis: Comparative Perspectives of Civil Procedure* (Oxford, UK: Oxford University Press, 1999).

Influential International Reform Initiatives

United Kingdom

Modern common law court reform really started more than 150 years ago with the efforts of Jeremy Bentham. In his studies of the then-existing British system, Bentham identified several (now very familiar) "mischiefs" with the "non-penal" (civil-side) branch of the court process, including: "Expense," "Delay" and "Complication" (among others).[103] Bentham's argument, then, was that all elements of a reform effort must be designed to address one or more of those "mischiefs":

> So many mischiefs as are liable to be found in a system of procedure, so many mischiefs to be avoided in every such system: so many mischiefs, the avoidance of which may in any such system be considered as respectively constituting so many ends to be kept in view … no provision that can be proposed can be entitled to a place in any such system, but in so far as it can be shown to be conducive to the attainment of one or more of these several ends.[104]

It was ultimately Bentham's efforts that influenced Henry Brougham and others to pursue the major court reforms that resulted in the *Judicature Acts* of 1873 and 1875 (which, together with subsequent rules reforms, provided the foundation for our modern common law codes of civil procedure and court processes).[105]

More than 100 years later, in 1996, Lord Woolf released his seminal report on civil justice reform in the UK: *Access to Justice*.[106] The *Woolf*

---

103 Jeremy Bentham, *Principles of Judicial Procedure, with the Outlines of a Procedural Code*, c. iii in *The Works of Jeremy Bentham*, ed. by John Bowring, vol. 2 (Edinburgh: William Tait, 1843) in Online Library of Liberty, ed., available online: Liberty Fund <http://oll.libertyfund.org/?option=com_staticxt&staticfile=show.php%3Ftitle=1921&chapter=113487&layout=html&Itemid=27>.

104 Ibid.

105 *Supreme Court of Judicature Act, 1873* (U.K.), 36 & 37 Vict., c. 66; *Supreme Court of Judicature Act, 1875* (U.K.), 38 & 39 Vict., c. 77. For a helpful discussion of this history, see Michael Lines, "Empirical Study of Civil Justice Systems: A Look at the Literature" (2005) 42 *Alta L. Rev.* 887 at 891–2.

106 Rt. Hon. Lord Woolf, M.R., *Access to Justice: Final Report to the Lord Chancellor on the civil justice system in England and Wales* (London: HMSO, 1996), available online: Department for Constitutional Affairs <http://webarchive.nationalarchives.gov.uk/+/http://www.dca.gov.uk/civil/final/contents.htm> [*Access to Justice* or the *Woolf Report*].

Report ultimately led to a new code of civil procedure for England and Wales.[107] Similar to previous major English reform proposals and rules restructurings, the *Woolf Report* and the new rules significantly influenced not only English procedural practices but also those that have subsequently been pursued throughout the entire common law world.[108] Many of the "problems" and "defects" identified by Lord Woolf were similar to those identified earlier by Bentham.[109] An underlying theme of Lord Woolf's approach, motivated primarily by fundamental access to justice concerns, was to recommend putting the courts more at the centre of how cases get managed or, as Lord Woolf put it, making "courts with the assistance of litigants" more "responsible for the management of cases."[110] Key elements of this approach included balancing expanded case management rules with the encouragement

---

107 The *Civil Procedure Rules 1998*, S.I. 1998/3132, as amended, available online: UK Government <http://www.justice.gov.uk/courts/procedure-rules/civil/stat_instr>.

108 For a leading collection of comments on the *Woolf Report* and subsequent rules reforms, see University of Oxford, Faculty of Law, "The Civil Procedure Rules Ten Years On" (a conference organized by the University of Oxford, Faculty of Law, British Academy, London, 1–2 December 2008), available online: University of Oxford <http://denning.law.ox.ac.uk/cpr10/home.php>. For further discussions of the *Woolf Report*, see, for example, Joshua Rosenberg, "Alternative Dispute Resolution in Public Law: Interview with Lord Woolf, C.J. Conducted by Joshua Rosenberg" in Richard Gordon, ed., *Judicial Review in the New Millennium* (London: Sweet & Maxwell, 2003) 109; and Suzanne Burn, "The Civil Justice Reforms in England and Wales: Will Lord Woolf Succeed Where Others Have Failed?" (1999) 17 *Windsor Y.B. Access Just.* 221.

109 According to Lord Woolf,

> The defects I identified in our present system were that it is too expensive in that the costs often exceed the value of the claim; too slow in bringing cases to a conclusion and too unequal: there is a lack of equality between the powerful, wealthy litigant and the under resourced litigant. It is too uncertain: the difficulty of forecasting what litigation will cost and how long it will last induces the fear of the unknown; and it is incomprehensible to many litigants. Above all it is too fragmented in the way it is organised since there is no one with clear overall responsibility for the administration of civil justice; and too adversarial as cases are run by the parties, not by the courts and the rules of court, all too often, are ignored by the parties and not enforced by the court.

Woolf, *Access to Justice*, supra note 106 at § 1(2).

110 Ibid. at § 1(3).

of ADR processes as mechanisms to improve efficiency and facilitate access to justice.[111] In the specific context of the report's approach to ADR, Lord Woolf made numerous major reform recommendations, which included a number of privatizing elements. For example, according to the report:

> Litigation will be avoided wherever possible.
> (a) People will be encouraged to start court proceedings to resolve disputes only as a last resort, and after using other more appropriate means when these are available.
> (b) Information on sources of alternative dispute resolution (ADR) will be provided at all civil courts.
> (c) Legal aid funding will be available for pre litigation resolution and ADR. …
> (e) Before commencing litigation both parties will be able to make offers to settle the whole or part of a dispute supported by a special regime as to costs and higher rates of interest if not accepted.
> Litigation will be less adversarial and more cooperative. …
> (b) The court will encourage the use of ADR at case management conferences and pre trial reviews, and will take into account whether the parties have unreasonably refused to try ADR or behaved unreasonably in the course of ADR.[112]

Other significant reform proposals dealt with various aspects of the system, including complexity, timeliness, cost, proportionality, accessibility, administration, structure, judicial training, and overall

---

111 As I have commented previously,

> The *Woolf Report* generally provided an expansive review and set of recommendations for increasing access to civil justice … it specifically considered the importance of ADR initiatives as tools for increasing access and efficiency. For example, when describing the "new landscape" of reformed civil justice, Lord Woolf stated that litigation "will be less adversarial and more co-operative." As such, the "court will encourage the use of ADR … and will take into account whether the parties have unreasonably refused to try ADR or behaved unreasonably in the course of ADR."

Farrow, "Dispute Resolution, Access to Civil Justice and Legal Education," supra note 43 at 749 [footnotes omitted].

112 Woolf, *Access to Justice*, supra note 106 at § 1(8)–(11) [emphasis omitted].

responsiveness.[113] All of these initiatives have been very influential on other countries' reform efforts. For example, the *Woolf Report*, as further discussed in the following, "was certainly the international study that was most influential in terms of subsequent civil justice reform thinking in Canada."[114]

Australia

Australia has also been significantly involved in civil justice reform, including major recent privatizing efforts. For example, shortly after the *Woolf Report* was released, the Australian Law Reform Commission released an influential discussion paper: *Review of the Federal Civil Justice System.*[115] As with Lord Woolf's approach, the terms of reference led the commission to have regard to "the need for a simpler, cheaper and more accessible legal system."[116] Following its review of the Australian system, the commission made recommendations that were also not dissimilar to those found in the *Woolf Report*. In particular, the commission's overall reform goals comprised several privatizing recommendations, including "emphasis[ing] dispute avoidance and prevention" and "encourage[ing] appropriate, effective and timely settlements."[117] Many of these efforts have been advanced through

---

113 Ibid. For a useful discussion of the English reform experience, see Advocates' Society, *Streamlining the Ontario Civil Justice System: A Policy Forum, Final Report* (9 March 2006) at 9–10, available online: Advocates' Society <http://www.advocates.ca/assets/files/pdf/publications/streamlining-justice.pdf>.

114 Farrow, "Dispute Resolution, Access to Civil Justice and Legal Education," supra note 43 at 749 [footnote omitted].

115 Australian Law Reform Commission (ALRC), "Review of the Federal Civil Justice System," Discussion Paper 62 (1999), available online: ALRC <www.austlii.edu.au/au/other/alrc/publications/dp/62/> ["ALRC Discussion Paper"]. See further ALRC, "Managing Justice: A Review of the Federal Civil Justice System," Report No. 89 (Sydney: ALRC, 1999), available online: ALRC <www.austlii.edu.au/au/other/alrc/publications/reports/89/>; and Murray Gleeson, "Managing Justice in the Australian Context" (Sydney: ALRC, 2000). The "ALRC Discussion Paper," in addition to its recommendations, is a very useful source for other Australian and international reports and literature on the subject of civil justice reform.

116 "ALRC Discussion Paper," supra note 115 at § 1(1.1) ("Introduction: Terms of Reference").

117 Ibid. at § 2(2.56) ("Change and Continuity in the Federal Civil Justice System: Reform Goals"). Although ultimately promoting the use of ADR, the commission took a balanced view in coming to the following position on ADR: "The Commission … makes suggestions to improve the utility of ADR … processes with the aim not

dispute resolution and access to justice initiatives being developed in the context of the Australian government's more recent civil justice and related advances and Access to Justice initiatives.[118]

United States

As with other common law systems, the United States has also, over the centuries, experienced its share of efficiency and other related civil justice systemic "mischiefs."[119] For example, early reports of civil justice in New York in the late 1600s and 1700s comment that litigation was becoming "lengthier and somewhat more complicated ... and ... complex."[120] At the same time, there were reports: of an "increase in delays in the court," that the court was "astonishingly inefficient and ineffective," and that "litigation was ... [in]convenient and ... expensive."[121] As a result (around the time that Bentham was making significant strides in the English context), major reform efforts were pursued in the United States.[122] A primary goal of those reforms was

---

simply to secure settlements but effective settlements." Ibid. at § 9(9.48) ("Issues in Case Management: ADR and Case Management"). For earlier comments on the "ALRC Discussion Paper," see, for example, Farrow, "Dispute Resolution, Access to Civil Justice and Legal Education," supra note 43 at 749–50, nn. 44–5. See further Lucille M. Ponte, "Reassessing The Australian Adversarial System: An Overview of Issues in Court Reform and Federal ADR Practice in the Land Down Under" (2000) 27:2 *Syracuse J. Int'l L. & Com.* 335; and Kathy Mack, *Court Referral to ADR: Criteria and Research* (Melbourne: Australian Institute of Judicial Administration Incorporated and the National Dispute Resolution Advisory Council, 2003).

118 See, for example, *Access to Justice (Federal Jurisdiction) Amendment Bill 2011* [Provisions] (29 March 2012), available online: Parliament of Australia <http://www.aph.gov.au/parliamentary_business/committees/senate_committees?url=legcon_ctte/completed_inquiries/2010-13/access_to_justice_federaljurisdiction/report/index.htm>.

119 Bentham, *Principles of Judicial Procedure, with the Outlines of a Procedural Code*, supra note 103 at c. iii.

120 Deborah A. Rosen, "The Supreme Court of Judicature of Colonial New York: Civil Practice in Transition, 1691–1760" (1987) 5 *L.H.R.* 213 at 218–9.

121 Ibid. at 220 and 227.

122 For example, in the mid-nineteenth century in the State of New York, significant reforms were pursued in the areas of both civil and criminal procedure. See, for example, *Act to Simplify and Abridge the Practice, Pleadings, and Proceedings of the Courts*, Laws N.Y. 1848, ch. 379 ("Field Code"). For a discussion of these reforms, see Friedman, A *History of American Law*, supra note 46 at c. 3; and Stephen N. Subrin, "David Dudley Field and the Field Code: A Historical Analysis of an Earlier Procedural Vision" (1988) 6:2 *L.H.R.* 311.

efficiency.[123] As part of those wide-ranging civil justice reform initiatives, several efforts to eliminate civil actions were made, including "extending the inducements to a compromise during … litigation" with the intention that "actions commenced may often be settled before a trial."[124] These reforms were specifically designed to reduce the number of cases needing a decision from the courts.[125] And over the next fifty years, further reforms were pursued that were designed to fill in gaps left by the "Field Code."[126] These efforts resulted in a new *Civil Procedure Act* and *Civil Procedure Rules*,[127] which were designed "not … for the benefit of the legal profession … but … to make the administration of justice more speedy, more certain and less expensive and thus advance the interests of the entire people of the state."[128] Key themes of the reforms were promptness and efficiency,[129] which were pursued in the spirit of "greater expedition, greater certainty and less expense in the administration of justice."[130] Ultimately, the *Federal Rules of Civil Procedure* were promulgated in 1938, which set up the modern civil practice throughout the federal court system in the United States.[131]

Notwithstanding these significant and ongoing efforts, the major modern ADR movement, which finds its roots in the United States, started more than a century after the Field Code was introduced in the context of widespread and growing dissatisfaction with the overall administration of civil justice.[132] Those early modern reform initiatives – notably including the 1976 Pound Conference convened by former

---

123 For example, according to the 31 December 1849 report from the commissioners responsible for presenting a reform report to the New York State Legislature, reforms to the civil procedure system of that state were pursued in the spirit of making "legal proceedings more intelligible, more certain, more speedy, and less expensive." See Commission on Practice and Pleadings (Arphaxed Loomis, David Graham and David Dudley Field), "Report of a Code of Civil Procedure" (Albany, NY: 1850) iii at v (HeinOnline).

124 Ibid. at viii.

125 Ibid.

126 See supra note 123.

127 Cited in Adolph J. Rodenbeck, "The New Practice in New York" (1916) 1:2 *Cornell L.Q.* 63 at 63–5.

128 Ibid. at 63.

129 Ibid. at 63, n. 2.

130 Ibid. at 75.

131 See Subrin, "David Dudley Field and the Field Code: A Historical Analysis of an Earlier Procedural Vision," supra note 122 at 311.

132 For further discussions of early ADR initiatives, see, for example, supra note 51 and accompanying text. See also infra Chapter 4.

chief justice Warren Burger that examined ways of improving the administration of justice and further discussions by Frank Sander and his colleagues[133] about a "multi-door courthouse"[134] – continue to drive modern thinking about ways of making the delivery of civil justice more accessible and efficient.[135] Around 1975, ADR was considered a "relatively obscure" concept.[136] Two years later, following the 1976 Pound Conference, the American Bar Association's dispute resolution committee was established. The committee was designed to examine the growing importance of alternative processes for the efficient delivery of justice.[137] It was also at that time that the current court-based and other ADR-related privatizing reform initiatives really took off.

---

133 See Jacqueline M. Nolan-Haley, *Alternative Dispute Resolution in a Nutshell*, 2nd ed. (St. Paul, Minn: West Group, 2001) at 5. For comment on the influence of these individuals on modern dispute resolution reforms, see, for example, Jay Folberg, "A Mediation Overview: History and Dimensions of Practice" in (1983) 1 *Mediation Q.*, c. 1, p. 3 at 7. For some of their ideas, see, for example, Frank E.A. Sander, "Varieties of Dispute Processing" (1976) 70 *F.D.R.* 111 in A. Leo Levin and Russell R. Wheeler, eds., *The Pound Conference: Perspectives on Justice in the Future* (St. Paul, MN: West Publishing, 1979), 65.

134 The concept of the "Multi-Door Courthouse" was developed in 1976 by Frank Sander of Harvard Law School. See, for example, ABA, Report of the American Bar Association Working Group on Civil Justice System Proposals, *ABA Blueprint for Improving the Civil Justice System* (Chicago: ABA, 1992) at 36 [*ABA Blueprint*]. See also Sander, "Varieties of Dispute Processing," supra note 133, also cited in Pirie, *Alternative Dispute Resolution: Skills, Science, and the Law*, supra note 88 at 396; and Jeffrey W. Stempel, "Reflections on Judicial ADR and the Multi-Door Courthouse at Twenty: Fait Accompli, Failed Overture, or Fledgling Adulthood?" (1996) 11 *Ohio St. J. Disp. Resol.* 297.

135 For further discussions of ADR's history, see, for example, Farrow, "Dispute Resolution, Access to Civil Justice and Legal Education," supra note 43 at pt. II.A-C; Farrow, "Thinking about Dispute Resolution," supra note 90 at pt. I; Farrow, "Negotiation, Mediation, Globalization Protests and Police: Right Processes; Wrong System, Issues, Parties and Time," supra note 92 at 667. See further, for example, Warren E. Burger, "Isn't There a Better Way?" (1982) 68 *A.B.A. J.* 274; Rt. Hon. Brian Dickson, P.C., "ADR, The Courts and The Judicial System: The Canadian Context" (1994) 28 *L. Soc'y Gaz.* 231 at 236; George W. Adams, *Mediating Justice: Legal Dispute Negotiations* (Toronto: CCH Canadian, 2003) at 12–15; D. Paul Emond, "Alternative Dispute Resolution: A Conceptual Overview," supra note 87; Pirie, "Critiques of Settlement Advocacy," supra note 43 at 290–2; Pirie, *Alternative Dispute Resolution: Skills, Science, and the Law*, supra note 88 at 1–33; and Carrie Menkel-Meadow, "Introduction: What Will We Do When Adjudication Ends? A Brief Intellectual History of ADR" (1997) 44 *UCLA L. Rev.* 1613. See also Lon L. Fuller, "The Forms and Limits of Adjudication" (1978) 92 *Harv. L. Rev.* 353.

136 *ABA Blueprint*, supra note 134 at 31. See further Stephen P. Johnson, *Just Solutions: Seeking Innovation and Change in the American Justice System* (Chicago: ABA, 1994).

137 *ABA Blueprint*, supra note 134 at 31.

Ten years later, the ADR movement in the United States was described as "dramatically different."[138] During that time, the ABA established goals to "integrate dispute resolution into every aspect of the legal system and society."[139] For example, between 1988 and 1989, the ABA adopted resolutions "[t]o promote continued use of and experimentation with ADR, both before and after suit is filed, as welcome components of the justice system" (adopted August 1989), and "[t]o support the increased use of ADR by federal agencies, which included support for the recently passed *Administrative Dispute Resolution Act* of 1990" (adopted August 1988).[140] In 1992, with a specific focus on legal education, the ABA – in Robert MacCrate's report on legal education and professional development[141] – strongly advocated for increased practical, clinical courses and approaches at law schools designed to "address the lack of competence among graduating lawyers."[142] Included in these recommendations (for improved lawyer skills training) was a focus on negotiation and litigation and ADR processes.[143] An underlying basis for this focus, according to the ABA, was its understanding that "continued public and professional education about ADR is necessary to

138 Ibid.

139 Ibid.

140 Ibid. at 35.

141 ABA, Section on Legal Education and Admissions to the Bar, *Legal Education and Professional Development – An Educational Continuum, The Report of the Task Force on Law Schools and the Profession: Narrowing the Gap* (Chicago: ABA, 1992) (Chair: Robert MacCrate) [*MacCrate Report*]. For earlier ABA teaching initiatives in the context of the development of ADR, see, for example, ABA, Section on Legal Education and Admissions to the Bar, *Report and Recommendations of the Task Force on Lawyer Competency: The Role of Law Schools* (1979) at 3–4; and ABA, *Law Schools and Professional Education: Report and Recommendations of the Special Committee for a Study of Legal Education of the American Bar Association* (1980) at 103, both cited in Robert B. Moberly, "Introduction: Dispute Resolution in the Law School Curriculum: Opportunities and Challenges" (1998) 50 *Fla. L. Rev.* 583 at 585.

142 Russell Engler, "The MacCrate Report Turns 10: Assessing its Impact and Identifying Gaps We Should Seek to Narrow" (2001) 8 *Clinical L. Rev.* 109 at 115. See further Daniel Gordon, "Does Law Teaching Have Meaning? Teaching Effectiveness, Gauging Alumni Competence, and the MacCrate Report" (1997) 25 *Fordham Urb. L.J.* 43.

143 See *MacCrate Report*, supra note 141 at 138–40, cited in Engler, "The MacCrate Report Turns 10," supra note 142 at 113, n. 13; and further in Robert MacCrate, "Yesterday, Today and Tomorrow: Building the Continuum of Legal Education and Professional Development" (New York Law School, Clinical Research Institute, Research Paper Series No. 03/04-1, September 2003) at 3, n. 6, online: Social Science Research Network Electronic Paper Collection <http://papers.ssrn.com/sol3/papers.cfm?abstract_id=444601> ["Yesterday, Today and Tomorrow"].

aid in the transformation of a legal system now centered around litigation into a system that includes non-adversarial ADR mechanisms."[144] Other influential reform-related ADR initiatives, at both the federal[145] and state[146] levels, also continued to develop in the United States after the publication of the 1992 *MacCrate Report*.[147]

---

144 *ABA Blueprint*, supra note 134 at 39. As a result, the ABA actively "promote[d] greater awareness of ADR through its publications, conferences, workshops and seminars" (ibid. at 38). In fact, as the ABA itself commented, in the context of its consideration of the report of the President's Council for Competitiveness (President's Council on Competitiveness, *Agenda for Civil Justice Reform in America* [Washington, DC, 1991]), it was "the prime mover in the creation of the Multi-Door Courthouse" (*ABA Blueprint*, ibid. at 35). For further background on the "Multi-Door Courthouse," see supra note 134 and accompanying text.

145 For example, on 5 February 1996, the president signed Executive Order 12988 on civil justice reform. The Preamble to Title 3 of the order highlights the federal government's intention "to improve access to justice for all persons who wish to avail themselves of court and administrative adjudicatory tribunals to resolve disputes, to facilitate the just and efficient resolution of civil claims involving the United States Government, ... to promote fair and prompt adjudication before administrative tribunals, and to provide a model for similar reforms of litigation practices in the private sector and in various states." EO 12988 – *Civil Justice Reform*, 66 Fed. Reg. 4727-4734 (1996), Title 3, p. 4729, s. 1, revoking EO 12778, 56 Fed. Reg. 55195 (1991), supplemented by EO 13083, 63 Fed. Reg. 27651 (1998) (which was suspended by EO 13095, 63 Fed. Reg. 42565 (1998)); EO 13132, 64 Fed. Reg. 43255 (1999). The order, among other things, provides that in the context of civil litigation involving the federal government in federal courts, ADR processes should be canvassed "[w]henever feasible"; EO 12988, ibid. at Title 3, p. 4729, s. 1(c)(1). Further, to "facilitate broader and effective use of informal and formal ADR methods," the Order provides that "litigation counsel should be trained in ADR techniques"; ibid. at Title 3, p. 4729, s. 1(c)(3). Finally, and importantly, although outside the specific federal government mandate, the order expressly contemplates acting as a "model" for litigation reform in both the private sector and in the various states; EO 12988, ibid. at Title 3, p. 4729, s. 1. For a general discussion, see, for example, Jeffrey M. Senger, "Turning the Ship of State" (2000) *J. Disp. Resol.* 79. For somewhat similar government preferences and initiatives in Canada, see infra Chapter 5.

146 For specific state initiatives, see, for example, Judge H.J. Fromholz, "The Los Angeles Superior Court Mediation Program" (conference presentation, Calgary, Alberta, 18 October 2001) in CFCJ et al., eds., "Negotiating the Future: A National Conference on Court-Annexed Mediation" (Calgary, Alberta, 15 November 2001) [unpublished conference materials] ["Negotiating the Future"]; and Sharon Press, "Florida Court-Connected Mediation Programs" (conference presentation, Calgary, Alberta, 18 October 2001), in ibid. [unpublished]; Stempel, "Reflections on Judicial ADR," supra note 134.

147 For general discussions, see, for example, MacCrate, "Yesterday, Today and Tomorrow," supra note 143; Engler, "The MacCrate Report Turns 10," supra note 143.

In sum, the post–Pound Conference ADR era amounted to a siren call for a massive rethinking of how civil disputes are resolved in the United States (and increasingly in other countries as well). Although initially stemming from the efforts of key individuals at elite institutions in the United States,[148] ADR quickly became seen as an elegant and deceptively simple[149] potential answer to the problems of increasingly inefficient and inaccessible public dispute resolution regimes. The bar – given dominant models of professionalism that continued to jealously guard visions of the zealous advocate trained in and working with the fine art of rights-based, client-centred advocacy – was initially generally resistant to a wholesale move to ADR. However, demands from various voices including rules reformers and clients continued to break down this initial practice-based resistance. Today, ADR is part of the mainstream diet of U.S. academics and practitioners.[150] Court-annexed ADR has become a fixture throughout the state and federal court systems.[151] It is clearly part of the plan for law schools going forward.[152] And as one source has noted, "[t]here is a growing sense … that it is time to look beyond adjudication as a single model for dispute

148 I am thinking here, for example, of people like Derek Bok, Frank Sander, and Roger Fisher at Harvard University.

149 See, for example, Roger Fisher and William Ury, *Getting to Yes: Negotiating Agreement without Giving In* (Boston: Houghton Mifflin, 1981).

150 See Farrow, "Dispute Resolution, Access to Civil Justice and Legal Education," supra note 43 at 745–6.

151 As one commentator noted several years ago, the ABA "Section on Dispute Resolution Conference, Only Three Years Old, Is Larger than the ABA Litigation Section Conference." Lela Porter Love, "Twenty-Five Years Later with Promises to Keep: Legal Education in Dispute Resolution and Training Mediators" (2002) 17 *Ohio St. J. Disp. Resol.* 597 at 601. See further Thomas J. Stipanowich, "ADR and the 'Vanishing Trial': The Growth and Impact of 'Alternative Dispute Resolution'" (2004) 1 *J. Emp. Leg. Stud.* 843. For a discussion of the state and federal court mediation initiatives, see, for example, Louise Phipps Senft and Cynthia A. Savage, "ADR in the Courts: Progress, Problems, and Possibilities" (2003) 108 *Penn St. L. Rev.* 327. See also Roselle L. Wissler, "Court-Connected Mediation in General Civil Cases: What We Know from Empirical Research" (2002) 17:3 *Ohio St. J. Disp. Resol.* 641.

152 See, for example, Roy Stuckey et al., *Best Practices for Legal Education: A Vision and a Road Map* (New York: Clinical Legal Education Association, 2007); and William M. Sullivan et al., *Educating Lawyers: Preparation for the Profession of Law* (San Francisco: Jossey-Bass, 2007) ["*Carnegie Report*"].

resolution, and to consider instead a spectrum of dispute resolution alternatives."[153] Similarly, according to another source,

> I see ADR as having become a part of the judicial system, perhaps inevitably and certainly for the present. Regardless of the effectiveness of ADR in particular situations, there is no doubt that socio-political forces will continue to promote it and will not be turned back by a call for adoption of (or a return to) a greater use of traditional, full-dress adjudication of disputes.[154]

Summary

With all of this international reform activity, the "face of the legal profession – and in particular the way modern disputes are thought about and resolved – has dramatically changed … over the past decade."[155] In sum, and put simply, as a further recent report confirmed, "[c]ivil justice reform initiatives are unfolding all around us in the Commonwealth … [and] throughout the common law world."[156] And clearly, based on the

---

153 Macfarlane, *Dispute Resolution: Readings and Case Studies* (2003), supra note 86 at xvii.

154 Stempel, "Reflections on Judicial ADR," supra note 134 at 305–6 [citations omitted]. See further Stephen N. Subrin, "A Traditionalist Looks at Mediation: It's Here to Stay and Much Better than I Thought" (2002/3) 3 *Nev. L.J.* 196, all discussed further in Farrow, "Dispute Resolution, Access to Civil Justice and Legal Education," supra note 43 at 745, n. 20 and accompanying text. See also Subrin, "David Dudley Field and the Field Code: A Historical Analysis of an Earlier Procedural Vision," supra note 122 at 311.

155 Farrow, "Dispute Resolution, Access to Civil Justice and Legal Education," supra note 43 at 746. Further, and put another way, the "lawyer's standard philosophical map" as described by Leonard Riskin is changing. See Leonard L. Riskin, "Mediation and Lawyers" (1982) 43 *Ohio St. L.J.* 29 at 43–4, cited in James R. Coben, "Summer Musings on Curricular Innovations to Change the Lawyer's Standard Philosophical Map" (1998) 50 *Fla. L. Rev.* 735 at 735. For other comments of mine on these issues, see, for example, Trevor C.W. Farrow, "Representative Negotiation" in Hanycz, Farrow, and Zemans, *The Theory and Practice of Representative Negotiation*, supra note 43 at c. 2; Trevor C.W. Farrow, "The Negotiator-as-Professional: Understanding the Competing Interests of a Representative Negotiator" (2007) 7 *Pepp. Disp. Resol. L.J.* 373. On the issue of lawyers' practices and preferences with respect to ADR, see further infra Chapter 5.

156 Editorial, "Entre Nous" (March 2007) 65:2 *Advocate* 153 at 153, 154.

international reform efforts discussed in this section, privatization is a common theme within this "global revolution."[157]

Canada

Reform initiatives across Canada – described recently as a "wave … sweeping across Canadian jurisdictions"[158] – have followed their English, Australian, and U.S. counterparts. Similar (and familiar) reform goals have also been pursued, and for some time. For example, as with the nineteenth-century reform initiatives in New York, early superior court rules initiatives in Canada – for example in 1842 in Upper Canada[159] – were made "for simplifying the proceedings … and rendering the same less expensive to Suitors."[160] Similarly, reports of the 1873 and 1881 reforms in Ontario[161] described these initiatives as being in pursuit of the "speedy, convenient and inexpensive administration of justice,"[162] which had been reported as being formerly "expensive and time-consuming."[163] Many of these early reforms, in response to criticisms of cumbersome and inefficient court procedures, came as a result of the modernization of early Canadian societies. For example, according to a dispatch from Sir Peregrine Maitland, lieutenant-overnor

157 Karl Mackie (referring specifically to mediation) in Economist Staff, "Knocking Heads Together" *Economist* (3 February 2007), available online: IADR Global <http://www.iadrglobal.org/newsitems/knockingheadstogether.php>. Further, according to Mackie, "Interest in mediation is rocketing, in countries of all legal traditions and none." See ibid.

158 Christopher Guly, "Alberta Leads the Way in Justice Reform" 28:15 *The Lawyers Weekly* (22 August 2008) 1 at 1.

159 See, for example, *Journals of the Legislative Assembly of … Canada* (1842), vol. 2, app. Q (p. 48). See also *Rules of Court, 1831–1895,* cited in William R. Riddell, *The Bar and the Courts of the Province of Upper Canada, or Ontario,* supra note 46 at 183–4, n. 4.

160 Riddell, *The Bar and the Courts of the Province of Upper Canada, or Ontario,* supra note 46 at 183.

161 See *Administration of Justice Act,* 36 Vict. (1873), c. 8 and Ontario *Judicature Act,* 44 Vict. (1881), c. 5, cited in Margaret A. Banks, "The Evolution of the Ontario Courts, 1788–1981" in David H. Flaherty, ed., *Essays in the History of Canadian Law* (Toronto, Buffalo, London: University of Toronto Press, 1983), vol. 2, c. 9 at 519 and 523.

162 Banks, "The Evolution of the Ontario Courts, 1788–1981" supra note 161 at 519.

163 Ibid. at 523.

of the province of Upper Canada, changes in the justice system were needed in order to accommodate the "rapid growth of the population, and the consequent increase in the number of commercial and other transactions."[164] As with their U.S. counterparts,[165] then, a key theme of these kinds of reforms was "efficiency."[166]

Modern National Initiatives

As the primary modern national starting point, in 1996, the Canadian Bar Association (CBA) engaged in a wide-ranging and influential review of the delivery of civil justice in Canada. The result was the CBA's "Systems of Civil Justice Task Force Report."[167] Numerous observations and recommendations made in that report have led to significant and

---

164 9 April 1827, cited in John Delatre Falconbridge, "Law and Equity in Upper Canada" (1914) 63:1 *U. Pa. L. Rev.* 1 at 9.

165 See, for example, the earlier discussion of U.S. reform initiatives.

166 See, for example, Paul Romney, "From Constitutionalism to Legalism: Trial by Jury, Responsible Government, and the Rule of Law in the Canadian Political Culture" (1989) 7:1 *L.H.R.* 121 at 141–2.

167 See Canadian Bar Association (CBA), Task Force on Systems of Civil Justice, "Systems of Civil Justice Task Force Report" (Ottawa: CBA, 1996), available online: CBA <http://www.cba.org/CBA/pubs/pdf/systemscivil_tfreport.pdf> ["CBA Task Force Report"]. The CFCJ and others held two "Into the Future" conferences to discuss the "agenda for civil justice reform" a decade after the publication of the "CBA Task Force Report," discussed further infra at note 176. Conference papers on file with author. For a further discussion of the CBA initiatives, see Farrow, "Dispute Resolution, Access to Civil Justice and Legal Education," supra note 43 at pt. II.C. For useful sources for civil justice reform initiatives, see CFCJ, "Inventory of Reforms," available online: CFCJ <http://www.cfcj-fcjc.org/inventory-of-reforms> (which includes reform initiatives in Canada from 1950–2009); and Canadian Judicial Council (CJC), Sub-Committee on Access to Justice (Trial Courts) of the Administration of Justice Committee, "Access to Justice: Report on Selected Reform Initiatives in Canada" (June 2008), available online: CJC <http://www.cjc-ccm.gc.ca/cmslib/general/2008_SelectedReformInitiatives_Report_final_EN.pdf> (which also includes a number of useful links to reform initiatives). For discussions of, and links to, many of the civil justice reform initiatives discussed in the following, see CFCJ, "Civil Justice News" ["Civil Justice News"] [archived with author]. This portion of this chapter is significantly influenced by those sources, discussions and links.

still ongoing reform initiatives in this country.[168] By way of background, the CBA task force was created "to inquire into the state of the civil justice system on a national basis and to develop strategies and mechanisms to facilitate modernization of the justice system so that it is better able to meet the current and future needs of Canadians."[169] As part of its inquiry, the CBA task force specifically focussed on the role that ADR methods can and should play in making the justice system more efficient and accessible.[170] The task force strongly encouraged the use of a "multi-option civil justice system."[171] In a multi-option civil justice system, according to the CBA, "litigation lawyers must move away from a focus on rights-based thinking and adopt a wider problem-solving approach."[172] This move – the "adoption of a dispute resolution approach" to "litigation practice"[173] – was described by the Task Force not only as desirable but also as a "new professional obligation."[174]

There were a number of key reform proposals in the "CBA Task Force Report" that were aimed at these overall reform goals, the summaries for many of which are set out in the following:

1. Every jurisdiction
   (a) make available as part of the civil justice system opportunities for litigants to use non-binding dispute resolution processes as early as possible in the litigation process and, at a minimum, at or shortly after the close of pleadings and again following completion of examinations for discovery; [and]

---

168 For a useful review of the CBA's recommendations and their subsequent implementation, see Margaret A. Shone, "Civil Justice Reform in Canada: 1996 to 2006 and Beyond" (December 2006), online: CFCJ <http://www.cfcj-fcjc.org/sites/default/files/docs/2006/shone-final-en.pdf>.

169 "CBA Task Force Report," supra note 167 at iii.

170 Ibid. at v–viii, "Summary of Task Force Recommendations" nos. 1–3, 5, 13, 26–7, 36, 38, and 49. For a discussion of the CBA Task Force Report recommendations, see, for example, CFCJ, "Civil Justice Reform Update," *News & Views Civ. Just. Reform* 2 (Fall 1999) 17. See also Pirie, *Alternative Dispute Resolution: Skills, Science, and the Law*, supra note 88 at 389–90. For earlier comments on these issues, see Farrow, "Dispute Resolution, Access to Civil Justice and Legal Education," supra note 43 at 750–4.

171 See, for example, "CBA Task Force Report," supra note 167 at c. 4.

172 Ibid. at 63.

173 Ibid. at 64.

174 Ibid. See generally Farrow, "Dispute Resolution, Access to Civil Justice and Legal Education," supra note 43 at 750–4.

(b) establish, as a pre-condition for using the court system after the close of pleadings, and later as a pre-condition for entitlement to a trial or hearing date, a requirement that litigants certify either that they have availed themselves of the opportunity to participate in a non-binding dispute resolution process or that the circumstances of the case are such that participation is not warranted or has been considered and rejected for sound reasons …

2. Each jurisdiction through its rules of procedure impose on all litigants a positive, early and continuing obligation to canvass settlement possibilities and to consider opportunities available to them to participate in nonbinding dispute resolution processes.
3. Every court undertake studies or pilot projects to determine best practices concerning the integration of non-binding dispute resolution processes in the post-discovery stages of litigation …

21. Every jurisdiction
    (a) develop a system of incentives and sanctions to encourage settlement and the prudent use of court time …

27. Every court provide point-of-entry advice to members of the public on dispute resolution options in the civil justice system and available community services …[175]

All of these reform recommendations, among others,[176] were clearly designed to promote greater efficiencies in the public justice system, primarily by actively encouraging the use of privatizing tools. Further,

175 "CBA Task Force Report," supra note 167 at v–vi, "Summary of Task Force Recommendations" nos. 1–3, 21, and 27. Other provisions included recommendations concerning professional responsibility obligations as well as legal education and training obligations. For a further discussion of the CBA's approach to reform and legal education, see infra Chapter 5.

176 Shortly after the task force published its report, and specifically pursuant to recommendation no. 52 of the report ("CBA Task Force Report," supra note 167 at 73–4), the Canadian Forum on Civil Justice was created. See CFCJ, available online: <http://www.cfcj-fcjc.org/> (I am the current chair of the CFCJ's board). Several of the primary purposes of the CFCJ, which has been very active and successful over the past decade, are to assist with the research about and dissemination of, court reform and court reform information at a national level. For example, a key national initiative organized by the CFCJ – in addition to its ongoing and significant research agenda – was its two-part national civil justice reform conference: "Into the Future: The Agenda for Civil Justice Reform" (Montréal, Québec, 30 April–2 May 2006; Toronto, Ontario, 8 December 2006), mentioned earlier at note 167.

in light of these significant reform initiatives, the CBA Task Force Report was followed four years later, in 2000, by the CBA's *Attitudes – Skills – Knowledge* report.[177] That report was generally a response to the CBA task force's recommendation no. 49, which was designed primarily to consider the creation of a "legal education plan to assist in civil justice reform."[178] More recently, further national reform initiatives continue to be pursued.[179]

Provincial and Territorial Initiatives

Notwithstanding these significant national initiatives, the same calls for reforms to address cost, speed, and backlogs continue to be made.[180] For example, in December 2006, former Ontario chief justice Roy McMurtry made the following comments:

> In Ontario, it has been recognized for some years that our civil justice system is in a crisis. …
>
> I became a judge in 1991 and very quickly learned that the issue of access to civil justice would be the principal justice challenge for the foreseeable future. In 1995, as the chief justice of the Superior Court, I referred to the crisis and stated publicly that:
>
> As well as the increasing cost, the system is labouring under the tremendous weight of a growing backlog of cases and a serious lack of adequate resources. Litigants must wait an inordinate length of time to resolve their civil disputes. Significant initiatives are absolutely essential if our court is to be able to provide timely and affordable justice to the citizens of this province.

---

177 CBA, Joint Multi-disciplinary Committee on Legal Education, *Attitudes – Skills – Knowledge: Recommendations for Changes to Legal Education to Assist in Implementing Multi-Option Civil Justice Systems in the 21st Century* (Ottawa: CBA, 2000).

178 "CBA Task Force Report," supra note 167 at 73. For a further discussion of the CBA's approach to reform and legal education, see infra Chapter 5.

179 See, for example, the 2008 establishment of the national "Action Committee on Access to Justice in Civil and Family Matters," the honourary chair for which is the Rt. Hon. Beverley McLachlin, P.C., chief justice of Canada. (I am currently a member of that committee.) For information on the Action Committee, see "Action Committee on Access to Justice in Civil and Family Matters," online: CFCJ <http://www.cfcj-fcjc.org/collaborations>.

180 For a report citing these factors, see Donalee Moulton, "Vanishing Trials: Out-of-Court Settlements on the Rise" 28:23 *The Lawyers Weekly* (17 October 2008) 22 at 22.

> Well, almost twelve years later, the crisis has deepened despite the best efforts of a lot of people, judges, lawyers and officials in the Ministry of the Attorney General.[181]

Because the administration of civil justice largely falls within the jurisdiction of the provinces,[182] the majority of the extensive and ongoing civil justice reform initiatives are being carried out at the provincial level. At this level, numerous ongoing efforts are being made to address the kinds of "crisis" that the former chief justice of Ontario described.[183] Put simply, every jurisdiction in Canada has been looking[184] – in some capacity – at ways of making civil dispute resolution processes more efficient and effective.[185] And it is largely in the context of these very

---

181 Hon. R. Roy McMurtry, CFCJ, Civil Justice Reform Conference: Phase II, "Remarks" (7 December 2006) at 3–4 ["McMurtry Remarks"] [archived with author]. For similar remarks by the chief justice of Canada commenting on the many challenges that face our systems of civil justice, see, for example, Rt. Hon. Beverley McLachlin, P.C., "The Challenges We Face" (remarks presented at Empire Club of Canada, Toronto, Ontario, 8 March 2007), available online: Supreme Court of Canada <http://www.scc-csc.gc.ca/court-cour/judges-juges/spe-dis/bm-2007-03-08-eng.aspx>.

182 See *Constitution Act, 1867* (U.K.), 30 & 31 Vict., c. 3, reprinted in R.S.C. 1985, App. II, No. 5, s. 92(14), which provides that

> [i]n each Province the Legislature may exclusively make Laws in relation to Matters coming within the Classes of Subjects next hereinafter enumerated; that is to say ... The Administration of Justice in the Province, including the Constitution, Maintenance, and Organization of Provincial Courts, both of Civil and of Criminal Jurisdiction, and including Procedure in Civil Matters in those Courts.

183 Not everyone believes there is a "crisis" in the civil justice system. According to Peter Lown, director of ALRI, who does certainly believe that civil justice – particularly in Alberta – is in need of reform, there has not been "a complete breakdown" or a "crisis" in the civil justice system. Peter J. M. Lown, Q.C., quoted in Guly, "Alberta Leads the Way in Justice Reform," supra note 158 at 15. For a different view, in the context of a comparative study of international reform initiatives, see Adrian Zuckerman, *Civil Justice in Crisis: Comparative Perspectives of Civil Procedure*, supra note 102 at v.

184 For a very useful and comprehensive study of, and recommendations regarding civil justice reform initiatives across Canada, see Shone, "Civil Justice Reform in Canada: 1996 to 2006 and Beyond," supra note 168. More generally, see CFCJ, "Inventory of Reforms," supra note 167. See also M. Jerry McHale, "Uniform Mediation Act: Discussion Paper" (paper presented at the Uniform Law Conference of Canada, Victoria, B.C., August 2000), available online: CFCJ <http://www.cfcj-fcjc.org/sites/default/files/docs/hosted/17494-uniform_mediation.pdf>.

185 For general summary discussions of various provincial initiatives, see, for example, Association of Canadian Court Administrators, "Dispute Resolution," materials

extensive and ongoing modern provincial reform efforts, many significant examples of which are discussed immediately next, that the privatization of the civil justice system in Canada is being heavily promoted and pursued today.[186] As one commentator recently described, "it is clear that there is a wholesale move toward alternative dispute resolution which will not disappear."[187] Similarly, according to Justice Eleanore Cronk of the Court of Appeal for Ontario, there has been a "spectacular growth of the alternative dispute resolution industry in

---

collected in *Can. Ct. Communiqué* (Winter 2011), supra note 89. See further CFCJ, "Cross Country Snapshot of Dispute Resolution" *News & Views Civ. Just. Reform* 4 (Spring 2002) 12 at 12–14; Graeme A. Barry, "In the Shadow of the Rule of Law: Alternative Dispute Resolution and Provincial Superior Courts" *News & Views Civ. Just. Reform* 8 (Fall 1999) 2; Patricia Hughes, "Mandatory Mediation: Opportunity or Subversion?" (2001) 19 *Windsor Y.B. Access Just.* 161; Joan I. McEwen, "JDR: Judicial Dispute Resolution" *National* 8:7 (November 1999) 36; David Orr, "Alternative Dispute Resolution in the Canadian Court System" (1999) 19:2 *The Court Manager* 36; and Michaela Keet and Teresa B. Salamone, "From Litigation to Mediation: Using Advocacy Skills for Success in Mandatory or Court-Connected Mediation" (2001) 64 *Sask. L. Rev.* 57. For general comments on governmental reform interests, see, for example, M. Jerry McHale, "8 Minute Round Table" in Justice Institute of B.C. et al., eds., "Shaping Directions in Policy, Research and Pedagogy," The First Annual B.C. Symposium on Conflict Resolution (Conference Materials, Vancouver, B.C., 25 April 2003). Many of these reform initiatives discussed in this note and note 167 and accompanying text are also discussed briefly in Farrow, "Dispute Resolution, Access to Civil Justice and Legal Education," supra note 43 at n. 46 and accompanying text. See also CFCJ, "Civil Justice News," supra note 167. Further, in terms of specific areas of law, ADR has taken strong hold with respect to family law matters in Canada, including custody, access, guardianship and child welfare. See, for example, Marion Boyd, "Dispute Resolution in Family Law: Protecting Choice, Promoting Inclusion" (December 2004), available online: Ontario Ministry of the Attorney General <http://www.attorneygeneral.jus.gov.on.ca/english/about/pubs/boyd/fullreport.pdf> ["Boyd Report"]. In turn, for commentary on the "Boyd Report," see, for example, John Jaffey, "Boyd Report Draws Mixed Reaction" *The Lawyers Weekly* (21 January 2005) 9; and Faisal Kutty, "Commentary: Boyd's Recommendations Balance Needs of Religious Communities with Rights of Vulnerable" *The Lawyers Weekly* (21 January 2005) 9.

186 Much of my awareness and understanding of these initiatives – including superior and inferior court reform initiatives and related materials, commentaries, and so on – have been directly influenced and assisted by the work of the CFCJ. See, for example, CFCJ, "Inventory of Reforms," supra note 167.

187 Ronalda Murphy, "Introduction" in Murphy and Molinari, eds., *Doing Justice: Dispute Resolution in the Courts and Beyond*, supra note 43 at xiii.

Canada. … The business community and individual litigants have seized upon ADR, almost with passionate abandon."[188]

I have chosen, in the following parts of this chapter, to document extensively many of the main provincial reform efforts, as opposed simply to providing a relatively brief summary. The reason for doing so is that, even if some of those provisions may change (or have changed since the research was done for this book), only with a relatively comprehensive picture of the collective of initiatives that have been developed over the last number of years does the depth and breadth of the current reform movement really become apparent.

British Columbia

B.C. has been engaged in a wide-ranging civil justice reform movement for several years. The B.C. Justice Review Task Force released its "Effective and Affordable Civil Justice" report[189] and proposed new rules of civil procedure, which came into force on 1 July 2010.[190] The basic premises behind these civil justice reforms are to provide people with ways to resolve legal problems more efficiently and affordably.[191] Building on current B.C. programs, including mediation[192] and other ADR-related

---

188 Hon. E. A. Cronk, "Examining Barriers that Prevent Litigants from Accessing the Civil Justice System" (paper given at CFCJ "Into the Future" conference, Montréal, Québec, 1 May 2006) at 6–7.

189 Civil Justice Reform Working Group to the Justice Review Task Force, "Effective and Affordable Civil Justice" (November 2006), available online: B.C. Justice Review Task Force <http://www.bcjusticereview.org/working_groups/civil_justice/cjrwg_report_11_06.pdf>. For a discussion of the B.C. reform process, see Allan Seckel, "Judicial Models: Can We Do Better? Proposed Reforms to Civil Procedure in British Columbia" in Murphy and Molinari, eds., *Doing Justice: Dispute Resolution in the Courts and Beyond*, supra note 43 at 19.

190 B.C. *Supreme Court Civil Rules*, B.C. Reg. 168/2009, as amended by B.C. Reg. 119/2010 (1 July 2010). See further B.C. Ministry of Attorney General, "New Supreme Court Civil and Family Rules," available online: B.C. Government <http://www.ag.gov.bc.ca/new-rules/>.

191 See generally B.C. Justice Review Task Force [archived with author].

192 See, for example, B.C.'s "Notice to Mediate" process, which allows a party to a proceeding to require another party to attend a mediation session. See "Bulletin: Notice to Mediate (General) Regulation," B.C. Reg. 4/2001 (effective 15 February 2001), available online: B.C. Dispute Resolution Office <http://www.bclaws.ca/EPLibraries/bclaws_new/document/ID/freeside/4_2001>. For a further description of the process, see B.C. Dispute Resolution Office, "Bulletin: Notice to Mediate, (General) Regulation" (June 2002), available online: Government of B.C. <http://www.ag.gov.bc.ca/dro/publications/bulletins/general.htm>.

options,[193] key aspects to these reforms include proposals for increasing tools for people to resolve their disputes before going to court, as well as tools to reduce costs for people who do go to court.[194] Regarding the first of these (out of court) aspects, the B.C. Justice Review Task Force stated that:

> The Working Group found that most citizens are seeking early and fair dispute resolution, not a costly and prolonged trial. The Working Group, therefore, proposed that citizens should be provided with the information and services they need to resolve their legal problems on their own before entering the court system.[195]

Proposals here include the creation of legal service "hubs," which are locations at which the public can obtain a variety of legal information regarding the potential resolution of their disputes, including information about available services, appropriate means of resolving disputes (specifically including meditation), and so on.[196]

With respect to in-court reforms, key aspects of the B.C. reforms include creating rules that, among other things, provide "judges with more authority to control the adversarial process so as to reduce complexity, cost and delay."[197] Particularly relevant to this book is part 9 of the new rules, which deals with "pre-trial resolution procedures."[198]

---

193 For a summary of some of B.C.'s dispute resolution options, see Hon. Marvyn Koenigsberg, "Access to Justice: A Survey of Reform Initiatives in British Columbia" (24 February 2006) (paper presented at "Streamlining the Ontario Civil Justice System: A Policy Forum," Advocates' Society, Toronto, 9 March 2006) [archived with author]. For a useful discussion of community-based mediation initiatives in B.C., see George C. Pavlich, *Justice Fragmented: Mediating Community Disputes under Postmodern Conditions* (London, New York: Routledge, 1996).

194 B.C. Justice Review Task Force, "Civil Justice Reform in British Columbia Supreme Court," supra note 191 at § III–IV. For a recent discussion, see *Vilardell v. Dunham*, 2012 BCSC 748.

195 Ibid. at § III.

196 Ibid. See further B.C. Ministry of Attorney General, Justice Access Centre, available online: Government of B.C. <http://www.ag.gov.bc.ca/justice-access-centre/>, which specifically includes information on mediation and other available legal services (in Nanaimo and Vancouver).

197 See B.C. Justice Review Task Force, "Civil Justice Reform in British Columbia Supreme Court," supra note 191 at § V.A.

198 B.C. *Supreme Court Civil Rules*, supra note 190 at pt. 9.

Included in these procedures are rules encouraging offers to settle and private settlement conferences run by judges or masters.[199] The new rules also provide for a case planning conference, an order from which can include

> requiring the parties of record to attend one or more of a mediation, a settlement conference or any other dispute resolution process, and giving directions for the conduct of the mediation, settlement conference or other dispute resolution process.[200]

Further, overlaying all of the proposed rules is an "interpretation" section, which provides, among other things, that cases should be dealt with "in ways that are proportionate to" the "amount involved," the "importance of the issues in dispute," and the "complexity of the proceeding."[201]

Taken together, the recent B.C. reforms – which are very wide-ranging in nature – contemplate significant in-court and out-of-court privatizing initiatives. In fact, the totality of the proposals that led to the reforms was at one point described by the president of the Trial Lawyers Association of B.C. as a "nuclear explosion" to "everything" in B.C.'s civil justice sector.[202]

---

199 Ibid. at rr. 9-1–9-2.

200 Ibid. at r. 5-3(1)(o). For judicial discussions of case planning conferences, see *Parti v. Pokorny*, supra note 66; *Shen v. Klassen* (2011), 17 B.C.L.R. (5th) 209, 2011 BCSC 234 (B.C.S.C.).

201 B.C. *Supreme Court Civil Rules*, supra note 190 at r. 1–3. For a recent discussion of proportionality, see Trevor C.W. Farrow, "Proportionality: A Cultural Revolution" (2012) 1 *J. Civ. Lit. & Practice* 151.

202 See Steve Frame (President of the Trial Lawyers Association of B.C.) in Christopher Guly, "Storm Erupts over B.C.'s Proposed Civil Reforms" 28:7 *The Lawyers Weekly* (13 June 2008) 1 at 1. As such, notwithstanding significant broad-based support for the recent reforms, there was also significant opposition to the proposed changes. For example, the Trial Lawyers Association of B.C. would have preferred a more "laser-guided" approach to reform (which is not necessarily surprising given the particular interest of this group). See Guly, "Storm Erupts over B.C.'s Proposed Civil Reforms," ibid. at 1. Individuals from other justice sectors also voiced criticism, including members of the judiciary and bar. See ibid. at 18. For a useful summary of the B.C. experience, see Advocates' Society, *Streamlining the Ontario Civil Justice System: A Policy Forum, Final Report*, supra note 113 at 4–7. For specific commentary on B.C.'s various reform initiatives over the past number of years, see, for example, Jill Leacock, "British Columbia Court of Appeal Judicial Settlement Conference Pilot Project" (2004) 62 *Advocate (B.C.)* 879; Gordon Turriff, "On the Road to Civil

Prairie Provinces and Territories

Alberta has recently been in the midst of a major civil justice system overhaul, which one report has described as "lead[ing] … the way in justice reform."[203] In fact, Alberta has been reworking several aspects of its superior court civil justice system over the last several decades. These reform efforts, taken together, all go to the promotion of early dispute resolution, primarily through privatization initiatives.

The first of these privatizing initiatives, which has been in place informally since the late 1970s and early 1980s and more formally since 1996,[204] is Alberta's judicial dispute resolution (JDR) initiative. The JDR program provides litigants with the opportunity to book a confidential dispute resolution session, often with a superior court judge of their choosing (or court of appeal judge, depending on the case).[205] This program – created largely through the initiative of Alberta's judiciary – has become extremely active and quite successful from a settlement perspective. For example, according to the recent "Alberta JDR Survey,"

Justice Reform in British Columbia" (2004) 62 *Advocate (B.C.)* 863; and Jack Giles, "The Compulsory Mediator" (2004) 62 *Advocate (B.C.)* 537. For earlier B.C. reform initiatives, see, for example, Hon. E.N. Hughes, *Access to Justice: Report of the Justice Reform Committee* (Victoria: Ministry of Attorney General, 1988).

203 Guly, "Alberta Leads the Way in Justice Reform," supra note 158 at 1. For a collection of materials, see Association of Canadian Court Administrators, "Dispute Resolution," materials collected in *Can. Ct. Communiqué* (Winter 2011), supra note 89.

204 See Hon. Allan H. Wachowich, "Court of Queen's Bench of Alberta, Judicial Dispute Resolution (JDR), Participant's Survey – Lawyers – 2007–2008" (cover letter to Hon. John D. Rooke's "Survey of Participants in the Court's JDR Program," September 2007) ["Alberta JDR Survey"] [unpublished, archived with author]. JDR is firmly part of Alberta's new rules of court (see *Alberta Rules of Court*, supra note 66 at rr. 4.17–4.21).

205 For a summary of the JDR process, see, for example, Alberta Court of Appeal, "Guidelines for Judicial Dispute Resolution (JDR)," available online: Alberta Courts <http://www.albertacourts.ab.ca/ca/practicenotes/1.pdf>. ALRI has also looked comprehensively at judicial dispute resolution initiatives – in the context of its Alberta Rules of Court revision project – designed to promote early settlement of disputes in Alberta through the use of ADR tools. See, for example, ALRI, "Promoting Early Resolution of Disputes," supra note 92. For a discussion of this Alberta study, see Margaret A. Shone, "Alberta Rules of Court Project: Promoting Early Dispute Resolution Through Settlement" *The Barrister* 68 (June 2003) 18. See further Christine E. Hart, "Draft Model Guidelines for Court-Connected Mediation Programs" (prepared for the CBA Systems of Justice Implementation Committee's Working Group on Dispute Resolution Standards, 3 September 1998).

the percentage of JDR settlements of parts or all of cases studied (between approximately 1 July 2007 and 30 June 2008) was reported at approximately 90 per cent.[206] Further anecdotal reports support these findings. For example, according to Belzil J. of the Alberta Court of Queen's Bench, "[o]ver the last number of years JDR has become hugely popular in the Province of Alberta. … Lawyers and clients report a high degree of satisfaction with the system, with ever increasing request for JDR."[207] Similarly, according to Wachowich C.J., "[t]o say the least, it [JDR in Alberta] has been an overwhelming success."[208]

Following the establishment of JDR in Alberta, civil mediation was developed as part of the toolkit available for litigants at the superior

---

206 Hon. John D. Rooke, "Interactive Survey Results – Excerpts (17 February 2009) (preliminary results from "Alberta JDR Survey," supra note 204) [unpublished, archived with author]. See further Hon. John D. Rooke, "The Multi-Door Courthouse is Open in Alberta: Judicial Dispute Resolution is Institutionalized in the Court of Queen's Bench" (LL.M. Thesis, University of Alberta, 2010), online: CFCJ <http://www.cfcj-fcjc.org/sites/default/files/docs/hosted/22471-multidoor_courthouse.pdf>.

207 Hon. R. Paul Belzil, "JDR (Judicial Dispute Resolution)" (14 November 2001) at 7–8 in CFCJ et al., eds., "Negotiating the Future," supra note 146.

208 Hon. Allan H. Wachowich, "Opening of the Court" (Calgary Courthouse, 2 September 2003) at 19–20 [unpublished] [archived with author]. See similarly Hon. Allan H. Wachowich, "Opening of the Court 2009" (Address by Chief Justice of Court of Queen's Bench of Alberta, 7 January 2009, Courtroom 317, Edmonton Law Courts, Alberta) at 4, available online: Alberta Courts <http://www.albertacourts.ab.ca/LinkClick.aspx?fileticket=lf4Lt8v3cmA%3d&tabid=69&mid=704>. For useful discussions of the JDR initiatives in the Alberta Court of Queen's Bench, see Hon. John A. Agrios, A *Handbook on Judicial Dispute Resolution for Canadian Lawyers* (Version 1.1, January 2004), online: Canadian Bar Association – Alberta <http://www.cba.org/alberta/PDF/JDR%20Handbook.pdf>; Hon. John A. Agrios, A *Handbook on Judicial Dispute Resolution for Law Students* (Version 3.7, July 2003); ALRI, "Promoting Early Resolution of Disputes," supra note 92 at 70–7; Hon. John A. Agrios, A *Handbook on Judicial Dispute Resolution for Canadian Judges* (Version 2.5, September 2002), cited in ibid. at 72, n. 175; Barry, "In the Shadow of the Rule of Law," supra note 185; "Negotiating the Future," supra note 146. See also Association of Canadian Court Administrators (ACCA), "Dispute Resolution," materials collected in *Can. Ct. Communiqué* (Winter 2011), supra note 89 at 7–9. It is important to note, however, that support for JDR is not universal. In addition to anecdotal (and confidential) comments I have heard from some members of the Alberta bench, see Hon. Hugh F. Landerkin and Andrew J. Pirie, "Judges as Mediators: What's the Problem with Judicial Dispute Resolution in Canada?" (2003) 82 *Can. Bar. Rev.* 249.

court in Alberta.[209] What has resulted is a program being offered in various local jurisdictions that provides private, user-pay, interest-based mediation.[210] Further, and perhaps most significantly, Alberta recently completed a total rewrite of its rules of court.[211] The new rules came into force on 1 November 2010.[212] The new rules are clearly designed to push efficiency, speed, cost-effectiveness and (at least to some extent) proportionality. For example, the "purpose and intention" section of the rules provides:

> 1.2(1) The purpose of these rules is to provide a means by which claims can be fairly and justly resolved in or by a court process in a timely and cost-effective way.

---

209 For a discussion of Alberta's mediation program, see Court of Queen's Bench, "Civil Mediation," available online: Alberta Courts <http://www.albertacourts.ab.ca/CourtofQueensBench/CivilMediation/tabid/74/Default.aspx>. By way of background to this mediation program, Alberta Justice sponsored a 2001 consultation session in Calgary that brought together ADR practitioners, court personnel, policy makers and academics. Behind this session was the provincial government's stated commitment "to improving access to courts and to simplifying our provincial justice system." See Hon. Dave Hancock, "Message from Alberta's Minister of Justice and Attorney General" in Alberta Justice, "Alberta Justice's Consultation on Court-Annexed Mediation" (Consultation Brochure, Calgary, 16 November 2001) [archived with author]. One of the outcomes of the 2001 Alberta consultation was the making of recommendations to the Minister of Justice concerning dispute resolution alternatives, including possible court-annexed mediation programs in civil cases. See ibid. See also ACCA, "Dispute Resolution," materials collected in *Can. Ct. Communiqué* (Winter 2011), supra note 89 at 6–7.

210 Court of Queen's Bench of Alberta, "Civil Practice Note No. 11: Court Annexed Mediation" (effective 1 September 2004), available online: Alberta Courts <http://www.albertacourts.ab.ca/qb/practicenotes/civil/pn11CourtAnnexedMediation.pdf>. For a recent survey of Alberta justice system stakeholders regarding the future of Alberta's court-annexed mediation program, see Alberta Court Services, "Online Survey Results: Court Annexed Dispute Resolution" (online responses to survey conducted 24 November 2008 – 8 December 2008) [archived with author].

211 See ALRI, *Rules of Court Project, Final Report No. 95* (Edmonton: ALRI, October 2008) at appendix H (available on CD), "Proposed Rules of Court," available online: ALRI <http://www.law.ualberta.ca/alri/docs/1.%20Appendix%20H%20-%20Proposed%20Rules%20of%20Court.pdf>. For a report on Alberta's initiatives, see Guly, "Alberta Leads the Way in Justice Reform," supra note 158. See also Peter J.M. Lown, "Rules of Court Project" (2005) 42 *Alta. L. Rev.* 907.

212 See *Alberta Rules of Court*, Alta. Reg. 124/2010 (mentioned supra note 66).

> (2) In particular, these rules are intended to be used …
> > (b) to facilitate the quickest means of resolving a claim at the least expense,
> > (c) to encourage the parties to resolve the claim themselves, by agreement, with or without assistance, as early in the process as practicable. …
>
> (3) To achieve the purpose and intention of these rules the parties must, jointly and individually during an action,
> > (a) identify or make an application to identify the real issues in dispute and facilitate the quickest means of resolving the claim at the least expense,
> > (b) periodically evaluate dispute resolution process alternatives to a full trial, with or without assistance from the Court. …
>
> (4) The intention of these rules is that the Court, when exercising a discretion to grant a remedy or impose a sanction, will grant or impose a remedy or sanction proportional to the reason for granting or imposing it.[213]

As part of these efforts, the new rules strongly promote private dispute resolution. According to ALRI, provincial reform initiatives are interested in the use of ADR as a tool for addressing the "timeliness, affordability and complexity of civil court proceedings."[214]

---

213 Ibid. at r. 1.2. For a recent discussion of proportionality, see Farrow, "Proportionality: A Cultural Revolution," supra note 201.

214 ALRI, "Promoting Early Resolution of Disputes by Settlement," supra note 92 at xiii. The new rules, taking these interests seriously, include significant sections on various dispute resolution tools, including the following dispute resolution dictate:

> The responsibility of the parties to manage their dispute includes good faith participation in one or more of the following dispute resolution processes with respect to all or any part of the action:
> (a) a dispute resolution process in the private or government sectors involving an impartial third person;
> (b) a court annexed dispute resolution process;
> (c) a judicial dispute resolution process …;
> (d) any program or process designated by the court for the purpose of this rule.

Alberta Rules of Court, supra note 66 at r. 4.16(1). See further ibid. at r. 8.4(3). In addition to the various Alberta reform initiatives discussed earlier, other initiatives include Alberta's new "law information centres," which are conceptually similar to B.C.'s legal information "hubs." For information on these services, see, for example,

Saskatchewan introduced an ambitious court-annexed mediation program in 1995.[215] The legislative debates surrounding the introduction of the program highlighted the motivations driving the initiatives, which focused largely on increasing the efficiency and reducing the costs of Saskatchewan's civil justice processes. According to the legislative report of the second reading of the proposed legislation, Justice Minister Robert Mitchell articulated some relative "failure[s]" of the "justice system ... to serve the needs of our citizens."[216] And in that context, he also articulated his view that "[i]n the best of all possible worlds, justice would be done efficiently, inexpensively and with minimal emotional pain to those involved."[217] What was required, in his view, was a court-annexed mediation program. According to Mitchell,

> Mr. Speaker, in an appropriate situation, mediation does provide a less costly and more effective method of solving problems. Mediation must be viewed as an integral part of the court process. To maximize its benefits, mediation must be a standard option in the early stages of litigation, an option to be explored before positions have become crystallized, before the parties have become inflexible.[218]

What followed was the creation of Saskatchewan's mandatory mediation program. First introduced as a pilot project in two centres, it

---

Alberta Justice and Attorney General, *Annual Report, 2007–2008* at 19, online: Alberta Justice <http://justice.alberta.ca/programs_services/about_us/Documents/2008_justice_annual_report.pdf>. Further, by way of important research initiatives, the CFCJ recently completed its "Alberta Legal Services Mapping Project," which maps and catalogues most of the legal services that are – and are not – available in Alberta. See CFCJ, "Alberta Legal Services Mapping Project," available online: CFCJ <http://www.cfcj-fcjc.org/alberta-legal-services>. For a comment on Alberta's mapping project, see Christopher Guly, "Project Set to 'Map' Services in Alberta" 28:15 *The Lawyers Weekly* (22 August 2008) 15.

215 For Saskatchewan's mediation provisions, see *Queen's Bench Act, 1998*, S.S. 1998, c. Q1.01, pt. vii.

216 Saskatchewan, Legislative Assembly, *Hansard* (18 March 1994) 997 at 998 [citation omitted] (Hon. R.W. Mitchell), cited in Julie Macfarlane and Michaela Keet, "Civil Justice Reform and Mandatory Civil Mediation in Saskatchewan: Lessons from a Maturing Program" (2005) 42 *Alta. L.R.* 677 at 678–9, nn. 2–4 and accompanying text (citations corrected).

217 Ibid.

218 Ibid. at 999.

now covers approximately 80 per cent of non-family cases in the province.[219] In line with Mitchell's view, the program requires that all parties to non-family civil actions "shall" proceed to a mediation session after the close of pleadings and before proceeding further in the litigation.[220] Further, as with other provinces, Saskatchewan has also recently revised its civil rules of court. Saskatchewan's new rules are designed "to facilitate the quickest means of resolving a claim at the least expense" and to encourage parties to resolve their matters "themselves, by agreement, with or without assistance, as early in the process as is practicable." As part of that settlement landscape, the rules include judicial case management provisions that contemplate judges assisting with settlement. Further, similar to B.C. and Ontario and to some extent Alberta, the rules also include a specific proportionality principle.[221]

Manitoba's Civil Justice Review Task Force reviewed the workings of its civil justice system more than ten years ago, including traditional and alternative methods of resolving disputes.[222] Currently, Manitoba judges have the power to engage in JDR initiatives pursuant to Manitoba's rules of court.[223] These powers have proved very effective in terms

219 See CFCJ, "Inventory of Reforms: Saskatchewan Queen's Bench Mandatory Mediation Program," available online: CFCJ <http://www.cfcj-fcjc.org/inventory-of-reforms/saskatchewan-queens-bench-mandatory-mediation>.

220 See *Queen's Bench Act, 1998*, supra note 215 at s. 42(1.1). For further descriptions of Saskatchewan's program, see Justice and Attorney General, Dispute Resolution Office, "Mediation," available online: Government of Saskatchewan <http://www.justice.gov.sk.ca/Mediation>; ACCA, "Dispute Resolution," materials collected in *Can. Ct. Communiqué* (Winter 2011), supra note 89 at 9–10. Evaluations of the program have generally been very positive. See, for example, Julie Macfarlane and Michaela Keet, *Learning from Experience: An Evaluation of the Saskatchewan Queen's Bench Mandatory Mediation Program* (Regina: Saskatchewan Justice Dispute Resolution Office, 2003); Macfarlane and Keet, "Civil Justice Reform and Mandatory Civil Mediation in Saskatchewan: Lessons from a Maturing Program," supra note 216; and Michaela Keet, "The Evolution of Lawyers' Roles in Mandatory Mediation: A Condition of Systemic Transformation" (2005) 68 *Sask. L. Rev.* 313. See also Julie Macfarlane, "Making Mediation Effective: Models for Best Practice" in Murphy and Molinari, eds., *Doing Justice: Dispute Resolution in the Courts and Beyond*, supra note 43 at 111.

221 *The Queen's Bench Rules* (effective 1 January 2012) at rr. 1-3(1)–(4), 4-7(1)(e). For a recent discussion of proportionality, see Farrow, "Proportionality: A Cultural Revolution," supra note 201.

222 See Manitoba, Civil Justice Review Task Force, *Manitoba Civil Justice Review Task Force Report* (Winnipeg: Department of Justice, 1996) (Chair: David Newman).

223 See *Court of Queen's Bench Rules*, Man. Reg. 553/88, r. 50.1, available online: Government of Manitoba <http://web2.gov.mb.ca/laws/rules/qbr1e.php>. For a discussion of Manitoba's approach to JDR, see Margaret A. Shone, "Law Reform

of settlements. For example, according to Schulman J. of the Manitoba Court of Queen's Bench,

> As a result of pre-trial procedures including Judicially Assisted Dispute Resolution Conferences the vast majority of civil actions in Manitoba are settled before trial. In our Court [Winnipeg Centre] fewer than 100 civil cases each year are brought to trial.[224]

Privatizing initiatives, through court-connected ADR programs, are also present in the Territorial systems of civil justice. For example, part 19 of the Northwest Territories rules of court[225] provides for a case management regime that affords parties to a civil dispute the assistance of a conference judge who can facilitate settlement through assisted settlement discussions, or a mini trial in which the conference judge may provide the parties with an "*in camera* ... non-binding advisory opinion" regarding a probable outcome on the merits, among others.[226] The Northwest Territories rules also apply to civil proceedings in Nunavut.[227] Yukon, as of 15 September 2008, adopted its own rules of court.[228] ADR plays a central role in these new rules.[229] For example,

---

and ADR: Pulling Strands in the Civil Justice Web" at n. 52 and accompanying text (paper presented at Australasian Law Reform Agencies Conference, Wellington, New Zealand, 13–16 April 2004), available online: New Zealand Law Commission <http://www.lawcom.govt.nz/sites/default/files/speeches/2004/04/Session%20 2B%20-%20ADR%20-%20Shone.pdf>. See further ACCA, "Dispute Resolution," materials collected in *Can. Ct. Communiqué* (Winter 2011), supra note 89 at 11–12.

224 *Semple v. Canada (Attorney General)*, [2006] M.J. No. 498 at para. 6.

225 *Rules of the Supreme Court of the Northwest Territories*, R-010-96 (in force 1 April 1996, as amended) at pt. 19, available online: Government of Northwest Territories <http://www.justice.gov.nt.ca/pdf/REGS/JUDICATURE/Rules_Supr_Crt_NWT_Pt_1.pdf>.

226 Ibid. at r. 292. See also Supreme Court of the Northwest Territories, Notice to the Profession, "Case Management Procedures, General Guidelines" (4 June 1996); and Supreme Court of the Northwest Territories, Notice to the Profession, "Case Management Guidelines (No. 2)" (22 December 1999).

227 See *Nunavut Judicial System Implementation Act*, S.N.W.T. 1998, c. 34, Sched. A, s. 59(2), available online: Nunavut Court of Justice <http://www.nucj.ca/rules.htm>.

228 *Rules of Court* (effective 15 September 2008), pursuant to *Judicature Act*, R.S.Y. 2002, c. 128, s. 38, available online: Yukon Courts <http://www.yukoncourts.ca/courts/supreme/ykrulesforms.html>. See also Yukon Government, News Release, "Government Modernizing Yukon Courts By Amending Three Acts" (31 October 2005), available online: Yukon Government <http://www.gov.yk.ca/news/2005/05-284.html>.

229 See, for example, *Rules of Court*, ibid. at r. 1(8)(e)–(f). See also the importance of proportionality: ibid. at r. 1(6).

a case management judge has the power to order parties to engage in ADR or JDR processes.[230] Further, private judicial settlement conferences can be scheduled at the request of a party and/or on order of a judge.[231]

Ontario

Ontario's first major modern ADR reform came in the form of a mandatory mediation pilot project, which was codified in Ontario's rules of court in 1999.[232] As of 2004, mandatory mediation provisions[233] (together with case management provisions[234]) apply to actions commenced in Toronto, Ottawa, and Essex County (with some exceptions).[235] Central to these mandatory mediation provisions, both in Toronto and elsewhere, is an attempt by the rules and by the court to encourage parties to settle their cases, in private, at the "earliest stage it is likely to be effective."[236] This process, typically requiring parties to submit to

230 Ibid. at r. 36(6)(i).

231 Ibid. at r. 37.

232 *Rules of Civil Procedure*, supra note 67 at r. 24.1. See further r. 75.1 ("Mandatory Mediation – Estates, Trusts and Substitute Decisions"). See further r. 76.08, which requires parties to an action under Ontario's Simplified Procedures regime to consider settlement.

233 See ibid. at rr. 24.1 (as amended by O/Reg. 438/08). See also former Superior Court of Justice, Practice Direction – Toronto Region, "Backlog Reduction / Best Practices Initiative" (in effect 31 December 2004, as renewed) at ss. 3–6, available online: Ontario Courts <http://www.ontariocourts.on.ca/scj/en/notices/pd/toronto/casemanagement.htm> ["Toronto 'Backlog Reduction / Best Practices Initiative'"].

234 See *Rules of Civil Procedure*, ibid. at r. 77. See also former r. 78, together with former "Toronto 'Backlog Reduction / Best Practices Initiative,'" ibid. at ss. 1, 16–23.

235 See *Rules of Civil Procedure*, ibid. at r. 24.1.04(2), which provides for certain proceedings to be exempted from the mandatory mediation rules, including, for example, actions on Toronto's Commercial List. For a further discussion of Ontario's case management regime, including proceedings that are exempted from that regime, see infra note 238 and accompanying text. For a discussion of Ontario's mandatory mediation program, see ACCA, "Dispute Resolution," materials collected in *Can. Ct. Communiqué* (Winter 2011), supra note 89 at 12–13.

236 See, for example, former "Toronto 'Backlog Reduction / Best Practices Initiative'," supra note 233 at "overview." See also ibid. at ss. 3–6, 28, 32, appendix ("Roster of Mediators") at s. 7(c)–(d); *Rules of Civil Procedure*, supra note 67 at r. 24.1 and r. 77. See also ibid. at r. 50 (Pre-Trial Conference) and r. 75.1 ("Mandatory Mediation – Estates, Trusts and Substitute Decisions).

a mediation service run by private, often roster-based mediators, has by and large been successful.[237] Notwithstanding some criticism of the mediation (and case management) provisions' (now former) across-the-board application in Toronto,[238] evaluations of the Ontario mediation

---

237 For judicial commentary on the purpose of R. 24.1, see, for example, *Hagel v. Giles* (2006), 80 O.R. (3d) 170 at paras. 27, 34 (S.C.J.), aff'd (2006), 82 O.R. (3d) 470 (C.A.). See also *Dicaro v. Wong*, [2001] O.J. No. 347 (Master). As is clear from the case law, courts are slow to exempt parties from these mandatory ADR requirements. See, for example, *O. (G.) v. H. (C.D.)* (2000), 50 O.R. (3d) 82 (S.C.J.).

238 Although many have viewed the Ontario initiatives as helpful, there have been numerous members of the Bar and Bench, particularly in Toronto, who have increasingly criticized the across-the-board application of Ontario's r. 24.1 and r. 77 mediation and case management provisions. See, for example, Martin Teplitsky, "Universal Mandatory Mediation: A Critical Analysis of the Evaluations of the Ontario Mandatory Mediation Program" (2001) 20:3 *Advocates' Soc. J.* 10; Martin Teplitsky, "Excessive Cost and Delay: Is There a Solution?" (2000) 19:2 *Advocates' Soc. J.* 5; John Jaffey, "Memo Suggests Axing Case Management, Mandatory Mediation" *The Lawyers Weekly* (1 October 2004) 3; and Jan Weir, "Mandatory Mediation Meltdown" *The Lawyers Weekly* (8 October 2004) 6. See also generally Hughes, "Mandatory Mediation: Opportunity or Subversion?," supra note 185. At least in part because of these criticisms, a practice direction – suspending the automatic operation of rr. 24.1 and 77 in Toronto – was published that revised the approach to ADR and case management in Toronto civil cases. See "Toronto 'Backlog Reduction / Best Practices Initiative'," supra note 233 at ss. 1–6. However, notwithstanding these significant changes, pre-trial mediation continued to be "mandatory" in Toronto. See ibid. at ss. 3–6. For a further discussion of the Toronto program, see Hon. Warren K. Winkler, "New Civil Case Management Pilot for Toronto Region: Rule 78 Cases" (paper given at CFCJ "Into the Future" conference, Montréal, Québec, 1 May 2006). Finally, as of 1 January 2010, Ontario *Rules of Civil Procedure*, r. 78 was revoked and r. 77 was amended – by O. Reg. 438/08, ss. 64, 65, 68(1) – to include many of the initiatives of the Toronto practice direction as well as revised versions of the purposes and practices of former rr. 77–8. The new r. 77 provides for a revised version of case management for cases subject to that rule. Currently, the rule applies to actions and applications commenced after 1 January 2010 in Ottawa, Toronto and Essex County, with certain exceptions, including proceedings under rr. 74–5 (estates); proceedings on the Commercial List in Toronto; simplified procedures actions (r. 76); and others. The general principles of new r. 77 are essentially both to keep a "greater share" of the responsibility for the case "with the parties" (as opposed to the court), and to be flexible enough to accommodate local "practices, traditions, customs or judicial resource[s]." These principles are specifically articulated as follows:

> 77.01 (1) The purpose of this Rule is to establish a case management system that provides case management only of those proceedings for which a need for the court's intervention is demonstrated and only to the degree that is appropriate, as determined in reliance on the criteria set out in this Rule.

initiative have generally been quite positive.[239] As such, according to Justice Chadwick of the Ontario Superior Court of Justice, "[i]n my view, mandatory mediation and case management is here to stay."[240]

More recently, Ontario has embarked on a further civil justice reform agenda.[241] Significantly based on the Honourable Coulter Osborne's

---

> 77.01 (2) This Rule shall be construed in accordance with the following principles:
>
> 1 Despite the application of case management under this Rule to a proceeding, the greater share of the responsibility for managing the proceeding and moving it expeditiously to a trial, hearing or other resolution remains with the parties.
>
> 2 The nature and extent of the case management provided by a judge or case management master under this Rule in respect of a proceeding shall be informed by any relevant practices, traditions, customs or judicial resource issues that apply locally in the region in which the proceeding is commenced or to which it is transferred. O. Reg. 438/08, s. 64.

Ontario *Rules of Civil Procedure*, r. 77, as amended by O. Reg. 438/08, s. 64.

239 For evaluations of Ontario's mandatory mediation program, see, for example, Julie Macfarlane, "Court-Based Mediation for Civil Cases: An Evaluation of the Ontario Court (General Division) ADR Centre" (Toronto: Ontario Ministry of the Attorney General, 1995); Robert Hann et al., "Evaluation of the Ontario Mandatory Mediation Program (Rule 24.1): Executive Summary and Recommendations" (Ontario: Queen's Printer, 12 March 2001), available online: Government of Ontario <http://www.attorneygeneral.jus.gov.on.ca/english/courts/manmed/exec_summary_recommend.pdf>. For an evaluation of the evaluation done by Macfarlane, supra, see Naomi Bussin, "Evaluating ADR Programs: The Ends Determine the Means" (2000) 22 *Advocates' Q.* 460 at 466. See further Colleen M. Hanycz, "Through the Looking Glass: Mediator Conceptions of Philosophy, Process and Power" (2005) 42 *Alta. L. Rev.* 819 at 823; Julie Macfarlane, "Making Mediation Effective: Models for Best Practice" in Murphy and Molinari, eds., *Doing Justice: Dispute Resolution in the Courts and Beyond*, supra note 43 at 111; and Julie Macfarlane, "Culture Change? A Tale of Two Cities and Mandatory Court-Connected Mediation" (2002) 2 *J. Disp. Resol.* 241.

240 Hon. Mr. Justice James B. Chadwick, "Court-Annexed Mediation in our Civil Courts" (14 November 2001) at 11 in "Negotiating the Future," supra note 146. For a summary of the program and related links, see Ministry of the Attorney General, "Mandatory Mediation Program," available online: Government of Ontario <www.attorneygeneral.jus.gov.on.ca/english/courts/manmed/>. See also Andrew C. Dekany, "Judges Increasingly Mediating in Ontario and Québec" *The Lawyers Weekly* (21 January 2005) 14.

241 Ministry of the Attorney General, News Release, "Resolving Lawsuits Faster and More Affordably, McGuinty Government Reforming Civil Justice For Ontarians" (11 December 2008), available online: Government of Ontario <http://www.attorneygeneral.jus.gov.on.ca/english/news/2008/20081211-civil-nr.asp>.

Civil Justice Reform Project,[242] Ontario adopted a number of rules-related and other reform proposals as of 1 January 2010.[243] As part of an overarching goal of dispute resolution proportionality,[244] which is expressly

242 Hon. Coulter A. Osborne, Q.C., *Civil Justice Reform Project* (November 2007), available online: Ontario Government <http://www.attorneygeneral.jus.gov.on.ca/english/about/pubs/cjrp/> [*Civil Justice Reform Project*]. See also the "Ontario Civil Legal Needs Project" (a joint initiative of the Law Society of Upper Canada ["LSUC"] and Pro Bono Law Ontario ["PBLO"]) in LSUC, Access to Justice Committee, "Report to Convocation" (26 June 2008), app. 1, available online: LSUC <http://www.lsuc.on.ca/media/convjun08_atj.pdf>. For earlier Ontario reform initiatives and reports, see, for example, Advocates' Society, *Streamlining the Ontario Civil Justice System: A Policy Forum, Final Report*, supra note 113; Zuber Commission Report: Ontario, *Report of Ontario Courts Inquiry*, by T. G. Zuber (Toronto: Ontario Ministry of Attorney General, 1987); LSUC, *Alternatives – The Report of the Dispute Resolution Subcommittee* (Toronto: LSUC, 1993); and Ontario Civil Justice Review, *Supplemental and Final Report* (Toronto: Ontario Civil Justice Review, 1996).

243 In addition to the reforms to Ontario's *Rules of Civil Procedure*, see the opening of the PBLO "Law Help Ontario" pilot project. This program – in a similar spirit to burgeoning self-help centres in B.C. and Alberta (discussed further supra) – is designed to assist people who cannot otherwise afford legal services with civil matters. For information on this program, see, for example, PBLO, "LawHelpOntario.org," available online: PBLO <http://www.lawhelpontario.org/>; and PBLO, Media Advisory, "Pro Bono Law Ontario to launch resource centre for unrepresented litigants" (28 November 2007) [archived with author]. For background reform material, see, for example, *Civil Justice Reform Project*, ibid. at § 6. For further comments, see Valerie Mutton, "Provincial Pro Bono Initiatives Get a Helping Hand from Firms" 27:32 *The Lawyers Weekly* (21 December 2007). Further, in a similar spirit to the Alberta Legal Services Mapping Project, discussed earlier (see supra note 214), a civil justice needs assessment and mapping project was recently completed in Ontario, which was designed to quantify and make recommendations about the "civil legal needs experienced by low and middle-income Ontarians." See Ontario Civil Legal Needs Project, "Listening to Ontarians" (Toronto: Ontario Civil Legal Needs Project Steering Committee, May 2010) at 2; and Jamie Baxter and Albert Yoon, *The Geography of Civil Legal Services in Ontario*, report of the mapping phase of the Ontario Civil Legal Needs Project (Toronto: Ontario Civil Legal Needs Project Steering Committee, November 2011). The project was co-sponsored by the Law Society of Upper Canada, Pro Bono Law Ontario, the Law Foundation of Ontario, and Legal Aid Ontario.

244 See *Civil Justice Reform Project*, ibid. supra note 242 at § 19. For one of the first treatments of this new rules-based concept of proportionality in Ontario, see *Moosa v. Hill Property Management Group Inc.*, [2010] O.J. No. 624 (Master). For another early treatment of the recent reforms in Ontario, specifically including the reforms to R. 20 (summary judgment), see *Healey v. Lakeridge Health Corp.*, [2010] O.J. No. 417 (Sup. Ct. Just.). See recently *Hryniak v. Mauldin*, 2014 SCC 7; *Bruno Appliance and Furniture, Inc. v. Hryniak*, 2014 SCC 8. For a further discussion of proportionality, see Farrow, "Proportionality: A Cultural Revolution," supra note 201. See also *2038724 Ontario Ltd. v. Quizno's Canada Restaurant Corp.*, 2012 ONSC 6549.

included in Ontario's new rule 1.04 (1.1),[245] the reform proposals included specific provisions directed at pre-trial settlement. For example, the *Civil Justice Reform Project* recommended reforming Ontario's pre-trial conference rule (rule 50) "to discuss settlement of some or all of the issues" and to ensure that "[j]udges skilled in negotiation and with expertise in the relevant subject matter should, where possible, preside over pre-trial conferences."[246] These judicial settlement-based proposals, which are in addition to Ontario's mandatory mediation provisions, have been expressly included in Ontario's new rule 50.[247]

Québec and the Atlantic Provinces

Québec has continued to take a serious look at its systems of civil justice following the time of the CBA task force. For example, the Civil

---

245 Ontario's *Rules of Civil Procedure*, as recently amended by O. Reg. 438/08, ss. 2, 68(1), provide – at r. 1.04 – an interpretation section with the following general principles:

> 1.04 (1) These rules shall be liberally construed to secure the just, most expeditious and least expensive determination of every civil proceeding on its merits.
> 1.04 (1.1) In applying these rules, the court shall make orders and give directions that are proportionate to the importance and complexity of the issues, and to the amount involved, in the proceeding.

246 *Civil Justice Reform Project*, supra note 242 at § 11.

247 Ontario's *Rules of Civil Procedure*, as recently amended by O. Reg. 438/08, ss. 47, provide – at r. 50 – among other things:

> 50.01 The purpose of this Rule is to provide an opportunity for any or all of the issues in a proceeding to be settled without a hearing and, with respect to any issues that are not settled, to obtain from the court orders or directions to assist in the just, most expeditious and least expensive disposition of the proceeding, including orders or directions to ensure that any hearing proceeds in an orderly and efficient manner. ...
> 50.06 The following matters shall be considered at a pre-trial conference:
> 1 The possibility of settlement of any or all of the issues in the proceeding.
> 2 Simplification of the issues. ...
> 11 Any other matter that may assist in the just, most expeditious and least expensive disposition of the proceeding.

See also the pre-trial settlement provisions provided for under r. 76 (Simplified Procedures).

Procedure Review Committee, established by the minister of justice, released its report in August 2001.[248] Efficiency was a primary driver of the initiative. According to the committee, its mandate "was to review ... civil procedure and propose measures that would [translation] 'implement a more rapid, efficient and reassuring justice [system], which is less time consuming and less expensive in terms of energy and money for both the person subject to trial and the justice system'."[249] Like other reform initiatives, and with a foundational concern for proportionality of proceedings, the committee identified a multifaceted vision for its revised civil procedure regime that included a focus on "respect of persons," "accountability of the parties," "increased intervention of the judge," "proportionality of the procedure," and the use of "information technologies."[250]

Of particular interest to this book were the committee's recommendations regarding settlement and ADR. One aspect to those recommendations was the adoption of a private mediation mechanism as a viable alternative process.[251] In addition, the committee, in furtherance of its vision for increasing the role of judges in civil proceedings, provided recommendations regarding the active involvement of judges in the settlement of disputes.[252] Although a judge-assisted settlement conference process existed in Québec from the late 1990s (prior to the revision of the rules of court coming out of the committee's recommendations[253]),

248 See Civil Procedure Review Committee, Report, A *New Judicial Culture* (Summary) (August 2001) at 1 [*A New Judicial Culture*], available online: Justice Québec <http://www.justice.gouv.qc.ca/english/publications/rapports/pdf/sommaire-a.pdf>.

249 Ibid. at 1 [citation omitted].

250 Ibid. at 3–4.

251 Ibid. at 10.

252 According to the committee,

> In order to allow the courts to play their full role in the proper conduct of the proceedings, the Committee considers it appropriate to plan measures that would allow a greater intervention of the judge in the administration of proceedings by allowing him, in addition to the pre-trial conferences, to hold case management conferences and settlement conferences.

Ibid. at 4. See also ibid. at 9.

253 For the new rules, see *Code of Civil Procedure*, R.S.Q., c. C-25 (updated to 18 February 2009), available online: Éditeur official du Québec <http://www2.publicationsduquebec.gouv.qc.ca/dynamicSearch/telecharge.php?type=2&file=/C_25/C25_A.HTM>. For commentary on Québec's civil justice reform process, see Justice Québec, "Reform of Civil Procedure" [archived with author].

the new rules specifically included judicial settlement provisions.[254] Those rules provide for a very flexible and confidential process.[255] They have also been considered to be very successful from a settlement perspective.[256] Québec's more recent reform agenda, its *Justice Access Plan*, contemplates a number of new initiatives including further powers for judges to promote settlement.[257]

254 *Code of Civil Procedure*, ibid. at div. IV, rr. 151.14–151.23. For useful background information on these reforms, see Hon. François Rolland, "Access to Justice: 3 Years After the Reform of the Code of Civil Procedure" (paper given at CFCJ "Into the Future" conference, Montréal, Québec, 1 May 2006) at section titled "Settlement Conference" [pagination for parts of the online version of this article are not available], available online: CFCJ <http://www.cfcj-fcjc.org/sites/default/files/docs/2006/rolland-en.pdf>. For further discussion of the "Into the Future" conference, see supra note 167.

255 See, for example, *Code of Civil Procedure*, supra note 253 at rr. 151.16–151.18, 151.21.

256 For example, according to François Rolland, chief justice of the Superior Court of Québec:

> This system is fabulous and facilitates access to justice. It has received an overwhelming reception from both the parties and their attorneys.
>
> However, in some ways, the Superior Court is now a victim of its own success. In fact, the problem is that we cannot keep up with the demand.
>
> Between 2001 and 2004, 1,295 settlement conferences were held throughout Québec. Last year, in the District of Montréal alone, we held close to 700 conferences. The delay to obtain a date was three weeks two years ago, and now it is seven months.
>
> Five judges are allocated full-time to preside over these conferences, plus judges who accept on a volunteer basis to preside over conferences. The success rate of these conferences is very impressive: 80% in civil matters and close to 70% in family matters.
>
> Obviously, the parties and the attorneys are extremely satisfied with these conferences because they have access to judges on an informal basis to explain their case and to settle their dispute. Normally, this is done quickly in the process.

Rolland, "Access to Justice: 3 Years After the Reform of the Code of Civil Procedure," supra note 254. Notwithstanding this positive support for judicial dispute resolution, perceptions of the overall results of the Québec reforms have been mixed. See, for example, ibid. at 5–6. For a summary of the Québec experience, see Advocates' Society, *Streamlining the Ontario Civil Justice System: A Policy Forum, Final Report*, supra note 113 at 8–9. See further Andrew C. Dekany, "Judges Increasingly Mediating in Ontario and Québec," supra note 240.

257 Justice Québec, *Justice Access Plan*, available online: Québec Government <http://www.justice.gouv.qc.ca/english/ministre/paj/index.htm>.

Nova Scotia, largely through the work of the Nova Scotia Civil Procedure Rules Revision Project, has also been engaged in a significant review of its civil justice system.[258] As with other provincial reform initiatives, efficiency has been a key driving theme underlying the project's efforts. For example, a specific focus of the project was how the rules of court "affect the speed, costs, and understandability of civil court proceedings."[259] According to the project, "[r]ules which are efficient, effective, and clear should reduce delays, lessen expenses and lead to more satisfactory results."[260] One of several key processes of interest to the project was "early dispute resolution." On this topic, the project examined the following questions:

- Should there be a rule regulating settlement conferences?
- Should the rules provide for a choice of process between pure mediation and a judge's second opinion?
- Should procedures be standardized for early dispute resolution?
- Should there be sanctions for a party who rejects a judge's suggested resolution and obtains a worse outcome after trial?[261]

Following the project's work, Nova Scotia's rules were revised and went into effect on 1 January 2009.[262] Many of the project's "early dispute resolution" issues are specifically contemplated by the settlement provisions of the new rules, which include a very comprehensive, flexible, and confidential judicial settlement conference regime.[263]

---

258 See Nova Scotia Civil Procedure Rules Revision Project, "Consultation with the Bar: Issues Memorandum" (Law Reform Commission of Nova Scotia, 16 June 2004) ["Issues Memorandum"], available online: Courts of Nova Scotia <http://www.courts.ns.ca/rules_revision/docs/final_bar_consult.pdf>. For commentary, see, for example, Courts of Nova Scotia, Civil Procedure Rules Nova Scotia, "Rules Revision Project," available online: Courts of Nova Scotia <http://www.courts.ns.ca/rules_revision/revision.htm>.

259 "Issues Memorandum," ibid. at 3.

260 Ibid.

261 Ibid. at 6.

262 See *Civil Procedure Rules of Nova Scotia*, supra note 66.

263 See *Civil Procedure Rules of Nova Scotia*, ibid. at pt. 4, rr. 10.11–10.16. For commentary on Nova Scotia's new rules, see Christopher Guly, "Bar-Bench Spar in NS over New Court Rules" *The Lawyers Weekly* (18 July 2008), available online: Lawyers Weekly <http://www.lawyersweekly.ca/index.php?section=article&articleid=725>.

ADR processes are also being used elsewhere in the Atlantic Provinces. For example, Newfoundland and Labrador has several ADR tools in its rules, including judicially assisted settlement conferences[264] as well as court-ordered mediation.[265] Prince Edward Island's rules of court provide for a judge assisted pre-trial conference.[266] New Brunswick's rules of court specifically provide for a comprehensive, flexible, and confidential judicial settlement conference regime as part of its pre-trial offerings.[267]

Other Courts

In addition to general superior courts of record, other courts in Canada – small claims courts, courts of appeal, and the federal court – are also experimenting with significant reform initiatives. Many of these efforts are pursuing the same reform goals of reduced cost and increased speed and efficiency. They are also resulting in similar privatizing trends.

Small claims courts have played an important role in the state's goal of providing a just, cost-effective, and accessible public venue for the resolution of many day-to-day disputes in society. According to Marvin Zuker, these courts "originated in response to a perception that the complex and technical regular civil procedure made it virtually impossible for wage earners and small businessmen to use the court system to collect wages or accounts which they were owed."[268] Key to these small claims court regimes are major efforts to reduce cost and delay by simplifying the processes by which disputes get resolved. Put simply, the basic purpose of these processes is to provide parties with a "quick, economical [dispute resolution] solution."[269] Badges of the small claims

264 See *Rules of the Supreme Court, 1986*, S.N.L. 1986, c. 42, sched. D, as amended at rr. 39, 18A.06(3), available online: Newfoundland and Labrador House of Assembly <http://www.assembly.nl.ca/Legislation/sr/regulations/RulesSC/Rc86ru18A.htm>.

265 See ibid. at r. 37A. For a discussion of these dispute resolution tools in Newfoundland and Labrador, see ACCA, "Dispute Resolution," materials collected in *Can. Ct. Communiqué* (Winter 2011), supra note 89 at 14.

266 Annotated *Rules of Civil Procedure* at r. 50.01(1), available online: Government of Prince Edward Island <http://www.gov.pe.ca/courts/supreme/rules/index.php3>.

267 See *Rules of Court*, N.B. Reg. 82-73 at rr. 50.07–50.15, available online: Government of New Brunswick <http://www.gnb.ca/0062/regs/Rule/rule_list.htm>.

268 Marvin A. Zuker, *Small Claims Court Practice* (Toronto: Carswell, 1998) 2–3, in Janet Walker, gen. ed., et al., *The Civil Litigation Process: Cases and Materials*, 6th ed. (Toronto: Emond Montgomery, 2005) at 27.

269 See Justice Québec, "Small Claims," available online: Government of Québec <http://www.justice.gouv.qc.ca/english/publications/generale/creance-a.htm>.

court system include less of a need for litigants to be represented by lawyers,[270] more interventionist judges (able to assist the parties when necessary to narrow the issues and move through the trial process), relaxed rules of evidence, and simplified rules of trial procedure.[271] In sum, again according to Zuker, the "crux of the small claims procedure is informality and simplicity."[272]

Informality, however, does not equal privacy. The traditional small claims court model still contemplates an open, public dispute resolution process. Having said that, for some years now small claims courts have also been experimenting with and implementing various alternative private process options. Many of these initiatives include case management and other ADR (typically mediation-oriented) regimes.[273] For example, Alberta's small claims regime includes a pre-trial conference and active mediation programs.[274] The first of several stated purposes of the pre-trial conference regime is to consider the "possibility of settling the claim."[275] The "aim" of the mediation program is to "increase

270 In Québec, lawyers are typically prohibited from acting. See *Code of Civil Procedure*, supra note 253 at s. 959.

271 See, for example, Ontario Small Claims Court Rules, O. Reg. 258/98, as amended. See also, for example, Ontario Ministry of the Attorney General, "Small Claims Court Guides to Procedures," available online: Ontario Government <http://www.attorneygeneral.jus.gov.on.ca/english/courts/guides/>.

272 Zuker, *Small Claims Court Practice*, supra note 268.

273 For a general discussion, see Shone, "Civil Justice Reform in Canada: 1996 to 2006 and Beyond," supra note 168 at 31–2. See also generally Janet Walker, gen. ed., et al., *The Civil Litigation Process: Cases and Materials*, 7th ed. (Toronto: Emond Montgomery, 2010) at 220–3.

274 See *Provincial Court Act*, R.S.A. 2000, P-31, ss. 64–5, available online: Alberta Queen's Printer <http://www.qp.alberta.ca/documents/Acts/P31.pdf>; *Provincial Court Act, Mediation Rules of the Provincial Court – Civil Division*, Alta. Reg. 271/97, online: Alberta Queen's Printer <http://www.albertacourts.ab.ca/pc/civil/publication/97_271.pdf>. See also Alberta Provincial Court, "Mediation and the Provincial Court," available online: Alberta Courts <http://www.albertacourts.ab.ca/pc/civil/publication/mediation_and_the_provincial_court.htm>; and Alberta Provincial Court, "Mediation and the Civil Courts," available online: Alberta Courts <http://www.albertacourts.ab.ca/go/ProvincialCourt/Civil/Mediation/FrequentQuestions/tabid/156/Default.aspx>. For a further discussion of the Provincial Court's mediation program, see ALRI "Promoting Early Resolution of Disputes," supra note 92 at 54–9.

275 *Provincial Court Act*, ibid. at s. 64(1)(a).

the number of civil cases resolved through mediation and reduce the number of civil cases that proceed to court."[276] For example, the 2007–2008 settlement ("success") rate for Alberta's program was 65 per cent, which was a 2 per cent increase over both the 2006–2007 settlement rate as well as the 2007–2008 target settlement rate.[277]

Other provincial small claims courts are pursuing similar initiatives. For example, Saskatchewan's Small Claims Court also offers a pre-trial case-management process.[278] As with the Alberta process, a primary motivation behind that process is to help the parties to settle their dispute with the assistance of a case-management judge.[279] B.C.'s small claims process includes a settlement conference regime and a multi-level mediation program for claims involving different amounts.[280] Québec's small claims regime includes a voluntary court-annexed mediation program.[281] Similarly, the Yukon's small claims regime also includes a voluntary court-annexed mediation option.[282] And other provinces have similar initiatives.[283] Further, although not a specific

276 See Alberta Justice and Attorney General, *Annual Report, 2007–2008* at 32, available online: Alberta Justice <http://justice.alberta.ca/programs_services/about_us/Documents/2008_justice_annual_report.pdf>.

277 Ibid.

278 *Small Claims Act, 1997*, S.S. 1997, c. S-50.11, s. 7.1 ("Case Management Conference"), available online: CanLII <http://www.canlii.org/en/sk/laws/stat/ss-1997-c-s-50.11/latest/ss-1997-c-s-50.11.html>.

279 Saskatchewan Justice and Attorney General, "The Small Claims Act 1997," available online: Government of Saskatchewan <http://www.justice.gov.sk.ca/Small-Claims-Act-1997>.

280 See *Court Rules Act; Small Claims Act, Small Claims Rules*, B.C. Reg. 261/93 (deposited 30 July 1993, effective 1 October 1993, as amended, B.C. Reg. 360/2007, 26 November 2007), rr. 7–7.4, available online: <http://www.bclaws.ca/EPLibraries/bclaws_new/document/ID/freeside/261_93_00b>. See also B.C. Dispute Resolution Office, "Bulletin: Court Mediation Program" (June 2002), online: Government of B.C. <http://www.ag.gov.bc.ca/dro/publications/bulletins/court-mediation.htm>. For B.C.'s current efficiency-seeking initiative in the small claims area, see *Civil Resolution Tribunal Act*, S.B.C. 2012, c. 25 (assented to 31 May 2012).

281 See, for example, *Code of Civil Procedure*, supra note 253 at s. 973.

282 See, for example, *Small Claims Court Regulations*, O.I.C. 1995/152, rr. 39–40, available online: Government of Yukon <http://www.gov.yk.ca/legislation/regs/oic1995_152.pdf>.

283 See, for example, Ontario's Small Claims Court Rules, supra note 271 at r. 13; Ontario Small Claims Court, "What Is Small Claims Court?," available online: Government of Ontario <http://www.attorneygeneral.jus.gov.on.ca/english/courts/guides/WhatisSCCJan08EN.pdf>.

focus of this book,[284] additional court initiatives include a wide range of mediation and case management programs in family law cases.[285]

In addition to small claims courts, courts of appeal in Canada have also, more recently, been experimenting with various forms of voluntary, court-annexed ADR processes. For example, as I mentioned previously,[286] the JDR program in Alberta is also available, in some cases, at the Court of Appeal.[287] The B.C. Court of Appeal offers a judicial settlement conference.[288] Similarly, some judges of the Court of Appeal for Ontario are also engaged in voluntary court-annexed mediation initiatives.[289] Other provincial courts of appeal also offer various ADR-related services, including Québec,[290] New Brunswick,[291] and Newfoundland and Labrador.[292]

Similarly, at the federal court level, case management and ADR – primarily through the court's "case management and dispute resolution services" program[293] – have been implemented for some years now and are being actively pursued as tools to reduce backlog and eliminate

---

284 As mentioned earlier, see supra note 86.

285 See, for example, Ontario *Family Law Rules*, O. Reg. 439/07, s. 40. For a comment, see Daryl-Lynn Carlson, "Family Lawyers Flocking to ADR" *Law Times* (18 June 2007).

286 See supra note 205 and accompanying text.

287 See, for example, Alberta Court of Appeal, "Guidelines for Judicial Dispute Resolution (JDR)," supra note 205.

288 The B.C. Court of Appeal's judicial settlement conference program commenced as a pilot project on 1 November 2004. See B.C. Court of Appeal, Practice Directive, "Judicial Settlement Conferences," available online: B.C. Government <http://www.courts.gov.bc.ca/court_of_appeal/practice_and_procedure/civil_practice_directives_/Civil-Judicial%20Settlement%20Conferences.htm>.

289 See, for example, "Brief Biographical Note of Justice Karen M. Weiler," available online: Court of Appeal for Ontario <http://www.ontariocourts.ca/coa/en/judges/weiler.htm>, which provides that "mediation" is "now offered by the Court of Appeal as a voluntary option to litigants who request it."

290 For a discussion of the Québec Court of Appeal's confidential judicial mediation program, see, for example, Court of Appeal of Québec, "Mediation," available online: Court of Appeal of Québec <http://www.tribunaux.qc.ca/c-appel/English/Altres/mediation/mediation.html>.

291 See *Rules of Court*, supra note 267 at r. 62.1, which provides for judicial "settlement conferences."

292 See *Rules of the Supreme Court, 1986*, supra note 264 at r. 57.22, which provides for a prehearing conference designed to canvass, in addition to other things, "the appropriateness of conducting a settlement of mediation hearing."

293 See *Federal Court Rules*, SOR/98-106, as amended, at pt. 9, rr. 380–91.

"dead wood" proceedings from the court's docket.[294] Dispute resolution services, performed by a case management judge or prothonotary, include confidential mediations, early neutral evaluations, and non-binding mini-trials designed to render an opinion as to the probable outcome of a proceeding.[295]

The Vanishing Trial

Settlement of civil cases is clearly not a new concept. As we saw, for example, in reports from the nineteenth-century court reforms in New York, "inducements to a compromise during a litigation" have been part of court reform initiatives for some time.[296] And these sorts of inducement regimes are certainly standard fare in modern civil court rules.[297] However, with all of the recent provincial and federal privatizing trends has come a concomitant phenomenon known as the "vanishing trial."[298] It is now widely recognized that fewer and fewer disputes that would typically proceed in the public civil courts are actually going to trial. As Julie Macfarlane notes, there are "fewer trials today than there were 10 years ago."[299] Although historically always present, settlement

294 Hon. Allan Lutfy, Swearing-in Ceremony, associate chief justice (as he then was) (7 January 2000), available online: Federal Court of Canada <http://cas-ncr-nter03.cas-satj.gc.ca/portal/page/portal/fc_cf_en/Speech>.

295 See *Federal Court Rules*, supra note 293 at rr. 386–8.

296 Commission on Practice and Pleadings (Arphaxed Loomis, David Graham and David Dudley Field), "Report of a Code of Civil Procedure," supra note 123 at viii.

297 See, for example, Ontario *Rules of Civil Procedure*, supra note 68 at r. 49.

298 See, for example, Special Issue, "The Vanishing Trial" (2004) 1 *J. Emp. Legal Stud.* 459–84. In particular, see Marc Galanter, "The Vanishing Trial: An Examination of Trials and Related Matters in Federal and State Courts" (2004) 1 *J. Emp. Legal Stud.* 459; and Stipanowich, "ADR and the 'Vanishing Trial': The Growth and Impact of 'Alternative Dispute Resolution'," supra note 151. In Canada, see, for example, Julie Macfarlane, *The New Lawyer: How Settlement Is Transforming the Practice of Law* (Vancouver: UBC Press, 2008). For recent comments, see Moulton, "Vanishing Trials: Out-of-Court Settlements on the Rise," supra note 180. For a criticism of the term vanishing, see Hon. Geoffrey L. Davies, "Civil Justice Reform: Some Common Problems, Some Possible Solutions" (paper presented at CFCJ "Into the Future" conference, Montréal, Québec, 1 May 2006) at 7, who prefers to argue that "trial rates have declined."

299 See Moulton (quoting Macfarlane), "Vanishing Trials: Out-of-Court Settlements on the Rise," supra note 180 at 22. See further Macfarlane, *The New Lawyer*, ibid. at 7.

through private means has become increasingly the norm in civil justice systems throughout the common law world. Put simply, almost all disputes settle; put differently, civil trials are "vanishing." As Chief Justice François Rolland of the Superior Court of Québec recently commented,

> The ... middle class has simply deserted the Common Law courtrooms. Most civil cases heard before the Superior Court in Montréal are filed by companies rather than individuals. This is with the exception of family matters, of course. At this rate, it looks as though, at least in the short term, a civil case between two individuals will become a rarity.[300]

In the United States, according to one recent report, 98.2 per cent of civil cases are settled before trial.[301] Similar trends are occurring elsewhere. For example, according to the ALRC, "[a]s the empirical data ... confirms, the vast majority of civil disputes commenced within the federal court and tribunal system are concluded by means other than formal adjudication. ... They are settled by negotiation or through other dispute resolution mechanisms (such as mediation, conciliation or arbitration)."[302] In addition, there is some further evidence relating to civil cases in the federal court system in the United States that points to an increasing number of cases that are also being resolved at the pre-trial stage by adversarial processes (summary judgment, dismissal, etc.).[303]

Settlement figures are similar in Canada, where the "vast majority [of cases] ... are ... resolved through a variety of related processes that have come to be grouped under the broad heading of 'alternative dispute resolution.'"[304] According to one report, approximately 95 to 96 per cent of civil cases settle prior to trial.[305] Paul Emond puts the high end of that settlement range even higher, with "the vast majority (95%

300 Rolland, "Access to Justice: 3 Years after the Reform of the Code of Civil Procedure," supra note 254 at 7.

301 See Moulton, "Vanishing Trials: Out-of-Court Settlements on the Rise," supra note 180 at 22. See further Special Issue, "Vanishing Trial," supra note 298.

302 ALRC, "Review of the Federal Civil Justice System," supra note 115 at c. 3, para. 3.40 [footnotes omitted], discussed further in Farrow, "Dispute Resolution, Access to Civil Justice and Legal Education," supra note 43 at n. 44 and surrounding text.

303 See Gillian K. Hadfield, "Where Have All the Trials Gone? Settlements, Non-Trial Adjudications and Statistical Artifacts in the Changing Disposition of Federal Civil Cases" (2004) 1 *J. Emp. Legal Stud.* 705.

304 Walker, gen. ed., et al., *The Civil Litigation Process*, 6th ed., supra note 268 at 525.

305 See Moulton, "Vanishing Trials: Out-of-Court Settlements on the Rise," supra note 180 at 22.

to 98%) of disputes" being "resolved through negotiation and not adjudication."[306] Julie Macfarlane puts it higher still, at 98.2 per cent.[307] Similarly, an Alberta study indicates that "current ratio of trials to filings in ... Canadian and foreign jurisdictions" is "less tha[n] 2%."[308] These numbers are in line with reports from other Canadian provincial jurisdictions. For example, the number of civil cases going to trial in B.C. is reportedly at an "all time low."[309] According to one B.C. source, 4 per cent of cases that are initiated in the civil justice system actually proceed to trial.[310] Another source puts the B.C. trial-to-filing ratio at 5 per cent.[311] Similar figures are coming out of Québec. Again according to Chief Justice Rolland, "in 2001, out of 100 cases filed in the Superior Court of Québec, seven cases ended with a judgment after a trial. On December 31st, 2005, out of 100 cases introduced in the Superior Court, 7% will still end with a judgment after a trial."[312]

Estimates as to the way, and at what stage of the process, disputes are resolved vary and are not precise. However, at least one Ontario report found that "approximately 55% of cases commenced never proceed to the point where a statement of defence is filed" and the "remaining 45% of the case load proceeds through various additional stages of litigation, with the vast majority settling at some point between the pleading stage and the eve or morning of trial."[313] Further, these general

306 See Emond, "A Conceptual Overview," supra note 87. For further discussions of these trends, see, for example, Julie Macfarlane, "Why Do People Settle?" (2001) 46 *McGill L.J.* 663 at 665; Farrow, "Dispute Resolution, Access to Civil Justice and Legal Education," supra note 43 at n. 43.

307 Macfarlane, *The New Lawyer*, supra note 298 at 7.

308 ALRI, "Promoting Early Resolution of Disputes by Settlement," supra note 92 at 8, n. 17.

309 Darrell Roberts (associate counsel with Miller Thomson LLP in Vancouver) in Guly, "Storm Erupts over B.C.'s Proposed Civil Reforms," supra note 202 at 18.

310 See Allan P. Seckel (B.C. Deputy A.G.), "Judicial Models: Can We Do Better? Proposed Reforms to Civil Procedure in British Columbia" (panel presentation at CIAJ, "Doing Justice: Dispute Resolution in the Courts and Beyond," CIAJ Annual Conference, Halifax, Nova Scotia, 11 October 2007). See generally Seckel, "Judicial Models: Can We Do Better? Proposed Reforms to Civil Procedure in British Columbia," supra note 189. See further B.C., "Effective and Affordable Civil Justice," supra note 189 at app. L.

311 See, for example, Guly, "Storm Erupts over B.C.'s Proposed Civil Reforms," supra note 202 at 18.

312 Rolland, "Access to Justice: 3 Years after the Reform of the Code of Civil Procedure," supra note 254.

313 Ontario Civil Justice Review, *First Report* (March 1995), online: Ontario Ministry of the Attorney General <http://www.attorneygeneral.jus.gov.on.ca/english/about/pubs/cjr/> at c. 13, n. 47 and surrounding text, also in Walker, gen. ed., et al., *The Civil Litigation Process*, 6th ed., supra note 268 at 529 [footnote omitted].

settlement figures blend different areas of practice, which are reported not to have uniform rates of settlement. For example, according to one lawyer practicing in the field of corporate dispute resolution, the number of cases involving commercial litigation issues that are settled prior to trial "is as high as 90 percent."[314]

Comprehensive longitudinal Canadian statistics for activity in the civil side of the justice system have been traditionally very hard to come by.[315] However, regardless of jurisdictional and subject matter differences, one thing is clear from these various studies and reports: almost all civil cases are resolved outside of court. Public civil trials are a "rarity"[316] and may be "vanishing."[317] And as we have seen in this chapter and as is further discussed in this book, the reduction of civil trials is clearly a major goal of the modern civil justice reform movement.

Overall Move to ADR and Related Private Processes

Many of the concerns raised by law commissions, law reformers, policy makers, and so on – identified earlier – regarding our current systems of civil justice continue to relate to what Adam Smith called the "expense

314 David Elliott in Moulton, "Vanishing Trials: Out-of-Court Settlements on the Rise," supra note 180 at 22.

315 A relatively recent initiative from Statistics Canada has started to collect data regarding the number of civil actions that are initiated or are active during a given calendar year. The statistics include information for several jurisdictions, including Nova Scotia, Ontario, British Columbia, Yukon, Northwest Territories, and Nunavut. Recent available results of this initiative are consistent with the anecdotes and annual trends from other jurisdictions. For example, but for the Northwest Territories, the number of cases that were initiated in each of the other five jurisdictions declined from the 2006/7 to the 2007/8 reporting periods. See Statistics Canada, "Initiated and Active Civil Court Cases," available online: Government of Canada <http://www.statcan.gc.ca/daily-quotidien/090120/t090120d1-eng.htm>. And although the number of filings rose generally between 2006/7 and 2010/11, the number of cases initiated in those jurisdictions between 2009/10 and 2010/11 declined (but for the Northwest Territories, which stayed constant). See Statistics Canada, "Initiated and Active Civil Court Cases by Type of Case, Selected Provinces and Territories, 2009/2010 and 2010/2011," available online: Government of Canada <http://www.statcan.gc.ca/pub/85-002-x/2012001/article/11634/tbl/tbl04-eng.htm>.

316 Rolland, "Access to Justice: 3 Years After the Reform of the Code of Civil Procedure," supra note 254 at 7.

317 See, for example, Special Issue, "Vanishing Trial," supra note 298 and accompanying text.

of a law-suit"[318]; to what Bentham subsequently identified as "mischiefs" within the civil-side of the court process including "Expense," "Delay" and "Complication"[319]; to what Lord Woolf more recently identified as "problems" and "defects" within the system including it being "too expensive," too "cost[ly]," "too slow," "too unequal," "too uncertain," "incomprehensible," "too fragmented" and "too adversarial"[320]; and to what former Ontario chief justice Roy McMurtry referred to as amounting to a "crisis," including the system's "increasing cost," "tremendous ... backlog," and "serious lack of adequate resources."[321] These are the kinds of concerns that have resulted in ongoing reform projects over the last centuries, including the recent modern civil justice reform movement over the last ten years or so. And based on a detailed review of the recent Canadian national and provincial reform initiatives,[322] there can be no doubt that a major goal of policymakers is to get cases out of the traditional public trial stream and into a variety of ADR settlement processes, including court-connected mediation,[323] judge-assisted and judicial dispute resolution programs,[324] specific family-related mediation services,[325] notice to mediate initiatives,[326] and so forth. Put simply, as the Honorable Roy McMurtry acknowledged,

---

318 Smith, *An Inquiry into the Nature and Causes of the Wealth of Nations*, supra note 11 at vol. 2, bk. V, c. I, pt. II, p. 240, discussed further supra note 101 and accompanying text.

319 Bentham, *Principles of Judicial Procedure, with the Outlines of a Procedural Code*, supra note 103 at c. iii, discussed further supra notes 103 and 120 and accompanying text.

320 Woolf, *Access to Justice*, supra note 106 at § 1(2), discussed further supra note 109 and accompanying text.

321 "McMurtry Remarks," supra note 181 at 3–4, discussed further ibid. and accompanying text.

322 See generally supra.

323 See, for example, the court-connected mediation programs in Alberta, Saskatchewan, and Ontario, discussed supra.

324 See, for example, the JDR programs in Alberta, Québec, and Nova Scotia, discussed supra.

325 Numerous family ADR services, which I do not specifically address in this research, are either in place and/or are being experimented with across the country. See, for example, Ontario Ministry of the Attorney General, "Family Mediation Services," available online: Ontario Government <http://www.attorneygeneral.jus.gov.on.ca/english/family/mediation.asp>; and Ontario Ministry of the Attorney General, "Family Mediation," online: Ontario Government <http://www.attorneygeneral.jus.gov.on.ca/english/family/divorce/mediation/>.

326 See, for example, B.C.'s "Notice to Mediate" regime, supra note 192 and accompanying text.

"we recognize that ADR is now firmly entrenched" in our modern, reforming systems.[327] Further, case management[328] and pre-trial conference[329] initiatives – together with incentives built into typical Canadian fee-shifting costs rules that provide parties with added legislatively sanctioned court-based incentives for private, non-trial-based settlements[330] – provide judges and parties with other robust mechanisms for the encouragement and facilitation of these ADR settlement procedures.

Taken together, these recent ADR and related litigation management and settlement initiatives are the sorts of civil justice tools that make up "all of the efforts over many years to encourage settlement between parties,"[331] or what one commentator, as mentioned earlier, referred to as a "global revolution."[332] They are also, taken together, what amounts to a major and systematic privatizing trend – as part of an increasingly widespread civil justice reform movement – throughout our public civil court system.

Before discussing the major preferences, influences and justifications behind this widespread privatizing trend, which I take up in Chapter 5, I now, in Chapter 4, turn to look at the significant privatization movement that is increasingly present in the administrative system as well as through the expansion of non-court or administrative-based legislative ADR processes.

---

327 "McMurtry Remarks," supra note 181 at 7.

328 See, for example, Ontario *Rules of Civil Procedure*, supra note 67 at r. 77. Further, see, for example, specifically ibid. at rr. 77.13(5)–(6), both of which provide for the referral of "any issue for alternative dispute resolution."

329 See, for example, ibid. at r. 50.

330 See, for example, ibid. at r. 49.

331 *Hagel v. Giles,* supra note 237 at para. 34, D.J. Power J.

332 Karl Mackie (referring specifically to mediation) in Economist Staff, "Knocking Heads Together," supra note 157. Further and as also mentioned earlier, according to Mackie, "[i]nterest in mediation is rocketing, in countries of all legal traditions and none." See ibid.

Chapter Four

Other State-Based or State-Sanctioned Dispute Resolution Regimes

Administrative System

Background

Over the years, administrative tribunals and related regimes[1] have developed largely as alternative, specialized dispute resolution forums. As Kaye Joachim commented, administrative tribunals "were created to provide a speedy, efficient, and more cost effective alternative to

1 Other regimes, which I do not generally discuss in this book (although many of the same issues apply), include ombud and related dispute resolution services. There are various ombud processes in Canada, including in the banking and insurance industries, as well as in other federal and provincial ombud regimes. In terms of the banking industry, see, for example, the Ombudsman for Banking Services and Investments (OBSI), which provides an optional dispute resolution process for disputes of less than $350,000 between customers and more than 600 participating organizations in the banking and investment industries. With respect to OBSI's dispute resolution services, see, for example, OBSI, "Our Work," available online: OBSI <http://www.obsi.ca/en/about-us>, which provides the following:

> We are independent and impartial, and our services are free to consumers. You must first complain to the firm involved, but if you remain unsatisfied you have a right to bring your case to us. As an alternative to the legal system, we work informally and confidentially to find a fair outcome. … If you don't like our findings in your case, you are still able to go to a lawyer or seek other ways of resolving your dispute.

For a discussion of these services, see Rob Carrick, "Ombudsman made headway" *The Globe and Mail* (14 May 2009) B14. In terms of the insurance industry, see, for

court adjudication."[2] Similarly, according to Régimbald, administrative "agencies, boards, commissions and tribunals," which are "often populated by experts in the area," provide

> specialized and technical resolutions to different situations, ensure greater innovation, flexibility and efficiency in the delivery of governmental programs and strategies, provide an informal and rapid forum for public hearings (thereby minimizing time and costs related to litigation before ordinary courts) and relieve politicians from what might be otherwise very sensitive political issues.[3]

However, notwithstanding their "alternative" position,[4] administrative regimes clearly perform central dispute resolution and societal regulation functions in Canada in many of the same ways that public courts do.[5] In fact, as the Supreme Court of Canada recently confirmed,

---

example, the General Insurance OmbudService (GIO), which provides non-binding conciliation, mediation, and senior adjudication processes for disputes between customers and participating insurance companies. See GIO, "How the Process Works," online: GIO <http://www.giocanada.org/helpyou.html>. Similarly, see Canadian Life and Health Insurance OmbudService (CLHIO), "Complaints," available online: CLHIO <http://www.olhi.ca/complaint_process.html>. For a further discussion of insurance dispute resolution processes in Ontario, see infra notes 51–5 and accompanying text. And for other provincial and federal regimes, see, for example, Office of the Procurement Ombudsman, online: Government of Canada <http://opo-boa.gc.ca/index-eng.html>; Office of the British Columbia Ombudsperson, online: <https://www.ombudsman.bc.ca/>; and Nova Scotia Office of the Ombudsman, online: Government of Nova Scotia <http://gov.ns.ca/ombu/>.

2 Kaye Joachim, "New Models in Administrative Hearings: The Human Rights Tribunal of Ontario" in Ronalda Murphy and Patrick A. Molinari, eds., *Doing Justice: Dispute Resolution in the Courts and Beyond* (Montréal: Canadian Institute for the Administration of Justice, 2009) at 89. See further generally Colleen M. Flood and Lorne Sossin, eds., *Administrative Law in Context* (Toronto: Emond Montgomery, 2008); David J. Mullan et al., *Administrative Law: Cases, Text, and Materials*, 5th ed. (Toronto: Emond Montgomery, 2003); Donald J.M. Brown and J.M. Evans, with the assistance of Christine E. Deacon, *Judicial Review of Administrative Action in Canada* (Toronto: Canvasback Publishing, 1998); Guy Régimbald, *Canadian Administrative Law* (Markham, ON: LexisNexis, 2008). For a useful background discussion, see Henry M. Hart, Jr. and Albert M. Sacks, *The Legal Process: Basic Problems in the Making and Application of Law*, ed. by William N. Eskridge, Jr. and Philip P. Frickey (Westbury, NY: Foundation Press, 1994) at c. 1, sec. 2, pp. 165–6.

3 Régimbald, *Canadian Administrative Law*, ibid. at 2–3.

4 Joachim, "New Models in Administrative Hearings: The Human Rights Tribunal of Ontario," supra note 2.

5 See further infra Chapter 2.

administrative panels, subject to express jurisdictional limitations, are considered to be "court[s] of competent jurisdiction"[6] for purposes of granting remedies pursuant to s. 24(1) of the *Charter*.[7] Administrative proceedings – such as courts – are also typically meant to be open to the public.[8] Further, in the same way that courts play a central role in our processes of democratic governance,[9] so too do administrative regimes. For example, according to David Mullan,

> [A]dministrative law ... is inevitably enmeshed in theoretical controversies about the legitimate roles of the state, the proper scope of individual autonomy, the content of democratic values, including the rule of law, and the ways in which they can best be realized. In addition ... administrative law raises ... some fundamental questions about the nature of law: the extent to which law is discrete and autonomous from other social phenomenon, on the one hand, or, on the other, is merely a vehicle for transporting to another forum debates about public policy and political power.[10]

An example of administrative law's democratic governance role can be seen clearly in the mission statement of the Québec Human Rights Tribunal (QHRT), which states that the QHRT "contributes in its own way, as part of the third pillar of government, to the building of an egalitarian society, with proper regard for the principles of fundamental justice and procedural fairness."[11]

Finally, as discussed further in this part of this chapter, in the same way that public civil courts are actively looking at ways of privatizing major aspects of their dispute resolution processes, again, so too are administrative regimes, which have embraced a similar ethos of reform.[12]

---

6 *R. v. Conway*, 2010 SCC 22, [2010] 1 S.C.R. 765 at para. 22.

7 *Canadian Charter of Rights and Freedoms, Part I of the Constitution Act, 1982*, being Schedule B to the *Canada Act 1982* (U.K.), 1982, c. 11. See further *Dunsmuir v. New Brunswick*, [2008] 1 S.C.R. 190 at para. 30.

8 See, for example, *Statutory Powers Procedure Act*, R.S.O. 1990, c. S.22 at s. 9. For a recent discussion of the open court process as it applies in the administrative context, see *Palkowski v. Ivancic* (2009), 100 O.R. (3d) 89 at 101–2 (C.A.).

9 See further infra Chapter 2.

10 Mullan et al., *Administrative Law: Cases, Text, and Materials*, supra note 2 at 3.

11 QHRT, "The Human Rights Tribunal," available online: Québec Government <http://www.tribunaux.qc.ca/mjq_en/TDP/index-tdp.html>.

12 For an earlier discussion of privatization in the context of administrative dispute resolution processes, which has significantly influenced this part of this chapter, see Trevor C.W. Farrow, "Public Justice, Private Dispute Resolution and Democracy" in

As one source notes, over the last ten to fifteen years, there has been "an explosion" in using ADR by various statutory bodies in Canada.[13] The research for this chapter turned up literally hundreds of provincial and federal statutes and legislative provisions in Canada regarding administrative-based dispute resolution processes, as well as hundreds of instances of discussions of the use of mediation, arbitration, and other forms of privatizing processes in publicly available materials for many of these administratively based privatizing regimes.[14]

Federal Processes

There are many examples of federal administrative processes that actively encourage and engage various privatizing processes.[15] According to Marian Robson, the former chair of the Canadian Transportation

---

Murphy and Molinari, eds., *Doing Justice: Dispute Resolution in the Courts and Beyond*, supra note 2 at 324–32. For a diagram contemplating the relationship between administrative processes and other dispute resolution processes discussed in this book, all of which are engaging privatizing procedures, see supra Chapter 1, Figure 1.1.

13 Genevieve A. Chornenki and Christine E. Hart, *Bypass Court: A Dispute Resolution Handbook*, 3rd ed. (Markham: LexisNexis, 2005) at 283. See also ibid. at 257. For judicial discussion of the issue, see, for example, *Reference re Amendments to the Residential Tenancies Act (N.S.)*, [1996] 1 S.C.R. 186.

14 For an early record of this research – much of which animated my thinking in Trevor C.W. Farrow, "Public Justice, Private Dispute Resolution and Democracy," supra note 12 – see Trevor C.W. Farrow and Ada Ho, "Canadian Federal and Provincial Administrative Legislation Containing ADR Processes" (September 2007), available online: CFCJ <http://www.cfcj-fcjc.org/sites/default/files/docs/2007/Admin_Legislation_Chart_(Sept_22,_2007).pdf>; and Trevor C.W. Farrow and Ada Ho, "Administrative Tribunals Using ADR" (May 2007), available online: CFCJ <http://www.cfcj-fcjc.org/sites/default/files/docs/2007/Administrative_Tribunal_Legislation_(May_17,_2007).pdf>. For an additional source of selected federal and provincial statutes that contain references to ADR, see Andrew J. Pirie, *Alternative Dispute Resolution: Skills, Science, and the Law* (Toronto: Irwin Law, 2000) at app. 1.

15 As mentioned, many federal administrative regimes actively promote and employ privatizing initiatives as part of their dispute resolution processes. In addition to those specifically discussed in this part of this chapter, see further, for example, the Immigration and Refugee Board of Canada, Immigration Appeal Division (IAD), "Alternative Dispute Resolution at the Immigration Appeal Division" (3 October 2003), available online: Government of Canada <http://www.irb-cisr.gc.ca/Eng/ImmApp/Pages/IadSaiAdrMarGuideApp.aspx> (ADR at the IAD is discussed briefly further at infra note 64 and accompanying text); Canadian Transportation Agency, "Canadian Transportation Agency Launches A New Pilot Project Offering Mediation Services," available online: Government of Canada <http://cta.gc.ca/eng/canadian-transportation-agency-launches-new-pilot-project-offering-mediation-services>.

Agency, "[i]n recent years, government tribunals that have introduced innovative mediation programs have seen a huge success rate among their clients."[16] For example, the Canadian Human Rights Commission (CHRC), established pursuant to the *Canadian Human Rights Act*,[17] has adopted a wide-ranging ADR program that actively promotes the simplification and privatization of many disputes brought to the CHRC.[18]

Within its former 1999 pilot project and now within its established ADR programs, which in 2005 were brought under the newly created Dispute Resolution Branch, the use of ADR has been quite widespread and reportedly successful. According to its 2006 annual report,

---

For a further example, see Public Works and Government Services Canada, "Conflict Management and Alternative Dispute Resolution (ADR) Services" [archived with author], which provides:

> The Conflict Management and ADR Services Group offers a range of options for managing conflict and resolving disputes – from providing advice and coaching in managing conflict, to facilitating voluntary processes for the resolution of disputes.
>
> Parties are encouraged to attempt to reach a solution through discussion and negotiation before seeking more-formal options. (Many contracts require that the parties attempt to resolve a dispute through alternative dispute resolution processes). Should negotiation and facilitated discussion fail to result in satisfactory agreement, parties may agree to enter into mediation. The Contract Conflict Resolution Board (CCRB arbitration boards) may also be an option. The most appropriate method to resolve any given dispute can only be chosen after a careful assessment of the facts and circumstances of the case. In making this evaluation, one must consider the interests of the parties, the nature of the dispute and any statutory or policy restrictions governing the use of a particular dispute resolution process.
>
> The consensual nature of most dispute resolution methods requires that the choice of process be made jointly by all parties. It is the ability of the parties to agree to which dispute resolution process best fits the case at hand that will improve the quality of and access to justice. Acceptable settlements, which may not be available through the litigation process, can be developed by the parties when using an ADR process.

16 See Canadian Transportation Agency, "Canadian Transportation Agency Launches a New Pilot Project Offering Mediation Services," supra note 15.

17 R.S.C. 1985, c. H-6, s. 26.

18 See, for example, CHRC, "Dispute Resolution Operating Procedures" [archived with author]. For further discussions about early settlement processes, including early resolution, mediation and facilitation, see CHRC, "What can I expect?", online: CHRC <http://www.chrc-ccdp.gc.ca/eng/content/what-can-i-expect>.

for example, nearly half of the cases dealt with by the CHRC in 2006 were settled, mostly using a CHRC-appointed conciliator or mediator.[19] Since that time, the CHRC "continues to place increased emphasis on early dispute resolution."[20] As is discussed further later,[21] one of the important aspects of the CHRC's approach to ADR is its recognition that not all cases are suitable for ADR. However, notwithstanding this recognition, it continues, as stated earlier, to make ADR an "increased" priority.[22]

There are many reasons cited for pursuing ADR in the administrative context, all of which are consistent with the general reasons behind most of the civil court reform initiatives discussed elsewhere in this book, including cost and efficiency-based reasons, among others.[23]

Another example of a federal process that actively promotes the use of ADR processes is the Commission for Public Complaints Against the RCMP (CPC), which was established in 1988 by the Federal Government. The CPC is designed to provide "civilian oversight" of the conduct of members of the Royal Canadian Mounted Police (RCMP).[24] According to the CPC, it actively promotes the use of ADR for the resolution of complaints:

> Once the CPC analyst determines the relevant facts and understands the goals of the complainant, the analyst explains the citizen's options for dealing with his or her concern. In appropriate cases, the analyst invites the complainant and the RCMP to work together informally to resolve the complaint. The complainant always retains the right to file a formal complaint.
>
> Where the complainant elects to resolve the complaint informally, the CPC analyst serves as a facilitator, helping the complainant obtain information by enlisting the aid of the senior RCMP officer in the jurisdiction where the problem arose. When facilitating in this manner, the analyst

---

19 CHRC, *2006 Annual Report* at 18 ("Effectiveness of the Business Model"), available online: CHRC <http://www.crr.ca/divers-files/en/publications/reports/diversReports/repAnnCHRC2006.pdf>.

20 CHRC, *2008 Annual Report* at 14 ("A Settlement through Mediation"), available online: CHRC <http://publications.gc.ca/collections/collection_2009/ccdp-chrc/HR1-2008E.pdf>.

21 See infra notes 22–7 and accompanying text.

22 CHRC, *2008 Annual Report* at 4 ("A Settlement through Mediation"), supra note 20.

23 See, for example, generally supra Chapter 3 and infra Chapter 5.

24 CPC, "About Us: Mission," available online: Government of Canada <http://www.cpc-cpp.gc.ca/cnt/wwa/index-eng.aspx>.

provides the RCMP with a summary of the concern expressed by the complainant, normally on the same day that the citizen raises the concern.[25]

Again, the merits of this process are well known. Speed, cost, and efficiency are important justifications for the CPC's use of alternative, more private, processes. However, it is clear that the CPC and the RCMP, particularly given budgetary realities, encourage the use of ADR to enable them to deploy their energies on matters that they view as more pressing. For example, according to the CPC,

> The informal resolution of complaints against members of the RCMP has been highly successful – the needs of complainants often can be addressed more quickly than through the formal process. *Informal resolution makes it possible for both the CPC and the RCMP to deploy scarce resources to higher priority work.*[26]

Provided other endeavours *are* more pressing and assuming the intake analyst who receives complaints gets the complaint-channelling process right, of course, that policy approach makes sense. However, to the extent that a case of significant public importance is run through the CPC's ADR channel, because of a bad decision by an intake analyst, bad faith on the part of the RCMP or the CPC, or simply because of "scarce resources" that are deemed to be needed for "higher priority work," concerns need to be raised.[27] These are the concerns of this book, which are further developed below.[28] Given the active promotion of ADR by the CPC, it is clear that, similar to the CHRC, its strong preference, which is also in line with the federal government's stated preferences,[29] is to try to resolve disputes using ADR.

---

25 CPC, *Annual Report, 2005–2006* at "Informal Resolution in Action," available online: Government of Canada <http://www.cpc-cpp.gc.ca/cnt/cr-ro/anr/2005-2006-eng.aspx#toc3.5.1>. See further CPC, *Annual Report, 2007–2008* at "Enquiries, Informal Resolutions and Complaints," available online: Government of Canada <http://www.cpc-cpp.gc.ca/cnt/cr-ro/anr/2007-2008-eng.aspx#a17>.

26 CPC, *Annual Report, 2005–2006* at "Informal Resolution in Action," ibid. [emphasis added].

27 According to the CPC, "It should be noted that the CPC does not resolve serious incidents informally." See CPC, *Annual Report, 2007–2008* at "Enquiries, Informal Resolutions and Complaints," supra note 25. What "serious" means, and whether it could include a pattern of less serious individual incidents that, taken together, amount to a serious problem, is not defined.

28 See generally infra Chapters 6 and 7.

29 See, for example, infra Chapter 5.

Provincial Processes

As with the federal administrative regime, provincial processes are increasingly promoting and employing privatizing initiatives as part of their dispute resolution systems.[30] As a preliminary matter, several provinces, including British Columbia and Ontario, have enacted administrative legislation of general application that allows for individual administrative regimes within those jurisdictions to create and administer ADR processes. These legislative initiatives are clearly in line with, and are in fact motivated by, the overall government preferences in these and other jurisdictions to promote the use of privatized dispute resolution mechanisms generally.[31] For example, according to the B.C. legislation, "[t]he chair of the tribunal may appoint a member or staff of the tribunal or other persons to conduct a dispute resolution process."[32] Similarly, in Ontario, tribunals are given broad authority to develop and administer privatizing ADR regimes, including mandatory regimes. According to the *Statutory Powers Procedure Act,*

> A tribunal may make rules ... classifying the types of proceedings that come before it and setting guidelines as to the procedural steps or processes (such as ... alternative dispute resolution mechanisms, expedited hearings) that apply to each type of proceeding and the circumstances in which other procedures may apply. ...
>
> A rule ... may provide that participation in an alternative dispute resolution mechanism is mandatory or that it is mandatory in certain specified circumstances.[33]

---

30 See Farrow and Ho, "Canadian Federal and Provincial Administrative Legislation Containing ADR Processes," supra note 14; and Farrow and Ho, "Administrative Tribunals Using ADR," supra note 14.

31 Discussed further at infra Chapter 5.

32 *Administrative Tribunals Act*, S.B.C. 2004, c. 45 at s. 28(1). For legislative commentary about this statute, see, for example, B.C., Legislative Assembly, *Hansard*, 37th Parl., 5th sess., vol. 25, No. 15 (18 May 2004) at 11191–6 (Hon. G. Plant). For B.C.'s current efficiency-seeking administrative initiative in the small claims area, see *Civil Resolution Tribunal Act*, S.B.C. 2012, c. 25 (assented to 31 May 2012).

33 R.S.O. 1990, c. S.22 at ss. 4.7, 4.8(4). To further the goal of efficiency, see Ontario's *Adjudicative Tribunals Accountability, Governance and Appointments Act*, 2009, S.O. 2009, c. 33, Sch. 5 at s. 1.

Of particular interest to the arguments presented in this book are administrative regimes that deal with significant public interest values and resources. One area of particular focus, in which these sorts of ADR mechanisms have been put in place, includes the various provincial human rights regimes. For example, the Manitoba Human Rights Commission (MHRC) "encourages" the use of ADR processes as part of its overall dispute resolution process.[34] Similarly, the B.C. Human Rights Tribunal (BCHRT) offers various forms of "off the record"[35] ADR settlement processes, including mediation, early evaluation, structured negotiation, and final determinations on the merits.[36]

The policy reasons behind the BCHRT initiatives, again, include speed, simplicity (often including reduced costs) and privacy. Specifically, according to the BCHRT, parties "may be interested in a settlement meeting for a number of reasons. Settlement meetings are often the quickest and simplest method of resolving disputes, and they are confidential. *If there is a settlement, there will not be a public hearing.*"[37]

Similar processes and policy advantages are identified as part of the ADR-based settlement initiatives of the Alberta Human Rights and Citizenship Commission (AHRCC) and the Nova Scotia Human Rights Commission (NSHRC). According to the AHRCC, for example, which provides for a "confidential" conciliation process, "[t]he success rate of conciliation is high: more than half of complaints are resolved through

---

34 MHRC, *Annual Report 2005* at 9 ("Complaint Process – Overview: Mediation"), available online: Manitoba Government <http://www.manitobahumanrights.ca/publications/annual_reports/annual_report_2005.pdf>.

35 BCHRT, "Guide 4 – The Settlement Meeting" at 2, available online: B.C. Government <http://www.bchrt.gov.bc.ca/guides_and_information_sheets/guides/English_Guide4.pdf>. For discussions of ADR processes in the context of the B.C. human rights regime, see Philip Bryden and William Black, "Designing Mediation Systems for Use in Administrative Agencies and Tribunals – The B.C. Human Rights Experience" in Anne L. Mactavish and Laverne A. Jacobs, *Dialogue between Courts and Tribunals: Essays in Administrative Law and Justice* (Montréal: Les Éditions Thémis, 2008) at 157; Philip Bryden and William Black, "Mediation as a Tool for Resolving Human Rights Disputes: An Evaluation of the B.C. Human Rights Commission's Early Mediation Project" (2004) 37 *U.B.C.L. Rev.* 73; and Heather M. MacNaughton, "The Role of Mediation in Human Rights Disputes" in Murphy and Molinari, eds., *Doing Justice: Dispute Resolution in the Courts and Beyond*, supra note 2 at 47.

36 BCHRT, "Guide 4 – The Settlement Meeting," ibid. at 1.

37 Ibid. at 2 [emphasis added].

conciliation."[38] Similarly, according to the NSHRC, the resolution of complaints is the "preferred way to settle human rights disputes."[39] If the dispute is settled before the commencement of a formal board of inquiry, the settlement is usually confidential.[40]

Other provincial administrative bodies that deal with significant public resource issues include environmental protection tribunals. Again, in this segment of the administrative law process, significant privatizing initiatives have been put in place. For example, the Alberta Environmental Appeals Board (AEAB) – an independent body that reviews decisions regarding development approval, water licenses, reclamation certificates, and enforcement orders[41] – actively encourages ADR. According to its materials, the AEAB "places a high value on its mediation program and encourages participants to use mediation as the *primary* way to resolve appeals that come before the Board."[42] In addition to its policy statements, the AEAB's preference for resolving disputes through its ADR process can also be seen from its settlement statistics. For example, according to the AEAB's available annual mediation information,

> From April 1, 2004 to March 31, 2005, the Board held 18 mediations, all of which were successfully resolved, resulting in a 100 percent success rate for this reporting year. Since the Board's inception in 1993, it has conducted 139 mediations with 116 being successfully resolved. This reflects an overall success rate of 83 percent.[43]

---

38 AHRCC, Information for Complainants, "How Does Conciliation Work?" [archived with author].

39 See NSHRC, "Settlement Summaries", online: NSHRC <http://humanrights.gov.ns.ca/settlement-summaries>. For a recent general discussion of Nova Scotia's human rights regime, see *Halifax (Regional Municipality) v. Nova Scotia (Human Rights Commission)*, [2012] 1 S.C.R. 364. Other provinces with human rights tribunal regimes that employ similar kinds of private ADR process include, for example, New Brunswick, Newfoundland and Labrador, P.E.I., and Saskatchewan. For a recent discussion of the Ontario regime, see Joachim, "New Models in Administrative Hearings: The Human Rights Tribunal of Ontario," supra note 2.

40 See NSHRC, "Settlement Summaries", ibid.

41 AEAB, "Welcome," available online: Alberta Government <http://www.eab.gov.ab.ca/index.htm>.

42 Ibid. [emphasis added].

43 AEAB, *2004–2005 Annual Report* at 24 ("Mediation Program"), available online: Alberta Government <http://www.eab.gov.ab.ca/pub/2004-05-AR.pdf>. By comparison, the settlement rates using these sorts of ADR-based processes in the

Similar environmental assessment and protection issues are dealt with by the Ontario Environmental Review Tribunal (OERT), which also actively deploys ADR techniques for the resolution of disputes. For example, according to the OERT,

> Parties are encouraged to narrow or settle their differences at an early stage of the hearing process. Mediation services are offered to the parties by the Tribunal following a preliminary hearing and generally 30 days prior to the commencement of the main hearing. ... The number[s] of required hearing days and issues to be adjudicated are often reduced, resulting in lower costs to the parties and taxpayers. ... The Tribunal will continue to offer these services in every appeal and, upon request, in all applications filed in order to encourage parties to resolve their issues.[44]

According to the OERT, its "target" in this regard is to "increase the number of mediation sessions."[45] Further, even after an initial settlement attempt, or if "parties choose not to participate" following the preliminary hearing, mediation services "are available throughout the hearing process, upon request."[46] Because a "number of the Tribunal Members are certified to conduct mediation,"[47] it is clear, even at the

---

human rights tribunal context are moderate to strong. For example, according to the AHRCC, more than 50 per cent (394 complaints) of the 749 complaints that were resolved in the 2005–2006 year (of a total of 778 complaint files opened) were resolved using the AHRCC's conciliation process. AHRCC, *Annual Review, April 1, 2005–March 31, 2006* at 10 ("Conciliated files"). Almost 60 per cent were resolved that way the previous year at the AHRCC. See ibid. Since that time, similar resolution rates are being achieved. For example, in 2007–2008, 52 per cent of the complaint files (378 of 733 files) were resolved with the assistance of a conciliator. In 2006–2007, 58 per cent of cases were resolved with a conciliator. All of these rates exceed the AHRCC's stated settlement goal of 50 per cent case closure through conciliation. See AHRCC, *Annual Review, April 1, 2007–March 31, 2008* at 10 ("Conciliated files") (on file with author).

44 OERT, *2008–2011Business Plan* at 4 and 11, available online: Government of Ontario <http://www.ert.gov.on.ca/files/Businessp/BusinessP_0811.pdf>. See similarly OERT, *2007–2010 Business Plan* at 4 and 10, available online: Government of Ontario <http://www.ert.gov.on.ca/files/Businessp/BusinessP_0710.pdf>.

45 OERT, *2008-2011 Business Plan*, ibid. at 19.

46 OERT, *Annual Report, April 1, 2007–March 31, 2008* at 4 ("Mediation"), available online: Government of Ontario <http://www.ert.gov.on.ca/files/AnnualR/Annual_Report_07-08.pdf>.

47 OERT, *2008–2011 Business Plan* at 4 ("Mediation"), supra note 44.

hearing stage, that mediation is actively considered and promoted by the OERT.

In addition to human rights and the environment, there are numerous other areas of administrative law in which ADR is playing an increasingly prominent role. For example, Ontario's new home warranty regime is governed by legislation[48] that includes various facilitation and mandatory arbitration provisions.[49] Another example includes the regulation of financial industries, specifically including disputes involving those industries, which are, in addition to ombud services,[50] actively using ADR techniques to resolve disputes. An example of this area of administrative regulation is the Financial Services Commission of Ontario (FSCO), which is an arm's-length body of the Ontario Ministry of Finance.[51] As of 1 March 2008, the FSCO reportedly regulated or registered: "394 insurance companies, 7,755 pension plans, 207 credit unions and caisses populaires, 55 loan and trust companies, 1,290 mortgage brokers, 1,610 co-operative corporations, as well as approximately 39,700 insurance agents, 4,040 corporate insurance agencies and 1,145 insurance adjusters."[52] As part of this extensive program, the FSCO has put in place a Dispute Resolution Group (DRG), which provides dispute resolution services for consumers and insurers in Ontario. It has been described as "the largest, most comprehensive dispute resolution system of any Ontario administrative agency, board or commission."[53]

48 *Ontario New Home Warranties Plan Act*, R.S.O. 1990, c. O.31.

49 See ibid. at ss. 17(1)–(4). For a different provincial initiative that promotes ADR (in the form of conciliation), see the Tribunal Administratif du Québec, online: <http://www.taq.gouv.qc.ca/en/>.

50 See, for example, supra note 1.

51 See FSCO, "About FSCO," online: Government of Ontario <http://www.fsco.gov.on.ca/english/about/>, which provides the following:

> The ... FSCO ... was created on July 1, 1998, as an arm's-length agency of the Ministry of Finance. The FSCO integrates the operations of the former Ontario Insurance Commission, Pension Commission of Ontario, and Deposit Institutions Division of the Ministry of Finance. FSCO comprises three key parts: the commission; the Financial Services Tribunal (Tribunal); and the Superintendent and Staff.

52 Ibid.

53 Hon. George W. Adams, "Ontario Insurance Commission Dispute Resolution Group Evaluation Report" (June 1998) in Naomi Bussin, "Evaluating ADR Programs: The Ends Determine the Means" (2000) 22 *Advocates' Q.* 460 at 463.

That regime, which has been reportedly quite successful in terms of resolving disputes,[54] provides several ADR processes, including a mandatory mediation regime.[55]

Settlements Involving Matters of Public Interest

There are policy-based provisions in various administrative regimes that encourage or require matters of "public interest" to proceed to a tribunal hearing,[56] or at least to be resolved pursuant to "public

---

54 See Adams, "Ontario Insurance Commission Dispute Resolution Group Evaluation Report" in Bussin, "Evaluating ADR Programs: The Ends Determine the Means," ibid. at 465. See further Elana Fleischmann and Naomi Bussin, "The Institutionalization of Alternative Dispute Resolution: A Case Study of the Ontario Insurance Commission" (1996) 6 *C.I.L.R.* 265.

55 According to the DRG's materials,

> The Dispute Resolution Group at the Commission provides mediation, neutral evaluation and arbitration services. There is also a process for appealing arbitration orders on a question of law, and a process for varying or revoking orders.
>
> If consumers and insurers are unable to resolve disputes about statutory accident benefits, the first step in the dispute resolution process is mediation. Mediation of such disputes is mandatory in Ontario and must be conducted through the Commission before the dispute can proceed to arbitration or court. The insured person is charged no fee for mediation. However, each party must pay for its own expenses, which may include lawyer's fees, travelling expenses, accounting services, and additional medical reports.
>
> Mediation is an informal process in which a mediator helps parties involved in a dispute to clarify issues and find solutions that lead to a satisfactory outcome. The Mediation Unit of the Dispute Resolution Group has established a successful record in mediation, achieving full or partial success in over 75 percent of mediations. In December 1998, the Unit was awarded the prestigious Amethyst Award for outstanding achievement by the Ontario Public Service.
>
> If the dispute remains unresolved after mediation at the Commission, the insured person has a number of choices. He or she can continue to negotiate directly with the insurance company. Alternatively, the insured person can opt for arbitration at the Commission, private arbitration, private neutral evaluation or a court action. Each option has its own rules, and the insured person may not be able to switch from one system to another. For example, once an action has been commenced in court, the insured person may not be able to switch to arbitration at the Commission, or vice versa.

56 See, for example, AEAB, "About Mediation: When Is Mediation not Appropriate?," available online: Alberta Government <http://www.eab.gov.ab.ca/mediation_about.htm>. See further infra nn. 59 and 63 and accompanying text.

interest" values.[57] Further, there exist annual lists of some tribunal settlement details and summaries, some of which are made public.[58] However, there remain numerous cases being settled using private ADR methods that involve matters of significant public interest and importance that receive little or no public scrutiny or attention. Some of these settlements involve matters that are discontinued and are not pursued at all through either the formal or the informal administrative processes.[59] Nothing further may be heard of these matters. Of those that do continue into the system, many are resolved based on confidential processes and are only reported in a very summary fashion, if at all, in the administrative regime's public materials. For example, private settlements at the administrative level over the past several years have involved matters of public interest such as subsidized housing discrimination[60]; physical disability and gender discrimination, often in the context of employment and services[61]; significant complaints about police mistreatment involving potential discrimination of members of First Nations[62]; environmental protection matters[63]; and immigration matters.[64] The public interest aspect of these privatized administrative settlements brings them within the scope of this book. Put simply, although there are clearly important and persuasive efficiency-based justifications underlying various federal and provincial administrative-based privatizing initiatives, they do not, as I argue later in this book, come without significant potential costs to both the dispute resolution and societal regulation purposes of public dispute resolution processes.

57 See, for example, the earlier discussion of the CHRC, supra note 18 and accompanying text.

58 See, for example, Ontario Human Rights Commission [OHRC], "Settlements and Decisions at the Human Rights Tribunal of Ontario" at apps., available online: OHRC <http://www.ohrc.on.ca/en/annual-report-2005-2006/appendices>, which were posted prior to the relatively recent and significant reforms to Ontario's human rights regime.

59 See, for example, AEAB, *2004–2005 Annual Report* at 36, supra note 43.

60 See, for example, MHRC, *Annual Report 2005* at 11, supra note 36.

61 See, for example, AHRCC, *Annual Review, April 1, 2005–March 31, 2006* at viii ("Resolution and Adjudication of Human Rights Complaints: Summary of Results"), supra note 44.

62 See, for example, CPC, *2006–2007 Annual Report*, app., "Informal Resolution of Complaints," available online: Government of Canada <http://www.cpc-cpp.gc.ca/cnt/cr-ro/anr/2006-2007-eng.aspx#toc8>.

63 See, for example, AEAB, *2004–2005 Annual Report* at 36, supra note 34.

64 See, for example, Immigration and Refugee Board of Canada, IAD, "Alternative Dispute Resolution at the Immigration Appeal Division," supra note 15.

However, before addressing those concerns, I first look at the final process of dispute resolution at stake in this book.

Non-Court or Administrative-Based Legislative ADR Processes

Introduction

The third aspect of the dispute resolution system that I focus on in this book, in addition to public courts and administrative regimes, is the increasingly important aspect of the system that lies in between those state-based dispute resolution regimes and the purely private realm of dispute resolution processes that occur completely outside of the state's influence.[65] This hybrid system typically involves arbitration processes that are set up pursuant to agreements between individuals or private entities but that are, at the same time, often enabled by (or at least contemplated by) federal[66] or provincial arbitration statutes.[67] The paradigmatic case is a private arbitration between two corporate entities, such as the Dealership case,[68] under the authority of federal or provincial arbitration legislation. This aspect of the discussion could also include non-court-annexed mediation processes under specific circumstances in which provincial mediation statutes are in force.[69] However, because provincial mediation legislation is less typical than is arbitration legislation (and for the sake of clarity), I generally refer to arbitration as the paradigmatic process for this aspect of the discussion.[70]

The arbitration processes at issue here are hybrid processes. They are partly public regimes, given the enabling and sanctioning arbitration legislation pursuant to which they receive much of their recognition and many of their powers. But they are primarily private regimes in the sense that they are initiated by private contractual agreement, and once underway, they allow parties essentially free reign to conduct

65 For a diagram contemplating the relationship between these processes, see supra Chapter 1, Figure 1.1.

66 See *Commercial Arbitration Act*, R.S.C. 1985 (2nd Supp.), c. 17.

67 See, for example, Alberta *Arbitration Act*, R.S.A. 2000, c. A-43.

68 See supra Chapter 1. However, a key distinguishing feature between the Dealership case and the paradigmatic case here is the fact that the Dealership case occurred in the U.S., and was subject to a U.S. commercial arbitration regime.

69 See, for example, Nova Scotia *Commercial Mediation Act*, S.N.S. 2005, c. 36; and Ontario *Commercial Mediation Act, 2010*, S.O. 2010, c. 16, sched. 3.

70 See further supra Chapter 1, Figure 1.1.

proceedings that are fully private and largely out of reach of all state actors (including the courts). Arbitration and related processes, therefore, are examples of what Hart and Sacks approvingly contemplated in their discussion about the "interplay of private and official [public] procedures of decisions."[71] According to Hart and Sacks,

> Not every question of group concern ... can be decided by officials. ... Every society necessarily assigns many kinds of questions to private decision, and then backs up the private decision, if it has been duly made, when and if it is challenged before officials. ... So may a host of ... matters be settled which are immediately of private, but potentially of public, concern. In a genuine sense, these procedures of private decision, too, become institutionalized. An understanding of how they work is vital to an understanding of the institutional system as a whole.[72]

The most important summary of the form of privatized dispute resolution processes – "back[ed] ... up" by public procedures[73] – that I am discussing in this part of this chapter is found in the relatively recent *Dell* case from the Supreme Court of Canada.[74] When describing arbitration clauses and the private jurisdiction they create, Justices Bastarache and LeBel stated:

> Exclusive arbitration clauses operate to create a "private jurisdiction" that implicates the loss of jurisdiction of state-appointed forums for dispute resolution, such as ordinary courts and administrative tribunals, rendering contractual arbitration both different and exclusive of the later entities. ... Contractual arbitration has also been described as creating a "private justice system" for the parties: ... "From a theoretical standpoint, arbitration is a private justice system that ordinarily arises out of an agreement. Thus, it has a contractual source and an adjudicative function" ....
>
> What makes contractual arbitration a "private jurisdiction" or "private justice system" is the degree of freedom the parties have in choosing the manner in which their dispute will be resolved:

---

71 Hart and Sacks, *The Legal Process: Basic Problems in the Making and Application of Law*, supra note 2 at c. 1, sec. 1, p. 6.

72 Ibid. at p. 7. See further ibid. at c. 2, sec. 2, pp. 309–21.

73 Ibid. at c. 1, sec. 1, p. 7.

74 *Dell Computer Corp. v. Union des consommateurs*, [2007] 2 S.C.R. 801.

> Arbitration is therefore the settling of disputes between parties who agree not to go before the courts, but to accept as final the decision of experts of their choice, in a place of their choice, usually subject to laws agreed upon in advance and usually under rules which avoid much of the formality, niceties, proof and procedure required by the courts. ...[75]

Also in the *Dell* case, Justices Bastarache and LeBel similarly stated that "the *effect* of exclusive arbitration clauses is to create a 'private jurisdiction' that implicates the loss of jurisdiction of state-appointed authorities for dispute resolution, such as domestic courts and administrative tribunals."[76]

As a final introductory comment, in addition to paradigmatic commercial arbitration proceedings, essentially any arbitration that is not excluded from the benefits and burdens of provincial arbitral statutory provisions could be contemplated in the context of this discussion. Examples of such arbitral proceedings could potentially include disputes involving consumer issues, contracts, property, tortious activity, and so forth. Potential notable exceptions, depending on the province, are some religious arbitral proceedings, specifically including those that do not accord with certain provincial or federal legal requirements. For example, religious arbitral proceedings in Ontario employing Sharia or other religious laws and customs, in ways that are not consistent with Ontario or federal family law, are not recognized under Ontario's arbitration legislation.[77] Other exceptions include arbitrations that are

---

75 Ibid. at paras. 132–3 [references omitted]. See also *Seidel v. Telus Communications Inc.*, 2011 SCC 15, [2011] 1 S.C.R. 531 at paras. 23 and 42 (majority), and 52, 89–103, 137, and 170–1.

76 *Dell Computer Corp. v. Union des consommateurs*, ibid. at para. 200. For commentary on the *Dell* case, see, for example, Jonnette Watson Hamilton, "Common Law Courts Interpret *Dell* Broadly" 28:7 *The Lawyers Weekly* (13 June 2008) 9.

77 For further discussions of these issues, see Trevor C.W. Farrow, "Re-Framing the Sharia Arbitration Debate" (2006) 15:2 *Const. Forum Const.* 79; Natasha Bakht, "Were Muslim Barbarians Really Knocking on the Gates of Ontario? The Religious Arbitration Controversy – Another Perspective" in Murphy and Molinari, eds., *Doing Justice: Dispute Resolution in the Courts and Beyond*, supra note 2 at 227; Jean-François Gaudreault-DesBiens, "On Private Choices and Public Justice: Some Microscopic and Macroscopic Reflections on the State's Role in Addressing Faith-Based Arbitration" in Murphy and Molinari, eds., *Doing Justice: Dispute Resolution in the Courts and Beyond*, supra note 2 at 247; and Julie Macfarlane, "Faith-Based Dispute Resolution" in Murphy and Molinari, eds., *Doing Justice: Dispute Resolution in the*

contemplated by other dispute resolution regimes, most notably including administrative proceedings[78] and many labour proceedings, which are typically governed by specific collective bargaining agreements and provincial labour codes.[79] Further, some provincial consumer legislation is also being amended to provide further protections for consumers in the form of limits to wide-ranging private arbitration regimes.[80]

Historical Background

Arbitration has a long history. For example, according to Thucydides's account of the Peloponnesian War, "arbitration" was proposed by the Athenians to the Spartans as the preferred method "to settle" their differences.[81] Centuries later, arbitration found its "modern" roots in the

---

Courts and Beyond, supra note 2 at 287. For the legislative debates surrounding the relatively recent amendments to Ontario's arbitration regime, which were primarily included in the *Family Statute Law Amendment Act, 2006*, S.O. 2006, c. 1 and which led to these religious exclusions, see, for example, Ontario, Legislative Assembly, *Official Report of Debates (Hansard)* (23, 28 November 2005); Ontario, Standing Committee on General Government, *Official Report of Debates (Hansard)* (16–18 January 2006). See further the related debates surrounding the enactment of the *Family Statute Law Amendment Act, 2006*, S.O. 2006, c. 1 at Ontario, Legislative Assembly, *Official Report of Debates (Hansard)* (1–3, 23 November 2005; 5 December 2005; 20, 28 February 2006; 1 March 2006). See also Marion Boyd, *Dispute Resolution in Family Law: Protecting Choice, Promoting Inclusion* (Toronto: December 2004), available online: Government of Ontario <http://www.attorneygeneral.jus.gov.on.ca/english/about/pubs/boyd/fullreport.pdf>.

78 Discussed supra.

79 See, for example, Ontario's *Labour Relations Act, 1995*, S.O. 1995, c. 1, sched. A, as amended, at ss. 48–50. For further commentary, see generally Donald J.M. Brown and David M. Beatty, with the assistance of Christine E. Deacon, *Canadian Labour Arbitration*, 4th ed. (Aurora, ON: Canada Law Book, 2006); and Morton G. Mitchnick and Brian Etherington, *Labour Arbitration in Canada* (Toronto: Lancaster House, 2006).

80 See infra note 124 and accompanying text. See further Chapters 5 and 6. See also generally *Seidel v. Telus Communications Inc.*, supra note 75 (discussed further below).

81 Thucydides, *History of the Peloponnesian War*, trans. by Rex Warner, rev. ed. (London: Penguin, 1972) at § 78, p. 82. The arbitration contemplated in that case was provided for by treaty. See ibid. For a brief world-wide review of the ancient roots of some alternative dispute resolution methods, specifically including mediation, see Jay Folberg, "A Mediation Overview: History and Dimensions of Practice" in (1983) 1 *Mediation Q.*, c. 1, p. 3 at 3–7.

work of canon lawyers in the later twelfth century in England[82] and subsequently in secular application in the middle of the fourteenth and fifteenth centuries.[83] By that time, and subsequently, arbitration had become an active part of the dispute resolution landscape.[84] In England, for example, non-court-based dispute resolution was regularly used during the 1500s and 1600s. According to James Jaffe, by the end of the Tudor and Stuart periods, "arbitration had become especially popular in the commercial sector, principally in order to avoid the costs and delays engendered by proceedings in the courts of common law and equity."[85] The *Arbitration Act*, for example, was enacted in 1698.[86] By the nineteenth century, again according to Jaffe,

> [L]ife and work in England had been penetrated by forms of dispute resolution that were meant to secure "order without law." Indeed the

---

82 James A. Jaffe, "Industrial Arbitration, Equity, and Authority in England, 1800–1850" (2000) 18:3 *L.H.R.* 525 at 529; Edward Powell, "Settlement of Disputes by Arbitration in Fifteenth-Century England" (1984) 2:1 *L.H.R.* 21 at 25. For further background commentary, see, for example, John S. Beckerman, "Procedural Innovation and Institutional Change in Medieval English Manorial Courts" (1992) 10:2 *L.H.R.* 197; and John S. Beckerman, "Toward a Theory of Medieval Manorial Adjudication: The Nature of Communal Judgments in a System of Customary Law" (1995) 13:1 *L.H.R.* 1.

83 Jaffe, "Industrial Arbitration, Equity, and Authority in England, 1800–1850," supra note 82 at 529; and Powell, "Settlement of Disputes by Arbitration in Fifteenth-Century England," supra note 82 at 25.

84 For further discussions of early attempts at ADR in the United States, Canada, and England, see, for example, Lawrence M. Friedman, *A History of American Law*, 3rd ed. (New York: Simon & Schuster, 2005) at 13–14, 22–3, and 405; Kermitt L. Hall, *The Magic Mirror: Law in American History* (New York and Oxford, UK: Oxford University Press, 1989) at 27, 86, 228, and 296; William R. Riddell, *The Early Courts of the Province* (Toronto?, 191? [specific publication details unknown]) at 8; Harry W. Arthurs, "Special Courts, Special Law: Legal Pluralism in Nineteenth Century England" in G.R. Rubin and David Sugarman, *Law, Economy and Society, 1750–1914: Essays in the History of English Law* (Oxford, UK: Professional Books Limited, 1984) at 380; and Katherine V.W. Stone, *Private Justice: The Law of Alternative Dispute Resolution* (New York: Foundation Press, 2000) at 10–12 [references omitted]. See also further supra Chapter 3.

85 Jaffe, "Industrial Arbitration, Equity, and Authority in England, 1800–1850," supra note 82 at 530. Further, see generally Powell, "Settlement of Disputes by Arbitration in Fifteenth-Century England," supra note 82.

86 Cited and discussed in Jaffe, "Industrial Arbitration, Equity, and Authority in England, 1800–1850," supra note 82 at 531. See also Stewart Kyd, A *Treatise on the Law of Awards*, 2nd ed. (Philadelphia: Farrand, 1808), also cited in Jaffe, "Industrial Arbitration, Equity, and Authority in England, 1800–1850," supra note 82 at 531, n. 22 and accompanying text.

arbitration of disputes by reference to independent individuals, frequently beyond the supervision or interference of the courts, was a well-recognized and common way to resolve contentious issues in many areas of English social life, including business ventures, contracts, property, and employment relations.[87]

Similar trends were occurring in the early United States and Canada in the late 1700s, 1800s and 1900s. According to one commentator, although U.S. "high courts" continued to develop and expand during that time as "busy institutions,"

> [M]ost ordinary business and nonbusiness disputes avoided the courts. The courts were too slow [and] … too expensive. … Delays piled up. … Aside from the expense and the delays, there was the problem of the law itself, and the judges who expounded it. They were men trained in the law; they did not necessarily understand what business people wanted or needed.[88]

For example, according to one report of civil dispute resolution in the State of New York in the 1750s, "[s]ince New Yorkers were familiar with the arbitration mechanism as a substitute for formal litigation, particularly for resolution of commercial disputes, it is not surprising that they were inclined to resort to some form of private settlement even after a lawsuit had been commenced."[89] Other reports of merchant trade in and near the border territories around Cornwall, Kingston, Detroit, Michillimackinac, and others – prior to the *Québec Act* of 1774 – discussed disputes being typically submitted either to military courts or courts of civil jurisdiction held by justices of the peace. However, "[t]hese failing," merchants were reported to "submit their differences to Arbitration."[90]

Again, almost a century later, reports of civil proceedings in the Court of Queen's Bench in Upper Canada, specifically in Cobourg,

87 Jaffe, "Industrial Arbitration, Equity, and Authority in England, 1800–1850," supra note 82 at 525 [citations omitted].

88 Friedman, *A History of American Law*, supra note 84 at 291.

89 Deborah A. Rosen, "The Supreme Court of Judicature of Colonial New York: Civil Practice in Transition, 1691–1760" (1987) 5 *L.H.R.* 213 at 227. See further ibid. at 240–2, 245.

90 William R. Riddell, *The Bar and the Courts of the Province of Upper Canada, or Ontario* (Toronto: Macmillan, 1928) at 48. See also ibid. at 52. For a brief discussion looking at early concerns about arbitration's fairness, see infra Chapter 6.

commented on actions started in that court that were "settled by reference to arbitration."[91] Similarly in the West, specifically in the 1820s and 1830s in Red River, Rupert's Land, Alexander Ross and the Reverend Roderick MacBeath (whose father was a magistrate in Assiniboia) described a "primitive" administration of justice "largely dependent on arbitration and equitable settlements."[92]

More recently, the introduction of a modern arbitration regime in Canada has largely tracked significant commercial arbitration developments on the international stage. This modern background has been recently and usefully summarized by Justice Deschamps of the Supreme Court of Canada:

> International arbitration law is strongly influenced by two texts drafted under the auspices of the United Nations: the *Convention on the Recognition and Enforcement of Foreign Arbitral Awards*, 330 U.N.T.S. 3 ("New York Convention"), and the *UNCITRAL Model Law on International Commercial Arbitration*, U.N. Doc. A/40/17 (1985) ("Model Law").
>
> The New York Convention entered into force in 1959. Article II of the Convention provides that a court of a contracting state that is seized of an action in a matter covered by an arbitration clause must refer the parties to arbitration. At present, 142 countries are parties to the Convention. The accession of this many countries is evidence of a broad consensus in favour of the institution of arbitration. … Canada acceded to the New York Convention on May 12, 1986.
>
> The Model Law is another fundamental text in the area of international commercial arbitration. It is a model for legislation that the UN recommends that states take into consideration in order to standardize the rules of international commercial arbitration. The Model Law was drafted in a manner that ensured consistency with the New York Convention. …
>
> The final text of the Model Law was adopted on June 21, 1985 by the United Nations Commission on International Trade Law ("UNCITRAL"). In its explanatory note on the Model Law, the UNCITRAL Secretariat states that it:
>
> … reflects a worldwide consensus on the principles and important issues of international arbitration practice. It is acceptable to States of all regions and the different legal or economic systems of the world.

91 Riddell, *The Bar and the Courts of the Province of Upper Canada, or Ontario*, ibid. at 184.

92 H. Robert Baker, "Creating Order in the Wilderness: Transplanting the English Law to Rupert's Land, 1835–51" (1999) 17:2 *L.H.R.* 209 at 217.

> (Explanatory Note by the UNCITRAL secretariat on the Model Law on International Commercial Arbitration, at para. 2)
>
> In 1986, Parliament enacted the *Commercial Arbitration Act*, R.S.C. 1985, c. 17 (2nd Supp.), which was based on the Model Law. ...[93]

Key motivating purposes for these internationally developed and accepted arbitral procedures include order, consistency, predictability, and efficiency in commercial affairs. These motivating purposes, particularly, although certainly not exclusively, at the international level, have been recently highlighted by the Federal Court of Australia:

> The New York Convention and the model law deal with one of the most important aspects of international commerce – the resolution of disputes between commercial parties in an international or multinational context. ... An ordered efficient dispute resolution mechanism leading to an enforceable award or judgment by the adjudicator, is an essential underpinning of commerce. Disputes arising from commercial bargains are unavoidable. They are part of the activity of commerce itself. Parties therefore often deal with the possibility of their occurrence in advance by the terms of their bargain. Unreliable or otherwise unsatisfactory decision making, or the fear of such, distorts commerce and makes markets less efficient, raising the cost of commerce. ... It is another illustration of the importance of consistency in the working of international commerce illuminated so clearly by Lord Diplock in *The "Maratha Envoy"* [1978] AC 1 at 8; [1977] 2 All ER 847 at 852 in his discussion of the role and place of well-known or usual forms of contract in international commerce and the place of courts in their consistent interpretation. The above considerations ground the importance to be given to party autonomy and holding parties to their bargains in international commerce. ...
>
> The recognition of the importance of international commercial arbitration to the smooth working of international commerce and of the importance of enforcement of the bilateral bargain of commercial parties in their agreement to submit their disputes to arbitration was reflected in both the New York Convention and the model law.[94]

---

93 *Dell Computer Corp. v. Union des consommateurs*, supra note 74 at paras. 38–41, Deschamps J. (majority). See further *Seidel v. Telus Communications Inc.*, supra note 75.

94 *Comandate Marine Corp. v. Pan. Australia Shipping Pty. Ltd.* (2006), 238 A.L.R. 457 at paras. 192–3; [2006] F.C.A.F.C. 192 at paras. 192–3, Allsop J. (F.C.A.).

Canada's federal arbitration regime reflects the policies and practices of this internationally accepted dispute resolution process.[95] So too do its provincial counterparts, which have been enacted across the country.[96]

Basic Characteristics

Arbitration is typically a private and confidential contractual arrangement determined and designed, in large measure, by individual disputing parties to fit the specific requirements and contexts of individual disputes. According to the Supreme Court of Canada:

> [A]rbitration is a creature that owes its existence to the will of the parties alone ... the parties to an arbitration agreement are free, subject to any mandatory provisions by which they are bound, to choose any place, form and procedures they consider appropriate ... The choice of procedure does not alter the institution of arbitration in any of these cases. The rules become those of the parties, regardless of where they are taken from.[97]

Given the importance of party autonomy, there really is no *single* model or format of arbitration. Each one is, at least in theory, unique. Having said that, given arbitration's increasing popularity and sophistication, there clearly are shared components, typically as provided for in Canadian arbitration statutes, including:

- broad subject matter coverage,
- significant ability to vary many provisions of the legislation,
- limited court intervention,
- wide procedural flexibility,
- binding awards,

---

95 See *Commercial Arbitration Act*, supra note 66.

96 For purposes of this discussion, I focus on domestic arbitration legislation. See, for example, Alberta *Arbitration Act*, supra note 67; Ontario *Arbitration Act, 1991*, S.O. 1991, c. 17, as amended; Nova Scotia *Arbitration Act*, R.S.N.S. 1989, c. 19; and so on.

97 *Dell Computer Corp. v. Union des consommateurs*, supra note 74 at paras. 51–2, Deschamps J. (majority). See further ibid. at para. 133, Bastarache and LeBel JJ. See further *Seidel v. Telus Communications Inc.*, supra note 75. For a commentary on the flexibility of arbitration, see Jennifer McPhee, "Arbitration Becoming the 'New' Civil Litigation" *Canadian Lawyer* (January 2008) 53 at 54.

- limited appeal rights,
- powers of enforcement, and
- powers to award costs.[98]

The ultimate touchstone of arbitration, therefore, is its significant respect for party autonomy. As a result, according to Frank Nussbaum and Meah Rothman Tell, "[a]rbitration, a privatization of civil justice, is a process … free of the constraints of certain constitutional rights."[99] Of particular significance to most arbitrating parties – and to this book – is the overwhelming purpose of arbitration legislation to provide parties with a powerful, flexible, private, and typically confidential dispute resolution process that is largely out of the reach of the public court system.[100]

---

98 See, for example, Alberta *Arbitration Act*, supra note 67 at ss. 2, 3, 6, 20, 37, 44–5, 48, 49, and 53. For general background discussions, see, for example, Julie Macfarlane, eds., *Dispute Resolution: Readings and Case Studies*, 3rd ed. (Toronto: Emond Montgomery, 2010) at c. 6; Stone, *Private Justice: The Law of Alternative Dispute Resolution*, supra note 84 at cc. 5–7; Hon. George W. Adams, *Mediating Justice: Legal Dispute Negotiation* (Toronto: CCH Canadian Limited, 2003) at 318–323; Pirie, *Alternative Dispute Resolution: Skills, Science, and the Law*, supra note 14 at c. 5; Desmond Ellis and Dawn Anderson, *Conflict Resolution: An Introductory Text* (Toronto: Emond Montgomery, 2005) at c. 3; and Stephen B. Goldberg, Frank E.A. Sander, and Nancy H. Rogers, *Dispute Resolution: Negotiation, Mediation, and Other Processes*, 3rd ed. (New York: Aspen Law, 1999) at c. 4.

99 Frank Nussbaum and Meah Rothman Tell, "General Practice, Solo and Small Firm: Arbitration and Attorney's Fees: A Pandora's Box" (2002) 76 *Fla. Bar. J.* 77 at 77.

100 This underlying policy, of putting arbitration largely out of the reach of the state's dispute resolution branches, can be seen in the many legislative debates that led to the development of these regimes. For example, according to the legislative debates regarding Alberta's arbitration legislation,

> [T]he purpose of the Act and the purpose of the arbitrating parties … is to avoid the courts. … The Bill provides limits on court intervention and prescribes grounds upon which an award may be appealed or set aside. Mr. Speaker, this Bill is … responsive to the marketplace, and it may very well assist our courts by assisting in reducing the backlog of cases before our courts.

Alberta, Legislative Assembly, *Official Report of Debates (Hansard)* (24 June 1991) at 1932–3 (Hon. Mr. Evans). Similarly, according to legislative debates regarding Ontario's arbitration legislation,

Judicial Deference to Arbitration

In recognition of these legislative intentions, which have found their way into the policies and provisions of Canadian arbitration statutes, courts have typically taken a very deferential approach to arbitration challenges. The *Dell* case provides the leading Canadian statement on

---

> The purpose of the Arbitration Act, 1991, is to provide a framework for the private settlement of disputes that will be as clear as possible for those who use it, while preserving the fairness of the process. The ability of an unwilling party to delay or derail an arbitration has been reduced to a minimum. The parties are generally free to set their own rules for arbitrations – that is, to override the act – so they have a great deal of flexibility. However, the law and the courts will ensure that the parties stick to their agreement to arbitrate, do not proceed unfairly, and abide by the result when it is given.

Ontario, Legislative Assembly, *Official Report of Debates (Hansard)* (5 November 1991) at 1550 (Hon. Howard Hampton) [emphasis added]. See further ibid. (19 June 1990) (Hon. Ian Scott). In the context of the debates leading to the enactment of Manitoba's arbitration legislation, equally supportive policy interests were articulated. As one legislator stated,

> I have always, Madam Speaker, and will continue to argue and articulate as to the benefits of arbitration as opposed to ultimately having to go to a court. Where we can provide an alternative to a courtroom setting, I think it is a very positive thing … the concept of anything that allows a larger role for arbitration over the court process is something I do not have any problem … being … supportive of. … I think far too often we underestimate the importance of arbitration and mediation as a viable positive alternative to the court system. That is in essence, as I say, the reason why, when I have looked at this particular piece of legislation, Madam Speaker, that I think it is a very positive move towards bringing more of a reliance on arbitration.

Manitoba, Legislative Assembly, *Official Report of Debates (Hansard)*, 36th Leg., 3d sess., No. 58 (10 June 1997) (Hon. Keven Lamoureux). For similar comments from legislative debates surrounding the enactment of other provincial arbitration legislation, see, for example, Saskatchewan, Legislative Assembly, *Official Report of Debates (Hansard)* (16 July 1992) at 1524 (Hon. Ms. Simard); Nova Scotia, Legislative Assembly, *Official Report of Debates (Hansard)*, 57th Gen. Ass., 1st sess. (25 May 1999) at 6188–93 (Hons. Robert Harrison, Kevin Deveaux, and Michael Baker). For an earlier national discussion, see, for example, Uniform Law Conference of Canada (ULCC), "Domestic Arbitrations" in ULCC, *Proceedings of the 71st Annual Meeting* (Yellowknife: August 1989) at 114, available online: ULCC <http://www.ulcc.ca/images/stories/Past_Proceedings_PDF/1989ULCC0071.pdf>.

this issue.[101] The dispute in *Dell* involved temporary discrepancies between the Internet prices of two different handheld computers. Specifically, for approximately one day, Dell advertised two computers at two low (incorrect) prices on its order Web page and at two higher (correct) prices on its product advertising webpage. After being notified about the discrepancy, Dell blocked access to the order pages through the usual address (although the pages were not removed from the website). Notwithstanding Dell's initial action, one of the respondents in the case, Olivier Dumoulin (who was identified by the court as a Québec "consumer"[102]), was able to order one of the products online at the lower price by accessing a "deep link" in Dell's Web system. The "deep link" enabled him to access to the incorrect order page without proceeding through the normal advertising links that had been corrected by Dell. Shortly after he made his order, Dell corrected the error and announced that it would not process orders made at the lower prices.[103] When Dell refused to honour Dumoulin's order at the lower price, Dumoulin – together with the Union des consommateurs – filed a motion seeking to bring a class proceeding against Dell. Because the conditions of purchase and sale included a mandatory arbitration clause, Dell sought to have the claim referred to arbitration (and not to court), as well as to have the motion seeking authorization to bring the claim by way of class proceeding dismissed (again pursuant to the conditions of purchase and sale).

Because the arbitration clause provided that disputes under it would be governed by the "National Arbitration Forum," which is located in the United States, and further, because Québec rules of private international law prohibit a waiver of Québec jurisdiction being set up against a consumer, the motions court found that the arbitration clause could not stand.[104] The Court of Appeal dismissed Dell's appeal, not based on the motion court's jurisdictionally driven decision but rather because the arbitration clause was contained in a hyperlinked contractual provision that did not, according to the Court of Appeal, adequately form part of the main contract to which the consumer was a party.[105] However, a majority of the Supreme Court of Canada allowed Dell's

101 See also *Seidel v. Telus Communications Inc.*, supra note 75 (discussed further below).
102 *Dell Computer Corp. v. Union des consommateurs*, supra note 74 at para. 4.
103 Ibid.
104 See ibid. at paras. 6, 128.
105 See ibid. at paras. 7, 129.

appeal, finding that the matter should have been referred to arbitration. The fact that the matter was initially brought to the lower court by way of class proceeding did not change the Supreme Court's view that, because of the mandatory arbitration clause, it should have proceeded by way of arbitration. As a threshold matter, the court recognized that

> It is ... well established that the effect of a valid undertaking to arbitrate is to remove the dispute from the jurisdiction of the ordinary courts of law. ... There is consequently no question that, if the arbitration agreement is valid and relates to the dispute, the Superior Court has no jurisdiction to hear the case and must refer the parties to arbitration.[106]

One of the central questions of the case, then, was whether a hyperlinked contractual provision in which the arbitration clause was located was valid. Both the majority and the dissenting judgments in *Dell* found that it was. The dissenting judges then went on to find against Dell, largely on private international law grounds.[107] The majority, however, rejected these private international law arguments and allowed Dell's appeal, finding no reason to deviate from a traditionally deferential approach to arbitration clauses. In addition to recognizing the well-established nature of valid contractual agreements to arbitrate, the majority confirmed that courts should only disrupt the jurisdiction of an arbitrator in limited circumstances. As Justice Deschamps stated,

> First of all, I would lay down a general rule that in any case involving an arbitration clause, a challenge to the arbitrator's jurisdiction must be resolved first by the arbitrator. A court should depart from the rule of systematic referral to arbitration only if the challenge to the arbitrator's jurisdiction is based solely on a question of law. ...
>
> If the challenge requires the production and review of factual evidence, the court should normally refer the case to arbitration, as arbitrators have, for this purpose, the same resources and expertise as courts. Where questions of mixed law and fact are concerned, the court hearing the referral application must refer the case to arbitration unless the questions of fact require only superficial consideration of the documentary evidence in the record.

106 Ibid. at para. 150, Bastarache and LeBel JJ.
107 See ibid. at paras. 179–217.

> Before departing from the general rule of referral, the court must be satisfied that the challenge to the arbitrator's jurisdiction is not a delaying tactic and that it will not unduly impair the conduct of the arbitration proceeding. This means that even when considering one of the exceptions, the court might decide that to allow the arbitrator to rule first on his or her competence would be best for the arbitration process.[108]

This approach by the Supreme Court of Canada, which has been the subject of a recent wave of significant judicial inquiry in several appellate courts in Canada since the judgment was released, clearly endorses a deferential approach to arbitration.[109] The court's approach in *Dell* aligns itself with, and thereby reinforces, the general and increasingly well-established domestic and foreign judicial landscape that fully recognizes arbitration as an important part of (and alternative to) the overall civil justice system.[110] For example, according to the Court of Appeal for Ontario, arbitration has clearly become a recognized, accepted, and now promoted method of dispute resolution. That court's position can be seen, for example, in Justice Finlayson's 1999 statement that "there has been a significant change since 1970 ... in the attitude of the courts and the legislature as to the desirability of encouraging the resolution of disputes between the parties other than by resort to the courts."[111]

108 Ibid. at paras. 84–6. See also *Rogers Wireless Inc. v. Muroff*, 2007 SCC 35, [2007] 2 S.C.R. 921 at para. 11; *Seidel v. Telus Communications Inc.*, supra note 75 at paras. 27–9.

109 See, for example, *Griffin v. Dell Canada Inc.* (2010), 98 O.R. (3d) 481 (C.A.), leave to appeal to S.C.C. refused, [2010] S.C.C.A. No. 75; *Smith Estate v. National Money Mart Co.* (2008), 92 O.R. (3d) 641 (C.A.), leave to appeal to S.C.C. refused, [2008] S.C.C.A. No. 535; *Dancap Productions Inc. v. Key Brand Entertainment, Inc.*, [2009] O.J. No. 572 (C.A.); *Jean Estate v. Wires Jolley LLP* (2009), 96 O.R. (3d) 171 (C.A.); *MacKinnon v. National Money Mart Co.*, [2009] B.C.J. No. 468 (C.A.). See also *Seidel v. Telus Communications Inc.*, supra note 75 (discussed further below).

110 It is important to recognize that some jurisdictions have taken legislative steps to limit the applicability of mandatory arbitration clauses in the context of consumer contracts (in order to provide increased protections to consumers in similar circumstances, including, for example, Québec, Ontario, Alberta and British Columbia). For further discussions on this point, see supra note 80 and infra note 124 and accompanying text (and further references mentioned therein).

111 *Canadian National Railway Co. v. Lovat Tunnel Equipment Inc.*, [1999] O.J. No. 2498 at para. 20; 174 D.L.R. (4th) 385 at para. 20 (C.A.). See also *Onex Corp. v. Ball Corp.*, [1994] O.J. No. 98, (1994), 12 B.L.R. (2d) 151 (Gen. Div.). This point is made quite clearly by the dissenting judgment in *Seidel v. Telus Communications Inc.*, supra note 75 at paras. 89–103 (with which the majority does not, in principle, disagree).

Similarly and more recently, according to Justice Feldman, agreements to arbitrate have "become a common and cost-effective method of dispute resolution."[112] These statements are also in line with other statements from the Supreme Court of Canada regarding arbitration. According to Justice LeBel,

> In general, arbitration is not part of the state's judicial system, although the state sometimes assigns powers or functions directly to arbitrators. Nonetheless, arbitration is still, in a broader sense, a part of the dispute resolution system the legitimacy of which is fully recognized by the legislative authorities.[113]

Taking this judicial recognition of arbitration one step farther, Justices Bastarache and LeBel also recognized the further policy of legislatures, building on *Desputeaux*, which "now accepts arbitration as a valid form of dispute resolution and, moreover, *seeks to promote its use*."[114] Recently, an Ontario court has confirmed, quoting from *Deluce Holdings Inc. v. Air Canada*[115] in the context of its discussion of Ontario's arbitration regime,

> This legislation represents a shift in policy towards the resolution of arbitrable disputes outside of court proceedings. Whereas prior to the enactment of this legislation the courts in Ontario had a broad discretion whether or not to stay a court action, the focus has now been reversed: the Court *must stay* the court proceedings and allow the arbitration to go ahead *unless* the matter either falls within one of the limited exceptions or is not a matter which the parties have agreed to submit to arbitration.
>
> The philosophy underlying the legislation is to encourage parties to submit their differences to a consensual dispute resolution process outside the regular court process and to hold them to that course once they have agreed to do so. ...[116]

---

112 *MDG Kingston Inc. v. MDG Computers Canada Inc.* (2008), 92 O.R. (3d) 4 at 14, para. 32 (C.A.).

113 *Desputeaux v. Éditions Chouette (1987) inc.*, 2003 SCC 17, [2003] 1 S.C.R. 178 at para. 41.

114 *Dell Computer Corp. v. Union des consommateurs*, supra note 74 at para. 143 [emphasis added].

115 (1992), 12 O.R. (3d) 131 (Ont. Gen. Div.) [Commercial List], Blair J.

116 *Bouchan v. Slipacoff*, [2009] O.J. No. 156 at paras. 18–19, A. J. O'Marra J. (Sup. Ct. Jus.). See further *Ontario Hydro v. Denison Mines Ltd.*, [1992] O.J. No. 2948 (Ont. Gen. Div.).

Similarly strong judicial support comes from other jurisdictions as well, including the United States,[117] the United Kingdom,[118] and Australia.[119] In light of this significant domestic and foreign judicial support, there can be no doubt that arbitration is a well-accepted and well-established alternative to the public dispute resolution processes.

As a final comment in this section, it is important to mention the Supreme Court of Canada's most recent statement on arbitration clauses, found in its 2011 *Seidel v. Telus Communications Inc.* decision.[120] That case, which originated out of British Columbia, dealt with a mediation-arbitration clause in a standard cellular phone contract. The contract provided that disputes were to be resolved by private and confidential mediation and, failing that, arbitration. The contract also purported to waive any rights to commence or participate in class proceedings. In addition to enacting typical provincial arbitration legislation,[121] British Columbia also subsequently enacted the *Business Practices and Consumer Protection Act* (*BPCPA*).[122] The *BPCPA* allows, through the operation of ss. 3, 8, and 172, for court actions (including class actions) to be brought by a person (other than a supplier) to enforce the legislation's consumer protection standards, whether or not the person making the claim has a special interest or is directly affected by the particular consumer

117 See, for example, *AT&T Mobility LLC v. Concepcion et ux.*, 131 S. Ct. 1740 (2011); *Equal Employment Opportunity Commission v. Waffle House, Inc.*, 534 U.S. 279 (2002); *Gilmer v. Interstate/Johnson Lane Corp.*, 500 U.S. 20 (1991); and *Mitsubishi Motors Corp. v. Soler Chrysler-Plymouth, Inc.*, 473 U.S. 614 (1985). See also *Arthur Andersen LLP v. Carlisle*, 556 U.S. 624 (2009); and *American Express Co.* v. *Italian Colors Restaurant*, 570 U.S. ____, slip op. 12–133 (2013).

118 See, for example, *Premium Nafta Products Limited (20th Defendant) and others (Respondents) v. Fili Shipping Company Limited (14th Claimant) and others (Appellants)*, [2007] UKHL 40; *Cable & Wireless PLC v. IBM United Kingdom Ltd.*, [2002] EWHC 2059 (Comm); *Sumukan Ltd. v. Commonwealth Secretariat*, [2007] EWCA Civ 243, [2007] 2 All ER (Comm) 23. For further commentary, see, for example, Simon Nesbitt and Henry Quinlan, "The Status and Operation of Unilateral or Optional Arbitration Clauses" (2006) 22:1 *Arb. Int'l.* 133; Thomas H. Webster, "Review of Substantive Reasoning of International Arbitral Awards by National Courts: Ensuring One-Stop Adjudication" (2006) 22:3 *Arb. Int'l.* 431; and Peter Aeberli, "Jurisdictional Disputes under the Arbitration Act 1996: A Procedure Route Map" (2005) 21:3 *Arb. Int'l.* 253.

119 See, for example, *Comandate Marine Corp. v. Pan. Australia Shipping Pty. Ltd*, supra note 94; and *Seeley International Pty. Ltd. (A.C.N. 054 687 035) v. Electra Air Conditioning B.V.* (2008), 246 A.L.R. 589; [2008] F.C.A. 29 (F.C.A.).

120 See supra note 75.

121 See *Commercial Arbitration Act*, R.S.B.C. 1996, c. 55.

122 S.B.C. 2004, c. 2.

transaction at issue (referred to in the judgment as "public interest" claims). The majority of the court interpreted this legislative regime as invalidating any arbitration contract provision that seeks to oust the court's jurisdiction in this particular public interest context. As such, to the extent that the claim in *Seidel* fell within s. 172 of the *BPCPA*, the arbitral provision that purported to govern that aspect of the claim was invalid. Importantly, however, the court also held that any claims governed by the mediation-arbitration agreement that did not fall within the specific s. 172 provisions of the *BPCPA* continued to be governed by the arbitration-mediation agreement.

The key, therefore, to the *Seidel* case is legislative intent. Put differently, unlike the view of the dissenting judges in that case, it is my view that nothing in the majority's decision in *Seidel* changes anything from the earlier *Dell* case with respect to the basic position of arbitration in the civil justice system. Both the wide-ranging acceptance of arbitration as a mainstream part of the dispute resolution landscape and the ability of arbitration agreements to oust the jurisdiction of courts remain in place. As the court in *Seidel* emphasized, "*Dell* and *Rogers Wireless* stand, as did *Desputeaux*, for the enforcement of arbitration clauses *absent legislative language to the contrary*."[123] In jurisdictions in which particular legislation has been enacted, particularly in the consumer protection sector, such limits have emerged.[124] Otherwise, the place of arbitration as an increasingly dominant player in the context of civil dispute resolution continues to be recognized and encouraged by courts.

---

123 *Seidel v. Telus Communications Inc.*, supra note 75 at para. 42.

124 In addition to B.C.'s *BPCPA* (discussed supra), see, for example, Québec's *Consumer Protection Act*, R.S.Q., c. P-40.1 and *An Act respecting the collection of certain debts*, R.S.Q., c. R-2.2; Ontario's *Consumer Protection Act*, 2002, S.O. 2002, c. 30, Sch. A; Alberta's *Fair Trading Act*, R.S.A. 2000, c. F-2, all discussed in *Seidel v. Telus Communications Inc.*, supra note 75 at paras. 25 (by the majority) and 173–4 (by the dissent). It is important to acknowledge that the dissenting judges of the Supreme Court in *Seidel* found that the majority's approach to arbitration contracts was inconsistent with the Court's recent line of cases (all of which – according to both the majority and the dissent – accept arbitration as a very viable dispute resolution alternative). See *Seidel v. Telus Communications Inc.*, ibid. at paras. 42 (by the majority) and 89–103 (by the dissent). It is important to acknowledge that the dissenting judges of the Supreme Court in *Seidel* found that the majority's approach to arbitration contracts was inconsistent with the Court's recent line of cases (all of which – according to both the majority and the dissent – accept arbitration as a very viable dispute resolution alternative). See *Seidel v. Telus Communications Inc.*, ibid. at paras. 42 (by the majority) and 89–103 (by the dissent).

Infrastructural Privatization

This strong legislative and judicial recognition and encouragement of arbitration, taken together, amounts to a clear example of general infrastructural privatization. Put simply, arbitration provides cost savings for the state. Policy debates leading to the enactment of various arbitration regimes highlight many legislators' intentions, in line with more typical privatization legislative intentions generally, to increase the use of arbitration as a way to offset the use of public resources in resolving certain civil matters. For example, in advance of amendments to Manitoba's arbitration legislation, one legislator commented that arbitration "[i]n the long run ... will provide ... the potential for savings."[125] In Ontario, prior to the enactment of Ontario's arbitration legislation, one legislator commented that the "use of ADR is widespread in the United States on the assumption that it reduces the financial burden on the justice system."[126] With a similar sensibility in mind, when Ontario legislators were debating Bill 101 (the *Franchises' Arbitration Act, 1996*), one legislator commented that, as a result of the legislation, "franchisees and franchisors" would save "not only their own money but ... also ... tax dollars, taxpayers' money in the form of not accessing court resources."[127] Similarly, in Alberta, one legislator acknowledged that ADR – specifically including mediation – results in a "win" situation for the courts because resources that "otherwise would be spent in the courts taking up time of ... the court staff at the counters or ... the court staff and the judge in the courtroom, can be spent on cases that, in fact, need be tried."[128] These sentiments have also led to the expression of some legislators' views that arbitration should be *mandated* for some commercial circumstances.[129]

---

125 Manitoba, Legislative Assembly, *Official Report of Debates (Hansard)*, 36th Leg., 3d sess., No. 58 (10 June 1997) at 1720 (Hon. Keven Lamoureux).

126 Ontario, Legislative Assembly, *Official Report of Debates (Hansard)* (27 March 1990) at 1350 (Hon. Ian Scott).

127 Ibid. (5 December 1996) at 1020 (Hon. Bruce Crozier).

128 Alberta, Legislative Assembly, Committee of Supply, *Alberta Hansard* (30 May 2007) at 1433 (Hon. Mr. Stevens).

129 For example, in the context of Manitoba's legislative debates leading up to amendments to its arbitration legislation, the Hon. Gord Mackintosh made the following statement:

To the extent calls prevail for limiting the state's involvement in the resolution of civil disputes for parties with "extensive resources,"[130] those calls are not new. Albeit without the revolutionary undercurrent, they echo sentiments expressed by Marx more than 150 years ago: "The administration of … civil justice is concerned almost exclusively with conflicts over property and hence affects almost exclusively the possessing classes. Are they to carry on their litigation at the expense of the national coffers?"[131] However, as I argue further in this book,[132] there are clearly good reasons for continuing to fund and to encourage the use of public dispute resolution processes for all kinds of public and

---

> We on this side acknowledge the value of arbitration as a way to resolve disputes. Arbitration usually costs less to the disputing parties. At least, we recognize that it can cut down on some costly legal costs and pretrial procedures. It certainly costs less to the taxpaying public, because the expensive judicial system is not called on to resolve the disputes. Arbitration is often, although not always – but usually faster than litigation. It is also informal, accessible and flexible, which meet the needs of the parties to a greater extent than formal litigation. Of course, arbitration also allows privacy. It is confidential, as long as one of the parties does not pursue an appeal.
>
> It is clear that arbitration does have a very important role in our society and, indeed, it is my firm belief that we should rely more on alternative dispute resolution. We should be looking for not only a greater reliance on arbitration but other ways of resolving disputes outside of the courts.
>
> I think one of the greatest arguments to support my belief is that when there are limited resources to deal with conflicts between individuals and limited resources to deal with Criminal Code infractions, we have to think why are we putting so many resources into the resolution of disputes between, for example, two large corporations that may have extensive resources and, yet, are going head to head in a battle over many years. … We really, I think, have to think in larger terms about how we are using public resources to solve disputes between certain kinds of parties and, in that regard, I wonder if we should not be looking towards a more affirmative statement or a more effective way of getting parties to use arbitration as an alternative to civil litigation, including *requiring* arbitration clauses in certain commercial contracts.

Manitoba, Legislative Assembly, *Official Report of Debates (Hansard)*, 36th Leg., 3d sess., No. 59, Orders of the Day (11 June 1997) at 1520 (Hon. Gord Mackintosh) [emphasis added]. For further treatment of this legislative statement, see infra Chapters 5 and 7.

130 Ibid.

131 Karl Marx, *Critique of the Gotha Program* (1875), pt. IV in Robert C. Tucker, ed., *The Marx-Engels Reader*, 2nd ed. (New York, London: W.W. Norton, 1978) 525 at 539.

132 See, for example, generally infra Chapter 7.

private disputes that engage, directly or indirectly, issues of significant importance to the public.

Popularity

Notwithstanding that calls for mandatory use in most circumstances have not succeeded, to date, the freedom and power that are clearly provided by arbitral legislative regimes have made arbitration increasingly popular, particularly as a method to resolve commercial disputes. As such, these processes have become the subject of increasing attention in academic[133] and popular commentary.[134] In the United States, for example, reports indicate that total case filings for the American Arbitration Association (AAA) dramatically increased over the ten-year period from 1993 to 2003 (from more than 60,000 cases in 1993 to more than 230,000 cases in 2003).[135] Reports from England suggest that there could be between 5,000 and 10,000 arbitrations every year, with these numbers increasing year after year.[136] Put simply, as I discuss further in Chapter 5, arbitration has become a preferred dispute resolution

---

133 In addition to the academic references included throughout this part of this chapter, see, for example, Jeffrey Barist, "Arbitration: The Privatization of the Judicial Process" (1996/1997) *Int'l Com. Lit.* 22; Nina Goswami, "A Game of Survival: Why the Bar Is Embracing Arbitration" *The Lawyer* (12 February 2007) 19; Thomas J. Stipanowich, "ADR and the 'Vanishing Trial': The Growth and Impact of 'Alternative Dispute Resolution'" (2004) 1 *J. Emp. Leg. Stud.* 843; Cindy Fazzi, "Lessons in ADR from Corporate America," Book Review of *Emerging Systems for Managing Workplace Conflict* by David B. Lipsky, Ronald L. Seeber, and Richard D. Fincher (2003–4) 58:4 *Disp. Resol. J.* 86; Marc Rose and Roger Suffling, "Alternative Dispute Resolution and the Protection of Natural Areas in Ontario, Canada" (2001) 56 *Landscape and Urb. Plan.* 1; William G. Horton, "ADR in Canada: Options for the Appropriate Resolution of Business Disputes" (2002) 21:2 *Advocates' Soc. J.* 11; and Randy A. Pepper, "Why Arbitrate?: Ontario's Recent Experience with Commercial Arbitration" (1998) 38 *Osgoode Hall L.J.* 807.

134 See, for example, Julius Melnitzer, "Arbitration Becomes More Like Litigation" *Law Times* (10 October 2011), available online: Law Times <http://www.lawtimesnews.com/Focus-On/Arbitration-becomes-more-like-litigation>; John Pepall, "Mundane disputes belong in court" *The Windsor Star* (8 January 1998) A4; Jackson Williams, "The Costs of Arbitration" *Public Citizen* (April 2002) 68.

135 Reported in Stipanowich, "ADR and the 'Vanishing Trial': The Growth and Impact of 'Alternative Dispute Resolution'," supra note 133 at 872.

136 See Goswami, "A Game of Survival: Why the Bar Is Embracing Arbitration," supra note 133 [references omitted].

process for disputing parties, and increasingly, for their lawyers. Not surprisingly, given their popularity, arbitration and other related ADR processes are now also being offered online.[137]

Taken together, the statutory, judicial, and popular sanctioning of, encouraging and preferencing of private arbitration evidence another very significant aspect of the overall trend of systematic efforts to privatize much of how we do civil dispute resolution today. Having now discussed the breadth and depth of that privatizing trend, it is to its underlying preferences, influences, and justifications to which I now turn in the next chapter.

137 For recent initiatives at the international level, see, for example, U.N. Commission on International Trade Law (UNCITRAL), Working Group III, "2010 to Present: Online Dispute Resolution," available online: UNCITRAL <http://www.uncitral.org/uncitral/commission/working_groups/3Online_Dispute_Resolution.html>. For a collection of background materials, see, for example, Ellen Zweibel, "Online Dispute Resolution" in Macfarlane et al., eds., *Dispute Resolution: Readings and Case Studies*, supra note 98 at c. 4; Christine E. Hart, "Online Dispute Resolution and Avoidance in Electronic Commerce" (August 1999), available online: Uniform Law Conference of Canada <http://www.ulcc.ca/en/1999-winnipeg-mb/359-civil-section-documents/356-online-dispute-resolution-and-avoidance-in-electronic-commerce-1999>; and Richard Susskind, *The End of Lawyers? Rethinking the Nature of Legal Services* (Oxford, UK, and New York: Oxford University Press, 2008) at c. 6, § 6.6 ("Online Dispute Resolution"). For further comments, see Teri A. Kirk, "Feds Finance Web Alternative to Commercial Litigation" 23:6 *The Lawyers Weekly* (6 June 2003); and W. Anthony Poland, "Electronic Courthouse a Timely, Affordable ADR Solution" 23:44 *The Lawyers Weekly* (26 March 2004).

Chapter Five

Preferences, Influences, and Justifications

Preferences and Influences for Privatization

Governments

There are several sources of influence and support for the current civil justice privatization movement and its driving ethos of reform. Because public regulation is a significant focus of this book, a good place to start is with governments. The introduction and encouragement of privatization initiatives in and through the civil, administrative and non-court or administrative-based legislative ADR regimes accord with, and in some cases are part of, general federal and provincial government dispute resolution strategies. These strategies are designed to encourage the privatization of dispute resolution in relation essentially to all activities in which governments are directly or indirectly involved. Put simply, governments and related public entities (rules committees, task forces, etc., which have been significant drivers of public privatization efforts) have become extremely active promoters of the privatization of dispute resolution. The primary justifications for this promotion, as I discuss further in this chapter, include increased efficiency and access to the instruments of justice.

At the federal level, the Dispute Resolution Service was established in 1992, under the watch of the Department of Justice.[1] Now under the name Dispute Prevention and Resolution Services (DPRS), the program

1 See Department of Justice, Audit and Management Studies Division, "Dispute Resolution Services" (July 2005), available online: Government of Canada <http://www.justice.gc.ca/eng/dept-min/pub/aud-ver/2005/drs-srd/>.

actively promotes ADR and related services in disputes relating to the affairs of the federal government.[2] Given the proliferation of privatization initiatives in the federal administrative regime, the goals and objectives of the DPRS are clearly materializing.[3]

At the provincial level, similar government initiatives have been actively pursued. In British Columbia, for example, the government, through the Ministry of Attorney General, has developed an active policy of ADR promotion through the 1996 creation of the Dispute Resolution Office (DRO).[4] The policy considerations behind these sorts of initiatives are animated largely by ADR-focused research,[5] anecdotal

2 According to the materials of the DPRS,

> DPRS ... is devoted to the prevention and management of disputes. Our mandate is to serve as a leading centre of dispute prevention and resolution (DPR) excellence within the Government of Canada and beyond. Our role is to promote a greater understanding of DPR and assist in the integration of DPR into the policies, operations and practices of departments and agencies of the Government of Canada, Crown corporations, federal tribunals and administrative agencies, and federally constituted courts.

Department of Justice, DPRS, "Services and Programs" (last updated: 13 February 2009), online: Government of Canada <http://www.justice.gc.ca/eng/pi/dprs-sprd/sp.html>.

3 Examples of these ADR-related initiatives in federal tribunals that are relevant to this book, which were discussed further in Chapter 4, include dispute resolution initiatives in the Canadian Human Rights Tribunal, the Canadian Transportation Agency, and others. See Department of Justice, DPRS, "DR Fund Evaluation: Overview of the Return on Investment from the DR Fund As of March 2004" [citation omitted], available online: Government of Canada <http://www.justice.gc.ca/eng/pi/dprs-sprd/ref/eval/peval-evalp.html>. Further, an example of ADR-related initiatives in the federal courts that accord with the principles of the DPRS objectives include, as were discussed in Chapter 3, the federal court of Canada's "case management and dispute resolution services" program. See *Federal Court Rules*, SOR/98-106, as amended, at pt. 9, rr. 380–91.

4 According to public materials of the DRO, " [t]he Ministry of Attorney General's ... [DRO] develops and promotes non-adversarial dispute resolution options within the justice system and government. Options such as mediation encourage early settlement of disputes and are less expensive than processes used in the formal court system." See B.C. Ministry of Attorney General, Dispute Resolution Office, available online: Government of B.C. <http://www.ag.gov.bc.ca/dro/>.

5 Often this kind of research is commissioned by governments, or research organizations at the behest of governments, to study ways to increase efficiencies and to

evidence, some empirical data,[6] and general reform trends. These policy considerations have been pursued over the past several decades – largely in pursuit of increased efficiencies – in various Commonwealth countries[7] towards simplified and privatized ADR initiatives across all aspects of the public civil dispute resolution spectrum.[8] The goals to promote and expand these sorts of initiatives are clear. For example, the Ministry of Attorney General states its intention to, among other things,

> Further develop the ADR policy to broaden and encourage the application of dispute resolution options through:

---

improve access to the tools of dispute resolution. I have recently been involved in some of this kind of research. See, for example, Trevor C.W. Farrow, "ADR in Canada: Courts and Administrative Tribunals" (a report prepared for the British Institute of International and Comparative Law, 2009) [unpublished]. Other significant funders in this area include various provincial law foundations. For important Canadian research that has benefitted significantly from law foundation and other funding, see, for example (among many others), the Canadian Forum on Civil Justice ("CFCJ"), "Research Projects," online: CFCJ <http://cfcj-fcjc.org/projects/>; Advocates' Society, *Streamlining the Ontario Civil Justice System: A Policy Forum, Final Report* (9 March 2006), available online: Advocates' Society <http://www.advocates.ca/assets/files/pdf/publications/streamlining-justice.pdf>. There is also a growing body of non-governmental, academically based research in this area. Much more, however (as I discuss further in Chapter 7), is needed. For a recent historical review of empirically-based civil justice and related research, see Carrie J. Menkel-Meadow and Bryant G. Garth, "Civil Procedure and Courts" in Peter Cane and Herbert M. Kritzer, eds., *Oxford Handbook of Empirical Legal Research* (Oxford, UK: Oxford University Press, 2010) 679.

6 For further discussions of ADR-related empirical research, see generally infra Chapter 6.

7 See, for example, supra Chapter 3.

8 The B.C. Ministry of Attorney General specifies that the DRO initiatives "are largely outcomes of considerable research and study carried out in the 1990's by organizations and professional groups across common law jurisdictions, for example, the Canadian Bar Association's Systems of Civil Justice Task Force Report, Lord Woolf's Report on Access to Justice, England, and Managing Justice: A Review of the Federal Civil Justice System, a report published by the Australian Law Reform Commission." See B.C. Ministry of Attorney General, "Alternative Dispute Resolution Policy and Design," available online: Government of B.C. <http://www.ag.gov.bc.ca/dro/policy-design/index.htm>. (Some of these reform initiatives are cited and discussed further earlier in this book. See, for example, supra Chapter 3.) Again according to the B.C. Ministry of Attorney General,

> There is considerable interest in resolving civil disputes outside of the formal court system. Options such as mediation are being employed by the courts,

a) continuing consultation with dispute resolution stakeholders and advocates;
b) promoting the use of alternative dispute resolution options among all ministries and agencies of government;
c) promoting the use of alternative dispute resolution techniques in neighbourhood or community disputes;
d) identifying and removing barriers to the understanding and use of alternative dispute resolution options;
e) supporting multi-party alternative dispute resolution processes such as land use planning, aboriginal treaty [*sic*].[9]

Other provincial governments have also been actively encouraging the use of ADR as a general policy matter in various areas.[10] For example, in 1998, Alberta's Department of Justice and Attorney General was "committed to working ... with the judiciary and the bar ... so

---

administrative tribunals, and ministries and agencies of the Government of BC to provide people with viable dispute resolution processes. ...

The Ministry of Attorney General has adopted an ADR Policy, signalling its commitment to a justice and conflict resolution environment which includes a wide range of dispute resolution options. In 1996, the ministry established the ... DRO ... to develop and implement dispute resolution options in the court system and in government.

Since 1996, the DRO has worked with a number of government ministries, boards, agencies and commissions to design and help implement [] dispute resolution processes. It has also helped organizations consider ways to improve existing processes to make them more efficient and effective.

B.C. Ministry of Attorney General, DRO, "Alternative Dispute Resolution Policy and Design," ibid.

9 Ibid. at "Alternative Dispute Resolution Policy and Design: Policy Statement, Objectives" (objective 12), available online: Government of B.C. <http://www.ag.gov.bc.ca/dro/policy-design/statement.htm>. Examples of B.C. court initiatives that were supported by the DRO include B.C.'s notice to mediate program (see supra Chapter 3) and its small claims mediation program (see ibid.; see further DRO, available online: Government of B.C. <http://www.ag.gov.bc.ca/dro/>). Its proposed new rules on expanded settlement powers, as also discussed earlier (see supra Chapter 3), are in line with these principles. Additionally, the ADR-enabling provisions of B.C.'s *Administrative Tribunals Act*, S.B.C. 2004, c. 45 at s. 28(1) (as discussed further, supra Chapter 4), as well as the various ADR provisions provided for by the B.C. Human Rights Tribunal (discussed further, supra Chapter 4), are in line with the objectives of B.C.'s DRO initiatives.

10 For further comments on specific provincial court and administrative regime initiatives, see additionally supra Chapters 3 and 4.

that we have an extensive [ADR] program."[11] Ten years later, similar legislative sentiments were continuing to be expressed in Alberta. For example, according to one legislator, "as a minister I feel that mediation is the way of the future. … I can tell you this: we continue to emphasize alternative dispute resolution."[12] Many (if not all) of Alberta's extensive privatization efforts, in its court and tribunal-based dispute resolution regimes (discussed earlier in this book[13]), are in line with the spirit of these various legislative statements.[14]

In addition to in-house government dispute resolution initiatives and facilities (including, for example, the federal government's DPRS and the B.C. government's DRO services), there are numerous other initiatives that have been put in place to study, make recommendations about, and assist with the implementation of dispute resolution reform in this country. Various law reform and rules committees,[15]

11 Alberta, Legislative Assembly, Designated Supply Committee – Justice and Attorney General, *Alberta Hansard* (23 February 1998) at DSS14 (Hon. Mr. Havelock).

12 Alberta, Legislative Assembly, Committee of Supply, *Alberta Hansard* (30 May 2007) at 1433 (Hon. Mr. Stevens). See similarly the legislative debates surrounding Alberta's Bill 216, *Crown Contracts Dispute Resolution Act, 1996*, in which one legislator commented, without taking away peoples' right to sue, that "[w]hat we need in this province is, yes, to facilitate arbitration, to facilitate mediation." Alberta, Legislative Assembly, *Alberta Hansard*, 23rd Leg. 4th sess. (14 August 1996) at 2146 (Hon. Mr. Dickson).

13 See supra Chapters 3 and 4.

14 Earlier, Ontario, which has also actively pursued numerous tribunal- and court-based privatizing dispute resolution initiatives (see ibid.), also examined ADR as a general governmental policy preference. Prior to the B.C. initiatives discussed immediately previously, the Ontario legislature engaged in a wide-ranging consideration of ADR and its promotion in the province. No significant dissenting views were noticed in the research for this book. For the Ontario Legislative Assembly's standing committee report, see Ontario, Legislative Assembly, Standing Committee on Administration of Justice, *Alternative Dispute Resolution 1990* (Toronto, June 1990). For transcripts of the Ontario Legislative Assembly's Standing Committee on Administration of Justice ADR debates, see, for example, the *Hansard* reports for 12–15, 19–22, and 26–7 February 1990.

15 See, for example, Alberta Law Reform Institute (ALRI), *Rules of Court Project, Final Report No. 95* (Edmonton: ALRI, October 2008) at appendix H (available on CD), "Proposed Rules of Court," online: ALRI <http://www.law.ualberta.ca/alri/docs/1.%20 Appendix%20H%20-%20Proposed%20Rules%20of%20Court.pdf>; ALRI, Consultation Memorandum No. 12.6, "Promoting Early Resolution of Disputes by Settlement" (Edmonton: ALRI, July 2003) at xiii, online: ALRI <http://www.law.ualberta.ca/alri/docs/cm0126.pdf>.

commissions,[16] task forces,[17] reviews[18] and reform projects[19] have actively encouraged some form of dispute resolution process privatization through the promotion of a number of ADR initiatives.[20]

Judges

In addition to governments, some of the most influential voices with respect to civil dispute resolution law reform have been (and continue to be) those of current and former judges. There is no doubt that Canadian judges are, at least as a comparative matter, typically of the view that Canada's justice system is a leader in the world.[21] And this view is clearly right. Having spent a significant amount of time working on legal and judicial education projects in various parts of the world, I can say that not only does Canada have a "strong and healthy" justice system,[22] but judges (and others) around the world also look to our system

16 See, for example, Nova Scotia Civil Procedure Rules Revision Project, "Consultation with the Bar: Issues Memorandum" (Law Reform Commission of Nova Scotia, 16 June 2004), available online: Courts of Nova Scotia <http://www.courts.ns.ca/rules_revision/docs/final_bar_consult.pdf>; and Law Commission of Canada, *Transforming Relationships Through Participatory Justice* (Ottawa: Law Commission of Canada, 2003), available online: Government of Canada <http://publications.gc.ca/collections/Collection/JL2-22-2003E.pdf>.

17 See, for example, B.C.'s Civil Justice Reform Working Group to the Justice Review Task Force, "Effective and Affordable Civil Justice" (November 2006), available online: B.C. Justice Review Task Force <http://www.bcjusticereview.org/working_groups/civil_justice/cjrwg_report_11_06.pdf>.

18 See, for example, Ontario Civil Justice Review, *First Report* (Toronto: Ontario Civil Justice Review, 1995) and Ontario Civil Justice Review, *Supplemental and Final Report* (Toronto: Ontario Civil Justice Review, 1996), available online: Government of Ontario <http://www.attorneygeneral.jus.gov.on.ca/english/about/pubs/cjr/>; and Québec's Civil Procedure Review Committee, Report, *A New Judicial Culture* (Summary) (August 2001), online: Justice Québec <http://www.justice.gouv.qc.ca/english/publications/rapports/pdf/sommaire-a.pdf>.

19 See, for example, Ontario Civil Justice Reform Project, online: Government of Ontario <http://www.attorneygeneral.jus.gov.on.ca/english/about/pubs/cjrp/>.

20 For further discussions of some of these initiatives, see supra Chapter 3.

21 As I noted earlier, the chief justice of Canada has recently commented that "Canada has a strong and healthy justice system. Indeed, our courts and justice system are looked to by many countries as exemplary." Rt. Hon. Beverley McLachlin, P.C., "The Challenges We Face" (remarks presented at Empire Club of Canada, Toronto, 8 March 2007), available online: Supreme Court of Canada <http://www.scc-csc.gc.ca/court-cour/ju/spe-dis/bm-2007-03-08-eng.aspx>, cited earlier in Chapter 2.

22 Ibid.

as a leader and as a source of inspiration for institutional thinking and reform.

Regardless of the recognized high quality of the Canadian justice system, there is also no doubt that our judiciary is increasingly concerned about efficiency and access to justice problems in our systems of civil justice and that, as a result, they are of the view that the system is in need of reform.[23] Further, more and more judges are publicly vocalizing these concerns. For example, the current chief justice of Canada has often acknowledged that "many Canadian men and women find themselves unable, mainly for financial reasons, to access the Canadian justice system."[24] Similarly, former chief justice of Canada Brian Dickson commented in 1989 that "[i]t is an unfortunate fact that legal proceedings in the civil ... courts ... have become increasingly lengthy and protracted."[25] Earlier in this book I cited the former chief justice of Ontario, Roy McMurtry, who stated that our civil justice system is in "crisis."[26]

As a result, notwithstanding strong judicial support for the open court principle,[27] judges are increasingly speaking up and encouraging lawyers and parties to make use of all sorts of private processes, including mediation, negotiation (either directly or through lawyers), other ADR settlement processes and cost-based settlement incentives. For example, when speaking generally about resolving disputes out of court, Justice Robert Armstrong of the Court of Appeal for Ontario stated that "Settlement discussion is something which pervades, and should pervade, almost every lawsuit."[28] According to Justice E.E. Gillese, also of the Court of Appeal for Ontario, the "policy of the courts is to encourage the settlement of litigation."[29] Justice G.E. Taylor similarly commented that "[o]ffers to settle are to be encouraged."[30] Finally,

---

23 See, for example, *Judges Act*, R.S.C. 1995, c. J-1, s. 60(1).

24 Hon. Beverley McLachlin, P.C., "The Challenges We Face," supra note 21.

25 Rt. Hon. Brian Dickson, P.C., "Access to Justice" (1989) 1 *Windsor Rev. Legal Soc. Issues* 1 at 2.

26 See supra Chapter 3.

27 See supra Chapter 2.

28 *Ristimaki v. Cooper* (2006), 79 O.R. (3d) 648 at para. 76 (C.A.) (QL).

29 *Olivieri v. Sherman* (2007), 86 O.R. (3d) 778 at para. 50 (QL).

30 *H.L. Staebler Company Ltd. v. Allen* (2008), 92 O.R. (3d) 788 at 791 (S.C.J.). For other judicial comments regarding settlement encouragement, see, for example, *Sable Offshore Energy Inc. v. Ameron International Corp.*, 2013 SCC 37; *M. (J.) v. B. (W.)* (2004), 71 O.R. (3d) 171 at 189–90, paras. 65–6 (C.A.), Cronk J.A.; *Heritage Duty Free Shop*

Justice Gonthier, when speaking about the modern, expansive role of the advocate, stated,

> [C]ontrary to popular belief, not only will a good advocate not foment dissension and promote disputes between parties, he will seek to reconcile opposing interests in order to avoid the ultimate confrontation of a trial. He will be called on to play the role of moderator, negotiator and conciliator. Indeed, it is his duty to facilitate a rapid solution to disputes and to avoid fruitless or frivolous actions. ... Thus, whenever it is appropriate to do so, the advocate must discuss alternative dispute resolution methods (mediation, conciliation and arbitration) with his client, and must properly advise the client regarding the benefits of settling disputes. He may also hold discussions with the opposing party and negotiate a resolution of the dispute between the parties.[31]

Put simply, judicial commentary from case law and from secondary literature demonstrates a general judicial view, as expressed perhaps most succinctly by former judge George Adams, that "ADR is an approach to justice whose time has come."[32] And it has come because not only of perceived crises in our civil justice systems, but also in response to the realities of our modern, complex administrative state. For example, when speaking about ADR in the administrative context, the

---

Inc. v. Canada (Attorney General), [2003] B.C.J. No. 1208 at paras. 17–18 (S.C.) (QL), aff'd [2005] B.C.J. No. 670 (C.A.); and *Guelph Centre Partners Inc. v. Guelph Storm Ltd.*, [2005] O.J. No. 458 at para. 10 (S.C.J.) (QL). See also the discussion of settlement in Trevor C.W. Farrow, "Ethics in Advocacy" in Alice Woolley et al., eds., *Lawyers' Ethics and Professional Regulation*, 2nd ed. (Markham, ON: LexisNexis, 2012) c. 6 at 372–3. See further *Rogacki v. Belz* (2003), 67 O.R. (3d) 330 (C.A.); and *Rudd v. Trossacs Investments Inc.* (2006), 79 O.R. (3d) 687 (Div. Ct.).

31 *Fortin v. Chrétien*, [2001] 2 S.C.R. 500 at para. 53. For comments on the importance of negotiation in the context of just settlements in the area of Aboriginal law, see, for example, *Delgamuukw v. British Columbia*, [1997] 3 S.C.R. 1010 at para. 186, Lamer C.J. For comments on the importance of alternatives to judicial determinations, specifically in the context of labour law, see, for example, *Reference Re Public Service Employee Relations Act, Labour Relations Act and Police Officers Collective Bargaining Act*, [1987] 1 S.C.R. 313 at 416–17, McIntyre J. (both discussed further in Trevor C.W. Farrow, "Dispute Resolution, Access to Civil Justice and Legal Education" (2005) 42 *Alta. L. Rev.* 741 at 745, n. 22).

32 Hon. George W. Adams & Naomi L. Bussin, "Alternative Dispute Resolution and Canadian Courts: A Time For Change" (1995) 17 *Advocates' Q.* 133 at 157.

Supreme Court of Canada has stated that "[a]s our society has become more urbanized, complex and regulated, the need for efficient and speedy dispute resolution has become an important goal of provincial administration."[33] Indeed, this observation from the Supreme Court of Canada tracks the primary underlying motivations for privatization generally,[34] as well as the privatization of civil dispute resolution more specifically.[35] Further, in addition to judicial commentary in the case law and literature, empirical research also evidences a general judicial support for ADR. For example, a recent U.S. report indicates that judges are supportive of, and further, are "usually" or "always" recommending ADR.[36] In Canada, a nationwide survey looking at specific aspects of court-annexed ADR and other programs confirmed much of the earlier case law and literature-based evidence regarding ADR preferences.[37]

---

33 *Reference re Amendments to the Residential Tenancies Act (N.S.)*, [1996] 1 S.C.R. 186 at para. 2, Lamer C.J. and Sopinka and Cory JJ.

34 Discussed further supra Chapter 3.

35 Discussed further generally supra Chapters 3 and 4.

36 Bobbi McAdoo, "All Rise, the Court Is in Session: What Judges Say about Court-Connected Mediation" (2007) 22:2 *Ohio St. J. Disp. Resol.* 377.

37 Margaret A. Shone, "Civil Justice Reform in Canada: 1996 to 2006 and Beyond" (December 2006), available online: CFCJ <http://www.cfcj-fcjc.org/sites/default/files/docs/2006/shone-final-en.pdf>. Although it is important to recognize that this survey canvassed many civil justice system participants, and not just judges, its results are instructive. The survey was based on 123 questionnaires, which were sent to "governments, Chief Justices of every Court, the Canadian Bar Association, Law Societies, the Association of Canadian General Counsel, law school deans, legal aid organizations and public legal education bodies throughout Canada, and to the Consumers Council of Canada." There were fifty-two questionnaires completed and returned. It is not clear how many of those fifty-two responses came from judges (see ibid. at 3–4). As such, I am including this survey in this book for information purposes only – I do not rely on it for the proposition that Canadian judges are definitively encouraging the use of ADR (other evidence for which I have presented earlier, for example, at nn. 28–36 and accompanying text). Regardless, in terms of the results of the study, it found that 89 per cent of the survey's respondents agreed – 53 per cent "strongly" and 36 per cent "somewhat" – that "[d]ispute resolution techniques should be promoted as integral components of the civil justice system, not alternatives to it." Similarly, 94 per cent of the survey's respondents agreed – 57 per cent "strongly" and 37 per cent "somewhat" – that the "court system should provide users with a broad array of integrated dispute resolution options focused on early settlement (e.g., mediation, early neutral evaluation, judicial settlement conferences and mini-trials, consensual arbitration and adjudication)." See ibid. at 147, 156–8, and 160–1.

Not only are many judges individually supportive of domestic privatizing reform initiatives, the judiciary as a whole is also actively involved in various international privatizing reform initiatives. For example, the National Judicial Institute (NJI),[38] together with three partners in the Philippines – the Supreme Court of the Philippines, the Philippine Judicial Academy, and the Alternative Law Groups Inc. (a coalition for access to justice advocacy) – was the Canadian executing agency for a five-year, $6.5-million project called the Justice Reform Initiatives Support Project (JURIS). The project started in 2003 and was funded by the Canadian International Development Agency (CIDA).[39] Other Canadian funded international administration of justice programs, which have included active court reform and ADR elements, have involved members of the Canadian judiciary.[40]

Notwithstanding the significant judicial support for ADR initiatives, it is important to recognize that this support is not without some reservation. For example, as I discussed in Chapter 3, prior to 2004, concerns were raised primarily by certain members of the "bench and bar" that the court-based management and mediation initiatives that had been in place for several years in Ontario, specifically in Toronto, were not improving but were in fact disrupting the efficient flow of certain civil

---

38 See NJI, "About the NJI," available online: NJI <http://www.nji-inm.ca/nji/inm/a-propos-about/index.cfm>, which provides:

> [b]ased in Ottawa, the … NJI … is an independent, not-for-profit institution [the Board of Governors for which is chaired by the Chief Justice of Canada] committed to building better justice through leadership in the education of judges in Canada and internationally.
>
> Since its inception in 1988, the NJI has continued to develop and deliver stimulating programs and a variety of electronic resources that foster judicial excellence. Alone or in partnership with courts and other organizations, the NJI is involved in the delivery of the majority of education taken by judges in Canada.

39 See NJI, NJI International Projects, available online: NJI <http://www.nji-inm.ca/nji/inm/collaboration-intl/projets-projects.cfm>.

40 See, for example, Judicial Development and Grassroots Engagement Project, a five-year, $12.5-million justice sector project in Vietnam funded primarily by CIDA as well as by the Vietnamese Government, available online: Agriteam Canada <http://www.agriteam.ca/projects/profile/judicial-development-and-grassroots-engagement-judge/> (I was part of the consulting team on that project).

justice cases.[41] Following the raising of these concerns, primarily on his own initiative but with the assistance of a working group, Justice Warren K. Winkler – as the senior regional justice of the Toronto region (before being appointed the chief justice of Ontario) – penned a practice direction[42] that exempted cases in Toronto from the universal application of Ontario rule 77.[43] The practice direction was implemented as a pilot project in Toronto in the form of former rule 78 and was co-signed by Justice Heather J. Smith, chief justice of the Superior Court of Justice. In a nutshell, the practice direction, through rule 78, provided for a more modest and flexible case management system for civil cases in Toronto as well as a longer time in which mandatory mediation was to occur.[44] However, although certainly reining in what some viewed as overly aggressive case management and ADR reform initiatives, even these more modest provisions in the Toronto region still maintained some case management provisions as well as mandatory mediation requirements. As such, notwithstanding incorrect assumptions at the time that court-annexed ADR was dead in civil cases in Toronto, even judicial critics of mandatory court-annexed ADR initiatives still

41 Superior Court of Justice, Practice Direction – Toronto Region, "Backlog Reduction/ Best Practices Initiative" (in force 31 December 2004) at para. 1, online: Ontario Courts <http://www.ontariocourts.on.ca/scj/en/notices/pd/toronto/casemanagement.htm> (discussed earlier, supra Chapter 3). See specifically Ontario *Rules of Civil Procedure*, R.R.O. 1990, Reg. 194, as amended, at r. 24.1 ("Mandatory Mediation") and r. 77 ("Civil Case Management") (again as discussed earlier, supra Chapter 3).

42 Practice directions are statements, typically from the court, designed to assist in the interpretation and efficient use of various processes found in rules of practice. They can be of wide, provincial application, or narrow, regional application. For a rules-based definition, see, for example, Ontario *Rules of Civil Procedure*, ibid. at r. 1.07.

43 Ibid. at r. 77. For a discussion of this process and the practice direction, see Hon. Warren K. Winkler, "Civil Justice Reform – The Toronto Experience" (The Warren Winkler Lectures on Civil Justice Reform, University of Ottawa, Faculty of Law, 12 September 2007), available online: Ontario Courts <http://www.ontariocourts.on.ca/coa/en/ps/speeches/civiljusticereform.htm>.

44 Rather than requiring mediation typically "within 90 days after the first defence has been filed" (Ontario *Rules of Civil Procedure*, supra note 41 at former r. 24.1.09(1)), mediation had to occur for typical cases in Toronto (as governed by former r. 78) much later in the life of a case: at least "within 90 days after the action is set down for trial ..." (ibid. at former r. 24.1.09.1(2)(c)). This change allowed parties and lawyers more time to develop their case, particularly in evidence-heavy proceedings, and as such more time to understand the dispute and whether, and if so, how the case could be resolved by ADR prior to trial.

supported versions of these privatizing initiatives. Finally, through very recent reforms in Ontario, a reformed rule 24.1 and a new rule 77 have been adopted, which, together, seek to balance many of the competing aspects of the former rules and practices.[45]

Lawyers

Largely in response to external criticism about the cost, speed and inefficiency of, and overall lack of access to, the civil justice system, bar associations have also actively been encouraging the use of privatizing dispute resolution processes. As I discussed at length in Chapter 3, the foundational civil justice reform report in Canada was done in 1996 by the Canadian Bar Association,[46] which described the "adoption of a dispute resolution approach" to "litigation practice" as a "new professional obligation."[47] Through the various rules reform projects and initiatives discussed earlier,[48] a huge number of the CBA's 1996 recommendations have been implemented, either fully or partially across Canada's court systems over the past ten or so years.[49] In line with this "new professional obligation," again at the national level, the CBA's *Code of Professional Conduct* provides model code provisions that encourage settlement and the use of ADR.[50] In addition, provincial bar

45 For a more fulsome discussion of these Ontario rules and recent reforms, see supra Chapter 3. For a critical discussion of judges and ADR, particularly judicial dispute resolution (JDR), see Hon. Hugh F. Landerkin, Q.C. and Andrew J. Pirie, "Judges as Mediators: What's the Problem with Judicial Dispute Resolution in Canada?" (2003) 82 *Can. Bar Rev.* 249.

46 Canadian Bar Association (CBA), Task Force on Systems of Civil Justice, "Systems of Civil Justice Task Force Report" (Ottawa: CBA, 1996), available online: CBA <http://www.cba.org/CBA/pubs/pdf/systemscivil_tfreport.pdf> ["CBA Task Force Report"] (discussed further, supra Chapter 3).

47 Ibid. at 62–3. For a discussion of these reforms and obligations, see, for example, Farrow, "Dispute Resolution, Access to Civil Justice and Legal Education," supra note 31 at 750.

48 See supra Chapter 3.

49 For a useful review of the CBA's recommendations and their subsequent implementation, see Shone, "Civil Justice Reform in Canada: 1996 to 2006 and Beyond," supra note 37.

50 According to the CBA's *Code of Professional Conduct*,

> Whenever the case can be settled reasonably, the lawyer should advise and encourage the client to do so rather than commence or continue legal proceedings. The lawyer should consider the use of alternative dispute resolution (ADR) for

associations are publishing publicly available best practice statements that discuss and encourage the use of ADR by their members on behalf of the members' clients.[51]

Similarly, law societies across the country are increasingly viewing alternative, private settlement methods as appropriate matters for professional regulation.[52] Following the CBA's model *Code of Professional Conduct*, law societies, through their own codes of professional conduct, have required lawyers to consider and potentially use ADR processes on behalf of their clients.[53] More recently, the Federation of Law Societies of Canada (FLSC) has published its *Model Code of Professional Conduct*.[54] The motivation behind producing the *Model Code*,

---

> every dispute and, if appropriate, the lawyer should inform the client of the ADR options and, if so instructed, take steps to pursue those options.

CBA, *Code of Professional Conduct*, rev. ed. (2009), c. IX.8, online: CBA <http://www.cba.org/CBA/activities/pdf/codeofconduct.pdf> [footnote omitted].

51 See, for example, CBA–British Columbia Branch, "Our Court System and Solving Disputes," available online: CBA–British Columbia Branch <http://www.cbabc.org/For-the-Public/Dial-A-Law/Scripts/Lawyers-Legal-Services-and-Courts/432>.

52 The regulation by law societies of lawyers and their ADR attitudes and practices was also a very specific goal of the "CBA Task Force Report," which recommended that "[e]very jurisdiction specify in its rules of professional conduct an obligation on lawyers to explore fully the prospects of settlement with their clients and an obligation to explain available dispute resolution options to clients in relation to litigation matters." See "CBA Task Force Report," supra note 46 at vii, "Summary of Task Force Recommendations" no. 38. See similarly the Law Commission of Canada's recommendation that provincial codes of professional conduct be reviewed in light of modern dispute resolution demands. See Law Commission of Canada, *Transforming Relationships Through Participatory Justice*, supra note 16 at 215–16.

53 For example, Ontario's Law Society of Upper Canada (LSUC), in its *Rules of Professional Conduct*, adopted the following dispute resolution provisions:

> A lawyer *shall* advise and encourage the client to compromise or settle a dispute whenever it is possible to do so on a reasonable basis and shall discourage the client from commencing useless legal proceedings.
>
> The lawyer *shall* consider the use of alternative dispute resolution (ADR) for every dispute, and, if appropriate, the lawyer shall inform the client of ADR options and, if so instructed, take steps to pursue those options.

LSUC, *Rules of Professional Conduct* (in effect 1 November 2000), r. 2.02(2)-(3), online: LSUC <http://www.lsuc.on.ca/with.aspx?id=671> [emphasis added]. For a further discussion, see Stephen G.A. Pitel, "Counseling and Negotiation" in Alice Woolley et al., eds., *Lawyers' Ethics and Professional Regulation*, supra note 30 at chapter 7.

54 FLSC, *Model Code of Professional Conduct* (adopted 2009 and 2011).

largely because of increasing lawyer mobility across the country, was to encourage the individual provincial law societies to adopt a new, relatively uniform set of ethical standards. That harmonization process is currently underway.[55] The *Model Code* (at r. 2.02(4) and commentary) includes the following provisions that encourage compromise and the use of ADR:

> A lawyer must advise and encourage a client to compromise or settle a dispute whenever it is possible to do so on a reasonable basis and must discourage the client from commencing or continuing useless legal proceedings.
>
> A lawyer should consider the use of alternative dispute resolution (ADR) when appropriate, inform the client of ADR options and, if so instructed, take steps to pursue those options.

The FLSC's *Model Code* provisions impose a duty on lawyers (by using the word *must*) to "advise and encourage" a client to settle a case in the appropriate circumstances. Further, the *Model Code* encourages lawyers (by using the word *should*) to consider using ADR. Ontario's rules also require lawyers (by using the word *shall*) to "advise and encourage" clients to settle their cases in appropriate circumstances.[56] However, they go further than the FLSC's *Model Code* by requiring lawyers (again by using the word *shall*) to consider the use of ADR whenever possible for "every" dispute.[57] Whether provincial codes will follow the FLSC's approach or the slightly more rigorous approach of Ontario will be seen as more and more law societies revise their codes over the coming years.[58] Either way, these various professional regulations provide clear encouragement as well as, at times, clear obligations for lawyers both to consider settlement as well as to use ADR processes on behalf of their clients.

55 For example, Alberta and Nova Scotia have recently adopted new codes of professional conduct. See Law Society of Alberta, *Code of Conduct* (version 2011_V1, in effect 1 November 2011); and Nova Scotia Barristers' Society, *Code of Professional Conduct* (approved by Council 23 September 2011, effective 1 January 2012). Ontario has also recently engaged in that process, with revised rules set to come into force in October 2014.

56 See supra note 53.

57 Ibid.

58 Nova Scotia's new *Code of Profession Conduct*, ibid. at r. 2.02(4) tracks the language of the FLSC's *Model Code*. Alberta's new *Code of Conduct*, ibid. at rr. 2.01(1) and 2.02(7) seems to walk slightly more of a middle road by including, in addition to similar language found in the FLSC's *Model Code* at r. 2.02(4), the skills of alternative dispute resolution in the definition of what counts as a "competent lawyer."

Put simply, they provide clear and important examples of privatization in action.[59]

In addition to the ADR initiatives of bar associations and the requirements of regulators discussed above, individual lawyers and firms are increasingly recognizing, and now espousing, the merits of ADR with their clients. This dramatic and ongoing opening up to ADR is occurring at one level as a practical, client-service matter. Lawyers are realizing the increased benefits for their clients in using ADR methods in terms of cost and time savings. They are also increasingly discovering their own economic opportunities and benefits that can result from expanding their practice skills to include ADR processes. Privatization of dispute resolution processes allows for an increased role for private, for-profit actors in the resolution of civil disputes. Obviously lawyers can be at the centre of this opportunity. As evidence of this new business

59 In line with these various law society initiatives, former chief justice Brian Dickson argued, in a similar vein, that protecting and fostering access to justice is not just about adequate institutional design. Rather, it is a lawyer's "professional duty, as an officer of the court, to ensure that matters proceed as expeditiously as possible." See Dickson, "Access to Justice," supra note 25 at 2. For Chief Justice Dickson, this may mean going even further than the basics set out in various code provisions: "While the Canadian Bar Association's *Code of Professional Conduct* states that lawyers should encourage clients to settle disputes on a reasonable basis and avoid useless legal proceedings, lawyers need to go further and should consider how ADR may best serve their clients." Rt. Hon. Brian Dickson, P.C., "ADR, the Courts and the Judicial System: The Canadian Context" (1994) 28 *L. Soc'y Gaz.* 231 at 238 [citation omitted]. For some further general discussions of lawyers' professional obligations in the context of ADR, see, for example, Trevor C.W. Farrow, "Representative Negotiation" in Colleen M. Hanycz, Trevor C.W. Farrow, and Frederick H. Zemans, *The Theory and Practice of Representative Negotiation* (Toronto: Emond Montgomery, 2008) [*The Theory and Practice of Representative Negotiation*] c. 2; Trevor C.W. Farrow, "The Negotiator-as-Professional: Understanding the Competing Interests of a Representative Negotiator" (2007) 7 *Pepp. Disp. Resol. L.J.* 373; and Frederick H. Zemans, "Representative Negotiators of Integrity" in *The Theory and Practice of Representative Negotiation*, supra at c. 5. See further Carrie Menkel-Meadow, "Ethics in ADR: The Many 'Cs' of Professional Responsibility and Dispute Resolution" (2001) 28 *Fordham Urb. L.J.* 979; Julie Macfarlane, gen. ed., et al., eds., *Dispute Resolution: Readings and Case Studies*, 2nd ed. (Toronto: Emond Montgomery, 2003) at 258–80, 482–515; and, more recently, Julie Macfarlane, gen. ed., et al., eds., *Dispute Resolution: Readings and Case Studies*, 3rd ed. (Toronto: Emond Montgomery, 2010) at 232–41, 390–417; Van A. Anderson, "Alternative Dispute Resolution and Professional Responsibility in South Carolina: A Changing Landscape" (2003) 55 *S.C.L. Rev.* 191. See also Farrow, "Dispute Resolution, Access to Civil Justice and Legal Education," supra note 31 at 786–7, n. 290.

Table 5.1. Mediation

Q. Do you ever recommend to your clients that they resolve a dispute using mediation?		
Yes:	179	(91.33%)
No:	17	(8.67%)
Total:	196	(not all lawyers responded to this question)
Q. How frequently do you make the recommendation that a client use mediation?		
Very frequently:	54	(33.33%)
Frequently:	53	(32.72%)
On occasion:	43	(26.54%)
Rarely:	12	(7.41%)
Total:	162	(not all lawyers responded to this question)

reality, one only needs to look at the front – "general display" – pages of various law reports to see that the number of lawyers and former judges advertising an expertise in all ADR areas and processes continues to expand in Canada.[60]

As part of the research for this book, I conducted a national survey of lawyers on the issue of ADR. This was a unique survey in Canada, the results of which provide a relatively current and very useful window onto the ADR practices and preferences of practicing litigation lawyers.[61] Set out in three tables – Tables 5.1 through 5.3 – are the survey results with respect to the use of mediation, arbitration, and dispute resolution clauses by lawyers, together with data regarding the frequency with which these processes are used.

The basic results of these aspects of the survey confirm a significant propensity for the lawyers who responded to use some form of ADR process in their practice. Of particular note was the fact that more than 90 per cent (179) of the lawyers who responded to the mediation questions recommended the use of mediation to their clients, with 92.59 per cent of those 179 lawyers making the recommendation either occasionally (43), frequently (53) or very frequently (54; see Table 5.1). In the case

60 See, for example, 116 O.R. (3d), pt. 5 (11 October 2013). For a discussion of this new lawyering reality, see Julie Macfarlane, *The New Lawyer: How Settlement is Transforming the Practice of Law* (Vancouver: UBC Press, 2008). See further Tamara Relis, *Perceptions in Litigation and Mediation: Lawyers, Defendants, Plaintiffs, and Gendered Parties* (Cambridge, UK and New York: Cambridge University Press, 2009).

61 See Trevor C.W. Farrow, "National Alternative Dispute Resolution Survey (2008)" (Toronto: University of Toronto Press, 2013), available online: University of Toronto Press <http://www.utppublishing.com/pdf/Farrow_LawyerSurvey.pdf>.

Table 5.2. Arbitration

Q. Do you ever recommend to your clients that they resolve a dispute using arbitration?		
Yes:	206	(80.47%)
No:	50	(19.53%)
Total:	256	
Q. How frequently do you make the recommendation that a client use arbitration?		
Very frequently:	12	(7.45%)
Frequently:	37	(22.98%)
On occasion:	87	(54.04%)
Rarely:	25	(15.53%)
Total:	161	(not all lawyers responded to this question)

Table 5.3. Dispute resolution clauses

Q. Do you recommend that your clients insert dispute resolution clauses into their contracts?		
Yes:	132	(74.16%)
No:	46	(25.84%)
Total:	178	(not all lawyers responded to this question)

of arbitration, more than 80 per cent (206) of the lawyers who responded to the arbitration questions recommended the use of arbitration to their clients, with 84.47 per cent making the recommendation either occasionally (87), frequently (37), or very frequently (12; see Table 5.2). Finally, more than 74 per cent (132) of the lawyers who responded to the dispute resolution clause questions recommended that their clients insert some form of dispute resolution clause into their contracts (see Table 5.3). In the case of lawyers (157) who recommend that clients insert dispute resolution clauses into their "business" contracts, more than 70 per cent of those 157 lawyers do so sometimes (71) or always (40).[62] The results of this portion of the survey confirm that lawyers who typically practice in the field of civil dispute resolution are making significant use of ADR procedures.

Further evidence of individual lawyers' enthusiastic acceptance and promotion of ADR, which is consistent with the responses from the

62 See Farrow, "National Alternative Dispute Resolution Survey (2008)," supra note 61. With respect to the dispute resolution clause questions, it should be noted that, because the survey was directed primarily at litigation lawyers, drafting contracts was reportedly not part of some of their practices (a fact that may have some impact on the results reported on these questions). See ibid.

lawyers who were surveyed for purposes of this book, can be seen in the number of firms that self-identify as promoting ADR. For example, 1,500 Canadian and international law firms, including 400 of the 500 largest law firms in the United States, have signed the "ADR Pledge" of the International Institute for Conflict Prevention & Resolution (CPR).[63]

Taken together, ADR's various privatizing influences and opportunities fit with, and are increasingly driven by, the skills and preferences of what one commentator has called the "new lawyer": one who is open to a dispute resolution world that is dominated by non-court-based venues, processes and sensibilities.[64] This new dispute resolution world of individual lawyers accords with the ADR preferences and initiatives of bar associations and law societies as well as judges.

Clients

Even if lawyers were not participating in the promotion of ADR initiatives, which we have now seen they very much are, lawyers would

---

63 The CPR's "ADR Pledge" provides that

> We recognize that for many disputes there may be methods more effective for resolution than traditional litigation. Alternative dispute resolution (ADR) procedures – used in conjunction with litigation or independently – can significantly reduce the costs and burdens of litigation and result in solutions not available in court.
>
> In recognition of the foregoing, we subscribe to the following statements of policy on behalf of our firm.
>
> First, appropriate lawyers in our firm will be knowledgeable about ADR.
>
> Second, where appropriate, the responsible attorney will discuss with the client the availability of ADR procedures so the client can make an informed choice concerning resolution of the dispute.

CPR, "Law Firm Policy Statement on Alternatives to Litigation," available online: CPR <http://www.cpradr.org/Portals/0/About_CPR/Pledge/CPR%20Law%20Firm%20Pledge%20on%20Alternatives%20to%20Litigation.pdf>. For law firms that have signed the "ADR Law Firm Pledge," see CPR <http://www.cpradr.org/About/ADRPledges/LawFirmPledgeSigners.aspx>. For further information, see "CPR's ADR Pledges," online: CPR <http://www.cpradr.org/About/ADRPledges.aspx>. I recognize that the "ADR Pledge" essentially tracks much of what at least most Canadian lawyers are now obligated to do pursuant to their codes of professional conduct. See, for example, supra notes 53–8 and accompanying text.

64 Macfarlane, *The New Lawyer: How Settlement is Transforming the Practice of Law*, supra note 60. See further Julie Macfarlane, "Demise of the 'Warrior Lawyer'" 28:7 *The Lawyers Weekly* (13 June 2008) 7 at 7, 11. See also Richard Susskind, *The End of Lawyers? Rethinking the Nature of Legal Services* (Oxford, UK: Oxford University Press, 2008) at c. 6.

find that clients are increasingly demanding these new skills from their legal representatives. Clients are "expecting lawyers to actively canvass methods of alternative dispute resolution – the alternative to the adversarial and costly litigation process."[65] According to another commentator, "clients are all demanding a problem-solving approach."[66] And while it is certainly the case that different types of clients are demanding the use of different types of ADR methods (a family law mediation, for example, is a very different process from either a contract negotiation or a commercial arbitration), the point that I am trying to make here is more of an aggregate argument. The preferences driving these client demands – albeit for different processes for different people – taken together provide persuasive evidence of a generalized (and increasing) client preference for ADR. And, as I've mentioned, it is a generalized preference that lines up with, as well as fuels, the preferences of other justice system stakeholders, including lawyers, law schools and elected officials.

As a general matter, international empirical research confirms these statements. For example, a survey in the United States, which examined "the use of ADR among 1,000 of the largest U.S. corporations," found that ADR is "widespread and likely to grow significantly in the foreseeable future."[67] Other international surveys report similar findings in terms of positive views towards ADR.[68] For example, a survey of

65 Trevor C.W. Farrow, "Sustainable Professionalism" (2008) 46:1 *Osgoode Hall L.J.* 51 at 54–5. For a discussion of other client demands that are contributing to the changing nature of the practice of law – specifically concerning the diversity of their legal counsel and firms – see, for example, Pamela McClintock, "Big Corporate Clients Demand Diversity" (1999) 221:99 *N.Y.L.J.* 5, discussed further in Farrow, "Sustainable Professionalism," supra at 65, n. 14 and accompanying text.

66 Dean Philip Bryden, cited in Donalee Moulton, "Vanishing Trials: Out-of-Court Settlements on the Rise" 28:23 *The Lawyers Weekly* (17 October 2008) 22 at 22.

67 David B. Lipsky and Ronald L. Seeber, "The Appropriate Resolution of Corporate Disputes: A Report on the Growing Use of ADR by U.S. Corporations" (Cornell/PERC Institute on Conflict Resolution, Summer 1998), available online: Cornell University, ILR School <https://www.ilr.cornell.edu/alliance/resources/Articles/approp_resol_corp_disputes.html> at "Description of Report." The study was based on a "phone and mail survey of 606 respondents."

68 Because of the relative lack of empirical research in Canada, combined with the similar ADR traditions that have grown up in Canada and the United States (and elsewhere), I am of the view that these sorts of international empirical studies – particularly from the United States and Commonwealth countries (set out here and elsewhere in this book) – are equally relevant and useful in Canada.

lawyers and parties involved in international private business arbitrations conducted through the American Arbitration Association (AAA) in 2000 revealed consistently high rankings in terms of lawyer and client opinions of the fairness of arbitral results.[69] Further, as we saw with their outside counsel,[70] corporate clients from the United States[71] and Canada[72] are also actively pledging their allegiance to ADR (even though they are under no similar professional obligation to do so).

---

69 Richard W. Naimark and Stephanie E. Keer, "International Private Commercial Arbitration: Expectations and Perceptions of Attorneys and Business People; A Forced-Rank Analysis" in Christopher R. Drahozal and Richard W. Naimark, eds., *Towards a Science of International Arbitration: Collected Empirical Research* (New York: Kluwer Law International, 2005) at 43.

70 See supra note 63 and accompanying text.

71 For example, 4,000 corporations, representing more than two thirds of the U.S. gross national product, have signed the CPR's "ADR Pledge," the corporate version of which provides:

> We recognize that for many disputes there is a less expensive, more effective method of resolution than the traditional lawsuit. Alternative dispute resolution (ADR) procedures involve collaborative techniques which can often spare businesses the high costs of litigation.
>
> In recognition of the foregoing, we subscribe to the following statements of principle on behalf of our company and its domestic subsidiaries:
>
> In the event of a business dispute between our company and another company which has made or will then make a similar statement, we are prepared to explore with that other party resolution of the dispute through negotiation or ADR techniques before pursuing full-scale litigation. If either party believes that the dispute is not suitable for ADR techniques, or if such techniques do not produce results satisfactory to the disputants, either party may proceed with litigation.

CPR, "Corporate Policy Statement on Alternatives to Litigation," online: CPR <http://www.cpradr.org/Portals/0/About_CPR/Pledge/CPR%20Corporate%20Pledge%20on%20Alternatives%20to%20Litigation.pdf>. For corporations that have signed the "ADR Pledge," see CPR, "Corporate Pledge Signers," online: CPR <http://www.cpradr.org/About/ADRPledges/CorporatePledgeSigners.aspx>. The CPR has also recently launched a new corporate pledge, the "21st Century Pledge," which is not limited to a two-party dispute resolution framework. Rather, the new pledge encourages signatories to become proactive in the development of policies and practices that encourage resolution over litigation. For further information, see CPR <http://www.cpradr.org/About/ADRPledges/21stCenturyPledgeFAQs.aspx>.

72 For example, a number of significant corporate entities – and leading Canadian law firms – have signed the ADR Institute of Canada's "Dispute Resolution Pledge." The "Dispute Resolution Pledge," in a similar fashion to the CPR's

In addition to these generalized views, client-based ADR preferences can be tracked from a more industry-specific perspective as well. For example, according to the lawyers surveyed for this book, clients in the commercial law context are increasingly demanding that the contracts by which they conduct their business affairs include some form of dispute resolution clause. As an AAA commentary noted, "[e]very year, millions of business contracts provide for mediation and arbitration as ways of resolving disputes."[73] Some industry sectors, particularly the financial services sector, have developed wide-ranging collective ombud and ADR services.[74] In addition, industry-specific practices have developed with respect to specialized dispute resolution contractual clauses.[75] Others, such as the labour sector, often primarily use arbitration processes as provided for under wide-ranging collective bargaining regimes.

---

pledge process (see, for example, supra notes 63 and 71), "commits signatories to willingly consider and suggest alternative dispute resolution processes in appropriate situations prior to turning to the courts." ADR Institute of Canada, Rules & Pledges, "Dispute Resolution Pledge: A Corporate Policy Statement," available online: ADR Institute of Canada <http://www.amic.org/>. For a list of signatory corporations and law firms, see ibid. at About Us, ADR Leaders, "Pledge Signatories." While the pledge is voluntary, signing it certainly indicates an institution's willingness to consider alternative private processes.

73 AAA, "Drafting Dispute Resolution Clauses – A Practical Guide" (1994), online: Cornell University, ILR School <https://www.ilr.cornell.edu/alliance/resources/Guide/drafting_dispres_clauses.html>.

74 See supra Chapter 4.

75 For example, given the complex regulatory and contractual nature of the construction industry, a sophisticated construction contract practice has developed, particularly with respect to construction dispute resolution clauses. For example, in the Canadian construction industry, the Canadian Construction Documents Committee (CCDC) has developed standard contractual documents that contain mandatory dispute resolution clauses that are specifically tailored to the Canadian construction industry. See CCDC, "Home," online: CCDC <http://www.ccdc.org/>. For a discussion of CCDC documents, see, for example, Donald E. Short, "New Approaches to Dispute Resolution in the Construction Sector" (November 2003), available online: Fasken Martineau <http://www.fasken.com/> at 3. See further Thomas J. Stipanowich, "Beyond Arbitration: Innovation and Evolution in the United States Construction Industry" (1996) 31 *Wake Forest L. Rev.* 169. Similarly, the AAA has developed significant resources specifically devoted to drafting ADR clauses in construction contracts. See AAA, National Construction Dispute Resolution Committee, "The AAA Guide to Drafting Alternative Dispute Resolution Clauses for Construction Contracts," online: AAA <http://www.adr.org/aaa/ShowPDF?doc=ADRSTG_002542>.

One area of particular interest to this book, which has witnessed a significant amount of legislative and judicial attention lately, is the consumer sector. Arbitration and other forms of non-court-based dispute resolution processes have been and continue to be used in many consumer contracts,[76] which now – as was the case in *Dell*[77] – also often include online contracts for the provision of goods and services. Arbitration in this sector is largely used as a class action risk management strategy. The consumer sector is singled out here because of its significant use of dispute resolution clauses as well as the significant number of people who are parties to consumer contracts. A typical example of a mandatory dispute resolution provision in a Canadian consumer contract is a recent mandatory arbitration clause found in Shaw's joint terms of service provisions, which provides:

> Any disputes or claims ("claims") whatsoever between Shaw and you will be referred to and determined by arbitration to the exclusion of the courts. ... You agree to waive any right you may have to commence or participate in any class action against Shaw related to any claim where such waiver is permitted, where applicable. You also agree to opt out of any class proceedings against Shaw.[78]

Other examples of recent mandatory dispute resolution clauses in familiar Canadian consumer contracts include clauses for Rogers,[79] Shaw

---

76 For a general study, see Susan Lott, Marie Hélène Beaulieu and Jannick Desforges, "Mandatory Arbitration and Consumer Contracts" (Public Interest Advocacy Centre (PIAC) and Option consommateurs, November 2004), online: PIAC <http://www.piac.ca/consumers/mandatory_arbitration_and_consumer_contracts/>. See further Ernst & Young, "Outcomes of Arbitration: An Empirical Study of Consumer Lending Cases" (2004), online: Ernst & Young <http://www.adrforum.com/rcontrol/documents/ResearchStudiesAndStatistics/2005ErnstAndYoung.pdf>. More recently, see Geneviève Saumier, "Consumer Dispute Resolution: The Evolving Canadian Landscape" (2007) 1 *Class Action Def. Q.* 52; and Theodore Eisenberg, Geoffrey P. Miller, and Emily Sherwin, "Arbitration's Summer Soldiers: An Empirical Study of Arbitration Clauses in Consumer and Nonconsumer Contracts" (2007–8) 41 *U. Mich. J. L. Ref.* 871.

77 *Dell Computer Corp. v. Union des consommateurs*, [2007] 2 S.C.R. 801. For a further discussion of *Dell*, see supra Chapter 4.

78 Shaw, "Joint Terms of Service" at "Disputes and Governing Law" (2012), available online: Shaw <http://www.shaw.ca/Terms-Of-Use/#section2>.

79 Rogers, "Rogers Terms of Service" at s. 34 ("Arbitration"), online: Rogers <https://your.rogers.com/about/legaldisclaimer/tos_eng.pdf>, which provides the following:

> To the extent permitted by applicable law, unless we agree otherwise, any claim, dispute or controversy, whether in contract or tort, pursuant to statute

Direct (formerly Star Choice),[80] Amazon.ca,[81] Direct Energy,[82] and Telus.[83] It was also this kind of mandatory arbitration clause that was at issue in the Dealership case.[84]

Notwithstanding their prevalence, however, recent legislative initiatives in some Canadian jurisdictions have limited the use of *mandatory*

> or regulation, or otherwise, and whether pre-existing, present or future, arising out of or relating to the following items will be determined by final and binding arbitration to the exclusion of the courts:
>
> - the Service Agreement;
> - the Services or Equipment;
> - oral or written statements, advertisements or promotions relating to the Service Agreement, the Services or Equipment; or
> - the relationships that result from the Service Agreement [emphasis omitted].

80 Shaw Direct (formerly Star Choice), "Shaw Direct Terms of Service – Residential Customer Agreement" at s. 29 ("Arbitration/No Class Action"), available online: Star Choice/Shaw Direct <http://www.shawdirect.ca/english/TermsofService.pdf>, which provides the following:

> Any claim or dispute (whether in contract or tort) arising out of or relating to these Terms of Service … (collectively a "Claim") will be referred to and determined by a sole arbitrator (to the exclusion of the courts) whose decision will be final and binding. Unless prohibited by law, Customer agrees to waive any right Customer may have to commence or participate in any class action suit or proceeding against Shaw Direct arising out of or relating to any Claim and you also agree to opt out of any class proceedings against us. … Any arbitration of a Claim will be pursuant to such rules as you and we agree and failing agreement will be conducted by a single arbitrator pursuant to the laws and rules relating to commercial arbitration in the province in which you reside that are in effect on the date of the notice to arbitrate.

81 Amazon.com.ca, Inc., "Conditions of Use" at "Disputes," available online: Amazon.ca <http://www.amazon.ca/gp/help/customer/display.html/702-0845219-5495233?ie=UTF8&nodeId=918816>, which provides the following:

> Any dispute relating in any way to your visit to the Amazon.ca site or to products you purchase through Amazon.ca shall be submitted to confidential arbitration in Seattle, Washington, United States, except that, to the extent that you have in any manner violated or threatened to violate the intellectual property rights of Amazon.ca or its affiliates, Amazon.ca or its affiliates may seek injunctive or other appropriate relief in any state or federal court in the state of Washington, and you consent to exclusive jurisdiction and venue in such courts. Arbitration under this agreement shall be conducted under the rules then prevailing of the American Arbitration Association. The arbitrator's award shall be binding and

dispute resolution clauses in consumer contracts. These are significant initiatives that somewhat temper (in specific circumstances) the otherwise overwhelming tendency to favour privatized dispute resolution processes and opportunities in consumer contracts. For example, according to Québec's amended *Consumer Protection Act*, consumer contracts

---

> may be entered as a judgment in any court of competent jurisdiction. To the fullest extent permitted by applicable law, no arbitration under this Agreement shall be joined to an arbitration involving any other party subject to this Agreement, whether through class arbitration proceedings or otherwise.

82 Direct Energy, "Web Site Terms of Use" at "Jurisdiction and Arbitration," available online: Direct Energy <http://www.directenergy.com/EN/Pages/TermsOfUse.aspx>, which provides the following:

> Access to this website is governed by all applicable federal, state, provincial and local laws, and, in the case of users resident outside of Canada or the United States, you may also be subject to additional laws of the country where you reside. You are responsible for compliance with the laws of your jurisdiction and other applicable law.
>
> The laws of the Province of Ontario, Canada shall govern any dispute arising out of the use of this website or these Terms of Use. You also agree to submit to the exclusive jurisdiction and venue of the courts located therein. In the event of any dispute with Direct Energy arising out of or related to these Terms of Use or your use of the Site you agree to submit such dispute to binding arbitration under the procedure provided by the Arbitration Act (Ontario).

83 Telus Communications Company, "Telus Standard Mobility Service Terms & Conditions" at s. 15 ("Arbitration") [archived with author] provides the following:

> Any claim, dispute or controversy (whether in contract or tort, pursuant to statute or regulation, or otherwise …) arising out of or relating to: (a) this agreement; (b) a phone or the service; (c) oral or written statements, or advertisements or promotions relating to this agreement or to a product or service; or (d) the relationships which result from this agreement (including relationships with third parties who are not parties to this agreement), (each, a "Claim") will be referred to and determined by private and confidential mediation before a single mediator chosen by the parties and at their joint cost. Should the parties after mediation in good faith fail to reach a settlement, the issue between them shall then be determined by private, confidential and binding arbitration by the same person originally chosen as mediator. Either party may commence court proceedings to enforce the arbitration result when an arbitration decision shall have been rendered. … By so agreeing, you waive any right you may have to commence or participate in any class action against TELUS related to any Claim and, where

that mandate arbitration by purporting to prohibit consumers from accessing public court processes are now prohibited.[85] Similar legislative amendments were also made several years earlier to Ontario's *Consumer Protection Act*.[86] As a result of these sorts of provisions, *mandatory* consumer arbitration clauses will no longer be permitted in jurisdictions in which either companies deem it not to be in their best interests and in which legislation prohibits them. In such cases, mandatory clauses are severed and deemed to be of no force and effect[87]; alternatively,

---

> applicable, you hereby agree to opt out of any class proceeding against TELUS otherwise commenced. … Mediation and arbitration of Claims will be conducted in such forum and pursuant to such rules as you and we agree upon, and failing agreement will be conducted by one mediator-arbitrator pursuant to the laws and rules relating to commercial arbitration in the province in which you reside that are in effect on the date of the notice to mediate and arbitrate. Some jurisdictions may not allow the use of compulsory mediation or arbitration or the waiver of rights to participate in a class action. If applicable law renders clauses requiring mandatory mediation or arbitration or the exclusion of the right to participate in a class action void, the provisions of this section shall be subject to severance. ...

It was Telus's standard form contract that was at issue in *Seidel v. Telus Communications Inc.*, 2011 SCC 15, [2011] 1 S.C.R. 531 at para. 13 (discussed further supra Chapter 4).

84 See supra Chapter 1.

85 *Consumer Protection Act*, R.S.Q., c. P-40.1. The relevant 2006 amendments to the legislation provide the following:

> Any stipulation that obliges the consumer to refer a dispute to arbitration, that restricts the consumer's right to go before a court, in particular by prohibiting the consumer from bringing a class action, or that deprives the consumer of the right to be a member of a group bringing a class action is prohibited. … If a dispute arises after a contract has been entered into, the consumer may then agree to refer the dispute to arbitration.

Ibid. at s. 11.1. For a further discussion of the new Québec regime and its application, see, for example, *Dell Computer Corp. v. Union des consommateurs*, supra note 77 (discussed further supra Chapter 4). Because the facts that triggered the arbitration clause at issue in *Dell* occurred prior to the coming into force of Québec's legislative amendments, they did not apply to the arbitration clause in that case.

86 See *Consumer Protection Act, 2002*, S.O. 2002, c. 30, sched. A at s. 7, the relevant provisions of which provide the following:

> 7(2) … any term … in a consumer agreement … that requires … that disputes arising out of the consumer agreement be submitted to arbitration is invalid insofar as it prevents a consumer from exercising a right to commence an action

companies may choose to include *voluntary* private dispute resolution clauses in their consumer contracts.[88]

Overall, based on anecdotal and empirical evidence, as well as a review of various client practices with respect to dispute resolution contractual clauses, there is no doubt that clients, in line with earlier findings with respect to their lawyers, are demonstrating a strong preference for using ADR in the context of resolving their civil disputes. Put simply, along with other dispute resolution participants discussed in this chapter, they are a significant source of momentum for the privatization movement that is at issue in this book.

Law Schools

Final sources of current (and future) privatizing preferences and influences are law schools. The legal academy, such as other justice system stakeholders, has significantly changed over the last number of years. A big part of this change includes a move towards actively embracing and promoting what have traditionally been thought of as practice-

---

> in the Superior Court of Justice given under this Act. …(3) … after a dispute over which a consumer may commence an action in the Superior Court of Justice arises, the consumer, the supplier and any other person involved in the dispute may agree to resolve the dispute using any procedure that is available in law. … (5) Subsection 7(1) of the *Arbitration Act, 1991* does not apply in respect of any proceeding to which subsection (2) applies unless, after the dispute arises, the consumer agrees to submit the dispute to arbitration. …

See further ibid. at s. 100(1), which provides that "[i]f a consumer has a right to commence an action under this Act, the consumer may commence the action in the Superior Court of Justice." Other provincial reform initiatives in this area include Alberta's *Fair Trading Act*, R.S.A. 2000, c. F-2 and British Columbia's *Business Practices and Consumer Protection Act*, S.B.C. 2004, c. 2. For a general discussion of these various provincial legislative initiatives, see *Seidel v. Telus Communications Inc.*, supra note 83 at paras. 25 (by the majority) and 173–4 (by the minority). See further supra Chapter 4.

87 See, for example, Telus Communications Company, "Telus standard mobility Service Terms & Conditions" at s. 15 ("Arbitration"), supra note 83, the relevant provision of which provides that "[i]f applicable law renders clauses requiring mandatory mediation or arbitration or the exclusion of the right to participate in a class action void, the provisions of this section shall be subject to severance."

88 An example of a recent voluntary dispute resolution clause in a Canadian consumer contract is the permissive mediation or arbitration clause found in National Money Mart's

oriented subjects, including clinical education, legal writing, ethics, professionalism, and – most relevant for this book – dispute resolution.[89] The shift towards ADR has been extremely noticeable in law schools over the last several decades. According to one report, in 1976, "there was no subject category for ADR or mediation"[90] in United States law schools whereas, in 1992, more than 94 per cent of those schools provided

---

B.C. contract for Fast Cash Advance customers for its "Payday Loans" services. See National Money Mart Company, Payday Loans, available online: Money Mart <http://www.moneymart.ca/paydayloans.asp>, specifically including the link for "Alternative Dispute Resolution Process for British Columbia Fast Cash Advance customers" at ibid. The specific "Dispute Process" clause provides that "[i]f you have a dispute regarding your Fast Cash Advance from us: i) you *may* mediate or arbitrate your dispute with us at no cost to you; and ii) as part of the mediation or arbitration we will provide you with a summary of your Fast Cash Advance transactions with us at no cost to you." National Money Mart Company, British Columbia, Fast Cash Advance Customers, "Dispute Process," available online: Money Mart <http://www.moneymart.ca/fca_disp_proc.asp> [emphasis added]. Customers who choose to mediate or arbitrate then are directed to complete a "Customer Application to Mediate or Arbitrate," which includes, among other things, the following customer acknowledgment:

> I understand, acknowledge and agree that any mediation or arbitration will be conducted privately and confidentially using rules to be mutually agreed upon by Money Mart and myself and that the results of any mediation or arbitration will also be private and confidential and will not be disclosed to any person who is not a party to the mediation or arbitration.

National Money Mart Company, British Columbia, "Customer Application to Mediate or Arbitrate," available online: Money Mart <http://www.moneymart.ca/ADRFORM.pdf> at s. 4.11.

89 For previous discussions, see Farrow, "Dispute Resolution, Access to Civil Justice and Legal Education," supra note 31 at 754–5 (and the references cited therein); Trevor C.W. Farrow, "Dispute Resolution and Legal Education: A Bibliography" (2005) 7 *Cardozo J. Conflict Resol.* 119; Joshua J.A. Henderson and Trevor C.W. Farrow, "The Ethical Development of Law Students: An Empirical Study" (2009) 72:1 *Sask. L. Rev.* 75; Farrow, "Sustainable Professionalism," supra note 65; Trevor C.W. Farrow, "The Negotiator-as-Professional: Understanding the Competing Interests of a Representative Negotiator," supra note 59; Trevor C.W. Farrow, "Globalizing Approaches to Legal Education and Training: Canada to Japan" (2005) 38 *Hosei Riron J. L. & Politics* 144; Trevor C.W. Farrow, "Thinking About Dispute Resolution," Review Essay (2003) 41:2 *Alta. L. Rev.* 559; Trevor C.W. Farrow, "Reviewing Globalization: Three Competing Stories, Two Emerging Themes, and How Law Schools Can and Must Participate" (2003) 13 *Meikei L. Rev.* 176, trans. into Japanese by M. Kuwahara, (2003) 44 *Aichigakuin L. Rev.* 29, repub'd (2004) 5 *J. Centre for Int'l Stud.* 1.

90 Lela Porter Love, "Twenty-Five Years Later with Promises to Keep: Legal Education in Dispute Resolution and Training Mediators" (2002) 17 *Ohio St. J. Disp. Resol.* 597 at 598 [citation omitted].

students with dispute resolution course offerings.[91] This upward trend of ADR interest and offerings has continued. Since 1999, according to one commentator, "the level of interest in dispute resolution – and in particular in the teaching of dispute resolution – has risen exponentially."[92] And this has not simply been a U.S. experience: a similar rise in dispute resolution teaching and learning has occurred in law schools in Canada[93] and elsewhere[94] over the last number of years.[95]

91 American Bar Association (ABA), Report of the ABA Working Group on Civil Justice System Proposals, *ABA Blueprint for Improving the Civil Justice System* (Chicago: ABA, 1992) at 31 [*ABA Blueprint*]. See further ABA, *Just Solutions: Seeking Innovation and Change in the American Justice System*, by Stephen P. Johnson (Chicago: ABA, 1994). For further foundational materials, see ABA, Section on Legal Education and Admissions to the Bar, *Legal Education and Professional Development – An Educational Continuum, The Report of the Task Force on Law Schools and the Profession: Narrowing the Gap* (Chicago: ABA, 1992) (Chair: Robert MacCrate). For earlier ABA teaching initiatives in the context of the development of ADR, see, for example, ABA, Section on Legal Education and Admissions to the Bar, *Report and Recommendations of the Task Force on Lawyer Competency: The Role of Law Schools* (1979) at 3–4; ABA, *Law Schools and Professional Education: Report and Recommendations of the Special Committee for a Study of Legal Education of the American Bar Association* (1980) at 103. See also Farrow, "Dispute Resolution, Access to Civil Justice and Legal Education," supra note 31 at 747.

92 Macfarlane, ed., *Dispute Resolution: Readings and Case Studies*, 2nd ed. (2003), supra note 59 at xvii. According to a 2002 U.S. commentary, "more than 500 law professors" self-identified as teaching ADR. Love, "Twenty-Five Years Later with Promises to Keep," supra note 90 at 598 [footnote omitted]. See also generally Frank E.A. Sander, "The Future of ADR" (2000) *J. Disp. Resol.* 3; Frank E.A. Sander and Robert H. Mnookin, "A Worthy Challenge: The Teaching of Problem Solving in Law Schools" *Dispute Resolution Magazine* 6 (Summer 2000) 21; and Robert B. Moberly, "Introduction: Dispute Resolution in the Law School Curriculum: Opportunities and Challenges" (1998) 50 *Fla. L. Rev.* 583.

93 An early driving force behind the increased interest in ADR in Canadian law schools came from the 1996 "CBA Task Force Report," supra note 46 (and generally supra Chapter 3). As part of its research and recommendations, the CBA Task Force specifically looked at ADR and its teaching in Canadian law schools. In its report, although commenting favourably on what had already been accomplished, the CBA Task Force found a need for significant further work in the area of ADR and legal education. Put simply, it suggested "revolutionizing" legal education in Canada. Ibid. at 72. Specifically, it pointed to a need to review current ADR course offerings by law schools, bar admission courses and continuing legal education providers to ensure that ADR "training and educational opportunities are widely available." Ibid. at 64. Further, it recommended that "law schools … offer education and training on dispute resolution options and on the means by which they can be integrated into legal practice, and … [that] such courses [should] be mandatory in Canadian law schools and Bar admission course programs." Ibid. at 65, rec. 39. Similar recommendations

Underlying all of these ADR developments at law schools are numerous preferences and influences. In addition to financial, reputational, research, and pedagogical interests of universities and their faculties,[96] several other preferences and influences are worthy of note. The first is a clear civil justice reform agenda that can be located, among other

---

were also made by the Law Commission of Canada (LCC) several years later. Specifically, in 2003, the LCC looked at the broad issue of dispute resolution in Canada in the context of restorative justice initiatives. See LCC, *Transforming Relationships Through Participatory Justice*, supra note 16. With a specific focus on the resolution of disputes and ADR, the LCC recommended that universities and colleges, "and law schools in particular," should "continue to expand the quality of teaching in alternative dispute resolution offered to law students." Ibid. at xxiv. Notwithstanding these efforts, certainly not all reform proposals have been implemented by Canadian law schools. In 2005, I conducted a survey of law school and related ADR programs. See Farrow, "Dispute Resolution, Access to Civil Justice and Legal Education," supra note 31 at 743–4, nn. 12–14. What I found, of particular relevance to this book, were essentially two things. First, in line with (although slightly behind) law schools in the United States, a significant amount of ADR research and teaching was going on at Canadian law schools. Many Canadian schools had developed at least some kind of ADR program, with many schools having more than one stand alone ADR course for example. Second, although strides had been made to introduce the topic, more was clearly needed and was going to be done. Some specific examples of areas of opportunity for further focus included the research and teaching of ADR and ethics, culture, power, poverty, and access to justice, industry differences, and so on. Further, focused clinical experiences in ADR were only just developing. See ibid. at 781–801. Since that 2005 research, many of these issues are being taken up and more is being done (including, for example, mediation clinical programs discussed earlier). For a discussion of an earlier survey of Canadian law schools, see CBA, *Attitudes – Skills – Knowledge*, infra note 95 at 20–5.

94 See Farrow, "Dispute Resolution, Access to Civil Justice and Legal Education," supra note 31 at pt. v.

95 Macfarlane, gen. ed., *Dispute Resolution: Readings and Case Studies* (2003), supra note 59 at xvii. See further Macfarlane, *The New Lawyer: How Settlement is Transforming the Practice of Law*, supra note 60 at 224–32. A 2000 statement by Justice Austin of the Court of Appeal for Ontario noted that, "until very recently, lawyers and judges in Canada were not generally trained in negotiation, mediation or arbitration. Only in the last 10 years has instruction in alternative dispute resolution become a necessity amongst lawyers and judges across Canada." *Canadian Union of Public Employees v. Ontario (Minister of Labour)* (2000), 51 O.R. (3d) 417 at para. 41 (C.A.). This point was consistent with research from a CBA survey conducted around the same time, which stated that: "it is clear that there is increased interest in and emphasis on [A]DR in all law schools." See CBA, Joint Multi-Disciplinary Committee on Legal Education, *Attitudes – Skills – Knowledge: Recommendations for Changes to Legal Education to Assist in Implementing Multi-Option Civil Justice Systems in the 21st Century*

places, in the "CBA Task Force Report." What law professors teach law students bears on what students do (or want to do) as lawyers.[97] In the context of civil dispute resolution, "the link is clear between what students are exposed to at law school and what new and future lawyers are inclined to develop and accomplish with their clients and through institutional reform at the Bar."[98] This link, between teaching ADR at law school and promoting civil justice law reform generally, was a driving influence behind much of the modern ADR movement in U.S. law schools. According to the ABA, for example, "continued public and professional education about ADR is necessary to aid in the transformation of a legal system now centered on litigation into a system that includes non-adversarial ADR mechanisms."[99] Similarly, there is no doubt that the modern Canadian civil justice reform agenda has had, and continues to have, a major impact on the development of ADR programs at law schools. And although much of the impetus for that reform agenda is practice related and efficiency based, and has therefore not – at least at the outset – been particularly pedagogically driven, what has now developed is the beginnings of a very interesting and critical mass of university-based research and teaching that is starting to move beyond its practice-based roots and define itself in terms of its own research and teaching agendas.

(Ottawa: CBA, 2000) at 25. For the background discussion paper that formed the basis for the CBA's *Attitudes – Skills – Knowledge* report, see CBA, "Attitudes – Skills – Knowledge: Proposals for Legal Education to Assist in Implementing a Multi-Option Civil Justice System in the 21st Century" (discussion paper, Ottawa: CBA, August 1999). See also CBA, Committee Responding to Recommendation 49 of the Systems of Civil Justice Task Force Report (Ottawa: CBA, 1996).

96 For two very recent and influential studies on legal education and curriculum reform, both of which strongly recommend a strengthened focus on skills-based training at law schools, see William M. Sullivan et al., *Educating Lawyers: Preparation for the Profession of Law* (San Francisco: Jossey-Bass, 2007); Roy Stuckey et al., *Best Practices for Legal Education: A Vision and A Road Map* (New York: Clinical Legal Education Association, 2007) [Stuckey Report]. For specific commentary on ADR, see, for example, the Stuckey Report at 77–9.

97 See, for example, Farrow, "Sustainable Professionalism," supra note 65; Henderson and Farrow, "The Ethical Development of Law Students: An Empirical Study," supra note 89.

98 Farrow, "Dispute Resolution, Access to Civil Justice and Legal Education," supra note 31 at 781–2.

99 *ABA Blueprint*, supra note 91 at 39.

Further influential factors, as I have commented elsewhere,[100] have included the preferences of law students. Law students are actively and increasingly pursuing and promoting practical courses at law schools, including courses in ADR. These preferences are driven by a perception, which is often justified, that these kinds of courses will help students to be more prepared and accomplished lawyers once they graduate and start practicing law. As one report has indicated, the growth of clinical legal education in the United States and in Canada stemmed, at least in part, from "student demands for relevance in the law school curriculum."[101] This demand for practical, "relevan[t]," courses includes courses in ADR.[102] As Catherine Morris noted, "dispute resolution education is in hot demand by law students."[103]

This strong student interest, which is resonating with increasing faculty and administrative support throughout the law school community, is part of what we are seeing as an overall collective of privatizing preferences and influences from a wide range of justice system stakeholders.

---

100 Farrow, "Dispute Resolution, Access to Civil Justice and Legal Education," supra note 31 at 755.

101 Margaret Martin Barry et al., "Clinical Education for this Millennium: The Third Wave" (2000) 7 *Clinical L. Rev.* 1 at 16.

102 Eric Atkins, "Courses on ADR becoming Popular in Canada's Law Schools" *The Lawyers Weekly* (3 November 2000) 24.

103 Catherine Morris, "The Moulding of Lawyers: ADR and Legal Education" (1999) 17 *Windsor Y.B. Access Just.* 271 at 271. A number of years ago, I recall seeing a poster for the "Student Arbitration and Mediation Society," which was, at least in 2003, one of the most recently formed student groups at the University of Alberta. The catch phrase on the poster was a question: "ADR, the fastest growing trend in the practice of law, are you prepared?" University of Alberta, Student Arbitration and Mediation Society (Lecture Poster, 24 March 2003) [archived with author], cited in Farrow, "Dispute Resolution, Access to Civil Justice and Legal Education," supra note 31 at 755, n. 79 and accompanying text. More recently, at my current faculty (Osgoode Hall Law School), a student-led ADR organization, the "ADR Project," successfully spearheaded, together with significant faculty support and interest, the creation of a new mediation clinic (which was in 2009 awarded a start-up grant of $170,000 by the Ontario Law Foundation). For information on Osgoode Hall Law School's mediation clinic, together with other ADR initiatives at Osgoode, see, for example, York University, "Helliwell Foundation Gift Supports a New Dispute Resolution Centre" *Y File* (31 March 2009), available online: York University <http://www.yorku.ca/yfile/archive/index.asp?Article=12327>. See generally Osgoode Hall Law School, "Mediation Intensive Program," online: <http://www.osgoode.yorku.ca/clinics-experiential/clinical-education/mediation-intensive-program>.

Taken together, the expression of this reform-oriented ethos from key justice system participants, including governments, judges, lawyers, clients, and law schools, has been a significant motivating force behind the unmistakable wave of dispute resolution privatization that is increasingly occurring throughout this country and in many parts of the world. There really is no corner of the civil justice landscape that is exempted from this active privatizing activity. Remarkably, it is occurring with very little public knowledge or understanding let alone active public engagement. Before getting to my concerns about the potential negative ramifications of this widespread privatization activity and the lack of public awareness or understanding of it,[104] I now turn to look at the primary justifications that are typically provided for these privatization preferences and influences.

Justifying Privatization

There are several different justifications that can be identified as animating the preferences and influences of the various justice system stakeholders that I discussed earlier in this chapter, which, taken together, militate in favour of the modern movement to privatize our systems of civil dispute resolution. These various contributing justifications include, for example, market optimality and efficiency; preferences for process flexibility, party autonomy, ownership and choice; desires for increased individual and group participation (which, on some readings, increases legitimacy); privacy; accessibility; and others. However, to my mind, there are two overriding justifications for a widespread privatization of dispute resolution in Canada that are most compelling in terms of the regulatory discussions at issue in this book (both of which draw on many of the various factors mentioned above). The first is what I call the "business case for privatization." The central animating force of the business case for privatization is efficiency. According to this argument, private justice, like privatization generally (as I discussed earlier[105]), is more efficient than public justice, both for the provider and for the consumer. Key indicators of efficiency include speed, cost, autonomy, flexibility, and so on. And to be clear, even though I use

104 See generally infra Chapters 6 and 7.
105 See supra Chapter 3.

the phrase *business case* (because of what has come to be seen as a generally shared understanding of the efficiency-based premises behind such arguments), this first overriding justification, as will be seen, obtains equally in the context of the preferences of both private and public stakeholders in the justice community.

The second overriding justification for privatization is what I call the "access to justice case for privatization." According to this argument, by aggressively pursuing privatizing alternatives through active civil justice system reforms, more members of the citizenry who have been previously excluded by the increasingly inaccessible public system will have greater access to much-needed legal services. Simply put, the second justification of privatization is that it purports to provide greater access to justice.

Given the common factor of efficiency, there is no doubt that these two overriding justificatory cases are not mutually exclusive; rather, they are in fact mutually supportive. Many of the factors that make the system more attractive from a business case perspective also make it more viable from an access to justice perspective. The more efficient a dispute resolution system is – faster, cheaper, understandable, and so on – typically the more accessible the system is. However, although clearly recognizing and acknowledging this overlap, there are also – at least for some stakeholders – distinct underlying motivations, which militate in favour of keeping separate my discussion of these two related justifications. For example, governments are typically interested in both saving money by reforming and, at times, outsourcing services (business case justifications) as well as making services more available (access justifications). Private clients, on the other hand, are typically motivated by self-interest (business case justifications), and are less interested – at least in this context – in the collective wellbeing of society (access justifications). And as I discuss later in this part of this chapter, although I strongly believe that lawyers, similar to governments, should be interested in both justifications (given the bargain they have struck with society, in return for self-regulation, to help facilitate access to justice for the members of the communities they serve), there is certainly a fairly strong public sentiment that the preferences of lawyers are driven, at least in large measure, by the self-interests of their clients (I will leave the lawyer jokes to others at this stage). So although sharing the significant animating factor of efficiency, I think of these two overriding justifications for privatization as conceptually distinct.

Business Case for Privatization

Many, if not all, users of and participants in the civil justice system have long been lamenting many of the system's challenges. Those challenges include the glacial pace at which it tends to operate. They include its crushing individual costs (including financial, emotional, reputational, and sometimes physical costs), and its systemic costs. The system's challenges also include its general inaccessibility (often in terms of complexity and comprehension; sometimes in terms of physical availability and openness; sometimes in terms of cultural, racial, language, and other barriers; and very often – again – financially), and its relative inflexibility (in terms of the kinds of remedies that might be available for dealing with litigants' actual interests, broadly put, rather than simply their stated or perceived rights).

To take an important example, on this last criticism of inflexibility, courts can deal, as we have seen,[106] with essentially any right that is at stake in a given case. To the extent that a tort, a contract, a property matter, or an estate issue is raised in a piece of litigation, the courts can understand the claim and craft an appropriate remedy. What courts do not do, and often cannot do, is help parties with issues that are less about legal "rights" and more about what their underlying core "interests" are. For example, when a news organization is sued by a businessperson over allegedly defamatory statements made about that person in the newspaper, often what is at stake is less about the person's actual financial loss and more about his or her business or personal reputational loss. An apology, properly placed in the newspaper, is often what is ultimately at stake in those kinds of cases. Although not entitled to it, as a "right," it is often what the aggrieved party wants (i.e., it is what he or she is really "interested" in). Courts are good at assessing a reasonable amount of "damages" (money) that the newspaper should pay. A solution amounting to forced speech is not typically within courts' jurisdiction as far as remedies are concerned. The courts cannot order the newspaper reporters and editor to look the aggrieved party in the eye and simply say (if this is the case), "We made a mistake, we are very sorry, and we will print a retraction right away." That apology (or similar result), however, is what often gets civil disputes settled by private processes. That is the difference between a remedy based on legal rights

106 See supra Chapter 2.

and a remedy that is extremely attentive to the disputants' interests. ADR processes often provide the informal, flexible, and sometimes supportive environments in which such exchanges can occur and remedies can be crafted. They are good at finding space for peoples' interests. That is what I mean, in this context, by the relative flexibility of ADR processes and the relative inflexibility of traditional litigation processes.[107]

As to criticisms of the traditional system's overall inaccessibility and inflexibility, when looking at alternatives, there is certainly no lack of support for the merits of private justice, from a variety of different stakeholders, especially regarding various forms of mediation and arbitration. For example, when writing about the benefits of mediation, Gary Furlong commented that "litigation, as a process, is often opaque, rigid and lacking 'common sense.'"[108] Mediation, on the other hand, delivers a "'just' and fair process" marked by "transparency, respect, justification, accuracy, and … a meaningful voice and input into the process" for participants.[109] According to George Pavlich, in the context of his research into community-based mediation programs in B.C., some informal mediation alternatives provide the potential to let "silenced voices speak" through "contextually sensitive (informal) dispute resolution settings" and flexible processes "that allow disputants to develop their own settlements" through "local" justice.[110] Further glowing support is often marshaled in favour of arbitration. For example, one recent report stated that a

> widely touted advantage of arbitration is that, unlike in civil litigation where dueling parties are stuck with the judge they're given, parties agreeing to arbitrate can pick the arbitrator or arbitrators who will determine their fate. … "People see how you can get an expert arbitrator deciding your case rather than some random judge who may or may not know anything about the issues in dispute."[111]

---

107 For a discussion of rights and interests in the context of ADR, see Macfarlane, *The New Lawyer: How Settlement is Transforming the Practice of Law*, supra note 60 at 49–54. See also ibid. at 178–81.

108 Gary Furlong, "Mediation Excels in Delivering Sense of Justice to Participants" 28:7 *The Lawyers Weekly* (13 June 2008) 8 at 8.

109 Ibid. at 8.

110 George C. Pavlich, *Justice Fragmented: Mediating Community Disputes under Postmodern Conditions* (London and New York: Routledge, 1996) at 41 [citation omitted].

111 Jennifer McPhee, "Arbitration Becoming the 'New' Civil Litigation" *Canadian Lawyer* (January 2008) 53 at 54 (paraphrasing and quoting Allan Stitt).

As such, according to Allan Stitt (speaking specifically about arbitration), "[p]eople are beginning to see the real benefits of arbitration over the court system."[112]

In addition to anecdotal evidence, there is a growing body of primary and secondary research supporting the merits of ADR (as broadly defined[113]). Specifically, there continues to be a general perception, supported by several empirical studies, that arbitration, mediation, and other privatizing processes can be faster,[114] cheaper,[115] and

---

112 Allan Stitt, quoted in ibid. at 54.

113 Recall my earlier discussion on the general terminology of ADR (supra Chapter 3). Further, as I mentioned earlier in this chapter, because of the relative lack of empirical research in Canada, combined with the similar ADR traditions that have grown up in Canada and elsewhere, international empirical studies (many examples of which are included in this section) are equally relevant to the Canadian context.

114 See, for example, John C. Carson, William C. Graham, and Wayne V. Carson, "Arbitration: The Proof of the Pudding, Results of the Carson / Graham Commercial Arbitration Survey, 1993" (1994) 13:1 *Advocates' Soc. J.* 16; Mark Fellows, "The Same Result as in Court, More Efficiently: Comparing Arbitration And Court Litigation Outcomes" (July 2006) *Metropolitan Corporate Counsel* 32; Harris Interactive, "Arbitration: Simpler, Cheaper, and Faster than Litigation" (April 2005), available online: USCILR <http://www.adrforum.com/rcontrol/documents/ResearchStudiesAndStatistics/2005HarrisPoll.pdf> at 5; Colleen M. Hanycz, "Through the Looking Glass: Mediator Conceptions of Philosophy, Process and Power" (2005) 42 *Alta. L. Rev.* 819 at 828; Lipsky and Seeber, "The Appropriate Resolution of Corporate Disputes: A Report on the Growing Use of ADR by U.S. Corporations," supra note 67 at 17; Shone, "Civil Justice Reform in Canada: 1996 to 2006 and Beyond," supra note 37 at 167; and Robert Hann et al., "Evaluation of the Ontario Mandatory Mediation Program (Rule 24.1): Executive Summary and Recommendations" (Ontario: Queen's Printer, 12 March 2001), available online: Government of Ontario <http://www.attorneygeneral.jus.gov.on.ca/english/courts/manmed/exec_summary_recommend.pdf>.

115 See, for example, Carson, Graham, and Carson, "Arbitration: The Proof of the Pudding, Results of the Carson / Graham Commercial Arbitration Survey, 1993," supra note 114; Thomas J. Stipanowich, "ADR and the 'Vanishing Trial': The Growth and Impact of 'Alternative Dispute Resolution'" (2004) 1:3 *J. of Emp. Legal Stud.* 843; and Hanycz, "Through the Looking Glass: Mediator Conceptions of Philosophy, Process and Power," supra note 114 at 828. See further Jackson Williams, "The Costs of Arbitration" (April 2002), available online: Public Citizen <http://www.citizen.org/documents/ACF110A.pdf>; Lipsky and Seeber, "The Appropriate Resolution of Corporate Disputes: A Report on the Growing Use of ADR by U.S. Corporations," supra note 67 at 17; Harris Interactive, "Arbitration: Simpler, Cheaper, and Faster Than Litigation," supra note 114 at 5; Shone, "Civil Justice Reform in Canada: 1996 to 2006 and Beyond," supra note 37 at 167; Hann et al., "Evaluation of the Ontario Mandatory Mediation Program (Rule 24.1): Executive Summary and Recommendations," supra note 114. For a recent review of literature relating to the cost of civil

simpler[116] than traditional court processes.[117] For instance, according to a 2005 study of approximately 600 individuals in the United States, arbitration was "widely" seen as faster (74 per cent), cheaper (51 per cent), and simpler (63 per cent) than was going to court.[118] Further reports indicate a general satisfaction with arbitration and other ADR processes and results.[119] In addition, several other benefits are also cited,

---

justice, see CFCJ, "What Does it Cost to Access Justice in Canada? How Much Is 'Too Much'? And How Do We Know?" (Literature Review) (31 August 2009) [unpublished, archived with author]. As I argue further below, more research on the topic of the cost of justice is clearly needed.

116 See, for example, Lott, Beaulieu, and Desforges, "Mandatory Arbitration and Consumer Contracts," supra note 76; Harris Interactive, "Arbitration: Simpler, Cheaper, and Faster Than Litigation," supra note 114 at 5; Stipanowich, "ADR and the 'Vanishing Trial': The Growth and Impact of 'Alternative Dispute Resolution'," supra note 115; and Hanycz, "Through the Looking Glass: Mediator Conceptions of Philosophy, Process and Power," supra note 114 at 828.

117 For a recent overview and critique of empirical studies and ADR, see Carrie Menkel-Meadow, "Dispute Resolution" in Peter Cane and Herbert M. Kritzer, eds., *Oxford Handbook of Empirical Legal Research* (Oxford, UK: Oxford University Press, 2010), 596, available online: SSRN <http://papers.ssrn.com/sol3/papers.cfm?abstract_id=1485563>.

118 See, for example, Harris Interactive, "Arbitration: Simpler, Cheaper, and Faster Than Litigation," supra note 114 at 5.

119 See, for example, Lipsky and Seeber, "The Appropriate Resolution of Corporate Disputes: A Report on the Growing Use of ADR by U.S. Corporations," supra note 67 at 17. See further Thomas J. Stipanowich, "Beyond Arbitration: Innovation and Evolution in the United States Construction Industry," supra note 75; Ernst & Young, "Outcomes of Arbitration: An Empirical Study of Consumer Lending Cases," supra note 76; Harris Interactive, "Arbitration: Simpler, Cheaper, and Faster Than Litigation," supra note 114 at 22–4, 27–9; Roselle L. Wissler, "Court-Connected Mediation in General Civil Cases: What We Know from Empirical Research" (2002) 17:3 *Ohio St. J. Disp. Resol.* 641; Michael A. Perino, "Report to the Securities and Exchange Commission Regarding Arbitrator Conflict Disclosure Requirements in NASD and NYSE Securities Arbitrations" (4 November 2005), available online: SEC <http://www.sec.gov/pdf/arbconflict.pdf>; Hanycz, "Through the Looking Glass: Mediator Conceptions of Philosophy, Process and Power," supra note 114 at 828; Kathy Mack, *Court Referral to ADR: Criteria and Research* (Melbourne: Australian Institute of Judicial Administration Incorporated and the National Dispute Resolution Advisory Council, 2003); Philip Bryden and William Black, "Mediation as a Tool for Resolving Human Rights Disputes: An Evaluation of the B.C. Human Rights Commission's Early Mediation Project" (2004) 37 *U.B.C. L. Rev.* 73; Bobbi McAdoo, "All Rise, the Court Is in Session: What Judges Say about Court-Connected Mediation" (2007) 22:2 *Ohio St. J. Disp. Resol.* 377; Hann et al., "Evaluation of the Ontario Mandatory Mediation Program (Rule 24.1): Executive

including the ability to tailor flexible outcomes (discussed earlier), increased voluntary compliance with results, freedom to choose laws and processes (all of which typically increase flexibility and predictability), and, of course, protection from public scrutiny through rules of privacy and confidentiality.[120] Finally, particularly from the systemic, supply side, the reduction of backlogs and costs, together with increased access for consumers of the system (discussed again further below) are also cited as benefits of ADR processes.[121]

In addition to these various generic advantages, there is also evidence of sector specific benefits. For example, again when looking at the

---

Summary and Recommendations," supra note 114; and Roselle L. Wissler, "The Effectiveness of Court-Connected Dispute Resolution in Civil Cases" (2004) 22 *Confl. Resol. Q.* 55 at 65–6.

120 See Trevor C.W. Farrow, "Public Justice, Private Dispute Resolution and Democracy" in Ronalda Murphy and Patrick A. Molinari, eds., *Doing Justice: Dispute Resolution in the Courts and Beyond* (Montréal: Canadian Institute for the Administration of Justice, 2009) 301 at 339; and Trevor C.W. Farrow, "Privatizing our Public Civil Justice System" (2006) 9 *News & Views on Civ. Just. Reform* 16 at 16. See also Andrew Pirie, "Critiques of Settlement Advocacy" in *The Theory and Practice of Representative Negotiation*, supra note 59 at c. 11, pp. 292–3, citing S.B. Goldberg, Frank E.A. Sander, and N.H. Rogers, *Dispute Resolution: Negotiation, Mediation, and Other Processes* (New York: Aspen Law and Business, 1999) at 8; and Randy A. Pepper, "Why Arbitrate?: Ontario's Recent Experience with Commercial Arbitration" (1998) 36:4 *Osgoode Hall L.J.* 807. See further my earlier discussion on privacy, confidentiality, and privilege in the context of ADR and related processes (supra Chapter 3).

121 See, for example, Farrow, "Public Justice, Private Dispute Resolution and Democracy" in Murphy and Molinari, eds., *Doing Justice: Dispute Resolution in the Courts and Beyond*, supra note 120 at 339. For example, in a recent discussion, George Adams commented:

> Fortunately, courts resolve only a small fraction of the disputes that are brought to their attention. ... In North America, only 3% to 5% of all civil cases filed proceed to trial. The vast majority are withdrawn or resolved through negotiated settlements or as a result of other settlement procedures. If this activity is to be considered private, there is clearly a public interest in it taking place.

George W. Adams, "The Privatization of Justice: Where Are We Going?" in Murphy and Molinari, eds., *Doing Justice: Dispute Resolution in the Courts and Beyond*, supra note 120 at 163. See also Christopher R. Drahozal and Samantha Zyontz, "An Empirical Study of AAA Consumer Arbitrations" (2009), available online: SSRN <http://papers.ssrn.com/sol3/papers.cfm?abstract_id=1365435>.

area of consumer law that I discussed previously, arbitration and other forms of non-court-based dispute resolution processes have been and continue to be used in many consumer contracts.[122] The reason, according to one Alberta legislator in the context of reforms to that province's fair trading regime, is familiar: "Both business and consumers told us that the court system for resolving disputes is crowded, cumbersome, and expensive."[123] By including dispute resolution clauses in contracts, parties can in effect contract out of the public court system and into a system of ADR. That ADR system is largely private and confidential, it is often seen to be more predictable (at least in terms of control over the choice of timing, rules and who the decision maker will be, etc.), and it is often considered to be more efficient. Arbitration and other ADR processes are also, as was discussed, often used in the consumer context as a form of class action risk management strategy (which is part of the predictability argument in favour of ADR).[124]

Earlier in this chapter, I discussed the privatizing preferences and influences of various justice system stakeholders, including governments, judges, lawyers, clients, and law schools. Clearly those stakeholders come at disputes and dispute resolution processes from different perspectives and for different reasons. However, there is a common thread that generally links the various justifications set out above with these various stakeholders, which is the "business case" justification for privatization. Put simply and very roughly: people typically want an efficient process that is (at least relatively) simple, cheap, and fast. That sensibility was certainly the case in the context of the legislative debates, just mentioned, which animated Alberta's reforms to its fair trading regime.[125] Other examples from legislative debates, along these lines, are discussed below, which provide additional evidence that it

---

122 For a general study, see Lott, Beaulieu, and Desforges, "Mandatory Arbitration and Consumer Contracts," supra note 76. See further Ernst & Young, "Outcomes of Arbitration: An Empirical Study of Consumer Lending Cases," supra note 76.

123 Alberta, Legislative Assembly, *Official Report of Debates (Hansard)* (2 March 1998) at 634 (Hon. Mr. Ducharme).

124 See, for example, Andrew D. Borrell, "Arbitration and Choice of Law Provisions as Class Action Risk Management Tools" (April 2002), available online: Fasken Martineau DuMoulin LLP <http://www.fasken.com/arbitration-and-choice-of-law-provisions-as-class-action-risk-management-tools-04-26-2002/>.

125 Alberta, Legislative Assembly, *Official Report of Debates (Hansard)* (2 March 1998) at 634 (Hon. Mr. Ducharme), supra note 123. See *Fair Trading Act*, supra note 86, which provides that "[d]espite any provision of this Act, neither a consumer nor the Director may commence or maintain an action or appeal under sections 13 to 15

Table 5.4. Moderate to critical factors for recommending arbitration

Factor	Lawyers (%)
Expertise of the arbitrator	90.91
Privacy	88.89
Reduces time	83.97
Greater control over procedure (simplification)	82.58
Fairness of the result	71.05
Finality of the decision	65.14
Reduces cost	62.83
Allows for a more amiable resolution	53.89
Avoids discovery	47.37
Encourages settlement	46.75
Allows parties to choose applicable law	37.50

is largely a business case analysis that, at least in large measure (in addition to the "access to justice" case that I discuss further below in this chapter) animates much of the government justifications for pursuing privatized initiatives in the civil justice and related sectors.[126]

Further, in addition to public sector preferences, there are clearly significant private interests at stake here as well, as I also discussed earlier in this chapter (which are at least in part driving those government choices). For example, as we saw, it has become very clear that clients and their lawyers, engaged in all sorts of different aspects of the civil justice system, are increasingly leaning towards private process initiatives. The views of the lawyers that I surveyed for the purpose of this book[127] with respect to the justifications for why they recommend (or do not recommend) ADR are largely in line with much of the earlier available anecdotal evidence and research.[128] For example, in the context of considering whether to recommend arbitration to their clients, Table 5.4 sets out the percentages of litigation lawyers who found the

if the consumer's cause of action under those sections is based on a matter that the consumer has agreed in writing to submit to arbitration and the arbitration agreement governing the arbitration has been approved by the Minister." Sections 13 to 15 deal with court actions brought by consumers as well as by the director of Fair Trading on behalf of consumers.

126 See, for example, Manitoba, Legislative Assembly, *Official Report of Debates (Hansard)*, 36th Leg., 3d sess., No. 59, Orders of the Day (11 June 1997) at 1520 (Hon. Gord Mackintosh); British Columbia, Legislative Assembly, *Hansard*, Vol. 25, No. 15 (18 May 2004) at 11192 (Hon. G. Plant).

127 See Farrow, "National Alternative Dispute Resolution Survey (2008)," supra note 61 and accompanying text and tables.

128 See, for example, supra notes 108–112 and accompanying text.

Table 5.5. Moderate to critical factors for recommending mediation

Factor	Lawyers (%)
Encourages settlement	96.95
Allows the parties to resolve the dispute	95.12
Reduces cost	93.37
Allows for a more amiable resolution	90.91
Reduces time	90.42
Expertise of the mediator	81.82
Privacy	79.27
Greater control over procedure (simplification)	78.89
Fairness of the result	71.16
Avoids discovery	55.21

justificatory factors canvassed in the survey to be of "moderate" (3) to "critical" (5) importance (on a 1–5 scale).[129]

In the responses, by far the two most important factors were seen as arbitrator expertise (90.91 per cent) and privacy (88.89 per cent). Interestingly, although a significant percentage of lawyers certainly saw a reduction in time as of moderate to critical importance (83.97 per cent), other factors – including arbitrator expertise (90.91 per cent), privacy (88.89 per cent), control (82.58 per cent), fairness (71.05 per cent), and finality (65.14 per cent) – were of more importance than was a reduction in cost (62.83 per cent). My sense of the primary reason for the relative "unimportance" of cost (it was obviously still important, just not *as* important as the other factors) is that of the lawyers who responded to the survey, many of them, based on their various stated practice areas, appear to act for larger, institutional clients or for clients who, again as a relative matter, are able to finance the various dispute resolution processes at issue. In the context of considering whether or not to recommend mediation to their clients, Table 5.5 sets out the percentages of respondents who found the justificatory factors canvassed in the survey to be of "moderate" (3) to "critical" (5) importance (again on a 1–5 scale).[130]

129 The specific survey question (question 4) was "Please rate the following factors on their importance to you when recommending whether to use arbitration to resolve a dispute." For survey responses to the reverse question (question 6) – "when you refrain from recommending arbitration to resolve a dispute, how important are the following factors?" – see Farrow, "National Alternative Dispute Resolution Survey (2008)," supra note 61.

130 The specific survey question (question 10) was: "Please rate the following factors on their importance to you when recommending whether to use mediation to resolve

Table 5.6. Lawyers recommending arbitration "sometimes or always"

Type of Dispute	Lawyers (%)
Company working with client (e.g. supplier)	89.26
Competitor	80.95
Other	72.98
Employee	66.66
Consumer	59.59

It is here, with mediation, where the more typical and oft-cited general ADR justifications really played out. The most important factors were encourages settlement (96.95 per cent), allows parties to resolve the dispute (facilitate consensus-style rather than command-style dispute resolution; 95.12 per cent), reduces cost (93.37 per cent), allows for more amiable resolutions (90.91 per cent), and reduces time (90.42 per cent).

Although the responses set out in Tables 5.4 and 5.5 give us a very good overall sense of the relative importance of various factors that motivate arbitration and mediation procedural advice and preferences among Canadian litigation lawyers, there is no doubt, based on the survey results, that specific dispute contexts are also important factors. Put simply, it matters in what business or other sector(s) a client operates, whether there is an underlying regulatory or other relevant external context, who the parties are, and what particular process is involved. For example, in the context of this discussion and according to the lawyers who responded to the survey, various factors that are often external to a dispute – including legislation, client needs, contractual requirements, court mandates, suggestions by opposing parties, client policies, and other ad hoc factors – all have different degrees of influence in terms of how often the various factors prompt lawyers to recommend arbitration.[131] Similar external factors influenced the lawyers' thinking in terms of how often they prompt the lawyers to recommend mediation.[132]

a dispute." For survey responses to the reverse question (question 12) – "When you refrain from recommending mediation to resolve a dispute, how important are the following factors?" – see Farrow, "National Alternative Dispute Resolution Survey (2008)," ibid.

131 See question 3 in ibid.

132 See question 9 in ibid.

Equally important, again according to the survey results, is the nature of the particular conflict.[133] For example, as set out in Table 5.6, the percentage of lawyers who would either "sometimes" or "always" recommend arbitration differed depending on the type of dispute in issue.[134]

Lawyers are much more likely to recommend arbitration for a dispute with a supplier (89.26 per cent) or a competitor (80.95 per cent) than they are for a dispute with an employee (66.66 per cent) or a consumer (59.59 per cent). This makes particular sense when one thinks of the kinds of ongoing relationships that are typically at stake with employers and employees. It is often easier to face an employee on Monday morning after a dispute has been resolved if the parties were somehow able to come to some kind of private resolution, rather than having a court impose a remedy on the situation only after a protracted public litigation battle.[135] The results with respect to disputes with consumers are less intuitive. There is often a preference among consumer industry providers to avoid significant lawsuits, including class action lawsuits, by employing ADR provisions and no-class action provisions in pre-dispute contractual arrangements. The *Dell* case is an example of such a situation.[136] In order to avoid major consumer tort claims, including class action proceedings, producers and service providers in the consumer sector have been actively using ADR clauses for some time.[137] As I discussed earlier, however, recent

133 For a brief note on conflict theory, together with some selected sources, see supra Chapter 1.

134 See question 5 in Farrow, "National Alternative Dispute Resolution Survey (2008)," supra note 61.

135 Having been involved – as a litigator – in both scenarios, I can say with first-hand experience that an ADR process in the employment law context can often make a significant difference in terms of salvaging some kind of ongoing relationship.

136 See *Dell Computer Corp. v. Union des consommateurs*, supra note 77, discussed further supra Chapter 4.

137 For a discussion of ADR clauses and class actions, see Myriam Gillies, "Opting Out of Liability: The Forthcoming, Near-Total Demise of the Modern Class Action" (2005) 104 *Mich. L. Rev.* 373. For further research on the issues of arbitration, consumer contracts and class actions (and access to justice), see, for example, Jonnette Watson Hamilton, "Pre-Dispute Consumer Arbitration Clauses: Denying Access to Justice?" (2006) 51 *McGill L.J.* 693; Geneviève Saumier, "Consumer Arbitration in the Evolving Canadian Landscape" (2008–9) 113 *Penn. St. L. Rev.* 1203; Geneviève Saumier, "Consumer Dispute Resolution: The Evolving Canadian Landscape," supra note 76; Shelley McGill, "The Conflict between Consumer Class Actions and Contractual Arbitration Clauses" (2006) 43:3 *Can. Bus. L.J.* 359; Shelley McGill, "Consumer Arbitration and Class Actions: The Impact of *Dell Computer Corp. v. Union des*

Table 5.7. Lawyers recommending mediation "sometimes or always"

Type of Dispute	Lawyers (%)
Company working with client (e.g. supplier)	89.31
Employee	83.85
Competitor	80.63
Consumer	80.63
Other	69.74

Table 5.8. Lawyers recommending dispute resolution clauses "sometimes or always"

Types of Parties	Lawyers (%)
Business	70.70
Employee	57.05
Consumer	52.35
Other	47.92

statutory amendments have an impact on the ability of goods and service providers to control some suits against them by consumers in this way.[138]

Similarly, according to Table 5.7, the percentage of lawyers who would either "sometimes" or "always" recommend mediation differed depending on the type of dispute in issue.[139]

Although all categories scored fairly highly, lawyers are more likely to recommend mediation for a dispute involving a supplier (89.31) than they are for a dispute involving a competitor (80.63) or a consumer (80.63). Again, ongoing relationships often play a significant factor here.

As is clear from Table 5.8, the types of parties at issue similarly have a significant impact on the percentage of lawyers who "sometimes" or "always" recommend various kinds of dispute resolution clauses.[140]

---

consommateurs" (2007) 45:3 *Can. Bus. L.J.* 334; Shelley McGill, "Consumer Arbitration Clause Enforcement: A Balanced Legislative Response" (2010) 47 *Am. Bus. L.J.* 361; and Jasminka Kalajdzic, "Consumer (In)Justice: Reflections on Canadian Consumer Class Actions" (2010) 50 *Can. Bus. L.J.* 356.

138 In addition to earlier comments in this chapter, see further supra Chapter 4, and infra Chapter 6. See also generally *Seidel v. Telus Communications Inc.*, supra note 83 (discussed further, for example, supra Chapter 4).

139 See question 11 in Farrow, "National Alternative Dispute Resolution Survey (2008)," supra note 61.

140 See questions 14 and 15 in ibid.

Notwithstanding the important factor of the type of dispute at issue, the survey results for both arbitration and mediation confirm significant support for the proposition that lawyers, on behalf of their clients, are actively recommending ADR processes in various disputing contexts (see Tables 5.6–5.7). Similarly, they are also actively recommending that clients include dispute resolution clauses in their contractual arrangements in order to ensure that those arrangements can be governed by, if disputed, the merits of private justice (see Table 5.8).

In addition to providing a relatively current window onto the ADR preferences of Canadian litigation lawyers, which – as well as assisting with this study – I hope will be useful for future conflict and conflict resolution thinking, this survey strengthens our understanding of the underlying justifications that animate the business case for privatization. Certainly, efficiency plays a factor, particularly when we look at responses that favour the cost and time savings of ADR processes. In addition, other factors that militate in favour of a client's "business" interests – privacy, flexibility, choice, and so on – are all present in the justifications that were articulated by the lawyers who responded to the survey.

Further, as will become clear with my arguments in Chapter 7, the fact that ADR preferences and choices differ depending on the nature and context of the dispute as well as the parties involved (as evidenced by the survey results in Tables 5.6–5.8) opens further possibilities for potentially being more nuanced in the way we think about how we resolve those disputes. Finally, by way of a cautionary conclusion to the discussion of the survey here, it is important to recognize, as I also discuss further in Chapter 6, that not everyone accepts the benefits of ADR. Many clearly do, as evidenced here in the survey results as well as in the context of other ADR research discussed in this book (often, although certainly not in the case of my survey, without any empirical basis or understanding of the underlying context).[141] However, not all commentators or practitioners see the benefits, nor do all studies support the merits of ADR (at least not in all circumstances).[142]

---

141 See, for example, supra notes 114–22 and accompanying text.

142 See, for example, Julius Melnitzer, "Arbitration Becomes More Like Litigation" *Law Times* (10 October 2011), available online: Law Times <http://www.lawtimesnews.com/Focus-On/Arbitration-becomes-more-like-litigation>; Daryl-Lynn Carlson, "Arbitrations versus Court" *Law Times* (20 April 2009); Mary Swanton, "System Slowdown: Can Arbitration be Fixed?" *InsideCounsel* (May 2007) 50. See further infra Chapter 6.

Business Case and Efficiency

A central underlying theme of many of the benefits of ADR (identified with the business case for privatization) sounds in the principle of efficiency, which has come essentially to define the modern discourse surrounding our civil justice systems and their reform. It also is, as we saw earlier and as I discuss again below, the siren call for modern trends towards privatization of all flavours, including the privatization of the civil justice system.[143] Recently, according to Marcel Storme, efforts to make civil procedure more "efficient" are "everywhere."[144] More fully, according to Héctor Fix-Fierro,

> [E]fficiency … has penetrated the legal and judicial systems at all levels and dimensions, from the level of society as a whole to the day-to-day operation of the judicial process, from the institutional role performed by adjudication in society to the organisational context of judicial decisions. … In other words: far from being an alien value with respect to the legal and judicial process, efficiency has simply become an inseparable part of the structure of expectations we address to the legal system.[145]

This efficiency-based argument, in the context of civil dispute resolution processes, essentially provides that dispute resolution is really no different than any other good or service. To the extent that we need a good or a service, all things being equal, we are typically willing to pay for it, at least on a basis that fits with our economic and other capacities and preferences. To the extent that there are options available (a factor that typically increases choice and decreases price), then so much the better. And when access to, and bargaining power within a given market are of relative parity, possibilities for optimal – or at least relatively acceptable – outcomes or solutions typically are realized. As far as dispute resolution is concerned, again as the argument goes, why should

143 See generally supra Chapter 3.

144 Marcel Storme, "Le Common Law / Civil Law Divide: An Introduction" in Janet Walker & Oscar G. Chase, eds., *Common Law, Civil Law and the Future of Categories* (Markham: LexisNexis, 2010) 23 at 25 (citing Mirjan Damaška).

145 Héctor Fix-Fierro, *Courts, Justice and Efficiency: A Socio-Legal Study of Economic Rationality in Adjudication* (Oxford, UK, and Portland, OR: Hart Publishing, 2003) at 235 [footnote omitted]. Note, however, that Fix-Fierro further comments that "economic rationality is not, and should not necessarily be, the prevalent value or the overriding concern in the context of legal decision-making." Ibid.

there not be a private market, and further, why should such a market operate significantly differently from any other market?[146]

Strong support for an efficiency-based argument for privatization comes from Gillian Hadfield. She provides a case for the privatization of law – particularly commercial law – in the overall spirit of "significantly decreasing the cost of law."[147] Hadfield – although recognizing that the justice system plays several important public roles in our modern democracies, including protecting "individual rights" – argues that when it comes to commercial law, the state should download, privatize, much of its dispute resolution functions. According to Hadfield, "the legal system ... performs important economic functions such as providing the structure and regulation necessary for the operation of efficient markets. The economic sphere of law regularly deals with relationships that involve only corporate entities. Private legal regimes could provide this law without raising legitimacy concerns."[148] Hadfield summarizes the basis for her argument as follows:

> The rules we want in these interactions [involving corporate entities] are the rules that promote and facilitate efficient market relationships between

146 As I have summarized this basic efficiency argument elsewhere,

> When a dispute involves the private rights of A v. B, and further, when two "consenting adults" (including corporations) have chosen to move their dispute off the busy docket of our public court system and into the private boardroom of an arbitrator or mediator, current views suggest that justice is being served. The argument is that the resolution of disputes – like other goods and services – should not be deprived of the benefits of freedom of movement and contract in an efficiency-seeking, innovative and expanding market economy.

See Farrow, "Privatizing our Public Civil Justice System," supra note 120 at 16. For a further discussion of ADR's purported efficiencies, see Fix-Fierro, *Courts, Justice and Efficiency*, supra note 145 at 123–5, 131–5. See also Colleen M. Hanycz, "More Access to Less Justice: Efficiency, Proportionality and Costs in Canadian Civil Justice Reform" (2008) 27 *C.J.Q.* 98. For a further discussion of dispute resolution processes that draws largely on the language of markets, see Maurits Barendrecht, "Understanding the Market for Justice" (2009), Tilburg University Legal Studies Working Paper No. 009/2009, available online: SSRN <http://papers.ssrn.com/sol3/papers.cfm?abstract_id=1416841>.

147 Gillian K. Hadfield, "Privatizing Commercial Law" (2001) 42:1 *Regulation* 40 at 40, available online: Cato Institute <http://object.cato.org/sites/cato.org/files/serials/files/regulation/2001/4/hadfield.pdf>. See also, for example, Gillian K. Hadfield and Eric Talley, "On Public versus Private Provision of Corporate Law" (2006) 22:2 *J.L. Econ. & Org.* 414; and Gillian K. Hadfield, "Exploring Economic and

> corporations. *In this setting, we are not interested in what is fair or just between two corporations; we are interested in what makes their economic relationship as productive and valuable as possible.* That goal suggests the need to look for ways to increase the role of markets in the process of developing and administering the legal regimes that govern the relationships between corporate entities.[149]

Put simply, Hadfield's argument set out earlier rests essentially on four points: corporate relationships are different than relationships involving "individual rights"; we need not be interested in the fairness of corporate relationships; cost reduction can be achieved through efficiency-seeking private dispute resolution mechanisms; and we should ultimately be guided by principles of efficiency – not what is "fair or just" – when making fundamental procedural policy choices in the context of commercial dispute resolution.[150]

To sustain this elegant, although ultimately problematic argument (as I discuss later[151]), Hadfield is guided by a fundamental process of categorization or distinction making. In order to make her case for the privatization of commercial law, Hadfield distinguishes between what she calls the "democratic function" of law and its "market function."[152] The "democratic function" of law "protects rights, structures the institutions of democratic governance, redistributes wealth, promotes social objectives such as equality or clean air, and resolves disputes among citizens."[153] The "market function" of law "provides the structure of markets – determining property rights, providing a means of

---

Democratic Theories of Litigation: Differences between Individual and Organizational Litigants in the Disposition of Federal Civil Cases" (2005) 57 *Stan. L. Rev.* 1275. For other efficiency-based arguments, see, for example, Richard Posner and William Landes, "Adjudication as a Private Good" (1979) 8 *J. Legal Stud.* 235; and Maurits Barendrecht and Berend R. de Vries, "Fitting the Forum to the Fuss with Sticky Defaults: Failure in the Market for Dispute Resolution Services?" (2005) 7 *Cardozo J. Confl. Resol.* 83. For further comments, see Richard A. Posner, *The Federal Courts: Challenge and Reform* (Cambridge, MA: Harvard University Press, 1985) c. 7.

148 Hadfield, "Privatizing Commercial Law," supra note 147 at 40.

149 Ibid. [emphasis added]. Not only does Hadfield contemplate the privatization of the procedural aspects of corporate dispute resolution, she also advocates for the privatization of substantive corporate law development. See ibid. at 41.

150 Ibid. at 40.

151 See generally infra Chapters 6 and 7.

152 Gillian K. Hadfield, "Privatizing Commercial Law: Lessons From ICANN" (2002) 6 *J. Small & Emerging Bus. L.* 258 at 263.

153 Ibid.

commitment through contract to support cooperative activity – and regulation to correct market failures in the achievement of efficiency."[154] For Hadfield, the "democratic function" of law "is one that must be accomplished through public institutions, accountable to the polity in order to preserve democratic legitimacy."[155] The "market function" of law "is a service – an input into the organization of transactions in markets" and, according to Hadfield, "is not so clearly a function that cannot be privatized."[156] The ultimate arbiter, for Hadfield, about whether the "democratic" or "market" function of law obtains in a given situation is which aspect of the "public interest" a given situation engages. Put simply, the distinction between the functions of law "rests not in the substance of a law per se, but rather more fundamentally in the public interest at stake in a given instance of law."[157] Law in its "market function" invokes "only a public interest in efficiency – creating wealth and maximizing the value of resources."[158] Law in its "democratic function" engages "any other value – redistribution, equality, autonomy, environmental preservation, public safety, human flourishing, participation, and so on."[159] To the extent that the functions of law, particularly in the context of dispute resolution, can be categorized and compartmentalized according to market or democratic aspects, then Hadfield's approach offers an intriguing way of sorting through what situations require the investment of the state's public system and what situations could be dealt with, more efficiently, through some form of private alternative. The problem, as I argue more fully in Chapter 7, is that there are very few functions of law that engage only a "public interest in efficiency." Almost all efficiency seeking situations, stereotypically (although not exclusively) involving corporate and commercial transactions, also engage issues of "redistribution," "autonomy," "participation," and so on.

Similar calls for privatizing the state's provision of public civil justice services come from Bryan Caplan and Edward Stringham.[160] Citing examples and studies that highlight high civil settlement rates

154 Ibid.
155 Ibid.
156 Ibid.
157 Ibid.
158 Ibid. [emphasis omitted].
159 Ibid. [emphasis omitted].
160 See Bryan Caplan and Edward P. Stringham, "Privatizing the Adjudication of Disputes" (2008) 9 *Theor. Inq. L.* 503.

and corporate preferences for arbitration, Caplan and Stringham ask, "Could private legal systems expand so that they continue to dismantle the near-monopoly of law that most governments possess?" In response to their own question, the authors argue that yes, a privatized system of justice, founded largely on economic principles of efficiency, could likely provide a superior system of dispute resolution. In the authors' own words, with a particular focus on the adjudication of disputes, they argue that "privatization of this area could occur with little difficulty."[161] The authors further argue that "if the government stopped interfering with people's voluntarily [chosen] ... [dispute resolution] contracts, a system of de facto privatization could come about. Even if the public courts continue to be subsidized with tax dollars ..., deregulated arbitrators might be in a position to outcompete public courts."[162] The tool by which the authors criticize the public court system and advocate for a private system is "economics."[163] Many of the economic benefits cited for private courts include, according to these authors, more "efficiently ration[ed] judicial services," flexibility that is responsive to the "different needs" of consumers, and, finally, what the authors call the "most impressive arguments for privatizing dispute resolution," which they acknowledge involve "the standard arguments for the prima facie superiority of private over public supply." Those arguments include the authors' views that "public bodies have no incentive to be efficient, and private ones do" and that "public bodies usually do not know what is efficient, while private bodies ... know better."[164]

All of these accounts are also in line with Richard Susskind's vision of lawyers and the legal system.[165] Susskind, who draws "heavily" on "information economists,"[166] essentially sees the future of legal services as a series of systems, information packages, and commodities.[167] According to Susskind's blunt and purposely provocative account, "the court system can be regarded, in large part, as a huge information system – an entity that receives, processes, stores, creates, monitors, and disseminates large quantities of documents and information."[168]

161 Ibid. at 508.
162 Ibid.
163 Ibid. at 510.
164 Ibid. at 518–9.
165 Susskind, *The End of Lawyers? Rethinking the Nature of Legal Services*, supra note 64.
166 Ibid. at 37.
167 Ibid. at cc. 2 and 6 (see, for example, p. 270).
168 Ibid. at 201.

It is his instrumental view of the judicial system that allows Susskind to muse about the possibility of "computers replacing judges" for non-"hard cases": those that do not involve "complex issues of principle, policy, and morality."[169] Beyond debt collection cases, nuisance cases, and the like, I wonder what those non-"hard cases" would actually look like. Many important policy issues lurk behind the façade of fights over contracts and property.[170] I return to this point later in the book.[171] Susskind's account is driven, in the end, by notions of "market ... efficiencies."[172] Like Hadfield and others, he sees the provision of law and legal services primarily in terms of systems, commodities and opportunities for increased efficiencies. He also thinks of the court more as a "service" than as a "place."[173]

In Chapter 3, in the context of my discussion of the basic underpinnings of the current privatization movement that forms an underlying context for essentially all of the issues raised in this book, I highlighted the specific connection between privatization and efficiency. Although other factors are relevant, efficiency is clearly the anchor of the privatization movement. In light of my earlier comments (which are more fully developed in Chapter 7), the arguments made by Hadfield, as well as those made by Caplan, Stringham, and Susskind, provide quintessential examples of the business case for privatization. Efficiency is the key criterion by which a dispute resolution system is judged.[174] Again

---

169 Ibid. at 217. But see ibid. at 274, where Susskind acknowledges that with respect to the work of barristers, which is "highly bespoke," it is "hard to see how oral advocacy and the dispensing of expert advice can be standardized or computerized."

170 For example, the ways in which commercial dealings and relationships are formed, maintained, and dismantled; how property is owned, leased, sold, and recovered; and so on, are all issues of fundamental interest – directly or indirectly – to most people in society. I acknowledge that Susskind's thesis is not simply about replacing legal work with computers, and that his musings about computers and judging must be put in the context of his overall arguments about "standardization, commoditization, and the transfer of many legal tasks from lawyers to non-lawyers." See ibid. at 274.

171 See generally infra Chapters 6 and 7.

172 See, for example, Susskind, *The End of Lawyers?*, supra note 64 at 270. See also ibid. at 237.

173 Ibid. at 218.

174 As I will discuss further in Chapter 7, efficiency considerations are key underlying components (along with access to justice concerns) that animate the proportionality considerations that are increasingly taking hold in civil justice reform initiatives.

put simply, according to Hadfield, efficiency trumps essentially all else, including what is "fair or just" as between two disputing corporate entities. On this reading, efficiency trumps justice – an argument to which I also return later on.[175]

Additional support for this kind of very strong, efficiency-based argument, particularly for corporations, comes from the legislative context. For example, the arguments for mandatory arbitration in some commercial contexts that were made leading up to amendments to Manitoba's arbitration legislation, discussed earlier, resonate strongly with the arguments advanced by Hadfield, Caplan, and Stringham.[176] Central to these approaches is an understanding of ADR's potential impact on reducing costs for both the private user and the public provider. Other key elements of the business case justification are speed, informality, flexibility, accessibility, and privacy[177] (all of which were raised in my lawyer survey). Based on these merits, proponents of privatization argue for increased use, as well as in some cases mandating the use of arbitration (and potentially other alternatives), all, in the end, in the name of the efficient use of limited public resources.[178]

A further public policy–based example of an argument that supports the business case for privatization comes from the report of the Institute of Law Research and Reform (ILRR; now the Alberta Law Reform Institute [ALRI]) in the context of the 1988 discussions surrounding the proposals for a then-new arbitration statute in Alberta.[179] As with a number of major preferences and influences that drove the enactment of most, if not all, provincial arbitration statutes (including Alberta's) that sounded in arguments of efficiency, flexibility, predictability and overall market efficiency,[180] it is clear that the ILRR was of the view that flexibility and choice, in the end, should prevail, even if it allowed

175 See infra Chapter 7.

176 See Manitoba, Legislative Assembly, *Official Report of Debates (Hansard)*, 36th Leg., 3d sess., No. 59, Orders of the Day (11 June 1997) at 1520 (Hon. Gord Mackintosh), discussed supra Chapter 4.

177 See, for example, ibid.

178 See, for example, ibid.

179 See ILRR, *Proposals for a New Alberta Arbitration Act*, Report No. 51 (Edmonton: ILRR, October 1988), available online: ALRI <http://www.law.ualberta.ca/alri/docs/fr51.pdf>.

180 See, for example, supra Chapter 4.

parties to dispense with law.[181] The reason the ILRR could say this, however, in addition to its clear preference for encouraging he efficiency aspects of arbitration legislation, was because it held the view that "there does not seem to be any public interest which will be injured if parties agree to dispense with law."[182] If adjudication were exclusively about dispute resolution, then, particularly in the confines of some private commercial or other cases, this statement might be justifiable. However, as I discussed in Chapter 2, adjudication is about much more than simply dispute resolution. I come back to this point below, and again in Chapter 6.

There is no doubt, generally, that saving time, money, relationships and reputations, while at the same time increasing flexibility, choice and market efficiencies, are all typically good things – for both consumers and providers. If one-off dispute resolution statistics and results were the only relevant factors by which to measure a dispute resolution regime, particularly involving private corporate entities, the discussion in this book would essentially be over. Unfortunately, this narrow, often litigant-based perspective is what currently drives much of our dispute resolution reform thinking and choices.[183] The problem,

---

181 According to the ILRR report,

> Occasionally, someone may want an arbitral tribunal which does not have to follow the law. The Model Law accommodates such wishes by providing that an arbitral tribunal "shall decide *ex aequo et bono* or as *amiable compositeur* only if the parties have expressly authorized it to do so," which makes it clear that they can so authorize it. Section 28 is not one of the provisions listed in section 4(1) of the draft Act, so that section 4(2) would apply and the parties could agree that a dispute is to be decided on principles other than law.
>
> Whether parties would ever be wise to dispense with law is doubtful. If an arbitrator's sense of fairness proves capricious or wrong-headed, there will be little that can be done about it if he is not obliged to follow the law, and an arbitrator might well feel uncomfortable about undertaking to adjudicate by anything so vague as his own subjective feelings. *However, there does not seem to be any public interest which will be injured if parties agree to dispense with law.*

ILRR, *Proposals for a New Alberta Arbitration Act*, Report No. 51, supra note 179 at 21 [emphasis added].

182 Ibid.

183 For example, when debating the addition of ADR into the B.C. *Administrative Tribunals Act*, S.B.C. 2004, c. 45 (discussed further supra Chapter 4), B.C.'s then attorney general argued that "*[w]hat citizens want more often than not is an outcome and a result rather than a process*. They want their problems solved. They want the relationship

however, is that although individuals and corporate citizens do typically care about the specific outcomes of their cases rather (or at least typically more) than about the general processes involved,[184] when we think about the system as a whole (which I did, for example, in Chapter 2), process is fundamental to a viable and democratic public justice system. Arguments that focus purely on efficiency or purely on individual, one-off interests and results lose this overall societal perspective. There is clearly more going on in dispute resolution regimes (including at the commercial level) than simply the resolution of one-off disputes. As we have seen, the fundamental and just regulation of society is also at stake.

For this reason, unlike Caplan, Stringham, and Hadfield, I am strongly of the view that the state should maintain not only a strong interest in the resolution of disputes involving "the lives and relationships of its citizens"; it should also do so in the context of resolving (at least some) disputes involving "corporate-to-corporate commercial dealings."[185] Although the state may not need to be involved in the resolution of every dispute, I am much slower to concede that the collective does not have a strong interest in the outcome of many dispute resolution processes. Because, unlike the ILRR's statements referenced previously,[186] I do think – particularly in a common law system – that some aspect of the public interest is engaged by essentially all disputes in society, including ones under arbitral regimes that are often (although clearly not always) limited to issues of a corporate or commercial nature. I have more to

---

improved, they want the benefit they believe they're entitled to, and they want government to stop doing what it is that is harming them." See British Columbia, Legislative Assembly, *Hansard*, Vol. 25, No. 15 (18 May 2004) at 11192 (Hon. G. Plant) [emphasis added]. As such, according to the same B.C. attorney general,

> Anything we can do to move forward dispute resolution so that it happens sooner is, in my view, a step in the right direction, and we are doing a lot as [a] government to try to encourage alternative dispute resolution not just in the administrative justice system but across the justice system as a whole. In fact, part of rethinking justice involves rethinking the idea of alternative dispute resolution so that it is no longer alternative but, rather, so that mediation, settlement, conciliation and settlement conferences are all part of the basic tools of all dispute resolution.

Ibid.

184 See, for example, ibid.

185 "Privatizing Commercial Law," supra note 147 at 45.

186 See supra note 181.

say on this point of efficiency preoccupation in light of my expansive vision of the purpose of dispute resolution, which I get to in Chapter 7. However, before I do, I now look at the second overriding justification for privatizing our dispute resolution systems: access to justice.

Access to Justice Case for Privatization

"Access to justice" means many things to many people.[187] In its narrow sense, the phrase often is collapsed with the notion of access to courts and/or access to lawyers. Arguments in favour, for example, of reducing legal fees, increasing small claims courts' monetary jurisdictional limits, or reforming civil justice procedural rules often sound in these kinds of immediate, narrow, access to justice justifications. The notion of justice, here, is typically equated with the justice (dispute resolution) system. And there is clearly an access to justice basis for these discussions, however narrow. In its broader sense, access to justice can be understood in much wider and more aspirational terms. These kinds of terms essentially frame the notion of justice as including much more of what are considered the basic processes of living and operating in a modern democratic society (including, for example, health care, food and housing, access to information and education, voting rights, and so on).[188] My own view is that thinking about access to justice in broadly, rather than in narrowly defined terms allows us to consider wider-ranging and more creative and innovative solutions to the everyday problems facing many Canadians today. As such, as I discuss further in Chapter 7, I am clearly a fan of thinking about justice, and access to it, broadly.[189]

The purpose of this part of this chapter, however, is to articulate the leading justifications for privatization. And the access to justice case

187 For an earlier discussion, as well as a representative list of sources, see supra Chapter 2. See further infra Chapter 7.

188 See ibid.

189 For some earlier comments, see, for example, Farrow, "Sustainable Professionalism," supra note 65 at 96; Farrow, "Dispute Resolution, Access to Civil Justice and Legal Education," supra note 31 at 798; Trevor C.W. Farrow, "What is Access to Justice?" (2014) *Osgoode Hall L.J.* (forthcoming); and Law Society of Upper Canada, "Accessing the Justice System: Exploring Perceptions" (Focus article on access to justice) *Gazette* 16:1 (Winter 2012) at 5. Improved access to justice is also raised as a justification for civil justice reform initiatives that are not directly equated with ADR, including self-help centres, proportionality efforts, rules simplification initiatives, and so on. Some of these initiatives were further discussed supra Chapter 3.

that is typically made in support of the privatization trends discussed in this book largely equates access to justice with access to courts and legal services. Specifically, what I am looking at here is what is widely seen as a second fundamental justification for why the various stakeholders identified earlier in this chapter – governments, judges, lawyers, clients, and the legal academy – are embracing privatization trends in our systems of civil justice.

Accessing the civil justice system, as well as any kind of methods of civil dispute resolution, particularly on a more affordable basis, has been one of the key reasons for the development and expansion of the modern ADR movement. Early U.S. proponents of ADR championed it as an accessible alternative to the costly, cumbersome court process. It was, and it still is. The "access to justice" basis for ADR, as it can be called here, is an extremely powerful justification for supporting privatized dispute resolution initiatives. It has also become a strong driving force behind the modern civil justice ethos of reform, most notably at the government, bar association and judicial levels. Most, if not all reforms to our modern systems of civil justice (more fully discussed in Chapter 3) have been largely based, and justified to the public, on the basis that they will improve access to justice. For example, the "CBA Task Force Report" contemplated increased "speed," "affordability" and "public understanding" as central factors to increasing access to civil justice.[190] In line with these early formulations, some of the public materials from the Ontario government supporting the more recent privatization reforms in Ontario sound largely in access to justice language and intent.[191] When discussing the various reforms, Ontario's

190 "CBA Task Force Report," supra note 46, discussed further supra Chapter 3.

191 For example, according to the Ministry of the Attorney General,

> Ontario's new civil justice reforms will make it less expensive to access justice and easier to use the courts to quickly resolve disputes.
>
> The province is increasing the monetary limit of the Small Claims Court from $10,000 to $25,000 effective January 1, 2010. This will provide a faster and more affordable option to Ontarians and businesses who are unable to resolve their own disputes.
>
> Additional civil justice reforms arising from twenty-five significant changes to the rules of Ontario's civil courts will simplify, speed up, and lower the costs of resolving disputes, including the following:
>
> - Making it easier and more affordable to resolve civil cases by raising the monetary limit for Simplified Procedure from $50,000 to $100,000, effective January 1, 2010.

former attorney general Chris Bentley stated that "[c]ivil justice needs to be accessible and affordable if it is to work for all Ontarians" and further that all of the proposed reforms "will help everyday Ontarians to fairly resolve disputes that they can't resolve on their own."[192] In the same Ontario context, former associate chief justice Coulter Osborne stated that by "acting on my recommendations, the Attorney General is reducing cost and delay for individuals and businesses who use our civil courts" and, further, that the "reforms reflect the need for proportionality in our civil justice, which means that straightforward, lower value cases should not take as long or cost as much as large, complex cases."[193]

Similarly, most of the justifications for pursuing alternatives that animate judicial calls for reform in this area rely on access to justice arguments. For example, as discussed earlier in Chapter 2, the current chief justice of Canada, when discussing reforms and civil justice options, acknowledged that "many Canadian men and women find themselves unable, mainly for financial reasons, to access the Canadian justice system."[194] Former chief justice of Canada Brian Dickson commented in 1989 that "[i]t is an unfortunate fact that legal proceedings in the civil … courts … have become increasingly lengthy and protracted."[195]

- Reducing pre-trial costs and delays by requiring advance timelines for sharing information between parties to a dispute and limiting pre-trial Examinations for Discovery to one day, unless the parties or the court decide that more time is needed.
- Lowering litigation costs and reducing the need for lengthy trials by making it easier to resolve cases earlier.

> The civil courts will now also be subject to the general principle of proportionality. This means the time and expense devoted to any case must reflect what is at stake in the proceedings. …

Ministry of the Attorney General, News Release, "Resolving Lawsuits Faster and More Affordably, McGuinty Government Reforming Civil Justice For Ontarians" (11 December 2008), online: Government of Ontario <http://www.attorneygeneral.jus.gov.on.ca/english/news/2008/20081211-civil-nr.asp>. See also the discussion of these materials at supra Chapter 3, and infra Chapter 7.

192 Ibid.

193 Ibid.

194 Rt. Hon. Beverley McLachlin, P.C., "The Challenges We Face," supra note 21, cited earlier in Chapter 2.

195 Rt. Hon. Brian Dickson, P.C., "Access to Justice," supra note 25 at 2.

As such, again according to former chief justice Dickson, "if ADR is handled carefully, then it holds the potential for substantial improvements to the manner in which justice is delivered in Canada."[196]

We can see from these statements, which are representative of the kinds of judicial statements made in support of the wide-ranging civil justice reforms that are now playing out across the country, that a – if not *the* – key argument justifying these forms of privatization and other initiatives is that they promote access to justice. Many similar justifications animate preferences from law societies, charged with a "duty" to "facilitate access to justice" for the citizens of the various provinces;[197] as well as from law schools.[198] This argument is also consistent with arguments that I and others have also made elsewhere:

> There are [several] reasons cited for this ADR "explosion." Speed, efficiency, cost, privacy, flexibility, choice of decision-maker, increased comfort

---

196 Rt. Hon. Brian Dickson, P.C., "ADR, The Courts and the Judicial System: The Canadian Context," supra note 59 at 242, cited in Farrow, "Dispute Resolution, Access to Civil Justice and Legal Education," supra note 31 at 746, n. 27 and accompanying text. Similarly, according to former justice George Adams and Naomi Bussin,

> [t]he problems afflicting the traditional court system stem from its total dependence on one dispute resolution mechanism. A more comprehensive dispute resolution response is required. Today many Canadians cannot afford a trial which means they cannot afford to have a dispute! ADR provides a necessary supplement to the traditional litigation process and builds on both previous court initiatives and the strengths of the legal profession. Most important, for the 21st century, ADR can restore the role of our courts as community centres for conflict resolution and thereby foster values fundamental to the well-being of contemporary Canadian society.

Adams and Bussin, "Alternative Dispute Resolution and Canadian Courts: A Time For Change," supra note 32 at 157.

197 See, for example, *Law Society Act*, R.S.O. 1990, c. L.8, s. 4.2, which provides the following:

> In carrying out its functions, duties and powers under this Act, the Society shall have regard to the following principles:
>
> 1. The Society has a duty to maintain and advance the cause of justice and the rule of law.
> 2. The Society has a duty to act so as to facilitate access to justice for the people of Ontario.
> 3. The Society has a duty to protect the public interest. …

198 See my earlier discussion of these preferences.

> with the processes, etc. are all familiar benefits. However, the primary basis for the development of ADR ... stems from the view that providing alternatives – through both court and non-court-based ADR initiatives – will provide civil justice system consumers with various cost-effective options that, ultimately, will increase overall access to the civil justice system.[199]

As can be seen, increasing "access to justice" is therefore a key justification behind many, if not most, of the widespread privatization initiatives that are discussed in this book. As I discuss further in Chapter 7, it is also, in my view, likely the most legitimate justification for ongoing and widespread civil justice reform. Put simply, it is clearly an important and compelling argument. It also, as can be seen, draws support largely from the foundations and arguments that ultimately drive what I have called, earlier in this chapter, the business case for privatization. And these foundations and arguments, of course, draw support in turn from the general privatization literature and discussions that I outlined earlier.[200] These new privatized processes typically cost the state (and in turn taxpayers) less in terms of time, space, human, and, ultimately, financial resources. They cost users of the system less on the same bases. Recent Canadian and international socio-legal studies also indicate that facilitating access to the civil justice system, and thereby allowing more of the traditionally unmet legal needs and disputes that exist in society to be addressed and resolved, will likely create further savings for the public collectively, and for private citizens individually, in terms of lost opportunities and other social and economic resources.[201] Further, to

---

199 Farrow, "Dispute Resolution, Access to Civil Justice and Legal Education," supra note 31 at 746.

200 See, for example, supra Chapter 3.

201 For some recent research on the issue of various societal impacts and costs of unmet legal needs, see, for example, Ab Currie, "A National Survey of the Civil Justice Problems of Low and Moderate Income Canadians: Incidence and Patterns" (April 2005), available online: CFCJ <http://www.cfcj-fcjc.org/sites/default/files/docs/2006/currie-en.pdf>; Pascoe Pleasence et al., *Causes of Action: Civil and Social Justice*, 2nd ed. (London: Legal Services Commission, 2006); Pascoe Pleasence et al., "The Health Cost of Civil Law Problems: Evidence of Links between Civil Law Problems, Morbidity, and the Consequential Use of Health Services" (First Annual Conference on Empirical Legal Studies Paper, 2006), available online: SSRN <http://papers.ssrn.com/sol3/papers.cfm?abstract_id=912478>. See further Hazel Genn, *Paths to Justice: What People do and Think about Going to Law* (Oxford, UK: Hart Publishing, 1999); and Rebecca L. Sandefur, ed., *Access to Justice* (Bingley, UK: JAI

the extent that disputes, resolved or unresolved, typically create huge amounts of stress and other physical and emotional impacts on users of the civil justice system, having a system that is more accessible for resolving disputes will also assist in reducing those other individual health-related costs, which in turn, ultimately, will save money in terms of public health care and other budgets.[202]

Finally, there is clearly an argument to be made for recognizing the benefits of increases to social and communal harmony that likely flow from accessible and affordable justice systems. Such systems of civil justice would not only promote the resolution of as many disputes as possible, but also hopefully – through transparency, contextual sensitivity[203] and (potentially) increased use – the avoidance of disputes through more proactive and effective dialogue and societal communication, education and understanding. This is certainly a significant part of Susskind's vision for the future of legal services, which recognizes that "what clients actually want is … to avoid legal problems, difficulties, and disputes."[204] Or put bluntly, "[c]lients prefer to have a fence at the top of a cliff rather than an ambulance at the bottom."[205] Access to justice, on this account, is "as much about dispute avoidance as it is about dispute resolution."[206]

Together, the two central justifications for privatization, the business case and the access to justice case, are found – to varying to degrees – at the core of the various preferences and influences discussed in the first part of this chapter. Systemic inefficiencies and access to justice challenges are demanding new and creative solutions. Clients are calling for more flexible, efficient, and cost-effective legal services (the business case).

Press, 2009). For a recent initiative, see CFCJ, "The Cost of Justice: Weighing the Costs of Fair and Effective Resolution to Legal Problems," available online: CFCJ <http://www.cfcj-fcjc.org/?q=cost-of-justice>. For a further discussion of these materials, see infra Chapter 7.

202 See again the various studies cited in ibid.

203 See, for example, Pavlich, *Justice Fragmented: Mediating Community Disputes under Postmodern Conditions*, supra note 110 at 41 [citation omitted].

204 Susskind, *The End of Lawyers?*, supra note 64 at 224 [emphasis omitted].

205 Ibid.

206 Ibid. at 231 [emphasis omitted].

At the same time, legal services need to be more accessible to more people (the access to justice case). There are obvious merits to all of these factors and arguments, which I fully acknowledge both here and in my final analysis of privatization in Chapter 7. Before getting there, however, I now turn to what I see as the five primary concerns about the privatization of civil justice.

Chapter Six

Five Concerns about Privatization

The purpose of much of the first five chapters in this book, and in particular Chapters 3 through 5, was to fairly and comprehensively document the current privatization movement that has engulfed the civil and administrative dispute resolution landscape and to put the arguments in favour of that movement at their highest. Having done that work, I now turn, in this chapter, to look at five specific areas of concern with respect to privatization that are, in my view, equally compelling but much less well documented. In a nutshell, these five concerns include my views that the privatization movement: tends to overstate ADR's benefits, has a negative impact on the development of the common law, results in a lack of procedural protections, leads to a negative impact on democracy, and is aggravated by globalization.

Overstating ADR's Benefits

My first concern with privatization – which is, in the end, my least concern – is that, as a threshold matter, even the many stated efficiency-related benefits of ADR (which I extensively discussed earlier in this book[1]) certainly have their doubters.

Arbitration

Some critics are of the view that, notwithstanding the legions of lawyers and clients lining up behind the arbitral process, arbitration is not

1 See, for example, generally supra Chapter 5.

all that it's cracked up to be, and certainly not in all cases, particularly major commercial cases. Mary Swanton, for example, has stated that "the speed and efficiency of arbitration has been oversold."[2] Other reports support her view. For example, according to a 2007 *Economist* report, arbitration "often proves no cheaper, fairer or even quicker."[3] These reports are consistent with the views of numerous arbitration practitioners. For example, Larry Schaner, a partner at the U.S. firm of Jenner & Block LLP, stated that in "some cases arbitration will be faster and cheaper, but in major commercial disputes that will not necessarily be the case."[4] Kathy Bryan, former head of litigation at Motorola who

---

2 Mary Swanton, "System Slowdown: Can Arbitration Be Fixed?" *InsideCounsel* (May 2007) 50 at 54. Similarly, John Laskin of Torys LLP in Toronto was quoted as saying that "[p]eople now realize more that some of the asserted advantages of arbitration were not real or at least a bit overblown." John Laskin, quoted in Julius Melnitzer, "Arbitration Becomes More Like Litigation" *Law Times* (10 October 2011), available online: Law Times <http://www.lawtimesnews.com/Focus-On/Arbitration-becomes-more-like-litigation>. See further Chris A. Carr and Michael R. Jencks, "The Privatization of Business and Commercial Dispute Resolution: A Misguided Policy Decision" (2000) 88 *Ky. L.J.* 183 at 202–4, nn. 51–4 and accompanying text.

3 See "Knocking Heads Together" *Economist* (1 February 2007), available online: IADR Global <http://www.iadrglobal.org/newsitems/knockingheadstogether.php>. According to another report,

> A[] commonly held fallacy is that arbitration is always faster and cheaper than the courts. ... Arbitration is faster to schedule in places where the courts are slow because parties don't have to wait around for an available judge. But parties pay arbitrators an hourly rate, and businesses with a tactical reason to delay arbitration still attempt to derail the process the same way they do in the courts.

Jennifer McPhee, "Arbitration Becoming the 'New' Civil Litigation" *Canadian Lawyer* (January 2008) 53 at 54 (paraphrasing Babak Barin). Similarly, again according to Mary Swanton, "[g]rumblings from in-house counsel about the cost and speed of domestic commercial arbitration are growing louder. Anecdotal evidence suggests that efficiency is highly variable, depending on arbitrators and the parties involved, and statistical proof of time and cost savings compared to litigation is scant." Swanton, "System Slowdown: Can Arbitration Be Fixed?," supra note 2 at 51. See further Jackson Williams, "The Costs of Arbitration" (April 2002), online: Public Citizen <http://www.citizen.org/documents/ACF110A.pdf>; and Jeffrey Barist, "Arbitration: The Privatization of the Judicial Process" (1996/7) *Int'l Com. Lit.* 22.

4 Larry Schaner, quoted in ibid. at 51. For Canadian judicial commentary on the issue of delay in arbitration, see, for example, *Flock v. Flock*, 2007 ABQB 307, 77 Alta. L.R. (4th) 20, leave to appeal to the C.A. refused, 2007 ABCA 287; *Flock v. Beattie*, 2010 ABQB 193, 25 Alta. L.R. (5th) 49.

subsequently moved to lead the International Institute for Conflict Prevention and Resolution, acknowledges that there is a growing concern over the cost and effectiveness of arbitration in the commercial context. According to Bryan, there is

> tremendous dissatisfaction with domestic arbitration. ... It's too expensive, too process oriented, not responsive enough and the quality of arbitrators is all over the map. General counsel after general counsel gets burned, and litigation lawyer after litigation lawyer gets burned. They are turning away from arbitration in droves.[5]

Gerald Ranking, former chair of the Canadian firm Fasken Martineau DuMoulin LLP's litigation department and former head of the firm's ADR group acknowledges that, depending on the nature of the case, arbitration can be a costly process. Ranking, who certainly recognizes the potential effectiveness of arbitration (particularly if "adverse parties genuinely want to resolve their disputes"), concedes that "arbitration can be almost like another form of court."[6] The costs of arbitration, again particularly in the commercial context, often increase as the stakes involved increase. Put simply, with more at stake and with limited rights of appeal, parties want more procedural safeguards, all of which typically increase time and expense. In those circumstances, as Ranking acknowledges, arbitration looks – and costs – a lot like court.

Eric Liebeler, chief litigation counsel at Honeywell International Inc., argues that the lack of speed in some commercial arbitration proceedings is the fault of arbitrators. According to Liebeler, because (at least some) arbitrators are paid by the hour and, as a result, fail to impose time limits on proceedings, there is "an incentive for them to spread it out."[7] Similarly, although clearly supportive of ADR, Claude Thomson, an arbitrator and ADR practitioner, recently stated:

> Over the last two or three months, I've had a number of meetings with lawyers who are prominent in both arbitration and litigation in order to explore with them why there aren't more commercial cases that are being resolved in arbitration rather than litigation and what I've been learning

5 Kathy Bryan, quoted in ibid. at 51.

6 Gerald Ranking, quoted in Daryl-Lynn Carlson, "Arbitrations versus Court" *Law Times* (20 April 2009) [archived with author].

7 Eric C. Liebeler, quoted in Swanton, "System Slowdown: Can Arbitration Be Fixed?," supra note 2 at 52.

is that too often, arbitration becomes an expensive form of litigation conducted before an arbitrator because the arbitrator tends to allow parties to manage the case without any particular kind of supervision.[8]

In addition to arbitrators, counsel also can be the cause of costs and delays in the process. According to Rick Jeydel, general counsel of Kanematsu USA Inc., the "inside counsel who are complaining about arbitration are people whose outside counsel have imported into the arbitration process all the bells and whistles that accompany a federal or state court litigation."[9] Claude Thomson has also indicated that "counsel themselves are somewhat to blame if they complain proceedings take too long."[10]

Other ADR Processes

Similarly, with respect to court-annexed and other ADR processes, some studies argue that purported reductions in cost and increases in speed and efficiency are not always present in those court-annexed ADR and related processes, and in any event, do not always militate in favour of increased efficiency of courts to which those ADR processes are annexed.[11] Some anecdotal experiences support the findings of these cautionary reports. For example, according to Martin Teplitsky (a mediator

8 Claude Thomson, quoted in Carlson, "Arbitrations versus Court," supra note 6.

9 Rick Jeydel, quoted in Swanton, "System Slowdown: Can Arbitration be Fixed?," supra note 2 at 52–3.

10 Claude Thomson, quoted in Carlson, "Arbitrations versus Court," supra note 6.

11 Héctor Fix-Fierro, *Courts, Justice and Efficiency: A Socio-Legal Study of Economic Rationality in Adjudication* (Oxford, UK, and Portland, OR: Hart Publishing, 2003) at 200–3, 236. See also Roselle L. Wissler "Court-Connected Mediation in General Civil Cases: What We Know from Empirical Research" (2002) 17:3 *Ohio St. J. Disp. Resol.* 641; Roselle L. Wissler, "The Effectiveness of Court-Connected Dispute Resolution in Civil Cases" (2004) 22 *Confl. Resol. Q.* 55 at 67–8, 78; Bobbi McAdoo, "All Rise, the Court Is in Session: What Judges Say About Court-Connected Mediation" (2007) 22:2 *Ohio St. J. Disp. Resol.* 377; Mark R. Sherman, "Mediation Hype & Hyperbole: How Much Should We Believe?" (2003) 58:3 *Disp. Resol. J.* 43; Randy A. Pepper, "Mandatory Mediation: Ontario's Unfortunate Experiment in Court-Annexed ADR" (1998) 20 *Advocates' Q.* 403; John Jaffey, "Memo Suggests Axing Case Management, Mandatory Mediation" *The Lawyers Weekly* (1 October 2004) 3; and Jan Weir, "Mandatory Mediation Meltdown" *The Lawyers Weekly* (8 October 2004) 6. See further Patricia Hughes, "Mandatory Mediation: Opportunity or Subversion" (2001) 19 *Windsor Y.B. Access Just.* 161; Hon. Hugh F. Landerkin and Andrew J. Pirie, "Judges as Mediators: What's the Problem with Judicial Dispute Resolution in Canada?" (2003) 82 *Can. Bar. Rev.* 249.

and litigator at the Toronto firm of Teplitsky Colson LLP), because most cases settle anyway, mediation does not significantly increase settlement rates, and further, in some cases it delays settlement.[12] According to Teplitsky, who argues that "only 15% of cases settle more quickly as a result of mandatory mediation,"[13] lawyers "stop settling cases once a third party is available."[14] Further, also according to Teplitsky, reported cost savings for mandatory mediation are not always present. For cases that are already going to settle, "mandatory mediation just costs money. ... It's just an extra hoop you have to jump through that adds to the total cost of the litigation process."[15]

Although the primary and secondary research presented earlier in this book generally and very strongly endorses the benefits of arbitration, mediation, and other court-annexed and related privatizing processes, support for these processes is not universal. Discussing the merits of ADR requires a more nuanced approach than is sometimes present in reports of the most ardent ADR supporters. Failing to fairly and critically assess the strengths and weaknesses of ADR risks undermining the accuracy and legitimacy of reform-oriented policy debates and thinking that are required for meaningful current and future reform efforts.

But even if we assume that all of ADR's efficiency benefits are present in most situations – and it is the case that they often (although certainly not always) are[16] – there are more fundamental concerns with the privatization movement, as set out below, that need to be seriously considered and discussed.

---

12 Martin Teplitsky, reported in Janice Mucalov, "Mediation: Like it or Not" *National* (January/February 2003) 26 at 27.

13 Teplitsky, reported in ibid. at 28. See further Martin Teplitsky, "Universal Mandatory Mediation: A Critical Analysis of the Evaluations of the Ontario Mandatory Mediation Program" (December 2001) *Advocates' Soc. J.* 12 at 10; Martin Teplitsky, "Excessive Cost and Delay: Is there a Solution?" (December 2000) *Advocates' Soc. J.* 5 at 6–10.

14 Martin Teplitsky, quoted in Mucalov, "Mediation: Like it or Not," supra note 12 at 27.

15 Ibid. at 28. See also Teplitsky, "Universal Mandatory Mediation: A Critical Analysis of the Evaluations of the Ontario Mandatory Mediation Program," supra note 13 at 10–11.

16 See, for example, McPhee, "Arbitration Becoming the 'New' Civil Litigation," supra note 3 at 55 (paraphrasing Allan Stitt).

Impoverished Development of the Common Law

A second concern I have about the privatization of the civil justice system is its potential long-term negative impact on the development of the common law. Put simply, the more we privatize our justice system, the less law we produce. Various critics of ADR and privatization have over the years pointed to the potential slow decline in the number of precedents created and the resulting erosion of the overall corpus of the common law as a result of ADR's popularity. An early but still authoritative example of this critique comes from Owen Fiss, who raised the concern that widespread settlement strategies would have a negative impact on the ability of courts, particularly appellate courts in public interest litigation, to develop the common law.[17] Tracy Walters McCormack has more recently raised similar concerns,[18] as has Peter Murray, who commented that the "high rate of settlement ... coupled with the wholesale pre-litigation diversion of disputes into private arbitration, means that public judgments are becoming a rarity."[19] Similarly, former B.C. attorney general Wally Oppal, a key proponent of the B.C. civil court reforms, commented on the increase in mediation and arbitration that has led to a "gigantic reduction in the number of civil trials."[20] According to Oppal, that reduction "is a very bad thing. ... We need to have more trials so we advance law to meet the needs of a changing society."[21]

Not everyone views ADR's eroding effect on the common law as a critical problem. For example, according to the B.C. Justice Review Task

17 See Owen M. Fiss, "Against Settlement" (1984) 93 *Yale L.J.* 1073. See further Owen M. Fiss, "Justice Chicago Style" (1987) *U. Chi. Legal F.* 1. For a recent discussion of Fiss's critique, see Andrew Pirie, "Critiques of Settlement Advocacy" in Colleen M. Hanycz, Trevor C.W. Farrow and Frederick H. Zemans, *The Theory and Practice of Representative Negotiation* (Toronto: Emond Montgomery, 2008) at c. 11, pp. 278–87. For a useful and recent collection of papers looking at the ideas raised by Fiss, see Symposium, "Against Settlement: Twenty-Five Years Later" (2009) 78:3 *Fordham L. Rev.*

18 Tracy Walters McCormack, "Privatizing the Justice System" (2006) 25 *Rev. Litig.* 735 at pt. vi.

19 Peter Murray, "The Privatization of Civil Justice" (May–June 2008) 91 *Judicature* 272 at 273.

20 Hon. Wally Oppal, quoted in Christopher Guly, "Storm Erupts over B.C.'s Proposed Civil Reforms" 28:7 *The Lawyers Weekly* (13 June 2008) 1 at 18.

21 Ibid.

Force, we need to keep in mind that, in the context of only a small handful of cases going to trial, "the setting of legal precedents occurs naturally as necessary to fill existing gaps."[22] The Task Force is right, at least on the status quo. However, to the extent that the small handful of cases going to trial becomes further and further diminished, then even in that small constellation, the resulting case law will vanish.

If the common law is being eroded by processes of privatization, which it is, that erosion is clearly a concern. As I discussed at length earlier, judge-made law is a central process of democratic governance.[23] Although there certainly is a robust amount of jurisprudence that continues to be produced by our trial and appellate courts every week, the phenomenon of the "vanishing trial"[24] will certainly, in the long run, have an impact on the production of law. For example, if the "fabulous" settlement rates from judge-assisted settlement processes described by Chief Justice François Rolland of the Superior Court of Québec are any indication,[25] trials and trial judgments in Canada do appear to be at least on the decline, if not vanishing. Further, to the extent that certain sectors of litigation lend themselves particularly well to ADR, the death of the common law will not be experienced equally by all sectors. Commercial law, for example, is an area of focused concern, particularly given calls for the privatization of wide swathes of commercial law by various academics and policy makers discussed earlier in this book.[26] This problem is further aggravated by the popularity of domestic and international arbitration in this area of law and practice.[27] Related areas of consumer law, as also discussed earlier in Chapter 5, are other areas of particular focus for privatization.

---

22 B.C. Civil Justice Reform Working Group to the Justice Review Task Force, "Effective and Affordable Civil Justice" (November 2006) at app. F, p. 76, available online: B.C. Justice Review Task Force <http://www.bcjusticereview.org/working_groups/civil_justice/cjrwg_report_11_06.pdf> [references omitted].

23 See supra Chapter 2. See recently *George Weston Ltd. v. Domtar Inc.* (2012), 112 O.R (3d) 190 (S.C.J.) at pt. II.A.

24 Discussed supra at Chapter 3.

25 Ibid.

26 See, for example, supra Chapter 5. Former Supreme Court of Canada Justice Ian Binnie recently commented that the rise of private arbitration in corporate disputes has the potential to "impoverish" the Court's influence in the area of business law. See Ian Binnie, quoted in Jacquie McNish, "Former Judge Laments Big Shifts in Legal Profession," *The Globe and Mail* (11 April 2012) B1.

27 See, for example, supra Chapter 5.

And let's be clear: although the lack of the production of precedents is a by-product of settlements, it is not always an unintended by-product. In some cases, it appears to be the primary goal. Take for example cases brought against the Ontario Lottery and Gaming Corporation (OLGC), which is a "provincial agency operating and managing province-wide lotteries, casinos and slots facilities at horse racing tracks."[28] Those lawsuits, which amounted apparently to approximately fifteen separate cases, alleged losses resulting from the fact that various Ontario casinos allowed gambling addicts to continue using their facilities notwithstanding that the plaintiffs had signed self-exclusion forms.[29] Far from an isolated problem, there are apparently almost 350,000 problem gamblers in Ontario.[30] Prior to the hearing of those cases, the Ontario government engaged in an active pattern of settlement, which was widely seen as an effort to avoid the setting of bad precedents that would further magnify OLGC's potential liability. According to one report in connection with the settlement of the *Treyes* case,[31] "[t]he Ontario Lottery and Gaming Corp. has settled out of court all of the major lawsuits launched against it in recent years by compulsive gamblers, avoiding any court ruling on its controversial program that offers addicts a chance to keep themselves out of casinos."[32] OLGC's lawyer reportedly emphasized that "there is no judicial precedent

28 OLGC, "Who We Are," available online: OLGC <http://www.olg.ca/about/who_we_are/index.jsp?ref=home_menu>.

29 See, for example, *Treyes v. Ontario Lottery and Gaming Corp.*, [2007] O.J. No. 2772 (Sup. Ct. Just.).

30 See William V. Sasso and Jasminka Kalajdzic, "Do Ontario and its Gaming Venues Owe a Duty of Care to Problem Gamblers?" (2006) 10 *Gaming L. Rev.* 552, which was referred to in *Treyes v. Ontario Lottery and Gaming Corp.*, supra note 29 at para. 12.

31 See supra note 29.

32 Andrew Chung, "Casinos Not Taking Chances in Court; Provincial Agency Settling Cases Brought by Problem Gamblers to Avoid Setting Precedents" *Toronto Star* (5 August 2007) A1. See further Victor Malarek, "A Gambler's Rehab Gone Horribly Wrong" *The Globe and Mail* (30 July 2003) A1. According to an earlier report of a different kind of settlement with a different claimant, OLGC "agreed to another last-minute financial settlement with a customer accusing it of wrongdoing, avoiding a potentially embarrassing trial." See Shannon Kari, "Lottery Corp Settles Lawsuit over Nine-Hour Error" *National Post* (26 March 2005) A5. See also Isabel Teotonio, "He's a Winner at Long Last as Lottery Settles out of Court" *Toronto Star* (18 March 2005) A18; Editorial, "Another Lottery Gamble" *The Globe and Mail* (26 October 2006)

to our knowledge right now anywhere in North America."[33] And although the same lawyer commented that these kinds of settlements do not in themselves indicate a pattern of precedent avoidance, he did acknowledge that a court ruling upholding a duty of care "obviously would have an impact on [OLGC's] ... operations."[34] A multibillion-dollar class action, potentially involving more than 10,000 class members, was subsequently filed.[35] However, certification was denied.[36]

The previously discussed OLGC settlements are confidential. In terms of judicial commentary, the most we probably know about these cases comes from a fortuitous ruling on a related contingency fee motion.[37] In that ruling, Justice MacDonald discussed one of the controversial cases, some of OLGC's policies, the fact of the lack of a precedent, and the confidential nature of the settlement.[38] Although there was no ruling on the merits in that case, this costs ruling still provides us with much more than would typically be available in the context of a confidential settlement of a controversial case, which is why it provides a useful example for this study. In sum, the OLGC gambling disputes provide a very instructive window onto the phenomenon of withering case law and purposeful precedent avoidance, all of which are provided for and, in fact actively encouraged, by the privatization of civil justice.

A20; Shannon Kari, "OLGC to Pay Legal Expenses" *National Post* (31 March 2007) A13; and News Staff, with a report from Chris Eby, "OLG Teaches One Settlement in Ticket Fiasco" *CTV News* (updated 7 January 2009), available online: CTV.ca <http://toronto.ctvnews.ca/olg-reaches-one-settlement-in-ticket-fiasco-1.358025>.

33 Chung, "Casinos Not Taking Chances in Court," supra note 32.

34 Ibid.

35 For a copy of the amended statement of claim, see online: Problem Gamblers Lawyer <http://www.problemgamblerslawyer.com/>.

36 See *Dennis v. Ontario Lottery and Gaming Corp.* (2010), 101 O.R. (3d) 23 (Sup. Ct. Just.), aff'd 2011 ONSC 7024 (Div. Ct.), aff'd 2013 ONCA 501, leave to appeal to S.C.C. filed, [2013] S.C.C.A. No. 373. For general media reports on the issues, see, for example, Lisa Priest, "The Big Bluff" *The Globe and Mail* (18 April 2009) A1; Jennifer MacMillan, "Ontario Rejects Blame for Gambler's Losses" *The Globe and Mail* (15 July 2009) A7; Shannon Kari, "Judge Rejects $3.5B Problem Gambling Class Action" *National Post* (20 March 2010) A10; and Jennifer Brown, "Appeal Court Grants Leave to Appeal in OLG Class Action," *InHouse* (20 August 2012), available online: <http://www.canadianlawyermag.com/4280/appeal-court-grants-leave-to-appeal-in-olg-class-action.html?utm_source=responsys&utm_medium=email&utm_campaign=20120820_CLNewswire>.

37 *Treyes v. Ontario Lottery and Gaming Corp.*, supra note 29.

The OLGC gambling settlements are not isolated examples. Other high-profile settlements reached involving cases against the Ontario Government and others[39] follow similar patterns of avoiding negative publicity regarding the alleged misconduct of government, police, public officials, and others through the use of private court settlements. Those cases include, for example, a settlement reached in the dispute revolving around the high profile termination of Kelly McDougald, former chief executive officer of OLG,[40] as well as a settlement reached with David Brown and Dana Chatwell, whose home was located in the midst of the February 2006 occupation of the Douglas Creek Estates development in Caledonia, Ontario, by members of the Six Nations and/or Haudenosaunee Six Nations Confederacy Council.[41] As one report commented about the McDougald settlement and its timing, which was announced by the Ontario government on 24 December 2009,

> It's conceivable that Ms. McDougald's wrongful-dismissal suit just happened to be settled on Christmas Eve, as officials claim. But if so, it was one hell of a coincidence. … There was no great urgency [in settling the case and announcing the settlement]. … But there was considerable upside for the government in making the announcement while most Ontarians were busy wrapping presents – right before the one day of the year that no major newspapers publish.[42]

38 Ibid.

39 For a report on examples of these cases, see Editorial, "Queen's Park Cash Deflects Blame: Critics" *National Post* (6 January 2010) [archived with author].

40 For reports, see, for example, Adam Radwanski, "A Cynical Lesson in How to Make Controversy Go Away" *The Globe and Mail* (5 January 2010), available online: <http://www.theglobeandmail.com/news/politics/a-cynical-lesson-in-how-to-make-controversy-go-away/article1419012/>; and Editorial, "Queen's Park Cash Deflects Blame: Critics," supra note 39.

41 For reports, see, for example, Christie Blatchford, "For Caledonia Couple, the Occupation Is Finally Over" *The Globe and Mail* (31 December 2009) A4; Editorial, "It's Simple, Really. Enforce the Law" *National Post* (2 January 2010) [archived with author]; and Barbara Brown, "Tab for Caledonia Dispute Soars; Taxpayers on the Hook for More than $64M Involving Land Fight with Native Protesters" *Toronto Star* (7 January 2010) A14. See further Christie Blatchford, "Just How Sensitive Is Canada's Native File?" *The Globe and Mail* (10 November 2010) A10; Christie Blatchford, "In a Corner, Crown Counters by Attacking the Plaintiffs" *The Globe and Mail* (24 November 2009); and Christie Blatchford, "Ontario Premier Wanted to Sweep Caledonia Issue 'Under the Rug', Court Told" *The Globe and Mail* (26 November 2009) A13.

42 Radwanski, "A Cynical Lesson in How to Make Controversy Go Away," supra note 40. The basic issue at stake in the McDougald case has been reported as follows:

Similarly, according to another report,

> Critics of the government of Premier Dalton McGuinty say the timing of the announcements displayed a new level of contempt for the public. … The settlement with Ms. McDougald was likely to prevent potentially embarrassing details from coming out about the government's role in the ongoing controversies at the lottery corporation.[43]

The Brown and Chatwell settlement was in connection with their law suit against the Ontario Government, members of the Ontario Provincial Police (OPP) and others, which involved allegations that the OPP "fail[ed]" to enforce court orders and the laws of Canada, the province of Ontario and the bylaws of the county of Haldimand in the context of the Caledonia occupation.[44] One report – which also highlights the retrospective and prospective functions of courts as well as the reality that individual disputants are typically only (or at least most) concerned about the immediate, dispute resolution function of courts – comments, as follows, on the settlement of the Brown and Chatwell dispute. The report also highlights the negative impact that a private settlement has

---

> The problem in question was that, hot on the heels of the eHealth scandal, another provincial agency was about to come under fire for its expenses. Never mind that some of the expenses were probably defensible in this instance, since OLG is expected to operate largely like a private company. The government had no interest in making that case – which admittedly would have been a tricky one to make – so instead it pre-emptively fired Ms. McDougald before the story had even properly broken.
>
> It also humiliated her, announcing that she had been fired "with cause" without bothering to specify what that cause was. (Ms. McDougald has claimed she was terminated because she refused to summarily fire other OLG executives, though that has not been proved.) All the Liberals did was point to the expenditures of various OLG employees, then subject the former CEO – along with the corporation's entire board of directors, which resigned the same day – to all manner of conjecture.

See ibid.

43 Editorial, "Queen's Park Cash Deflects Blame: Critics," supra note 39.

44 See, for example, the Brown and Chatwell Amended Statement of Claim (Court file no. 172/2006, 18 July 2007) [archived with author].

on the public interest behaviour modification and societal regulation aspects of the court process:

> From Dave Brown's and Dana Chatwell's perspective, settling their lawsuit against the Ontario Provincial Police and provincial government, as they did Wednesday, makes perfect sense. The Caledonia, Ont., couple only ever wanted the means to move out of the Douglas Creek Estates subdivision, which the government essentially ceded to native protesters in 2006. They've already bought a new house, and Mr. Brown says he hopes never again to see the old one. (The actual amount of the settlement won't be disclosed.)
>
> For society at large, however, this is a most unsatisfying outcome. The Liberal government has never been able to argue coherently, in or out of court, against Mr. Brown's and Ms. Chatwell's basic version of events: that their family and home were abandoned to … protesters whose … conduct the police refused to … well, to police. This shocking abdication of the government's most basic responsibilities deserves a stern rebuke from the highest court available: The government cannot decline to enforce the law and protect its citizens simply because it might anger a certain segment of society or create an uncomfortable political situation.
>
> We weren't going to get that satisfaction from the civil suit, of course, but a humiliating finding against the government and in Mr. Brown's and Ms. Chatwell's favour would have been gratifying. Now we won't get it. And we won't hear allegedly damning testimony from OPP officers that they had indeed been given orders to stand back and let events unfold as they may. That testimony, which was to be heard next week, is the best explanation available as to why the government suddenly decided to settle.[45]

45 Editorial, "It's Simple, Really. Enforce the Law," supra note 41. Similar sentiments were raised in a letter to the editorial board of the *Toronto Star*:

> While I am pleased for David Brown and his family, it is unfortunate that we may never find out who directed the OPP to stand down in Caledonia and abandon the rule of law in the face of … criminal acts.
>
> The timing of the settlement was curious, coming just before police officers were to testify. Did the Premier or his minister responsible for the OPP interfere in an operational policing matter contrary to the Police Services Act?
>
> We may never know. Money has been thrown at the problem and the truth has been stifled.

Gord Marshall, "Truth Stifled in Caledonia Case," Letter to the Editor, *Toronto Star* (4 January 2010) A14 [archived with author].

Other recent high-profile cases and secret settlements, involving significant public interest issues and concerns, reportedly include confidential settlements reached with Scouts Canada over child sex-abuse incidents. Scouts Canada has reportedly made confidential settlements with more than a dozen child sex-abuse victims over the last number of years. Many of the agreements, through confidentiality clauses, prevent victims from revealing the amounts of the settlements, and some prevent the disclosure of the existence of the settlements themselves. Further, at least one agreement bars a former Boy Scout from publicly stating that the abuse even happened. According to one victim, "Scouts Canada was interested in minimizing the financial cost to them [*sic*] and to making sure that nobody else ever found out about it."[46]

Notwithstanding the immediate concerns of these and other private civil settlements, which involve significant public interest issues, it is the continued production of jurisprudence by our courts that makes this discussion so difficult, and the potential problem so deceptive. Put simply, it is not easy to see the eroding effects of privatization on a weekly (or even yearly) basis. One of the tough things about this discussion is that it is a bit like concerns over climate change. It takes a long time for glaciers to melt or sea levels to rise. It also often takes the diligence and patience of several generations to track, understand, and address some of these slow-moving, long-term issues. But when the impacts are seen and felt, they are clearly significant. Having recently returned from Tanzania, where one of the most famous glaciers

---

46 CBC News, "Scouts Canada Sex Settlements Kept Secret" (24 October 2011) [archived with author]. According to this report, twenty-four lawsuits have been filed across Canada against Scouts Canada since 1995. Of those cases, settlements including confidentiality provisions have been reached with thirteen plaintiffs. See ibid. For further reports, see CBC News, "Sex-Abuse Victim Breaks Silence on Scouts Settlement" (24 October 2011) [archived with author]; CBC News, "Scouts Lawsuits over Prolific Pedophile Quietly Settled" (24 October 2011) [archived with author]. See recently KPMG, *Scouts Canada: Review of Suspension and Termination Files* (21 June 2012), available online: Scouts Canada <http://www.scouts.ca/cys/sc-kpmg-report.pdf>; and Oliver Moore and Kim Mackrael, "Scouts Canada Confronts its Troubling Past," *The Globe and Mail* (26 June 2012) A3. Similar issues and concerns were raised with settlements involving sex-abuse cases within the Catholic Church. See Hon. G. Normand Glaude, Commissioner, *Report of the Cornwall Inquiry* (2009), available online: Government of Ontario <http://www.attorneygeneral.jus.gov.on.ca/inquiries/cornwall/en/report/index.html>.

in the world – the Furtwängler Glacier on Mount Kilimanjaro – is dramatically disappearing, the comparison seems particularly apposite at the moment. And there are certainly similar examples much closer to home. The Crowfoot Glacier in Banff National Park is a particularly obvious example.

When discussing the risk to the "right to a trial" caused by mandatory court-annexed ADR programs, G. Thomas Eisele, judge of the U.S. District Court for the Eastern District of Arkansas, recollected an expression from his father: "You know you can be nibbled to death by ducks." Judge Eisele added that "[o]f course, once dead it may not be too important to determine the cause of death or whether we lost our life through one fatal blow or by being nibbled to death over a protracted period of time."[47] Judge Eisele was speaking about the right to trial itself. However, to the extent that trials are vanishing, it follows that judgments from those trials are also vanishing. And like with the trial itself, it likely will not matter that the death occurred by one "fatal blow" or by "being nibbled to death." The erosion of publicly available judge-made law, which is clearly aggravated by the privatization movement, is an ongoing and troubling concern that needs to be further researched, monitored, and addressed. I fear at the moment that it is being nibbled to death.

Lack of Procedural Protections

A third concern associated with private civil justice processes involves their procedural protections, or more specifically, their potential lack thereof. Clearly, one of the main benefits of ADR, as was expressly recognized, for example, in the 1991 legislative debates surrounding Ontario's arbitration legislation, is its wide-ranging flexibility through party autonomy, whereby parties are "generally free to set their own rules ... so they have a great deal of flexibility."[48] However, with flexibility comes a potential significant cost. Specifically, my concern here, as I have argued elsewhere, is that without adequate public scrutiny, primarily through open court processes and the publication of

47 G. Thomas Eisele, "The Case against Mandatory Court-Annexed ADR Programs" (1991–2) 75 *Judicature* 34 at 40.

48 Ontario, Legislative Assembly, *Official Report of Debates (Hansard)* (5 November 1991) at 1550 (Hon. Howard Hampton), discussed supra at Chapter 4.

precedents, there is a real danger that parties, particularly including those with power, will use the private system to circumvent public policies, accountability, and basic notions of procedural fairness.[49]

Concerns about the fairness of private dispute resolution processes have been around for some time.[50] For example, in the context of arbitration and perceptions of its preferred status in North America over the previous centuries, William Robertson (a commissioned justice in the late 1700s), commented that, although the "Committee or Court of Arbitration" was "very impartial and fair," in Robertson's view it was a "local temporary expedient, dictated by extreme necessity" without "coercive authority to carry its judgments into execution. ..."[51] Further, and specifically in terms of fairness, the prevalence of arbitration at that time, which corresponded to significant developments in the industrial relations sectors, did not necessarily reflect a universal belief in its fairness, equity or neutrality. According to Chitty, for example, "[W]e cannot ever anticipate a certain[,] just and correct decision upon any subject, by *one* or *two* individuals ... and hence, men naturally prefer an open trial by jury ... to a private decision by an arbitrator."[52]

---

49 See Trevor C.W. Farrow, "Privatizing our Public Civil Justice System" (2006) 9 *News & Views on Civ. Just.* Reform 16, available online: CFCJ <http://www.cfcj-fcjc.org/sites/default/files/docs/news_and_views/newsviews09-en.pdf>. For further procedural concerns, see, for example, Eisele, "The Case against Mandatory Court-Annexed ADR Programs," supra note 47. See further the Australian Law Reform Commission [ALRC], which has acknowledged that "ADR in a sense 'privatises' dispute resolution which limits its precedent value and means that issues of public interest can be taken off the public agenda and become, in part immune, from public scrutiny." ALRC, "Review of the Federal Civil Justice System," Discussion Paper 62 (1999) at 9 (9.36) ("ADR and case management"), available online: ALRC <www.austlii.edu.au/au/other/alrc/publications/dp/62/> [footnote omitted].

50 For a discussion of the long and extensive history of private dispute resolution, particularly arbitration, see supra Chapter 4. For a specific discussion about procedural concerns, see, for example, Richard Delgado et al., "Fairness and Formality: Minimizing the Risk of Prejudice in Alternative Dispute Resolution" (1985) *Wis. L. Rev.* 1359.

51 William R. Riddell, *The Bar and the Courts of the Province of Upper Canada, or Ontario* (Toronto: Macmillan, 1928) at 56–7, n. 14. The reference to "extreme necessity" appears to result from distances between courts and trading centres in the region and availability of court alternatives, etc. See generally ibid. at c. iv.

52 Joseph Chitty, *The Practice of Law in All its Departments; with a View of Rights, Injuries, and Remedies, as Ameliorated by Recent Statutes, Rules, and Decisions* (London: Henry Butterworth, 1834) 2, 73–4, cited in James A. Jaffe, "Industrial Arbitration, Equity, and Authority in England, 1800–1850" (2000) 18:3 *L.H.R.* 525 at 539–40.

As James Jaffe subsequently commented, "it has been suggested … that systems of arbitration were not neutral; instead, they were the result of struggles for authority in industry."[53] The acceptance of arbitral settlements or awards, therefore, was "based less upon an unarticulated equity promise than it was upon an understanding of who was implementing the system and who was writing the 'rules of the game.'"[54]

These early comments and examples raising concerns about the fairness of private justice do not simply involve quaint reminiscences of early procedural struggles. They reflect concerns that are very much alive today in the context of modern Canadian procedural debates. For example, concerns about power and procedural fairness in the context of ADR were the central issues in the debates surrounding Ontario's amendments to its arbitration legislation in the area of family law. Because I have written elsewhere on this subject, I only very briefly develop this example of procedural concern further here.[55] In a nutshell,

---

53 Jaffe, "Industrial Arbitration, Equity, and Authority in England, 1800–1850," ibid. at 558 [references omitted].

54 Ibid.

55 For my earlier comments, see Trevor C.W. Farrow, "Re-Framing the Sharia Arbitration Debate" (2006) 15:2 *Const. Forum Const.* 79. For other commentaries, see, for example, Natasha Bakht, "Were Muslim Barbarians Really Knocking at the Gates of Ontario?: The Religious Arbitration Controversy – Another Perspective" in Ronalda Murphy and Patrick A. Molinari, eds., *Doing Justice: Dispute Resolution in the Courts and Beyond* (Montréal: Canadian Institute for the Administration of Justice [CIAJ], 2009) at 227; Jean-François Gaudreault-DesBiens, "On Private Choices and Public Justice: Some Microscopic and Macroscopic Reflections on the State's Role in Addressing Faith-Based Arbitration" in Murphy and Molinari, eds., *Doing Justice: Dispute Resolution in the Courts and Beyond*, supra at 247; and Julie Macfarlane, "Faith-Based Dispute Resolution" in Murphy and Molinari, eds., *Doing Justice: Dispute Resolution in the Courts and Beyond*, supra at 287. See further Catherine Morris, "Media's Mediation and Other Matters: Faith-Based Dispute Resolution in Canada" (speaking notes for a panel presentation, ADR Subsection, B.C. Branch, Canadian Bar Association [CBA], Vancouver, Canada, 25 January 2006), available online: CBA <http://www.cba.org/CBA/newsletters/pdf/ADR-Morris_presentation.pdf>; Catherine Morris, "Arbitration of Family Law in British Columbia" (paper presented for the Ministry of Attorney General of British Columbia, 7 July 2004), available online: B.C. Justice Review Task Force <http://www.bcjusticereview.org/working_groups/family_justice/paper_07_07_04.pdf>; Caryn Litt Wolfe, "Faith-Based Arbitration: Friend or Foe? An Evaluation of Religious Arbitration Systems and their Interaction with Secular Courts" (2006) 75 *Fordham L. Rev.* 427; Natasha Bakht, "Family Arbitration Using Sharia Law: Examining Ontario's Arbitration Act and its Impact on Women" (2004) 1 *Muslim World J. H.R.* art. 7; Almas Khan, "The Interaction between Shariah and International Law in Arbitration" (2005–6) 6 *Chi. J. Int'l L.* 791; and Michael

prior to 2006, parties could use Ontario's *Arbitration Act, 1991* for the resolution of a wide variety of disputes, including family law disputes. In so doing, they could essentially contract out of the application of progressive substantive and procedural family law protections. Relatively recently, the Ontario government, following significant public debate regarding the use of Ontario's arbitration legislation to sanction faith-based dispute resolution processes that potentially discriminated against women and children, sought to limit those opportunities through amendments to its arbitration legislation contained in the *Family Statute Law Amendment Act, 2006*.[56] The result of the amendments essentially was to exclude family disputes from the benefits of arbitration legislation unless the process employed by the parties complied with "the law of Ontario or another Canadian jurisdiction."[57]

This move by the Ontario government was clearly made given the obvious public interest issues engaged in family law disputes, and in particular, gender, religious, child-welfare, and community-welfare interests. As such, there is at least a relatively clear argument for why Ontario decided to privilege substantive equality rights, through robust procedural protections, over the promotion of choice, diversity, and religious freedom in the context of the Sharia arbitration debate. However, in cases outside of the family law context, do concerns for procedural protections and potential power imbalances still obtain? In my view, absolutely. One only needs to look as far as the *Dell* case[58] and its progeny,[59] for example, as well as recent amendments to various provincial

---

C. Grossman, "Is This Arbitration? Religious Tribunals, Judicial Review, and Due Process" (2007) 107 *Colum. L. Rev.* 169. See also Marion Boyd, "Dispute Resolution in Family Law: Protecting Choice, Promoting Inclusion" (Executive Summary) (report prepared for Ministry of Attorney General of Ontario, December 2004), available online: Government of Ontario <http://www.attorneygeneral.jus.gov.on.ca/english/about/pubs/boyd/executivesummary.pdf>; and Standing Committee on General Government, Consideration of Bill 27 (16 January 2006), available online: Government of Ontario <http://www.ontla.on.ca/committee-proceedings/transcripts/files_html/2006-01-16_G011.htm>.

56 S.O. 2006, c. 1.

57 Ibid. at s. 2.2(1). See further *Arbitration Act, 1991*, S.O. 1991, c. 17.

58 *Dell Computer Corp. v. Union des consommateurs*, [2007] 2 S.C.R. 801, discussed further at supra Chapter 4.

59 See, for example, *Griffin v. Dell Canada Inc.* (2010), 98 O.R. (3d) 481 (C.A.), leave to appeal to S.C.C. refused, [2010] S.C.C.A. No. 75; *Smith Estate v. National Money Mart Co.* (2008), 92 O.R. (3d) 641 (C.A.), leave to appeal to S.C.C. refused, [2008] S.C.C.A. No. 535; *Dancap*

consumer protection statutes,[60] for procedural protection discussions in a different context. And the reason why we should care about protecting parties in these kinds of cases is bound up in my argument that all sorts of cases, not simply family law cases, engage issues of strong interest to the public.

To develop my procedural protection concern further, I start with an example: the Dealership case.[61] I do so for two reasons. First, on its face, the Dealership case arguably engages issues that are more in line with what Hadfield refers to as the "market function" of law, rather than its "democratic function."[62] Recall that, according to Hadfield, the "democratic function" of law "protects rights, structures the institutions of democratic governance, redistributes wealth, promotes social objectives such as equality or clean air, and resolves disputes among citizens" whereas the "market function" of law "provides the structure of markets – determining property rights, providing a means of commitment through contract to support cooperative activity – and regulation to correct market failures in the achievement of efficiency."[63] As such, again on its face, the Dealership case is the toughest case for my procedural protection concern in that it is the kind of case that, if we need to make choices based on Hadfield's calculus, we would probably be less concerned about the fairness of the proceeding than one involving, for example, individual equality rights. Again recall Hadfield's argument that "we are not interested in what is fair or just between two corporations; we are interested in what makes their economic relationship as productive and valuable as possible."[64] Second, and perhaps more important, I use the Dealership case to illustrate my concerns here because

---

Productions Inc. v. Key Brand Entertainment, Inc., [2009] O.J. No. 572 (C.A.); *Jean Estate v. Wires Jolley LLP* (2009), 96 O.R. (3d) 171 (C.A.); *MacKinnon v. National Money Mart Co.*, [2009] B.C.J. No. 468 (C.A.); and *Seidel v. Telus Communications Inc.*, 2011 SCC 15, [2011] 1 S.C.R. 531, all of which cases are also mentioned earlier in Chapter 4.

60 See, for example, Québec's *Consumer Protection Act*, R.S.Q., c. P-40.1; Ontario's *Consumer Protection Act, 2002*, S.O. 2002, c. 30, sched. A; Alberta's *Fair Trading Act*, R.S.A. 2000, c. F-2; and British Columbia's *Business Practices and Consumer Protection Act*, S.B.C. 2004, c. 2. For further discussions of these legislative initiatives, see, for example, supra Chapters 4 and 5; and infra Chapter 7.

61 See further supra Chapter 1.

62 See Gillian K. Hadfield, "Privatizing Commercial Law: Lessons from ICANN" (2002) 6 *J. Small & Emerging Bus. L.* 258 at 263, discussed further supra Chapter 5.

63 Ibid.

64 Gillian K. Hadfield, "Privatizing Commercial Law" (2001) 42:1 *Regulation* 40 at 40,

in it I witnessed, first-hand, numerous violations of basic procedural protections that militated to the significant detriment of John (one of the main players in the case).

Numerous procedural protection problems occurred in the Dealership case. I discuss three of them here and a fourth in the next section of this chapter. All three of the examples that I use in this section arose in the context of the discovery phase of the proceeding, which is the primary evidentiary gathering phase of the civil litigation process. Under the rules laid out in the U.S. *Federal Rules of Civil Procedure*,[65] which the parties in the Dealership case agreed would primarily govern their arbitral proceeding, discovery evidence is primarily gathered by way of the exchange of documents, as well as through oral examinations for discovery ("depositions" in the United States). In addition to the rules of civil procedure that governed the case (by agreement), all lawyers involved in the case were also governed by their various home jurisdictional codes of professional conduct.[66]

The first example arose during one part of the defendant's deposition of one of the officers of the Corporation, after repeated requests for a series of documents and repeated denials by the Corporation's lawyers about their existence or relevance. During the deposition, the officer for the Corporation inadvertently (although properly) disclosed the fact that the documents, with knowledge of their lawyers, were in the trunk of his car that was parked just outside of the office in which the deposition was taking place. After a break to retrieve the documents (which turned out to be relevant), it became clear that the lawyers for the Corporation were actively concealing the existence of those documents,

---

available online: Cato Institute <http://www.cato.org/sites/cato.org/files/serials/files/regulation/2001/4/hadfield.pdf> [emphasis added], discussed further supra Chapter 5.

65 See, for example, online: U.S. Government <http://www.uscourts.gov/rules/CV2008.pdf> at r. 26.

66 In my case, see Law Society of Upper Canada (LSUC), *Rules of Professional Conduct* (in effect 1 November 2000), available online: LSUC <http://www.lsuc.on.ca/WorkArea/DownloadAsset.aspx?id=2147486159>. To avoid breaching any confidentiality or other obligations (discussed supra at Chapter 1), I do not identify the home state of the Corporation's lawyers. For relevant professional code obligations, however, see American Bar Association [ABA], *Model Rules of Professional Conduct* (adopted 1983), available online: ABA <http://www.americanbar.org/groups/professional_responsibility/publications/model_rules_of_professional_conduct/model_rules_of_professional_conduct_table_of_contents.html>.

which contained several problematic statements relating to the corporate structure of the Corporation that undermined their theory of the case. The non-disclosure by the Corporation's lawyers was a clear violation of procedural and ethical rules: they should have been produced.

A second example involved a much more subtle violation of the Corporation's ethical rules. Some of the depositions in the Dealership case occurred in the defendant's home state; others, in the plaintiff's home state. When I flew to the home state of the Corporation to take the deposition of one its officers, we agreed to hold the deposition in the offices of the Corporation's lawyers. I arrived alone (the cost of flying more than one lawyer was prohibitive). I was faced, on the other side of the table, by six or seven people: two or three lawyers, the deponent (a senior officer of the Corporation), and two or three other senior officers of the Corporation. The number of people on the other side of the table, in itself, was not a violation of any rule. Bringing that many people to the deposition for the sole purpose of intimidation, together with continued rude treatment and interruptions by various members of the group during the course of the deposition, clearly was. I quickly realized, like Dorothy in the *Wizard of Oz*, that I was "not in Kansas anymore." The lawyers for the Corporation had orchestrated the deposition process in a way that was obviously designed to intimidate me and to influence the way in which deposition evidence was given by the Corporation's own witness. Again, the conduct on the other side of the table was a clear violation of professional obligations.[67]

The third example of problematic procedural issues in the Dealership case, which was clearly the most concerning of the three, involved the suppression of evidence later in the same deposition that I just described. Notwithstanding efforts of intimidation, the deposition of the Corporation's officer continued. I was pursuing a line of questioning with the deponent that went to the heart of both sides' theory of the case. Specifically, one of the key points in issue in the dispute was

67 See, for example, LSUC, *Rules of Professional Conduct*, supra note 66 at r. 4.01(6) and r. 4.06(1), which provide, respectively, that a lawyer "shall be courteous, civil, and act in good faith to the tribunal and with all persons with whom the lawyer has dealings in the course of litigation" and "shall encourage public respect for and try to improve the administration of justice." The conduct was also contrary to the spirit of pre-trial ABA rules, which provide, for example, that a "lawyer shall not … unlawfully obstruct another party's access to evidence. …" ABA, *Model Rules of Professional Conduct*, supra note 66 at r. 3.4.

whether, and how much, John knew about the corporate reorganization deal that involved the Manufacturer and the newly created Corporation.[68] It appeared that the Corporation (and the Manufacturer) had worked very hard to conceal the fact and extent of the reorganization (to maintain and encourage company and brand loyalty, etc.). An admission by the Corporation that the reorganization was not a matter of public knowledge would have been very problematic for its case. During the deposition of the Corporation's officer, the following exchange of questions and answers occurred (as recorded in the deposition transcript)[69]:

Q. [By Mr. Farrow, counsel for the Dealership] And so it was a new company set up to buy the __ division?
A. [By Mr. __, Corporate Officer] Yes.
Q. Were you involved at all with the transition of the division from __ to __?
A. Yes.
Q. Tell me about that transition.
A. Well, it was all effective, really, in a day. I believe the day to be __ … The existing employees of __ … that were … "assigned" to the __ branch that they had worked for, became __ employees in our company effectively that date. And, really, it was rather a transparent change. ...
Q. What do you mean by "transparent change"?
Q. [By Mr. __, counsel for the Corporation] Let me talk to my witness a minute.
Q. [By Mr. Farrow] Excuse me for a minute before you go out.
Q. [By Mr. __, counsel for the Corporation] He can talk to me anytime he wants. I want to talk to my witness.

[*Brief recess.*]
…

Q. [By Mr. Farrow] … I do note for the record that the break was as a result of counsel for Mr. __ asking to speak with him in private after his response just before the break.
Q. [By Mr. __, counsel for the Corporation] Objection. …

---

68 See supra Chapter 1.
69 Again, I have made all necessary deletions (which are marked either by "__" or "…") in order to comply with my professional, ethical, and legal obligations under the circumstances of this case.

Q. … You told me that the transition from __ to __ was meant to be transparent. …

Q. … First of all, I want to say, I *don't like being told what I'm supposed to do or not to do by either one of you guys*. So if you want this to continue … then … both of you need to watch it, because I have about this much left of my patience from either one of you ([Witness] indicates [to Mr. Farrow and to Mr. __, counsel for the Corporation]). … As far as the transparency issue I was talking about, I was talking about from a service standpoint. … And that's the end of what I have to say about that. …

Q. [By Mr. Farrow] I note for the record that this deposition has completely changed since Mr. __'s break with his witness. The tone of the witness has changed. He is nonresponsive and clearly, in my view, has been instructed to change the way he is proceeding at this stage.[70]

What happened in that deposition was truly remarkable from the standpoint of legal ethics. Essentially, my line of deposition questions was improperly interrupted by counsel for the Corporation, who proceeded to insist on taking a break "to talk to [his] … witness." After the break, the witness returned to the room and started to answer my questions with a very different, much less forthcoming demeanour. He then quickly lost his temper, pointed at his own lawyer and at me, and said, in a loud, flustered, and almost panicked voice, that he was tired of "being told what … to do or not to do" by either his lawyer or by me in the context of his testimony during the deposition. Notably at that stage, I had not told him to do or not to do anything. As such, what he was really saying, on the transcript, was that his lawyer had been instructing him over the break how to answer my questions to tailor the evidentiary process in favour of the Corporation.

Never has there been clearer evidence on a deposition transcript of a lawyer being caught having coached a witness during a break to change or tailor the witness' evidence. That kind of overly zealous lawyering is clearly improper under any rules of professional conduct. According to standards set by the ethical rules that govern lawyers in Ontario, for example, the lawyer for the Corporation clearly acted unprofessionally when he interrupted my line of examination questions. For example, the rule on "communication with witnesses giving evidence," which

70 Dealership Case, confidential Deposition Transcript, pp. 28–31 [archived with author] [emphasis added].

"applies with necessary modifications to examinations out of court" (including depositions),[71] provides that "during cross-examination by an opposing licensee, the witness's own lawyer ought not to have any conversation with the witness about the witness's evidence or any issue in the proceeding. ..."[72] Similarly, according to the *Model Code of Professional Conduct* of the Federation of Law Societies of Canada,

> Subject to the direction of the tribunal, a lawyer must observe the following rules respecting communication with witnesses giving evidence: ...
>
> (b) during cross-examination of the lawyer's own witness, the lawyer must not discuss with the witness the evidence given in chief or relating to any matter introduced or touched on during the examination-in-chief. ...
>
> The term "cross-examination" means the examination of a witness or party adverse in interest to the client of the lawyer conducting the examination. It therefore includes an examination for discovery, examination on affidavit or examination in aid of execution. The rule prohibits obstruction or improper discussion by any lawyer involved in a proceeding and not just by the lawyer whose witness is under cross-examination.
>
> The opportunity to conduct a fully ranging and uninterrupted cross-examination is fundamental to the adversarial system. It is counterbalanced by an opposing advocate's ability to ensure clarity of testimony through initial briefing, direct examination and re-examination of that lawyer's witnesses. There is therefore no justification for obstruction of cross-examination by unreasonable interruptions, repeated objection to proper questions, attempts to have the witness change or tailor evidence, or other similar conduct while the examination is ongoing. ...
>
> This rule applies with necessary modifications to examinations out of court.[73]

Although the Dealership case was not a Canadian case, equally apposite ethical obligations obtain in the United States. For example, the ABA's *Model Rules of Professional Conduct* provide the following:

---

71 LSUC, *Rules of Professional Conduct*, supra note 66 at r. 4.04 (commentary).

72 Ibid. at r. 4.04 (d). See similarly Canadian Bar Association [CBA], *Code of Professional Conduct*, rev. ed. (2009), c. IX.18, available online: CBA <http://www.cba.org/CBA/activities/pdf/codeofconduct.pdf>.

73 Federation of Law Societies of Canada, *Model Code of Professional Conduct* (adopted 2009 and 2011) at r. 4.04(2) and commentary.

> R. 3.4 A lawyer shall not:
> (a) unlawfully obstruct another party's access to evidence or unlaw fully alter, destroy or conceal a document or other material having potential evidentiary value. A lawyer shall not counsel or assist another person to do any such act;
> (b) falsify evidence, counsel or assist a witness to testify falsely, or offer an inducement to a witness that is prohibited by law …
> (d) in pretrial procedure, make a frivolous discovery request or fail to make reasonably diligent effort to comply with a legally proper discovery request by an opposing party. …[74]

The conduct of the lawyer for the Corporation clearly offended against any one of these versions of the ethical obligation not to obstruct the evidentiary process. As the record made clear, he obviously coached his witness to tailor his evidence in line with the Corporation's theory of its case.

Because the Dealership case was being dealt with pursuant to a private arbitration regime, the typical procedural safeguards provided for by a court were not immediately present to curb or punish the behaviour of the Corporation or its lawyers in the context of any of these problematic procedural occurrences, including the hiding of documents in the witness's car, the improper intimidation deposition tactics, or the flagrant witness coaching. However, notwithstanding the absence of immediate judicial recourse, pre-hearing procedures to raise the issues with the arbitrator were available, which we pursued. Following written and oral presentations on the various violations, the arbitrator was clearly unmoved to do anything about them. As such, he decided to do nothing. And given the lack of a requirement to provide written reasons (either for any interlocutory rulings or for the final arbitral decision in that case),[75] it was not clear on what basis he dismissed

74 See, for example, ABA, *Model Rules of Professional Conduct*, supra note 66 at r. 3.4. For a general discussion of legal ethics in the context of a lawyer's role as a civil advocate, see Trevor C.W. Farrow, "Ethics in Advocacy" in Alice Woolley et al., *Lawyers' Ethics and Professional Regulation*, 2nd ed. (Markham, ON: LexisNexis, 2012) c. 6. For my recent views on legal ethics and professionalism generally, see Trevor C.W. Farrow, "Sustainable Professionalism" (2008) 46:1 *Osgoode Hall L.J.* 51; Trevor C.W. Farrow, "The Good, the Right, and the Lawyer" (2012) 15:1 *Legal Ethics* 163.

75 Arbitration statutes and rules typically contemplate the issue of arbitrators giving reasons. The default position is often that the arbitrator will give reasons to support

the complaints. The ethical violations could not have been clearer. The fact that the arbitrator was a roster arbitrator, who presumably hoped to be retained in future cases (and therefore was perhaps less willing to make negative rulings about a lawyer's ethical conduct), may have had something to do with it. We will never know. Regardless, at that point it became patently clear to me what it means that, at least in some arbitral circumstances, there is a real potential for inadequate procedural protection and abuse that can militate against the realization of fair and just dispute resolution outcomes.

The Dealership case is certainly not the only arbitral proceeding in which at least some participants have been concerned about the lack of available procedural protections. Another – high profile – illustrative example involves a relatively recent employment termination arbitration. The employer in the case was Washington state–based Vulcan, Inc. Vulcan is a corporation started by Paul G. Allen – co-founder of the Microsoft Corporation – to manage his business and charitable affairs.[76] The employees were two investment managers with Vulcan's

his or her award. That is the case, for example, under Canada's *Commercial Arbitration Act*, R.S.C. 1985, c. 17 (2nd Supp.), art. 31(2) and Ontario's *Arbitration Act, 1991*, supra note 57 at s. 38. However, both statutes allow parties to agree otherwise. See *Commercial Arbitration Act*, ibid. at 31(2); *Arbitration Act, 1991*, ibid. at s. 3. By comparison, the U.S. *Federal Arbitration Act*, U.S.C. tit. 9 § 1–14 is silent on the issue. In terms of arbitration rules, the *Commercial Arbitration Rules* of the American Arbitration Association (AAA), for example, provide that arbitrators must issue "awards" (decisions). However, according to the AAA Rules, an arbitrator "need not render a reasoned award unless the parties request such an award in writing prior to appointment of the arbitrator or unless the arbitrator determines that a reasoned award is appropriate." See AAA, *Commercial Arbitration Rules* (amended and effective 1 June 2009), r. 42, available online: AAA <http://www.adr.org/aaa/ShowProperty?nodeId=/UCM/ADRSTG_004103&revision=latestreleased>. In practice, reasons are often, although not always, given in support of arbitral awards. For example, although a reasoned award was not issued in the Dealership case, a reasoned award was given in the Vulcan case, which I discuss below. The key to this issue is the will and agreement of the parties. Finally, even if an award is given with reasons, those reasons are usually kept confidential by the parties, which is again typically at the will and agreement of the parties. For a further discussion of the privacy and confidentiality of arbitration, see supra Chapter 3. For a recent case that looks at the issue of arbitrator reasons, see *ACTIV Financial Systems, Inc. v. Orbixa Management Services, Inc.* (2011), 109 O.R. (3d) 385 (Sup. Ct.).

76 Vulcan, Inc., online: <http://www.vulcan.com/TemplateHome.aspx?contentId=1>.

private equity group. The dispute was about the employees' exit compensation. Their compensation agreement included a profit sharing formula, which increased if the employees were not terminated before the disposition of various managed investments. Both employees were terminated prior to the investment disposition date. They were provided with exit compensation under the terms of their compensation package, but were not provided with the full amount as if the investments had been disposed. Whether they were entitled to the difference in compensation – altogether reportedly amounting to approximately $20 million USD – was the issue in the case.

The Vulcan employment contract included a mandatory arbitration agreement. The rules governing the arbitration were the *Commercial Arbitration Rules* of the American Arbitration Association (AAA). The agreement provided for a three-person arbitration panel. Each side picked one of the three arbitrators, the two of whom picked the third. The employees selected a Seattle lawyer named Arthur W. Harrigan, Jr. Vulcan did not object (which it could have done). Vulcan selected Judge Robert H. Alsdorf (ret.). James A. Smith, Jr. was selected as the third arbitrator. The arbitration proceeded from 22 to 25 June 2009, following which the panel substantially found in favour of the employees in its arbitration award dated 29 July 2009. After the arbitration, when counsel for Vulcan received the legal bills of the employees in support of their claim for attorneys' fees, Vulcan learned for the first time that one of the arbitrators, Mr. Harrigan, had issued an invoice to the employees for $3,355 USD for 5.5 hours of time spent allegedly reviewing pleadings, evidence, and arguments with the employees and/or their representatives. The meetings for which the bill was issued occurred prior to the arbitration (apparently nearly two months before he was appointed as an arbitrator). The meetings also apparently occurred approximately two weeks before the employees served their arbitration demand and prior to the arbitrator declaring that he did not have "any 'present or past personal or business relationship'" with the employees and prior to declaring that he had no "entanglement with the parties of the subject matter of the case 'that may give rise to a justifiable doubt as to [his] impartiality or independence.'"[77]

77 See Vulcan's Motion to Vacate Arbitration Award, filed in the Superior Court for the State of Washington, County of King (8 March 2010), pt. I. For arguments from

Under the governing AAA arbitration rules, each side was allowed to meet with potential arbitrators in order to determine the fitness of the arbitrator for the case. Specifically, the rules provide that

> [A] party, or someone acting on behalf of a party, may communicate ex parte with a candidate for direct appointment … in order to advise the candidate of the general nature of the controversy and of the anticipated proceedings and to discuss the candidate's qualifications, availability, or independence in relation to the parties or to discuss the suitability of candidates for selection as a third arbitrator where the parties or party-designated arbitrators are to participate in that selection.[78]

However, there is a difference between meeting with an arbitrator to determine whether his or her prior contacts or experiences militate in favour or against his or her appointment and meeting with an arbitrator to discuss the merits of a case, draft court documents, clarify facts, and so forth. In its motion materials, Vulcan alleged that the employees and Mr. Harrigan crossed that line in this case, that Mr. Harrigan was therefore not "impartial and independent" as required by the AAA rules,[79] and that, therefore, the arbitration award should be set aside.[80] Without having received and carefully reviewed the legal bills, which were disclosed by the employees for a different purpose, Vulcan would have never learned about those confidential meetings.[81]

Notwithstanding its arguments and objections, Vulcan was unsuccessful at all levels of this matter. Following the various arbitral proceedings,[82] Vulcan's appeals to the Washington state courts for relief against both the underlying employment arbitral decision as well as

---

the employees, see, for example, Petitioners' Joint Reply in Support of Motion to Confirm Arbitration Awards (18 March 2010).

78 AAA, *Commercial Arbitration Rules*, supra note 75 at r. 18.

79 See ibid. at r. 17. See further Vulcan's Motion to Vacate Arbitration Award, supra note 77 at pt. II.B.

80 See Vulcan's Motion to Vacate Arbitration Award, ibid. at pt. II.C.

81 See ibid. at pt. II.D.

82 The arbitration panel's initial arbitration award, finding for the employees, is dated 29 July 2009. Its final arbitration award, largely specifying the monetary amounts in the initial award and the amounts of legal and arbitration fees and costs owed to the employees, is dated 9 February 2010. The arbitral decision on the issue of arbitrator neutrality, issued by Judge Terry Lukens (ret.), arbitrator, in his Decision Regarding Disqualification of Arbitrator (No. 1160017635), is dated 8 January 2010.

the arbitral decision concerning arbitrator neutrality were dismissed.[83] Vulcan's further appeals, to the Washington State Court of Appeals and Supreme Court, were also dismissed, largely based on deference to the decisions of the early panels and the permissive nature of the arbitral rules provided by the AAA.[84] All of these issues were also the subject of high-profile media attention.[85]

It stretches the imagination to think of the same kind of thing happening if the matter had initially been before a judge (as opposed to an arbitration panel). Judges are not chosen or paid by the parties and, given the strength of the open court principle (discussed earlier in Chapter 2), do not meet with parties alone. For purposes of this book, what particularly interests me about the Vulcan case (as well as the Dealership case) is the fact that, even in the context of extremely sophisticated business parties, potential procedural fairness issues are at play in the context of private arbitration processes. And although the dealership case and the Vulcan case provide just two examples of arbitral proceedings in which significant concerns about procedural protections have been raised, they clearly are not the only cases in which such concerns have been raised. According to one report, people are "turning away" from commercial arbitration "because they believe any benefits of domestic commercial arbitration are outweighed by the risks of forfeiting protections inherent in the ... judicial system: rules of evidence, reasoned judgments and the right to appeal."[86] Further, according to David Schlecker, a partner at the U.S. firm of Anderson Kill & Olick, P.C.,

83 See *Capobianco and Thukkaram v. Vulcan et al.*, Judgment, No 10-2-09609-4SEA (30 April 2010) (Wash. Sup. Ct.).

84 See *Capobianco v. Vulcan, Inc.*, 2011 Wash. App. LEXIS 840 (11 April 2011) (Wash. C.A., Div. One); aff'd *Capobianco v. Vulcan, Inc.*, 2011 Wash. LEXIS 841 (1 November 2011) (Wash. Sup. Ct.), citing, among other things, r. 18 of the AAA, *Commercial Arbitration Rules* (supra note 75).

85 See, for example, Dionne Searcey, "Vulcan Capital Challenges Arbitrator's Impartiality" *The Wall Street Journal* (11 March 2010), available online: Wall Street Journal <http://online.wsj.com/article/SB10001424052748704655004575113961030321200.html>; Brier Dudley, "Allen Loses Bid to Block $20M for 2 Fired Vulcan Staffers" *The Seattle Times* (6 April 2010, page modified 7 April 2010), online: The Seattle Times Company <http://seattletimes.com/html/businesstechnology/2011540336_paulallen07.html>; and Dionne Searcey, "Allen's Vulcan Capital Loses Ruling" *The Wall Street Journal* (9 April 2010), online: Wall Street Journal <http://online.wsj.com/article/SB10001424052702304830104575172122413363024.html>.

86 Swanton, "System Slowdown: Can Arbitration Be Fixed?," supra note 2 at 51. See further ibid. at 51–2.

"[a]rbitrators don't have to have reasoned decisions and sometimes the parties are left scratching their heads. … Then you are essentially stuck with the decision because the right of appeal is very limited."[87] In line with these concerns, according to Vulcan spokesperson David Postman, as a result of the company's experience, "we don't have faith in arbitration."[88] Reports of Vulcan's business practices indicate that it has removed employment contract clauses that require mandatory arbitration processes to settle disputes.[89]

The point of this discussion is not to say that all arbitration procedures (and arbitrators) fail to ensure adequate procedural protections for the litigants; or, for that matter, to say that all judicial procedures (and judges) always get it right. My point, however, through these examples, is to highlight an important procedural concern with arbitration's lack of established procedural protections, which is aggravated by the process's typical secrecy and lack of robust appeal routes. Similar concerns also obtain for other private processes involving third-party neutrals. Mediation, for example, can suffer from many of the same procedural concerns (although, given the typically more voluntary nature of mediation, the severity of the consequences can, in some circumstances, be less acute). So it is one thing for George Adams to claim, as a retired judge and experienced mediator, that mediation settlements are often, in his experience, "principled," "professional" and "elegant."[90] And often he is right. However, particularly with court-annexed mediation, Adams's observation is also dependent on his acknowledgment that "[o]f course, it doesn't work if there aren't consequences to not agreeing and these settlements being driven by very ethical professional courts that are there so if you don't settle, you're going to be visiting the judge and she is going to decide who wins and who loses and it's going to be quite costly."[91] The problem in the Dealership case, for example, was that there was no easy recourse to a judge, and further, as it turned out, the arbitrator was not effective at ensuring procedural fairness.

Finally, in addition to generic procedural fairness issues that can potentially come up in any privatized procedural process (including

87 David Schlecker, quoted in ibid. at 51.

88 David Postman, quoted in Searcey, "Vulcan Capital Challenges Arbitrator's Impartiality," supra note 85.

89 Searcey, "Vulcan Capital Challenges Arbitrator's Impartiality," ibid.

90 Carlson, "Arbitrations versus Court," supra note 6.

91 Ibid.

evidentiary and professional issues, and the like), there also exist a host of other procedural fairness issues that can potentially arise in private processes that negatively and disproportionately impact on certain groups or litigants, including women, young people, minority groups, and other equity-seeking participants. These procedural concerns can include potential power imbalances resulting from differences in class, wealth and other resources, gender and age, cultural inequities resulting from ignorance or system bias, language issues, and a host of other potential challenges. Admittedly these issues can (and do) also come up in the context of public judicial proceedings.[92] And when they do,

92 The Supreme Court of Canada has variously discussed some of these issues in the context of the judicial process. See, for example, *Baker v. Canada (Minister of Citizenship and Immigration)*, [1999] 2 S.C.R. 817 (headnote), which provides that "Procedural fairness ... requires that decisions be made free from a reasonable apprehension of bias, by an impartial decision-maker. ... They require a recognition of diversity, an understanding of others, and an openness to difference." See further *R. v. S. (R.D.)*, [1997] 3 S.C.R. 484 (headnote), which provides the following:

> Judicial inquiry into context provides the requisite background for the interpretation and the application of the law. ... This process of enlargement is a precondition of impartiality. A reasonable person, far from being troubled by this process, would see it as an important aid to judicial impartiality. ... The reasonable person approaches the question of whether there exists a reasonable apprehension of bias with a complex and contextualized understanding of the issues in the case. He or she understands the impossibility of judicial neutrality but demands judicial impartiality. This person is cognizant of the racial dynamics in the local community, and, as a member of the Canadian community, is supportive of the principles of equality.

Finally, see *R. v. Lavallee*, [1990] 1 S.C.R. 852, sec. 5, Wilson J., which provides – in the context of recognizing both the reality, gravity and ongoing stigma of gendered violence (and in particular the "battered wife syndrome"), and the judicial system's obligation to recognize and make space for those gendered issues in the judicial decision-making process through an openness to differences and discrimination based on gender – that:

> [t]he gravity, indeed, the tragedy of domestic violence can hardly be overstated. Greater media attention to this phenomenon in recent years has revealed both its prevalence and its horrific impact on women from all walks of life. Far from protecting women from it the law historically sanctioned the abuse of women within marriage as an aspect of the husband's ownership of his wife and his "right" to chastise her. ... Laws do not spring out of a social vacuum. ... The definition of what is reasonable must be adapted to circumstances which are, by and large, foreign to the world inhabited by the hypothetical "reasonable man."

there is at least, in theory (as I discussed in Chapter 2), an openness to the process that allows for outside scrutiny and critique, as well as a right of appeal. One of the stated benefits of ADR is that, given its flexibility and informality, it can be extremely sensitive to the social context needs of and issues facing the participants. And when ADR processes work, they work well on this front.[93] I fully acknowledge that fact. However, given the typical secrecy, lack of formal procedural protections and limited rights of appeal discussed earlier, the concern about these procedural issues can be significantly heightened in the context of private processes. Put simply, the rights and interests of vulnerable people participating in private and informal processes can be very much at risk in the face of inexperienced neutrals and powerful opponents. Because this issue is the focus of a significant body of literature and ongoing debate,[94] which I have touched on (very briefly)

For other relevant cases, see, for example, *M. v. H.*, [1999] 2 S.C.R. 3; *Eldridge v. British Columbia (Attorney General)*, [1997] 3 S.C.R. 624; *R. v. D.B.*, [2008] 2 S.C.R. 3; *R. v. Gladue*, [1999] 1 S.C.R. 688.

93 For a useful discussion on this point, in the context of community-based mediation, see George C. Pavlich, *Justice Fragmented: Mediating Community Disputes under Postmodern Conditions* (London, New York: Routledge, 1996).

94 See, for example, Eric K. Yamamoto, "ADR: Where Have All the Critics Gone?" (1995–6) 36 *Santa Clara L. Rev.* 1055, who also cites a number of useful sources (see, for example, ibid. at nn. 17 and 44), including Penelope E. Bryan, "Killing Us Softly: Divorce Mediation and the Politics of Power" (1992) 40 *Buff. L. Rev.* 441; Kim Dayton, "The Myth of Alternative Dispute Resolution in the Federal Courts" (1991) 76 *Iowa L. Rev.* 889; Richard Delgado, "ADR and the Dispossessed: Recent Books About the Deformalization Movement" (1988) 13 *Law & Soc. Inquiry* 45; Delgado et al., "Fairness and Formality: Minimizing the Risk of Prejudice in Alternative Dispute Resolution," supra note 50; Harry T. Edwards, "Alternative Dispute Resolution: Panacea or Anathema?" (1986) 99 *Harv. L. Rev.* 668; Owen M. Fiss, "Against Settlement," supra note 17; Trina Grillo, "The Mediation Alternative: Process Dangers for Women" (1991) 100 *Yale L.J.* 1545; Michele G. Hermann, "The Dangers of ADR: A Three-Tiered System of Justice" (1989–90) 3 *J. Contemp. Legal Issues* 117; David Luban, "Bargaining and Compromise: Recent Work on Negotiation and Informal Justice" (1985) 14 *Phil. & Pub. Aff.* 397; Carrie Menkel-Meadow, "Pursuing Settlement in an Adversary Culture: A Tale of Innovation Co-Opted or 'The Law of ADR'" (1991) 19 *Fla. St. U. L. Rev.* 1; Marjorie A. Silver, "The Uses and Abuses of Informal Procedures in Federal Civil Rights Enforcement" (1987) 55 *Geo. Wash. L. Rev.* 482; Jana B. Singer, "The Privatization of Family Law" (1992) *Wis. L. Rev.* 1443; Bruce E. Barnes, "Conflict Resolution Across Cultures: A Hawaii Perspective and a Pacific Mediation Model" (1994) 12 *Mediation Q.* 117; Robert D. Garrett, "Mediation in Native America" (1994) 49 *Disp. Resol. J.* 38; Isabelle R. Gunning, "Diversity Issues in Mediation: Controlling Negative Cultural Myths" (1995) *J. Disp. Resol.* 55; Mori Irvine, "Mediation: Is

elsewhere,[95] I do not spend much further time on the specific issue here, other than to raise its importance and relevance for this discussion as well as to mentioned that it was exactly these concerns that ultimately governed Ontario's approach in the Sharia arbitration debate that I discussed earlier in this chapter. As such, these specific equality

---

it Appropriate in Sexual Harassment Grievances?" (1993) 9 *Ohio St. J. Disp. Resol.* 27; Stephen Meili and Tamara Packard, "Alternative Dispute Resolution in a New Health Care System: Will it Work for Everyone?" (1994) 10 *Ohio St. J. Disp. Resol.* 23, 30–5; and Larry R. Spain, "Alternative Dispute Resolution for the Poor: Is It an Alternative?" (1994) 70 *N.D. L. Rev.* 269. See also Yamamoto, "ADR: Where Have All the Critics Gone?," supra at 1065, n. 49–50.

For further sources looking at the issues of power, gender, culture and other equity issues in the context of ADR and process, see, for example, Jennifer P. Maxwell, "Mandatory Mediation of Custody in the Face of Domestic Violence: Suggestions for Courts and Mediators" (1999) 37:3 *Fam. Concil. Cts. Rev.* 335 (now *Fam. Ct. Rev.*); Jordi Agusti-Panareda, "Power Imbalances in Mediation: Questioning Some Common Assumptions" (2004) 59:2 *Disp. Resol. J.* 24; Colleen M. Hanycz, "Through the Looking Glass: Mediator Conceptions of Philosophy, Process and Power" (2005) 42 *Alta. L. Rev.* 819; Philip Bryden and William Black, "Mediation as a Tool for Resolving Human Rights Disputes: An Evaluation of the B.C. Human Rights Commission's Early Mediation Project" (2004) 37 *U.B.C. L. Rev.* 73; McAdoo, "All Rise, the Court Is in Session: What Judges Say about Court-Connected Mediation," supra note 11; Sherman, "Mediation Hype & Hyperbole: How Much Should We Believe?," supra note 11; John Lande, "Commentary: Focusing on Program Design Issues in Future Research on Court-Connected Mediation" (2004) 22 *Confl. Resol. Q.* 89; Julie Macfarlane, gen. ed., et al., *Dispute Resolution: Readings and Case Studies*, 3rd ed. (Toronto: Emond Montgomery, 2010) at 56–81, 184–204, 371–90; Catherine E. Bell and David Kahane, eds., *Intercultural Dispute Resolution in Aboriginal Contexts* (Vancouver: University of British Columbia Press, 2004); Michelle LeBaron and Zena D. Zumeta, "Windows on Diversity: Lawyers, Culture, and Mediation Practice" (2003) 20 *Conflict Res. Q.* 463; Michelle LeBaron, *Bridging Troubled Waters: Conflict Resolution from the Heart* (San Francisco: Jossey-Bass, 2002); Jennifer J. Llewellyn, "Dealing With the Legacy of Native Residential School Abuse in Canada: Litigation, ADR, and Restorative Justice" (2002) 52 *U.T.L.J.* 253; Cynthia Ford, "Including Indian Law in a Traditional Civil Procedure Course: A Reprise, Five Years Later" (2001) 37 *Tulsa L. Rev.* 485; Ian Morrison and Janet Mosher, "Barriers to Access to Civil Justice for Disadvantaged Groups" in Ontario Law Reform Commission, *Rethinking Civil Justice: Research Studies for the Civil Justice Review* (Toronto: Ontario Law Reform Commission, 1996) 637 at 663–74; Judith Resnik, "Revising the Canon: Feminist Help in Teaching Procedure" (1993) 61 *U. Cin. L. Rev.* 1181; and Elizabeth M. Schneider, "Gendering and Engendering Process" (1993) 61 *U. Cin. L. Rev.* 1223.

95 See, for example, Trevor C.W. Farrow, "Dispute Resolution, Access to Civil Justice and Legal Education" (2005) 42 *Alta. L. Rev.* 741 at 786, nn. 286–9 and accompanying text; Trevor C.W. Farrow, "Public Justice, Private Dispute Resolution and Democracy"

and related concerns are clearly part of the overall concern about the potential lack of procedural protections that can be associated with private dispute resolution processes.

Negative Impact on Democracy

My fourth concern, which is the most significant concern that I have regarding the privatization of civil justice, is an issue that relates to the second concern that I raised earlier (regarding the development of the common law) and is one that weaves its way through this entire project. Specifically, this fourth concern relates to the fundamental purpose of the public dispute resolution process not only as a method for resolving individual disputes, but also as a norm-creating instrument of societal regulation, and the eroding impact that the privatization of civil dispute resolution has on this foundational democratic function.

Recalling the discussions from Chapters 2 through 4, there are at least three key components to the public adjudicative system. First, public civil justice systems are clearly central actors in the adjudicative process. As S.M. Waddams has summarized, in addition to "statutes," the "study of law is, to a large extent, the study of … judicial decisions."[96] Second, in our highly complex and regulated democracies, the administrative system plays an equally, if not more important role. Again as Waddams has discussed, in a "highly regulated state … there are thousands of administrative bodies exercising very important regulatory and adjudicative powers. … [A]s a practical matter, the direct effect of regulatory tribunals is often of more importance than the direct effect of legislation or of judicial decisions."[97] Third, in addition to the state-funded civil courts and administrative processes, there is a vast body of "alternative" justice – largely in the form or arbitration,

in Murphy and Molinari, eds., *Doing Justice: Dispute Resolution in the Courts and Beyond*, supra note 55 at 301, 343–6; Farrow, "Privatizing our Public Civil Justice System," supra note 49 at 16; and Farrow, "Re-Framing the Sharia Arbitration Debate," supra note 55.

96 S. M. Waddams, *Introduction to the Study of Law*, 3rd ed. (Toronto: Carswell, 1987) at 19.

97 Ibid. at 19. For a negative commentary on the importance and role of administrative tribunals, see Ezra Levant, *Shake Down: How Our Government is Undermining Democracy in the Name of Human Rights* (Toronto: McClelland & Stewart, 2009).

mediation, and so forth – that, as the Supreme Court of Canada recognized in *Desputeaux*, forms a "fully recognized" part of a state's overall adjudicative process.[98] The first two of these adjudicative processes, public courts and tribunals, not only resolve individual disputes as well as keep legislation in check through hearings, trials, and processes of judicial review[99]; they also create a body of law that directly governs and indirectly guides, through both the full light and the shadow of the common law, much of what we do in our daily lives, including both individual and corporate actors.[100] As such, far from simple mechanical dispute ending procedures, civil dispute resolution regimes play a central role in the regulatory processes of modern Western democracies. Given this central role, the move to privatize public civil dispute resolution regimes has profound implications for how we govern ourselves in a free and democratic society. Put simply, to the extent that we are privatizing public civil dispute resolution systems, we are essentially

98 *Desputeaux v. Éditions Chouette (1987) inc.*, [2003] 1 S.C.R. 178 at para. 41, LeBel J.

99 For some foundational works and statements on judicial review, see, for example, Alexander M. Bickel, *The Least Dangerous Branch: The Supreme Court at the Bar of Politics*, 2nd ed. (New Haven, CT, and London: Yale University Press, 1986); Robert K. Carr, *The Supreme Court and Judicial Review* (New York: Holt, Rinehart and Winston, 1942); Arthur A. North, *The Supreme Court: Judicial Process and Judicial Politics* (New York: Merredith, 1966); and Rt. Hon. Lord Denning, M.R., *The Discipline of Law* (London: Butterworths, 1979) at 133. See more recently Gerald Baier, *Courts and Federalism: Judicial Doctrine in the United States, Australia, and Canada* (Vancouver: UBC Press, 2006).

100 For relevant discussions, see, for example, Owen Fiss, "The Forms of Justice" (1979) 93 *Harv. L. Rev.* 1, reprinted in Owen Fiss, *The Law as It Could Be* (New York: New York University Press, 2003) 1; Fiss, "Against Settlement," supra note 17; David Luban, "Settlements and the Erosion of the Public Realm" (1995) 83 *Geo. L.J.* 2619; Robert H. Mnookin and L. Kornhauser, "Bargaining in the Shadow of the Law: The Case of Divorce" (1979) 88 *Yale L.J.* 950; Carr and Jencks, "The Privatization of Business and Commercial Dispute Resolution: A Misguided Policy Decision," supra note 2; Russell B. Korobkin, "The Role of Law in Settlement" in Michael L. Moffitt and Robert C. Bordone, eds., *The Handbook of Dispute Resolution* (San Francisco: Jossey-Bass, 2005) 254; Judith Resnik, "Courts: In and Out of Sight, Site, and Cite" (2008) 53 *Vill. L. Rev.* 771. See also Kent Roach, "Teaching Procedures: The Fiss/Weinrib Debate in Practice" (1991) 41 *U.T.L.J.* 247; Erik S. Knutsen, "Secret Settlements in Canada" (2009), in Janet Walker, gen. ed., et al., *The Civil Litigation Process: Cases and Materials*, 7th ed. (Toronto: Emond Montgomery, 2010) 859.

privatizing, and in the process largely eliminating, a significant part of the way democracy is realized.[101]

To illustrate this concern, I am again going to return to the Dealership case, and in particular, to the fourth procedural problem that occurred in that dispute. Now my reader might ask at this stage: What does the Dealership case have to do with societal regulation and democracy? In my view, as I now discuss, everything. Because as it turned out, the Dealership case was not at its core an isolated dispute, but rather the result of a pattern of potentially fraudulent conduct on the part of the Corporation. Throughout our retainer with John, we received a relatively steady stream of anecdotal information about similarly situated dealers in the United States who had found themselves in the same position vis-à-vis the Corporation and its deceptive and aggressive business practices. We also learned, again anecdotally, about a number of similar arbitrations being aggressively pursued by or against the Corporation. Because of the strict confidentiality provisions surrounding those proceedings, however, we were not able to obtain evidence about those other arbitrations, either through informal inquiries or through repeated efforts through the production and deposition stages of the proceeding. Overt denials of other proceedings were all that were forthcoming from the Corporation's officers and its lawyers.

However, approximately two weeks before our arbitration hearing was set to begin, I received in the mail a list of approximately thirty or forty similar, active arbitral proceedings in which the Corporation was involved. The list, which was included as part of a report to the Corporation's auditors, established clearly that the conduct engaged in by the Corporation with John was a pattern of repeated conduct that had led to similar disputes with numerous other dealers across the United States. The only reason we received it was because it was mistakenly sent to me by office staff of the Corporation's lawyers. In the face of this list, it seemed difficult for the Corporation to continue to voice, in good faith, its denial of the existence of these proceedings or their relevance. Unfortunately, because of professional and evidentiary reasons that prohibited us from leading the evidence in the arbitration,

101 For a further discussion of the court's regulatory role and its relationship to the state's legislative function, see W. Kip Viscusi, ed., *Regulation through Litigation* (Washington, DC: AEI-Brookings Joint Center for Regulatory Studies, 2002). See also supra Chapter 2.

that is exactly what the Corporation did: it proceeded at the arbitration as though those other proceedings did not exist. And the arbitrator's judgment did not take into account the fact that the conduct about which John was complaining was a course of conduct in which the Corporation was engaging with dozens of other dealers across the United States.

If we saw the dealership case as simply an A v. B case, or as what Fiss called the typical "dispute resolution story" involving a "quarrel between two neighbors"[102] that involves only limited private (in this case commercial) interests, there might be no need to concern ourselves with the procedural violations that occurred in that case or even the potentially fraudulent conduct that had a negative impact on John and thirty or forty similarly situated U.S. dealers. Recall again Hadfield's argument, for example, that we are not to concern ourselves with the "fair[ness]" of these sorts of commercial cases.[103] However, if we see the Dealership case, instead, as a potential opportunity not only to shut down the problematic conduct of a significant U.S. goods and services provider but also to send a significant signal to other similarly situated individual and corporate actors (and lawyers) in society about the negative repercussions of engaging in that sort of conduct, then opinions, policies, resource allocation, overall corporate behaviour, and potentially relevant regulatory policies (governing both corporations and lawyers) might be modified or at least influenced. That is the power of the adjudicative aspects of our processes of democratic governance. That is what the Dealership case has to do with the processes of regulation and democracy. Our system of democratic governance, which delegates much of its authority and policy-making functions to the adjudicative process, depends heavily on the direct and indirect regulatory effects of public dispute resolution processes.

Further, even absent situations involving fraudulent corporate behaviour, in many ways we are all like John in the Dealership case. Every time we automatically agree to a standard form contract provision (for a cell phone, Internet service, a car rental, an airline ticket, etc.) we essentially enter into contractual arrangements similar to the one at issue

102 Fiss, "Against Settlement," supra note 17 at 1076.

103 Hadfield, "Privatizing Commercial Law," supra note 64 at 40, discussed further at supra Chapter 5.

in the Dealership case. Privatizing the dispute resolution instruments of societal regulation, which allow us to challenge and look into those everyday relationships and agreements when they are of concern, risks losing important aspects of our public regulatory process that affect us all.

Public policy is made through civil disputes all the time, including in corporate and commercial matters. And these matters raise issues of public interest. If the directors of corporation A conduct its operations in such a way as to oppress the rights of its minority shareholders, then those shareholders typically have a right to the court's assistance pursuant to provincial or federal business corporations legislation. That court process is designed to resolve that individual dispute. It will also, however, set the ground rules, through public precedent and public scrutiny, for the future actions and expectations of directors, officers, employees, regulators, and clients of corporations B, C, D, E, F, and so on. And those ground rules will include policies about how to hire and fire employees, whether corporate wage and other policies negatively affect a certain class or group of employees, whether a corporation should reduce short-term share value in order to invest in the long term sustainability of its production processes, and so on. For example, according to Robert Vischer, when discussing the collapse of Enron following its improper use of off-balance sheet partnership structures to pursue transactions that would not have passed public disclosure scrutiny:

> Make no mistake, Enron's demise is a tale steeped in moral claims. The transactions on which Enron's skyrocketing share price was built were made possible only by the distinct acts and omissions of the company's managers, directors, accountants, and lawyers. The creation and treatment of these transactions constituted an unmistakable moral perspective: that profit trumps principle, that public perception of profit is a matter for advocacy and manipulation, that the corporation's only duty to its shareholders is the maximization of share price, and that it owes no duties to the public at large whatsoever. This perspective is helpfully illustrated by a former Enron employee's infamous explanation of the company's approach to the governing rules:
>
> Say you have a dog, but you need to create a duck on the financial statements. Fortunately, there are specific accounting rules for what constitutes a duck: yellow feet, white covering, orange beak. So you take the dog and paint its feet yellow and its fur white and you paste an orange plastic beak

> on its nose, and then you say to our accountants, "This is a duck! Don't you agree that it's a duck?" And the accountants say, "Yes, according to the rules, this is a duck." Everybody knows that it's a dog, not a duck, but that doesn't matter, because you've met the rule for calling it a duck.[104]

In Canada, one only needs to look as far back as 2008 in the Supreme Court of Canada's *BCE* judgment to see how significant public interest issues, located exclusively in corporate law contexts, get dealt with by the court in a way that has dramatic impacts not just for the immediate parties but for all of those affected by corporate and commercial activity as well.[105] The basic dispute in that case was about the value of debentures of a small group of debenture holders following a planned leveraged buyout of BCE Inc. On its face, therefore, the case was all about money. From a different perspective, however, the case was all about public policy: policies dealing with the management of corporations; duties of corporate decision makers to third parties; what it means to act in the "best interests of the corporation" (as opposed to simply acting in the best financial interests of its shareholders); and what the "business judgment rule" could mean, including, potentially, for modern, socially conscious directors, and so on. A lot was at stake in the *BCE* case that, given the wide swathe that corporate activity cuts through the everyday lives of regular citizens, was of interest – directly or indirectly – to that citizenry.

However, to the extent that the resolution of these disputes gets pushed behind closed doors, which is what we are actively doing, whatever decisions get made, if any, are made by those parties in accordance with their chosen processes as driven by their private interests. As the Supreme Court of Canada has acknowledged, private litigants "are normally presumed to be pursuing their own interests rather than those of the public at large."[106] Settlements are brokered on grounds of

104 Robert K. Vischer, "Legal Advice as Moral Perspective" (2006) 19:1 *Geo. J. Legal Ethics* 225 at 244.

105 *BCE Inc. v. 1976 Debentureholders*, [2008] 3 S.C.R. 560. For other relevant cases, see, for example, *Peoples Department Stores Inc. (Trustee of) v. Wise*, [2004] 3 S.C.R. 461; *Revlon, Inc. v. MacAndrews & Forbes Holdings, Inc.*, 506 A.2d 173 (1986); *Unocal Corp. v. Mesa Petroleum Co.*, 493 A.2d 946 (1985). For a discussion of some of the issues raised in these cases, see Ed Waitzer and Johnny Jaswal, "*Peoples, BCE*, and the Good Corporate 'Citizen'" (2009) 47:3 *Osgoode Hall L. J.* 439.

106 *RJR – MacDonald Inc. v. Canada (Attorney General)*, [1994] 1 S.C.R. 311 at pt. D.1.

business efficiencies and acceptable line-item entries, rather than on the bases of principles that militate in favour of justice and the strong pursuit of the public interest. And even if a decision gets reached, for example, in a private commercial arbitration setting, there is no guarantee, from a legitimacy perspective, that the process by which that decision got made accorded with basic public interest values. See the Dealership case for but one example.

And, of course, the democratic function of civil dispute resolution does not only reside in the world of corporate law. In fact, that is where some may also think it does not generally belong.[107] Ever since (and, of course, before) Lord Atkin's judgment in *Donoghue v. Stevenson*,[108] which – basing an assessment of reasonable conduct on the foundation of the "neighbor principle" – essentially founded our modern law of negligence, all sorts of areas of judge made civil law continue to engage critical public interest policies and distributional arrangements. Examples of that law include cases involving police misconduct,[109] employment and pay equity rights,[110] same-sex marriage,[111] insurance company misconduct,[112] defamation,[113] and so on. The list could be endless, even without class action cases, which are, by their very nature, designed to modify behaviour "by ensuring that actual and potential wrongdoers modify their behaviour to take full account of the harm they are causing, or might cause, to the public."[114]

---

107 See, for example, Chapter 5.

108 [1932] A.C. 562 (H.L.).

109 See, for example, *Jane Doe v. Board of Commissioners of Police for the Municipality of Metropolitan Toronto* (1990), 74 O.R. (2d) 225 (Div. Ct.). For a recent discussion of the *Jane Doe* case, see Trevor C.W. Farrow, "Five Pleadings Cases Everyone Should Read" (2009) 35:4 *Advocates' Q.* 466 at 478–80.

110 See, for example, *Public Service Alliance of Canada v. Canada Post Corporation*, 2011 SCC 57; *Ontario Nurses' Assn. v. Ontario (Pay Equity Hearings Tribunal)* (1995), 23 O.R. (3d) 43 (C.A.), leave to appeal to S.C.C. refused, *Glengarry Memorial Hospital v. Ontario (Pay Equity Hearings Tribunal) (S.C.C.)*, [1995] S.C.C.A. No. 259.

111 See, for example, *Halpern v. Canada (Attorney General)* (2003), 65 O.R. (3d) 161 (C.A.). See further *Halpern v. Canada (Attorney General)*, [2003] S.C.C.A. No. 337.

112 See, for example, *Whiten v. Pilot Insurance Co.*, [2002] 1 S.C.R. 595.

113 *Hill v. Church of Scientology of Toronto*, [1995] 2 S.C.R. 1130.

114 *Hollick v. Toronto (City)*, [2001] 3 S.C.R. 158, para. 15, McLachlin C.J. For a general background discussion, see Garry D. Watson, "Class Actions: The Canadian Experience" (2001) 11 *Duke J. Comp. & Int'l L.* 269.

But I have chosen to focus specifically on more typical corporate cases above to demonstrate that even in what would usually be thought of as cases invoking what Hadfield refers to as the "market function" of law, rather than its "democratic function,"[115] major public interest values can be at stake. As such, our current, almost knee-jerk reaction to privatizing these and other cases all over the justice system needs to be questioned and reconsidered. Sound policy bases, as I discuss in the next chapter, need to be identified and considered before we continue down a road, the end of which sees essentially the death of the court's role in framing important public interest policies.

This privatization cycle is equally present within state regulatory agencies. For example, as also discussed at length earlier in Chapter 4, various provincial and federal tribunals now have the mandate to seek to resolve complaints by using private dispute resolution mechanisms before moving to full-panel processes. To the extent that the private resolution of these administrative disputes is successful, their processes and results – designed to move our administrative law forward in ways that will better protect human rights and interests and influence expectations of the rest of us for how societal relationships should and must be conducted – are swept under the carpet. Even if there is an immediate and satisfactory resolution to the dispute at hand (and we cannot always be confident of that), we do not get the benefit of publicly scrutinized hearings and results that fill the increasingly influential space between private affairs and public legislation. That is a key role for public courts and tribunals, which needs to be jealously guarded.[116]

115 See Hadfield, "Privatizing Commercial Law: Lessons from ICANN" supra note 62 at 263, discussed further supra Chapter 5.

116 For recent comments on the potential problematic nature of secret settlements involving human rights tribunal matters, see, for example, John Cotter (Canadian Press), "Fired Transgendered Teacher Rejects Deal that Would Muzzle Him" *The Toronto Star* (10 April 2011), available online: <http://www.thestar.com/news/canada/2011/04/10/fired_transgendered_teacher_rejects_deal_that_would_muzzle_him.html>; and Metro News, "Transgendered Teacher Rejects Muzzle Offer" *Metro* (11 April 2011) 11.

Globalization

The final concern I raise in this chapter about the process of privatizing our systems of civil justice deals not so much with a specific incident or procedural issue, but rather with how the process of privatization, and in particular its problematic implications for democracy, are aggravated by globalization.

As a threshold question, what do I mean by globalization? Because I have discussed the phenomenon of globalization at some length elsewhere,[117] I will be relatively brief here. Globalization means many things to many people. It is a notoriously thorny and elusive concept, or as Brodie and Trimble have stated, its "meaning and implications ... remain elusive and contested."[118] As I have stated elsewhere,

> More than simply an historically-contingent event, globalization is a nuanced and expansive process involving a wide range of geographically-relevant political, economic, social and cultural connections and changes that are being created by and visited upon our personal and community

117 See, for example, Trevor C.W. Farrow, "Globalization, International Human Rights, and Civil Procedure" (2003) 41:3 *Alta. L. Rev.* 671; Trevor C.W. Farrow, "Negotiation, Mediation, Globalization Protests & Police: Right Processes; Wrong System, Parties, Issues & Time" (2003) 28 *Queen's L.J.* 665; Trevor C.W. Farrow, "Globalizing Approaches to Legal Education and Training: Canada to Japan" (2005) 38 *Hosei Riron J. L. & Pol.* 144; and Trevor C.W. Farrow, "Reviewing Globalization: Three Competing Stories, Two Emerging Themes, and How Law Schools Can and Must Participate" (2003) 13 *Meikei L. Rev.* 176, trans. (into Japanese) by M. Kuwahara, (2003) 44 *Aichigakuin L. Rev.* 29, rep'd (2004) 5 *J. Centre Int'l Stud.* 1. See further Trevor C.W. Farrow, "Regional Integration and Dispute Resolution in the Free Trade Area of the Americas" in Andy Knight et al., eds., *Re-Mapping the Americas: Globalization, Regionalization and the FTAA* (Edmonton: University of Alberta Press, forthcoming); Farrow, "Dispute Resolution, Access to Civil Justice and Legal Education," supra note 95 at 742, n. 5 and 787, n. 292, and accompanying text; and Trevor C.W. Farrow and Sheilah L. Martin, "Globalization & the Law: An Introduction" (2003) 41:3 *Alta. L. Rev.* 657. For an early formulation of my views on globalization, see Trevor C.W. Farrow, *Embracing the Complex Personality of International Law: Formalism, Anti-Formalism and the Globalization Construct* (LL.M. Thesis, Harvard Law School, 2000) [unpublished, archived at Harvard University Library]. See also recently Trevor C.W. Farrow, "Ethical Lawyering in a Global Community"(2013) 36:1 *Man. L. J.* 141.

118 Janine Brodie and Linda Trimble, "Reinventing Canada, An Overview" in Janine Brodie and Linda Trimble, eds., *Reinventing Canada: Politics of the 21st Century* (Toronto: Prentice Hall, 2003) 1 at 5.

> affairs. It therefore involves – in this broad sense – much more than what is often seen largely as a process of increased and interconnected trade, technology, and the movement of capital.[119]

However, for purposes of this book, what I am primarily interested in is only part of this more wide-ranging picture of globalization: international commerce and, in particular, the ability of commercial activity to operate within and move between domestic jurisdictions all over the world. As I have also commented elsewhere, a "defining characteristic of this narrow aspect of globalization has been the internationalization of commercial affairs, largely through the presence of MNCs [multinational corporations] ... in various jurisdictions around the world."[120] Further, as Andrew Bell has commented,

---

119 Farrow, "Globalization, International Human Rights, and Civil Procedure," supra note 117 at 675. For further sources on the topic of globalization and related governance issues, see, for example, Janine Brodie, "Introduction: Globalization and Citizenship beyond the National State" (December 2004) 8:4 *Citizenship Studies* 323; Brodie and Trimble, "Reinventing Canada, An Overview," supra note 118 at 5; Elizabeth Smythe, "Canadian Sovereignty and Global Trade and Investment Rules" in Brodie and Trimble, eds., *Reinventing Canada: Politics of the 21st Century*, supra note 118 at c. 21; David Schneiderman, *Constitutionalizing Economic Globalization: Investment Rules and Democracy's Promise* (Cambridge, UK and New York: Cambridge University Press, 2008); Erin A. O'Hara and Larry E. Ribstein, *The Law Market* (Oxford, UK, and New York: Oxford University Press, 2009); John H. Dunning, ed., *Making Globalization Good: The Moral Challenges of Global Capitalism* (Oxford, UK, and New York: Oxford University Press, 2003); Alfred C. Aman, *The Democracy Deficit: Taming Globalization through Law Reform* (New York: New York University Press, 2004); David Held et al., *Global Transformations: Politics, Economics and Culture* (Stanford, CA: Stanford University Press, 1999); William Twining, *Globalisation and Legal Theory* (London: Butterworths, 2000); Paul Hirst and Grahame Thompson, *Globalization in Question: The International Economy and the Possibilities of Governance*, 2nd ed. (Cambridge, UK: Polity Press, 1999). See also Dani Rodrik, *Has Globalization Gone Too Far?* (Washington, DC: Institute of International Economics, 1997); Joseph E. Stiglitz, *Globalization and its Discontents* (New York: W.W. Norton, 2002); A.S. Bhalla, ed., *Globalization, Growth and Marginalization* (Ottawa: International Development Research Centre, 1998); and Barry B. Hughes, *International Futures: Choices in the Creation of a New World Order*, 2nd ed. (Boulder, CO: Westview Press, 1996).

120 Farrow, "Globalization, International Human Rights, and Civil Procedure," supra note 117 at 675. See further Schneiderman, *Constitutionalizing Economic Globalization: Investment Rules and Democracy's Promise*, supra note 119; Stiglitz, *Globalization and its Discontents*, supra note 119 at 8–10; and Thomas L. Friedman, *The Lexus and the Olive Tree: Understanding Globalization* (New York: Anchor Books, 2000).

> One feature of economic globalization has been the great diversification of corporate holdings, both in terms of commodity portfolios and geographical spheres of operation, and a company's plant, equipment, and other assets will frequently be located in a strategic range of countries. Such diversification characterizes the corporate behaviour of vast multinational corporations. ... This collective burgeoning of transnational activity is seen most clearly in ... international commerce.[121]

We live in a world that is significantly dominated by corporate activity, and more specifically, corporate activity that engages or has an impact on the people, resources, and norms of more than one jurisdiction. According to Jeffrey Sachs, "[w]e live in revolutionary times, a revolution of global capitalism."[122] And the nature of this global revolution, according to Sachs, is "the intertwining and intensification of two profound trends: the globalization of society and the diffusion of capitalism."[123] From the perspective of democratic accountability, it is clear that commercial actors, and often and significantly international commercial actors, are playing increasingly powerful roles in the ordering of domestic affairs. As Andrew Canon has argued, the "nation state is consciously giving more power to industry groups. Globalisation has resulted in the concentration of actual power in corporate groups, which are independent of the nation state."[124] Sachs agrees: the spread of capitalism has become "the organizing principle of national economies."[125] Given this state of affairs, Marx was clearly right about a number of things. He appreciated the "gigantic"[126] power of capitalism.[127] He also clearly appreciated the growing phenomenon of globalization. As he put it,

---

121 Andrew Bell, *Forum Shopping and Venue in Transnational Litigation* (Oxford, UK: Oxford University Press, 2003) at 3, 5.

122 Jerrfey D. Sachs, "Globalization and the Rule of Law" (remarks to Yale Law School alumni weekend, Yale University, 16 October 1998) [archived with author].

123 Ibid.

124 Andrew J. Canon, "A Pluralism of Private Courts" (2004) 23 *C.J.Q.* 309 at 310.

125 Ibid.

126 Karl Marx and Frederich Engels, *Manifesto of the Communist Party* (1848) in Robert C. Tucker, ed., *The Marx-Engels Reader*, 2nd ed. (New York and London: W.W. Norton, 1978) 473 at 478.

127 See generally Karl Marx, *Capital: A Critique of Political Economy*, vols. 1 and 2 (London: Penguin Books, 1976).

> National differences and antagonisms between peoples are daily more and more vanishing, owing to the development of the bourgeoisie, to freedom of commerce, to the world-market, to uniformity in the mode of production and in the conditions of life corresponding thereto.[128]

With respect to "National differences and antagonisms," Marx was in essence noticing (with respect to the bourgeois beneficiaries of globalization) what Thomas Friedman – an extremely unlikely bedfellow – called 150 years later his "Golden Arches Theory of Conflict Prevention." Friedman's Golden Arches theory is that no two countries "that both had McDonald's had fought a war against each other since each got its McDonald's."[129] And as the recent world economic crisis demonstrated, Marx was also largely right (although for different reasons) about the fact that the world capital economy is controlled to a great extent by forces beyond the direct control of the state. According to Marx, modern capitalism ("bourgeois society") is "like the sorcerer, who is no longer able to control the powers of the nether world whom he has called up by his spells."[130] What Marx was obviously not correct about was the "fall"[131] or "d[ying] off"[132] (which he called "inevitable"[133]) of the bourgeois system. Marx saw that "fall" as the "end of capitalism,"[134] which would come through the production "of its own grave-diggers."[135] Put bluntly (and very simply), looking to Friedman again, the "free market" – due to the "Darwinian brutality of … capitalism" – is the "only ideological

128 Marx and Engels, *Manifesto of the Communist Party*, supra note 126 at 488. See also ibid. at 475–7.

129 Friedman, *The Lexus and the Olive Tree*, supra note 120 at c. 12, p. 248. Friedman also acknowledges several things: first, he is not the first to notice the effect that commerce and globalization have on the potential to increase peace (see, for example, Montesquieu and Norman Angell), and, second, that "globalization does not, and will not, end geopolitics." Ibid. at 249–50. For Friedman's further thinking on globalization, see Thomas L. Friedman, *The World Is Flat: A Brief History of the Twenty-First Century* (New York: Farrar, Straus and Giroux, 2005).

130 Marx and Engels, *Manifesto of the Communist Party*, supra note 126 at 478.

131 Ibid. at 483.

132 Karl Marx, *Critique of the Gotha Program* (1875), pt. IV in Tucker, ed., *The Marx-Engels Reader*, supra note 126 at 525, 537.

133 Marx and Engels, *Manifesto of the Communist Party*, supra note 126 at 483.

134 Karl Marx, *The Grundrisse* (1857–8) at pt. H in Tucker, ed., *The Marx-Engels Reader*, supra note 126 at 221, 291.

135 Marx and Engels, *Manifesto of the Communist Party*, supra note 126 at 483.

alternative left" in the struggle for prominence between "free-market capitalism" and "communism, socialism and fascism."[136] And although the current economic crisis has witnessed an increased role for the state in the way of calls for greater regulatory oversight and greater financial involvement through, for example, massive bailout and other injections, the ongoing and deepening privatization phenomenon discussed earlier[137] continues to strengthen the power and upward trajectory of the free-market economy.

So what does all of this have to do with the privatization of the civil justice system? We have established that international economic actors have an increasing presence domestically, including through the use of processes and means of production (including information technology, natural and manufactured resources, and human capital), through access to domestic markets (through retailers and consumers, etc.), and so on. And we typically expect that, at least in theory, international actors who operate within our local jurisdictions will play by the rules that we set for ourselves in those jurisdictions. Environmental standards, labour standards, equality and other human rights standards, securities regulations, competition standards, and fair advertising requirements, among others, are all examples of the kinds of rules we set for ourselves and for those who operate within our local jurisdictions.

To the extent that violations of those rules occur, we have public dispute resolution processes available to deal with those violations. Given economic globalization, these domestic civil dispute resolution processes have become increasingly populated by foreign actors. As the Supreme Court of Canada has acknowledged, "the business of litigation, like commerce itself, has become increasingly international."[138] For some time now, however, international commercial actors have been increasingly seeking out ADR proceedings, as opposed to courts, for the resolution of their domestic disputes.[139] These often include

136 Friedman, *The Lexus and the Olive Tree*, supra note 120 at 104.

137 See, for example, supra Chapter 3.

138 *Amchem Products Inc. v. British Columbia (Workers' Compensation Board)*, [1993] 1 S.C.R. 897 at 911, Sopinka J.

139 As I have commented elsewhere, "[i]n an age where commercial relationships are increasingly complex and globalized … ADR … has become an attractive option for almost all types of disputes and disputants. ADR often provides tools that are flexible, cost-effective, private and, generally, preferred by dispute resolution consumers." Trevor C.W. Farrow, "The Rule of Law in Developing Countries Is Not Just about Courts" 26:31 *The Lawyers Weekly* (15 December 2006) 11.

arbitration[140]; however, mediation is also increasingly being used as well.[141] And not only are parties expressing these ADR preferences, courts are encouraging them.[142] In addition to the typical benefits that flow from private ADR processes (that I discussed at length earlier in Chapter 4), international commercial actors are pursuing ADR for actively sidestepping domestic processes and, often, domestic substantive legal rights and obligations.[143] If we are fine with this trend, then privatize away! However, to the extent that we want to ensure: that violations by international actors of domestic laws, customs, and regulations are resolved in accordance with those accepted local rules (as well as established international standards); that current and future commercial actors – both domestic and international – operating within our borders know that their activities and affairs will be regulated by

---

140 See, for example, Christopher R. Drahozal and Richard W. Naimark, eds., *Towards a Science of International Arbitration: Collected Empirical Research* (The Hague: Kluwer, 2005); Richard Boivin and Nicola Mariani, "International Arbitration in Canada: Highest Court Rules in Favour of Broad Interpretation of Arbitrability" (2003) *J. Int'l Arb.* 507; Andreas F. Lowenfeld, *International Commercial Litigation and Arbitration* (St. Paul, MN: West Publishing, 1993); Dora M. Gruner, "Accounting for the Public Interest in International Arbitration: The Need for Procedural and Structural Reform" (2002–3) 41 *Colum. J. Transnat'l L.* 923; Yves Dezalay, *Dealing in Virtue: International Commercial Arbitration and the Construction of a Transnational Legal Order* (Chicago: University of Chicago Press, 1996); and Fernando Mantilla-Serrano, "Towards a Transnational Procedural Public Policy" (2004) 20:4 *Arb. Int'l* 333. See further Donalee Moulton, "Flying the Friendly Skies: Lawyers Arbitrate Internationally" 28:7 *The Lawyers Weekly* (13 June 2008) 7; Jennifer McPhee, "Arbitration Becoming the 'New' Civil Litigation," supra note 3.

141 See, for example, Linda C. Reif, "The Use of Conciliation or Mediation for the Resolution of International Commercial Disputes" (2007) 45 *Can. Bus. L.J.* 20; and Daryl-Lynn Carlson, "Worldwide Mediation" 13:7 *National* (November 2004) 30.

142 For example, according to the Supreme Court of Canada,

> [t]his Court has often stressed the importance of such clauses ["arbitration clause[s] or … choice of forum clause[s]"] … and the need to encourage them, because they provide international commercial relations with the stability and foreseeability required for purposes of the critical components of private international law, namely order and fairness. …

GreCon Dimter inc. v. J. R. Normand inc., [2005] 2 S.C.R. 401 at para. 22, LeBel J. [citations omitted].

143 See Farrow, "The Rule of Law in Developing Countries Is Not Just about Courts," supra note 139.

principled and consistent legal standards; and that those actors know what those standards are so that they, and others, can govern their arrangements and relationships accordingly, then putting the resolution of disputes behind closed doors, with no resulting body of publicly available law being produced, will not help us achieve our regulatory objectives. Doing otherwise, or put differently, allowing international actors to sidestep local policy arrangements and distributional choices through the promotion and use of private dispute resolution mechanisms, permits private international market arrangements facilitated by globalization to trump domestic public democratic processes.

This is what we are currently and actively promoting with domestic ADR processes that allow and encourage international actors to resolve their disputes within domestic borders. And again, if all that was at stake was the resolution of Fiss's "quarrel between two neighbors,"[144] then we might not be so concerned. However, as we saw earlier, what we are more often talking about are major cases involving environmental issues, employment issues, human rights issues, and so forth. When non-domestic norms and values, particularly ones driven by corporate efficiency-based interests, are driving the litigation strategies of international disputants in cases that can have significant impacts on the current and future lives and distributional arrangements of local citizens and industries, some sense of public scrutiny and awareness of and deliberation about those cases is warranted. Doing otherwise not only loses the benefit of creating important law in a given commercial area (for the benefit of both the immediate parties as well as others who are similarly situated), it also moves the site of norm-creation and societal regulation one step farther up the global ladder and away from the local communities that are, in the end, directly and indirectly affected by the actions and distributional choices of those international actors. It cuts the citizenry out of the deliberative law-making potential of the open judicial process, thereby delegitimizing the process and the result.[145] It also, as Frank Michelman has commented, creates a situation

144 Fiss, "Against Settlement," supra note 17 at 1076, discussed supra at note 102 and accompanying text.

145 An example of a step toward more openness and transparency, in the context of international arbitration, was the Free Trade Commission's 2001 commitment to make arbitration documents in NAFTA investor-state proceedings accessible to the public. See Foreign Affairs and International Trade Canada, "Dispute Settlement:

in which the law and norms at play in society "that people would regularly confront" would increasingly be regulatory processes "with whose creation they have had nothing whatsoever to do."[146]

To illustrate my point, I now look at one of the most infamous cases of economic globalization gone wrong: the Bhopal gas leak disaster. As I have discussed more thoroughly elsewhere,[147] the event involved thousands and thousands of residents of the city of Bhopal in central India who suffered injury and death on the night of 2–3 December 1984. The tragedy resulted from a massive leak of the highly toxic methyl isocyanate gas, which was used to make Sevin and Temik pesticides, at the Union Carbide Corporation (UCC) Bhopal chemical plant. When a corporation such as UCC, through its transnational holdings, is able to capitalize on the comparative advantages of foreign labour and environmental standards for the benefit of its shareholders and international clientele, one would expect it also to take the burden of remedying negative local impacts such as the 1984 environmental and human rights disaster that occurred in Bhopal as a result of that capitalization. That did not happen. As such, litigation, which was largely unsuccessful on a number of fronts,[148] was subsequently brought against UCC and others in the United States.[149]

NAFTA – Chapter 11 – Investment" (last updated 17 May 2002), available online: Government of Canada <http://www.international.gc.ca/trade-agreements-accords-commerciaux/topics-domaines/disp-diff/nafta.aspx>. See further ibid. at "General Information on NAFTA Chapter 11" (last modified 30 November 2011), available online: Government of Canada <http://www.international.gc.ca/trade-agreements-accords-commerciaux/topics-domaines/disp-diff/nafta-general-alena-generale.aspx?lang=eng>. It is important to acknowledge, however, that this particular sort of "sunshine" approach to investor-state arbitration in NAFTA is very much the exception and not the norm in the context of thousands of other investor-state arbitration treaties and agreements in which confidentiality is still very much the rule. I am grateful to my colleague Gus Van Harten for useful assistance on this point.

146 Frank I. Michelman, "W(h)ither the Constitution?" (1999–2000) 21 *Cardozo L. Rev.* 1063 at 1071 (discussed further supra Chapter 2). For a further discussion on the connection between privatization and globalization, see generally ibid.

147 Farrow, "Globalization, International Human Rights, and Civil Procedure," supra note 117.

148 See ibid.

149 See, for example, *In re Union Carbide Corp. Gas Plant Disaster at Bhopal, India*, 634 F.Supp. 842 at 844 (S.D.N.Y. 1986), Keenan Dist. J., mod'd & aff'd 809 F.2d 195 (2d Cir. 1987), cert. den'd 484 U.S. 871 (1987). See also subsequent related cases including *In re Union Carbide Corp. Gas Plant Disaster*, [1992] U.S. Dist. LEXIS 1909

Despite the disappointing and problematic results of the litigation (and subsequent settlements, treatment of survivors, site cleanup, and so on, all of which unsatisfactorily continued more than twenty-five years later[150]), there was one positive aspect of the Bhopal litigation: its publicity. This publicity, at least in part, fostered public awareness of the disaster. And through this awareness, increased pressure has been brought, and continues to be brought, upon (and now from within) the international corporate community in an effort to improve corporate social responsibility in all sorts of areas of commercial activity.[151] Further, important international initiatives also continue to develop in the area.[152] Regardless of the success or failure of the Bhopal case from a dispute resolution perspective, it was, in my view, at least a partial success from a non-party future regulatory perspective, even without a finding of liability on the merits. That, again, is the power of public process. If all of that litigation had occurred behind closed doors pursuant to private arbitration, much of the benefit of that public scrutiny and

---

(S.D.N.Y. 1992), aff'd *Bi v. Union Carbide Chems. and Plastics Co.*, 984 F.2d 582 (2d Cir. 1993), cert. den'd 510 U.S. 862 (1993). See also *Bano v. Union Carbide Corp.*, [2000] U.S. Dist. LEXIS 12326 (S.D.N.Y. 2000), aff'd, vac'd in part & remanded 273 F.3d 120 (2d Cir. 2001), claim dis'd and motion grant'd [2003] U.S. Dist. LEXIS 4097 (S.D.N.Y. 2003).

150 See, for example, Suketu Mehta, "A Cloud Still Hangs over Bhopal" *The New York Times* (2 December 2009) [archived with author].

151 See, for example, Ilias Bantekas, "Corporate Social Responsibility in International Law" (2004) 22 *B.U. Int'l L.J.* 309; and Halina Ward, "The Interface Between Globalization, Corporate Responsibility, and the Legal Profession" (2004) 1 *U. St. Thomas L.J.* 813.

152 See, for example, United Nations, *Report of the Special Representative of the Secretary-General on the Issue of Human Rights and Transnational Corporations and other Business Enterprises, John Ruggie*, "Guiding Principles on Business and Human Rights: Implementing the United Nations 'Protect, Respect and Remedy' Framework," HRC, 17th Sess., Agenda Item 3, UN Doc. A/HRC/17/31 (21 March 2011) (endorsed by UNHRC 16 June 2011), available online: OHCHR <http://www.ohchr.org/documents/issues/business/A.HRC.17.31.pdf>; U.N. Global Compact, available online: United Nations <http://www.unglobalcompact.org/>; U.N. Global Compact, Business Leaders Initiative on Human Rights, "A Guide for Integrating Human Rights into Business Management," available online: United Nations <http://www.unglobalcompact.org/docs/issues_doc/human_rights/Resources/guide_hr.pdf>. See further Amnesty International et al., "Joint Civil Society Statement on the Draft Guiding Principles on Business and Human Rights" (January 2011), available online: Business & Human Rights Resource Centre <http://www.fidh.org/IMG/pdf/Joint_CSO_Statement_on_GPs.pdf>; and Global Reporting Initiative (GRI), "Sustainability Reporting Guidelines" (G3.1, 2011) [archived with author].

active international and political engagement surrounding that case would have certainly been lost or greatly reduced.[153]

Privatizing these globalized processes further will only magnify the already existing democratic deficit caused by the privatization of dispute resolution processes involving solely domestic parties. Not only does the state lose control of who gets to play in its backyard; it also loses one of its strongest processes to help control how those games are played. And when those games involve the lives and property of local citizens, through employment contracts, the use of resources, activities with major environmental impacts, and so on, then we should care whether or not we maintain some degree of oversight, influence, control over, and engagement with the rules and norms by which those activities are pursued. Privatizing these processes cuts the citizenry out of those deliberative democratic discussions.

153 For further commentary, see Gruner, "Accounting for the Public Interest in International Arbitration: The Need for Procedural and Structural Reform," supra note 140; Farrow, "Globalization, International Human Rights, and Civil Procedure," supra note 117; S. Bottomley and D. Kinley, eds., *Commercial Law and Human Rights* (Aldershot, UK: Ashgate Publishing, 2002); Bell, *Forum Shopping and Venue in Transnational Litigation*, supra note 121; Jonnette Watson Hamilton, "The Impact of International Commercial Arbitration on Canadian Law and Courts" in Patricia Hughes and Patrick A. Molinari, eds., *Participatory Justice in a Global Economy: The New Rule of Law* (Montréal: Les Éditions Thémis, 2004) 125; and Patricia Hughes, "The Rule of Law: Challenges in a Global Economy" in Hughes and Molinari, eds., *Participatory Justice in a Global Economy: The New Rule of Law*, ibid.

Chapter Seven

Challenges and the Future of Reform

The focus of this book is the privatization trajectory of modern civil justice practice and reform. Through this focus of attention, the overall goal of this book is to notice, and in turn to unpack, understand, question, and *at times* argue for the redirection of what has become the largely unwavering nature of that civil justice privatization trajectory. However, by calling for a questioning of the trajectory "at times" (rather than "at *all* times" or something similarly absolute), I want to make clear, as I stated in the introductory chapter, that my overall goal is *not* to do away with privatization all together. As I have tried to articulate, there are many sound legal, political, and social policy reasons, as supported by the voices of practicing stakeholders from all corners of the dispute resolution system, to support some aspects of current privatization initiatives.

As such, the difficult question for this book, as I earlier acknowledged (in Chapter 1), becomes one of balance. If I am right that some privatization is desirable, but that the current trajectory of privatized civil dispute resolution practice and reform is highly problematic in that, in sum, it is at odds with fundamental notions of public democratic governance, then the discussion must move to the question of how to balance the protection of public law-making functions (Chapter 2) and the preferences and justifications for privatization at all levels of civil and related dispute resolution processes (Chapters 3–5) with my concerns about privatization and its potential negative impacts on democracy (Chapter 6). The key to that balancing process, in my view, is a shift in how we understand, evaluate, and legitimize the civil dispute resolution process in the first place. What I am talking about here, to avoid further jeopardizing the regulatory power of public adjudication, is shifting the ultimate source for how we think about, legitimize, evaluate and practice civil justice away from ground-level preferences based primarily on *efficiency*, where, as Héctor Fix-Fierro has recognized,[1] the legitimizing source currently lies, and towards ground-level preferences based primarily on *justice*.

I recognize at this stage that for my argument, which advocates for a shift in the current understanding of the fundamental justifications for civil justice practice and reform to be persuasive, it must address the strongest challenges – the counterarguments that seek to justify privatization – that line up against it. And the strongest of those justifications, as I developed earlier (in Chapter 5) involve, in a nutshell, privatization's tendency towards efficiency and its purported (and related) ability to facilitate access to justice. Therefore, I develop my argument in this final chapter not by sidestepping those strong counterarguments but rather by taking this opportunity to frame my argument as a direct response to, as well as a conversation with, those important counterarguments.

The Business Case Revisited

Efficiency and Justice

As I discussed earlier in Chapter 5, one of the two primary justifications for current privatization preferences is premised on a basic business case analysis, which in turn, at its core, sounds in principles of efficiency. According to these policy and practice preferences, privatization is good from a business case perspective largely because it is demonstrably more efficient. Now it is important to concede, right off the bat, that the two premises at play in this discussion – efficiency and justice – are clearly not necessarily or always mutually exclusive. Often when disputes are resolved more efficiently, justice obtains. However, on occasions when they are mutually exclusive, *and in any event*, justice must be the ultimate source of legitimacy and indicator of success when it comes to making significant policy choices and resource allocations at all levels and regarding all players, individual and collective,

1 See Héctor Fix-Fierro, *Courts, Justice and Efficiency: A Socio-Legal Study of Economic Rationality in Adjudication* (Oxford, UK, and Portland, OR: Hart Publishing, 2003) at 235, discussed further at supra Chapter 5.

within our public systems of civil justice. When the two premises are at odds, justice must trump efficiency.[2] To do otherwise risks one of the very foundational aspects of our processes of public governance in a democracy. As I argued earlier in this book (in Chapters 2 and 4), through the public court and administrative tribunal systems, citizens have downloaded major aspects of the public law-making and regulatory functions. This delegation has been done on the premise, and trust, that citizens can rely on the form and substance of these methods of public regulation. In this sense, the operation of democracy, which very much relies on the various branches of government, would be impossible without a robust rule of law system that is operationalized through our public judicial and quasi-judicial bodies. So although efficiency is clearly a good thing and must be encouraged, at the end of the day, efficiency cannot be the endgame of the process. Rather, justice must be – that is the ultimate promise of the public justice system. Further, to the extent that these principles do collide, justice, and not efficiency, must be the ultimate guiding consideration for how we legitimize, evaluate, practice and reform public civil justice.

What I mean by justice (and access to it) is developed in several layers – at both the individual and collective levels of society – over the course of this chapter. To the extent that this book is premised on a vision of civil justice that seriously engages both its retrospective and prospective elements (discussed in Chapter 2), the idea of justice that I am developing further in this chapter must operate at both levels. At the retrospective, dispute resolution level, clearly fair, predictable, and accessible processes are needed in order to provide for an efficient, but ultimately just, system of dispute resolution in society. Justice in this sense is about the fair workings of the civil dispute resolution system largely in the context of individual cases. At the prospective, regulatory level, justice draws in broader, public interest notions of redistribution, participation, social ordering, and equality. Because civil justice

2 For an earlier discussion on this issue, see Trevor C.W. Farrow, "Public Justice, Private Dispute Resolution and Democracy" in Ronalda Murphy and Patrick A. Molinari, eds., *Doing Justice: Dispute Resolution in the Courts and Beyond* (Montréal: Canadian Institute for the Administration of Justice, 2009) 301 at 357–8. See further Nancy A. Welsh, "Remembering the Role of Justice in Resolution: Insights from Procedural and Social Justice Theories" (2004) 54 *J. Legal Educ.* 49; Jacqueline M. Nolan-Haley, "Court Mediation and the Search for Justice Through Law" (1996) 74 *Wash. U.L.Q.* 47; and Colleen M. Hanycz, "More Access to Less Justice: Efficiency, Proportionality and Costs in Canadian Civil Justice Reform" (2008) 27 *C.J.Q.* 98.

fundamentally involves conversations about procedure, what I am largely talking about in this chapter ultimately takes up justice very much in its procedural workings and effects. This is the case through this part of this chapter, in which I come back to efficiency arguments underpinning the various functions of law that I developed and challenged earlier in Chapters 5 and 6. I then return to the access to justice discussion that I developed earlier in Chapter 5, this time looking at how notions of procedural justice animate both the narrow and broad versions of that discussion. In the end, as I develop through the final parts of this chapter, what I care about is largely a procedural notion of justice that operates through the civil justice system to enable not only the fair resolution of disputes, but also the substantive well-being of society.

Categorizing Cases

To start this discussion, I first turn to the notion of categorizing cases based on the aspect or function of law that they engage. Here is where my argument runs up against the various policy and practice-related arguments, discussed earlier in Chapter 5, which support the current and very robust efficiency-driven privatization ethos. Several versions of those counterarguments include, from an academic perspective for example, the arguments made by Hadfield, Caplan, and Stringham, and from a public policy-making perspective, for example, from the Hon. Gord Mackintosh of the Manitoba Legislative Assembly (all discussed earlier in Chapter 5). For example, recall that, according to Hadfield, the "democratic function" of law "protects rights, structures the institutions of democratic governance, redistributes wealth, promotes social objectives such as equality or clean air, and resolves disputes among citizens," whereas the "market function" of law "provides the structure of markets – determining property rights, providing a means of commitment through contract to support cooperative activity – and regulation to correct market failures in the achievement of efficiency."[3]

At this initial point of the discussion, I quickly concede that I agree on one level with Hadfield: the "democratic function" of law, as I essentially articulate in Chapter 2, is "one that must be accomplished

3 See Gillian K. Hadfield, "Privatizing Commercial Law: Lessons from ICANN" (2002) 6 *J. Small & Emerging Bus. L.* 258 at 263, discussed further supra Chapters 5 and 6.

through public institutions, accountable to the polity in order to preserve democratic legitimacy."[4] What I fail to see, however, is how many disputes – specifically including commercial disputes in the context of the arguments, for example, made expressly by Hadfield and, in essence, by Mackintosh – only engage "a public interest in efficiency" that involves "creating wealth and maximizing the value of resources,"[5] while not at the same time engaging other "democratic" values that include "redistribution, equality, autonomy, environmental preservation, public safety, human flourishing, participation" and the like.[6] Although Hadfield does acknowledge the possibility of an economic activity implicating "both efficiency and nonefficiency values,"[7] where we differ is the extent to which that situation of dual implication will obtain. I fail to see how many, if not most, disputes – and again specifically including commercial disputes for purposes of this part of the discussion – do not invoke principles that go beyond the purview of what Hadfield calls the "market function" of law, or what Mackintosh contemplates as its pure "commercial" aspects.

This discussion has an impact at two levels. First, at the ground level of individual disputes, the discussion engages the question of what cases should or should not go to court. Second, at a more general and collective level, the discussion engages policy choices about civil justice processes and reform and how much those choices should be influenced by efficiency-driven principles as opposed to justice-driven principles.

Individual Disputes

As to the first level, the question essentially boils down to this: Can we categorize civil justice disputes as ones that should go a private route as opposed to ones that should go to a public hearing? Simply put, what I am talking about here is looking at which of the cases, for example, that the litigators in the survey that I conducted for purposes of this

---

4 Ibid.

5 Ibid. [emphasis omitted].

6 Ibid. [emphasis omitted].

7 Ibid. See further Gillian K. Hadfield, "Privatizing Commercial Law" (2001) 42:1 *Regulation* 40, available online: Cato Institute <http://object.cato.org/sites/cato.org/files/serials/files/regulation/2001/4/hadfield.pdf>.

book[8] are involved in "should" go to court. The current reality, based on my survey and other studies,[9] is that most civil justice stakeholders think that most cases should go the private route. That is certainly, in fact, what is happening at the moment (see Chapters 3–5). And this reality is consistent with the following observation from the chief justice of Canada regarding approaches by the courts to this question (which is also consistent with my earlier discussion about court-based preferences in Chapters 3 and 5): "Courts have been promoting various forms of out-of-court mediation and arbitration as a more effective way of achieving settlement and dealing with many civil cases. This is good."[10] However, as the chief justice also remarks, "The fact is, some cases should go to court. They raise legal issues that should be considered by the courts for the good of the litigants and the development of the law."[11]

In light of this statement from the chief justice, the categorization question now becomes reframed as what cases are included in those "some cases" that "should go to court"? Or put slightly differently, Carri Menkel-Meadow questions "when and how … we use adjudication and when … we use something else."[12] To address these questions, in light of earlier discussions in this book, we need essentially to think about whether we can reasonably and meaningfully categorize cases, as Hadfield, Mackintosh and others essentially try to do, as ones that involve public interest values that engage the "democratic function" of law as opposed to ones whose public interest values extend only to a "public interest in efficiency" and as such essentially engage only the "market function" of law. The former cases, in this line of thinking, are more likely candidates for proceeding in the public dispute resolution system, whereas the latter are more likely candidates for a private system.

8 See supra Chapter 5.

9 See generally ibid.

10 Rt. Hon. Beverley McLachlin, P.C., "The Challenges We Face" (remarks presented at Empire Club of Canada, Toronto, 8 March 2007), available online: Supreme Court of Canada <http://www.scc-csc.gc.ca/court-cour/judges-juges/spe-dis/bm-2007-03-08-eng.aspx>.

11 Ibid. For a report of these remarks, see Kirk Makin, "Top Judge Sounds Alarm on Trial Delays" *The Globe and Mail* (9 March 2007) A1. See recent *George Weston Ltd. v. Domtar Inc.* (2012), 112 O.R (3d) 190 (S.C.J.) at pt. II.A.

12 Carri Menkel-Meadow, "Introduction: What Will We Do When Adjudication Ends? A Brief Intellectual History of ADR" (1996–7) 44 *UCLA L. Rev.* 1613 at 1623.

There is clearly an appeal to this bifurcated approach. And in the end, to the extent that I will argue for a retained (and fairly robust) place for efficiency considerations in how we think about civil justice reform going forward, this kind of categorization *sensibility* (as opposed to an actual system) may be helpful. But it only gets us so far. Because, as I also argue, it is extremely difficult to see how a bifurcated system would work, either procedurally as a practical matter or, more importantly, from the perspective of the aspects of law that cases, substantively, actually engage. As a threshold practical matter, Owen Fiss, when challenging the ADR movement early on, considered this categorization question as well. In so doing, he rejected this approach of sorting cases into "tracks," one for (private) settlement and one for (public) judgment.[13] He essentially questioned whether a procedure could be articulated that could provide a meaningful and workable criteria-based system. According to Fiss, such a system could likely not be "sensibly implemented" because of his view that it is "impossible to formulate adequate criteria for prospectively sorting cases."[14] I tend to agree, for some of the reasons articulated immediately above.

However, let us assume that such a system could be objectively articulated. My bigger concern is that even if a criteria-based system were practically formulated, I find it hard to see whether many cases at all, in terms of the legal issues that they engage or the public policy issues on which they potentially have an impact, would clearly involve "market" rather than "democratic" criteria as set up pursuant to a function-of-law analysis envisioned by Hadfield or, for that matter, Mackintosh. Another person who also, in essence, contemplates a bifurcated approach to evaluating cases is Richard Susskind. For Susskind, there is merit in thinking about cases in terms of "hard" cases and non-"hard" cases. Hard cases are those that involve "complex issues of principle, policy, and morality."[15] The others presumably do not. For Susskind, judges are still required for the determination of at least some of these

---

13 See Owen M. Fiss, "Against Settlement" (1984) 93 *Yale L.J.* 1073 at 1087–9.

14 Ibid. at 1088.

15 Richard Susskind, *The End of Lawyers? Rethinking the Nature of Legal Services* (Oxford, UK: Oxford University Press, 2008) at 217. See further Richard Susskind, *Expert Systems in Law* (Oxford, UK: Oxford University Press, 1987; paperback ed., 1989) at 249–51, cited in ibid. at 217, n. 41.

hard cases. However, for non-hard cases, Susskind paints a scenario that contemplates, albeit provocatively, "computers replacing judges."[16] This, for Susskind, would be a quintessential – online – version of privatization.[17]

If most disputes really did engage fully private A v. B scenarios,[18] what Susskind categorizes as non-hard cases,[19] or what Fiss called the typical "dispute resolution story" that involved a lawsuit as a simple "quarrel between two neighbors" (a "story" told, according to Fiss, by the ADR movement in order to justify its increased prominence),[20] then an exercise in categorization along "hard" vs. non-"hard" cases, or public interest vs. private (or market-based) interest might make significant sense. As I have argued elsewhere, to the extent that

> a dispute involves the private rights of A v. B, and further, when two "consenting adults" (including corporations) have chosen to move their dispute off the busy docket of our public court system and into the private boardroom of an arbitrator or mediator, current views suggest that justice is being served. The argument is that the resolution of disputes – like other goods and services – should not be deprived of the benefits of freedom of movement and contract in an efficiency-seeking, innovative and expanding market economy.[21]

However, in addition to the "costs"[22] associated with this kind of approach that I discussed earlier (see, e.g., Chapter 6), the concern that

---

16 Susskind, *The End of Lawyers?*, ibid. at 217. But see ibid. at 274, where Susskind acknowledges that with respect to the work of barristers, which is "highly bespoke," it is "hard to see how oral advocacy and the dispensing of expert advice can be standardized or computerized."

17 As I mentioned earlier (supra Chapter 5), I acknowledge that Susskind's thesis is not simply about replacing legal work with computers and that his musings about computers and judging must be put in the context of his overall arguments about "standardization, commoditization, and the transfer of many legal tasks from lawyers to non-lawyers." See ibid. at 274.

18 See, for example, Trevor C.W. Farrow, "Privatizing our Public Civil Justice System" (2006) 9 *News & Views Civ. Just. Ref.* 16 at 16.

19 Susskind, *The End of Lawyers?*, supra note 15 at 217.

20 Fiss, "Against Settlement," supra note 13 at 1076.

21 Farrow, "Privatizing our Public Civil Justice System," supra note 18 at 16.

22 I am thinking here of the costs associated with privatization's negative impact on democracy. See ibid. See further supra Chapter 6.

I am raising here is that, like Fiss, I think the number of cases that involve more than simply the "market" or non-hard aspects of law is likely not negligible. In fact, many cases engage elements of both the market and democratic aspects of law. The kinds of cases Fiss was interested in included "those cases in which there are significant distributional inequalities ... and those in which justice needs to be done, or to put it more modestly, where there is a genuine social need for an authoritative interpretation of law." As with Fiss, I agree that "the number of cases that satisfy one of these ... criteria is considerable. ... [T]hey probably dominate the docket of a modern court system."[23] My position here is based on my view that many cases that might look to be market-related cases in fact engage much more than those efficiency-premised issues. Often important public policy issues lurk behind the façade of fights over private property and contracts.

The Dealership Case

A good example that supports this position is the Dealership case. As I argued earlier,[24] the Dealership case was a commercial case that, on first blush, very much engaged the "market function" of law as contemplated by Hadfield, or the flavor of "commercial" cases contemplated by Mackintosh for which, in his view, private dispute resolution processes should be "require[d]."[25] On one level, the case was about "determining property rights," "providing a means of commitment through contract to support cooperative activity" and "correct[ing] market failures in the achievement of efficiency."[26] It also, along these market-oriented lines, engaged what Hadfield identifies as "a public interest in efficiency," which involves "creating wealth and maximizing the value of resources."[27] On these levels, the Dealership case was very much a case that engaged the non-"hard," "commercial," and "market function" of law and therefore should take seriously ways in which its resolution could have maximized the efficient use (or, in fact, non-use) of state resources as well as being efficient in terms of its distributional outcome(s).

---

23 Fiss, "Against Settlement," supra note 13 at 1087.

24 See supra Chapter 6.

25 Manitoba, Legislative Assembly, *Official Report of Debates (Hansard)*, 36th Leg., 3d sess., No. 59, Orders of the Day (11 June 1997) at 1520 (Hon. Gord Mackintosh).

26 Hadfield, "Privatizing Commercial Law: Lessons from ICANN," supra note 3 at 263.

27 Ibid. [emphasis omitted].

Given the privatized nature of how the case proceeded, that is in fact what did occur. It was treated, in the end, as a non-hard case. And in my view, that treatment resulted in a serious miscarriage of justice. Because, on further reflection (as I discussed in Chapter 6), the Dealership case also engaged many aspects of what I would identify with Hadfield's notion of the "democratic function" of law, including issues of "redistribution" (in the context of corporate and consumer affairs), "public safety" (not from a personal security point of view but rather from the point of view of protecting society from fraud, misrepresentation and other unfair and harmful business practices), "human flourishing" (broadly defined to include the business-related interests of consumers and providers), "participation" (again broadly defined to include consumer and provider participation in and protection from meaningful corporate and market arrangements), and the like.[28] It also engaged aspects of what qualify, for Susskind, as hard cases: cases that involve issues of "principle, policy, and morality."[29] As such, the Dealership case, which on its face looks very much like a non-hard case, but on reflection engages many if not most aspects of what would be considered to be hard cases that perhaps "should go to court,"[30] very much challenges the notion that cases can be easily categorized as involving only one or another aspect of law.

Three Hypothetical Examples

While the Dealership case is a particularly useful case for this discussion, it is not the only case (or kind of case) that engages and potentially challenges a bifurcated approach to thinking about ground-level dispute resolution choices. Many examples – real or hypothetical, caricatures or not, and which could support the "business case" for privatization that I discussed earlier[31] – also illustrate the point. For further animating this discussion, I have crafted three other civil cases (which specifically do not, in line with the overall focus of this book, directly involve family law issues). Although these examples are all hypothetical cases, they are based on real examples with which I have some direct knowledge or familiarity. And in case it is not already clear, the purpose

28 Ibid. [emphasis omitted].

29 Susskind, *The End of Lawyers?*, supra note 15 at 217.

30 McLachlin, "The Challenges We Face," supra note 10.

31 See supra Chapter 5.

of setting out these cases is, as with the Dealership case, to demonstrate how very market, commercial, non-hard or private-looking cases that many would say should not go to court can, on further reflection or with only slight factual variations, engage some very important, hard and public interest values.

The first example contemplates a private commercial law dispute between a supplier and a manufacturer over a supply contract. The supplier supplies parts for a given manufacturing process. Both supplier and manufacturer are of similar size and of similar financial strength. The parts in question are relatively specialized, and are not the subject of many other similar supply contacts for similarly situated manufacturers. Neither the supplier nor the manufacturer depends, for its financial future or viability, on the outcome of this one contract. As such, while clearly important, financial futures are not at stake. Further, because there are not many (if any) similarly situated parties with similar relationships or contracts (again, the parts here are specialized), there is less of a need for a well-publicized precedent to guide the resolution of similar future disputes across a broad industry sector (although the result of this dispute could, arguably, be useful for other general supply disputes). Finally, again given the relative uniqueness of this relationship and the small market, there is less of a need for a public process, perhaps reported on by the press, and precedent – including perhaps some significant damage award – to guide (and perhaps deter) future behaviour along similar lines. Based on these facts alone, the case looks very much like a case that would be a good candidate for a privatized dispute resolution process.

My second hypothetical example comes from the franchise sector. One dispute of which I have recently become aware almost crushed an extremely successful small restaurant business. The dispute involved an alleged agreement between the restaurant chain (the "Restaurant") and one of its franchisees. Specifically, what was in essence at issue was the ownership of a particular location of the Restaurant and its profits. Often, franchisees in Canada, particularly in the restaurant industry, have been seen to be in a less powerful position than franchisors.[32]

32 See, for example, *887574 Ontario Inc. v. Pizza Pizza Ltd.*, [1995] O.J. No. 936, 23 B.L.R. (2d) 259 (Gen. Div., Com. List), leave to appeal to Ont. C.A. refused, [1995] O.J. No. 1645, in which Justice Macpherson remarked, at para. 4, that:

> [t]he fifty plaintiffs in this case are all franchise owners ("franchisees") who operate Pizza Pizza stores in Ontario. Many of these people have come to Canada as

However, in this case, the relative size and strength of the two parties was essentially equal. Both were small. Both were private. The type of restaurant at issue was relatively (although not totally) unique. And as such, again, although a precedent would not be irrelevant to other franchise disputes, given the relatively unique circumstances of this case, the need for a precedent was not as great as it might be with a much more run-of-the-mill franchise dispute. The dispute at issue here lasted several years. Both sides retained counsel. Counterclaims were made. Counsel for the Restaurant ultimately got off the file because of a potential negligence claim against him. New counsel was retained. Professional and private insurers were involved. Experts were retained. Many hundreds of thousands of dollars were spent on legal and other fees. The financial impact on the parties was enormous. The emotional and other impacts on the individuals involved and their day-to-day operations were equally if not more significant. After years of litigation, the case was settled for essentially what the parties first discussed right at the time that the dispute arose. Had an early privatized process been used, much of the financial, emotional, health-related, and other business damage would have been avoided. Again, the dispute described here would have been an ideal candidate for early ADR (it ultimately settled in any event using a private mediation process).

A final example involves a very basic, private dispute between two neighbours over the height that one of the neighbours wants to build an adjoining fence (this case is largely in line with what Fiss described as the typical "dispute resolution story" involving a "quarrel between two neighbors"[33]). Imagine a community that is not governed by

---

> immigrants or refugees, worked hard and saved money scrupulously, and then invested their life savings in the purchase of a Pizza Pizza outlet. Having obtained a franchise, they then work long hours, often in arduous conditions, in an attempt to earn a living from their stores. Anyone who has stood at the counter of a Pizza Pizza store and peered into the kitchen behind, or watched a Pizza Pizza delivery car push through the snow of unploughed streets to beat the advertised 30 minute delivery time (it's free if it's late) must know that the operation of a Pizza Pizza franchise is difficult and stressful work indeed.

Because of various pressures, including from court-based precedents, legislative initiatives – such as Ontario's *Arthur Wishart Act (Franchise Disclosure), 2000*, S.O. 2000, c. 3 – have been pursued in order to address some of these franchise-related working conditions, contractual arrangements, and power imbalances.

33 Fiss, "Against Settlement," supra note 13 at 1076 (discussed further supra note 20 and accompanying text).

uniform appearance codes (e.g., certain condominiums, cooperative apartments, or exclusive housing communities). Unlike those more specialized housing types, this is a regular pair of houses on a regular street in a regular neighbourhood. Also imagine that the local building code allows for a fence to be built at the different heights that the two neighbours are proposing. It also happens that the fence separates the neighbours' backyards and is not visible to any other person in the neighbourhood. It is a truly private fence. One neighbour wants a ten-foot tall, full barrier against which children can play ball. The other neighbour wants an extremely low, chain-linked fence through which climbing shrubs can grow (to give more of a sense of space, light, and nature). Clearly, this is not a unique dispute, and a precedent could be of use to some similarly situated neighbours in some similarly situated communities. However, notwithstanding the potential precedential benefit of a case such as this (assuming, for the moment, that a precedent from a dispute such as this, which would likely occur, if at all, in a small claims court, would get published in the first place), there is a serious question – an overriding question – about whether the cost of such a dispute could ever justify taking it to court (either in monetary terms, or, even if it were to go to small claims court, in terms of the time and resources used to pursue it). Again, this dispute would be a very good candidate to be resolved by a private ADR process: an ongoing relationship is involved, a relative equality of power exists between the parties, the monetary value is low, and interests, rather than rights, are likely what are ultimately driving this dispute.

The common element of these three hypothetical cases is the fact that all of them would likely be good candidates for a privatized dispute resolution process. Although certainly engaging important issues for the immediate disputants, the resolution of each of these cases will not likely have a significant impact on parties other than those immediately involved in the dispute. As such, they are good candidates for ADR, or put differently, they are cases that perhaps "should [not] go to court."

However, if the factual premises of the cases were very slightly altered, they could equally become cases that are good candidates for a public dispute resolution process. In the first case, if the supply parts in question were slightly less specialized, all of a sudden the precedential value of the case becomes significantly greater. And further, if the conduct of one of the parties in the dispute involved some kind of ongoing bad faith, fraud or other kind of unfair or sharp business practice, then the precedential value of the case for similarly-situated manufacturers or suppliers would be greater still (not to mention the public protection function of law as well). At its core, the case would still involve the private corporate interests of A v. B. However, once slightly modified as I have just suggested, the case now also engages significant public interest issues that go beyond simply the private interests of the immediate corporate disputants. And like with the Dealership case, these important factual nuances and variances are not always apparent at the outset of a case. In the Dealership case, for example, it took months to start to understand the full nature and extent of the misconduct that had been and was still occurring on the other side of the table.

In the second hypothetical case, a similar shift would occur if the type of restaurant at issue were slightly less unique. All of a sudden, the case, which potentially involves labour rights, human rights, corporate arrangements and distributional choices, would be of significant interest to a wide variety of public and private individuals and entities. Finally, a similar shift would also occur in the third hypothetical scenario. Even if one fact – the fence's visibility to passersby on surrounding public walkways – were to change (i.e., the fence was slightly more visible), all of a sudden the nature of the case shifts from one that engages largely individual private interests to one that equally engages other, more public elements. And all it takes to change this kind of fact, for example, is for the case to be initiated not during the summer months, but rather during the winter months, when leaves and other foliage no longer shade the fence from public view.

There are several points to make here. The first is to acknowledge that there certainly are cases that are good candidates for privatized processes. These three cases, as initially presented, are such cases. They involve matters that, at their core, are primarily and largely of concern only to the immediate parties. These cases also do not involve significant power imbalances in terms of financial or litigation resources or capacities. The second point, however, is to emphasize that it does not take much at all to change these cases into potentially good candidates for a more public dispute resolution setting. As I have argued earlier, my sense is that many cases that are seen as good cases for private processes in fact involve facts and issues that make them perhaps equally good (and sometimes better) candidates for a public process. Seeing these three hypothetical cases (as slightly revised as discussed earlier), as well as the Dealership case, all as cases that could, on one level, fit the "market function" criteria of law and, at the same time, could fit the "democratic function" criteria of law demonstrates how problematic it would be to rely on a criteria or "track"-based system. In particular, the risk is, as we have seen, that such a system would categorize cases at the outset in ways that would arbitrarily classify those cases or, worse, in ways that would risk putting them into a market, non-hard, commercial, or private track instead of a democratic, hard, or public track (and perhaps vice versa). A simple track-based system for categorizing which cases, at the front-end of the ground-level of individual disputes, "should" go to court and which cases should not go to court does not, therefore, seem to be workable.

Retained Party Autonomy

However, by recognizing the difficulty of *imposing* a track-based system at the dispute resolution level – for example by requiring individual parties to certify at the court clerk's office that their case involves matters that engage the "democratic function" of law and legal process, or to confirm that their case is of a "hard" nature – I am *not* suggesting that parties should be deprived absolutely of the *choice* to proceed by way of public or private processes. First, to do so would be equally unworkable. It would be difficult to imagine a world, at present and under present economic circumstances, in which parties were forced to take all (or even most) disputes to court, no matter what or who was involved. For example, forcing the neighbours in my third hypothetical case to take what could be a totally private dispute to court would not be workable or desirable.

While some societies in which I have worked in the context of civil justice and judicial reform do seem, at least at the moment, to favour taking disputes to court as opposed to trying to settle them by way of ADR and related privatized processes, litigants in those public-process-heavy systems still retain the *choice* to go the public or the private route. I am thinking here, for example, of work that I have done with several development projects over the past ten years in post-war Bosnia and Herzegovina, in the context of which I discovered, first-hand, that parties in that country still largely pursue the resolution of civil disputes in the public court system as opposed to private ADR regimes.

Further, even if it were possible to require all parties to take all cases to court as opposed to pursuing the resolution of their disputes in one of a variety of alternative private processes, doing so would fly in the face of current democratic principles of freedom of choice and contract. Put simply, ADR is one of the beneficiaries of the free market economy. As I have noticed elsewhere (and previously) regarding arguments allowing for and favouring private processes, "the resolution of disputes – like other goods and services – should not be deprived of the benefits of freedom of movement and contract in an efficiency-seeking, innovative and expanding market economy."[34]

Finally, requiring all disputes to go to court would make a mess of the public court docket. Again, I need only reflect on my relatively recent work in Bosnia and Herzegovina to find a case study of that problem. Because of the typical preference of Bosnian citizens for taking their disputes to court as opposed to settling them through private processes, the courts in Bosnia and Herzegovina have been saddled with huge and crushing case backlogs. And while it is certainly important to acknowledge that, given the intervention of various Canadian, U.S., and other international donor and development organizations and projects, Bosnia and Herzegovina's court delays and backlogs are starting to be positively addressed (largely through court administration and technology-based innovations as well as ADR-related initiatives), there is still a long way to go to overcome what is a deep-rooted culture that prefers to litigate rather than to settle.

So where does that leave us? At the ground level of individual civil disputes, it seems to me that it would be very difficult to contemplate a workable system in which cases are sorted into public or private tracks based on how hard, commercial, market-oriented or democratic-oriented they are, and equally unworkable and difficult to imagine forcing all parties to engage the public system for all cases. As such, parties who are left to their own devices (which is a significant goal of liberal democratic justice systems) will choose a process that is right and expedient for them and their disputes. However, the ground level of individual disputes is not the only relevant level of discussion. And in fact, for purposes of this book, it is not the primary level of focus. Because where I do feel that there is significant room for discussion and rethinking is at the higher level of collective policy choices regarding civil justice process and reform. This level is important on its own. It is also important in that it will often directly influence how parties deal with their cases at the level of individual dispute resolution as well.

Civil Justice Process and Reform

So although the ground, retail level of civil dispute resolution still involves a significant amount of free market choice about how disputes

34 Farrow, "Privatizing our Public Civil Justice System," supra note 18 at 16.

should and do get resolved (i.e., publicly or privately), there is certainly more to be said regarding how we think about civil justice process and reform from a general, system-wide, wholesale level of policy.[35] The discussion here focuses not on individual cases, but rather on collective policy choices about civil justice process and reform and how much those choices should be influenced by efficiency-driven principles as opposed to justice-driven principles. This discussion directly engages some of the institutional stakeholders that were discussed earlier in Chapter 5, including governments and policy-making bodies such as law commissions and law reform institutes, courts, law societies, bar associations, law schools, and the like. It is here where I think a fundamental shift does need to be made – a shift in the overall ethos of those who work with and think about public civil dispute resolution processes and reform. Put simply, all civil justice policy, reform thinking and implementation needs to start from bottom-line legitimizing and evaluating premises based not on notions of efficiency but rather on robust notions of justice.

As I discussed earlier in Chapter 5, the civil justice system, and in particular those who use, provide and reform that system, are preoccupied with efficiency. As Mirjan Damaška has argued,

> [T]here is … a ubiquitous concern with increased efficiency. In the midst of this concern, a tendency is discernible to de-emphasize preoccupations with procedural form … and to concentrate instead on measures likely to contribute to the efficient functioning of civil justice. But consider that efficiency, properly understood, is a measure of the relation of the valued output, or goal of an activity, to the cost of achieving it. The speed and cost at which a justice system disposes of ingested cases tell us little about its efficiency unless we include its goals into the efficiency equation: without reference to them, efficiency is a countless ideal.[36]

Similar observations are made by Janice Gross Stein – about society generally – in her observation that recently "My ear has caught more and more public talk about efficiency, accountability, and choice, and

35 The "retail" and "wholesale" metaphor comes, albeit in a different context, from Rob Atkinson, "How the Butler Was Made to Do It: The Perverted Professionalism of *The Remains of the Day*" (1995) 105 *Yale L.J.* 177 at 188.

36 Mirjan Damaška, "The Common Law / Civil Law Divide: Residual Truth of a Misleading Distinction" in Janet Walker and Oscar G. Chase, eds., *Common Law, Civil Law and the Future of Categories* (Markham: LexisNexis, 2010) 3 at 20 [citation omitted].

less and less about equity and justice."[37] I do not think it is an overstatement to say that current civil justice practices and policy thinking have focused their sights largely on efficiency alone, as opposed to the goal of justice that might be obtained in various ways, including, but not limited to, ways that maximize efficiency. The important difference is, in line with the observations of both Damaška and Janice Gross Stein, that the current ethos of reform looks at efficiency largely and increasingly for efficiency's sake, whereas a justice-seeking sensibility looks at efficiency as a way to help achieve the end goal of justice. However, before pursuing this discussion further, it is illustrative to recognize that, although I articulated numerous examples in Chapter 5 of how governments, courts, tribunals and the like are tending to focus on efficiency essentially as an end in itself, there are also helpful examples of where these civil justice stakeholders are engaged in policy choices that go beyond a simple efficiency-based threshold.

Take for example the relatively recent decision by the Ontario Government to prohibit the application of its *Arbitration Act* to family law arbitrations that do not proceed in a manner that is consistent with Ontario or Canadian family law and *Charter*-related values.[38] That decision was clearly made in light of the obvious public interest issues engaged in family law disputes, and in particular, gender, religious, child-welfare, and community-welfare interests, among others. Although purely efficiency-related considerations might have yielded a different result, what animated the government's decision – which was made in the context of an extremely lively public deliberative process – was a sense of the underlying equality and justice issues that were at stake in these sorts of proceedings. Similar balancing exercises were clearly at play in the context of procedurally based reforms to consumer protection legislation and investor-state arbitration processes that I also discussed earlier.[39]

---

37 Janice Gross Stein, *The Cult of Efficiency* (Toronto: House of Anansi Press, 2001) at xi.

38 For a further discussion of this issue, see supra Chapter 6. See also, in particular, Trevor C.W. Farrow, "Re-Framing the Sharia Arbitration Debate" (2006) 15:2 *Const. Forum Const.* 79.

39 For discussions about consumer protection legislative reforms, see, for example, supra Chapters 4–6. For a brief discussion of reforms to Canada's approach to investor-state arbitration under NAFTA, see supra Chapter 6.

Similarly, in the operation of civil courts, all players – specifically including masters and judges – should not be overly pressured into realizing economic efficiencies as ends in themselves, including, for example, backlog and cost-reduction goals and initiatives. Although backlog and cost-reduction initiatives are important, they are only important if they assist in the furthering of the ultimate business of courts, namely, resolving disputes as well as, more generally, setting society-wide expectations and assisting with the modification of individual and community relationships and distributional arrangements. Public decision makers need to have the power to make procedural decisions and encourage procedural choices that privilege justice-seeking considerations over purely efficiency-seeking ones. Given that courts are in the business of delivering justice, while at the same time are becoming increasingly active in the promotion of settlements and other private processes, they cannot, as Galanter and Cahill have cautioned, be agnostic to the impact of those private processes, the processes by which those settlements are reached, or the outcomes they produce. With respect to settlement, for example, according to Galanter and Cahill, "[o]nce we apprehend the multiplex connection between court and settlement, ensuring the quality of these processes and the settlements they produce is a central task of the administration of justice."[40]

I am aware, as I briefly discussed in Chapter 6, that judges in class action cases, because of the public nature of those kinds of proceedings, engage in these sorts of considerations all the time. Indeed, a key animating aspect of all class action proceedings is a public, behaviour modification component.[41] This behaviour modification or deterrence

---

40 Marc Galanter and Mia Cahill, "'Most Cases Settle': Judicial Promotion and Regulation of Settlements" (1993–4) 46 *Stan. L. Rev.* 1339 at 1390–1.

41 For example, as the Supreme Court of Canada stated in *Western Canadian Shopping Centres Inc. v. Dutton,*

> [C]lass actions serve efficiency and justice by ensuring that actual and potential wrongdoers do not ignore their obligations to the public. Without class actions, those who cause widespread but individually minimal harm might not take into account the full costs of their conduct, because for any one plaintiff the expense of bringing suit would far exceed the likely recovery. Cost-sharing decreases the expense of pursuing legal recourse and accordingly deters potential defendants who might otherwise assume that minor wrongs would not result in litigation. …

Western Canadian Shopping Centres Inc. v. Dutton, [2001] 2 S.C.R. 534 at para. 29, McLachlin C.J. See also *Hollick v. Toronto (City),* [2001] 3 S.C.R. 158 at para. 15.

aspect of dispute resolution plays an underlying role in judicial deliberations. It helps determine whether or not – through the certification process[42] – a class action should be allowed to proceed.[43] These kinds of behaviour modification considerations also play an underlying role in whether or not judges will approve particular settlements in class action proceedings[44] (a step that is required under various class proceedings statutes[45]).

However, in addition to class proceedings, which are relatively specialized in that they are self-consciously designed to take up these collective, public interest aspects of law, I am also clearly aware that masters and judges already have the power to – and do – make decisions that privilege a legitimizing sensibility of justice over that of pure efficiency in contexts involving other procedural aspects of the civil dispute resolution system. An example of such a procedural context – one that particularly resonates with the arguments at issue in this book – involves judicial decisions about whether to promote or not to promote the use of mandatory ADR provisions in the context of a piece of civil litigation. For example, when deciding on whether to exempt a case from mandatory mediation, the court has the power to move a case off a mediation list for several reasons, including where matters of significant public interest are involved. In *O. (G.) v. H. (C.D.)*, Kiteley J. articulated the following considerations in these sorts of circumstances:

> At the risk of generalizing from the few reasons for decision and from the somewhat cryptic explanation made by the local mediation co-ordinators in the list tracking exemptions, it would appear that the following criteria are relevant to whether an exemption order should be granted:
>
> - whether the parties have already engaged in a form of dispute resolution, and, in the interests of reducing cost and delay, they ought not to be required to repeat the effort; [and]

42 See, for example, the requirements of Ontario's *Class Proceedings Act, 1992*, S.O. 1992, c. 6, s. 5.

43 See, for example, *Western Canadian Shopping Centres Inc. v. Dutton*, supra note 41; *Hollick v. Toronto (City)*, supra note 41; *AIC Limited v. Fischer*, 2013 SCC 69. See further the discussion of behavior modification in the majority's judgment in *Seidel v. Telus Communications Inc.*, 2011 SCC 15, [2011] 1 S.C.R. 531 (discussed further supra Chapter 4).

44 See, for example, *Semple v. Canada (Attorney General)*, [2006] M.J. No. 498 (Q.B.).

45 See, for example, Ontario's *Class Proceedings Act, 1992*, supra note 42 at s. 29.

- whether the issue involves a matter of public interest or importance which requires adjudication in order to establish an authority which will be persuasive if not binding on other cases. ...[46]

It was the second of these types of considerations – considerations involving matters of public interest – that animated Master Beaudoin's reasons in the earlier case of *Wilson v. Canada (Attorney General)*.[47] In that case, the applicants challenged s. 25(4) of the *Public Services Superannuation Act*, R.S.C 1985 c. P-36 – regarding the definition of a "surviving spouse," which included the words "opposite sex" – as violating s. 15 of the *Charter*. The moving parties in the particular motion before the master sought leave to have the proceedings exempted from a mandatory referral to mediation, as, in their view, it would "not be productive given the subject matter of the Application."[48] Master Beaudoin, when granting the motion, gave the following reasons:

> The Ottawa Practice Direction with respect to mandatory referral to mediation contemplates a referral to interest-based mediation. Through the intervention of a third party neutral, the parties are encouraged to consider a resolution of their dispute on terms that consider their broader interests rather than a strict consideration of their rights; often requiring the parties to arrive at a form of compromise. In this instance, the resolution of this application requires the determination of the rights of the individual applicants, not only for themselves but for all others who are similarly situated.
>
> There is no precedent to guide the court in this matter. An article entitled The Adequacy of the Adversarial System in Charter Litigation by Robin S. Sharma in the National Journal of Constitutional Law [3 N.J.C.L.], in my view, correctly sets out the approach to be taken. At p. 119 the author cites two reasons why Alternative Dispute Resolution techniques may not be appropriate in resolving *Charter* disputes. With regard to the second reason the author states that
>
>> constitutional cases, so often involving issues of paramount societal concern, must have the ability to influence and shape future conduct and to prompt necessary behavioural changes. This requires

46 *O. (G.) v. H. (C.D.)* (2000), 50 O.R. (3d) 82 (Sup. Ct.) at para. 13.
47 [1998] O.J. No. 1780 (Master) (QL). *Wilson* was cited in the *O. (G.) v. H. (C.D.)* case.
48 *Wilson v. Canada (Attorney General)*, supra note 47 at para. 2.

> adjudication within a public forum such as a law court where the public interest is represented and binding, effective decisions are rendered.
>
> Although the author goes on to suggest that certain cases exist where compromise/settlement procedures should be considered seriously, this is not one of those cases. The ultimate disposition of this application will have implications for same sex couples throughout the country and accordingly, leave to be exempted from the referral is granted.[49]

Masters and judges, in line with Master Beaudoin's approach in *Wilson*, should base their decisions about the use and encouragement of mediation and other private dispute resolution processes on considerations animated primarily by principles of justice, not efficiency. To the extent that the two principles obtain, so much the better. But the first must trump the second in terms of an animating force for public decision-making processes and approaches. Such an approach should clearly be pursued in these sorts of high profile public interest cases. However, what counts as "public interest" should not be viewed so narrowly as only to include the sorts of *Charter* issues that were at stake in the *Wilson* case. While those cases are clearly important, they are not the only cases that act to shape the conduct and relationships of day-to-day people on day-to-day issues. As I discussed previously, particularly in the context of the Dealership case, almost all cases can be seen as *potential* candidates to be moved off the privatization track and onto a public track. Current and overwhelming preferences for efficiency, particularly in the moments of a civil case when decisions about case management or court-annexed ADR processes are made, militate against considering, let alone encouraging, the use of public processes for more than the most obvious of public interest cases.

The same shift in sensibility from preferring efficiency over justice as the ultimate source of evaluation and legitimacy needs to obtain at the administrative tribunal level as well. Clearly, to date, government preferences for including and encouraging ADR at all levels of operation, expressly in pursuit of efficiency-related factors, has resulted in the significant use of ADR throughout the federal and provincial administrative system.[50] According to the settlement rates and statistics of some of

49 Ibid. at paras. 3–4.
50 See supra Chapter 4.

those tribunals, the use of ADR is becoming the norm. As with the court system, the problem is not that procedures do not exist for these sorts of justice-based considerations. They do. For example, notwithstanding the Canadian Human Rights Commission's (CHRC) preference and active promotion of ADR when resolving complaints,[51] it still retains the jurisdiction to review complaints on a case-by-case basis to determine whether public policy considerations militate against the use of ADR:

> The Commission's focused litigation strategy allows it to support the parties at pre-tribunal mediation, while it concentrates on vigorously pursuing high-impact, public interest cases before the Canadian Human Rights Tribunal. On a case-by-case basis, the Commission determines the scope and nature of its participation before the Tribunal after assessing such factors as whether the case raises broad policy issues, relates to major policy concerns, or raises new points of law. The Commission can also intervene in precedent-setting cases before courts and administrative tribunals dealing with human rights issues.[52]

Of course "high-impact" cases that involve the "public interest" and "major policy concerns" should, typically, be subject to the scrutiny and rigour of the public tribunal (or court) process. As I discussed in Chapter 4, they could do so by not being diverted to mediation or other private processes. Further, even if such a case is settled using a tribunal's ADR regime, employing the retained jurisdiction of a tribunal to review the settlement, combined with a summary "sunshine" report of the result, would provide at least some level of scrutiny for these kinds of public interest cases.[53] However, as argued earlier in the context of the Dealership case (although admittedly not an administrative case), there are many instances in which cases that are not self-consciously high impact or high profile (particularly on their face) turn out to be significant in terms of overall societal regulation. Those cases, too, should become

---

51 See, for example, CHRC, *2008 Annual Report* ("Respect, Protection, Promotion, Equality") at 14 ("Resolving Disputes"), online: CHRC <http://publications.gc.ca/collections/collection_2009/ccdp-chrc/HR1-2008E.pdf>.

52 CHRC, *2006 Annual Report* at 22 ("Public Interest Litigation"), available online: CHRC <http://www.crr.ca/divers-files/en/publications/reports/diversReports/repAnnCHRC2006.pdf>.

53 For a discussion of public interest cases and settlements at tribunals, including the idea of settlement lists, see supra Chapter 4. See also infra notes 53 and 90, and accompanying text.

candidates for staying on the public track. At the moment, my fear is that the sensibility of privatization at the tribunal level systematically leads these sorts of cases to the private track. Again, the guiding sensibility in these sorts of determinations should be guided by principles of open justice, not private efficiency. Cases going to ADR need to be very carefully considered to ensure that they are not being sent there for reasons of expediency or efficiency, notwithstanding that they engage important democratic functions of law. Further, to the extent that cases are sent to ADR, mediators and other neutrals need to ensure that any settlements are consistent with justice-based public interest values, and that those settlements are properly approved by the commission or tribunal in question and published in as clear and informative a way as possible.[54]

So it is these and other examples of government, court, tribunal, and other stakeholder-related initiatives that challenge the current trends of making efficiency the endgame of civil justice practice and reform. Efficiency for efficiency's sake is not the answer. Efficiency must remain the handmaiden of justice, and not vice versa. We have now seen several examples where this has successfully occurred. We have also now seen why the efficiency-focused, business-case analyses that I developed in this book, on their own, are not able to provide an adequate framework by which to evaluate, practice, and reform civil justice. The failure of these analyses to deal with the several faces of the Dealership case, for example, articulates this deficiency. However, before we get to a further discussion of the road ahead, there is the other primary justification for privatization that needs to be addressed, namely, access to justice.

Access to Justice Revisited

The other major justification for privatization is that it militates in favour of promoting access to justice. Here is where the efficiency argument, coupled with the realities of the inaccessibility of our current justice system, is at its strongest in my view. Put simply, making the current public system more efficient and affordable, as well as by providing dispute resolution avenues that are alternative to the public system, improves access to the procedures of civil dispute resolution, which is certainly a good thing on any account. To the extent that

54 For a useful source and discussion of some of these ideas, see Philip Bryden and William Black, "Mediation as a Tool for Resolving Human Rights Disputes: An Evaluation of the B.C. Human Rights Commission's Early Mediation Project" (2004) 37 *U.B.C. L. Rev.* 73 at paras. 33–42 (QL).

studies, for example, by Ab Currie, Pascoe Pleasence, and others (discussed earlier in Chapter 5) confirm that people with unmet legal needs typically suffer significant legal, social and personal problems (including health-related problems), there is no doubt that making procedures that can assist with those problems more accessible will be a good thing for those individuals, as well as for society. So here is where, at a systemic level, I do leave significant room for discussion, debate and continued policy thinking that follow some trajectories of privatization in the name of providing more access to civil justice for more people. And this is particularly the case with processes (public legal information, self-help, etc.) that assist the public with both preventing, and if necessary, dealing with disputes before they find themselves involved in the formal dispute resolution system.

However, before stopping here, it is extremely important to notice what we are doing by pursuing these trajectories. Choices within the civil justice system that involve efficiency-driven privatization initiatives are designed to increase access to the processes and gatekeepers of civil justice (lawyers, judges, small claims and other courts, simplified procedures, etc.). Whether these choices increase access to *justice* depends entirely on whether what has been increased does, in fact, amount to an increase in justice, or, instead, simply a tool of procedure.

In Chapter 5, I identified many of the current arguments surrounding access to justice initiatives. Recall, for example, the public materials from the Ontario government supporting the recent civil justice reforms in that province, which sound ultimately in access to justice language and intent.[55] When discussing these various reforms, Ontario's former attorney general Chris Bentley stated that "[c]ivil justice needs to be accessible and affordable if it is to work for all Ontarians" and that "[e]ach of these changes – and particularly the Small Claims or 'people's court' reform – will help everyday Ontarians to fairly resolve disputes that they can't resolve on their own."[56] It is clear from these and other statements[57] that, in essence, what the government is calling

55 Ministry of the Attorney General, News Release, "Resolving Lawsuits Faster and More Affordably, McGuinty Government Reforming Civil Justice For Ontarians" (11 December 2008), available online: Government of Ontario <http://www.attorneygeneral.jus.gov.on.ca/english/news/2008/20081211-civil-nr.asp> (discussed supra Chapters 3 and 5).

56 Ibid.

57 See further supra Chapter 6.

increased "access to justice" really involves an effort to increase access to the tools of civil dispute resolution. Specifically, these reform initiatives are designed to provide faster, cheaper and more accessible court processes, among other civil justice procedures. Although these are certainly laudable goals, they do not automatically amount to an increase in access to *justice*.

If we return to the discussion I started earlier regarding the difference between the narrow and broader senses of access to justice,[58] what we certainly are doing in the context of the modern civil justice reform movement is, at best, increasing access to justice in its narrow sense. And my worry here is that by framing current reform movements in the terms we do (i.e., as increasing "access to justice"), I fear that we are obfuscating what are at core much deeper justice-related problems in society. In its broader sense, access to justice has been discussed in much wider and more aspirational terms. These kinds of terms essentially frame the notion of justice as including much more of what are considered the basic tools of living and operating in a modern democratic society. These kinds of considerations include the potential for access to the processes of power in society, which can, broadly conceived, include, for example, meaningful and representational voting rights; access to the necessities of life, including food, housing, education, and health care; and the processes of meaningful justice, including not only dispute resolution but also powers of dispute avoidance, relationship building, the ability to understand and engage with rules, laws, policies and legal practices, and the ability to have those rules, laws, policies, and practices take into account relevant cultural or other important personal considerations.[59] One vocal proponent is Roderick Macdonald, who has argued very strongly for a wide, participatory

---

58 See ibid. See also further comments on this issue earlier in this chapter.

59 See Trevor C.W. Farrow, "Sustainable Professionalism" (2008) 46:1 *Osgoode Hall L.J.* 51 at 96; Trevor C.W. Farrow, "Dispute Resolution, Access to Civil Justice and Legal Education" (2005) 42 *Alta. L. Rev.* 741 at 798. Trevor C.W. Farrow, "What is Access to Justice?" (2014) *Osgoode Hall L.J.* (forthcoming). See also Action Committee on Access to Justice in Civil and Family Matters, Final Report, *Access to Civil & Family Justice: A Roadmap for Change* (Ottawa, October 2013) at 2, online: CFCJ <http://www.cfcj-fcjc.org/sites/default/files/docs/2013/AC_Report_English_Final.pdf>. For further access to justice materials and discussions, see the materials noted in Chapter 2, note 3 and accompanying text. See also supra Chapter 5.

vision of access to justice.[60] Similarly, for Jürgen Habermas, the "interactions with others" of the sort contemplated by Macdonald become, as part of Habermas' discourse theory of law and democracy,[61] a central element to a meaningful notion of access to justice. Like Macdonald, Habermas also looks at the notion of access to justice in broad terms,

---

60 According to Macdonald,

> Experience has shown that true access to justice means more than overcoming the time, cost and complex barriers that limit people's ability to deploy official institutions to help resolve a legal problem. Making dispute-resolution institutions more objectively accessible will not overcome the main failings of official law simply because official law is, in myriad ways, the cause of these failings. Subjective, not objective, barriers bulk largest. Words like disenchantment, disenfranchisement and disempowerment best capture how many citizens view the justice system.
>
> Our systems of civil justice are not designed to contest or disrupt the existing distributions of social power that stand in the way of broader access. Access to justice will never be achieved through reactive adjudicative institutions that are meant to find justice in relationships by simply restoring an unjust status quo ante. Efficiency in the service of injustice is not a social good. So the core access to justice challenge is:
>
> How do we give as much emphasis to the "justice" component of the phrase "access to justice" as we do to the "access" component so that citizens will actually want to pursue justice in courts?...
>
> [I]t is time to jettison the belief that a lack of access to justice can be remedied principally by systemic reform and by institutional redesign. Law is a precious resource for mediating human relationships. A failure to ask what we expect of our law is a failure to ask what we expect of ourselves. Every day we consciously disengage from the hard work of building a more just society. This disengagement is the greatest barrier to access to justice.
>
> True access to justice requires us to seek and to find meaning in our interactions with others by discovering and nurturing just relationships. In the end, we vindicate the goal of a just and accessible law by making it just and accessible in our own lives.

Roderick A. Macdonald, "Access to Justice and Law Reform #2" (2001) 19 *Windsor Y.B. Access Just.* 317 at 320, 325, cited in Farrow, "Dispute Resolution, Access to Civil Justice and Legal Education," supra note 59 at 798, n. 368 and accompanying text. See further Roderick A. Macdonald, "Access to Justice and Law Reform" (1990) 10 *Windsor Y.B. Access Just.* 287; Roderick A. Macdonald, "Whose Access? Which Justice?" (1992) 7 *Can. J.L. & Soc.* 175; and Roderick A. Macdonald, "Access to Justice in Canada Today: Scope, Scale and Ambitions" in Julia Bass, W.A. Bogart and Frederick H. Zemans, eds., *Access to Justice for a New Century – The Way Forward* (Toronto: Law Society of Upper Canada, 2005) at 19–31, 99–101.

61 For a brief discussion of Habermas' discourse theory of justice, in the context of this book, see supra Chapter 2.

and certainly beyond a simple notion of access to courts and lawyers. For Habermas, access to justice includes access to processes that "involve" clients in "the organized perception, articulation, and assertion of their own interests."[62] Interests are not synonymous with narrow legal rights. Rather, what is at stake here, in this broad sense of access to justice, really amounts to access to the processes of meaningful community participation and of citizenship.[63]

The importance of the participatory aspect of Habermas' vision of access to justice is also heightened under his discourse theory of law given the pluralism of norms that exist in modern globalized societies (discussed briefly in Chapter 6), in what Habermas describes as pluralistic communities in which "comprehensive worldviews and collectively binding ethics have disintegrated" or in "societies in which the surviving posttraditional morality of conscience no longer supplies a substitute for the natural law that was once grounded in religion or metaphysics."[64] Under these pluralistic and globalized social conditions, the "democratic procedure for the production of law ... forms the only postmetaphysical source of legitimacy."[65] Here again, in the context of this discussion of access to justice, we see the connections, as I discussed more fully in Chapter 2, between the judicial function, a pluralistic citizenry's role vis-à-vis that function, and the resulting legitimacy of law in the form of legal decisions. As such, meaningful access to justice, and in particular access to the processes of law broadly defined – as a form of participatory norm creation in globalized communities – provides a legitimating force for modern notions of participatory and pluralistic community membership.

---

62 According to Habermas,

> [A]ffected citizens must experience the organization of legal protection as a political process, and they themselves must be able to take part in the construction of countervailing power and the articulation of social interests. Participation in legal procedures could then be interpreted as collaboration in the process of realizing rights, thus linking positive legal status with the status of active citizenship.

Jürgen Habermas, *Between Facts and Norms: Contributions to a Discourse Theory of Law and Democracy*, trans. by William Rehg (Cambridge, MA: MIT Press, 1996) at § 9.2.1, p. 411.

63 Ibid. [emphasis omitted].

64 Ibid. at Postscript (1994) § 1, p. 448.

65 Ibid. For a recent discussion of pluralism, see Trevor C.W. Farrow, "Ethical Lawyering in a Global Community" (2013) 36:1 *Man. L. J.* 141.

My own view of these issues, as partly developed elsewhere,[66] is that thinking about access to justice in broadly, rather than in narrowly defined terms allows us to think of broader, wider ranging solutions to the many everyday problems facing many Canadians today. As such, I am clearly in favour of thinking about justice, and access to it, broadly, along the lines that Macdonald and Habermas have articulated. This kind of engaged, broad-based thinking about access to justice can go on at the same time as more narrow and modest efforts to increase access to the processes of civil procedure continue. However, my concern about the current, more narrow initiatives is not what they *are* trying to do; rather, it is what they are *not* trying to do. By calling these efforts initiatives to improve access to justice, not only are we misnaming the project and misleading the public in so doing; we also risk failing to engage in the broader, deeper, and ultimately more meaningful work that truly will bring more justice – not more efficient processes – to more people. Current "access to justice"–related trajectories fail to do that deeper work. So although I certainly think we should continue to pursue efficiency-based improvements to the way we deliver civil justice processes, if we use these efforts to bandage over much deeper wounds, then I do not think they are worth pursuing. At some point, the underlying disease will need to be addressed, and the longer we wait, the worse it is likely to get.[67]

---

66 See, for example, Farrow, "Sustainable Professionalism," supra note 59 at 96; Farrow, "What is Access to Justice?," supra note 59; and Farrow, "Dispute Resolution, Access to Civil Justice and Legal Education," supra note 59 at 798.

67 For research on the issue of various societal impacts and costs of unmet legal needs, see, for example, Ab Currie, "A National Survey of the Civil Justice Problems of Low- and Moderate-Income Canadians: Incidence and Patterns" (2006) 13 *Int'l J. Legal Prof.* 217; Pascoe Pleasence et al., *Causes of Action: Civil and Social Justice*, 2nd ed. (London: Legal Services Commission, 2006); and Pascoe Pleasence et al., "The Health Cost of Civil Law Problems: Evidence of Links Between Civil Law Problems, Morbidity, and the Consequential Use of Health Services" (First Annual Conference on Empirical Legal Studies Paper, 2006), available online: SSRN <http://papers.ssrn.com/sol3/papers.cfm?abstract_id=912478>. See further Hazel Genn, *Paths to Justice: What People Do and Think about Going to Law* (Oxford, UK: Hart Publishing, 1999); Rebecca L. Sandefur, ed., *Access to Justice* (Bingley, UK: JAI Press, 2009). For a recent initiative, see Canadian Forum on Civil Justice, "The Cost of Justice: Weighing the Costs of Fair and Effective Resolution to Legal Problems," available online: CFCJ <http://www.cfcj-fcjc.org/?q=cost-of-justice>. For an earlier discussion of these materials, see supra Chapter 5.

What we are left with now is an understanding of the two principal justifications for privatization that, while maintaining some merits on their own, do not – either individually or collectively – amount to adequate ends in themselves as goals of or justifications for the practice or reform of civil justice. As I have argued, these justifications are, in the end, built on arguments that sound in efficiency as an end in itself, as opposed to efficiency as a tool for justice. As I discussed earlier in this book,[68] when thinking about privatization and its promotion in society, we tend to focus on efficiency alone. For example, as Megginson and Netter argue, "[t]o a large extent we ignore the arguments concerning the importance of equitable concerns ... The effect[] of privatization on productive efficiency ... is the focus of most of the empirical literature we review."[69]

And it is here were we return to where I started this chapter. What we need in the context of civil justice reform is a shift in how we understand, evaluate and legitimize the civil dispute resolution process in the first place, which involves a shift away from thinking about efficiency as an end in itself and towards a notion of efficiency that is simply one of many tools, or put differently, one of many lenses through which to view the provision of meaningful civil justice. As Andrew Pirie has noticed, "what may be missing in promoting or advocating for settlement is a concern for quality justice."[70] It is this final discussion to which I now turn.

The Future of Civil Justice Reform

Proportionality and Justice

One of the most significant developments in the recent civil justice reform movement is the addition of the notion of "proportionality" as a foundational consideration for how we practice and reform civil justice. Although efficiency is part of proportionality, the latter has become the new lens through which to view and evaluate processes

68 See supra Chapter 3.

69 William L. Megginson and Jeffry M. Netter, "From State to Market: A Survey of Empirical Studies on Privatization" (2001) 39:2 *J. Econ. Lit.* 321 at pt. 3.1. This statement is discussed and contextualized further at supra Chapter 3.

70 Andrew Pirie, "Critiques of Settlement Advocacy" in Colleen M. Hanycz, Trevor C.W. Farrow, and Frederick H. Zemans, eds., *The Theory and Practice of Representative Negotiation* (Toronto: Emond Montgomery, 2008) c. 11 at p. 295.

and proceedings. One of the key initiatives coming out of Lord Woolf's seminal reform proposals in England and Wales was the simple but powerful proposition that the "cost of litigation will be more affordable, more predictable, and more *proportionate* to the value and complexity of individual cases."[71] The initiative essentially provides that all aspects of a civil proceeding, including each step as well as the overall proceeding itself, must be justifiable essentially on a cost-benefit – efficiency-based – calculus. The time, money, and effort spent on steps in a proceeding, as well as on overall cases, must be proportionate to the ends that they are designed to achieve.

In a nutshell, the reform proposal provides a slight variation of the typical utilitarian calculus of the means must be justified by the ends. As I discussed further in Chapter 3, subsequent civil justice reforms have adopted this proportionality approach. For example, the reforms to Ontario's *Rules of Civil Procedure*, which came into force on 1 January 2010, provide that when applying the Ontario rules, "the court shall make orders and give directions that are proportionate to the importance and complexity of the issues, and to the amount involved, in the proceeding."[72] Similar reforms occurred in Québec several years earlier,[73] and now more recently in B.C., Alberta, and Saskatchewan.[74]

---

71 Rt. Hon. Lord Woolf, M.R., *Access to Justice: Final Report to the Lord Chancellor on the civil justice system in England and Wales* (London: HMSO, 1996) at sec. I.9, available online: Department for Constitutional Affairs <http://webarchive.nationalarchives.gov.uk/+/http://www.dca.gov.uk/civil/final/index.htm>, discussed further at supra Chapter 3.

72 Ontario *Rules of Civil Procedure*, R.R.O. 1990, Reg. 194 at r. 1.04 (1.1). For previous comments, see Trevor C.W. Farrow, "Proportionality: A Cultural Revolution" (2012) 1 *J. Civ. Lit. & Practice* 151. For other discussions of proportionality in the civil justice system, see Hon. François Rolland, "Access to Justice: 3 Years After the Reform of the Code of Civil Procedure" (address given at CFCJ "Into the Future" conference, Montréal, Québec, 1 May 2006), available online: CFCJ <http://www.cfcj-fcjc.org/sites/default/files/docs/2006/rolland-en.pdf>; Hanycz, "More Access to Less Justice: Efficiency, Proportionality and Costs in Canadian Civil Justice Reform," supra note 2. See also Ministry of the Attorney General, News Release, "Resolving Lawsuits Faster and More Affordably, McGuinty Government Reforming Civil Justice for Ontarians," supra note 55.

73 See supra Chapter 3.

74 Ibid.

Proportionality provisions on their own leave room for significant conversations to occur about what kind of process should be dispensed for what kind of issue. On their face, therefore, there is certainly room for optimism that a robust discussion about just results, and not simply efficient means, can obtain. We saw this in a different context in the *Wilson* case.[75] Proportionality discussions leave room for these kinds of conversations and thinking at all levels of the practice and reform of civil justice. However, to the extent that proportionality discussions collapse simply into means-ends evaluations of economic expenditures based on an assessment of the damages claimed in a given proceeding, without also looking at the underlying law-making and societal regulation functions and possibilities of a given case, then we are back to current tendencies to fetishize efficiency above all else. And although proportionality assessments might be relatively straightforward when viewing cases in light of the "market function" of law, they may become much more difficult when looking at cases in light of the "democratic function" of law. Given that, at least in Ontario, the rule has only relatively recently come into force, it remains to be seen how this calculus will play out in particular cases in that province.[76] And British Columbia, Alberta, and Saskatchewan, for example, in light of their recent reforms, will be watching closely as well (and vice versa).

However, we do have some anecdotal evidence from Québec that both makes the case for proportionality thinking as well as justifies my concern. As I discussed earlier in Chapter 3, Québec's proportionality and related judicial dispute resolution (JDR) initiatives, according to Chief Justice François Rolland of the Superior Court of Québec, have been a "success" in that province in terms of moving cases off the trial list and onto the settlement list.[77] To be clear, what Chief Justice Rolland was talking about is the increased amount of settlement activity that is

---

75 See supra note 47 and accompanying text.

76 For one of the first treatments of this new rules-based concept of proportionality in Ontario, see *Moosa v. Hill Property Management Group Inc.*, [2010] O.J. No. 624 (Master). See more recently *2038724 Ontario Ltd. v. Quizno's Canada Restaurant Corp.*, 2012 ONSC 6549. For a discussion of other recent cases, see Farrow, "Proportionality: A Cultural Revolution," supra note 72.

77 Rolland, "Access to Justice: 3 Years after the Reform of the Code of Civil Procedure," supra note 72. Notwithstanding this positive support for judicial dispute resolution, perceptions of the overall results of the Québec reforms have been mixed. See, for example, ibid. at 5–6. For earlier discussions of these comments, see supra Chapter 3.

resulting from several reform initiatives in Québec, including proportionality, and even more importantly, JDR. However, the sensibility of proportionality is certainly an underlying factor that drives much of the reform trajectories and "success" in Québec.

So it is clear that proportionality and related initiatives have been effective in Québec in terms of reducing the number of trials. That is an efficiency-based calculus. What we do not know is whether reducing the number of cases proceeding along the trial list is militating in favour of increased justice. That is my concern. In line with Damaška's earlier caution, efficiency for the sake of efficiency, or indeed proportionality for the sake of proportionality (or efficiency), is "a countless ideal."[78] And it is here, among other places, where I think the importance of the shift in preferences from efficiency to justice, called for by this book, comes into sharp relief. When masters or judges are looking at the relative proportionality of a given step or a given proceeding, it is my view that robust notions of justice should, in the end, form the ultimate justifying and legitimizing source for those sorts of assessments. Of course efficiency, among other factors, will play a role. But the ultimate assessment must be justice based. And because proportionality looks like it will become a significant principle across the modern civil justice reform movement, this shift in focus – from efficiency to justice – must take on an increased importance.

Of course, just saying that "justice should obtain" does not mean that it will automatically happen. First, as a threshold matter, we need to think about what we mean when referring to justice in this context. Many of the foundational democratic premises that help realize meaningful opportunities for justice were discussed earlier in Chapter 2. But what I am talking about here, in the context of individual disputes (as opposed to the broader discussion of access to justice that I developed earlier), is a procedural notion of justice that ensures that opportunities and protections provided for by rules of civil procedure operate in ways that assist parties to realize on the substantive rights and remedies to which they are entitled.

There are two central benefits to this aspect of justice. First, it resonates with the retrospective function of law, which I developed when discussing the purpose of courts in Chapter 2, by providing a just

78 Damaška, "Residual Truth of a Misleading Distinction," supra note 36 at 13 [citation omitted].

framework in which disputes can be fairly, predictably, and efficiently resolved. Second, and equally if not more important, procedural justice also allows for cases to be resolved in ways that actively and self-consciously recognize that their results will speak to similarly situated individuals and collectives beyond the confines of the immediate dispute at hand. This aspect of justice resonates with the prospective function of law that I also developed in Chapter 2. In this sense, rules of procedure become the processes by which human flourishing is encouraged through the civil justice system at both the individual and collective levels of society.

To the extent that compromises or trade-offs need to be made in terms of procedural choices or availabilities, they need to be made in ways that, in the end, are defensible on more than a simple efficiency calculus (whether guised in language of proportionality or not). For example, whether or not a person or organization is allowed to be added to a proceeding as a party in order to make sure that public interest issues at stake in a case litigated otherwise by parties with private interest standing form part of the court's evidentiary record, or alternatively, are added as an intervener so that those public interest issues are at least argued before a judge[79]; whether a party is allowed to discover another party for more than the minimum amount of time[80]; whether a party is entitled to move a case in or out of a private stream[81]; whether one or more lay or expert witnesses is required for the proof of a given issue[82]; whether a plaintiff is allowed to pursue a novel cause of action with significant evidentiary burdens[83]; and whether a party will be successful in moving for summary judgment,[84] all are the kinds of questions and determinations that can be

79 See, for example, Ontario *Rules of Civil Procedure*, supra note 72 at r. 13. See also, for example, *Canada (Attorney General) v. Downtown Eastside Sex Workers United Against Violence Society*, 2012 SCC 45; *Canadian Council of Churches v. The Queen*, [1992] 1 S.C.R. 236; *Canadian Blood Services v. Freeman*, [2004] O.J. No. 4519 (Master).

80 See, for example, Ontario *Rules of Civil Procedure*, supra note 72 at r. 31.

81 See, for example, *Wilson v. Canada (Attorney General)*, supra note 47.

82 See, for example, Ontario *Rules of Civil Procedure*, supra note 72 at r. 53.

83 See, for example, *Jane Doe v. Board of Commissioners of Police for the Municipality of Metropolitan Toronto* (1990), 74 O.R. (2d) 225 (Div. Ct.).

84 See, for example, *Hryniak v. Mauldin*, 2014 SCC 7; *Bruno Appliance and Furniture, Inc. v. Hryniak*, 2014 SCC 8; *George Weston Ltd. v. Domtar Inc.*, supra note 11; *1318214 Ontario Ltd. v. Sobeys Capital Inc.* (2012), 112 O.R. (3d) 190 (Sup. Ct.).

looked at through different lenses. And although decisions should be made on reasonable grounds, which can certainly include considerations of efficiency and proportionality, at the end of the day decisions need to be made that accord with fundamental notions of just procedural dealings.

Further, at the collective level of civil justice reform thinking, all choices that governments, law reform commissions, rules committees, and the like make with respect to civil procedure reform must be made in the spirit of the arguments I am advancing in this book. To do otherwise would jeopardize the significant, forward-looking, societal-regulating aspects of law and legal process that are so fundamental to our democratic systems of governance. This larger landscape must be kept in view. Civil justice is a precious good that we need to cherish. And the important roles of our judges and courts, as ambassadors of justice and key sites of the democratic regulatory process, need also to be cherished and nurtured. Courts, as we have seen, play a foundational role in how we regulate our affairs in society, either through the direct light of precedent or through the long shadow it casts on similarly situated members of a community.[85] Relegating (and cheapening) these processes to a simple utilitarian calculus of efficiency very much puts that foundational role in jeopardy.

Another point that should be made at this juncture is that what I am talking about does not necessarily need to be seen as threatening to all current preferences and stakeholders. On many occasions, front-line decisions will not change. I am certainly not advocating for an unsustainable approach to civil procedure. Having worked and taught in the area for almost twenty years, I am certainly aware of the practical, economic, and access challenges that face modern civil courts and litigants. Law reform commissions, rules committees, and the like have spent a lot of time, in good faith, trying to make the procedures of the system more accessible to more people. And we need to harness much of that good work. But we are at a juncture where we need to make a decision. Is the civil justice system going to continue to play a meaningful role in our modern systems of democratic governance; or are we going to let it die a relatively slow death in the face of current and future preferences for efficiency-based private processes? I clearly am of the view that we

85 For the article that articulated the notion of the "shadow" of the law in terms of the modern ADR movement, see Robert H. Mnookin and L. Kornhauser, "Bargaining in the Shadow of the Law: The Case of Divorce" (1979) 88 *Yale L.J.* 950.

need to maintain and increase our public dispute resolution capacity. But, as I discussed in Chapters 3 through 5, our current trajectories and preferences paint a very different picture. A move to proportionality-based thinking across the civil justice system is going to force us to make hard choices about how to preference justice over efficiency when it comes to thinking about the legitimacy and success of a procedural regime. Ontario, Saskatchewan, Alberta, and B.C. are, as of recently, now facing exactly that choice. And other jurisdictions are in the same boat. Now is the time to make those decisions.

But to be clear, preferences for justice over efficiency, as the ultimate indicator of a system's legitimacy or success, do not require the elimination of private procedural options. As I argued previously, such a scenario – even if desirable, which it is not – would be unworkable. As we have seen, there are incredibly important and positive aspects to the ADR movement. Similarly as with my discussion earlier about mixed public and private partnerships generally,[86] there will, of course, be ongoing and meaningful space for creative private solutions in the context of the public civil justice system. Again, not everything will or should change. However, we do need to take serious stock of what our current voracious appetite for privatization will mean for civil justice and democracy in five, ten, fifteen, or twenty years. Again, my climate change analogy obtains.[87] I worry, as discussed earlier, that although the efficient use of resources will occur, not much will be left of the public civil justice system. As the former chief justice of Ontario stated, "We should not attempt to create a justice system where efficiency is our No. 1 priority … When you are dealing with human factors, you are never going to achieve a particularly high level of efficiency."[88] Although we can (and should) always strive for efficient justice, it must be justice that prevails as the ultimate source of a system's legitimacy as well as the ultimate metric by which to judge a system's success.

Further, even within current preferences for ADR, the survey that I conducted for the purpose of this book confirmed that not all sectors and stakeholders view and use ADR in the same way. The survey confirmed, as discussed in Chapter 5, that some issues and some parties are more suited to different private processes. What this highlights, for the

86 See, for example, supra Chapter 3.

87 See supra Chapter 6.

88 Hon. Roy McMurtry, quoted in Kirk Makin, "The Regrets of a Consensus-Building Chief Justice" *The Globe and Mail* (4 April 2007) A10.

purpose of this discussion, is that judges, parties and rules committees need to be more nuanced in their thinking about when and if to recommend, deploy or mandate the use of privatized processes. Further, given that, at least according to some parts of the survey, confidentiality was not as important as other factors, it may be that ADR procedural reform initiatives at the court and tribunal levels that increase transparency and publicity, including, for example, more detailed and far-reaching public settlement lists at tribunals and potentially at courts,[89] would not be as difficult to implement as some might have thought. For example, settlements using court-annexed mediation services, JDR efforts, tribunal-related ADR services and the like, all might come with an obligation (or at least a threshold expectation) to provide even a bare minimum of detail as to the nature of the case, the parties involved, and the settlement reached. The privacy of the proceeding would not be overly jeopardized, nor would the confidentiality of the actual settlement discussions. However, the ultimate secrecy of the result could be balanced with the significant public interest values that are often at stake.[90] And even if not all court or tribunal-connected settlements involving all parties were reported on in this fashion (at least not right away), I could imagine starting this kind of reform effort with cases involving certain kinds of litigants (perhaps including, for example, governments, public officials, and even publicly traded companies). I recognize that this would not cover all cases, particularly including the majority of disputes, which involve purely private negotiated settlements that never proceed to the formal system and that are therefore generally beyond the immediate reach of this discussion.[91] However,

89 See, for example, supra Chapter 4.

90 For an earlier discussion on this point, see supra nn. 52–3 and accompanying text. See also my previous discussion on privacy, confidentiality, and privilege in the context of arbitration and other ADR processes, supra Chapters 3–5. In those discussions, for example, it was acknowledged that even in the typical private context of commercial arbitration, parties do not always enjoy an absolute ability to keep proceedings, and particularly their results, confidential. See, for example, *Esso Australia Resources Ltd. and Others v. Plowman (Minister for Energy and Minerals) and Others* (1995), 128 A.L.R. 391 at 400–1. For a different but relevant discussion of reforms to Canada's approach to investor-state arbitration under NAFTA, which were designed to bring more transparency to NAFTA arbitral processes and results, see supra note 39 and accompanying text and, further, Chapter 6.

91 See further Chapter 1 at Figure 1.1.

just because some cases are not within reach (even if a majority) does not mean that we should stop trying to improve the circumstances involving those that are.

Public Funding and Access to Justice

A further systemic concern that I only briefly touch on here is the concern that if we are serious about maintaining a meaningful civil justice system, then we need, as a society, to appropriately budget for it. One of the most significant reasons for the growth of private justice is the lack of public commitment, primarily financial, made in this sector. We need to encourage meaningful investment in the public civil justice system, which has traditionally not been a popular topic amongst voters, and therefore not a line item high on government budgets. Susskind is probably right to assume that public funding for civil justice will likely at least not increase over the foreseeable future.[92] However, such a situation does not have to be, and should not be, the case.

Now I am certainly aware, based on conversations I have had at the ministerial and assistant deputy ministerial levels of attorneys general's offices, that money for civil justice, particularly in light of the current economic climate, is not in abundance – quite the opposite. However, practical realities and politically expedient budgetary choices and preferences do not replace principled bases for decision making when it comes to public resources as important as civil justice. According to Lord Neuberger, given the foundational role that property and contractual rights play in the ongoing development of modern societies, civil justice systems that deal with the resolution of disputes involving those rights should have priority in terms of public funding.[93] And although more money simply for the processes of civil dispute resolution will not directly assist with the broader access to justice discussion raised earlier, it certainly would help with the narrower (but still critically important) project of assisting more people to access the procedures of the civil justice system more easily. We could learn from Finland, for example, which instituted significant legal aid reforms in 2002.[94] The

92 Susskind, *The End of Lawyers?*, supra note 15 at 236–7.

93 Lord Neuberger (speech at Property Association Dinner, 2 October 2007) [unpublished], cited in Susskind, *The End of Lawyers?*, supra note 15 at 236, n. 10 and accompanying text.

94 For information on these reforms, see, for example, Ministry of Justice, Finland, "Legal Aid, Legislation," available online: <http://www.oikeus.fi/20630.htm>.

purpose of those reforms was reportedly to "transform public legal aid from a right for people with limited means toward a civil right."[95]

When I am watching the efforts that development projects are making in countries in which civil justice systems have been compromised by war, by corruption, or for other reasons, it quickly becomes apparent – although those countries are working hard to move towards versions of our public systems – that we really do have systems that should be cherished and championed.[96] The price for not having a robust public system for resolving civil disputes – one in which people have trust – is too high. Simply put, a country's social and economic well-being depends on it. It is for this reason, again in the context of my work in the former Yugoslavia, that I recall that one of the first justice-related investments in Bosnia and Herzegovina after the recent and devastating war involved the creation and implementation of a new code of civil procedure. Without dependable and predictable civil justice, there was little chance of stable and active economic activity and investment (domestic and foreign) in that country. And without that economic activity and investment, sustainable growth and development was seen essentially as an impossibility.[97]

---

95 Marjukka Litmala and Kari Alasaari, "Follow-Up Study on the Reform of Public Legal Act (2002), Part 1 (National Research Institute of Legal Policy ["NRILP"], Publication no. 211, Helsinki, 2004), available online: NRILP <http://www.optula.om.fi/uploads/euph7b.pdf>. See further Ministry of Justice, Finland, "Legal Aid," supra note 94. For further commentary on Finland's reforms, see Alex Hutchinson, "Access to Justice: Foreign Countries Offer Lessons to Canada" *The Lawyers Weekly* (24 October 2008), available online: Lawyers Weekly <http://www.lawyersweekly.ca/index.php?section=article&articleid=787>. For an argument for "universal legal care" in Canada, see Alex Hutchinson, "The People's Court" *The Walrus* (20 January 2009), available online: Walrus <http://walrusmagazine.com/article.php?ref=2008.09-law-the-peoples-court-universal-legal-care-alex-hutchinson&page=>. To date, the Supreme Court of Canada has not been willing to find the existence of a general constitutional right to legal assistance in Canada. See *British Columbia (Attorney General) v. Christie*, [2007] 1 S.C.R. 873. See also *Canadian Bar Assn. v. British Columbia*, [2008] B.C.J. No. 350 (C.A.), leave to appeal to S.C.C. refused, [2008] S.C.C.A. No. 185.

96 I recognize that part of the justice development efforts of some of those countries includes developing innovative private processes as well. See, for example, Trevor C.W. Farrow, "The Rule of Law in Developing Countries Is Not Just about Courts" 26:31 *The Lawyers Weekly* (15 December 2006) 11. These privatizing efforts are important for all sorts of reasons – many of which resonate with the benefits of ADR discussed earlier in this book (see, for example, generally Chapter 3). However, to the extent that countries are concerned about corruption, moving the resolution of disputes farther away from public venues and public scrutiny certainly raises potential concerns.

97 For a further discussion on this issue, see ibid.

Finally, systemic efforts need to be made beyond the civil justice system itself in terms of making good on promises to make justice, broadly defined, accessible to more people. We cannot continue to think about access to courts and lawyers as proxies for access to the things that make membership and participation in society a meaningful reality. Law is not an end in itself. As the motto of my law school – *"Per jus ad justitiam:* Through law to justice" – suggests,[98] law is a process for realizing on other social goods. And as part of law, civil procedure is a process for realizing other social goods. Access to law and the procedures of law, although sometimes a precondition for justice, do not equate with access to and the delivery of justice.

Conclusion

Fundamentally changing a central aspect of a democracy's regulatory structure, one would think, should require significant debate and far-reaching public consultation. To date, no such wide-ranging and robust debate or consultation, on a fully informed basis, has characterized the modern and wide-ranging tendency to privatize our public systems of civil justice. On my reading of the policy thinking and legislative history of this overall trend of privatization, although there has been some significant discussion *within* the justice system particularly concerning the *merits* of ADR, there is little or no awareness at the level of the general public about the significance of these issues or their potential concerns as they relate to the overall workings of society. As was recognized during legislative standing committee statements surrounding Ontario's approach to ADR in 1990, "[b]ecause of arbitration being a private matter, most members of the public are unaware of the many matters that are resolved by this technique and this mechanism."[99] This statement is still by and large true today, and it could equally apply to the public's understanding of ADR processes more generally. Put simply, the public is unaware of the breadth and depth of the privatizing forces at play in the modern civil justice reform movement.

---

98 See Osgoode Hall Law School, York University, "Coat of Arms," available online: Osgoode <http://www.osgoode.yorku.ca/history-archives/coat-of-arms>.

99 Ontario, Legislative Assembly, *Official Report of Debates (Hansard)*, (14 February 1990) at J-102 (Gordon F. Henderson).

There continues to be ongoing debate about how the common law is created and administered in the public sphere, often through discussions framed in support or critique of "judicial activism."[100] As Roberto Unger has commented, "The proper extent of revisionary power – the power to declare some portion of received legal opinion mistaken – remains among the most controversial legal topics, as the American debates about judicial 'activism' and 'self-restraint' show."[101] Ironically, however, the public is generally ignorant of a much more prevalent trend away from an accountable form of adjudicative governance (in terms of our public civil justice system, in which 95 to 98 per cent of cases settle or are resolved by some alternative, private process).[102] As I have said elsewhere, "it never ceases to amaze me that the public, while typically up in arms about the 'activism' of our public judges, is largely silent (or ignorant) about the significant decisions made every day by private decision-makers behind closed-doors."[103]

Fundamentally, privatizing our public civil dispute resolution systems merits significantly more public debate, and understanding, than what has to date occurred. Whether and how we continue actively to privatize our procedures of civil justice are questions that will have a dramatic impact not only on how people resolve individual disputes but also on how we as a collective govern ourselves. The current move to privatize much of what counts as civil justice is being conducted without adequate public debate about, let alone public understanding of, all of the implications – positive and negative – of this clear policy choice.[104] We must recognize the potential strengths of private dispute

100 See, for example, Farrow, "Re-Framing the Sharia Arbitration Debate," supra note 38 at 86, n. 50.

101 Roberto M. Unger, *The Critical Legal Studies Movement* (Cambridge, MA: Harvard University Press, 1986) 10. In Canada, see, for example, generally Kent Roach, *The Supreme Court on Trial: Judicial Activism or Democratic Dialogue* (Toronto: Irwin Law, 2001).

102 Discussed supra Chapter 3. I recognize that most of these settlements do not involve third-party mediators or decision makers. Further, I also recognize that some of these cases are not settled but simply do not proceed to a trial or any other form of resolution. Further research is needed to better understand this important issue.

103 Farrow, "Re-Framing the Sharia Arbitration Debate," supra note 38 at 82 [footnote omitted]. See further Farrow, "Public Justice, Private Dispute Resolution and Democracy," supra note 2 at 357–8.

104 See ibid. The Supreme Court of Canada's judgment in *Seidel v. Telus Communications Inc.*, supra note 43, is a useful place to look for a discussion of some of the potential implications of privatization in the context of civil dispute resolution dealing

resolution alternatives. However, only through responsible, public participation in the development of these processes will we avoid a silent erosion of our core democratic values significantly embodied in a strong rule of law system, simply in the name of efficiency and proportionality. We cannot treat justice simply as an externality. Again quoting from the chief justice of Canada,

> In this country, we realize that without justice, we have no rights, no peace, no prosperity. We realize that, once lost, justice is difficult to reinstate. We in Canada are the inheritors of a good justice system, one that is the envy of the world. Let us face our challenges squarely and thus ensure that our justice system remains strong and effective.[105]

Ensuring that our justice system remains "strong and effective" does not mean selling it out to the lowest bidder. Whether we are talking about courts, tribunals or legislatively sanctioned private arbitration panels that enjoy the coercive enforcement powers of the state, justice – not efficiency – must be our fundamental guide in determining how those bodies operate, how they are legitimized and evaluated, and how they will be reformed going forward.

Ensuring this result will require allies as well as what has been described as important "sites of change."[106] It is here where I see an important series of intersections at play. First, in terms of people and groups, the shift that is contemplated by this book will require buy-in from a number of the civil justice stakeholders that were discussed earlier,[107] including government officials and policy makers, judges, lawyers and clients, law societies and bar associations, law schools, and, ultimately, the public. Collaboration amongst these stakeholders is important, as is cooperation with other agencies and interested parties.[108] Further, there

---

with public interest values (in that case involving consumer protection). However, the fact that the Court was so sharply (and narrowly) divided (5–4) regarding the overall role and benefit of private dispute resolution processes in that context also shows how difficult this discussion can potentially be. For a further discussion of the *Seidel* case, see, for example, supra Chapter 4.

105 McLachlin, "The Challenges We Face," supra note 10 at "Conclusion."

106 See Julie Macfarlane, *The New Lawyer: How Settlement Is Transforming the Practice of Law* (Vancouver: UBC Press, 2008) at c. 9.

107 See generally supra Chapter 5.

108 For a particularly important and current initiative, see the work of the Action Committee on Access to Justice in Civil and Family Matters (online: CFCJ <http://www.cfcj-fcjc.org/?q=collaborations>).

will also be an important intersection created between the practice and reform of civil justice and the fundamental process of lawyering. These intersections will require new partnerships and allies. They will require new ways of thinking about what it means to be a judge and a lawyer. And they will require creative policy and research initiatives and collaborations to explore the possibilities of what, for example, judging and practicing in the spirit of "proportionality" might look like in terms of recognizing efficiency while pursuing justice. These are all relatively new concepts in light of modern civil justice reform initiatives that are being pursued in the context of current and very challenging economic times. In addition, thinking about access to justice in ways that meaningfully address real societal vulnerabilities and weaknesses, as opposed to simply covering them over with the provision of cheaper and faster courts and procedures, will take new and creative ways of thinking.

One important place that provides significant foundational opportunities for thinking about the roles of civil justice and civil justice reform is law school. As I have said elsewhere,

> There are many moments within the profession at which the possibility of change can occur, including at law schools, bar admission programs, mentoring initiatives, continuing education courses, judicial speeches and judgments, discipline rulings, bencher directives, and in professional rules and commentaries. Of course external sources for change also obtain, including legislative limits …, public opinion, client demands, and others. However, it is at the initial stage of the professional experience that a sensibility of openness to alternative discourses is most palpable, possible, and important. How we see ourselves individually as lawyers and how we see ourselves collectively as a profession are foundational questions that must be addressed in legal education.[109]

Law students and new lawyers need to understand not only the nuts and bolts of how the various procedures operate, but more importantly, we need to help our students think further about the purpose, goals and possibilities of the system in the first place. Courses on civil

109 Farrow, "Sustainable Professionalism," supra note 59 at 100–1. Although for different purposes, Julie Macfarlane has similarly noticed the power of law schools and legal education as important "sites of change." See Macfarlane, *The New Lawyer: How Settlement Is Transforming the Practice of Law*, supra note 106 at 224–32.

procedure, legal process, and indeed ADR do not always encourage such foundational and theoretical thinking. Equally important will be the inclusion of these sorts of conversations in the context of teaching ethics and professionalism. The practice and reform of civil procedure along justice-seeking lines needs to be seen as part of a modern notion of ethical lawyering and sustainable professionalism.[110]

In addition, this educational continuum needs to not stop at law school graduation. With increased opportunities and requirements for continuing professional education, these discussions need to animate the lifelong learning opportunities[111] of practicing lawyers[112] and sitting judges.[113] Further, adequate research and support for policy makers will also be necessary as we try to understand and shape the power and purpose of the modern civil justice reform agenda. Again, these will be extremely important "sites of change" as we chart a new course for what it means to practice and reform civil procedure in a proportional, just, and progressive way.[114]

Given what is at stake, these are clearly important, challenging and very exciting times. The future of civil justice and civil justice reform, along with what it means to think about and practice civil justice and

110 See Farrow, "Sustainable Professionalism," supra note 59. See further Joshua J.A. Henderson and Trevor C.W. Farrow, "The Ethical Development of Law Students: An Empirical Study" (2009) 72:1 *Sask. L. Rev.* 75; Farrow, "Ethical Lawyering in a Global Community," supra note 65. See also my earlier discussion of law schools in the context of this book at supra Chapter 5.

111 See, for example, Trevor C.W. Farrow and Stephen G.A. Pitel, guest eds., "Lifelong Learning in Professionalism," Special Feature, (2010) *Can. Legal Educ. Ann. Rev.*

112 See, for example, Law Society of British Columbia (LSBC), "Continuing Professional Development: Overview," available online: LSBC <http://www.lawsociety.bc.ca/licensing_membership/profdev/overview.html>; Law Society of Upper Canada (LSUC), Professional Development & Competence Committee and Paralegal Standing Committee, Joint Report to Convocation (29 October 2009), available online: LSUC <http://www.lsuc.on.ca/media/convoct09_joint_report.pdf>; and Law Society of Upper Canada, News Release, "Continuing Professional Development Requirement Supports Professional Competence" (25 February 2010), available online: LSUC <http://www.lsuc.on.ca/media/feb10_finalcpd requirementrelease.pdf>.

113 See, for example, National Judicial Institute (NJI), "Building Better Justice," available online: NJI <http://www.nji-inm.ca/nji/inm/accueil-home.cfm?lang=en>.

114 See, for example, Canadian Forum on Civil Justice, "The Cost of Justice: Weighing the Costs of Fair and Effective Resolution to Legal Problems," supra note 67.

civil justice reform, are at stake. Further, a central pillar of democracy is currently in question. Given privatization trajectories and preferences, pushing for change in individual and institutional thinking along the lines proposed in this book will not be easy. It will take hard work, dedication, significant public debate, resources, and – most importantly – imagination and a commitment to the ideals that underlie a robust public civil justice system. However, given what is at stake, this work must be done. In the words of Roberto Unger and Cornel West, we must do the following:

> [U]se the tools of institutional experimentalism to rethink and rebuild … the hope that under democracy individual men and women can achieve … [a] largeness of vision and experience. … It is not enough to rebel against the lack of justice unless we also rebel against the lack of imagination. The structure of society matters … Practices and institutions make this structure what it is.[115]

Civil justice involves practices and institutions that contribute to the fundamental structure of society. To the extent that those practices and institutions are challenged by the current privatization movement, which they clearly are, we need to harness "tools of institutional experimentalism" in the spirit of "rethink[ing] and rebuild[ing]" a better, more progressive and ultimately more just system of civil dispute resolution. Why? Because the practices and institutions at issue go to the bedrock of who we are and how we govern ourselves in modern society.

115 Roberto M. Unger and Cornel West, *The Future of American Progressivism: An Initiative for Political and Economic Reform* (Boston: Beacon Press, 1998) at 23–4.

Selected Bibliography

Outline of Selected Bibliographic Materials

Books, Chapters, and Articles

Ackerman, Bruce, "Why Dialogue?" (1989) 86 *J. Phil.* 5.

Acorn, Annalise E., *Compulsory Compassion: A Critique of Restorative Justice* (Vancouver: UBC Press, 2004).

Adams, Hon. George W., and Naomi L. Bussin, "Alternative Dispute Resolution and Canadian Courts: A Time for Change" (1995) 17 *Advocates' Q.* 133.

Adams, Hon. George W., "Ontario Insurance Commission Dispute Resolution Group Evaluation Report" (June 1998) in Naomi Bussin, "Evaluating ADR Programs: The Ends Determine the Means" (2000) 22 *Advocates' Q.* 460.

Adams, Hon. George W., *Mediating Justice: Legal Dispute Negotiations* (Toronto: CCH Canadian, 2003).

Adams, Hon. George W., "The Privatization of Justice: Where Are We Going?" in Ronalda Murphy and Patrick A. Molinari, eds., *Doing Justice: Dispute Resolution in the Courts and Beyond* (Montréal: Canadian Institute for the Administration of Justice, 2009).

Aeberli, Peter, "Jurisdictional Disputes under the Arbitration Act 1996: A Procedure Route Map" (2005) 21:3 *Arb. Int'l.* 253.

Agrios, Hon. John A., *A Handbook on Judicial Dispute Resolution for Law Students* (Version 3.7, July 2003)

Agusti-Panareda, Jordi, "Power Imbalances in Mediation: Questioning Some Common Assumptions" (2004) 59:2 *Disp. Resol. J.* 24.

Aman, Alfred C., *The Democracy Deficit: Taming Globalization through Law Reform* (New York: New York University Press, 2004).

Anderson, Van A., "Alternative Dispute Resolution and Professional Responsibility in South Carolina: A Changing Landscape" (2003) 55 *S.C.L. Rev.* 191.

Aquinas, St. Thomas, *Selected Writings*, ed. by Rev. M.C. D'Arcy (London: J.M. Dent, 1946).

Aquinas, St. Thomas, *Summa Theologica*, in A.P. D'Entrèves, ed., *Aquinas: Selected Political Writings*, trans. by J.G. Dawson, 6th imp. (Oxford: Basil Blackwell, 1974).

Aquinas, St. Thomas, *On Politics and Ethics* (Selections from the Work of St. Thomas Aquinas), trans. and ed. by Paul E. Sigmund (New York and London: Norton, 1988).

Archibald, Bruce P., "Progress in Models of Justice: From Adjudication/Arbitration through Mediation to Restorative Conferencing (and Back)" in Ronalda Murphy and Patrick A. Molinari, eds., *Doing Justice: Dispute Resolution in the Courts and Beyond* (Montréal: Canadian Institute for the Administration of Justice, 2009).

Archibald, Todd et al., *Ontario Superior Court Practice* (Markham, Ontario: LexisNexis, 2008).

Aristotle, *The Politics*, ed. by Richard McKeon (New York: Random House, 1941).

Aristotle, *The Politics* in *The Politics of Aristotle*, ed. and trans. by Ernest Barker (Oxford, UK: Oxford University Press, 1969).

Aristotle, *The Politics*, trans. by Carnes Lord (Chicago and London: University of Chicago Press, 1984).

Aristotle, *The Politics*, trans. by William Ellis (Buffalo: Prometheus, 1986).

Aristotle, *The Politics*, ed. by Stephen Everson (Cambridge: Cambridge University Press, 1988).

Aristotle, *The Art of Rhetoric*, trans. by H.C. Lawson-Tancred (London: Penguin, 1991).

Arthurs, Harry W., and Robert Kreklewich, "Law, Legal Institutions, and the Legal Profession in the New Economy" (1996) 34 *Osgoode Hall L.J.* 1.

Arthurs, Harry W., "Special Courts, Special Law: Legal Pluralism in Nineteenth Century England" in G.R. Rubin and David Sugarman, *Law, Economy and Society, 1750–1914: Essays in the History of English Law* (Oxford, UK: Professional Books Limited, 1984).

Atkinson, Rob, "How the Butler Was Made to Do It: The Perverted Professionalism of *The Remains of the Day*" (1995) 105 *Yale L.J.* 177.

Austin, John, *Lectures on Jurisprudence Or the Philosophy of Positive Law*, rev. ed. by Robert Campbell (London: John Murray, 1885).

Austin, John, *The Province of Jurisprudence Determined* in *The Province of Jurisprudence Determined Etc.* (London: Weidenfeld and Nicolson, 1954).

Baier, Gerald, *Courts and Federalism: Judicial Doctrine in the United States, Australia, and Canada* (Vancouver: UBC Press, 2006).

Bailey, Martha J., "Unpacking the 'Rational Alternative': A Critical Review of Family Mediation Claims" (1989) 8 *Can. J. Fam. L.* 61.

Baker, G. Blaine, "The Reconstitution of Upper Canadian Legal Thought in the Late-Victorian Empire" (1985) 3 *L.H.R.* 219.

Baker, H. Robert, "Creating Order in the Wilderness: Transplanting the English Law to Rupert's Land, 1835–51" (1999) 17:2 *L.H.R.* 209.

Bakht, Natasha, "Family Arbitration Using Sharia Law: Examining Ontario's Arbitration Act and its Impact on Women" (2004) 1 *Muslim World J. H.R.* art. 7.

Bakht, Natasha, "Were Muslim Barbarians Really Knocking at the Gates of Ontario?: The Religious Arbitration Controversy – Another Perspective" in Ronalda Murphy and Patrick A. Molinari, eds., *Doing Justice: Dispute Resolution in the Courts and Beyond* (Montréal: Canadian Institute for the Administration of Justice, 2009).

Ballati, Deborah S., ed., *Privatizing Governmental Functions* (New York: Law Journal Press, 2001).

Banks, Margaret A., "The Evolution of the Ontario Courts, 1788–1981" in David H. Flaherty, ed., *Essays in the History of Canadian Law* (Toronto; Buffalo, NY; and London: University of Toronto Press, 1983).

Bantekas, Ilias, "Corporate Social Responsibility in International Law" (2004) 22 *B.U. Int'l L.J.* 309.

Barendrecht, Maurits, and Berend R. de Vries, "Fitting the Forum to the Fuss with Sticky Defaults: Failure in the Market for Dispute Resolution Services?" (2005) 7 *Cardozo J. Confl. Resol.* 83.

Barendrecht, Maurits, "Understanding the Market for Justice" (2009) Tilburg University Legal Studies Working Paper No. 009/2009, available online: SSRN <http://papers.ssrn.com/sol3/papers.cfm?abstract_id=1416841>.

Barist, Jeffrey, "Arbitration: The Privatization of the Judicial Process" (1996/7) *Int'l Com. Lit.* 22.

Barnes, Bruce E., "Conflict Resolution across Cultures: A Hawaii Perspective and a Pacific Mediation Model" (1994) 12 *Mediation Q.* 117.

Barry, Graeme A., "In the Shadow of the Rule of Law: Alternative Dispute Resolution and Provincial Superior Courts" *News & Views Civ. Just. Reform* 8 (Fall 1999) 2.

Barry, Margaret Martin et al., "Clinical Education for this Millennium: The Third Wave" (2000) 7 *Clinical L. Rev.* 1.

Baruch Bush, Robert A., and Joseph P. Folger, "Changing People, Not Just Situations: A Transformative View of Conflict and Mediation" in Robert A. Baruch Bush and Joseph P. Folger, *The Promise of Mediation: Responding to Conflict through Empowerment and Recognition* (San Francisco: Jossey-Bass, 1994).

Beckerman, John S., "Procedural Innovation and Institutional Change in Medieval English Manorial Courts" (1992) 10:2 *L.H.R.* 197.

Beckerman, John S., "Toward a Theory of Medieval Manorial Adjudication: The Nature of Communal Judgments in a System of Customary Law" (1995) 13:1 *L.H.R.* 1.

Bell, Andrew, *Forum Shopping and Venue in Transnational Litigation* (Oxford, UK: Oxford University Press, 2003).

Bell, Catherine E., and David Kahane, eds., *Intercultural Dispute Resolution in Aboriginal Contexts* (Vancouver: University of British Columbia Press, 2004).

Bentham, Jeremy, "Draught of a New Plan for the Organization of the Judicial Establishment in France: With Critical Observations on the Draught Proposed by the National Assembly Committee, in the Form of a Perpetual Commentary" (1790) in *The Works of Jeremy Bentham*, published under the superintendence of his executor, John Bowring (Edinburgh: Tait, 1843).

Bentham, Jeremy, *Principles of Judicial Procedure, with the Outlines of a Procedural Code* in *The Works of Jeremy Bentham*, ed. by John Bowring (Edinburgh: William Tait, 1843) in Online Library of Liberty, ed., available online: Liberty Fund <http://oll.libertyfund.org/?option=com_staticxt&staticfile=show.php%3Ftitle=1921&chapter=113487&layout=html&Itemid=27>.

Berlins, Marcel, and Clare Dyer, *The Law Machine*, 3rd ed. (London: Penguin, 1989).

Bhalla, A.S., ed., *Globalization, Growth and Marginalization* (Ottawa: International Development Research Centre, 1998).

Bickel, Alexander M., *The Least Dangerous Branch: The Supreme Court at the Bar of Politics*, 2nd ed. (New Haven, CT, and London: Yale University Press, 1986).

Birch, Anthony H., *The British System of Government*, 7th ed. (London: Allen & Unwin, 1986).

Black, Henry Campbell, *Black's Law Dictionary*, 6th ed. by Joseph R. Nolan and Jacqueline M. Nolan-Haley, coauthors et al. (St. Paul, MN: West Publishing, 1990).

Blackstone, William, *Commentaries on the Laws of England* (Oxford, UK: Clarendon Press, 1765–9), elec. ed. (Novi, MI: Lonang Institute, 2005), available online: Lonang <http://www.lonang.com/exlibris/blackstone/>.

Bogart, W., *Courts and Country* (Toronto: Oxford University Press, 1994).

Boivin, Richard, and Nicola Mariani, "International Arbitration in Canada: Highest Court Rules in Favour of Broad Interpretation of Arbitrability" (2003) *J. Int'l Arb.* 507.

Borrell, Andrew D., "Arbitration and Choice of Law Provisions as Class Action Risk Management Tools" (April 2002), available online: Fasken Martineau DuMoulin LLP <http://www.fasken.com/arbitration-and-choice-of-law-provisions-as-class-action-risk-management-tools-04-26-2002/>.

Bottomley, S. and D. Kinley, eds., *Commercial Law and Human Rights* (Aldershot: Ashgate Publishing, 2002).

Boulle, Laurence, and Kathleen J. Kelly, *Mediation: Principles, Processes, Practice*, Cdn. ed. (Toronto and Vancouver: Butterworths, 1998).

Brada, Josef C., "Privatization Is Transition – Or Is It?" (1996) 10:2 *J. Econ. Perspectives* 67.

Brazil, Wayne D., "Hosting Mediations as a Representative of the System of Civil Justice" (2007) 22 *Ohio St. J. Disp. Resol.* 227.

Brodie, Janine, "Introduction: Globalization and Citizenship Beyond the National State" (December 2004) 8:4 *Citizenship Studies* 323.

Brodie, Janine and Linda Trimble, eds., *Reinventing Canada: Politics of the 21st Century* (Toronto: Prentice Hall, 2003).

Brown, Donald J.M., and David M. Beatty, with the assistance of Christine E. Deacon, *Canadian Labour Arbitration*, 4th ed. (Aurora, ON: Canada Law Book, 2006).

Brown, Donald J.M., and J.M. Evans, with the assistance of Christine E. Deacon, *Judicial Review of Administrative Action in Canada* (Toronto: Canvasback Publishing, 1998).

Bryan, Penelope E., "Killing Us Softly: Divorce Mediation and the Politics of Power" (1992) 40 *Buff. L. Rev.* 441.

Bryden, Philip, and William Black, "Mediation as a Tool for Resolving Human Rights Disputes: An Evaluation of the B.C. Human Rights Commission's Early Mediation Project" (2004) 37 *U.B.C. L. Rev.* 73.

Bryden, Philip, and William Black, "Designing Mediation Systems for Use in Administrative Agencies and Tribunals – The B.C. Human Rights Experience" in Anne L. Mactavish and Laverne A. Jacobs, *Dialogue between Courts and Tribunals: Essays in Administrative Law and Justice* (Montréal: Les Éditions Thémis, 2008).

Burbank, Stephen B., "Implementing Procedural Change: Who, How, Why, and When" (1997) 49 *Ala. L. Rev.* 221.

Burger, Warren E., "Isn't There a Better Way?" (1982) 68 *A.B.A. J.* 274.

Burn, Suzanne, "The Civil Justice Reforms in England and Wales: Will Lord Woolf Succeed Where Others Have Failed?" (1999) 17 *Windsor Y.B. Access Just.* 221.

Bussin, Naomi, "Evaluating ADR Programs: The Ends Determine the Means" (2000) 22 *Advocates' Q.* 460.

Canon, Andrew J., "A Pluralism of Private Courts" (2004) 23 *C.J.Q.* 309.

Caplan, Bryan, and Edward P. Stringham, "Privatizing the Adjudication of Disputes" (2008) 9 *Theor. Inq. L.* 503.

Carmichael, Don, "Liberalism" in Janine Brodie and Sandra Rein, eds., *Critical Concepts: An Introduction to Politics*, 3rd ed. (Toronto: Prentice Hall, 2005).

Carr, Chris A., and Michael R. Jencks, "The Privatization of Business and Commercial Dispute Resolution: A Misguided Policy Decision" (2000) 88 *Ky. L.J.* 183.

Carr, Robert K., *The Supreme Court and Judicial Review* (New York: Holt, Rinehart and Winston, 1942).

Carson, John C., William C. Graham, and Wayne V. Carson, "Arbitration: The Proof of the Pudding, Results of the Carson / Graham Commercial Arbitration Survey, 1993" (1994) 13:1 *Advocates' Soc. J.* 16.

Castels, Francis G., *Comparative Public Policy: Patterns of Post-war Transformation* (Cheltenham, UK: Edward Elgar, 1998).

Chitty, Joseph, *The Practice of Law in All its Departments; with a View of Rights, Injuries, and Remedies, as Ameliorated by Recent Statutes, Rules, and Decisions* (London: Henry Butterworth, 1834).

Chornenki, Genevieve A., and Christine E. Hart, *Bypass Court: A Dispute Resolution Handbook*, 3rd ed. (Markham: LexisNexis, 2005).

Coben, James R., "Summer Musings on Curricular Innovations to Change the Lawyer's Standard Philosophical Map" (1998) 50 *Fla. L. Rev.* 735.

Cohn, Daniel, "Changing Conceptions of the Public Interest" in Janine Brodie and Linda Trimble, eds., *Reinventing Canada: Politics of the 21st Century* (Toronto: Prentice Hall, 2003).

Constant, Benjamin, "Liberty of the Ancients Compared with That of the Moderns" (1819) in Benjamin Constant, *Political Writings*, trans. and ed. by Biancamaria Fontana (New York: Cambridge University Press, 1988).

Coombs, Clyde H., and George S. Avrunin, *The Structure of Conflict* (Hillsdale, NJ: Lawrence Erlbaum Associates, 1988).

Crane, Peter, and Herbert M. Kritzer, eds., *Oxford Handbook of Empirical Legal Research* (Oxford, UK: Oxford University Press, 2010).

Currie, Ab, "A National Survey of the Civil Justice Problems of Low- and Moderate-Income Canadians: Incidence and Patterns" (2006) 13 *Int'l J. Legal Prof.* 217.

Damaška, Mirjan, "The Common Law / Civil Law Divide: Residual Truth of a Misleading Distinction" in Janet Walker and Oscar G. Chase, eds., *Common Law, Civil Law and the Future of Categories* (Markham: LexisNexis, 2010).

Damaška, Mirjan R., *The Faces of Justice and State Authority: A Comparative Approach to the Legal Process* (New Haven, CT: Yale University Press, 1986).

Dayton, Kim, "The Myth of Alternative Dispute Resolution in the Federal Courts" (1991) 76 *Iowa L. Rev.* 889.

Delgado, Richard, "ADR and the Dispossessed: Recent Books about the Deformalization Movement" (1988) 13 *Law & Soc. Inquiry* 45.

Delgado, Richard et al., "Fairness and Formality: Minimizing the Risk of Prejudice in Alternative Dispute Resolution" (1985) *Wis. L. Rev.* 1359.

Delgado, Richard, and Jean Stefancic, *Critical Race Theory: An Introduction* (New York and London: New York University Press, 2001).

Denning, M.R., Rt. Hon. Lord, *The Discipline of Law* (London: Butterworths, 1979).

Dezalay, Yves, *Dealing in Virtue: International Commercial Arbitration and the Construction of a Transnational Legal Order* (Chicago: University of Chicago Press, 1996).

Di Luca, Joseph, "Expedient McJustice or Principled Alternative Dispute Resolution? A Review of Plea Bargaining in Canada" (2005) 50 *Crim. L.Q.* 14.

Dicey, Albert Venn, *Introduction to the Study of the Law of the Constitution*, 10th rev. ed. (London: Palgrave Macmillan, 1961).

Dicey, Albert Venn, *Lectures on the Relation between Law and Public Opinion in England during the Nineteenth Century*, 2nd ed. (London: Macmillan, 1919).

Dickson, P.C., Rt. Hon. Brian, "Access to Justice" (1989) 1 *Windsor Rev. Legal Soc. Issues* 1.

Dickson, P.C., Rt. Hon. Brian, "ADR, the Courts and the Judicial System: The Canadian Context" (1994) 28 *L. Soc'y Gaz.* 231.

Drahozal, Christopher R., and Richard W. Naimark, eds., *Towards a Science of International Arbitration: Collected Empirical Research* (New York: Kluwer Law International, 2005).

Dobuzinskis, Laurent, Michael Howlett, and David Laycock, eds., *Policy Analysis in Canada: The State of the Art* (Toronto: University of Toronto Press, 2007).

Dunning, John H., ed., *Making Globalization Good: The Moral Challenges of Global Capitalism* (Oxford, UK, and New York: Oxford University Press, 2003).

Duxbury, Neil, *The Nature and Authority of Precedent* (Cambridge, UK and New York: Cambridge University Press, 2008).

Dworkin, Ronald M., "Is Law a System of Rules?" in Ronald M. Dworkin, ed., *The Philosophy of Law* (Oxford, UK: Oxford University Press, 1977).

Dworkin, Ronald M., *Taking Rights Seriously* (London: Duckworth, 1977).

Dworkin, Ronald M., A *Matter of Principle* (Cambridge, MA: Harvard University Press, 1985).

Dworkin, Ronald M., *Law's Empire* (London: Fontana, 1986).

Dworkin, Ronald M., ed., *The Philosophy of Law* (Oxford: Oxford University Press, 1986).

Dworkin, Ronald M., *Freedom's Law: The Moral Reading of the American Constitution* (Cambridge, MA: Harvard University Press, 1996).

Edwards, Harry T., "Alternative Dispute Resolution: Panacea or Anathema?" (1986) 99 *Harv. L. Rev.* 668.

Eisele, G. Thomas, "The Case against Mandatory Court-Annexed ADR Programs" (1991–2) 75 *Judicature* 34.

Eisenberg, Theodore, Geoffrey P. Miller, and Emily Sherwin, "Arbitration's Summer Soldiers: An Empirical Study of Arbitration Clauses in Consumer and Nonconsumer Contracts" (2007–8) 41 *U. Mich. J. L. Ref.* 871.

Ellis, Desmond, and Dawn Anderson, *Conflict Resolution: An Introductory Text* (Toronto: Emond Montgomery, 2005).

Ely, John Hart, *Democracy and Distrust: A Theory of Judicial Review* (Cambridge, MA: Harvard University Press, 1980).

Emond, D. Paul, "Alternative Dispute Resolution: A Conceptual Overview" in D. Paul Emond, ed., *Commercial Dispute Resolution: Alternatives to Litigation* (Aurora, ON: Canada Law Book, 1989).

Engler, Russell, "The MacCrate Report Turns 10: Assessing its Impact and Identifying Gaps We Should Seek to Narrow" (2001) 8 *Clinical L. Rev.* 109.

English, Christopher, "From Fishing Schooner to Colony: The Legal Development of Newfoundland, 1791–1832" in Louis A. Knafla and Susan W.S. Binnie, eds., *Law, Society, and the State: Essays in Modern Legal History* (Toronto; Buffalo, NY; and London: University of Toronto Press, 1995).

Falconbridge, John Delatre, "Law and Equity in Upper Canada" (1914) 63:1 *U. Penn. L. Rev.* 1.

Farrow, Trevor C.W., "Ethics in Advocacy" in Alice Woolley et al., eds., *Lawyers' Ethics and Professional Regulation*, 2nd ed. (Markham, ON: LexisNexis, 2012) c. 6.

Farrow, Trevor C.W., *Embracing the Complex Personality of International Law: Formalism, Anti-Formalism and the Globalization Construct* (LL.M. Thesis, Harvard Law School, 2000) [unpublished, archived at Harvard University Library].

Farrow, Trevor C.W., "Globalization, International Human Rights, and Civil Procedure" (2003) 41:3 *Alta. L. Rev.* 671.

Farrow, Trevor C.W., "Negotiation, Mediation, Globalization Protests and Police: Right Processes; Wrong System, Issues, Parties and Time" (2003) 28 *Queen's L.J.* 665.

Farrow, Trevor C.W., "Reviewing Globalization: Three Competing Stories, Two Emerging Themes, and How Law Schools Can and Must Participate" (2003) 13 *Meikei L. Rev.* 176, trans. into Japanese by M. Kuwahara, (2003) 44 *Aichigakuin L. Rev.* 29, repub'd (2004) 5 *J. Centre for Int'l Stud.* 1.

Farrow, Trevor C.W., "Thinking about Dispute Resolution," Review Essay (2003) 41:2 *Alta. L. Rev.* 559.

Farrow, Trevor C.W., "Dispute Resolution, Access to Civil Justice and Legal Education" (2005) 42 *Alta. L. Rev.* 741.

Farrow, Trevor C.W., "Dispute Resolution and Legal Education: A Bibliography" (2005) 7 *Cardozo J. Conflict Resol.* 119.

Farrow, Trevor C.W., "Globalizing Approaches to Legal Education and Training: Canada to Japan" (2005) 38 *Hosei Riron J. L. & Pol.* 144.

Farrow, Trevor C.W., "Privatizing our Public Civil Justice System" (2006) 9 *News & Views on Civil Justice Reform* 16.

Farrow, Trevor C. W., "Re-Framing the Sharia Arbitration Debate" (2006) 15:2 *Const. Forum Const.* 79.

Farrow, Trevor C.W., "The Negotiator-as-Professional: Understanding the Competing Interests of a Representative Negotiator" (2007) 7 *Pepp. Disp. Resol. L.J.* 373.

Farrow, Trevor C.W., "National Alternative Dispute Resolution Survey (2008)" (Toronto: University of Toronto Press, 2012), available online: University of Toronto Press <http://www.utppublishing.com/pdf/Farrow_LawyerSurvey.pdf>.

Farrow, Trevor C.W., "Representative Negotiation" in Colleen M. Hanycz, Trevor C.W. Farrow, and Frederick H. Zemans, *The Theory and Practice of Representative Negotiation* (Toronto: Emond Montgomery, 2008) c. 2.

Farrow, Trevor C.W., "Sustainable Professionalism" (2008) 46:1 *Osgoode Hall L.J.* 51.

Farrow, Trevor C.W., "Five Pleadings Cases Everyone Should Read" (2009) 35:4 *Advocates' Q.* 466.

Farrow, Trevor C.W, "Public Justice, Private Dispute Resolution and Democracy" in Ronalda Murphy and Patrick A. Molinari, eds., *Doing Justice: Dispute Resolution in the Courts and Beyond* (Montréal: Canadian Institute for the Administration of Justice, 2009) 301.

Farrow, Trevor C.W., *Civil Justice, Privatization and Democracy* (PhD Thesis, University of Alberta, Department of Political Science, 2011) [unpublished, archived at University of Alberta Library and York University (Osgoode Hall Law School) Library].

Farrow, Trevor C.W., "What is Access to Justice?" (2014) *Osgoode Hall L.J.* (forthcoming).

Farrow, Trevor C.W., "Ethical Lawyering in a Global Community" (2013) 36:1 *Man. L.J.* 141.

Farrow, Trevor C.W., "The Good, the Right, and the Lawyer" (2012) 15:1 *Legal Ethics* 163.

Farrow, Trevor C.W., "Proportionality: A Cultural Revolution" (2012) 1 *J. Civ. Lit. & Practice* 151.

Farrow, Trevor C.W., "Regional Integration and Dispute Resolution in the Free Trade Area of the Americas" in Andy Knight et al., eds., *Re-Mapping the Americas: Globalization, Regionalization and the FTAA* (Edmonton: University of Alberta Press, forthcoming).

Farrow, Trevor C.W., and Ada Ho, "Administrative Tribunals Using ADR" (May 2007), available online: CFCJ <http://www.cfcj-fcjc.org/sites/default/files/docs/2007/Administrative_Tribunal_Legislation_(May_17,_2007).pdf>.

Farrow, Trevor C.W., and Ada Ho, "Canadian Federal and Provincial Administrative Legislation Containing ADR Processes" (September 2007), available online: CFCJ <http://www.cfcj-fcjc.org/sites/default/files/docs/2007/Admin_Legislation_Chart_(Sept_22,_2007).pdf>.

Farrow, Trevor C.W., and Sheilah L. Martin, "Globalization & the Law: An Introduction" (2003) 41:3 *Alta. L. Rev.* 657.

Farrow, Trevor C.W., and Stephen G.A. Pitel, guest eds., "Lifelong Learning in Professionalism," Special Feature, (2010) *Can. Legal Educ. Ann. Rev.*

Farrow, Trevor C.W., and Garry D. Watson, Q.C., "Courts and Procedures: The Changing Roles of the Participants" in Janet Walker and Oscar G. Chase, eds., *Common Law, Civil Law and the Future of Categories* (Markham: LexisNexis, 2010) 155, reprinted in (2010) 49 *Sup. Ct. L. Rev.* (2d) 155.

Fazzi, Cindy, "Lessons in ADR from Corporate America," Book Review of *Emerging Systems for Managing Workplace Conflict* by David B. Lipsky, Ronald L. Seeber, and Richard D. Fincher, (2003–4) 58:4 *Disp. Resol. J.* 86.

Fellows, Mark, "The Same Result as in Court, More Efficiently: Comparing Arbitration And Court Litigation Outcomes" (July 2006) *Metropolitan Corporate Counsel* 32, available online: <http://www.metrocorpcounsel.com/articles/6988/same-result-court-more-efficiently-comparing-arbitration-and-court-litigation-outcomes>.

Finnis, John, *Natural Law and Natural Rights* (Oxford, UK, and New York: Oxford University Press, 1989).

Fisher, Roger, and William Ury, *Getting to Yes: Negotiating Agreement Without Giving In* (Boston: Houghton Mifflin, 1981).

Fisher, Ronald J., *Interactive Conflict Resolution* (Syracuse, NY: Syracuse University Press, 1997).

Fishkin, James S., and Peter Laslett, eds., *Debating Deliberative Democracy* (Malden, MA: Blackwell, 2003).

Fiss, Owen M., "Against Settlement" (1984) 93 *Yale L.J.* 1073.

Fiss, Owen M., "Justice Chicago Style" (1987) *U. Chi. Legal F.* 1.

Fiss, Owen, "The Forms of Justice" (1979) 93 *Harv. L. Rev.* 1.

Fiss, Owen, *The Law as it Could Be* (New York: New York University Press, 2003).

Fix-Fierro, Héctor, *Courts, Justice and Efficiency: A Socio-Legal Study of Economic Rationality in Adjudication* (Oxford, UK, and Portland, OR: Hart Publishing, 2003).

Fleischmann, Elana, and Naomi Bussin, "The Institutionalization of Alternative Dispute Resolution: A Case Study of the Ontario Insurance Commission" (1996) 6 *C.I.L.R.* 265.

Flood, Colleen M., and Lorne Sossin, eds., *Administrative Law in Context* (Toronto: Emond Montgomery, 2008).

Folberg, Jay, "A Mediation Overview: History and Dimensions of Practice" in (1983) 1 *Mediation Q.*

Ford, Cynthia, "Including Indian Law in a Traditional Civil Procedure Course: A Reprise, Five Years Later" (2001) 37 *Tulsa L. Rev.* 485.

Friedman, Lawrence M., *A History of American Law*, 3d ed. (New York: Simon & Schuster, 2005)

Friedman, Milton, *Capitalism and Freedom* (Chicago: University of Chicago Press, 1962).

Friedman, Thomas L., *The Lexus and the Olive Tree: Understanding Globalization* (New York: Anchor Books, 2000).

Friedman, Thomas L., *The World Is Flat: A Brief History of the Twenty-First Century* (New York: Farrar, Straus and Giroux, 2005).

Fuller, Lon, *The Morality of Law*, rev. ed. (New Haven, CT, and London: Yale University Press, 1969).

Fuller, Lon L., "Mediation – Its Forms and Functions" (1971) 44 *S. Cal. L. Rev.* 305, reprin'd in Kenneth I. Winston, ed., *The Principles of Social Order: Selected Essays of Lon L. Fuller*, rev. ed. (Oxford, UK: Hart Publishing, 2001).

Fuller, Lon L., "The Forms and Limits of Adjudication" (1978) 92 *Harv. L. Rev.* 353.

Galanter, Marc, and Mia Cahill, "'Most Cases Settle': Judicial Promotion and Regulation of Settlements" (1993–4) 46 *Stan. L. Rev.* 1339.

Galanter, Marc, "Access to Justice as a Moving Frontier" in Julia Bass, W.A. Bogart, and Frederick H. Zemans, eds., *Access to Justice for a New Century – The Way Forward* (Toronto: Law Society of Upper Canada, 2005).

Galanter, Marc, "The Vanishing Trial: An Examination of Trials and Related Matters in Federal and State Courts" (2004) 1 *J. Emp. Legal Stud.* 459.

Garber, Judith, "Community" in Janine Brodie and Sandra Rein, eds., *Critical Concepts: An Introduction to Politics*, 3rd ed. (Toronto: Prentice Hall, 2005).

Garrett, Robert D., "Mediation in Native America" (1994) 49 *Disp. Resol. J.* 38.

Garth, Bryant G., "Privatization and the New Formalism: Making the Courts Safe for Bureaucracy" (1988) 13 *Law & Soc. Inquiry* 157.

Garth, Bryant G., "From Civil Litigation to Private Justice: Legal Practice at War with the Profession and its Values" (1993–4) 59 *Brook L. Rev.* 931.

Gaudreault-DesBiens, Jean-François, "On Private Choices and Public Justice: Some Microscopic and Macroscopic Reflections on the State's Role in Addressing Faith-Based Arbitration" in Ronalda Murphy and Patrick A. Molinari, eds., *Doing Justice: Dispute Resolution in the Courts and Beyond* (Montréal: Canadian Institute for the Administration of Justice, 2009).

Genn, Hazel, *Paths to Justice: What People Do and Think about Going to Law* (Oxford, UK: Hart Publishing, 1999).

Gerencser, Alison E., "Alternative Dispute Resolution Has Morphed Into Mediation: Standards of Conduct Must Be Changed" (1998) 50 *Fla. L. Rev.* 843.

Giles, Jack, "The Compulsory Mediator" (2004) 62 *Advocate* (B.C.) 537.

Gillies, Myriam, "Opting Out of Liability: The Forthcoming, Near-Total Demise of the Modern Class Action" (2005) 104 *Mich. L. Rev.* 373.

Gleeson, Murray, "Managing Justice in the Australian Context" (Sydney: Australian Law Reform Commission, 2000).

Goldberg, Stephen B. et al., eds., *Dispute Resolution: Negotiation, Mediation, and Other Processes* (New York: Aspen Law and Business, 1999).

Goldberg, Stephen B. et al., eds., *Dispute Resolution: Negotiation, Mediation, and Other Processes*, 4th ed. (New York: Aspen Law & Business, 2003).

Gordon, Daniel, "Does Law Teaching Have Meaning? Teaching Effectiveness, Gauging Alumni Competence, and the MacCrate Report" (1997) 25 *Fordham Urb. L.J.* 43.

Green, L.C., *Law and Society* (Dobbs Ferry, NY: Oceana Publications, 1975).

Greene, Ian, "The Courts and Democracy" in Ian Greene, *The Courts* (Vancouver: UBC Press, 2006).

Grillo, Trina, "The Mediation Alternative: Process Dangers for Women" (1991) 100 *Yale L.J.* 1545.

Grossman, Michael C., "Is This Arbitration? Religious Tribunals, Judicial Review, and Due Process" (2007) 107 *Colum. L. Rev.* 169.

Gruner, Dora M., "Accounting for the Public Interest in International Arbitration: The Need for Procedural and Structural Reform" (2002–3) 41 *Colum. J. Transnat'l L.* 923.

Gunning, Isabelle R., "Diversity Issues in Mediation: Controlling Negative Cultural Myths" (1995) *J. Disp. Resol.* 55.

Habermas, Jürgen, *Legitimation Crisis*, trans. by Thomas McCarthy (Boston: Beacon Press, 1975).

Habermas, Jürgen, *Between Facts and Norms: Contributions to a Discourse Theory of Law and Democracy*, trans. by William Rehg (Cambridge, MA: MIT Press, 1996).

Habermas, Jürgen, "Paradigms of Law" (1996) 17 *Cardozo L. Rev.* 771.

Hadfield, Gillian K., "Privatizing Commercial Law" (2001) 42:1 *Regulation* 40, online: Cato Institute <http://object.cato.org/sites/cato.org/files/serials/files/regulation/2001/4/hadfield.pdf>.

Hadfield, Gillian K., "Privatizing Commercial Law: Lessons from ICANN" (2002) 6 *J. Small & Emerging Bus. L.* 258.

Hadfield, Gillian K., "Where Have All the Trials Gone? Settlements, Non-Trial Adjudications and Statistical Artifacts in the Changing Disposition of Federal Civil Cases" (2004) 1 *J. Emp. Legal Stud.* 705.

Hadfield, Gillian K., "Exploring Economic and Democratic Theories of Litigation: Differences between Individual and Organizational Litigants in the Disposition of Federal Civil Cases" (2005) 57 *Stan. L. Rev.* 1275.

Hadfield, Gillian K., and Eric Talley, "On Public versus Private Provision of Corporate Law" (2006) 22:2 *J.L. Econ. & Org.* 414.

Hajer, Maarten, and Hendrik Wagenaar, eds., *Deliberative Policy Analysis: Understanding Governance in the Network Society* (Cambridge, UK: Cambridge University Press, 2003).

Hall, Kermit L., *The Magic Mirror: Law in American History* (New York and Oxford, UK: Oxford University Press, 1989).

Hallevy, Gabriel, "Is ADR (Alternative Dispute Resolution) Philosophy Relevant to Criminal Justice? – Plea Bargains as Mediation Process between the Accused and the Prosecution" (2008), available online: SSRN <http://papers.ssrn.com/sol3/papers.cfm?abstract_id=1315984>.

Hamilton, Jonnette Watson, "The Impact of International Commercial Arbitration on Canadian Law and Courts" in Patricia Hughes and Patrick A. Molinari, eds., *Participatory Justice in a Global Economy: The New Rule of Law* (Montréal: Les Éditions Thémis, 2004).

Hanycz, Colleen M., "Through the Looking Glass: Mediator Conceptions of Philosophy, Process and Power" (2005) 42 *Alta. L. Rev.* 819.

Hanycz, Colleen M., "More Access to Less Justice: Efficiency, Proportionality and Costs in Canadian Civil Justice Reform" (2008) 27 *C.J.Q.* 98.

Hanycz, Colleen M., Trevor C.W. Farrow, and Frederick H. Zemans, *The Theory and Practice of Representative Negotiation* (Toronto: Emond Montgomery, 2008).

Hart, Gerald E., *The Québec Act, 1774* (Montreal: Gazette Printing, 1891).

Hart, H.L.A., *The Concept of Law* (Oxford, UK: Clarendon Press, 1961).

Hart, H.L.A., *The Concept of Law*, 2nd ed. (Oxford, UK, and New York: Oxford University Press, 1994).

Hart, Jr., Henry M., and Albert M. Sacks, *The Legal Process: Basic Problems in the Making and Application of Law*, ed. by William N. Eskridge, Jr. and Philip P. Frickey (Westbury, NY: Foundation Press, 1994).

Hayek, Friedrich A. von, *The Road to Serfdom* (London: Routledge Press; Chicago: University of Chicago Press, 1944).

Held, David et al., *Global Transformations: Politics, Economics and Culture* (Stanford, CA: Stanford University Press, 1999).

Henderson, Joshua J.A., and Trevor C.W. Farrow, "The Ethical Development of Law Students: An Empirical Study" (2009) 72:1 *Sask. L. Rev.* 75.

Hermann, Michele G., "The Dangers of ADR: A Three-Tiered System of Justice" (1989–90) 3 *J. Contemp. Legal Issues* 117.

Hirst, Paul, and Grahame Thompson, *Globalization in Question: The International Economy and the Possibilities of Governance*, 2nd ed. (Cambridge, UK: Polity Press, 1999).

Hobbes, Thomas, *Leviathan*, ed. by Richard Tuck (Cambridge, UK: Cambridge University Press, 1991).

Holmes, Oliver Wendell, "Law and the Court" (1913) in Oliver Wendell Holmes, *Collected Legal Papers* (New York: Peter Smith, 1952).

Horkheimer, Max, and Theodor W. Adorno, *Dialectic of Enlightenment*, trans. by John Cumming (London and New York: Verso, 1979).

Hornblower, William B., "A Century of Judge-Made Law" (1907) 7:7 *Colum. L. Rev.* 453.

Horton, William G., "ADR in Canada: Options for the Appropriate Resolution of Business Disputes" (2002) 21:2 *Advocates' Soc. J.* 11.

Horwitz, Morton J., *The Transformation of American Law, 1780–1860* (Cambridge, MA: Harvard University Press, 1977).

Hughes, Barry B., *International Futures: Choices in the Creation of a New World Order*, 2d ed. (Boulder, CO: Westview Press, 1996).

Hughes, Patricia, "Mandatory Mediation: Opportunity or Subversion?" (2001) 19 *Windsor Y.B. Access Just.* 161.

Hughes, Patricia, "The Rule of Law: Challenges in a Global Economy" in Patricia Hughes and Patrick A. Molinari, eds., *Participatory Justice in a Global Economy: The New Rule of Law* (Montréal: Les Éditions Thémis, 2004).

Hughes, Patricia, and Janet E. Mosher, guest eds., "Access to Justice," Special Issue, (2008) 46:4 *Osgoode Hall L. J.*

Hutchinson, Allan C., ed., *Access to Civil Justice* (Toronto: Carswell, 1990).

Jaffe, James A., "Industrial Arbitration, Equity, and Authority in England, 1800–1850" (2000) 18:3 *L.H.R.* 525.

Jenkinson, Tim, and Colin Mayer, "The Privatisation Process in France and the U.K." (1988) 32 *Eur. Econ. Rev.* 482.

Jennings, W.H., *Canadian Law: For Business & Personal Use* (Toronto: The Ryerson Press, 1951).

Joachim, Kaye, "New Models in Administrative Hearings: The Human Rights Tribunal of Ontario" in Ronalda Murphy and Patrick A. Molinari, eds., *Doing Justice: Dispute Resolution in the Courts and Beyond* (Montréal: Canadian Institute for the Administration of Justice, 2009).

Kalajdzic, Jasminka, "Consumer (In)Justice: Reflections on Canadian Consumer Class Actions" (2010) 50 *Can. Bus. L.J.* 356.

Keet, Michaela, and Teresa B. Salamone, "From Litigation to Mediation: Using Advocacy Skills for Success in Mandatory or Court-Connected Mediation" (2001) 64 *Sask. L. Rev.* 57.

Keet, Michaela, "The Evolution of Lawyers' Roles in Mandatory Mediation: A Condition of Systemic Transformation" (2005) 68 *Sask. L. Rev.* 313.

Kellogg, Catherine, "Ideas of Justice: Natural and Human" in Austin Sarat et al., eds., *Law and the Humanities, An Introduction* (Cambridge, UK: Cambridge University Press, 2010).

Kellogg, Catherine, "Democracy" in Janine Brodie and Sandra Rein, eds., *Critical Concepts: An Introduction to Politics*, 4th ed. (Toronto: Pearson, 2009).

Kelman, Herbert C., and V. Lee Hamilton, *Crimes of Obedience: Toward a Social Psychology of Authority and Responsibility* (New Haven, CT: Yale University Press, 1989).

Kennedy, David, "Receiving the International" (1994) 10 *Conn. J. Int'l L.* 1.

Kennedy, Duncan, *A Critique of Adjudication (fin de siècle)* (Cambridge, MA: Harvard University Press, 1997).

Kerelis, Kim, "Private Justice: How Civil Litigation Is Becoming a Private Institution – The Rise of Private Dispute Centres" (1993–1994) 23 *Sw. U.L. Rev.* 621.

Keynes, John Maynard, *The General Theory of Employment, Interest and Money*, new ed. (New York: Palgrave Macmillan, 2007).

Khan, Almas, "The Interaction between Shariah and International Law in Arbitration" (2005–6) 6 *Chi. J. Int'l L.* 791.

Kikeri, Sunita, and John Nellis, "Privatization in Competitive Sectors: The Record to Date" (World Bank Policy Research Working Paper 2860, June 2002), available online: World Bank <http://www-wds.worldbank.org/servlet/WDSContentServer/WDSP/IB/2002/08/02/000094946_02072209183311/Rendered/INDEX/multi0page.txt>.

Kikeri, Sunita, John Nellis, and Mary Shirley, *Privatization: The Lessons of Experience* (Washington, DC: World Bank, 1992).

Kikeri, Sunita, and Verena Phipps, "Privatization Trends: A Record Year in 2006" (13 January 2008), available online: World Bank <http://rru.worldbank.org/documents/publicpolicyjournal/317Kikeri_Phipps.pdf>.

Klement, Alon, and Zvika Neeman, "Civil Justice Reform: A Mechanism Design Framework" (2008) 164 *J. of Institutional and Theoretical Econ.*, available online: SSRN <http://papers.ssrn.com/sol3/papers.cfm?abstract_id=998028>.

Knafla, Louis A., and Susan W.S. Binnie, "Beyond the State: Law and Legal Pluralism in the Making of Modern Societies" in Louis A. Knafla and Susan W.S. Binnie, eds., *Law, Society, and the State: Essays in Modern Legal History* (Toronto; Buffalo, NY; and London: University of Toronto Press, 1995).

Knutsen, Erik S., "Secret Settlements in Canada" (2009), in Janet Walker, gen. ed., et al., *The Civil Litigation Process: Cases and Materials*, 7th ed. (Toronto: Emond Montgomery, 2010).

Korobkin, Russell B., "The Role of Law in Settlement" in Michael L. Moffitt and Robert C. Bordone, eds., *The Handbook of Dispute Resolution* (San Francisco: Jossey-Bass, 2005).

Kyd, Stewart, *A Treatise on the Law of Awards*, 2nd ed. (Philadelphia: Farrand, 1808).

Kymlicka, Will, *Contemporary Political Philosophy*, 2nd ed. (Oxford, UK, and New York: Oxford University Press, 2002).

Kymlicka, Will, *Liberalism, Community and Culture* (Oxford, UK: Clarendon Press, 1989).

Lande, John, "Commentary: Focusing on Program Design Issues in Future Research on Court-Connected Mediation" (2004) 22 *Confl. Resol. Q.* 89.

Landerkin, Hon. Hugh F., and Andrew J. Pirie, "Judges as Mediators: What's the Problem with Judicial Dispute Resolution in Canada?" (2003) 82 *Can. Bar. Rev.* 249.

Leacock, Jill, "British Columbia Court of Appeal Judicial Settlement Conference Pilot Project" (2004) 62 *Advocate* (B.C.) 879.

LeBaron, L. Michelle, and Venashri Pillay, eds. *Conflict across Cultures: A Unique Experience of Bridging Differences* (Boston: Intercultural Press, 2006).

LeBaron, Michelle, and Zena D. Zumeta, "Windows on Diversity: Lawyers, Culture, and Mediation Practice" (2003) 20 *Conflict Res. Q.* 463.

LeBaron, Michelle, *Bridging Troubled Waters: Conflict Resolution from the Heart* (San Francisco: Jossey-Bass, 2002).

Levant, Ezra, *Shake Down: How our Government Is Undermining Democracy in the Name of Human Rights* (Toronto: McClelland & Stewart, 2009).

Levin, A. Leo, and Russell R. Wheeler, eds., *The Pound Conference: Perspectives on Justice in the Future* (St. Paul, MN: West Publishing, 1979).

Lines, Michael, "Empirical Study of Civil Justice Systems: A Look at the Literature" (2005) 42:3 *Alta L. Rev.* 887.

Llewellyn, Jennifer J., "Dealing With the Legacy of Native Residential School Abuse in Canada: Litigation, ADR, and Restorative Justice" (2002) 52 *U.T.L.J.* 253.

Llewellyn, Jennifer J., "Doing Justice: New Directions in Restorative Justice" in Ronalda Murphy and Patrick A. Molinari, eds., *Doing Justice: Dispute Resolution in the Courts and Beyond* (Montréal: Canadian Institute for the Administration of Justice, 2009).

Locke, John, *Second Treatise of Government* (1690), ed. by C.B. Macpherson (Indianapolis, IN: Hackett Publishing, 1980).

Locke, John, *The Second Treatise of Government: An Essay Concerning the True Origin, Extent, and End of Civil Government* in John Locke, *Two Treatises of Government*, ed. by Peter Laslett, stud. ed. (Cambridge, UK: Cambridge University Press, 1990).

Love, Lela Porter, "Twenty-Five Years Later with Promises to Keep: Legal Education in Dispute Resolution and Training Mediators" (2002) 17 *Ohio St. J. Disp. Resol.* 597.

Lowenfeld, Andreas F., *International Commercial Litigation and Arbitration* (St. Paul, MN: West Publishing, 1993).

Lown, Peter J.M., "Rules of Court Project" (2005) 42 *Alta. L. Rev.* 907.

Luban, David, "Bargaining and Compromise: Recent Work on Negotiation and Informal Justice" (1985) 14 *Phil. & Pub. Aff.* 397.

Luban, David, "Settlements and the Erosion of the Public Realm" (1995) 83 *Geo. L.J.* 2619.

Lund, Michael S., *Preventing Violent Conflicts: A Strategy for Preventive Diplomacy* (Washington, DC: United States Institute of Peace Press, 1996).

MacCrate, Robert, "Yesterday, Today and Tomorrow: Building the Continuum of Legal Education and Professional Development" (New York Law School, Clinical Research Institute, Research Paper Series No. 03/04–1, September 2003), available online: SSRN <papers.ssrn.com/sol3/papers.cfm?abstract_id=444601>.

Macdonald, Roderick A., "Access to Justice and Law Reform" (1990) 10 *Windsor Y.B. Access Just.* 287.

Macdonald, Roderick A., "Whose Access? Which Justice?" (1992) 7 *Can. J.L. & Soc.* 175.

Macdonald, Roderick A., "Access to Justice and Law Reform #2" (2001) 19 *Windsor Y.B. Access Just.* 317.

Macdonald, Roderick A., "Access to Justice in Canada Today: Scope, Scale and Ambitions" in Julia Bass, W.A. Bogart, and Frederick H. Zemans, eds., *Access to Justice for a New Century – The Way Forward* (Toronto: Law Society of Upper Canada, 2005).

Macfarlane, Julie, ed., *Rethinking Disputes: The Mediation Alternative* (Toronto: Emond Montgomery, 1997).

Macfarlane, Julie, "What Does the Changing Culture of Legal Practice Mean for Legal Education?" (2001) 20 *Windsor Y.B. Access Just.* 191.

Macfarlane, Julie, "Why Do People Settle?" (2001) 46 *McGill L.J.* 663.

Macfarlane, Julie, "Culture Change? A Tale of Two Cities and Mandatory Court-Connected Mediation" (2002) 2 *J. Disp. Resol.* 241.

Macfarlane, Julie, "Mediating Family Disputes" in Julie Macfarlane, gen. ed., et al., eds., *Dispute Resolution: Readings and Case Studies*, 2nd ed. (Toronto: Emond Montgomery, 2003).

Macfarlane, Julie, "Collaborative Family Lawyering" in Julie Macfarlane, gen. ed., et al., eds., *Dispute Resolution: Readings and Case Studies*, 2nd ed. (Toronto: Emond Montgomery, 2003).

Macfarlane, Julie, *The New Lawyer: How Settlement Is Transforming the Practice of Law* (Vancouver: UBC Press, 2008).

Macfarlane, Julie, "Faith-Based Dispute Resolution" in Ronalda Murphy and Patrick A. Molinari, eds., *Doing Justice: Dispute Resolution in the Courts and Beyond* (Montréal: Canadian Institute for the Administration of Justice, 2009) 287.

Macfarlane, Julie, "Making Mediation Effective: Models for Best Practice" in Ronalda Murphy and Patrick A. Molinari, eds., *Doing Justice: Dispute Resolution in the Courts and Beyond* (Montréal: Canadian Institute for the Administration of Justice, 2009) 111.

Macfarlane, Julie, gen. ed., et al., eds., *Dispute Resolution: Readings and Case Studies*, 2nd ed. (Toronto: Emond Montgomery, 2003).

Macfarlane, Julie, gen. ed., et al., eds., *Dispute Resolution: Readings and Case Studies*, 3rd ed. (Toronto: Emond Montgomery, 2010).

Macfarlane, Julie, and Michaela Keet, "Civil Justice Reform and Mandatory Civil Mediation in Saskatchewan: Lessons from a Maturing Program" (2005) 42 *Alta. L.R.* 677.

Machiavelli, Niccolo, *Discourses*, intro. by Max Lerner (New York: Random House, 1950).

MacIntyre, Alisdair, *After Virtue*, 2nd ed. (Notre Dame, IN: University of Notre Dame Press, 1984).

MacIntyre, Alisdair, *Whose Justice? Which Rationality* (Notre Dame, IN: University of Notre Dame Press, 1988).

Mack, Kathy, *Court Referral to ADR: Criteria and Research* (Melbourne: Australian Institute of Judicial Administration Incorporated and the National Dispute Resolution Advisory Council, 2003).

MacNaughton, Heather M., "The Role of Mediation *in* Human Rights Disputes" in Ronalda Murphy and Patrick A. Molinari, eds., *Doing Justice: Dispute Resolution in the Courts and Beyond* (Montréal: Canadian Institute for the Administration of Justice, 2009) 47.

Macpherson, C.B., *The Real World of Democracy* (Toronto: Canadian Broadcasting Corporation, 1965).

Madison, James, "The Particular Structure of the New Government and the Distribution of Power Among Its Different Parts" *The New York Packet* (1 February 1788) in *The Federalist* (New York: J. and M. McLean, 1788) ("*The Federalist Papers*") at Federalist No. 47 in *The Federalist Papers*, ed. by Clinton Rossiter (New York: Mentor, 1961).

Malin, Martin H., and Robert F. Ladenson, "Privatizing Justice: A Jurisprudential Perspective on Labor and Employment Arbitration from the *Steelworkers Trilogy* to *Gilmer*" (1992–3) 44 *Hastings L.J.* 1187.

Malone, Albert P., and Allan Karnes, *The American Legal System: Perspectives, Politics, Processes, and Policies*, 2nd ed. (Lanham, MD: Rowman & Littlefield Publishers, 2008).

Maltby, Lewis L., "Private Justice: Employment Arbitration and Civil Rights" (1998) 30 *Colum. Human Rights L. Rev.* 29.

Mantilla-Serrano, Fernando, "Towards a Transnational Procedural Public Policy" (2004) 20:4 *Arb. Int'l* 333.

Marcuse, Herbert, *Eros and Civilization* (London: Sphere Books, 1969).

Marx, Karl, *Capital: A Critique of Political Economy*, vols. 1 and 2 (London: Penguin Books, 1976).

Marx, Karl, "Critique of the Gotha Program" (1875) in Robert C. Tucker, ed., *The Marx-Engels Reader*, 2nd ed. (New York and London: W.W. Norton, 1978).

Marx, Karl, *The German Ideology* (1845–6) in Robert C. Tucker, ed., *The Marx-Engels Reader*, 2nd ed. (New York and London: W.W. Norton, 1978).

Marx, Karl, *The Grundrisse* (1857–8) in Robert C. Tucker, ed., *The Marx-Engels Reader*, 2nd ed. (New York and London: W.W. Norton, 1978).

Marx, Karl, "On the Jewish Question" (1843) in Robert C. Tucker, ed., *The Marx-Engels Reader*, 2nd ed. (New York and London: W.W. Norton, 1978).

Marx, Karl, and Frederich Engels, *Manifesto of the Communist Party* (1848) in Robert C. Tucker, ed., *The Marx-Engels Reader*, 2nd ed. (New York and London: W.W. Norton, 1978).

Maxwell, Jennifer P., "Mandatory Mediation of Custody in the Face of Domestic Violence: Suggestions for Courts and Mediators" (1999) 37:3 *Fam. Concil. Cts. Rev.* 335 (now *Fam. Ct. Rev.*).

Mayer, Bernard S., *The Dynamics of Conflict Resolution: A Practitioner's Guide* (San Francisco: Jossey-Bass, 2000).

McAdoo, Bobbi, "All Rise, the Court Is in Session: What Judges Say about Court-Connected Mediation" (2007) 22:2 *Ohio St. J. Disp. Resol.* 377.

McClintock, Pamela, "Big Corporate Clients Demand Diversity" (1999) 221:99 *N.Y.L.J.* 5.

McCormack, Tracy Walters, "Privatizing the Justice System" (2006) 25 *Rev. Litig.* 735.

McGill, Shelley, "The Conflict between Consumer Class Actions and Contractual Arbitration Clauses" (2006) 43:3 *Can. Bus. L.J.* 359.

McGill, Shelley, "Consumer Arbitration and Class Actions: The Impact of *Dell Computer Corp. v. Union des consommateurs*" (2007) 45:3 *Can. Bus. L.J.* 334.

McGill, Shelley, "Consumer Arbitration Clause Enforcement: A Balanced Legislative Response" (2010) 47 *Am. Bus. L.J.* 361.

McLaren, John, Hamar Foster, and Chet Orloff, eds., *Law for the Elephant, Law for the Beaver: Essays in the Legal History of the North American West* (Pasadena, CA: Ninth Judicial Circuit Historical Society, 1992).

Megginson, William L., and Jeffry M. Netter, "From State to Market: A Survey of Empirical Studies on Privatization" (2001) 39:2 *J. Econ. Lit.* 321.

Meili, Stephen, and Tamara Packard, "Alternative Dispute Resolution in a New Health Care System: Will it Work for Everyone?" (1994) 10 *Ohio St. J. Disp. Resol.* 23.

Menkel-Meadow, Carrie, "Pursuing Settlement in an Adversary Culture: A Tale of Innovation Co-Opted or 'The Law of ADR'" (1991) 19 *Fla. St. U. L. Rev.* 1.

Menkel-Meadow, Carrie, "Introduction: What Will We Do When Adjudication Ends? A Brief Intellectual History of ADR" (1997) 44 *UCLA L. Rev.* 1613.

Menkel-Meadow, Carrie, "Ethics in ADR: The Many 'Cs' of Professional Responsibility and Dispute Resolution" (2001) 28 *Fordham Urb. L.J.* 979.

Menkel-Meadow, Carrie, "Dispute Resolution" (2009) in Peter Cane and Herbert M. Kritzer, eds., *Oxford Handbook of Empirical Legal Research* (Oxford, UK: Oxford University Press, 2010), available online: SSRN <http://papers.ssrn.com/sol3/papers.cfm?abstract_id=1485563>.

Menkel-Meadow, Carrie, and Bryant G. Garth, "Civil Procedure and Courts" (2009) in Peter Cane and Herbert M. Kritzer, eds., *Oxford Handbook of Empirical Legal Research* (Oxford, UK: Oxford University Press, 2010), available online: SSRN <http://papers.ssrn.com/sol3/papers.cfm?abstract_id=1537448>.

Michelman, Frank I., "Democracy and Positive Liberty" (1996) 21 *Boston Rev.* 3.

Michelman, Frank I., "Constitutional Authorship by the People" (1999) 74 *Notre Dame L. Rev.* 1605.

Michelman, Frank I., "W(h)ither the Constitution?" (1999–2000) 21 *Cardozo L. Rev.* 1063.

Michelman, Frank I., "Morality, Identity and 'Constitutional Patriotism'" (2001) 14 *Ratio Juris* 253.

Mill, James, "Liberty of the Press" in *Essays on Government, Jurisprudence, Liberty of the Press, and Law of Nations* (London: J. Innes, 1825), reprint ed. (New York: A.M. Kelley, 1967).

Mill, John Stuart, "Bentham" (August 1838) *London and Westminster Review* in John Stuart Mill, *Utilitarianism, On Liberty, Essay on Bentham*, ed. by Mary Warnock (New York: Meridian, 1962).

Mill, John Stuart, *On Liberty* in John Stuart Mill, *Utilitarianism, On Liberty, Essay on Bentham*, ed. by Mary Warnock (New York: Meridian, 1962).

Mill, John Stuart, *Utilitarianism* (1863) in John Stuart Mill, *Utilitarianism, On Liberty, Essay on Bentham*, ed. by Mary Warnock (New York: Meridian, 1962).

Miller, Sidney T., "The Development of the Canadian Legal System" (1913) 61:9 *U. Pa. L. Rev.* 625.

Milton, John, *Samson Agonistes* (1671) in *The Poetical Works of John Milton*, with a memoir, and critical remarks on his genius and writings, by James Montgomery (London: Tilt and Bogue, 1843).

Mitchnick, Morton G., and Brian Etherington, *Labour Arbitration in Canada* (Toronto: Lancaster House, 2006).

Mnookin, Robert H., and L. Kornhauser, "Bargaining in the Shadow of the Law: The Case of Divorce" (1979) 88 *Yale L.J.* 950.

Moberly, Robert B., "Introduction: Dispute Resolution in the Law School Curriculum: Opportunities and Challenges" (1998) 50 *Fla. L. Rev.* 583.

Moffitt, Michael L., and Robert C. Bordone, eds., *The Handbook of Dispute Resolution* (San Francisco: Jossey-Bass, 2005).

Moran, Michael, Martin Rein, and Robert E. Goodin, eds., *The Oxford Handbook of Public Policy* (Oxford, UK: Oxford University Press, 2006).

Mori, Irvine, "Mediation: Is it Appropriate in Sexual Harassment Grievances?" (1993) 9 *Ohio St. J. Disp. Resol.* 27.

Morris, Catherine, "The Moulding of Lawyers: ADR and Legal Education" (1999) 17 *Windsor Y.B. Access Just.* 271.

Mullan, David J. et al, *Administrative Law: Cases, Text, and Materials*, 5th ed. (Toronto: Emond Montgomery, 2003).

Murphy, Ronalda, and Patrick A. Molinari, eds., *Doing Justice: Dispute Resolution in the Courts and Beyond* (Montréal: Canadian Institute for the Administration of Justice, 2009).

Murray, John S., Alan Scott Rau, and Edward F. Sherman, *Processes of Dispute Resolution: The Role of Lawyers*, 3rd ed. (Westbury, NY: The Foundation Press, 2002).

Murray, Peter, "The Privatization of Civil Justice" (May–June 2008) 91 *Judicature* 272.

Murray, Stuart, "Value for Money? Cautionary Lessons about P3s from British Columbia" (Summary), available online: Canadian Centre for Policy Alternatives, B.C. Office <http://www.policyalternatives.ca/sites/default/files/uploads/publications/BC_Office_Pubs/bc_2006/P3_vfm_summary.pdf>.

Naimark, Richard W., and Stephanie E. Keer, "International Private Commercial Arbitration: Expectations and Perceptions of Attorneys and Business People; A Forced-Rank Analysis" in Christopher R. Drahozal and Richard W. Naimark, eds., *Towards a Science of International Arbitration: Collected Empirical Research* (New York: Kluwer Law International, 2005).

Nesbitt, Simon, and Henry Quinlan, "The Status and Operation of Unilateral or Optional Arbitration Clauses" (2006) 22:1 *Arb. Int'l.* 133.

Neuman, W. Lawrence, and Karen Robson, *Basics of Social Research: Qualitative and Quantitative Approaches*, Cdn. ed. (Toronto: Pearson Education Canada, 2009).

Noble, Cinnie, L. Leslie Dizgun, and D. Paul Emond, *Mediation Advocacy: Effective Client Representation in Mediation Proceedings* (Toronto: Emond Montgomery, 1998).

Nolan-Haley, Jacqueline M., "Court Mediation and the Search for Justice through Law" (1996) 74 *Wash. U. L. Q.* 47.

Nolan-Haley, Jacqueline M., *Alternative Dispute Resolution in a Nutshell*, 2nd ed. (St. Paul, MN: West Group, 2001).

North, Arthur A., *The Supreme Court: Judicial Process and Judicial Politics* (New York: Merredith, 1966).

Nozick, Robert, *Anarchy, State and Utopia* (New York: Basic Books, 1974).

Nussbaum, Frank, and Meah Rothman Tell, "General Practice, Solo and Small Firm: Arbitration and Attorney's Fees: A Pandora's Box" (2002) 76 *Fla. Bar. J.* 77.

O'Hara, Erin A., and Larry E. Ribstein, *The Law Market* (Oxford, UK, and New York: Oxford University Press, 2009).

Ogilvie, M.H., "Recent Developments in Canadian Law: Legal History" (1987) 19 *Ottawa L. Rev.* 225.

Olson, Kelly Browe, "Lessons Learned from a Child Protection Mediation Program: If at First You Succeed and Then You Don't …" (2003) 41:4 *Fam. Ct. Rev.* 480.

Orr, David, "Alternative Dispute Resolution in the Canadian Court System" (1999) 19:2 *The Court Manager* 36.

Pavlich, George, "Critical Policy Analysis, Power and Restorative Justice" (March 2009) 75 *Crim. Just. Matters* 24.

Pavlich, George, *Justice Fragmented: Mediating Community Disputes under Postmodern Conditions* (London and New York: Routledge, 1996).

Pavlich, George, "The Art of Critique or How Not to be Governed Thus" in Gary Wickham and George Pavlich, eds., *Rethinking Law, Society and Governance: Foucault's Bequest* (Oxford, UK, and Portland, OR: Hart Publishing, 2001).

Pavlich, George, *Governing Paradoxes of Restorative Justice* (London: Glass-House Press, 2005).

Pavlich, George, "Restorative Justice and Its Paradoxes" (Winter 2005–6) 22 *Connections* 1.

Pavlich, George, "The Law of Subaltern Discipline" in Augustine Brannigan and George Pavlich, eds., *Governance and Regulation in Social Life: Essays in Honour of W.G. Carson* (Abingdon, UK; Oxon, UK; and New York: Routledge-Cavendish, 2007).

Pepper, Randy A., "Mandatory Mediation: Ontario's Unfortunate Experiment in Court-Annexed ADR" (1998) 20 *Advocates' Q.* 403.

Pepper, Randy A., "Why Arbitrate?: Ontario's Recent Experience with Commercial Arbitration" (1998) 38 *Osgoode Hall L.J.* 807.

Picard, Cheryl et al., *The Art and Science of Mediation* (Toronto: Emond Montgomery, 2004).

Pirie, Andrew J., *Alternative Dispute Resolution: Skills, Science, and the Law* (Toronto: Irwin Law, 2000).

Pirie, Andrew, "Critiques of Settlement Advocacy" in Colleen M. Hanycz, Trevor C.W. Farrow, and Frederick H. Zemans, *The Theory and Practice of Representative Negotiation* (Toronto: Emond Montgomery, 2008).

Plato, *The Laws* in *The Dialogues of Plato*, trans. by B. Jowett, 3rd ed. (London: Oxford University Press, 1931 imp.)

Plato, *The Laws*, trans. by Trevor J. Saunders (London: Penguin, 1970).

Plato, *Republic*, trans. by Robin Waterfield (Oxford, UK, and New York: Oxford University Press, 1993).

Pleasence, Pascoe et al., *Causes of Action: Civil and Social Justice*, 2nd ed. (London: Legal Services Commission, 2006).

Ponte, Lucille M., "Reassessing the Australian Adversarial System: An Overview of Issues in Court Reform and Federal ADR Practice in the Land Down Under" (2000) 27:2 *Syracuse J. Int'l L. & Com.* 335.

Posner, Richard A., and William Landes, "Adjudication as a Private Good" (1979) 8 *J. Legal Stud.* 235.

Posner, Richard A., *The Federal Courts: Challenge and Reform* (Cambridge, MA: Harvard University Press, 1985).

Powell, Edward, "Settlement of Disputes by Arbitration in Fifteenth-Century England" (1984) 2:1 *L.H.R.* 21.

Pruitt, Dean G., and Peter J. Carnevale, *Negotiation in Social Conflict* (Buckingham: Open University Press, 1993).

Pruitt, Dean G., Jeffrey Z. Rubin, and Sung Hee Kim, *Social Conflict: Escalation, Stalemate, and Settlement*, 2nd ed. (New York: McGraw-Hill, 1994).

Rawls, John, A *Theory of Justice*, rev. ed. (Cambridge, MA: Belknap Press, 1999).

Rawls, John, *Justice as Fairness, a Restatement* (Cambridge, MA: Belknap Press, 2001).

Raz, Joseph, *The Concept of a Legal System: An Introduction to the Theory of Legal System*, 2nd ed. (Oxford, UK: Oxford University Press, 1983).

Raz, Joseph, *The Authority of Law: Essays on Law and Morality* (Oxford, UK, and New York: Oxford University Press, 1986).

Raz, Joseph, *Ethics in the Public Domain: Essays in the Morality of Law and Politics* (Oxford, UK: Clarendon Press, 1994).

Read, David B., Q.C., *The Lives of the Judges of Upper Canada and Ontario, From 1791 to the Present Time* (Toronto: Rowsell & Hutchison, 1888).

Régimbald, Guy, *Canadian Administrative Law* (Markham, ON: LexisNexis, 2008).

Reif, Linda C., "The Use of Conciliation or Mediation for the Resolution of International Commercial Disputes" (2007) 45 *Can. Bus. L.J.* 20.

Relis, Tamara, *Perceptions in Litigation and Mediation: Lawyers, Defendants, Plaintiffs, and Gendered Parties* (Cambridge, UK and New York: Cambridge University Press, 2009).

Resnik, Judith, "Courts: In and Out of Sight, Site, and Cite" (2008) 53 *Vill. L. Rev.* 771.

Resnik, Judith, "Interdependent Federal Judiciaries: Puzzling about Why & How to Value the Independence of Which Judges" (2008) 137 *Daedalus* 28.

Resnik, Judith, "Revising the Canon: Feminist Help in Teaching Procedure" (1993) 61 *U. Cin. L. Rev.* 1181.

Reuben, Richard C., "Public Justice: Toward a State Action Theory of Alternative Dispute Resolution" (1997) 85 *Cal. L. Rev.* 577.

Riddell, William R., *Some Early Legislation and Legislators in Upper Canada* (Toronto: Carswell, 1913).

Riddell, William R., *The Early Courts of the Province* (Toronto?, 1916? [specific publication details unknown]).

Riddell, William R., "The First Court of Chancery in Canada" (1922) 2 *B.U.L. Rev.* 231.

Riddell, William R., "The Prerogative Court in Upper Canada" in Ontario Historical Society, *Papers and Records* (Toronto: Ontario Historical Society, 1926), vol. xxii.

Riddell, William R., *The Bar and the Courts of the Province of Upper Canada, or Ontario* (Toronto: Macmillan, 1928).

Riddell, William R., *The Court of King's Bench in Upper Canada, 1824–1827* (Toronto? [specific publication details unknown]).

Riddell, William R., *How the King's Bench Came to Toronto* (Toronto? [specific publication details unknown]).

Riskin, Leonard L., "Mediation and Lawyers" (1982) 43 *Ohio St. L.J.* 29.

Roach, Kent, *The Supreme Court on Trial: Judicial Activism or Democratic Dialogue* (Toronto: Irwin Law, 2001).

Roach, Kent, "Teaching Procedures: The Fiss/Weinrib Debate in Practice" (1991) 41 *U.T.L.J.* 247.

Rodenbeck, Adolph J., "The New Practice in New York" (1916) 1:2 *Cornell L.Q.* 63.

Rodrik, Dani, *Has Globalization Gone Too Far?* (Washington, DC: Institute of International Economics, 1997).

Romney, Paul, "From Constitutionalism to Legalism: Trial by Jury, Responsible Government, and the Rule of Law in the Canadian Political Culture" (1989) 7:1 *L.H.R.* 121.

Rooke, Hon. John D., "The Multi-Door Courthouse is Open in Alberta: Judicial Dispute Resolution is Institutionalized in the Court of Queen's Bench" (LL.M. Thesis, University of Alberta, 2010), available online: CFCJ <http://www.cfcj-fcjc.org/sites/default/files/docs/hosted/22471-multidoor_courthouse.pdf>.

Rose, Marc, and Roger Suffling, "Alternative Dispute Resolution and the Protection of Natural Areas in Ontario, Canada" (2001) 56 *Landscape and Urb. Plan.* 1.

Rosen, Deborah A., "The Supreme Court of Judicature of Colonial New York: Civil Practice in Transition, 1691–1760" (1987) 5 *L.H.R.* 213.

Rosenberg, Joshua, "Alternative Dispute Resolution in Public Law: Interview with Lord Woolf, C.J. Conducted by Joshua Rosenberg" in Richard Gordon, ed., *Judicial Review in the New Millennium* (London: Sweet & Maxwell, 2003) 109.

Rousseau, Jean-Jacques, *Discourse on the Origin and Basis of Inequality Among Men* (1754) in *The Essential Rousseau*, trans. by Lowell Bair (New York: Meridian, 1974).

Rousseau, Jean-Jacques, *The Social Contract or Principles of Political Right* in Jean-Jacques Rousseau, *The Social Contract and Discourses*, trans. by G.D.H. Cole, rev. by J.H. Brumfitt and John C. Hall (London and Melbourne: J.M. Dent, 1973).

Rubin, G.R. and David Sugarman, *Law, Economy and Society, 1750–1914: Essays in the History of English Law* (Oxford, UK: Professional Books Limited, 1984).

Russell, Peter H., "Judicial Power in Canada's Political Culture" in F.L. Morton, ed., *Law, Politics and the Judicial Process in Canada* (Calgary: University of Calgary Press, 1989).

Russell, Peter H., *The Judiciary in Canada: The Third Branch of Government* (Toronto: McGraw-Hill Ryerson, 1987).

Saaty, Thomas L., and Joyce M. Alexander, *Conflict Resolution: The Analytic Hierarchy Approach* (New York: Praeger, 1989).

Sabatier, Paul A., ed., *Theories of the Policy Process*, 2nd ed. (Boulder, CO: Westview Press, 2007).

Sabine, George H., A *History of Political Theory* (New York: Henry Holt, 1948).

Sandefur, Rebecca L., ed., *Access to Justice* (Bingley, UK: JAI Press, 2009).

Sandel, Michael J., *Liberalism and the Limits of Justice* (Cambridge, UK: Cambridge University Press, 1982).

Sandel, Michael J., "Political Liberalism," Review Essay (1994) 107 *Harv. L. Rev.* 1765.

Sandel, Michael J., *Democracy's Discontents: America in Search of a Public Philosophy* (Cambridge, MA: Belknap, 1996).

Sandel, Michael J., *Justice: A Reader* (Oxford, UK; New York: Oxford University Press, 2007).

Sandel, Michael J., *Justice: What's the Right Thing to Do?* (New York: Farrar, Straus and Giroux, 2009).

Sander, Frank E.A., "Varieties of Dispute Processing" (1976) 70 *F.D.R.* 111.

Sander, Frank E.A., "The Future of ADR" (2000) *J. Disp. Resol.* 3.

Sasso, William V., and Jasminka Kalajdzic, "Do Ontario and its Gaming Venues Owe a Duty of Care to Problem Gamblers?" (2006) 10 *Gaming L. Rev.* 552.

Saumier, Geneviève, "Consumer Dispute Resolution: The Evolving Canadian Landscape" (2007) 1 *Class Action Def. Q.* 52.

Saumier, Geneviève, "Consumer Arbitration in the Evolving Canadian Landscape" (2008–9) 113 *Penn. St. L. Rev.* 1203.

Savas, E.S., "A Taxonomy of Privatization Strategies" (1989–90) 18:2 *Pol'y Stud. J.* 343.

Schelling, Thomas C., *The Strategy of Conflict* (Cambridge, MA: Harvard University Press, 1960, repr. 1997).

Schneider, Elizabeth M., "Gendering and Engendering Process" (1993) 61 *U. Cin. L. Rev.* 1223.

Schneiderman, David, *Constitutionalizing Economic Globalization: Investment Rules and Democracy's Promise* (Cambridge, UK and New York: Cambridge University Press, 2008).

Schor, Miguel, "Judicial Review and American Constitutional Exceptionalism" (2008) 46:3 *Osgoode Hall L.J.* 535.

Seckel, Allan, "Judicial Models: Can We Do Better? Proposed Reforms to Civil Procedure in British Columbia" in Ronalda Murphy and Patrick A. Molinari, eds., *Doing Justice: Dispute Resolution in the Courts and Beyond* (Montréal: Canadian Institute for the Administration of Justice, 2009).

Senft, Louise Phipps, and Cynthia A. Savage, "ADR in the Courts: Progress, Problems, and Possibilities" (2003) 108 *Penn St. L. Rev.* 327.

Senger, Jeffrey M., "Turning the Ship of State" (2000) *J. Disp. Resol.* 79.

Shepard, Benjamin, and Ronald Hayduk, eds., *From ACT UP to the WTO: Urban Protest and Community Building in the Era of Globalization* (London and New York, Verso, 2002).

Sherman, Mark R., "Mediation Hype & Hyperbole: How Much Should We Believe?" (2003) 58:3 *Disp. Resol. J.* 43.

Sheshinski, Eytan, and Luis F. López-Calva, "Privatization and its Benefits: Theory and Evidence" (2003) 49:3 *CESifo Econ. Stud.* 429.

Shone, Margaret A., "Civil Justice Reform in Canada: 1996 to 2006 and Beyond" (December 2006), available online: CFCJ <http://www.cfcj-fcjc.org/sites/default/files/docs/2006/shone-final-en.pdf>.

Short, Donald E., "New Approaches to Dispute Resolution in the Construction Sector" (November, 2003), available online: Fasken Martineau <http://www.fasken.com/>.

Silver, Marjorie A., "The Uses and Abuses of Informal Procedures in Federal Civil Rights Enforcement" (1987) 55 *Geo. Wash. L. Rev.* 482.

Silver, Michael P., *Mediation and Negotiation: Representing Your Clients* (Toronto, Vancouver: Butterworths, 2001).

Singer, Jana B., "The Privatization of Family Law" (1992) *Wis. L. Rev.* 1443.

Slaughter, Anne-Marie, "International Law and International Relations Theory: A Dual Agenda" (1993) 87 *Am. J. Int'l L.* 205.

Smith, Adam, *An Inquiry into the Nature and Causes of the Wealth of Nations*, ed. by Edwin Cannan (Chicago: University of Chicago Press, 1967).

Smythe, Elizabeth, "Canadian Sovereignty and Global Trade and Investment Rules" in Janine Brodie and Linda Trimble, eds., *Reinventing Canada: Politics of the 21st Century* (Toronto: Prentice Hall, 2003) c. 21.

Solum, Lawrence B., "Alternative Court Structures in the Future of the California Judiciary: 2020 Vision" (1993) 66 *S. Cal. L. Rev.* 2121.

Sossin, Lorne, "The Public Interest, Professionalism, and Pro Bono Publico" (2008) 46:1 *Osgoode Hall L.J.* 131.

Spain, Larry R., "Alternative Dispute Resolution for the Poor: Is it an Alternative?" (1994) 70 *N.D. L. Rev.* 269.

Spencer, J.R., ed., *Jackson's Machinery of Justice* (Cambridge, UK: Cambridge University Press, 1989).

Stein, Janice Gross, *The Cult of Efficiency* (Toronto: House of Anansi Press, 2001).

Stempel, Jeffrey W., "Reflections on Judicial ADR and the Multi-Door Courthouse at Twenty: Fait Accompli, Failed Overture, or Fledgling Adulthood?" (1996) 11 *Ohio St. J. Disp. Resol.* 297.

Stiglitz, Joseph E., *Globalization and its Discontents* (New York: W.W. Norton, 2002).

Stipanowich, Thomas J., "ADR and the 'Vanishing Trial': The Growth and Impact of 'Alternative Dispute Resolution'" (2004) 1 *J. Emp. Leg. Stud.* 843.

Stipanowich, Thomas J., "Beyond Arbitration: Innovation and Evolution in the United States Construction Industry" (1996) 31 *Wake Forest L. Rev.* 169.

Stone, Katherine Van Wezel, *Private Justice: The Law of Alternative Dispute Resolution* (New York: Foundation Press, 2000).

Stone, Marcus, *Representing Clients in Mediation* (London, Edinburgh, and Dublin: Butterworths, 1998).

Storme, Marcel, "Le Common Law / Civil Law Divide: An Introduction" in Janet Walker and Oscar G. Chase, eds., *Common Law, Civil Law and the Future of Categories* (Markham: LexisNexis, 2010).

Strauss, Leo, and Joseph Cropsey, eds., *History of Political Philosophy*, 3rd ed. (Chicago and London: University of Chicago Press, 1987).

Stuart, Henry, *Private Justice: Towards Integrated Theorising in the Sociology of Law* (London; Boston: Routledge & Kegan Paul, 1983).

Subrin, Stephen N., "A Traditionalist Looks at Mediation: It's Here to Stay and Much Better than I Thought" (2002/3) 3 *Nev. L.J.* 196.

Subrin, Stephen N., "David Dudley Field and the Field Code: A Historical Analysis of an Earlier Procedural Vision" (1988) 6:2 *L.H.R.* 311.

Susskind, Richard, *Expert Systems in Law* (Oxford, UK: Oxford University Press, 1987; paperback ed., 1989).

Susskind, Richard, *The End of Lawyers? Rethinking the Nature of Legal Services* (Oxford, UK, and New York: Oxford University Press, 2008).

Symposium, "Against Settlement: Twenty-Five Years Later" (2009) 78:3 *Fordham L. Rev.*

Taylor, Charles, *Philosophical Arguments* (Cambridge, MA: Harvard University Press, 1995).

Teplitsky, Martin, "Excessive Cost and Delay: Is there a Solution?" (2000) 19:2 *Advocates' Soc. J.* 5.

Teplitsky, Martin, "Universal Mandatory Mediation: A Critical Analysis of the Evaluations of the Ontario Mandatory Mediation Program" (2001) 20:3 *Advocates' Soc. J.* 10.

Thucydides, *History of the Peloponnesian War*, trans. by Rex Warner, rev. ed. (London: Penguin, 1972).

Tocqueville, Alexis de, *Democracy in America*, trans. by George Lawrence, ed. by J.P. Mayer (New York: Perennial, 2000).

Turpel-Lafond, Mary-Ellen, "Justice for Aboriginal Communities: Sharing the Ways" in Ronalda Murphy and Patrick A. Molinari, eds., *Doing Justice: Dispute Resolution in the Courts and Beyond* (Montréal: Canadian Institute for the Administration of Justice, 2009).

Turriff, Gordon, "On the Road to Civil Justice Reform in British Columbia" (2004) 62 *Advocate (B.C.)* 863.

Twining, William, *Globalisation and Legal Theory* (London: Butterworths, 2000).

Unger, Roberto M., *The Critical Legal Studies Movement* (Cambridge, MA: Harvard University Press, 1986).

Unger, Roberto M., *Democracy Realized: The Progressive Alternative* (London and New York: Verso, 1998).

Unger, Roberto M., *The Self Awakened: Pragmatism Unbound* (Cambridge, MA and London: Harvard University Press, 2007).

Unger, Roberto M., and Cornel West, *The Future of American Progressivism: An Initiative for Political and Economic Reform* (Boston: Beacon Press, 1998).

Urquhart, Ian, "Constitutions and the Rule of Law" in Janine Brodie and Sandra Rein, eds., *Critical Concepts: An Introduction to Politics*, 3rd ed. (Toronto: Prentice Hall, 2005).

Vischer, Robert K., "Legal Advice as Moral Perspective" (2006) 19:1 *Geo. J. Legal Ethics* 225.

Viscusi, W. Kip, ed., *Regulation through Litigation* (Washington, DC: AEI-Brookings Joint Center for Regulatory Studies, 2002).

Waddams, S.M., *Introduction to the Study of Law*, 3rd ed. (Toronto: Carswell, 1987).

Waitzer, Ed, and Johnny Jaswal, "*Peoples, BCE*, and the Good Corporate 'Citizen'" (2009) 47:3 *Osgoode Hall L. J.* 439.

Walker, Janet, gen. ed., et al., *The Civil Litigation Process: Cases and Materials*, 7th ed. (Toronto: Emond Montgomery, 2010).

Walker, Janet, gen. ed., et al., *The Civil Litigation Process: Cases and Materials* 6th ed. (Toronto: Emond Montgomery, 2005).

Walker, Janet and Oscar G. Chase, eds., *Common Law, Civil Law and the Future of Categories* (Markham: LexisNexis, 2010).

Walker, Janet and Lorne Sossin, *Civil Litigation* (Toronto: Irwin Law, 2010).

Walzer, Michael, *Spheres of Justice: A Defence of Pluralism and Equality* (New York: Basic Books, 1983).

Walzer, Michael, "The Communitarian Critique of Liberalism" (1990) 18 *Political Theory* 6.

Ward, Halina, "The Interface between Globalization, Corporate Responsibility, and the Legal Profession" (2004) 1 *U. St. Thomas L.J.* 813.

Watson, Garry D., and Michael McGowan, *Ontario Civil Practice, 2010* (Toronto: Carswell, 2009).

Watson, Garry D., "Class Actions: The Canadian Experience" (2001) 11 *Duke J. Comp. & Int'l L.* 269.

Watson Hamilton, Jonnette, "Pre-Dispute Consumer Arbitration Clauses: Denying Access to Justice?" (2006) 51 *McGill L.J.* 693.

Webster, Thomas H., "Review of Substantive Reasoning of International Arbitral Awards by National Courts: Ensuring One-Stop Adjudication" (2006) 22:3 *Arb. Int'l.* 431.

Weiler, Paul, *In the Last Resort: A Critical Study of the Supreme Court of Canada* (Toronto: Carswell, 1974).

Weinstein, Jack B., "Some Benefits and Risks of Privatization of Justice through ADR" (1996) 11 *Ohio St. J. Disp. Resol.* 241.

Weinstein, Jack B., and Catherine Wimberly, "Secrecy in Law and Science" (2001–2) 23 *Cardozo L. Rev.* 1.

Welsh, Nancy A., "Remembering the Role of Justice in Resolution: Insights from Procedural and Social Justice Theories" (2004) 54 *J. Legal Educ.* 49.

Wissler, Roselle L., "Court-Connected Mediation in General Civil Cases: What We Know from Empirical Research" (2002) 17:3 *Ohio St. J. Disp. Resol.* 641.

Wissler, Roselle L., "The Effectiveness of Court-Connected Dispute Resolution in Civil Cases" (2004) 22 *Confl. Resol. Q.* 55.

Wolfe, Caryn Litt, "Faith-Based Arbitration: Friend or Foe? An Evaluation of Religious Arbitration Systems and Their Interaction with Secular Courts" (2006) 75 *Fordham L. Rev.* 427.

Woolley, Alice et al., eds., *Lawyers' Ethics and Professional Regulation*, 2nd ed. (Markham, ON: LexisNexis Canada, 2012).

Wylie, William N.T., "Instruments of Commerce and Authority: The Civil Courts in Upper Canada, 1789–1812" in David H. Flaherty, ed., *Essays in the History of Canadian Law* (Toronto; Buffalo, NY; and London: University of Toronto Press, 1983).

Yamamoto, Eric K., "ADR: Where Have the Critics Gone?" (1995–6) 36 *Santa Clara L. Rev.* 1055.

Zemans, Frederick H., "Representative Negotiators of Integrity" in Colleen M. Hanycz, Trevor C.W. Farrow, and Frederick H. Zemans, *The Theory and Practice of Representative Negotiation* (Toronto: Emond Montgomery, 2008).

Zuker, Marvin A., *Small Claims Court Practice* (Toronto: Carswell, 1998).

Zuckerman, Adrian, *Civil Justice in Crisis: Comparative Perspectives of Civil Procedure* (Oxford, UK: Oxford University Press, 1999).

Zweibel, Ellen, "Online Dispute Resolution" in Julie Macfarlane, gen. ed., et al., eds., *Dispute Resolution: Readings and Case Studies*, 2nd ed. (Toronto: Emond Montgomery, 2003).

Reports, Letters, Statements, Presentations, and Conferences

Action Committee on Access to Justice in Civil and Family Matters, Final Report, *Access to Civil & Family Justice: A Roadmap for Change* (Ottawa, October 2013), available online: CFCJ <http://www.cfcj-fcjc.org/sites/default/files/docs/2013/AC_Report_English_Final.pdf>.

Adams, Douglas S., "Alternative Dispute Resolution Programs in Law School Curricula – What's Next?" (A project for the American Bar Association Section of Dispute Resolution, 24 August 2001).

ADR Institute of Canada, Rules & Pledges, "Dispute Resolution Pledge: A Corporate Policy Statement," available online: ADR Institute of Canada <http://www.amic.org/>.

Advocates' Society, *Streamlining the Ontario Civil Justice System: A Policy Forum, Final Report* (9 March 2006), available online: Advocates' Society <http://www.advocates.ca/assets/files/pdf/publications/streamlining-justice.pdf>.

Alberta Court Services, "Online Survey Results: Court Annexed Dispute Resolution" (online responses to survey conducted 24 November 2008–8 December 2008).

Alberta Environmental Appeals Board, *2004–2005 Annual Report*, available online: Alberta Government <http://www.eab.gov.ab.ca/pub/2004-05-AR.pdf>.

Alberta Human Rights Commission, *Annual Review, April 1, 2005–March 31, 2006.*

Alberta Human Rights Commission, *Annual Review, April 1, 2007–March 31, 2008.*

Alberta Justice and Attorney General, *Annual Report, 2007–2008*, available online: Alberta Justice <http://justice.alberta.ca/programs_services/about_us/Documents/2008_justice_annual_report.pdf>.

Alberta Law Reform Institute, Consultation Memorandum No. 12.6, "Promoting Early Resolution of Disputes by Settlement" (Edmonton: ALRI, July 2003), available online: ALRI <http://www.law.ualberta.ca/alri/>.

Alberta Law Reform Institute, *Rules of Court Project, Final Report No. 95* (Edmonton: ALRI, October 2008), app. H (available on CD), "Proposed Rules of

Court," available online: ALRI <http://www.law.ualberta.ca/alri/docs/1.%20Appendix%20H%20-%20Proposed%20Rules%20of%20Court.pdf>.

Alberta Provincial Court, "Mediation and the Civil Courts," available online: Alberta Courts <http://www.albertacourts.ab.ca/go/ProvincialCourt/Civil/Mediation/FrequentQuestions/tabid/156/Default.aspx>.

Alberta Provincial Court, "Mediation and the Provincial Court," available online: Alberta Courts <http://www.albertacourts.ab.ca/pc/civil/publication/mediation_and_the_provincial_court.htm>.

American Arbitration Association, "Drafting Dispute Resolution Clauses – A Practical Guide" (1994), available online: Cornell University, ILR School <https://www.ilr.cornell.edu/alliance/resources/Guide/drafting_dispres_clauses.html>.

American Bar Association, *Law Schools and Professional Education: Report and Recommendations of the Special Committee for a Study of Legal Education of the American Bar Association* (1980).

American Bar Association, Report of the American Bar Association Working Group on Civil Justice System Proposals, *ABA Blueprint for Improving the Civil Justice System* (Chicago: American Bar Association, 1992).

American Bar Association, Report of the American Bar Association Working Group on Civil Justice System Proposals, *Just Solutions: Seeking Innovation and Change in the American Justice System* (Chicago: American Bar Association, 1994).

American Bar Association, Section of Dispute Resolution, *State and Local Bar Alternative Dispute Resolution Survey, 2001 Edition* (Washington: ABA, Section of Dispute Resolution, 2001).

American Bar Association, Section on Legal Education and Admissions to the Bar, *Legal Education and Professional Development – An Educational Continuum, the Report of the Task Force on Law Schools and the Profession: Narrowing the Gap* (Chicago: ABA, 1992) (Chair: Robert MacCrate).

American Bar Association, Section on Legal Education and Admissions to the Bar, *Report and Recommendations of the Task Force on Lawyer Competency: The Role of Law Schools* (1979).

Amnesty International et al., "Joint Civil Society Statement on the Draft Guiding Principles on Business and Human Rights" (January 2011), available online: Business and Human Rights Resource Centre <http://www.fidh.org/IMG/pdf/Joint_CSO_Statement_on_GPs.pdf>.

Australian Law Reform Commission, "Managing Justice: A Review of the Federal Civil Justice System," Report No. 89 (Sydney: ALRC, 1999), available online: ALRC <www.austlii.edu.au/au/other/alrc/publications/reports/89/>.

Australian Law Reform Commission, "Review of the Federal Civil Justice System," Discussion Paper 62 (1999), available online: ALRC <www.austlii.edu.au/au/other/alrc/publications/dp/62/>.

Baxter, Jamie, and Albert Yoon, *The Geography of Civil Legal Services in Ontario*, report of the mapping phase of the Ontario Civil Legal Needs Project (Toronto: Ontario Civil Legal Needs Project Steering Committee, November 2011).

B.C. Civil Justice Reform Working Group to the Justice Review Task Force, "Effective and Affordable Civil Justice" (November 2006), available online: B.C. Justice Review Task Force <http://www.bcjusticereview.org/working_groups/civil_justice/cjrwg_report_11_06.pdf>.

B.C. Dispute Resolution Office, "Bulletin: Court Mediation Program" (June 2002), available online: Government of B.C. <http://www.ag.gov.bc.ca/dro/publications/bulletins/court-mediation.htm>.

B.C. Dispute Resolution Office, "Bulletin: Notice to Mediate, (General) Regulation" (June 2002), available online: Government of B.C. <http://www.ag.gov.bc.ca/dro/publications/bulletins/general.htm>.

B.C. Justice Review Forum, "Effective and Affordable Civil Justice System," available online: B.C. Justice Review Forum <http://www.bcjusticereview.org/working_groups/civil_justice/cjrwg_report_11_06.pdf>.

B.C. Justice Review Task Force, "Civil Justice Reform in British Columbia Supreme Court" (9 April 2008) ("Fact Sheet").

Belzil, Hon. R. Paul, "JDR (Judicial Dispute Resolution)" (14 November 2001) in Canadian Forum on Civil Justice et al., eds., "Negotiating the Future: A National Conference on Court-Annexed Mediation" (Calgary, Alberta, 15 November 2001).

Boyd, Marion, "Dispute Resolution in Family Law: Protecting Choice, Promoting Inclusion" (December 2004), available online: Ontario Ministry of the Attorney General <http://www.attorneygeneral.jus.gov.on.ca/english/about/pubs/boyd/fullreport.pdf>.

Canadian Bar Association, "Attitudes – Skills – Knowledge: Proposals for Legal Education to Assist in Implementing a Multi-Option Civil Justice System in the 21st Century" (discussion paper, Ottawa: CBA, August 1999).

Canadian Bar Association, Committee Responding to Recommendation 49 of the Systems of Civil Justice Task Force Report (Ottawa: CBA, 1996).

Canadian Bar Association, Joint Multi-disciplinary Committee on Legal Education, *Attitudes – Skills – Knowledge: Recommendations for Changes to Legal Education to Assist in Implementing Multi-Option Civil Justice Systems in the 21st Century* (Ottawa: CBA, 2000).

Canadian Bar Association, Task Force on Systems of Civil Justice, "Systems of Civil Justice Task Force Report" (Ottawa: CBA, 1996), online: CBA <http://www.cba.org/CBA/pubs/pdf/systemscivil_tfreport.pdf>.

Canadian Forum on Civil Justice, "Alberta Legal Services Mapping Project," available online: CFCJ <http://www.cfcj-fcjc.org/sites/default/files/docs/2011/mapping-final-en.pdf>.

Canadian Forum on Civil Justice, "Cross Country Snapshot of Dispute Resolution" *News & Views Civ. Just. Reform* 4 (Spring 2002) 12.

Canadian Forum on Civil Justice, "Inventory of Reforms: Saskatchewan Queen's Bench Mandatory Mediation Program," available online: CFCJ <http://cfcj-fcjc.org/inventory/reform.php?id=8>.

Canadian Forum on Civil Justice, "What Does it Cost to Access Justice in Canada? How Much Is 'Too Much'? And How Do We Know?" (Literature Review) (31 August 2009) [unpublished].

Canadian Human Rights Commission, *2006 Annual Report*, available online: CHRC <http://www.ohrc.on.ca/sites/default/files/attachments/Annual_report_2006-2007.pdf>.

Canadian Human Rights Commission, *2008 Annual Report* ("Respect, Protection, Promotion, Equality"), available online: CHRC <http://www.ohrc.on.ca/sites/default/files/attachments/Annual_report_2008-2009.pdf>.

Canadian Judicial Council, Sub-Committee on Access to Justice (Trial Courts) of the Administration of Justice Committee, "Access to Justice: Report on Selected Reform Initiatives in Canada (June 2008), available online: CJC <http://www.cjc-ccm.gc.ca/cmslib/general/2008_SelectedReformInitiatives_Report_final_EN.pdf>.

Chadwick, Hon. Mr. Justice James B., "Court-Annexed Mediation in our Civil Courts" (14 November 2001) in Canadian Forum on Civil Justice et al., eds., "Negotiating the Future: A National Conference on Court-Annexed Mediation" (Calgary, Alberta, 15 November 2001).

Civil Procedure Review Committee, Report, *A New Judicial Culture* (Summary) (August 2001), available online: Justice Québec <http://www.justice.gouv.qc.ca/english/publications/rapports/pdf/sommaire-a.pdf>.

Commission for Public Complaints Against the RCMP, *2006–2007 Annual Report*, available online: Government of Canada <http://www.cpc-cpp.gc.ca/cnt/af-fr/ar-ra/AR2007_e.pdf>.

Commission for Public Complaints Against the RCMP, *Annual Report, 2005–2006*, available online: Government of Canada <http://www.cpc-cpp.gc.ca/cnt/af-fr/ar-ra/AR0506_e.pdf>.

Commission for Public Complaints Against the RCMP, *Annual Report, 2007–2008*, available online: Government of Canada <https://www.cpc-cpp.gc.ca/cnt/af-fr/ar-ra/0708_ar_eng.pdf>.

Commission on Practice and Pleadings (Arphaxed Loomis, David Graham, and David Dudley Field), "Report of a Code of Civil Procedure" (Albany, NY: 1850) (HeinOnline).

Court of Appeal of Québec, "Mediation," available online: Court of Appeal of Québec <http://www.tribunaux.qc.ca/c-appel/English/Altres/mediation/mediation.html>.

Court of Queen's Bench, "Civil Mediation," available online: Alberta Courts <http://www.albertacourts.ab.ca/CourtofQueensBench/CivilMediationProgram/tabid/74/Default.aspx>.

Courts of Nova Scotia, "Civil Procedure Rules Nova Scotia," available online: Courts of Nova Scotia <http://www.courts.ns.ca/Rules/toc.htm>.

Courts of Nova Scotia, Civil Procedure Rules Nova Scotia, "Rules Revision Project," available online: Courts of Nova Scotia <http://www.courts.ns.ca/rules_revision/revision.htm>.

Cronk, Hon. E.A., "Examining Barriers that Prevent Litigants from Accessing the Civil Justice System" (paper given at Canadian Forum on Civil Justice, "Into the Future" conference, Montréal, Québec, 1 May 2006).

Davies, Hon. Geoffrey L., "Civil Justice Reform: Some Common Problems, Some Possible Solutions" (paper given at Canadian Forum on Civil Justice, "Into the Future" conference, Montréal, Québec, 1 May 2006).

Denham, Susan, "Launch of the Report on Multi-Party Litigation" (Irish Law Reform Commission (ILRC), 27 September 2005), available online: ILRC <http://www.courts.ie/courts.ie/library3.nsf/16c93c36d3635d5180256e3f003a4580/97b4a7362c75858f8025708f002f964e?OpenDocument>.

Drahozal, Christopher R., and Samantha Zyontz, "An Empirical Study of AAA Consumer Arbitrations" (2009), available online: SSRN <http://papers.ssrn.com/sol3/papers.cfm?abstract_id=1365435>.

Ernst & Young, "Outcomes of Arbitration: An Empirical Study of Consumer Lending Cases" (2004), available online: Ernst & Young <http://www.adrforum.com/rcontrol/documents/ResearchStudiesAndStatistics/2005ErnstAndYoung.pdf>.

Farrow, Trevor C.W. et al., *Addressing the Needs of Self-Represented Litigants in the Canadian Justice System*, a white paper prepared for the Association of Canadian Court Administrators (ACCA) (Toronto and Edmonton: ACCA, 2012), available online: ACCA <http://www.acca-aajc.ca/portals/0/repository/Addressing%20the%20Needs%20of%20SRLs%20ACCA%20White%20

Paper%20March%202012%20Final%20Revised%20Version.f4bd3c5b-e062-4678-aff2-7fd2ac0c6772.pdf>.

Farrow, Trevor C.W., "ADR in Canada: Courts and Administrative Tribunals" (a report prepared for the British Institute of International and Comparative Law, 2009) [unpublished].

Fromholz, Judge H.J., "The Los Angeles Superior Court Mediation Program" (conference presentation, Calgary, Alberta, 18 October 2001) in Canadian Forum on Civil Justice et al., eds., "Negotiating the Future: A National Conference on Court-Annexed Mediation" (Calgary, Alberta, 15 November 2001).

Gilroy, Leonard C., "Reason Foundation's 22nd Annual Analysis of Privatization and Outsourcing" (1 August 2008), available online: Reason Foundation <http://reason.org/news/show/annual-privatization-report-20-27>.

Glaude, Hon. G. Normand, Commissioner, *Report of the Cornwall Inquiry* (2009), available online: Government of Ontario <http://www.attorneygeneral.jus.gov.on.ca/inquiries/cornwall/en/report/index.html>.

Global Reporting Initiative, "Sustainability Reporting Guidelines" (G3.1, 2011), available online: GRI <https://www.globalreporting.org/resourcelibrary/G3.1-Guidelines-Incl-Technical-Protocol.pdf>.

Hancock, Hon. Dave, "Message from Alberta's Minister of Justice and Attorney General" in Alberta Justice, "Alberta Justice's Consultation on Court-Annexed Mediation" (Consultation Brochure, Calgary, 16 November 2001).

Hann, Robert et al., "Evaluation of the Ontario Mandatory Mediation Program (Rule 24.1): Executive Summary and Recommendations" (Ontario: Queen's Printer, 12 March 2001), available online: Government of Ontario <http://www.attorneygeneral.jus.gov.on.ca/english/courts/manmed/exec_summary_recommend.pdf>.

Harris Interactive, "Arbitration: Simpler, Cheaper, and Faster Than Litigation" (April 2005), available online: USCILR <http://www.adrforum.com/rcontrol/documents/ResearchStudiesAndStatistics/2005HarrisPoll.pdf>.

Hart, Christine E., "Draft Model Guidelines for Court-Connected Mediation Programs" (Prepared for the CBA Systems of Justice Implementation Committee's Working Group on Dispute Resolution Standards, 3 September 1998).

Hart, Christine E., "Online Dispute Resolution and Avoidance in Electronic Commerce" (August 1999), available online: Uniform Law Conference of Canada <http://www.ulcc.ca/en/1999-winnipeg-mb/359-civil-section-documents/356-online-dispute-resolution-and-avoidance-in-electronic-commerce>.

Hughes, Hon. E.N., *Access to Justice: Report of the Justice Reform Committee* (Victoria: Ministry of Attorney General, 1988).

Institute of Law Research and Reform (now Alberta Law Reform Institute), *Proposals for a New Alberta Arbitration Act*, Report No. 51 (Edmonton: ILRR, October 1988), available online: ALRI <http://www.law.ualberta.ca/alri/docs/fr51.pdf>.

International Institute for Conflict Prevention & Resolution (CPR), "Law Firm Policy Statement on Alternatives to Litigation," available online: CPR <http://www.cpradr.org/Portals/0/About_CPR/Pledge/CPR%20Law%20Firm%20Pledge%20on%20Alternatives%20to%20Litigation.pdf>.

International Institute for Conflict Prevention & Resolution (CPR), "Law Firm Pledge Signers," available online: CPR <http://www.cpradr.org/AboutCPR/TheCPRADRPledge/WhoHasSignedThePledgeLawFirms/tabid/292/Default.aspx>.

International Institute for Conflict Prevention & Resolution (CPR), Frequently Asked Questions, "The ADR Pledge," available online: CPR <http://www.cpradr.org/Portals/0/21st%20Century%20Pledge.pdf>.

International Institute for Conflict Prevention & Resolution (CPR), "Corporate Policy Statement on Alternatives to Litigation," available online: CPR <http://www.cpradr.org/Portals/0/About_CPR/Pledge/CPR%20Corporate%20Pledge%20on%20Alternatives%20to%20Litigation.pdf>.

International Institute for Conflict Prevention & Resolution (CPR), "Corporate Pledge Signers," available online: CPR <http://www.cpradr.org/AboutCPR/TheCPRADRPledge/WhoHasSignedThePledgeCorporations/tabid/169/Default.aspx>.

Justice and Attorney General, Dispute Resolution Office, "Mediation," available online: Government of Saskatchewan <http://www.justice.gov.sk.ca/Mediation>.

Justice Québec, "Reform of Civil Procedure," available online: Justice Québec <http://www.justice.gouv.qc.ca/english/ministere/dossiers/crpc/crpc-a.htm>.

Justice Québec, "Small Claims," available online: Government of Québec <http://www.justice.gouv.qc.ca/english/publications/generale/creance-a.htm>.

Koenigsberg, Hon. Marvyn, "Access to Justice: A Survey of Reform Initiatives in British Columbia" (24 February 2006) (paper presented at "Streamlining the Ontario Civil Justice System: A Policy Forum," Advocates' Society, Toronto, 9 March 2006).

KPMG, *Scouts Canada: Review of Suspension and Termination Files* (21 June 2012), available online: Scouts Canada <http://www.scouts.ca/cys/sc-kpmg-report.pdf>.

Law Commission of Canada, ed., *New Perspectives on the Public-Private Divide* (Vancouver: UBC Press, 2003).

Law Commission of Canada, *Transforming Relationships through Participatory Justice* (Ottawa: Law Commission of Canada, 2003), available online:

Government of Canada <http://dalspace.library.dal.ca/bitstream/handle/10222/10290/Participatory%20Justice%20Report%20EN.pdf?sequence=1>.

Law Society of British Columbia, "Continuing Professional Development: Overview," available online: LSBC <http://www.lawsociety.bc.ca/licensing_membership/profdev/overview.html>.

Law Society of Upper Canada and Pro Bono Law Ontario, "Ontario Civil Legal Needs Project" in LSUC, Access to Justice Committee, "Report to Convocation" (26 June 2008), app. 1, available online: LSUC <http://www.lsuc.on.ca/media/convjun08_atj.pdf>.

Law Society of Upper Canada, *Alternatives – The Report of the Dispute Resolution Subcommittee* (Toronto: LSUC, 1993).

Law Society of Upper Canada, News Release, "Continuing Professional Development Requirement Supports Professional Competence" (25 February 2010), available online: LSUC <http://www.lsuc.on.ca/media/feb10_finalcpdrequirementrelease.pdf>.

Law Society of Upper Canada, Professional Development & Competence Committee and Paralegal Standing Committee, Joint Report to Convocation (29 October 2009), available online: LSUC <http://www.lsuc.on.ca/media/convoct09_joint_report.pdf>.

Lipsky, David B., and Ronald L. Seeber, "The Appropriate Resolution of Corporate Disputes: A Report on the Growing Use of ADR by U.S. Corporations" (Cornell/PERC Institute on Conflict Resolution, Summer 1998), available online: Cornell University, ILR School <https://www.ilr.cornell.edu/alliance/resources/Articles/approp_resol_corp_disputes.html>.

Litmala, Marjukka, and Kari Alasaari, "Follow-Up Study on the Reform of Public Legal Act (2002), Part 1 (National Research Institute of Legal Policy, Publication no. 211, Helsinki, 2004), available online: NRILP <http://www.optula.om.fi/uploads/euph7b.pdf>.

Lott, Susan, Marie Hélène Beaulieu, and Jannick Desforges, "Mandatory Arbitration and Consumer Contracts" (Public Interest Advocacy Centre (PIAC) and Option consommateurs, November 2004), available online: PIAC <http://www.piac.ca/consumers/mandatory_arbitration_and_consumer_contracts/>.

Lutfy, Hon. Allan, Swearing-in Ceremony, associate chief justice (as he then was) (7 January 2000), available online: Federal Court of Canada <http://cas-ncr-nter03.cas-satj.gc.ca/portal/page/portal/fc_cf_en/Speech>.

Macfarlane, Julie, and Michaela Keet, *Learning from Experience: An Evaluation of the Saskatchewan Queen's Bench Mandatory Mediation Program* (Regina: Saskatchewan Justice Dispute Resolution Office, 2003).

Macfarlane, Julie, "Court-Based Mediation for Civil Cases: An Evaluation of the Ontario Court (General Division) ADR Centre" (Toronto: Ontario Ministry of the Attorney General, 1995).

Maitland, Sir Peregrine (Lieutenant-Governor of the Province of Upper Canada), Dispatch (9 April 1827) in John Delatre Falconbridge, "Law and Equity in Upper Canada" (1914) 63:1 *U. Pa. L. Rev.* 1.

Manitoba Human Rights Commission, *Annual Report 2005*, available online: Manitoba Government <http://www.manitobahumanrights.ca/publications/annual_reports/annual_report_2005.pdf>.

Manitoba, Civil Justice Review Task Force, *Manitoba Civil Justice Review Task Force Report* (Winnipeg: Department of Justice, 1996) (Chair: David Newman).

McHale, M. Jerry, "8 Minute Round Table" in Justice Institute of B.C. et al., eds., "Shaping Directions in Policy, Research and Pedagogy," The First Annual B.C. Symposium on Conflict Resolution (conference materials, Vancouver, B.C., 25 April 2003).

McHale, M. Jerry, "Uniform Mediation Act: Discussion Paper" (paper presented at the Uniform Law Conference of Canada, Victoria, B.C., August 2000), available online: ULCC <http://www.cfcj-fcjc.org/sites/default/files/docs/hosted/17494-uniform_mediation.pdf>.

McLachlin, P.C., Rt. Hon. Beverley, "The Challenges We Face" (remarks presented at Empire Club of Canada, Toronto, Ontario, 8 March 2007), available online: Supreme Court of Canada <http://www.scc-csc.gc.ca/court-cour/judges-juges/spe-dis/bm-2007-03-08-eng.aspx>.

McLachlin, P.C., Rt. Hon. Beverley, "Welcome," available online: Supreme Court of Canada <http://www.scc-csc.gc.ca/home-accueil/index-eng.asp>.

McLachlin, P.C., Rt. Hon. Beverley, "Judges in a Multicultural Society" (paper presented at Chief Justice of Ontario's Advisory Committee on Professionalism, First Colloquium on the Legal Profession, "Inaugural Colloquium on the Legal Profession," 20 October 2003, Faculty of Law, University of Western Ontario), available online: LSUC <http://www.lsuc.on.ca/media/mclachlin_judges_multicultura_society.pdf>.

McLachlin, P.C., Rt. Hon. Beverley, "Lawyers' Professional Obligations, Public Service and Pro Bono Work (remarks made during a question-and-answer session following her presentation at the University of Alberta, Faculty of Law, 19 September 2008).

McMurtry, Hon. R. Roy, Canadian Forum on Civil Justice, Civil Justice Reform Conference: Phase II, "Remarks" (7 December 2006), available online: CFCJ <http://www.cfcj-fcjc.org/sites/default/files/docs/2006/mcmurtry-en.pdf>.

Ministry of the Attorney General, "Mandatory Mediation Program," available online: Government of Ontario <www.attorneygeneral.jus.gov.on.ca/english/courts/manmed/>.

Ministry of the Attorney General, News Release, "Resolving Lawsuits Faster and More Affordably, McGuinty Government Reforming Civil Justice for Ontarians" (11 December 2008), available online: Government of Ontario <http://www.attorneygeneral.jus.gov.on.ca/english/news/2008/20081211-civil-nr.asp>.

Morris, Catherine, "Arbitration of Family Law in British Columbia" (paper presented for the Ministry of Attorney General of British Columbia, 7 July 2004), available online: B.C. Justice Review Task Force <http://www.bcjusticereview.org/working_groups/family_justice/paper_07_07_04.pdf>.

Morris, Catherine, "Media's Mediation and Other Matters: Faith-Based Dispute Resolution in Canada" (speaking notes for a panel presentation, ADR Subsection, B.C. Branch, Canadian Bar Association, Vancouver, Canada, 25 January 2006), available online: CBA <http://www.cba.org/CBA/newsletters/pdf/ADR-Morris_presentation.pdf>.

Morrison, Ian, and Janet Mosher, "Barriers to Access to Civil Justice for Disadvantaged Groups" in Ontario Law Reform Commission, *Rethinking Civil Justice: Research Studies for the Civil Justice Review* (Toronto: Ontario Law Reform Commission, 1996) 637.

Neuberger, Lord (speech at Property Association Dinner, 2 October 2007) [unpublished], cited in Richard Susskind, *The End of Lawyers? Rethinking the Nature of Legal Services* (Oxford, UK and New York: Oxford University Press, 2008) 236.

Nova Scotia Civil Procedure Rules Revision Project, "Consultation with the Bar: Issues Memorandum" (Law Reform Commission of Nova Scotia, 16 June 2004), available online: Courts of Nova Scotia <http://www.courts.ns.ca/rules_revision/docs/final_bar_consult.pdf>.

Number 10, "Global Plan for Recovery and Reform" (2 April 2009), available online: Government of United Kingdom <http://webarchive.nationalarchives.gov.uk/+/number10.gov.uk/news/statements-and-articles/2009/04/g20-leaders-joint-communique-18914#skip_to_content>.

Office of the Prime Minister, Stephen Harper, Prime Minister of Canada, "Priorities," available online: Government of Canada <http://www.pm.gc.ca/eng/feature.asp?pageId=133&featureId=4>.

Ontario Civil Justice Review, *First Report* (Toronto: Ontario Civil Justice Review, 1995), available online: Government of Ontario <http://www.attorneygeneral.jus.gov.on.ca/english/about/pubs/cjr/>.

Ontario Civil Justice Review, *Supplemental and Final Report* (Toronto: Ontario Civil Justice Review, 1996), available online: Government of Ontario <http://www.attorneygeneral.jus.gov.on.ca/english/about/pubs/cjr/>.

Ontario Environmental Review Tribunal, *2007–2010 Business Plan*, available online: Government of Ontario <http://www.ert.gov.on.ca/files/Businessp/BusinessP_0710.pdf>.

Ontario Environmental Review Tribunal, *2008–2011 Business Plan*, available online: Government of Ontario <http://www.ert.gov.on.ca/files/Businessp/BusinessP_0811.pdf>.

Ontario Environmental Review Tribunal, *Annual Report, April 1, 2007–March 31, 2008*, available online: Government of Ontario <http://www.ert.gov.on.ca/files/AnnualR/Annual_Report_07-08.pdf>.

Ontario Human Rights Commission, "Settlements and Decisions at the Human Rights Tribunal of Ontario," available online: OHRC <http://www.ohrc.on.ca/ko/node/9909>.

Ontario Ministry of the Attorney General, "Small Claims Court Guides to Procedures," available online: Ontario Government <http://www.attorneygeneral.jus.gov.on.ca/english/courts/guides/>.

Ontario Small Claims Court, "What Is Small Claims Court?," available online: Government of Ontario <http://www.attorneygeneral.jus.gov.on.ca/english/courts/guides/WhatisSCCJan08EN.pdf>.

Ontario, Legislative Assembly, Standing Committee on Administration of Justice, *Alternative Dispute Resolution 1990* (Toronto, June 1990).

Osborne, Hon. Coulter A., *Civil Justice Reform Project* (November 2007), available online: Ontario Government <http://www.attorneygeneral.jus.gov.on.ca/english/about/pubs/cjrp/>.

Parliament of Australia, Senate Standing Committee on Legal and Constitutional Affairs, "Access to Justice" (8 December 2009), available online: Government of Australia <http://www.aph.gov.au/parliamentary_business/committees/senate_committees?url=legcon_ctte/completed_inquiries/2008-10/access_to_justice/info.htm>.

Perino, Michael A., "Report to the Securities and Exchange Commission Regarding Arbitrator Conflict Disclosure Requirements in NASD and NYSE Securities Arbitrations" (4 November 2005), available online: SEC <http://www.sec.gov/pdf/arbconflict.pdf>.

Pleasence, Pascoe et al., "The Health Cost of Civil Law Problems: Evidence of Links Between Civil Law Problems, Morbidity, and the Consequential Use of Health Services" (First Annual Conference on Empirical Legal Studies

Paper, 2006), available online: SSRN <http://papers.ssrn.com/sol3/papers.cfm?abstract_id=912478>.

President's Council on Competitiveness, *Agenda for Civil Justice Reform in America* (Washington, DC, 1991).

Press, Sharon, "Florida Court-Connected Mediation Programs" (conference presentation, Calgary, Alberta, 18 October 2001), in Canadian Forum on Civil Justice et al., eds., "Negotiating the Future: A National Conference on Court-Annexed Mediation" (Calgary, Alberta, 15 November 2001).

Pro Bono Law Ontario, Media Advisory, "Pro Bono Law Ontario to launch resource centre for unrepresented litigants" (28 November 2007), available online: CNW Group <http://www.pblo.org/news/article.172718-Pro_Bono_Law_Ontario_to_launch_resource_centre_for_unrepresented_litigants>.

Rolland, Hon. François, "Access to Justice: 3 Years after the Reform of the Code of Civil Procedure" (paper given at Canadian Forum on Civil Justice, "Into the Future" conference, Montréal, Québec, 1 May 2006), available online: CFCJ <http://www.cfcj-fcjc.org/sites/default/files/docs/2006/rolland-en.pdf>.

Sachs, Jerrfey D., "Globalization and the Rule of Law" (remarks to Yale Law School alumni weekend, Yale University, 16 October 1998).

Saskatchewan Justice and Attorney General, "The Small Claims Act 1997," available online: Government of Saskatchewan <http://www.justice.gov.sk.ca/Small-Claims-Act-1997>.

Seckel, Allan P., "Judicial Models: Can we do better? Proposed Reforms to Civil Procedure in British Columbia" (panel presentation at Canadian Institute for the Administration of Justice, "Doing Justice: Dispute Resolution in the Courts and Beyond," CIAJ Annual Conference, Halifax, Nova Scotia, 11 October 2007).

Shone, Margaret A., "Law Reform and ADR: Pulling Strands in the Civil Justice Web" (paper presented at Australasian Law Reform Agencies Conference, Wellington, New Zealand, 13–16 April 2004), available online: New Zealand Law Commission <http://www.lawcom.govt.nz/sites/default/files/speeches/2004/04/Session%202B%20-%20ADR%20-%20Shone.pdf>.

Spragge, John Godfrey, "A Letter on the subject of the Courts of Law of Upper Canada addressed to the Attorney General and Solicitor General" (1847) in John Delatre Falconbridge, "Law and Equity in Upper Canada" (1914) 63:1 *U. Penn. L. Rev.* 1.

Statistics Canada, "Initiated and Active Civil Court Cases," available online: Government of Canada <http://www.statcan.gc.ca/daily-quotidien/090120/t090120d1-eng.htm>.

Statistics Canada, "Initiated and Active Civil Court Cases by Type of Case, Selected Provinces and Territories, 2009/2010 and 2010/2011," available online: Government of Canada <http://www.statcan.gc.ca/pub/85-002-x/2012001/article/11634/tbl/tbl04-eng.htm>.

Stuckey, Roy et al., *Best Practices for Legal Education: A Vision and A Road Map* (New York: Clinical Legal Education Association, 2007).

Sullivan, William M. et al., *Educating Lawyers: Preparation for the Profession of Law* (San Francisco: Jossey-Bass, 2007).

Trebilcock, Michael, "Report of the Legal Aid Review 2008" (2008), available online: Legal Aid Ontario <http://www.legalaid.on.ca/en/publications/downloads/advisorygroups/transform-poverty_trebilcock.pdf>.

U.N., *Report of the Special Representative of the Secretary-General on the issue of human rights and transnational corporations and other business enterprises, John Ruggie*, "Guiding Principles on Business and Human Rights: Implementing the United Nations 'Protect, Respect and Remedy' Framework," HRC, 17th Sess., Agenda Item 3, UN Doc. A/HRC/17/31 (21 March 2011) (endorsed by UNHRC 16 June 2011), available online: OHCHR <http://www.ohchr.org/documents/issues/business/A.HRC.17.31.pdf>.

U.N. Commission on International Trade Law (UNCITRAL), Working Group III, "2010 to Present: Online Dispute Resolution," available online: UNCITRAL <http://www.uncitral.org/uncitral/commission/working_groups/3Online_Dispute_Resolution.html>.

U.N. General Assembly, Human Rights Council, "Promotion of All Human Rights, Civil, Political, Economic, Social and Cultural Rights, Including the Right to Development" (Report of the Special Representative of the Secretary-General on the issue of human rights and transnational corporations and other business enterprises), 11th Sess., Item 3, UN Doc. A/HRC/11/13 (22 April 2009), available online: U.N. <http://www2.ohchr.org/english/bodies/hrcouncil/docs/11session/A.HRC.11.13.pdf>.

U.N. Global Compact, Business Leaders Initiative on Human Rights, "A Guide for Integrating Human Rights into Business Management," available online: U.N. <http://www.unglobalcompact.org/docs/issues_doc/human_rights/Resources/guide_hr.pdf>.

U.N., Economic and Social Council, Commission on Human Rights, Sub-Commission on the Promotion and Protection of Human Rights, "Economic, Social and Cultural Rights: Norms on the responsibilities of transnational corporations and other business enterprises with regard to human rights," 55th Sess., Item 4, UN Doc. E/CN.4/Sub.2/2003/12/Rev.2 (26 August 2003), available online: U.N. <http://www.unhchr.ch/huridocda/huridoca.nsf/(Symbol)/E.CN.4.Sub.2.2003.12.Rev.2.En>.

Uniform Law Conference of Canada (ULCC), "Domestic Arbitrations" in ULCC, *Proceedings of the 71st Annual Meeting* (Yellowknife: August 1989), available online: ULCC <http://www.ulcc.ca/images/stories/Past_Proceedings_PDF/1989ULCC0071.pdf>.

United States General Accounting Office (GAO), Report to the Chairman, House Republican Task Force on Privatization, "Privatization: Lessons Learned by State and Local Governments" (GAO/GGD-97-48) (Washington, DC: March 1997), available online: Government of United States <http://www.gao.gov/archive/1997/gg97048.pdf>.

University of Alberta, Student Arbitration and Mediation Society (Lecture Poster, 24 March 2003) [unpublished].

University of Oxford, Faculty of Law, "The Civil Procedure Rules Ten Years On" (a conference organized by the University of Oxford, Faculty of Law, British Academy, London, 1–2 December 2008), available online: University of Oxford <http://denning.law.ox.ac.uk/cpr10/home.php>.

Victorian Law Reform Commission (VLRC), "Civil Justice Review: Report 14" (2009), available online: VLRC <http://www.lawreform.vic.gov.au/sites/default/files/VLRC%2BCivil%2BJustice%2BReview%2B-%2BReport.pdf>.

Wachowich, Hon. Allan H.J., "Opening of the Court 2009" (address by chief justice of Court of Queen's Bench of Alberta, 7 January 2009, Courtroom 317, Edmonton Law Courts, Alberta), available online: Alberta Courts <http://www.albertacourts.ab.ca/LinkClick.aspx?fileticket=lf4Lt8v3cmA%3d&tabid=69&mid=704>.

Wachowich, Hon. Allan H.J., "Court of Queen's Bench of Alberta, Judicial Dispute Resolution (JDR), Participant's Survey – Lawyers – 2007–2008" (cover letter to Hon. John D. Rooke's "Survey of Participants in the Court's JDR Program," September 2007).

Wachowich, Hon. Allan H.J., "Opening of the Court" (Calgary Courthouse, 2 September 2003).

Williams, Jackson, "The Costs of Arbitration" (April 2002), available online: Public Citizen <http://www.citizen.org/documents/ACF110A.pdf>.

Winkler, Hon. Warren K., "Civil Justice Reform – The Toronto Experience" (The Warren Winkler Lectures on Civil Justice Reform, University of Ottawa, Faculty of Law, 12 September 2007), available online: Ontario Courts <http://www.ontariocourts.on.ca/coa/en/ps/speeches/civiljusticereform.htm>.

Winkler, Hon. Warren K., "New Civil Case Management Pilot for Toronto Region: Rule 78 Cases" (paper given at Canadian Forum on Civil Justice, "Into the Future" conference, Montréal, Québec, 1 May 2006).

Woolf, Rt. Hon. Lord, M.R., *Access to Justice: Final Report* (Final report to the Lord Chancellor on the civil justice system in England and Wales) (July 1996), available online: Department for Constitutional Affairs <http://webarchive.nationalarchives.gov.uk/+/http://www.dca.gov.uk/civil/final/contents.htm>.

York University, "Helliwell Foundation Gift Supports a New Dispute Resolution Centre" *Y File* (31 March 2009), available online: York University <http://www.yorku.ca/yfile/archive/index.asp?Article=12327>.

Yukon Government, News Release, "Government Modernizing Yukon Courts by Amending Three Acts" (31 October 2005), available online: Yukon Government <http://www.gov.yk.ca/news/2005/05-284.html>.

Zuber Commission Report: Ontario, *Report of Ontario Courts Inquiry*, by T.G. Zuber (Toronto: Ontario Ministry of Attorney General, 1987).

Statutes, Rules, Regulations, Codes, Practice Directions, and Treaties

Access to Justice (Civil Litigation Reforms) Amendment Bill 2009 (Cth), No. 117, 2009 (assented to 4 December 2009).

Act to Simplify and Abridge the Practice, Pleadings, and Proceedings of the Courts, Laws N.Y. 1848, ch. 379 ("Field Code").

Adjudicative Tribunals Accountability, Governance and Appointments Act, 2009, S.O. 2009, c. 33, Sch. 5.

Administration of Justice Act, 36 Vict. (1873).

Administrative Tribunals Act, S.B.C. 2004, c. 45.

Alberta Rules of Court, Alta. Reg. 124/2010.

Alberta Court of Appeal, "Guidelines for Judicial Dispute Resolution (JDR)," available online: Alberta Courts <http://www.albertacourts.ab.ca/ca/practicenotes/l.pdf>.

American Bar Association, *Model Rules of Professional Conduct* (adopted 1983), available online: ABA <http://www.americanbar.org/groups/professional_responsibility/publications/model_rules_of_professional_conduct/model_rules_of_professional_conduct_table_of_contents.html>.

An Act Respecting the Collection of Certain Debts, R.S.Q., c. R-2.2.

Annotated *Rules of Civil Procedure*, available online: Government of Prince Edward Island <http://www.gov.pe.ca/courts/supreme/rules/index.php3>.

Arbitration Act, 1991, S.O. 1991, c. 17.

Arbitration Act, R.S.A. 2000, c. A-43.

Arbitration Act, R.S.N.S. 1989, c. 19.

Arthur Wishart Act (Franchise Disclosure), 2000, S.O. 2000, c. 3.

B.C. *Supreme Court Civil Rules*, B.C. Reg. 168/2009, as amended by B.C. Reg. 119/2010 (1 July 2010).

B.C., "Notice to Meditate (General) Regulation," B.C. Reg. 4/2001 (effective 15 February 2001), available online: B.C. Dispute Resolution Office <http://www.bclaws.ca/EPLibraries/bclaws_new/document/ID/freeside/4_2001>.

B.C. Court of Appeal, Practice Directive, "Judicial Settlement Conferences," available online: B.C. Government <http://www.courts.gov.bc.ca/court_of_appeal/practice_and_procedure/civil_practice_directives_/Civil-Judicial%20Settlement%20Conferences.htm>.

Business Practices and Consumer Protection Act, S.B.C. 2004, c. 2.

Canadian Bar Association, *Code of Professional Conduct*, rev. ed. (2009), available online: CBA <http://www.cba.org/CBA/activities/pdf/codeofconduct.pdf>.

Canadian Charter of Rights and Freedoms, Part I of the Constitution Act, 1982, being Schedule B to the *Canada Act 1982* (U.K.), 1982, c. 11.

Canadian Human Rights Act, R.S.C. 1985, c. H-6.

Civil Procedure Act 2010 (Vic.), No. 47 of 2010.

Civil Procedure Rules 1998, S.I. 1998/3132, as amended, available online: UK Government <http://www.legislation.gov.uk/uksi/1998/3132/contents/made>.

Civil Procedure Rules of Nova Scotia (effective 1 January 2009), available online: Courts of Nova Scotia <http://www.courts.ns.ca/Rules/toc.htm>.

Civil Resolution Tribunal Act, S.B.C. 2012, c. 25 (assented to 31 May 2012).

Class Proceedings Act, 1992, S.O. 1992, c. 6.

Code of Civil Procedure, R.S.Q., c. C-25.

Commercial Arbitration Act, R.S.B.C. 1996, c. 55.

Commercial Arbitration Act, R.S.C. 1985 (2nd Supp.), c. 17.

Commercial Mediation Act, S.N.S. 2005, c. 36.

Commercial Mediation Act, 2010, S.O. 2010, c. 16, sched. 3.

Constitution Act, 1867, 30 & 31 Victoria, c. 3 (U.K.)

Constitution Act, 1982, being Schedule B to the *Canada Act 1982* (U.K.), 1982, c. 11.

Consumer Protection Act, 2002, S.O. 2002, c. 30.

Consumer Protection Act, R.S.Q., c. P-40.1.

Convention on the Recognition and Enforcement of Foreign Arbitral Awards, 330 U.N.T.S. 3 ("New York Convention").

Court of Queen's Bench Act, R.S.A. 2000, c. C-31.

Court of Queen's Bench of Alberta, "Civil Practice Note No. 11: Court Annexed Mediation" (effective 1 September 2004), available online: Alberta Courts <http://www.albertacourts.ab.ca/qb/practicenotes/civil/pn11CourtAnnexedMediation.pdf>.

Court of Queen's Bench Rules, Man. Reg. 553/88.

Court Rules Act; Small Claims Act, Small Claims Rules, B.C. Reg. 261/93 (deposited 30 July 1993, effective 1 October 1993, as amended, B.C. Reg. 360/2007, 26 November 2007).

Courts of Justice Act, R.S.O. 1990, c. C.43.

Fair Trading Act, R.S.A. 2000, c. F-2.

Family Law Rules, O. Reg. 439/07.

Family Statute Law Amendment Act, 2006, S.O. 2006, c. 1.

Federal Arbitration Act, U.S.C. tit. 9 § 1–14.

Federal Court Rules, SOR/98–106, as amended.

Federation of Law Societies of Canada, *Model Code of Professional Conduct* (adopted 2009 and 2011).

Human Rights Code, R.S.O. 1990, c. H.19.

Judges Act, R.S.C. 1985, c. J-1.

Judicature Act, R.S.A. 2000, c. J-2.

Labour Relations Act, 1995, S.O. 1995, c. 1, sched. A.

Law Society Act, R.S.O. 1990, c. L.8.

Law Society of Alberta, *Code of Conduct* (version 2011_V1, in effect 1 November 2011).

Law Society of Upper Canada (LSUC), *Rules of Professional Conduct* (in effect 1 November 2000), available online: LSUC <http://www.lsuc.on.ca/with.aspx?id=671>.

Legal Aid Services Act, 1998, O. Reg. 107/99, as amended by O. Reg. 151/10.

Magna Carta, or *The Great Charter of King John* (15 June 1215).

Nova Scotia Barristers' Society, *Code of Professional Conduct* (approved by Council 23 September 2011, effective 1 January 2012).

Nunavut Judicial System Implementation Act, S.N.W.T. 1998, c. 34, Sched. A.

Ontario *Judicature Act*, 44 Vict. (1881).

Ontario New Home Warranties Plan Act, R.S.O. 1990, c. O.31.

Ontario Small Claims Court Rules, O. Reg. 258/98, as amended.

Ontario, "Mediators' Fees (rule 24.1, *Rules of Civil Procedure*)," O. Reg. 451/98.

Provincial Court Act, Mediation Rules of the Provincial Court – Civil Division, Alta. Reg. 271/97.

Provincial Court Act, R.S.A. 2000, P-31.

Public Services Superannuation Act, R.S.C 1985 c. P-36.

Queen's Bench Act, 1998, S.S. 1998, c. Q1.01, pt. vii.

Queen's Bench Rules (Saskatchewan) (effective 1 January 2012).

Rules of Civil Procedure, R.R.O. 1990, Reg. 194, as amended.

Rules of Court (effective 15 September 2008), pursuant to *Judicature Act*, R.S.Y. 2002, c. 128, s. 38.

Rules of Court, N.B. Reg. 82–73.

Rules of the Supreme Court of the Northwest Territories, R-010–96 (in force 1 April 1996, as amended).

Rules of the Supreme Court, 1986, S.N.L. 1986, c. 42, sched. D, as amended.

Small Claims Act, 1997, S.S. 1997, c. S-50.11.

Small Claims Court Regulations, O.I.C. 1995/152, available online: Government of Yukon <http://www.gov.yk.ca/legislation/regs/oic1995_152.pdf>.

Statutory Powers Procedure Act, R.S.O. 1990, c. S.22.

Superior Court of Justice, Practice Direction – Toronto Region, "Backlog Reduction / Best Practices Initiative" (in effect 31 December 2004, as renewed), available online: Ontario Courts <http://www.ontariocourts.on.ca/scj/en/notices/pd/toronto/casemanagement.htm>.

Supreme Court of Judicature Act, 1873 (U.K.), 36 & 37 Vict., c. 66.

Supreme Court of Judicature Act, 1875 (U.K.), 38 & 39 Vict., c. 77.

Supreme Court of the Northwest Territories, Notice to the Profession, "Case Management Procedures, General Guidelines" (4 June 1996), available online: Northwest Territories Courts <https://www.nwtcourts.ca/directives/np1.pdf>.

Supreme Court of the Northwest Territories, Notice to the Profession, "Case Management Guidelines (No. 2)" (22 December 1999), available online: Northwest Territories Courts <https://www.nwtcourts.ca/directives/np8.pdf>.

UNCITRAL Model Law on International Commercial Arbitration, U.N. Doc. A/40/17 (1985) ("Model Law").

U.S. *Federal Rules of Civil Procedure*, available online: U.S. Government <http://www.uscourts.gov/rules/CV2008.pdf>.

U.S., EO 12988 – *Civil Justice Reform*, 66 Fed. Reg. 4727–4734 (1996), Title 3, p. 4729, s. 1, revoking EO 12778, 56 Fed. Reg. 55195 (1991), supplemented by EO 13083, 63 Fed. Reg. 27651 (1998) (which was suspended by EO 13095, 63 Fed. Reg. 42565 (1998)); EO 13132, 64 Fed. Reg. 43255 (1999).

Legislative Debates

Alberta, Legislative Assembly, *Alberta Hansard*, 23rd Leg. 4th sess. (14 August 1996) at 2146 (Hon. Mr. Dickson).

Alberta, Legislative Assembly, Committee of Supply, *Alberta Hansard* (30 May 2007) at 1433 (Hon. Mr. Stevens).

Alberta, Legislative Assembly, Designated Supply Committee – Justice and Attorney General, *Alberta Hansard* (23 February 1998) at DSS14 (Hon. Mr. Havelock).

Alberta, Legislative Assembly, *Official Report of Debates (Hansard)* (2 March 1998) at 634 (Hon. Mr. Ducharme).

Alberta, Legislative Assembly, *Official Report of Debates (Hansard)* (24 June 1991) at 1932–1933 (Hon. Mr. Evans).

British Columbia, Legislative Assembly, *Hansard*, Vol. 25, No. 15 (18 May 2004) at 11192 (Hon. G. Plant).

Journals of the Legislative Assembly of … Canada (1842).

Manitoba, Legislative Assembly, *Official Report of Debates (Hansard)*, 36th Leg., 3rd sess., No. 58 (10 June 1997) at 1720 (Hon. Keven Lamoureux).

Manitoba, Legislative Assembly, *Official Report of Debates (Hansard)*, 36th Leg., 3rd sess., No. 59, Orders of the Day (11 June 1997) at 1520 (Hon. Gord Mackintosh).

Nova Scotia, Legislative Assembly, *Official Report of Debates (Hansard)*, 57th Gen. Ass., 1st sess. (25 May 1999) at 6188–6193 (Hons. Robert Harrison, Kevin Deveaux, and Michael Baker).

Ontario, Legislative Assembly, *Official Report of Debates (Hansard)* (1–3, 23, 28 November 2005; 5 December 2005; 20, 28 February 2006; 1 March 2006).

Ontario, Legislative Assembly, *Official Report of Debates (Hansard)* (5 November 1991) at 1550 (Hon. Howard Hampton).

Ontario, Legislative Assembly, *Official Report of Debates (Hansard)* (27 March 1990, 19 June 1990) (Hon. Ian Scott).

Ontario, Legislative Assembly, *Official Report of Debates (Hansard)* (14 February 1990) at J-102 (Gordon F. Henderson).

Ontario, Legislative Assembly, *Official Report of Debates (Hansard)* (5 December 1996) at 1020 (Hon. Bruce Crozier).

Ontario, Standing Committee on Administration of Justice, *Official Report of Debates (Hansard)* (12–15, 19–22, and 26–7 February 1990).

Ontario, Standing Committee on General Government, Consideration of Bill 27 (16 January 2006), available online: Government of Ontario <http://www.ontla.on.ca/committee-proceedings/transcripts/files_html/2006-01-16_G011.htm>.

Ontario, Standing Committee on General Government, *Official Report of Debates (Hansard)* (16–18 January 2006).

Saskatchewan, Legislative Assembly, *Hansard* (18 March 1994) at 997 (Hon. R.W. Mitchell).

Saskatchewan, Legislative Assembly, *Official Report of Debates (Hansard)* (16 July 1992) at 1524 (Hon. Ms. Simard).

Jurisprudence

80 Wellesley St. East Ltd. v. Fundy Bay Builders Ltd. et al., [1972] 2 O.R. 280 (C.A.)

887574 Ontario Inc. v. Pizza Pizza Ltd., [1995] O.J. No. 936, 23 B.L.R. (2d) 259 (Gen. Div., Com. List), leave to appeal to Ont. C.A. refused, [1995] O.J. No. 1645.

1318214 Ontario Ltd. v. Sobeys Capital Inc. (2012), 112 O.R. (3d) 190 (Sup. Ct.).
A.B. v. Bragg Communications Inc., 2012 SCC 46.
ACTIV Financial Systems, Inc. v. Orbixa Management Services, Inc. (2011), 109 O.R. (3d) 385 (Sup. Ct.).
AIC Limited v. Fischer, 2013 SCC 69.
A.M. v. Ryan, [1997] 1 S.C.R. 157.
Amchem Products Inc. v. British Columbia (Workers' Compensation Board), [1993] 1 S.C.R. 897.
American Express Co. v. Italian Colors Restaurant, 570 U.S. ____, slip op. 12–133 (2013).
Arthur Andersen LLP v. Carlisle, 556 U.S. 624 (2009).
AT&T Mobility LLC v. Concepcion et ux., 131 S. Ct. 1740 (2011).
Attorney General of Nova Scotia v. MacIntyre, [1982] 1 S.C.R. 175.
Baker v. Canada (Minister of Citizenship and Immigration), [1999] 2 S.C.R. 817.
Bano v. Union Carbide Corp., [2000] U.S. Dist. LEXIS 12326 (S.D.N.Y. 2000), aff'd, vac'd in part & remanded 273 F.3d 120 (2d Cir. 2001), claim dis'd and motion grant'd [2003] U.S. Dist. LEXIS 4097 (S.D.N.Y. 2003).
BCE Inc. v. 1976 Debentureholders, [2008] 3 S.C.R. 560.
Black v. Canada (Prime Minister) (2001), 54 O.R. (3d) 215.
Blank v. Canada (Minister of Justice), 2006 SCC 39, [2006] 2 S.C.R. 319.
Board v. Board, [1919] A.C. 956, 48 D.L.R. 13 (P.C.).
Bouchan v. Slipacoff, [2009] O.J. No. 156 (Sup. Ct. Jus.).
Boucher v. The King, [1951] S.C.R. 265.
British Columbia (Attorney General) v. Christie, [2007] 1 S.C.R. 873.
British Columbia v. Imperial Tobacco Canada Ltd., [2005] 2 S.C.R. 473.
Bruno Appliance and Furniture, Inc. v. Hryniak, 2014 SCC 8.
Cable & Wireless PLC v. IBM United Kingdom Ltd., [2002] EWHC 2059 (Comm).
Canada (Attorney General) v. Downtown Eastside Sex Workers United Against Violence Society, 2012 SCC 45.
Canadian Bar Assn. v. British Columbia, [2008] B.C.J. No. 350 (C.A.), leave to appeal to S.C.C. refused, [2008] S.C.C.A. No. 185.
Canadian Blood Services v. Freeman, [2004] O.J. No. 4519 (Master).
Canadian Broadcasting Corp. v. Canada (Attorney General), 2011 SCC 2.
Canadian Broadcasting Corp. v. New Brunswick (Attorney General) (Re R. v. Carson), [1996] 3 S.C.R. 480.
Canadian Council of Churches v. The Queen, [1992] 1 S.C.R. 236.
Canadian National Railway Co. v. Lovat Tunnel Equipment Inc., [1999] O.J. No. 2498; 174 D.L.R. (4th) 385 (C.A.).
Canadian Union of Public Employees v. Ontario (Minister of Labour) (2000), 51 O.R. (3d) 417 (C.A.).

Capobianco and Thukkaram v. Vulcan et al., Judgment, No 10–2-09609–4SEA (30 April 2010) (Wash. Sup. Ct.).
Capobianco v. Vulcan, Inc., 2011 Wash. App. LEXIS 840 (11 April 2011) (Wash. C.A., Div. One); aff'd *Capobianco v. Vulcan, Inc.*, 2011 Wash. LEXIS 841 (1 November 2011) (Wash. Sup. Ct.).
Charkaoui v. Canada (Citizenship and Immigration), [2007] 1 S.C.R. 350.
Comandate Marine Corp. v. Pan. Australia Shipping Pty. Ltd. (2006), 238 A.L.R. 457, [2006] F.C.A.F.C. 192 (F.C.A.).
Dagenais v. Canadian Broadcasting Corp., [1994] 3 S.C.R. 835.
Delgamuukw v. British Columbia, [1997] 3 S.C.R. 1010.
Dancap Productions Inc. v. Key Brand Entertainment, Inc., [2009] O.J. No. 572 (C.A.).
Dell Computer Corp. v. Union des consommateurs, 2007 SCC 34, [2007] 2 S.C.R. 801.
Deluce Holdings Inc. v. Air Canada, (1992), 12 O.R. (3d) 131 (Gen. Div., Com. List).
Dennis v. Ontario Lottery and Gaming Corp. (2010), 101 O.R. (3d) 23 (Sup. Ct. Just.), aff'd 2011 ONSC 7024 (Div. Ct.), aff'd 2013 ONCA 501, leave to appeal to S.C.C. filed, [2013] S.C.C.A. No. 373.
Desputeaux v. Éditions Chouette (1987) inc., 2003 SCC 17, [2003] 1 S.C.R. 178.
Dicaro v. Wong, [2001] O.J. No. 347 (Master).
Donaghy v. Scotia Capital Inc./Scotia Capitaux Inc. (2009), 93 O.R. (3d) 776 (C.A.), leave to appeal to S.C.C. refused, 33068 (May 28, 2009), [2009] S.C.C.A. No. 92.
Donoghue v. Stevenson, [1932] A.C. 562 (H.L.).
Dunsmuir v. New Brunswick, [2008] 1 S.C.R. 190.
Edmonton Journal v. Alberta (Attorney General), [1989] 2 S.C.R. 1326.
Eldridge v. British Columbia (Attorney General), [1997] 3 S.C.R. 624.
Equal Employment Opportunity Commission v. Waffle House, Inc., 534 U.S. 279 (2002).
Esso Australia Resources Ltd. and Others v. Plowman (Minister for Energy and Minerals) and Others (1995), 128 A.L.R. 391 (H.C.).
Expedition Helicopters Inc. v. Honeywell Inc. (2010), 100 O.R. (3d) 241 (C.A.).
Flock v. Flock, 2007 ABQB 307, 77 Alta. L.R. (4th) 20, leave to appeal to C.A. refused, 2007 ABCA 287.
Flock v. Beattie, 2010 ABQB 193, 25 Alta. L.R. (5th) 49.
Fortin v. Chrétien, [2001] 2 S.C.R. 500.
George Weston Ltd. v. Domtar Inc. (2012), 112 O.R (3d) 190 (S.C.J.).
Gilmer v. Interstate/Johnson Lane Corp., 500 U.S. 20 (1991).
Grant v. Torstar, 2009 SCC 61, [2009] 3 S.C.R. 640.
GreCon Dimter inc. v. J. R. Normand inc., [2005] 2 S.C.R. 401.
Griffin v. Dell Canada Inc. (2010), 98 O.R. (3d) 481 (C.A.), leave to appeal to S.C.C. refused, [2010] S.C.C.A. No. 75.
Guelph Centre Partners Inc. v. Guelph Storm Ltd., [2005] O.J. No. 458 (S.C.J.).
H.L. Staebler Company Ltd. v. Allen (2008), 92 O.R. (3d) 788 (S.C.J.).

Hagel v. Giles (2006), 80 O.R. (3d) 170 (S.C.J.), aff'd (2006), 82 O.R. (3d) 470 (C.A.).
Halifax (Regional Municipality) v. Nova Scotia (Human Rights Commission), [2012] 1 S.C.R. 364.
Halpern v. Canada (Attorney General) (2003), 65 O.R. (3d) 161 (C.A.).
Halpern v. Canada (Attorney General), [2003] S.C.C.A. No. 337.
Healey v. Lakeridge Health Corp., [2010] O.J. No. 417 (Sup. Ct. Just.).
Heritage Duty Free Shop Inc. v. Canada (Attorney General), [2003] B.C.J. No. 1208 (S.C.), aff'd [2005] B.C.J. No. 670 (C.A.).
Hill v. Church of Scientology of Toronto, [1995] 2 S.C.R. 1130.
Hollick v. Toronto (City), [2001] 3 S.C.R. 158.
Hryniak v. Mauldin, 2014 SCC 7.
In re Union Carbide Corp. Gas Plant Disaster at Bhopal, India, 634 F.Supp. 842 at 844 (S.D.N.Y. 1986), mod'd & aff'd 809 F.2d 195 (2d Cir. 1987), cert. den'd 484 U.S. 871 (1987).
In re Union Carbide Corp. Gas Plant Disaster, [1992] U.S. Dist. LEXIS 1909 (S.D.N.Y. 1992), aff'd *Bi v. Union Carbide Chems. and Plastics Co.*, 984 F.2d 582 (2d Cir. 1993), cert. den'd 510 U.S. 862 (1993).
Jane Doe v. Board of Commissioners of Police for the Municipality of Metropolitan Toronto (1990), 74 O.R. (2d) 225 (Div. Ct.).
Jean Estate v. Wires Jolley LLP (2009), 96 O.R. (3d) 171 (C.A.).
Juman v. Doucette, 2008 SCC 8, [2008] 1 S.C.R. 157.
M. (J.) v. B. (W.) (2004), 71 O.R. (3d) 171 (C.A.).
M. v. H., [1999] 2 S.C.R. 3.
MacIntyre v. Nova Scotia (Attorney-General), [1982] 1 S.C.R. 175.
MacKinnon v. National Money Mart Co., [2009] B.C.J. No. 468 (C.A.).
Manitoba Language Rights Reference, [1985] 1 S.C.R. 721.
Manor of London v. Cox (1867), 1 E. & I. App. 239.
MDG Kingston Inc. v. MDG Computers Canada Inc. (2008), 92 O.R. (3d) 4 (C.A.)
Mitsubishi Motors Corp. v. Soler Chrysler-Plymouth, Inc., 473 U.S. 614 (1985)
Moore v. Bertuzzi (2007), 88 O.R. (3d) 499 (Master).
Moosa v. Hill Property Management Group Inc., [2010] O.J. No. 624 (Master).
Named Person v. Vancouver Sun, [2007] 3 S.C.R. 252.
O. (G.) v. H. (C.D.) (2000), 50 O.R. (3d) 82 (S.C.J.).
Olivieri v. Sherman (2007), 86 O.R. (3d) 778 (C.A.).
Onex Corp. v. Ball Corp., [1994] O.J. No. 98, (1994), 12 B.L.R. (2d) 151 (Gen. Div.).
Ontario Hydro v. Denison Mines Ltd., [1992] O.J. No. 2948 (Gen. Div.).
Ontario (Liquor Control Board) v. Magnotta Winery Corp., 2010 ONCA 681, 102 O.R. (3d) 545 (C.A.).

Ontario Nurses' Assn. v. Ontario (Pay Equity Hearings Tribunal) (1995), 23 O.R. (3d) 43 (C.A.), leave to appeal to S.C.C. refused, *Glengarry Memorial Hospital v. Ontario (Pay Equity Hearings Tribunal) (S.C.C.)*, [1995] S.C.C.A. No. 259.
OPSEU v. Ontario (Attorney General), [1987] 2 S.C.R. 2.
Palkowski v. Ivancic (2009), 100 O.R. (3d) 89 (C.A.).
Parti v. Pokorny, 2011 BCSC 955, [2011] B.C.J. No. 1362 (B.C.S.C.).
Peoples Department Stores Inc. (Trustee of) v. Wise, [2004] 3 S.C.R. 461.
Premium NAFTA Products Limited (20th Defendant) and others (Respondents) v. Fili Shipping Company Limited (14th Claimant) and others (Appellants), [2007] UKHL 40.
Pritchard v. Ontario (Human Rights Commission), 2004 SCC 31, [2004] 1 S.C.R. 809.
Provincial Judges Reference, [1997] 3 S.C.R. 3.
Public Service Alliance of Canada v. Canada Post Corporation, 2011 SCC 57.
RJR – MacDonald Inc. v. Canada (Attorney General), [1994] 1 S.C.R. 311.
R. v. Baltovich [re Canadian Broadcasting Corp.], [2008] O.J. No. 2307 (S.C.J.).
R. v. Carswell, [2008] O.J. No. 4242 (Ont. C.J.).
R. v. Conway, 2010 SCC 22, [2010] 1 S.C.R. 765.
R. v. D.B., [2008] 2 S.C.R. 3.
R. v. Gladue, [1999] 1 S.C.R. 688.
R. v. Lavallee, [1990] 1 S.C.R. 852.
R. v. Mentuck, [2001] 3 S.C.R. 442.
R. v. O.N.E., [2001] 3 S.C.R. 478.
R. v. Oakes, [1986] 1 S.C.R. 103.
R. v. S. (R.D.), [1997] 3 S.C.R. 484.
R. v. Salituro, [1991] 3 S.C.R. 654.
Re Southam Inc. and The Queen (No.1) (1983), 41 O.R. (2d) 113 (C.A.).
Re: Resolution to amend the Constitution, [1981] 1 S.C.R. 753.
Reference re Alberta Statutes, [1938] S.C.R. 100.
Reference re Amendments to the Residential Tenancies Act (N.S.), [1996] 1 S.C.R. 186.
Reference re Manitoba Language Rights, [1985] 1 S.C.R. 721.
Reference Re Public Service Employee Relations Act, Labour Relations Act and Police Officers Collective Bargaining Act, [1987] 1 S.C.R. 313.
Reference re Remuneration of Judges of the Provincial Court of Prince Edward Island, [1997] 3 S.C.R. 3.
Reference re Secession of Québec, [1998] 2 S.C.R. 217.
Revlon, Inc. v. MacAndrews & Forbes Holdings, Inc., 506 A.2d 173 (1986).
Ristimaki v. Cooper (2006), 79 O.R. (3d) 648 (C.A.).
Rogacki v. Belz (2003), 67 O.R. (3d) 330 (C.A.).
Rogers Wireless Inc. v. Muroff, 2007 SCC 35, [2007] 2 S.C.R. 921.

Roncarelli v. Duplessis, [1959] S.C.R. 121.
Rudd v. Trossacs Investments Inc. (2006), 79 O.R. (3d) 687 (Div. Ct.).
Sable Offshore Energy Inc. v. Ameron International Corp., 2013 SCC 37.
Saumur v. City of Québec, [1953] 2 S.C.R. 299.
Sauvé v. Canada (Chief Electoral Officer), 2002 SCC 68, [2002] 3 S.C.R. 519.
Scott v. Scott, [1913] A.C. 419 (H.L.).
Seeley International Pty. Ltd. (A.C.N. 054 687 035) v. Electra Air Conditioning B.V. (2008), 246 A.L.R. 589; [2008] F.C.A. 29 (F.C.A.).
Seidel v. Telus Communications Inc., 2011 SCC 15, [2011] 1 S.C.R. 531, appeal from [2009] B.C.J. No. 469 (C.A.).
Semple v. Canada (Attorney General), [2006] M.J. No. 498 (Q.B.).
Shen v. Klassen (2011), 17 B.C.L.R. (5th) 209, 2011 BCSC 234 (B.C.S.C.).
Sierra Club of Canada v. Canada (Minister of Finance), [2002] 2 S.C.R. 522.
Smith Estate v. National Money Mart Co. (2008), 92 O.R. (3d) 641 (C.A.), leave to appeal to S.C.C. refused, [2008] S.C.C.A. No. 535.
Sumukan Ltd. v. Commonwealth Secretariat, [2007] EWCA Civ 243, [2007] 2 All ER (Comm) 23.
Switzman v. Elbling, [1957] S.C.R. 285.
TeleZone Inc. v. Canada (Attorney General), 2008 ONCA 892, 94 O.R. (3d) 19, aff'd *Canada (Attorney General) v. TeleZone Inc.*, 2010 SCC 62, [2010] 3 S.C.R. 585.
The "Maratha Envoy" [1978] AC 1.
Tolofson v. Jensen; Lucas (Litigation Guardian of) v. Gagnon, [1994] 3 S.C.R. 1022.
Toronto Star Newspapers v. Ontario, [2005] 2 S.C.R. 188.
Treyes v. Ontario Lottery and Gaming Corp., [2007] O.J. No. 2772 (S.C.J.).
Unocal Corp. v. Mesa Petroleum Co., 493 A.2d 946 (1985).
Van Breda v. Village Resorts Limited, [2010] O.J. No. 402 (C.A.), aff'd *Club Resorts Ltd. v. Van Breda*, 2012 SCC 17.
Vancouver Sun (Re), [2004] 2 S.C.R. 332.
Vilardell v. Dunham, 2012 BCSC 748.
Western Canadian Shopping Centres Inc. v. Dutton, [2001] 2 S.C.R. 534.
Whiten v. Pilot Insurance Co., [2002] 1 S.C.R. 595.
Wilson v. Canada (Attorney General), [1998] O.J. No. 1780 (Master).
Z.I. Pompey Industrie v. ECU-Line N.V., [2003] 1 S.C.R. 450.

Index